Fundamentals of
Family Law

Editorial Advisors

Deborah E. Bouchoux, Esq.
Georgetown University

Therese A. Cannon
Higher Education Consultant

Katherine A. Currier
Chair, Department of Paralegal and Legal Studies
Elms College

Susan M. Sullivan
Director, Graduate Career Programs
University of San Diego

Laurel A. Vietzen
Professor Emeritus
Elgin Community College

ASPEN COLLEGE SERIES

Fundamentals of Family Law

J. Shoshanna Ehrlich

Professor of Women's and Gender Studies
College of Liberal Arts
University of Massachusetts — Boston

Wolters Kluwer

Published by Wolters Kluwer in New York.

Wolters Kluwer serves customers worldwide with CCH, Aspen Publishers, and Kluwer Law International products. (www.wolterskluwerlb.com)

To contact Customer Service, e-mail customer.service@wolterskluwer.com, call 1-800-234-1660, fax 1-800-901-9075, or mail correspondence to:

Wolters Kluwer
Attn: Order Department
PO Box 990
Frederick, MD 21705

Printed in the United States of America.

1 2 3 4 5 6 7 8 9 0

ISBN 978-1-4548-5095-3

Library of Congress Cataloging-in-Publication Data

Ehrlich, J. Shoshanna, author.
   Fundamentals of family law / J. Shoshanna Ehrlich, Professor of Women's and Gender Studies, College of Liberal Arts, University of Massachusetts, Boston.
      pages cm. — (Aspen college series)
   Includes bibliographical references and index.
   ISBN 978-1-4548-5095-3 (alk. paper)
   1. Domestic relations—United States. 2. Legal assistants—United States—Handbooks, manuals, etc. I. Title.
   KF505.E375 2015
   346.7301'5—dc23
                                        2015023679

About Wolters Kluwer Law & Business

Wolters Kluwer Law & Business is a leading global provider of intelligent information and digital solutions for legal and business professionals in key specialty areas, and respected educational resources for professors and law students. Wolters Kluwer Law & Business connects legal and business professionals as well as those in the education market with timely, specialized authoritative content and information-enabled solutions to support success through productivity, accuracy and mobility.

Serving customers worldwide, Wolters Kluwer Law & Business products include those under the Aspen Publishers, CCH, Kluwer Law International, Loislaw, ftwilliam.com and MediRegs family of products.

CCH products have been a trusted resource since 1913, and are highly regarded resources for legal, securities, antitrust and trade regulation, government contracting, banking, pension, payroll, employment and labor, and healthcare reimbursement and compliance professionals.

Aspen Publishers products provide essential information to attorneys, business professionals and law students. Written by preeminent authorities, the product line offers analytical and practical information in a range of specialty practice areas from securities law and intellectual property to mergers and acquisitions and pension/benefits. Aspen's trusted legal education resources provide professors and students with high-quality, up-to-date and effective resources for successful instruction and study in all areas of the law.

Kluwer Law International products provide the global business community with reliable international legal information in English. Legal practitioners, corporate counsel and business executives around the world rely on Kluwer Law journals, looseleafs, books, and electronic products for comprehensive information in many areas of international legal practice.

Loislaw is a comprehensive online legal research product providing legal content to law firm practitioners of various specializations. Loislaw provides attorneys with the ability to quickly and efficiently find the necessary legal information they need, when and where they need it, by facilitating access to primary law as well as state-specific law, records, forms and treatises.

ftwilliam.com offers employee benefits professionals the highest quality plan documents (retirement, welfare and non-qualified) and government forms (5500/PBGC, 1099 and IRS) software at highly competitive prices.

MediRegs products provide integrated health care compliance content and software solutions for professionals in healthcare, higher education and life sciences, including professionals in accounting, law and consulting.

Wolters Kluwer Law & Business, a division of Wolters Kluwer, is headquartered in New York. Wolters Kluwer is a market-leading global information services company focused on professionals.

To Alan, Emma, my father, and the memory of my mother

Summary of Contents

Contents

Preface

Welcome to the study of family law. This book is intended to provide you with a thorough working knowledge of this exciting area of the law. Along with its in-depth topical coverage, the book also addresses the important skills that a family law paralegal is likely to need in an active law office, such as client interviewing and legal drafting. However, in my view, it is not enough for a textbook simply to cover the topics and skills that a student will need in order to work effectively in a law office. Accordingly, the book also introduces you to some of the critical and often controversial issues in the field today so that you can be an informed and engaged member of the legal community.

This book is divided into 13 chapters, each of which follows the same basic format. Most chapters begin with a brief introduction to the covered topic, and the material is then presented in headed subsections. Throughout each chapter, key terms are bolded and then defined in the margins of the text. At the end of the chapters, you will find a chapter summary, list of key terms, review questions, discussion questions, and assignments. To help orient yourself, you may find it helpful to read the summary before you read the chapter. The review questions follow the order of the chapter and are designed to help you determine how well you understood the chapter. They are a useful self-testing device. The discussion questions frame some of the more controversial and less settled aspects of the law discussed in the chapter. The assignments are designed to help you apply and further develop your understanding of the law.

The companion website for *Fundamentals of Family Law* at www .aspenlawschool.com/books/ehrlich_fundamentals includes additional resources for students and instructors.

In using this book, you should keep a few important points in mind. First, although every effort has been made to ensure that this book is current, the law is always changing, and that which is current today may be obsolete tomorrow based on a new court decision or statute. Second, this book is written for a national audience and is not geared to the law of any particular state. In the course of your studies, you may want to learn more about the law of your state. Third, although I hope that this book will continue to be a resource for you when you leave school, it should be clear from the first two points that when working on an actual case, this book should not be your primary source of legal information. No book can substitute for the legal research required to ensure a current and comprehensive understanding of the applicable law in your jurisdiction. Good luck, and I hope you enjoy your entry into this fascinating area of the law!

July 2015   *J. Shoshanna Ehrlich*

Acknowledgments

This development of this book has benefited greatly from the contribution of many wonderful people who have given generously of both their time and their expertise. And although I certainly hope that it is free of errors, if any do exist, I take full responsibility for them.

I would specifically like to thank the following students, whose outstanding research helped to shape this book: Janice Babcock, Stephanie Bonvissuto, Alexi Ehrlich, Kayla Getchell, Vicki Kelleher, Barry Kilroy, Jolie Main, John Martin, Andrea Martinez, Sarah Mcdougall, Darryl Palmer, Sabah Uddin, Lizzy Wolozin, and Frank Wood. I would also like to extend a special thanks to David Kelly.

Many others contributed to the shaping of this book, and I am deeply grateful to the following persons for their support and guidance: Sarah Bartlett, Jacquelynne Bowman, Lynne Dahlborg, Janet L. Dolgin, Brad Honoroff, Judith Lennett, Jennifer Levi, David Matz, Terry McLarney, Mary E. O'Connell, Paula Roberts, David Rubin, Jamie Ann Sabino, Stephen N. Subrin, Ann Withorn, and Joan Zora.

On a more personal note, a number of very special people in my life deserve mention. To my husband, Alan Stoskopf, and my daughter, Emma Stoskopf-Ehrlich, thank you for your love and support throughout the years. You are my center. To my father, Fred Ehrlich, thank you for being there; and to the memory of my mother, who loved the written word. Thank you also to my siblings and dear friends, for being such an important part of my life.

I would also like to thank the editorial team for all of their hard work on bringing this book to fruition, including Elizabeth Kenny, Angela Dooley, Sarah Hains, and Renee Cote.

Chapter One

Marriage and the Legal Recognition of Nonmarital Couples

When people think about marriage, they usually think of it as a private, intimate relationship shaped by the love, commitment, and needs of two individuals. However, this understanding of marriage as an essentially private relationship fails to account for the fact that the state also has an interest in marriage—an interest that is grounded in the belief that the exclusivity, permanence, and procreative potential of the marital bond promotes social cohesion and stability. To promote this interest, states traditionally have exercised considerable control over marriage. As an important corollary, states have historically denied legal recognition to unmarried couples in order to buttress the privileged status of marriage, although, as we will see, the traditional bright-line distinction between married and unmarried couples has blurred a bit over time.

Although the modern trend has been away from state control over marriage in favor of greater individual autonomy, state laws continue to structure this relationship. They determine who is eligible to marry, what the rights, entitlements, and obligations of spouses are during the marriage, and what their continuing responsibilities are toward one another should the marriage fail. In short, marriage is a legally transformative act:

- With marriage, each partner becomes formally connected to the family of the other. One literally acquires a "family-in-law." Mirror relationships are created such that the mother of one spouse becomes the mother-in-law of the other.
- Upon marriage, spouses automatically acquire the right to a wide range of entitlements, such as Social Security and workers' compensation benefits, health insurance coverage, beneficial immigration status, and statutory rights of inheritance.
- With marriage, each spouse acquires a legal obligation to support the other. Historically, this obligation was imposed only upon husbands, but this obligation is now mutual.
- If a marriage ends, rights to property and support are automatically triggered, and state law provides a structured framework within

which competing claims can be resolved. Although one does not usually think of divorce as a "benefit" that comes with marriage, it is important to recognize that divorce provides married couples with a structured dissolution process that is not available to unmarried couples.

Reflecting the multidimensional importance of marriage as both a private and a public relationship, a critical recent development has been the struggle by gay men and lesbians for equal marriage rights. Dividing the nation, this struggle has raised critical questions about notions of fairness and the meaning of family.

Regulation of the Relationship: A Brief History

Our original marriage laws were based upon English law. As eloquently expressed by William Blackstone, a famed English legal commentator, a defining aspect of this tradition was the legal subordination of married women:

> By marriage, the husband and wife are one person in law; that is, the very being or legal existence of the woman is suspended during the marriage, or at least is incorporated and consolidated into that of the husband; under whose wing, protection, and *cover*, she performs everything. . . . Upon this principle, of a union of person in husband and wife, depend almost all the legal rights, duties, and disabilities, that either one of them acquire by the marriage.[1]

Outwardly manifested by the requirement that she take her husband's last name as her own, marriage altered a woman's legal status; rights that she possessed as a single woman were transferred to her husband in exchange for his support and protection. For example, she lost the right to own **personal property**, and any such property a woman owned at the time of marriage or subsequently acquired became her husband's. **Real property**—land and whatever is grown on or fixed to it—was treated differently. Title did not pass to the husband, but he acquired the exclusive right to manage and control the realty together with the right to all rents and profits derived from it, and a married woman could not convey her realty without the consent of her husband.

A married woman was also regarded as legally incompetent. Accordingly, any **contracts** that she entered into were null and void. She also lost her **testamentary capacity**—the ability to make a will—and any wills she had made prior to marriage were automatically revoked. She could not sue or be sued in her own name. As the owner of her legal claims, her husband had to be joined as a party and was entitled to collect any damages.

Personal Property:
All property owned by an individual other than real property; includes both tangible and intangible assets

Real Property:
Refers to land and that which is growing upon or affixed to it

Contracts:
Legally enforceable agreements between two or more parties

Testamentary Capacity:
The legal ability to dispose of one's property at death through the execution of a will

A married woman also lost the right to her own labor, and a husband acquired the right to his wife's services both at home and as performed for third parties. Because her labor belonged to him, he acquired an interest in the fruits of her labor, and monies paid to her for services she rendered became his.

In exchange for the loss of her legal persona, a married woman was entitled to be supported by her husband, and he became responsible for her debts, including those she came into the marriage with. This exchange of services for support lay at the heart of the traditional legal concept of marriage and resulted in the husband's unquestioned status as the head of household, with the right to make all major family decisions, including where the family was to live. This core dimension of the marriage relationship endured well into the twentieth century, long after other traditional features had been replaced by more modern rules.

It should be noted that based upon patterns of colonization and territorial acquisition, eight states (Arizona, California, Idaho, Louisiana, Nevada, New Mexico, Texas, and Washington) were influenced by Spanish civil law rather than English common law.[2] Known as **community property** states, at least in theory, the status of married women was different in these jurisdictions. Here, a wife's legal identity did not merge into her husband's. Instead, each spouse retained his or her separate identity, and marriage was viewed as a partnership. Subject to limited exceptions, property acquired during marriage was considered community property and belonged to both partners; however, the husband was given complete authority over the community property, including his wife's earnings.

Community Property: A system of property ownership between husband and wife in which each spouse has a vested one-half ownership interest in all marital property regardless of title

Married Women's Property Acts

Beginning in the late 1830s, states began passing laws known as the **Married Women's Property Acts**, which led to a gradual improvement in the legal status of married women.[3] Interestingly, the first such Acts were enacted in the South and appear to have been motivated by economic concerns, rather than by a desire to emancipate married women. Prompted by the economic panic of 1837, in which many southern plantation owners faced bankruptcy and loss of property — including slaves — to their creditors, legislators passed laws giving married women rights of ownership over their own property, which served to protect it from being seized by their husbands' creditors. Husbands, however, retained their common law right of management and control over their wives' property.

In other regions of the country, most notably the Northeast, the passage of these Acts responded more directly to concerns being voiced by the newly emerging women's rights movement about the legal subordination of married women. Seeking greater equality within the domestic realm, reformers demanded "(1) full control over their property with the

Married Women's Property Acts: The series of statutory reforms that gradually improved the legal status of married women

powers to contract, will, and sue regarding it; (2) the right to their own wages; (3) recognition of the wife's joint right to the earnings of the co-partnership; and (4) equal guardianship of their children."[4]

Striking at the heart of the traditional marital relationship and the husband's privileged position within the home, these demands were seen as radical and were often greeted with scorn and apprehension that women were seeking to rule their husbands. However, over the last half of the nineteenth century, states responded to these demands in halting fashion. By the turn of the century, married women had many more rights than they had previously possessed, and in some states, they could own property, enter into contracts, and sue and be sued in their own name. However, in no state did these laws recognize married women as the legal equals of their husbands, who continued to enjoy their status as the legal head of household.

The Move to Legal Equality

Reflecting the deeply entrenched nature of gender norms in our marriage laws, in 1940, a federal district court in Michigan refused to uphold an agreement between a husband and wife in which the husband agreed to quit his job and follow his wife in her travels in exchange for a monthly sum of money, explaining that:

> As a result of the marriage contract . . . the husband has a duty to support and to live with his wife and the wife must contribute her services and society to the husband and follow him in his choice of domicile. The law is well settled that a private agreement between persons married or about to be married which attempts to change the essential obligations of the marriage contract as defined by the law is contrary to public policy and unenforceable.
>
> Even in the states with the most liberal emancipation statutes, . . . the law has not gone to the extent of permitting husbands and wives by agreement to change the essential incidents of the marriage contract.[5]

Equal Protection Clause:
A clause in the fourteenth amendment to the U.S. Constitution that prevents states from imposing arbitrary and discriminatory legislative classifications

However, in the late 1960s, as the feminist movement gained strength, women again began challenging existing marriage (and other) laws that limited their rights based on fixed notions of appropriate female behavior, by, for example, requiring them to take their husbands' name or to follow them in their choice of domicile, or by limiting their right to freely dispose of property or obtain credit in their own right. Relying primarily on the **equal protection clause** of the fourteenth amendment of the U.S. Constitution (or analogous provisions in state constitutions), courts gradually began striking down most of the remaining sex-based laws on the ground that it was improper for states to assign rights and responsibilities based on fixed assumptions about the proper roles of men and women.

Illustrative of this approach, in 1979, the U.S. Supreme Court invalidated Alabama's alimony law because it imposed a support obligation only on men:

> [T]he "old notion" that "generally it is the man's primary responsibility to provide a home and its essentials," can no longer justify a statute that discriminates on the basis of gender. "No longer is the female destined solely for the home and the rearing of a family, and only the male for the marketplace and world of ideas. . . ."
>
> Legislative classifications which distribute benefits and burdens on the basis of gender carry the inherent risk of reinforcing stereotypes about the "proper place" of women and their need for special protection. Whereas here, the State's . . . purposes are well-served by a gender-neutral classification . . . the State cannot be permitted to classify on the basis of sex.[6]

In addition to relying on equality principles to invalidate these laws, some courts also looked to the Supreme Court's decision in Griswold v. Connecticut, in which it struck down a Connecticut statute prohibiting the use of contraceptives by married couples based on a protected right of marital privacy under the **due process clause** of the fourteenth amendment.[7] Following suit, courts similarly limited the authority of states to structure the terms of the marital relationship in accordance with fixed understandings of spousal roles without regard for the wishes and interests of the marriage partners themselves.

Due Process Clause:
A clause found in both the fifth and fourteenth amendments to the U.S. Constitution that protects persons from arbitrary or intrusive governmental actions

Entrance into Marriage: Choosing a Spouse

Although state laws no longer define marital rights and obligations based upon gender, they continue to play an important role in shaping our understanding of the marital relationship by imposing certain restrictions on an individual's choice of marital partner. Although state laws no longer define marital rights and obligations based upon gender, they continue to play a role in shaping our understanding of the marital relationship by imposing certain restrictions on an individual's choice of marital partner. Most of these restrictions, such as those that prohibit close family members from marrying, are not terribly controversial. However, one of the most heated issues of our time has been whether states can prohibit same-sex partners from marrying. As discussed below, after decades of struggle, in June of 2015, the Supreme Court, in the seminal Obergefell v. Hodges decision,[8] declared that these bans are unconstitutional.

We begin this section by looking at leading Supreme Court cases, including *Obergefell*, that impose constitutional limits on the authority of state to regulate marital partner choice. We then turn our attention to the most common marriage restriction laws that remain in effect today.

Marriage as a Fundamental Right

In 1967, the U.S. Supreme Court, in the case of Loving v. Virginia,[9] struck down Virginia's anti-miscegenation law, which prohibited interracial marriage between white and "colored" persons. Reflective of their racist origins, anti-miscegenation laws date back to the time of slavery and were once in effect in a majority of states. When *Loving* was decided, Virginia was one of 16 states that still prohibited interracial marriage. Virginia's law was challenged by a couple who had been convicted of violating the ban on interracial marriage. They were given a one-year jail sentence, which was suspended on the condition that they leave Virginia and not return for 25 years.

On appeal, Virginia's highest court upheld the Lovings' conviction, concluding that the law was a valid exercise of "'preserve the racial integrity of its citizens'" and prevent "'the corruption of blood'" and a "'mongrel breed of citizens.'"[10] The Supreme Court disagreed. Focusing on the racial hatred that had motivated the passage of anti-miscegenation laws, the Court held that Virginia had violated the equal protection clause of the fourteenth amendment by restricting an individual's choice of marriage partner based on racial classifications. It also held that, under the due process clause of the fourteenth amendment, marriage is a *fundamental right*: "The freedom to marry has long been recognized as one of the vital personal rights essential to the orderly pursuit of happiness by free men. Marriage is one of the 'basic civil rights of man,' fundamental to our very existence and survival."[11] This case marks the first time that the Supreme Court limited the authority of a state to regulate entry into marriage.

Eleven years later, in the case of Zablocki v. Redhail,[12] the Court again invalidated a state law that restricted an individual's right to marry. In question was a law passed by the state of Wisconsin that prohibited noncustodial parents who were behind in child support payments from marrying. In support of the law, the state argued that it was necessary to ensure that noncustodial parents met existing child support obligations. In striking down the law, the Court, building upon *Loving*, held that marriage is a fundamental right and that a state may not impinge on this right in order to collect child support, especially since other collection mechanisms are available. However, it also stated that the right to marry, although fundamental, is not absolute, and that some restrictive laws would most likely withstand constitutional scrutiny. Subsequently, in the case of Turner v. Safley, the Court invalidated a Missouri law prohibiting inmates from marrying, finding that the state's interest in rehabilitation and security did not justify this limitation on an individual's fundamental right to marry.[13]

Marital Rights of Same-Sex Partners

Gay men and lesbians have been fighting for the right to marry since the early 1970s, when a number of same-sex couples who were denied marriage licenses brought lawsuits challenging the fairness of restricting marriage to heterosexual couples. Citing Loving, they argued that with marriage now firmly established as a fundamental right, states no longer had a valid basis for excluding same-sex couples who, like their heterosexual counterparts, were seeking the acceptance and benefits that derive from state recognition.

In this early round of cases, courts did not take this assertion seriously. They consistently concluded that the fundamental right to choose one's marital partner did not extend to same-sex partners because marriage has always been between a man and a woman. The courts similarly concluded that because same-sex couples are critically different from heterosexual couples, particularly with respect to procreative potential, the denial of marital rights did not violate the equal protection clause.

Following these defeats, gay rights activists turned to other approaches, such as domestic partnership initiatives (discussed next), to obtain recognition of their relationships and access to family benefits.

Some also hoped that a more gradualist approach would lead to a greater acceptance of gay couples, which in turn would eliminate social hostility to the idea of same-sex marriage.

The Renewed Struggle for Marriage Equality

In the late 1980s, prompted in part by the AIDS epidemic and bolstered by gains in civil rights protections for gay men and lesbians, activists again began to focus on securing equal marriage rights. Once again, same-sex couples who were denied marriage licenses, this time in Hawaii and Alaska, brought lawsuits arguing that the denial deprived them of the right to privacy and equal protection under their respective state constitutions. Courts in both states appeared on the brink of extending marital rights to same-sex couples; however, while the cases were winding their way through the courts, opponents waged successful campaigns to amend their respective state constitutions to define marriage as being between one man and one woman, thus effectively bringing the court challenges to an end.

The Backlash: The Campaign to Preserve Marriage as a Heterosexual Institution

When it looked as if same-sex marriage might become a reality in Hawaii and Alaska, opponents of marriage equality launched a fierce campaign to formally encode the traditional meaning of marriage as an exclusive relationship between a man and a woman into law at both the state and federal levels. At the federal level, this opposition was encoded into law with the enactment of Defense of Marriage Act (DOMA). DOMA both authorized states to deny recognition to valid same-sex marriages that were entered into in states where they were permitted and defined marriage for purposes of federal law as being exclusively between a man and a woman. Following the lead of the federal government, a majority of states enacted laws or amended their constitutions to define marriage as exclusively being between a man and a woman. In addition to banning marriages between same-sex partners in the enacting states, these "mini-DOMAs" also withheld recognition to marriages between same-sex partners that were validly entered into in a state permitting such unions.

Marriage Equality Becomes a Reality

In 2003, in the groundbreaking case of Goodridge v. Department of Public Health, the Massachusetts Supreme Judicial Court ruled that same-sex couples have a constitutional right to marry.[14] In reaching this decision, the court focused on the profound importance of the marital relationship, stating:

> Without question, civil marriage enhances the 'welfare of the community.' It is a 'social institution of the highest importance.' Civil marriage anchors society by encouraging stable relations over transient ones. . . .
>
> Marriage also bestows enormous private and social advantages on those who choose to marry. Civil marriage is at once a deeply personal commitment to another human being and a highly public celebration of the ideals of mutuality, companionship, fidelity, and family. . . . Because it fulfills yearnings for security, safe haven, and connection that express our common humanity, civil marriage is an esteemed institution, and the decision whether and whom to marry is among life's momentous acts of self-definition.[15]

In deciding for the plaintiffs, the court rejected the state's assertion that the marriage ban is necessary to ensure a favorable setting for procreation and child rearing, concluding that there is no reasonable connection between protecting the welfare of children and barring same-sex couples from marrying. The court also rejected the state's argument that allowing same-sex marriage would trivialize or even destroy "the institution of marriage as it has historically been fashioned." Instead, the court stated that "[i]f anything, extending civil marriage to same-sex couples reinforces the importance of marriage to individuals and communities . . . [and] is a testament to the enduring place of marriage in our laws and in the human spirit."[16]

Making clear that Massachusetts was not simply an outlier, in less than a decade after the Goodridge decision, marriage equality had become a reality in eight states as well as in the District of Columbia. In some jurisdictions, this was similarly accomplished by a ruling from the state's highest court, while in others, it was accomplished by way of a legislative enactment or voter-approved ballot initiatives.

Marriage Equality: The Law of the Land

In 2013, in the case of United States v. Windsor, the Supreme Court invalidated the section of DOMA that defined marriage for purposes of federal law as being exclusively between a man and a woman on the grounds that the denial of federal recognition to intimate relationships that states had "deemed . . . worthy of dignity in the community equal with all other marriages" in accordance with "evolving understandings of the meaning of equality," injured the very group of people that states were seeking to protect by placing "same-sex couples in an unstable position of being in a second-tier marriage."[17] In reaching this decision, the Court made clear that this differentiation was demeaning to same-sex couples and humiliating to their children by making it "more difficult for [them] to understand the integrity and closeness of their own family and its concord with other families in their community and in their daily lives."[18]

Although *Windsor* did not speak directly to the constitutionality of state marriage bans, the decision accelerated the pace of change as state and federal courts relied on its powerful language to strike down existing state marriage bans. Thus, for example, in concluding that "Virginia's same-sex marriage bans impermissibly infringe on its citizens' fundamental right to marry," the federal appeals court relied on *Windsor* for the proposition that laws that evince "disrespect for the 'moral and sexual choices' that accompany a same-sex couple's decision to marry" are constitutionally infirm.[19] Accordingly, by the time the *Obergefell* case reached the United States Supreme Court, a majority of states had embraced marriage equality.

The case of Obergefell v. Hodges was brought by 14 same-sex couples and two men whose partners had died. The plaintiffs were from the states of Ohio, Tennessee, Michigan, and Kentucky, which all had laws defining marriage as being exclusively between one man and one woman. The parties argued that their rights had been violated under the fourteenth amendment either because their state had barred them from marrying or had failed to recognize the validity of a marriage entered into in another state.

James Obergefell's story poignantly captures the impact of this definition of marriage on the lives of the parties. James had been with his partner, John Arthur, for more than two decades. When John was diagnosed with amyotrophic lateral sclerosis (ALS) in 2011, the parties decided to marry before he died. Since their home state of Ohio did not allow marriage between same-sex partners, they flew to Maryland in a medical transport plane and were wed in the plane on the tarmac as John was too ill to leave the plane. After his death three months later, the state of Ohio refused to list James as his surviving spouse on the death certificate, which meant, as the Court put it, that they "must remain strangers"even in death.[20]

In its landmark ruling in favor of the plaintiffs, the Court began by explaining that the "history of marriage is one of both continuity and change."[21] It thus noted that marriage had once been viewed as an "arrangement by the couple's parents based on political, religious, and financial concerns," and that in the not too distant past, "a married man and woman were treated by the State as a single male-dominated legal entity."[22] Paralleling these developments, the Court also underscored the changing legal and social status of gay men and lesbians, remarking that until recently, "many persons did not deem homosexuals to have dignity in their own distinct identity."[23]

Rooting its decision in the above-discussed line of fundamental right to marry cases, the Court held that the well-established constitutional rule that marriage is fundamental applies with "equal force to same-sex couples" based on four essential principles, namely that:

1. "the right to personal choice regarding marriage is inherent in the concept of individual autonomy" and is "among the most intimate that an individual can make;"
2. marriage dignifies the commitment of two persons by offering "the hope of companionship and understanding and assurance that while both still live there will be someone to care for the other;"
3. marriage "safeguards children and families" by affording material benefits and protections to children as well as by offering them "permanency and stability" and the security of knowing that their families are accepted;
4. "marriage is the keystone of our social order."[24]

In so holding, the Court rejected the argument made by the defending states that the plaintiffs were not seeking to "exercise the right to marry but rather a new and nonexistent 'right to same-sex marriage.'"[25] In repudiating this assertion, the Court thus made clear that there is but a single category of marriage that includes both heterosexual and same-sex couples, alike.

As in *Loving*, the Court also held that the ban on same-sex marriage violated the equal protection clause. Explaining that the rights of liberty and equality as respectively embedded in the due process and the equal protection clauses often worked hand in hand, it concluded that restricting the freedom of gay men and lesbians to marry the person of their choosing also abridged "central precepts of equality" that constituted a "grave and continuing harm" in an established realm of fundamental importance.[26]

Restrictions on Entry into Marriage

Although the right to marry is now constitutionally protected, all states still have laws in effect that restrict an individual's choice of marriage partner. These laws have either not been challenged or have been upheld on the grounds that they promote important state interests. We now consider some of the more common **marriage restriction laws** in effect today.

Incest

All states have **incest** laws that make it a crime for family members within a certain degree of kinship to engage in sexual relationships with one another. Running along parallel lines, marriage restriction laws generally prohibit these same relatives from marrying.

These laws have religious roots and can be traced back to the book of Leviticus. At one time, based on the view that a husband and wife were a single person, incest laws applied equally to persons related by marriage (affinity) and those related by blood (consanguinity); in effect, the blood relatives of one spouse were treated as the blood relatives of the other. Today, most states no longer prohibit marriages between persons related by affinity but retain the prohibition against marriage between stepparents and stepchildren to protect children from sexual exploitation.

In terms of specific prohibitions, all states forbid marriage between a parent and child, a grandparent and grandchild, and a brother and sister of whole or half blood. Most states treat sibling relationships created through adoption as a blood relation, and thus prohibit marriage between adopted siblings, and most, if not all, states prohibit marriage between an uncle and a niece and between an aunt and a nephew. With respect to first cousins, the trend is in favor of lifting this restriction, and many states now permit first cousin marriages. This trend reflects the fact that concerns about the genetic risks of "inbreeding" have turned out to be less significant than once believed, at least where first cousins are concerned. According to a report of the National Society of Genetic Counselors, studies indicate that "the increased risk for a significant birth defect in offspring of a first cousin union range between 1.7 and 2.8% above the risk of the general population."[27] However, some states permit first cousins to marry only where the parties are over procreative age or provide evidence of genetic counseling.

Given that marriage is a fundamental right, some commentators have questioned the appropriateness of state laws that prevent consenting adults from marrying one another based on family ties. As expressed by one author:

> All too often . . . society is merely trying to save the individual from conduct that society finds repulsive. State intervention into adult decision-making must be restricted to those instances where the danger

Marriage Restriction Laws: Laws that prevent certain people, such as close relatives, from marrying each other

Incest: Unlawful sexual relations between persons who are closely related to each other

of imminent bodily harm is readily demonstrable and marriage between adults related by consanguinity or affinity does not meet this requirement.[28]

Although there has been some loosening of incest-based restrictions, most notably with respect to first-cousin marriages, there does not appear to be any real movement favoring the elimination of this category of marriage restriction laws.

Multiple Marriages

Bigamy:
The unlawful act of contracting a second marriage while one or both of the partners is already married to someone else

Polygamy:
The situation where an individual has multiple spouses at the same time

All states prohibit a person from having more than one spouse at a time. The term **bigamy** describes the situation where a person enters into a second marriage while his or her first marriage is still in effect; the term **polygamy** applies to the situation where an individual (most commonly a man) has multiple spouses at the same time. A marriage contracted in violation of the "more than one spouse at a time" prohibition is void and may subject the participants to criminal prosecution.

Like incest prohibitions, these laws have religious underpinnings: Monogamy is a central tenet of the Judeo-Christian belief structure. However, unlike the incest taboo, the prohibition against multiple spouses has far less universal reach. For example, in this country, Mormon settlers in what is now Utah regarded the taking of multiple wives as a matter of divine right based on a revelation of the religion's founder, Joseph Smith. In 1890, the Mormon Church repudiated the practice as a condition of Utah's admission as a state; however, since then Mormon fundamentalists have revived the practice.

Although rooted in religious principles, the prohibition of multiple spouses has been justified on a number of policy grounds. Perhaps most important, it has been regarded as essential to preserving the integrity of families by limiting an individual's financial and emotional commitments to a single spouse and their offspring. However, since the Court's decision in *Zablocki*, some commentators have questioned the validity of this rationale, noting that these laws do not really promote the state's interest in protecting family integrity since the same concerns about financial and emotional instability are present with remarriage (or as it is sometimes called, sequential polygamy) and no limits are placed on the number of times a person can remarry and reproduce with each successive spouse.

Marital Age

Age of Capacity:
The minimum age below which a young person may not marry

Complex rules govern the ability of young people to marry. Most states set a minimum age, referred to as the **age of capacity**, below which a young person may not marry. Commonly, this age is 14. Some laws contain exceptions for circumstances such as pregnancy, but the exception usually confers a conditional rather than an absolute right of marriage since most states require a minor to first obtain parental and/or judicial consent. Most states also set an age at which a person becomes eligible to consent to his or her own marriage. This is referred to as the age of consent, and it is usually set at 18—the age of majority.

For young people below the age of consent and, where applicable, above the age of capacity, the right to marry is usually conditional upon obtaining parental and/or judicial consent. Generally, states allow minors who are close to the age of consent to marry with the permission of a parent only, but in the case of younger teens, states may require authorization from both a parent and a judge. In some states, if a parent withholds permission, a minor can petition the court for permission to marry.

These laws were designed to serve at least two state interests. First, by requiring parental participation and approval, they support the traditional authority of parents over their children. Second, and perhaps more importantly, they are thought to protect minors from making ill-advised decisions with potentially long-term harmful consequences for themselves and future offspring. Although there has been a growing trend toward granting minors greater legal autonomy, challenges to these laws have not generally been successful.[29] One important reason is that unlike other decisions, such as whether to terminate a pregnancy, the marriage decision can be postponed without any lasting harmful consequences. Moreover, unlike anti-miscegenation laws or laws prohibiting marriage between same-sex partners, age-restriction laws are not an absolute barrier to marrying one's chosen partner; they simply require deferral of the marriage date.

■ Marriage Formalities

State control over marriage, particularly in structuring the terms of the marital relationship, has diminished over time. However, as clearly evidenced by the requirement that a couple must obtain a license in order to be recognized as legally wed, marriage continues to be a state-sanctioned and regulated relationship.

Thus, although we tend to think of a marriage ceremony as a private event, it is actually compliance with state licensing procedures, rather than saying "I do," that makes one married.

Obtaining a Marriage License

Although the requirements vary from state to state, the differences are generally minor. Allowing for variation, the following discussion provides

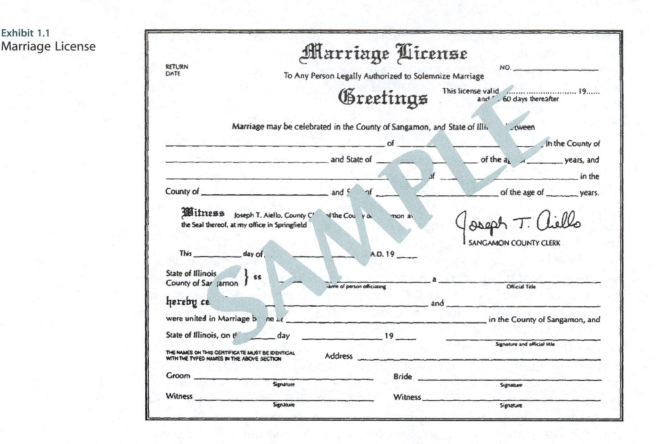

an overview of the steps a couple must follow in order to establish a valid marriage, as well as and the rationale behind these requirements.

First, a couple must obtain a marriage license (Exhibit 1.1). Licenses are usually issued by a county or municipal officer, such as a clerk. Application is made by providing information under oath about age, prior marriages, and possibly also the legal relationship between the intended spouses. In some states, the clerk simply approves or denies the license based on the information as it appears on the face of the application. In other states, the clerk has some responsibility to assess whether the information provided is correct—for example, by requiring the production of a birth certificate or a divorce decree. This application process is a mechanism for enforcing a state's substantive restrictions on who can marry, as the information enables a clerk to determine if, for example, the applicants are underage, married to someone else, or close relatives. Disclosure of these circumstances would result in denial of the license. It also enables a state to collect vital statistics about its citizens as it does with birth and death certificates. Additionally, all states now require both parties to provide their Social Security numbers, which, in the event of divorce or separation, can be used to track down an absent parent for child support collection purposes.

Most states impose a waiting period, ranging from 24 hours to five days, between the time of application and the issuance of the license, although in some states, the waiting period is between issuance of the license and performance of the ceremony. It is hoped that this pause will deter couples from rushing into marriage, as it gives them time to reflect on the seriousness of their decision.

As a condition of eligibility for a marriage license, a few states also require that a doctor perform a blood test and certify that neither party has a venereal disease. The rationale of this requirement is to protect the health of the non-infected spouse and potential offspring. The measure assumes, however, that the parties have not had premarital intercourse, and in recognition of changed social reality, most states have abandoned this requirement. Other less common requirements include the provision of birth control information, premarital counseling for couples under a certain age, and the distribution of information regarding the availability of AIDS and HIV testing.

Once the license is issued, a marriage ceremony must be performed by an authorized person. States usually authorize religious leaders as well as civil officers, such as justices of the peace, to perform marriage ceremonies. Beyond perhaps requiring an oath or acknowledgment of consent to become husband and wife, the presence of witnesses, and a statement by the officiator to the effect that the parties are now lawfully wed, states do not generally regulate the form, content, or manner of the ceremony. Following the ceremony, the license must be recorded in a timely manner. This is usually done by the person who officiated at the wedding.

Consequences of Failing to Comply with Licensing Requirements

In most states, a technical failure to comply with an entry requirement (e.g., if the ceremony is performed by someone claiming to be authorized to perform weddings but who, in fact, lacked such authority) will not invalidate the marriage. The public policy in favor of marriage will usually override any such procedural flaw. In states that recognize common law marriages, a common law marriage rather than a formal marriage may be the result, but, as discussed next, this distinction has no real practical significance.

▪ Common Law Marriage

A **common law marriage** is created by the conduct of the parties in the absence of a formal ceremony. A well-established English practice,

Common Law Marriage: A marriage created by the conduct of the parties rather than through a formal ceremony

common law marriage was accepted by most American colonies as a practical reality in a new country whose scattered populace made access to religious and civil officials difficult. But by the close of the nineteenth century, common law marriage came under increasing attack. Reformers complained that the modern American family had lost its moral footing and that overly relaxed marriage and divorce laws were leading to social decay and promiscuity. They feared that by treating these "irregular" relationships like true marriages, the law was condoning immoral conduct, especially on the part of women, as it was mostly economically dependent wives who sought to establish the existence of a common law marriage following the death of their spouses. As a result of these challenges and increased urbanization, most, but not all, states abolished common law marriages.

Formation Requirements and Consequences

Where still permitted, establishment of a valid common law marriage generally requires proof of three elements:

- a mutual agreement to become spouses;[30]
- cohabitation, and
- reputation in the community as spouses. (In some states, this third element is expressed as a requirement that the parties hold themselves out as spouses; see element one above.)

Because it can be difficult to prove that the parties agreed to become spouses, especially since many disputes over whether a valid common law marriage existed arise after the death of one partner, some courts will infer agreement from the fact of cohabitation and reputation, thus obviating the need for direct proof.

Once a valid common law marriage is established, the parties are considered married for all intents and purposes. They are entitled to all the benefits afforded to spouses, and dissolution of the relationship requires the filing of a divorce action. Once created, the status cannot be informally terminated. Accordingly, it is very important to distinguish common law marriage from "mere" cohabiting relationships; cohabitation may give rise to certain entitlements, but it does not lead to the creation of a spousal relationship.

Given that common law marriage predates the marriage equality movement, most statutes as well as cases not surprisingly speak in terms of the formation of a common law marriage between persons who hold themselves out as and/or establish a reputation in the community as a *husband* and *wife*. However, in light of the *Obergefell* decision, same-sex couples should be able to establish a common law marriage in the same manner as heterosexual couples. In short, although this is a new and untested proposition, it is hard to imagine any legitimate basis for differential treatment.

Interstate Recognition

What happens if a couple establishes a common law marriage in a state that allows them and then moves to a jurisdiction that does not allow such marriage? Will their marriage be accepted in the second state, or will they be considered married in their home state and unmarried in the second state? Almost all states will recognize the marriage so long as the parties satisfied the requirements of the state in which they were originally domiciled. This comports with the general rule that a validly contracted marriage will be recognized in all states, including a state that it could not have been entered into in the first place, unless it is in breach of that state's public policy.

The question of recognition becomes more complex when a couple from a state that does not allow common law marriage spends time in a second state that does, satisfies the requirements for establishing a common law marriage there, and then returns home. Some states will not recognize the marriage unless the parties have established a new domicile in the second state. Other states are looser and will extend recognition simply based on visits made to a jurisdiction that allows common law marriage. Other states take a middle position and will accept the marriage if the parties had sufficient contact with the second state to give rise to evidence of their relationship and reputation in that community.

Legal Recognition of Nonmarital Couples

As noted in the introduction to this chapter, states traditionally have drawn a bright line between marriage and other forms of intimate association. This fixed demarcation has long been considered necessary in order to safeguard the state's interest in marriage as a vital social institution. Placed outside the realm of sanctioned family life, unwed couples have accordingly been excluded from the rights and privileges of marriage. Needless to say, this exclusion has had the greatest impact on same-sex couples who historically, unlike committed heterosexual couples, have not had the choice to formalize their relationships through marriage.

Since the 1970s, however, the law has begun moving away from a strict reliance on marriage as the exclusive marker for determining family status and the corresponding entitlement to benefits. To some extent, this shift responds to the marriage equality movement. Although unwilling to grant formal legal equality to same-sex couples, some states instead were willing to extend partial rights based on a growing awareness of the hardships caused by a nonrecognition policy, such as, for example, where a life partner is denied hospital visitation rights because he or she is not considered family. Moreover, as exemplified by the case of Marvin v. Marvin discussed later in this chapter, this trend also responds to concerns of fairness raised by heterosexual couples who, for a variety of reasons, choose to live together rather than to marry.

In this section, we consider three approaches that courts and lawmakers have taken with respect to the extension of rights and obligations to unmarried couples: namely, permitting cohabitants to sue for property and support rights upon the dissolution of their relationship, the establishment of domestic partnership registries, and the formal protection of relational interests. Although each approach is distinct, a commonality is that unlike with marriage, none of these approaches provides an unmarried couple with an across-the-board family status; rather, rights and recognition are partial and generally limited to particular contexts.[31]

Cohabitation:
Two unmarried persons living together in an intimate relationship; the term applies to both same-sex and heterosexual couples

Cohabitation

Before 1976, courts generally refused to get involved in dissolution disputes between cohabiting partners over money and the allocation of accumulated property. Judges did not want to appear to be sanctioning nonmarital sexual relationships, and they worried that recognizing rights between cohabiting partners would diminish the importance of marriage. However, in 1976, in the landmark case of Marvin v. Marvin,[32] the door to the courthouse was opened for the first time to cohabiting partners seeking to sort out their affairs upon the dissolution of a relationship.

The Marvin *Decision*

Actor Lee Marvin and Michelle Triola lived together for more than seven years, accumulating assets worth more than $1 million in the name of Marvin alone. Following their breakup, Triola sued for support and a share of accumulated assets, based on what she said was an express agreement between the parties that she would give up her musical career and provide domestic services to Marvin in exchange for his financial support and a shared interest in accumulated assets. Marvin, on the other hand, argued that any agreement between the parties was void because it was inextricably bound up with the sexual aspect of their relationship — a traditional barrier to the enforcement of these claims.

Focusing on what it saw as the inherent unfairness of Marvin's position, the California Supreme Court held that unless sexual services are the sole contribution that one party makes to the relationship (thus making the relationship akin to prostitution), the fact that cohabiting partners are engaged in a nonmarital sexual relationship should not prevent the enforcement of agreements between them: "Although we recognize the well-established public policy to foster and promote the institution of marriage, perpetuation of judicial rules which result in an inequitable distribution of property accumulated during a nonmarital relationship is neither a just nor an effective way of carrying out that policy."[33]

Post-*Marvin*, most, if not all, states have opened their doors to cohabiting partners who are seeking to resolve support and property disputes upon the dissolution of their relationships. However, some courts have remained reluctant to hear cases involving disputes between same-sex partners — a reluctance that in some instances may have been attributable to the influence of a state's marriage ban. However, now that marriage equality is the law of the land, it seems unlikely that courts will persist in this approach.

In *Marvin*, Triola based her claim to support and a division of assets on the fact that the parties had entered into an express contract, which is an actual, articulated agreement. In holding that these agreements should be honored, the *Marvin* court also recognized that most cohabiting couples do not formalize their relational expectations, and it urged other courts to consider a variety of contractual and equitable approaches when seeking to resolve claims stemming from a failed cohabiting relationship.

Accordingly, in addition to upholding express agreements, many courts will infer that there was a sharing agreement between the parties based on their conduct during their relationship, much as a court might infer an agreement to pay based on the acceptance of a paper that is delivered to one's door on a daily basis.[34] In contract parlance, an agreement that is inferred from conduct is referred to as an **implied-in-fact contract**. In the context of cohabitation, a court might find an implied agreement to share accumulated assets based on the fact that a couple made purchases from a shared account or commingled their possessions. Some courts might also consider a partner's nonfinancial contribution (e.g., homemaking services) that preserves and enhances the value of the couple's property as evidence of an intent to share in the accumulation.

Implied-in-Fact Contract: A contract that is inferred from the conduct of the parties

Courts have been more reluctant to find implied support agreements based on two traditional barriers. First, it has long been assumed that household services have no real monetary worth. Second, there is a long-standing legal presumption that household services are provided gratuitously or as a gift, without expectation of compensation. These barriers, however, are breaking down. Based in part on the work of economists who have estimated what it would cost to purchase the services of a homemaker in the marketplace, courts have begun to recognize that household services have economic value and that they usually are not provided as a gift but rather, as acknowledged by the *Marvin* court, with the expectation that the parties intended a fair exchange.

Finally, some courts have gone beyond contract law to resolve disputes between cohabiting parties. For example, some have relied upon trust theories to distribute property from one partner to the other based on a showing that the titled partner was either actually holding it for the benefit of his or her partner or had engaged in some kind of fraud or overreaching. Others have treated the relationship like a business partnership that is winding down its affairs and distributing the accumulated assets.

In resolving disputes between cohabiting couples, most courts have been reluctant to treat cohabitation as a status relationship. Accordingly, in contrast to a divorce case where the post-dissolution rights and obligations flow from the existence of the relationship itself, in most states, a cohabitant who seeks support or a share of accumulated assets must establish that his or her claim is grounded in contract or some other legal approach, such as trust or partnership theories. In short, rather than creating a formal legal status for cohabitants, what courts have done is to have removed "a relationship-based impediment to their contractual freedom."[35] However, a distinct minority of jurisdictions have taken this extra step and now treat cohabitation as a status relationship. Accordingly, as with marriage, parties may be found to have post-dissolution obligations to one another based on the existence of the relationship itself.

Although the majority of states continue to use "contract as the conceptual underpinning for claims between intimate partners,"[36] in 2002 the prestigious American Law Institute (ALI) recommended, in its influential *Principles of the Law of Family Dissolution* ("Principles"), that status replace contract as the dominant paradigm. Accordingly, upon dissolution, cohabitants who have shared a "primary residence and a life together as a couple" for a significant period of time would be treated like a married couple with respect to post-relationship rights and obligations.[37]

Family law experts are sharply divided over the ALI recommendation.[38] Supporters argue that a status approach is a fairer way to resolve disputes because most couples simply do not think about their relationship in contractual terms. As a consequence, if there is no agreement to enforce, the economically more vulnerable partner may end up with nothing — a particularly harsh result in the context of a long-term relationship structured along traditional gender lines. Supporters also argue that this approach advances the goal of equality by honoring a broader range of relationship choices in accordance with how people are actually living their lives, rather than simply privileging marriage above all other forms of intimate association.

Others, however, worry that recognizing cohabitation as a formal status will weaken the institution of marriage. One fear is that recognition will blur the distinction between cohabitation and marriage, thus detracting from the unique nature of the marital bond and making it more likely that couples will simply choose to live together because marriage will no longer seem so special. Another concern is that the imposition of post-relationship obligations may contravene the actual intentions of the parties, who, in choosing cohabitation over marriage, may have purposefully been seeking to avoid the legal consequences of marriage. Of course, this argument does not apply to same-sex couples living in states in which marriage is not an option.

Domestic Partnerships and Civil Unions

Starting in the mid-1980s, a number of towns and cities across the country responded to the changing reality of family life by enacting domestic partnership ordinances.[39] More recently, a few states have also passed domestic partnership laws. Also, although not our focus, it should be noted that a growing number of employers now provide workplace benefits to the domestic partners of their employees, often utilizing a registration system similar to that described next.

Domestic Partnership: Refers to a municipal ordinance allowing unmarried couples to register as domestic partners; provides some legal recognition and possible eligibility for benefits; also recognized by some private employers

As usually structured, domestic partnership laws authorize the creation of a central registry at which a qualified unmarried couple can register their relationship. Once registered, the couple may then be eligible for designated benefits, although, as discussed next, these are usually quite limited. As used in this text, the term "domestic partnership" will refer to this limited form of relationship recognition, as distinguished from civil unions, which, as discussed later in this chapter, typically provide partners with the full range of state rights and benefits that are provided to married couples. However, you should be aware that the nomenclature varies from place to place, and some jurisdictions may use the term "domestic partnership" to refer to a more inclusive civil union–type status.

To register as domestic partners, partners typically must complete an affidavit that requires them to attest to the following:

- that they are over the age of 18 and competent to enter into such a relationship;
- that they are cohabiting;
- that their relationship is exclusive and that neither person is married or has another domestic partner;
- that they are responsible for one another's welfare and share basic living expenses;
- that they are not related such that a marriage between them would violate state incest provisions;
- that neither has, within the preceding six months, filed a statement of domestic partnership with anyone else; and
- that if they end the relationship, they will file a certificate of dissolution.

In addition to these qualifying factors, some states and municipalities restrict eligibility to public employees, thus significantly limiting the pool of potential registrants. Additionally, in some locales where same-sex marriage has not been an option, registration has been limited to gay and lesbian couples as a way to provide them with at least some benefits. Although it is too early to tell, it is not clear what impact, if any, the Obergefell decision will have on the domestic partnership registries. On the one hand, some may believe that now that marriage is available to all couples, such measures are no longer needed. On the other hand, some couples may opt not to marry, and thus still be in need of at least the limited benefits offered by domestic partnership registries.

Once registered, partners become eligible for designated benefits. In the municipal context, benefits are notably limited because municipalities have narrow legislative authority. A city or town cannot require private employers to extend benefits to domestic partners, nor can it compel a state to extend state-conferred benefits, such as inheritance rights, if a partner dies without a will. Consequently, unless one partner is a municipal employee, the only benefit of registration may be that it provides some degree of formal relationship recognition, although in some locales, limited benefits, such as jail and hospital visitation rights and tenancy protections, may be available. Where, however, one partner is a municipal employee, registration typically offers some tangible gains, such as the ability to provide health insurance coverage for his or her partner, just as a married employee can do for his or her spouse. However, this move toward workplace equality between married couples and domestic partners has been undercut by the federal tax code. Under the code, an employer's contribution to health insurance coverage for an employee's spouse is not included in the employee's taxable income; in contrast, the amount contributed toward the coverage of the domestic partner of an employee must be included in the taxable income of that employee.[40] A domestic partner may also be entitled to other benefits granted to spouses, such as the right to take time off to care for a domestic partner (or a member of his or her family) on the same basis that allows a married employee to take time off to care for an ill spouse or a member of his or her family.

The picture is quite different in the context of *state* domestic partnership registries. Here, given the far greater regulatory power of the state as compared to the authority of a town or municipality, the benefits tend to be far more extensive, with some states offering registered couples virtually all of the rights and benefits of marriage that accrue under state law. However, as in the municipal context, some states may limit all or some of the available benefits to public employees.

In addition, a few states have enacted what are known as "civil union laws," which effectively create a parallel status to marriage (Hawaii uses the term "reciprocal beneficiaries"). Again, it is not clear what impact the *Obergefell* decision will have on these registries.

Protecting Relational Interests

Another approach that some courts have used to extend rights to cohabitants is to look beyond the lack of a formal status and instead focus on the relational interests that exist between committed cohabiting partners. At the heart of these cases is a judicial willingness to look beyond legal formalities in order to protect the integrity of a committed union. The first case to exemplify this approach is the landmark Braschi v. Stahl Associates Co. decision, in which New York's highest court held that the term "family" could be defined to include same-sex life partners.[41] In *Braschi*, a landlord sought to evict a tenant following the death of his life partner who had been the named tenant on the lease. The surviving partner sought protection under the non-eviction provisions of New York's rent control law that prevent a landlord from evicting the "surviving spouse of the deceased tenant or some other member of the deceased tenant's *family* who has been living with the tenant."[42] The court rejected the landlord's argument that the term "family" should be limited to persons related by blood, marriage, or adoption. Instead, the court said that in defining "family" for the purposes of the rent control statute, one must look beyond "fictitious legal distinctions or genetic history" to the "reality of family life."[43] Accordingly, where an unmarried couple's relationship partakes of the qualities that have made the traditional family a valued and protected social unit, the couple should be recognized as a family.

Since *Braschi*, courts have been particularly receptive to the "relational interest" approach in tort cases where one partner has suffered a financial or emotional loss (or both) following the injury or death of his or her partner. In the influential case of Dunphy v. Gregor,[44] the New Jersey Supreme Court allowed a woman to recover damages for the emotional distress she suffered after witnessing the man she was living with and engaged to marry die after being struck by a car while helping a friend to change a tire. Rejecting the defendant's argument that only family members who are related by marriage or blood should be allowed to recover for "bystander" injuries, the court focused on the nature of the relationship: "Central to a claim under bystander liability is the existence of an intimate familial relationship and the strength of the emotional bonds that surround that relationship. The harm . . . must be so severe that it destroys the emotional security derived from a relationship that is deep, enduring, and intimate. The quality of the relationship creates the severity of the loss."[45] So viewed, it is the quality and nature of the relationship, rather than simply the existence of a formal legal bond, that is important when determining if an individual is entitled to recover for bystander injuries.

Looking to *Dunphy*, New Mexico subsequently became the first state to allow a cohabiting partner to sue for loss of consortium (which generally encompasses the loss of material services, love, companionship, and sexual

Relational Interests: An approach used by some courts to extend rights/benefits to nonmarital couples based on the nature of their relationship

relations) occasioned by an injury to her life-partner, stating that "a person brings this claim to recover for damage to a relational interest, not a legal interest. . . . The use of legal status necessarily excludes many persons whose loss of a significant relational interest may be just as devastating as the loss of a legal spouse."[46] In keeping with *Dunphy*, the court concluded that where a cohabiting couple has a "close familiar relationship" based on factors such as "the degree of mutual dependence, the extent of common contributions to a life together . . . [and] their emotional reliance on each other," it is as deserving of protection as a relationship between married partners.[47]

With respect to expanding the rights of nonmarital partners, the relational interest approach has two inherent limitations. First, to qualify for family status, a couple must offer up the inner workings of their private life to a court for review. This disclosure can be expensive, time-consuming, and highly intrusive. Second, unmarried couples may be held to a higher standard of family life than married couples. Married couples automatically qualify for status and benefits, regardless of how they treat one another or the degree to which their relationship conforms to a domestic norm, whereas a nonmarital couple must show that their relationship satisfies specific criteria in order to be recognized as a family unit.

Chapter Summary

Although we generally think of marriage as a purely private matter, states have actively sought to shape and preserve marriage as a vital social institution. Although laws no longer mandate prescribed roles based on highly gendered notions of proper marital conduct, states still regulate who can marry and the formalities that must be complied with to establish a valid marriage. However, marriage is now recognized as a fundamental right, and laws that burden an individual's right to marry will be subjected to careful judicial review.

Since the 1970s, gay men and lesbians have actively fought for the right to marry, and in 2003, in a historic first, the Massachusetts Supreme Judicial Court ruled that it was unconstitutional to bar same-sex couples from marrying; since then, a growing number of other jurisdictions followed suit and, whether by judicial decision, voter-approved ballot measure, or legislative action, also extended marital rights to same-sex couples, and in 2013 the Supreme Court invalidated the provision of DOMA that had defined marriage for federal purposes as being exclusively between a man and a woman. Marking the culmination of this growing movement in favor of marriage equality, in June of 2015, the Supreme Court held that same-sex couples have a fundamental right to marry, thus making equal marriage rights the law of the land.

Most states have abolished common law marriage. However, most, if not all, states will recognize a common law marriage that was entered into in a state that still permits them.

Today, marriage is no longer the only way that a couple can obtain rights and be formally recognized as a family unit. Most jurisdictions no longer deny legal access to cohabiting couples who seek to resolve property and support disputes when they dissolve their relationships. In some towns, and in a few states as well, a cohabiting couple may be able to register as domestic partners, thus acquiring a formal status and qualifying for benefits that, unless available at the state level, are usually quite limited. Under the functional family approach, the focus is on the reality of a couple's life rather than on its legal form. In carefully defined contexts, courts may protect the relational interests of cohabiting couples where their relationship partakes of many of the qualities traditionally associated with marriage.

Key Terms

Personal Property
Real Property
Contracts
Testamentary Capacity
Community Property
Married Women's
    Property Acts

Equal Protection Clause
Due Process Clause
Marriage Restriction
    Laws
Incest
Bigamy
Polygamy

Age of Capacity
Age of Consent
Defense of
    Marriage Act
    (DOMA)
Domestic
    Partnership

Common Law
    Marriage
Cohabitation
Implied-in-Fact
    Contract
Relational
    Interests

Review Questions

1. What was the status of married women under common law?
2. What were a husband's legal responsibilities under common law?
3. How was marriage seen in community property states?
4. What prompted the passage of the Married Women's Property Acts?
5. What reforms did the Acts accomplish? What aspects of the common law marital relationship did they leave untouched?

6. When and how was the transition to gender-neutral marriage laws accomplished?
7. What did the Supreme Court decide in the case of Loving v. Virginia? Why is this case so important?
8. What kinds of marriage restriction laws are in effect today?
9. What arguments have same-sex couples made in support of their position that they are legally entitled to marry?
10. What arguments have states made against their position?
11. What did the Massachusetts high court decide in the case of Goodridge v. Department of Public Health? What was the basis of its ruling?
12. What is DOMA? As enacted, what were the Act's two provisions?
13. What did the U.S. Supreme Court decide in the *Obergefell* case?
14. What steps must a couple follow to create a formal marriage? What purposes are served by these requirements?
15. What is the effect of a technical failure to comply with these requirements?
16. What is a common law marriage?
17. What elements are necessary to establish a valid common law marriage?
18. Why did courts traditionally deny relief to cohabiting couples upon dissolution of their relationship?
19. What was the result of the *Marvin* decision?
20. What is an implied-in-fact agreement, and under what circumstances might one arise in the cohabitation context?
21. What is the ALI approach to resolving dissolution disputes between cohabitants? Explain how this approach differs from the approach that most states use in resolving these disputes.
22. What is a domestic partnership?
23. What kinds of benefits might be offered under a domestic partnership law?
24. What is the "relational interest" approach? In what kinds of cases might this approach be used?

Discussion Questions

1. Since the U.S. Supreme Court's decision in *Zablocki*, some commentators have suggested that all restrictions on an individual's right to marry are unconstitutional. Do you think states should be able to impose restrictions on a person's choice of a marital partner? If so, what restrictions do you think are appropriate? What arguments support your position?
2. What do you think of the Supreme Court's decision in *Obergefell?*
3. What does the concept of "family" mean to you? Is marriage a central aspect of your definition? Why or why not?
4. Should the law extend marital-like rights to cohabiting couples, or should they be required to marry if they want legal recognition of their relationships? What concerns are at stake in this debate?

Assignments

1. Locate your state's marriage statutes and answer the following questions: a. What restrictions, such as closeness of relationship, does your state use to limit entry into marriage? b. What steps must a couple take in order to establish a formal marriage? c. What are the consequences of failing to comply with these requirements?
2. Assume that a client who is in the process of ending a long-term cohabiting relationship has come into the firm where you work. Your supervising attorney has asked you to research the

laws in your state regarding the rights of cohabiting partners and then write up your results in a short in-house memorandum. The purpose of the memo is to provide the attorney with an overview of the law in your jurisdiction.

3. Select a major employer in your community. Develop a set of questions and then interview the appropriate person in human resources regarding the company's policy on providing benefits to unmarried partners. (Note: Most companies do not presently offer such benefits, so be sure to include questions regarding any future plans and the impact that extending benefits could have on the company.)

4. A local trial judge is considering a case with the following facts:

Mary works as a salesclerk at Green's, a major department store. Green's allows employees to make purchases at a 15 percent discount. It also issues discount cards to the families of their salesclerks that entitle them to the same discount. The store defines "family" as the spouse and children of an employee.

Mary has lived with Julie for eight years. They own a house together. They maintain a joint checking and savings account. They are committed to one another and are regarded as a family by their friends.

Mary applied for a family discount card for Julie. Green's denied the card because Julie was not a member of the family. As a result, Mary has decided to sue her employer.

Assume that you are a paralegal working in a firm that represents either Mary or Green's and that you have been asked to do the following:

a. Read Braschi v. Stahl (543 N.E.2d 49 (N.Y. 1989)) in its entirety and evaluate your client's case in light of this decision.

b. Write an interoffice memo in which you explore the applicability of *Braschi* to the present facts, and develop an argument in which you urge the court (depending on whom you represent) to either accept or reject *Braschi*.

Endnotes

1. William Blackstone, Commentaries on the Laws of England 441-442 (15th ed. A. Strahan ed., 1809) (citations omitted).

2. It should be noted that in Louisiana, the law was shaped by both Spanish and French civil law principles.

3. This section is based mainly on the following works: Norma Basch, In the Eyes of the Law: Women, Marriage, and Property in Nineteenth-Century New York (1982), and Elizabeth Bowles Warbassee, The Changing Legal Rights of Married Women 1800-1861 ch. 1 (1987).

4. Warbassee, *supra* note 3, at 273.

5. Graham v. Graham, 33 F. Supp. 936, 938-939 (E.D. Mich. 1940).

6. Orr v. Orr, 440 U.S. 268, 279-280, 283 (1979), quoting Stanton v. Stanton, 421 U.S. 7, 10, 14-15 (1975).

7. Griswold v. Connecticut, 381 U.S. 479 (1965).

8. 576 U.S._____(2015)

9. Loving v. Virginia, 388 U.S. 1 (1967).

10. *Id*. at 7, citing Naim v. Naim, 197 Va. 80, 90, 87 S.E.2d 749, 756 (1955).

11. *Id*. at 13, citing Skinner v. Oklahoma, 316 U.S. 535, 541 (1942).

12. 434 U.S. 374 (1978).

13. Turner v. Safley, 428 U.S. 78 (1987).

14. 440 Mass. 309, 798 N.E.2d 941 (2003).

15. Id. at 955-956 (internal citations omitted).

16. Id. at 966.

17. United States v. Windsor, 133 S. Ct. 2675, 2693 (2013).

18. Id. at 2695.

19. Bostic v. Schaefer, United States Court of Appeals for the Fourth Circuit, No. 14-1167, 20 & 37 (2014).

20. Obergefell, 576 U.S. at ____.

21. Id.

22. Id.

23. Id.

24. Id.

25. Id.

26. Id.

27. Robin L. Bennett et al., Genetic Counseling and Screening of Consanguineous Couples and Their Offspring: Recommendations of the National Society of Genetic Counselors, 11 J. Genetic Counseling 97 (2002).

28. Carolyn Bratt, Is Oedipus Free to Marry? 18 Fam. L.Q. 267, 288-289 (1984) (citations omitted).

29. *See, e.g.*, Moe v. Dinkins, 669 F.2d 67 (2d Cir. 1982).

30. As noted below, this requirement has traditionally referred to a mutual agreement to become husband and wife, but in light of the *Obergefell* decision, same-sex couples should now also have the right to enter into a common law marriage on the same basis as a heterosexual couple.

31. Because of the partial nature of these approaches, there had previously been some limited interest in adult adoption as a way to create a relationship that encompasses all of the legal attributes of a fully conferred family status.

However, because the drawbacks—including the fact that many states do not recognize these adoptions, the lack of a means to dissolve the relationship, and the difficulties associated with trying to shoehorn an adult relationship into a parent-child structure—outweigh the benefits, this approach really never gained traction.

32. 18 Cal. 3d 660, 557 P.2d 106, 134 Cal. Rptr. 815 (1976).

33. *Id.* at 122.

34. Some couples do enter into formal cohabitation agreements in order to structure their post-dissolution rights and obligations. Some couples also execute a variety of additional legal documents, such as wills and durable powers of attorney, in order to create rights between them similar to those that the law grants to married couples.

35. Margaret M. Mahoney, Forces Shaping the Law of Cohabitation for Opposite Sex Couples, 7 J.L. Fam. Stud. 135, 161 (2005). Cohabitation is treated as a formal legal status in a few states. As with marriage, then, rights and obligations flow from the existence of the relationship itself, thus eliminating the need to prove the existence of an agreement.

36. Mark Ellman, Unmarried Partners and the Legacy of Marvin v. Marvin: "Contract Thinking" Was Marvin's, 76 Notre Dame L. Rev. 1365 (2001).

37. American Law Institute, Principles of the Law of Family Dissolution: Analysis and Recommendations (2002), §6.03(1). The Principles provide detailed guidelines for "identifying those nonmarital relationships which bear a sufficient resemblance to marriage to justify and require similar post-relationship obligations between the parties, whom the Institute refers to as "domestic partners." Ellman, *supra* note 37, at 1378-1379.

38. In addition to Ellman, *see* Nancy D. Polikoff, Making Marriage Matter Less: The ALI Domestic Partner Principles Are One Step in the Right Direction, 2004 U. Chi. Legal F. 353 (2004); Marsha Garrison, Is Consent Necessary? An Evaluation of the Emerging Law of Cohabitation Obligation, 52 UCLA L. Rev. 815 (2005).

39. A growing number of private employers now provide domestic partner benefits.

40. The only exception is if the partner qualifies as a dependent.

41. 74 N.Y.2d 201, 543 N.E.2d 49, 544 N.Y.S.2d 784 (1989).

42. *Id.* at 50.

43. *Id.* at 53. *See also* In re Guardianship of Sharon Kowalski, Ward, 478 N.W.2d 790 (Minn. Ct. App. 1991), *rev. denied* (Feb. 10, 1992). Here, the court described a lesbian couple as a "family by affinity."

44. 136 N.J. 99, 642 A.2d 372 (N.J. 1994).

45. *Id.* at 378-379.

46. Lozoya v. Sanchez, 133 N.M. 579, 66 P.3d 948, 956 (2003).

47. *Id.* at 958, citing Dunphy v. Gregor, 642 A.2d at 378.

Chapter Two

Premarital and Postmarital Agreements

In Chapter 1, we saw that the trend has been away from state regulation of marriage and toward a legal model that emphasizes individual choice. With this increased emphasis on private ordering, **premarital agreements** have gained in both legal and social acceptance. More recently, **postmarital agreements** have also become somewhat more common. These arrangements allow couples to control the terms of their dissolution in the event the marriage ends in divorce.[1] Accordingly, these agreements are often particularly attractive to wealthy individuals who are entering into a marriage with substantial income and assets. They may also be attractive to individuals who have children from a previous relationship, as they allow a parent to protect assets intended for his or her children from claims of the new spouse in the event of a divorce.

Premarital agreements have become an increasingly important dimension of the private ordering of marriage; however, they have not been accepted without controversy and some judicial ambivalence. Accordingly, as discussed in this chapter, in many states, premarital contracts are reviewed more carefully than ordinary contracts. The standard of review may be higher, and certain types of provisions, particularly those involving children, are likely to be unenforceable even if the parties knowingly and voluntarily agreed to the terms. However, the trend is clearly in favor of treating these agreements like other contracts.

Premarital Agreements: A contract entered into by prospective spouses in which they seek to establish their respective rights in the event the marriage fails

Postmarital Agreements: Similar to a premarital agreement, but entered into after rather than before a marriage

The Traditional Approach

Until the early 1970s, premarital agreements made in contemplation of a possible divorce were generally considered void as being against public policy. Although courts no longer disfavor such agreements, the public policy concerns that historically led states to withhold recognition from premarital agreements continue to inform the ongoing debate over whether these agreements should be treated like "ordinary" contracts or whether, because of their unique nature, they should occupy a special place in the law. Historically, the most significant fear was that premarital agreements would encourage divorce because the party who stood to benefit from the agreement would have less incentive to remain in the marriage when things got rocky. According to this way of thinking, a wealthy man whose wife had waived her right to support would be more inclined to walk away from a troubled marriage than a man who knew he would be burdened with alimony payments, thus undermining the state's interest in preserving marriage as a fundamental social unit.

A related fear was that the enforcement of premarital contracts would lead to the post-divorce impoverishment of women. In opinion after opinion, judges expressed the concern that women would be pushed into signing agreements by financially secure and sophisticated men, and they would give up future rights they did not even know they possessed. As discussed next, this protective impulse has shaped much of the present law regarding enforceability. Another concern was that if couples entering into a marriage were allowed to contract with one another, marriage would be reduced to a commercial enterprise. The vision of couples participating in protracted financial negotiations in contemplation of a possible divorce was an uncomfortable one suggesting that the world of family was no different from the world of commerce and that spouses were more like business associates than intimate companions.

The Growing Acceptance of Premarital Agreements

In 1970, the Florida Supreme Court, in the landmark case of Posner v. Posner,[2] held that premarital agreements made in contemplation of divorce are not per se invalid, and other states soon followed suit. This trend corresponded with changing notions about marriage and divorce. As individuals acquired greater legal freedom to structure the terms of their marriage, it was a logical development that they be permitted to structure the terms of marital dissolution. The acceptance of no-fault divorce, which eliminated many of the traditional barriers to marital dissolution, also contributed to the acceptance of premarital agreements. With the increased acceptability and availability of divorce, the argument that premarital agreements would facilitate marital dissolution no longer carried the same weight that it had when divorces were more difficult to obtain. (See Chapter 4 for more detail on "no-fault" divorce reform.)

Another key factor underlying the acceptance of premarital agreements was the changing status of women. Today, courts no longer assume, as they once did, that women are so financially unsophisticated that they will not be able to comprehend the significance of these agreements and will be taken advantage of by prospective husbands. Nor is the financial dependence of married women assumed. In short, as explained by the Pennsylvania Supreme Court in the case of Simeone v. Simeone: "[P]aternalistic presumptions and protectors that arose to shelter women . . . have, appropriately, been discarded."[3]

Legal Requirements

Threshold Considerations

Premarital agreements are contracts. Accordingly, to be enforceable, they must, at a minimum, satisfy certain threshold requirements generally applicable to all contracts. However, as discussed later in this chapter, unlike with most other contracts, satisfying these requirements may not be enough to make a premarital agreement enforceable. These threshold requirements are:

1. There must be an offer and an acceptance of the offer.
2. The contract must be supported by **consideration**. Consideration is the bargained-for exchange of something of value—here, the mutual promise of marriage.
3. The parties must have the capacity to enter into a contract.
4. The subject matter of the agreement cannot be illegal.

Consideration:
The bargained-for exchange that underlies the formation of an enforceable contract; consideration served to distinguish a contract from a promise

Additionally, in most jurisdictions, premarital contracts come within the **statute of frauds**, which is a rule specifying that certain types of contracts must be in writing in order to be enforceable. Most likely, the agreement will also need to be signed by both parties, and the signatures may need to be both witnessed and notarized.

Statute of Frauds:
A rule requiring that certain kinds of contracts be in writing in order to be enforceable

The Fairness Requirement

As a general rule, our legal system emphasizes **freedom of contract**—the right of each individual to freely structure his or her affairs. A corollary of this principle is that once parties have entered into a contract, they are entitled to rely upon it, and courts will protect the expectancies that arise from the terms of the agreement. Without proof of conduct that rises to the level of fraud, misrepresentation, duress, or the like, courts typically will not refuse to enforce a contract because it is more favorable to one party. Unless these more serious kinds of concerns can be established, considerations of fairness with respect to either the process by which the contract was negotiated, such as where a party felt rushed into signing it, or the resulting terms, such as where a person agrees to

Freedom of Contract:
The right of each individual to freely structure his or her own affairs

Unconscionability:
When a contract is grossly unfair to one side; usually involves parties with a significant disparity in bargaining power

Procedural Fairness:
Fairness of the parties in their treatment of one another in the process of negotiating an agreement

Substantive Fairness:
Fairness of the actual terms of an agreement

pay more for a painting than it is worth, are essentially irrelevant. Thus, as a general rule, adherence to the freedom-of-contract principle means that an individual cannot avoid contractual obligations because he or she realizes that the deal is unfair or more favorable to the other side. The primary exception to this rule is the doctrine of **unconscionability**, which allows a court to inquire into issues of fairness in outrageous situations; for this doctrine to apply, there usually must be gross overreaching by a party who is in a vastly superior bargaining position.

However, when a dispute involves a premarital contract, courts typically review the agreement for evidence of unfairness in either the process of negotiating the agreement, referred to as **procedural fairness**, or in the resulting terms, referred to as **substantive fairness**. This hands-on approach, as distinct from the traditional hands-off approach to contract review, flows from a number of considerations. First, by entering into a premarital contract, parties are substituting their own terms for state laws that determine rights of support and property distribution between divorcing spouses. In effect, these agreements create private law in an area long considered to be under the exclusive authority of the state because of its special interest in marriage. Thus, the subject matter of premarital agreements is quite different from that of more ordinary contracts, such as those governing the purchase and sale of real estate.

Second, parties to a typical contract stand at "arm's-length" distance from one another — they are generally not intimately connected and each party can be assumed to be acting in his or her own self-interest. In contrast, parties to a premarital agreement are in an intimate relationship, or what the courts refer to as a "confidential relationship," and are thought to be more vulnerable to being unduly influenced by each other. This risk is compounded by the fact that the parties often are negotiating from positions of unequal bargaining power. Premarital agreements are usually proposed by the prospective spouse with greater wealth who stands to gain more from avoiding state divorce laws, and the other party may feel that she or he has no choice but to sign or face the cancellation of the wedding. Closely related, at least in the early days of recognition, were lingering concerns about the inability of prospective brides to comprehend the details of the financial terms being proposed by her future husband, particularly where differences in wealth were pronounced.

Third, the performance of contractual obligations usually begins within a reasonably short and clearly defined time period after the contract is executed. In contrast, with premarital contracts, the time of performance is uncertain or may never come to be, since the triggering event is divorce. Performance of the terms could thus come several years, or even several decades, after execution of the contract. With the passage of time, unforeseen events may intervene that would make performance of the original terms unfair.

Finally, perhaps this heightened standard of review reflects a continued uneasiness about the contractualization of family life, rooted in a sense that the domestic realm should remain distinct from the commercial realm. Courts may be reluctant to fully import legal standards developed in the realm of impersonal dealings into the realm of intimate relationships.

Requirements of Procedural Fairness

Although the clear trend is in favor of treating premarital contracts more like ordinary agreements, with a corresponding emphasis upon individual autonomy and choice, most courts still look to see if the parties treated each other fairly when negotiating the terms of the agreement. If a court determines that in the course of negotiating the agreement, one party did not treat the other fairly, such as by not fully disclosing assets, it may invalidate the agreement.

The requirement of full and fair disclosure is usually the most important consideration, and the general rule is that both parties have an affirmative duty to make full disclosure even if this information is not requested. Although the standard for determining what constitutes adequate disclosure varies from state to state, more than a mere estimation of the value of existing assets is most likely to be required. Thus, for example, a party may be required to determine the actual value of his or her property and to disclose assets that he or she is entitled to receive in the future. If disclosure is not adequate, entry into the agreement is generally not considered to be voluntary, based on the view that a party cannot freely relinquish assets or income without knowing their correct value or even knowing that they existed.

In some states, a limited exception to the disclosure requirement may be made where one party has actual and specific knowledge of the other potential spouse's assets. However, a general familiarity with the other's financial reputation is unlikely to justify the failure to disclose.

In preparing premarital agreements, even if not specifically required by state law, most attorneys will prepare a full schedule of their client's income and assets, which is attached to the agreement as an exhibit (see Exhibit 2.1). Frequently, paralegals will be asked to assist in this process. Great care must be taken to obtain complete and accurate information, as the adequacy and accuracy of disclosure may determine the subsequent enforceability of the agreement. Often a client is given a written questionnaire to complete regarding his or her income and assets.

In evaluating procedural fairness, some courts also consider factors such as whether the party challenging the agreement understood its provisions at the time of signing, whether she or he was made aware of the legal rights being waived (e.g., the right to spousal support) by entry into the agreement, and whether she or he had the opportunity to review the agreement with an independent attorney. Most jurisdictions require only that a party have the opportunity to review the agreement with an attorney; actual consultation is not required. The primary objective is to prevent one partner from presenting the other with an agreement for the first time at the rehearsal dinner and telling him or her that it must be signed if the wedding is to proceed as planned. As with the requirement of financial disclosure, these elements also relate to whether entry into the agreement was free and voluntary.

SAMPLE QUESTIONS FOR COMPILING A SCHEDULE OF ASSETS

1. Do you own any real estate or have an interest in any realty? If yes, please provide a detailed list, including location of the real estate, nature of your interest, purchase date, purchase amount and amount of your down payment, current fair market value, and the amount of your equity in the real estate.
2. Please provide an itemized list of all household furnishings and effects you own, including the fair market value of each item.
3. Please provide an itemized list of all artwork you own, including the date of purchase, the purchase price, and the fair market value of each item.
4. Please provide an itemized list of all collections you own, including but not limited to collection items such as stamps, coins, cards, antiques, rare books, guns, and records. Include the fair market value of each collection.
5. Please provide an itemized list of all jewelry you own, including the fair market value of each item.
6. Please provide a detailed list of all stocks, bonds, retirement accounts, pension plans, and profit-sharing plans, including the nature of your interest, identifying information for each item, and the current value of your interest in each.
7. Please provide a detailed list of any other asset owned by you that is not set out above, together with the fair market value of each asset.

However, it is important to be aware that some jurisdictions have begun to emphasize the importance of contractual freedom over strict conformity to the requirements of procedural fairness, thus viewing premarital contracts increasingly like ordinary agreements. Still other jurisdictions employ a somewhat flexible approach to evaluating formation fairness.

	FAIR MARKET VALUE	ENCUMBRANCE	NET VALUES
	$	$	$
REAL ESTATE			
Location: 16 Armand Rd. *Recorded at*: Norfolk County, Registry of Deeds; Book No. 814, Page No. 9	$240,000	$170,000	$70,000
PERSONAL PROPERTY			
Household Furnishings:			
Complete set of bedroom, living room, dining room, and kitchen furniture	$3,800	$0	$3,800
Other Household Items (list all worth more than $100):			
Tiffany lamp	$600	$0	$600
Indoor gym equipment	$1,500	$0	$1,500
Computer	$2,500	$0	$2,500
Kitchen appliances (including refrigerator and microwave)	$1,100	$0	$1,100
Antique phonograph	$1,200	$0	$1,200
Collections:			
Rare jazz records	$3,500	$0	$3,500
Jewelry (list all worth more than $100):			
Antique diamond ring	$1,200	$0	$1,200
Rolex watch	$1,400	$0	$1,400
Automobiles:			
2001 VW Bug	$16,000	$4,000	$12,000
Bank Accounts:			
Savings account, Union Federal Bank, account no. 1743	$4,000	—	—
Individual Retirement Account, Union Federal Bank, account no. 97363	$12,000	—	—
Stocks and Bonds:			
80 shares of General Utility Stock	$800	—	—

Note: This sample Schedule of Assets is for one party only. In actuality, both parties would complete one.

Exhibit 2.1
Schedule of Assets for Sandra Lopez

For example, a reviewing judge may be stricter if the parties do not stand on equal footing, such as where one partner is much wealthier or better educated than the other. However, if they stand on relatively equal footing with respect to income, assets, and education, the court may be less concerned with procedural irregularities. Also, as discussed next, if the outcome is fair, courts may be less concerned with procedural irregularities. This may also be the case in jurisdictions that place a great emphasis on the importance of contractual freedom.

Requirements of Substantive Fairness

In addition to reviewing whether the process of contract formation was fair, courts in most jurisdictions will also review the actual terms of the agreement to see if they are fair. However, the *Simeone* decision is illustrative of the growing emphasis on considerations of contractual freedom over contractual fairness. In *Simeone*, the Pennsylvania high court not only limited the scope of review for procedural fairness to considerations of adequate disclosure but also held that the terms of an agreement should not be reviewed to determine if they are fair:

> The reasonableness of a prenuptial bargain is not a proper subject for judicial review. . . . By invoking inquiries into reasonableness, . . . the functioning and reliability of prenuptial agreements is severely undermined. Parties would not have entered into such agreements, and indeed may not have entered into their marriages, if they did not expect the agreements to be strictly enforced.[4]

Fairness can be measured as it existed at the time the contract was executed, as it exists at the time of performance, or both. Again, this kind of review is a substantial departure from the usual contract law approach that gives individuals "freedom" to make bad deals. Subject to the limited unconscionability exception, a person cannot avoid an ordinary contract because he or she subsequently realizes that it is unfair or one-sided.

At Formation.   In jurisdictions where the terms of a premarital agreement are reviewed for fairness, a court would first evaluate them in light of the circumstances as they existed at the time the contract was executed. For example, looking back to the time of contract formation, the waiver of alimony by a two-career couple not intending to have children appears equitable, whereas a waiver by a woman planning to stay home and raise a large family would not. At this phase of the review, events taking place after execution are not considered.

States differ in the standards they use to determine if the terms were fair at the time of execution. Some will not enforce provisions that are "unreasonable," such as a waiver of support by a spouse with a good job but with a much lower earning potential than his or her partner, although something more than a mere inequality of result is generally required. Other states will strike only clauses that are unconscionable or so unfair that they "shock the conscience." In a few jurisdictions, alimony waivers are considered per se unfair and will not be enforced, although this is a minority approach.

At Performance. In addition to determining if the terms were fair at the time the contract was executed, some courts will review them to see if they are fair at the time of divorce. This is sometimes referred to as the second glance doctrine. Here, traditional freedom of contract principles are clearly subordinated in favor of protecting an economically vulnerable spouse. By way of example, let us return to our two-career couple who did not plan to have children and included an alimony waiver in their prenuptial agreement. Assuming that this was fair at the time of execution, if the parties subsequently changed their minds and decided to have children, the waiver might be deemed unfair at the time of performance if one parent had cut back on employment to care for them. At second glance, terms that appeared fair at the time of contract formation would now work a hardship because of changed circumstances.

Second Glance Doctrine: Review by a court of the terms of a premarital agreement to determine whether they are fair as of the time of enforcement

However, many courts consider this too great an interference with rights of contractual freedom, based on the view that once parties have made an agreement that is fair at the time of execution, they are entitled to rely on it regardless of subsequent events. So viewed, the only proper role of the court is to protect legitimate expectations arising from the agreement.

Courts will usually take a second glance only at support-related clauses, and they tend to employ a very high standard of review in order to strike a balance between avoiding hardship and honoring contractual expectations. At this stage, many courts will invalidate a term waiving or limiting support rights only where enforcement would leave a party unable to meet basic needs or would force him or her onto public assistance. Other courts are less strict and will invalidate a clause if enforcement would result in a substantial reduction in a party's standard of living, even if actual poverty is not threatened.

The Interdependence of Procedural and Substantive Fairness

Although the previous discussion treats the requirements of procedural and substantive fairness as independent variables, many courts regard them as interdependent. Accordingly, where the substantive terms are fair, a court may choose to overlook procedural deficiencies; for example, financial disclosure will not be insisted on as a pure formality. Likewise, if the result is clearly unfair, a court may presume that the procedure was inherently flawed and proceed to review the agreement with particular care.

Common Types of Provisions

In light of this history, it is not surprising that even in more liberal jurisdictions, courts may be reluctant to accept certain types of provisions. Moreover, as discussed later in this chapter, with respect to clauses involving children, traditional family law principles also factor into the general rule of non-enforceability. Although the discussion is far from exhaustive, we now consider the kinds of provisions that many couples include in their premarital agreements.[5]

Property

Perhaps the most common and generally least controversial type of premarital provisions are those that address how the property that the parties accumulated over the marriage is to be allocated in the event of divorce. In effect, these provisions allow a couple to opt out of the legal rules that would otherwise control the disposition of their property (see Chapter 8).

Most significant here is a determination of what assets will be regarded as separate, and thus unreachable by the other spouse in the event of a divorce, and what is to be considered marital property that is subject to distribution under applicable state rules. The ability to insulate property from the potential divorce claims of a spouse can be particularly important to an individual who already has children, as it enables him or her to preserve and eventually bequeath the intended assets to them.

Many patterns are possible here. Parties might simply seek to ensure that assets they come into the marriage with will continue to be defined as their sole and separate property, regardless of how they might otherwise be classified at the time of divorce under state law. Parties might also seek to classify all assets purchased during the marriage as the separate property of the acquiring spouse, free from any claims of the other, or they might set out a schema for determining which assets are to be considered separate and which are to be considered marital that differs from the classification pattern under state law.

Spousal Support

Courts have typically been more wary of provisions in which one or both spouses waive their right to spousal support. Of particular concern is that a spouse might find herself unable to make ends meet, and thus end up on public assistance. Accordingly, some courts will not enforce alimony waivers, often based on the view that they are "void as against public policy," although this traditional approach is now a distinctly minority position.

In the majority of states that now permit parties to waive spousal support rights, many have addressed concerns about potential post-divorce impoverishment through rules governing the review process. Accordingly, in some states, precise language must be in strict accordance with statutory or case law requirements in order for a waiver to be effective. Moreover, as discussed earlier in this chapter, many require that the terms of the waiver be closely examined to ensure that they are fair, even if such a substantive review is not required for the property provisions. Some also mandate a second glance (as discussed previously) to ensure that even if fair at the time of enactment, the waiver is still fair at the time of divorce. In addition to or in lieu of substantive fairness requirements, some states also employ heightened procedural fairness requirements to ensure that a support waiver is truly free and voluntary.

Child Custody and Child Support

Despite the clear trend in favor of allowing spouses to structure in advance the consequences of divorce, this trend stops when it comes to provisions regarding children. Reflecting long-standing family law principles, this general proscription on the enforceability of child-related provisions is unlikely to change.

With respect to premarital efforts to determine custodial arrangements in the event of divorce, courts are in accord that spouses cannot determine in advance what would be in the "best interest" of their future offspring were they to eventually divorce (see Chapter 5). Although, as we have been discussing, parties can opt out of other rules, such as those governing the distribution of assets, through private ordering, the state retains a duty to ensure that custodial arrangements are carefully tailored to promote the well-being of children at the time of divorce.

Similarly, courts will not enforce provisions intended to modify or eliminate either party's child support obligations. Mandated by state law, the right to support runs to the child, not to the custodial parent, and thus cannot be waived or limited by a "third party."

Postmarital Contracts

Although far less common than premarital agreements, postmarital (or postnuptial) contracts have slowly become more popular. Consistent with the trend in favor of private ordering, many states now recognize the validity of postmarital agreements. However, other jurisdictions have not yet addressed the issue of their enforceability, and a few states have determined, either by statute or legislative enactment, that they are not enforceable. Moreover, as noted next, where allowed, their enforceability may be governed by stricter standards than those governing premarital agreements.

Postnuptial contracts typically serve the same general purpose as premarital contracts: namely, allowing spouses to set the terms of a subsequent divorce. However, commentators have suggested two primary reasons for why they may be regarded as somewhat more attractive than contracts of the prenuptial variety. First, because the parties are already married, the dreaded last-minute situation where one party presents the other with an agreement at the rehearsal dinner and says "Sign, or the wedding is off" is avoided, thus potentially making them less coercive.

Countering this view, however, some courts have noted that the potential for coercion is also present in the postnuptial context, as one spouse may threaten divorce if his or her spouse refuses to sign an agreement that is presented unilaterally at a rocky moment in the relationship. Moreover, the fact of marriage does not obviate the problem that the spouse with greater wealth—typically the husband in a heterosexual union—usually has greater bargaining power. Reflecting these types of concerns, some courts actually hold these contracts to a higher standard of fairness and review them more carefully than premarital agreements.[6]

Second, and perhaps more importantly, the actual circumstances of a couple's life together may be clearer, thus enabling them to more carefully tailor an agreement to their actual, as distinct from their projected, needs. For example, as has been noted, "if a couple's first child has autism, the wife may choose to forgo a career opportunity to care for her child. A postnuptial contract would allow her to tailor her rights upon divorce to ensure that her sacrifice is borne equally by both parents."[7]

Chapter Summary

Until the 1970s, premarital agreements made in contemplation of divorce were generally considered void as against public policy, in large part because they were thought to encourage divorce. Nonrecognition was also thought necessary to protect women from being taken advantage of by financially savvy prospective spouses, as well as from post-divorce impoverishment. Influenced by the growing acceptance of no-fault divorce and the changing socioeconomic status of women, the majority of jurisdictions now recognize these agreements. Although less common, many states now also recognize postmarital agreements.

Although now generally accepted, many courts still treat premarital and postmarital agreements differently from ordinary contracts and, in the event of a dispute, emphasize fairness over strict adherence to freedom of contract principles. A near-universal rule is that for a premarital agreement to be enforceable, the parties must have entered into it freely and with full knowledge of the other spouse's financial circumstances. Beyond this, courts may review other procedural elements as well, such as whether the parties understood the terms of the agreement at the time of execution. Some courts will also look to see if the terms of the agreement were fair at the time of execution, and some will also take a "second glance" to determine if the terms are fair at the time of enforcement. However, the clear trend is to treat premarital agreements more like ordinary contracts, resulting in a growing emphasis on contractual freedom over contractual fairness.

Key Terms

Premarital Agreements	Freedom of Contract	Substantive Fairness	Postmarital
Consideration	Unconscionability	Second Glance	Agreements
Statute of Frauds	Procedural Fairness	Doctrine	

Review Questions

1. What is a premarital contract?
2. Why would someone enter into one?
3. In what ways are premarital contracts treated differently from ordinary contracts?
4. Why are they treated differently?
5. What might a court look to in determining procedural fairness?
6. What might a court look to in determining substantive fairness?
7. What is the "second glance" doctrine?
8. How are the concepts of procedural and substantive fairness interrelated?
9. What direction are courts moving in with respect to reviewing premarital contracts? What considerations underlie this shift?
10. What kinds of provisions do couples typically include in a prenuptial agreement?
11. What is the general approach that courts take with respect to each type of provision?
12. What are postnuptial contracts? How do they different from premarital agreements?

Discussion Questions

1. In the event of a dispute over the enforcement of a premarital contract, do you think the agreement should be treated like an ordinary contract or do you think the court should review it for procedural unfairness? For substantive unfairness? Why or why not?
2. If you were planning to get married, would you want to enter into a premarital contract? Why or

why not? What kinds of considerations would you take into account? How would you feel if the person you were intending to marry insisted on entry into a premarital agreement? In formulating your answer, think about the economic as well as the emotional issues.

Assignments

1. Answer the following questions based on the law of your jurisdiction:
   • What is required for premarital agreements to be enforceable? For example, what kind of disclosure is required?
   • What is the applicable standard of review for premarital agreements? Are they treated like ordinary contracts?
   • Do courts consider procedural fairness when reviewing these agreements? Substantive fairness?

   • Will courts take a "second glance" at any of the terms of the agreement to see if they are fair at the time of execution? How is the concept of fairness defined?
2. Building on the Sample Questions for Compiling a Schedule of Assets form earlier in this chapter, develop a comprehensive intake form for use in an interview with a client who is coming to the office you work in to have a prenuptial agreement drafted.

Endnotes

1. Synonymous terms are "prenuptial agreement" and "antenuptial agreement." Note that the focus in this chapter is on premarital agreements, which are made in contemplation of divorce, not death. Agreements that spell out rights upon the death of one or both spouses generally have been accepted by the courts because there are no countervailing policy considerations.
2. 233 So. 2d 381 (Fla. 1970).
3. 525 Pa. 392, 581 A.2d 162 (1990).
4. *Id*. at 167.

5. For further detail on other types of provisions, *see* Jonathan E. Fields, Forbidden Provisions in Prenuptial Agreements: Legal and Practical Considerations for the Matrimonial Lawyer, 21 J. Am. Acad. Matrimonial Law. 413 (2008).
6. Sean Hannon Williams, Postnuptial Agreements, 2007 Wis. L. Rev. 827. *See also* M. Neil Browne and Katherine S. Fister, The Intriguing Potentials of Postnuptial Contract Modifications, 23 Hastings Women's L.J. 187 (2012).
7. Williams, *supra* note 6, at 828.

Chapter Three

Domestic Violence

All states have enacted laws that enable victims of **domestic violence** (also referred to as **domestic abuse** or **intimate partner violence**) to obtain civil orders of protection from abuse. These laws came about largely as a result of the women's movement, which focused public attention on the extent and seriousness of violence directed toward women by their male partners. Insisting that partner violence was not simply a private matter, activists successfully campaigned for laws that would allow victims to seek legal protection from abuse.

Domestic Violence: Abusive behavior toward someone with whom one is in a dating, familial, household, or intimate relationship

These laws are the focus of this chapter. To put them into context, we first briefly examine the historical approach of the law to spousal abuse. This history reveals a tradition of support for a husband's right of physical authority over his wife; however, it also reveals challenges to the social acceptance of male physical dominance over their spouses.[1]

The Traditional Approach: A Brief History

The Roman law of marriage required that "married women . . . conform themselves entirely to the temper of their husbands and the husbands to rule their wives as necessary and inseparable possessions."[2] Charged with the responsibility of maintaining domestic order, a husband with an "unruly" wife was considered derelict in his obligations.

The right of a husband to use physical force against his wife was carried forward into English common law and then into early American law. As the legal head of the household, a husband was generally assumed to have a right to use the degree of force necessary to make his wife obey. Wives who disobeyed or displayed bad temper were blamed for causing the violent reaction in their husbands through their disregard for his authority.

This traditional understanding is captured by the following passage from an 1862 decision from North Carolina, in which the court denied the wife's divorce petition because she did not explain the circumstances giving rise to the blows administered by her husband, thus failing to prove they were not her fault:

> [W]e are of the opinion that it was necessary to state the circumstances under which the blow with the horse-whip, and the blows with the switch were given; for instance, what . . . had she done, or said to induce such violence on the part of the husband? . . .
>
> The wife must be subject to the husband. Every man must govern his household, and if by reason of an unruly temper, or an unbridled tongue, the wife persistently treats her husband with disrespect, and he submits to it, he . . . loses the respect of the other members of his family, without which he cannot expect to govern them. . . . It follows that the law gives the husband power to use such a degree of force as is necessary to make the wife behave herself and know her place. . . . [S]o that there are circumstances under which a husband may strike his wife with a horse-whip or may strike her several times with a switch, so hard as to leave marks on her person, and these acts do not furnish sufficient grounds for divorce.[3]

The court here draws a distinction between "justifiable" and unjustifiable beatings, thus indicating that the law did not grant husbands unlimited authority over their wives. Beatings that were "unprovoked" by the wife, or involved more force than necessary to secure her obedience, might furnish grounds for a divorce on the basis of cruelty, or possibly subject a husband to criminal prosecution.

Although the idea that a husband had the right to use force against his wife gradually lost its force, courts were nonetheless loathe to intervene in what was largely regarded as a private matter that spouses should work out on their own. This framing of domestic violence as a personal matter outside the reach of the law was challenged in the 1960s by women's rights activists, who insisted that the law recognize that battering, as it came to be called, was anchored in the history of male domestic authority over women. Seeking to reallocate this historical imbalance of power, they successfully called for states to adopt **abuse prevention laws.**

Abuse Prevention Laws: Laws that enable domestic violence victims to obtain emergency protective orders

Before looking at these laws, it is important to recognize that domestic violence remains a serious problem. Although the rate of "non-fatal intimate partner violence" has been declining steadily since the mid-1990s, the gendered nature of partner violence has remained largely unchanged. According to U.S. Department of Justice figures, between 1994 and 2010, "about 4 in 5 victims of intimate partner violence were female."[4]

Obtaining Civil Orders of Protection Under Abuse Prevention Laws

To understand generally how abuse protection laws work, it is helpful to consider a number of basic questions. These questions can also be used to analyze the provisions of an individual state's law. They include the following:

- What kinds of relationships qualify for a protective order?
- What kinds of harm entitle a victim to obtain a protective order?
- What kinds of protection are available?
- What is the process for obtaining an order?
- How is the order enforced?

Protective Order:
A court order to protect the victim from harm; although civil in nature, violation of these orders is a criminal offense in many states

These questions will guide our discussion, but keep in mind that the precise answers vary from state to state.

Qualifying Relationships

Abuse prevention laws are intended to provide protection to persons who are being abused by someone with whom they have an intimate, family, or familylike relationship. When parties are in a more distant relationship, such as that of neighbor or coworker protection cannot usually be obtained through an abuse prevention law, although other remedies, such as a criminal action, may be available. In addition, a number of states now have harassment laws that permit an individual who is being harassed to seek a civil **harassment order** without the requirement of a special qualifying relationship.

Harassment Order:
A civil order that can be obtained by an individual who is being harassed without the requirement of a special qualifying relationship

However, the trend is in favor of expanding the pool of parties against whom an individual may seek a protective order. For example, some states allow a protective order to be obtained against the current spouse of one's ex-spouse, while some allow a party who is assisting a victim of violence to obtain an order against the abuser despite the lack of a direct relationship. Going well beyond this, a few states have eliminated the relationship requirement altogether; however, the available protections may be more limited if the parties are not in a "qualifying" type of relationship.

The statutes in some states are fairly comprehensive and allow someone to seek protection from abuse by a range of persons with whom they have a "special" relationship. An inclusive statute might permit someone to seek protection from:

- a spouse or former spouse;
- a cohabiting partner or former cohabiting partner (but some statutes frame this category more broadly to include all household members even if there is no family or intimate relationship);

- family members related by blood and possibly by marriage;
- a dating or an intimate partner (a topic discussed next);
- a party with whom one has a child in common, regardless of whether there is or has been an ongoing relationship.

As states have sought to determine which relationships should qualify for protection, some tension has existed around the inclusion of dating relationships and same-sex couples, which, of course, can be overlapping categories.

Dating Relationships

At first, abuse prevention laws did not address dating violence, which was not considered to be a serious or common problem. However, as it became increasingly apparent that intimate partner abuse is not limited to marital or cohabiting relationships, but also occurs within the context of dating relationships, many states amended their abuse protection laws to include individuals in dating or engagement relationships. Some statutes refer simply to dating relationships, while others impose specific definitional requirements, such as that the relationship be substantial in nature and/or one that is sexually intimate. These kinds of definitional limitations seek to make clear that an individual may not seek protection from someone who is a friend or work associate.

Teen Dating Relationships. Teen dating violence raises some particular concerns. To begin with, adults may discount the potential gravity of the situation based on the view that romantic relationships between teenagers are not very serious and can easily be ended.[5] However, there is an increased awareness of the extent and seriousness of teen dating violence, and the fact that teen girls who are in an abusive dating relationship are at particular risk for compounding problems, including eating disorders, drug and alcohol abuse, and suicidality.[6]

Teens also face legal barriers that adults usually do not have to contend with. First, if a statute excludes dating relationships altogether or limits them to adult dating relationships, most teens will not be able to obtain a protective order unless they are in another qualifying relationship, such as when they are seeking protection from a family member or the father of a "child in common." Second, if there is a "sexual intimacy" requirement, it is possible that a teen dating relationship will not qualify. Moreover, even if a teen is sexually active within the meaning of the statute, she may be more reluctant than an adult would be to share this with a judge. This is particularly likely to be true if a parent has accompanied her to court. Third, many statutes do not permit a minor to seek a protective order on his or her own, but require that it be filed on the minor's behalf by a parent or other responsible adult. Alternatively, a statute might permit a minor to file for a protective order on his or her own, but then require the court to notify the minor's parents that he or she has done so. Although the involvement of a parent or other caring adult can provide a minor with much-needed support, these adult involvement requirements may deter some teens from seeking help due to a sense of shame or the need to keep their dating relationship a secret. Also, some statutes do not permit a party to obtain an order of protection from an abuser who is under the age of 18, thus significantly limiting the availability of protection to teens who are in peer dating relationships. Finally, in addition to facing age-based obstacles to obtaining relief, teens who are in an abusive dating relationship with a same-sex partner may well face another separate set of barriers based on their sexual orientation.

Same-Sex Couples

Intimate partner violence is not limited to heterosexual couples; however, the law has been slower to respond to victims who experience violence within the context of same-sex relationships. In large part, this reflects the legal system's traditional reluctance to take same-sex relationships seriously. Additional complicating factors include fear within the gay and lesbian community that disclosure of abuse within same-sex relationships will exacerbate existing negative stereotypes, and an apprehension that judges will not respond to these cases with the seriousness and sensitivity that they merit.

Abuse prevention laws take a variety of approaches toward same-sex couples. A few statutes expressly limit the availability of the law to "opposite-sex couples." However, the continued validity of this approach has certainly been thrown into question by the Supreme Court's recent marriage equality decision (see Chapter 1). At the other end of the continuum, some expressly extend protections to same-sex couples, thus formally equalizing the treatment of same-sex and heterosexual relationships. In many states, however, the abuse prevention law does not either expressly include or expressly exclude same-sex couples; accordingly, where an abuse victim can demonstrate that he or she is in a qualifying relationship, there should not be doubt about the applicability of the law.

Covered Conduct

What types of abusive behavior trigger eligibility for protection? There is less variability here than there is with respect to who is entitled to seek protection, but some statutes are more comprehensive than others and include types of conduct, such as the malicious destruction of property, that are usually not covered by abuse prevention laws. The following discussion focuses on the kinds of behaviors that are covered in most states.

Most often, petitioners are seeking protection from *physical abuse*, and all states authorize the issuance of protective orders in this situation. Protection usually can also be sought for *attempted physical harm*, such as where someone throws a rock at someone but misses. Most statutes also cover *threatened physical harm*. Generally, a petitioner must show that he or she was placed in fear of imminent bodily harm — the definition of criminal assault. However, as a practical matter, some judges are reluctant to issue orders for threats of harm in the absence of a history of physical abuse. This reluctance can put a victim at great risk because threats often escalate into violence; for instance, research indicates that up to 50 percent of battered women who are murdered by their partners had previously been threatened with death.[7]

Some states also authorize relief for *emotional* or *verbal abuse*, which does not involve threats of physical harm, although these provisions are less common. Courts tend to interpret these provisions narrowly, and may, for instance, grant relief only where there has been a prior history of abuse or where an intent to harm can be inferred from accompanying conduct. An order may also be based on *stalking* (see the section entitled "Supplementing the Enforcement Process: Criminal Anti-Stalking Laws," later in this chapter).

Orders also may be granted based on *harassment* or *interference with an individual's liberty*, although many states do not recognize these as separate qualifying behaviors, but subsume them into another category of harm, such as threatened physical harm. Harassment has been defined to include a range of conduct, such as preventing a person from leaving a room, pulling the telephone out of the wall or cutting the wires, or slashing the tires of someone's car. Based on an understanding of domestic violence as an expression of power, some commentators have pushed for an expanded recognition of these types of harm in order to fully account for the complex array of strategies that abusers use to gain control over a partner's or former partner's life.[8]

Many statutes also expressly authorize the granting of protective orders based on sexual assault. In states where sexual assault is not specifically mentioned, judges are likely to include this conduct in their working definition of physical abuse. *Sexual assault* is generally understood to involve coercing someone to engage in sexual relations against his or her will through force, threats of force, or, possibly, duress, such as where someone says, "If you do not have sex with me, you'll never see your children again." In such cases, the consent is negated by the coercion.

Available Remedies

Most abuse prevention laws authorize a fairly broad range of specific remedies, including a "catchall" provision that allows a judge to tailor the remedy to the circumstances of the case before him or her. In this section, we look at the generally available remedies.

Before doing so, however, a brief word is in order about a supplemental approach that has slowly been gaining traction in same states: turning to tort law as a way of obtaining compensation for injuries caused by domestic violence beyond what may be awarded under a state's abuse prevention law. In this regard, the ability to seek compensation for emotional pain and suffering may be of particular relevance. Highlighting this trend, according to one report, "the majority of interspousal tort actions involve domestic violence."[9]

A number of traditional tort actions are potentially available to domestic violence victims, depending, of course, on the circumstances of the case. These include assault and battery, false imprisonment, and the intentional infliction of emotional distress. In addition, a few states now recognize domestic violence as a distinct form of tortious conduct. This approach often provides a more generous statute of limitations than is typically available in tort actions, which can be particularly beneficial to domestic violence victims who, due to the fear of reprisal, may well delay the initiation of legal proceedings beyond the usual time limits.[10]

Refraining from Further Abuse

Judges in all states can enjoin the abusive party from engaging in conduct that places the victim at risk of harm. This is often expressed as a requirement that the abuser refrain from committing any further acts of abuse, as defined by the applicable abuse prevention law. This provision is commonly referred to as a **restraining order**. By itself, a restraining order does not usually prohibit contact between the parties; it simply prohibits abusive behavior.

Restraining Order: A court order directing a perpetrator to refrain from committing further acts of domestic violence against the party seeking protection from abuse

Vacate and Stay-Away Orders

In most, if not all, states, a judge can issue a **vacate order**, which requires a batterer to leave the parties' home. In many instances, removal of the perpetrator is an important step in securing the safety of the abuse victim, but in other cases, this remedy is worth little because it leaves the victim living in a place that is known to the abuser. Thus, despite the fact that the law may require the perpetrator to depart the premises, safety concerns may force the victim to vacate the shared premises. The issuance of a vacate order does not affect the vacated party's title to the property.

Vacate Order: A court order requiring a perpetrator of domestic violence to move out of the home he or she shares with the party who has been abused

Stay-Away Order:
A court order requiring the perpetrator to keep away from the victim's home or from other places where the victim regularly goes

When the parties do not live together, a judge can issue a **stay-away order**, which requires the abuser to keep away from the victim's home. This stay-away order can be supplemented by language that further requires the abuser to stay away from other places, such as the victim's place of work, her parents' house, and her neighborhood. Stay-away provisions can also be used to supplement a vacate order.

No-Contact Orders

No-Contact Order:
A protective order that prohibits someone from having any contact with the party that he or she has abused

Most abuse prevention laws expressly authorize a judge to issue a **no-contact order**. Where not expressly authorized, a no-contact order can issue under a law's "catchall" provision. When drafted with care and specificity, no-contact orders can greatly enlarge the scope of available protection because they can be used to prohibit the abusive party from seeking any contact with the victim through any means or in any place. No-contact orders also can be drafted to prevent individuals who are acting on the abuser's behalf from contacting the victim.

Custody and Visitation

Most abuse prevention laws authorize judges to include temporary custody awards of minor children in a protective order. In some states, custody can be awarded only to the person seeking relief, while others employ a rebuttable presumption against awarding custody to the perpetrator of violence.

Some statutes permit a judge to fashion a temporary visitation order; however, recognizing that visitation often carries with it a serious risk of continued abuse, judges frequently impose specific conditions to help ensure the safety of the victim as well as the children, and in some states, this is statutorily required. Accordingly, supervised visitation may be ordered, or the parties may be required to drop off and pick up the children at the home of a third party or other neutral location, such as a police station or social service agency. Such arrangements may need to be made through an intermediary. By so structuring visitation, the need for contact between the parties is minimized, which, in turn, reduces the risk of continued abuse. Despite the availability of these preventive measures, some judges are reluctant to interfere with a parent's visitation rights and hesitate to impose restrictions except in the most egregious circumstances.

It is important to be aware that these custody and visitation orders are temporary in nature and may be superseded by orders entered in a subsequent divorce, custody, or separation proceeding. Moreover, if such an action is pending at the time a protective order is sought, the judge in the abuse action may be required to defer to this proceeding in matters of custody and visitation. If you are assisting someone who is seeking a restraining order, it is important to be aware of how the various statutory provisions governing custody and visitation interact in your jurisdiction. The interactive patterns are often complex and can result in conflicting orders that must be properly prioritized so the controlling order can be determined. The failure to do this can leave a client unprotected and at risk of violating a court order that has been superseded by a subsequent one.

Protection of Pets

Based on studies documenting the close connection between domestic violence and cruelty to animals, as well as a growing awareness that a victim of domestic violence may be reluctant to leave an abusive relationship based on fears for the safety of pets they may be forced to leave behind, starting with the state of Maine in 2006, a growing number of jurisdictions have amended their abuse protection laws to provide for the safety and well-being of household pets. Most commonly, these provisions allow a judge to order a defendant to stay away from and to refrain from abusing or injuring a pet and/or to grant the exclusive care, custody, and possession of the pet to the petitioner. In addition, some statutes now also define the term "domestic violence" to include the abuse of a pet.[11]

Support and Monetary Compensation

Most states authorize the inclusion of a temporary child support and/ or a temporary spousal support award in a protective order. However, even where allowed, some judges are reluctant to make support awards, perhaps believing that financial matters are best addressed in a divorce proceeding. The failure to provide financial support, whether through a statutory exclusion or a judicial omission, can compromise a battered woman's safety. If she is unable to provide for herself and her children, she may feel that she has no choice but to return to the abuser.

Distinct from support, most statutes enable a judge to order the abuser to compensate the victim for any financial loss suffered due to the abuse. Compensation might include out-of-pocket medical expenses, the repair or replacement of damaged property, lost wages, and moving costs. However, frequently fearful that the court action will provoke retaliation, many victims are reluctant to request relief not directly related to securing their safety and the safety of their children.

Treatment/Counseling

Although many experts in the field are at best cautiously optimistic about whether batterer intervention programs are effective in changing

Batterer Intervention Program:
A treatment or counseling program that works specifically with abusers

behavior, most abuse prevention laws authorize a judge to order an abuser to participate in a treatment or counseling program that works specifically with batterers. **Batterer intervention programs**, as they are generally called, usually target men who abuse female intimate partners, but some now provide services to women who abuse their male partners and to gay men and lesbians. A growing number of states have adopted mandatory guidelines that batterer intervention programs must follow. These guidelines allow for state oversight of the quality and effectiveness of the program. Guidelines often relate to matters such as staff qualifications, intake and discharge procedures, and the intervention approach.

Unlike the previously discussed remedies, a judge may have the authority to order a party into a batterer intervention program only after a violation of the protective order has occurred. However, a judge may be able to *recommend* that an abuser seek help as part of the initial order. Where intervention is ordered rather than just recommended, the abuser's attendance is monitored, often by having the program send periodic reports back to the judge; if sessions are missed, the judge can impose sanctions.

Relinquishment of Firearms

The use of a firearm significantly increases the chance of a violent death. According to one study, "family and intimate assaults with firearms are 12 times more likely to result in death than non-firearm assaults."[12] In households where there is a history of domestic abuse, the presence of a gun increases the risk of murder by 20 times; this compares to the threefold increase in the risk of murder where a gun is present in a household but there is no history of abuse.[13]

Given these potentially deadly consequences, many abuse prevention laws now include gun (and other weapon) possession provisions that restrict an abuser's access to firearms and ammunition. In some states, the entry of a protective order based on specific criteria, such as that the abuser poses a credible threat to the safety of the petitioner, results in a mandatory prohibition on the possession of a firearm. More commonly, however, a judge is given the discretion to enter an order prohibiting the abuser from possessing a firearm. Additionally, some abuse prevention laws allow a judge to revoke the abuser's license to carry a firearm for the duration of the protective order.

Supplementing these state law provisions, in 1994, based on a recognition of the increased risk of lethality when domestic violence involves firearms, Congress, in addition to passing the Violence Against Women Act (discussed later in this chapter), amended the Federal Gun Control Act of 1968 to criminalize the possession of a firearm or ammunition by a party who is already subject to a qualifying restraining order.[14] In 1996, Congress further amended the Gun Control Act by approving the Domestic Violence

Offender Gun Ban, which makes it illegal for any person who has been convicted of a misdemeanor crime of domestic violence to possess a firearm.[15] Unlike the 1994 Act, which provides limited exceptions to the possession ban for certain governmental employees, such as police officers and military personnel who are required to carry a weapon as part of their official duties, this amendment does not contain any such exceptions. Accordingly, much to the chagrin of many gun rights advocates, it effectively disqualifies "people with domestic violence misdemeanor convictions from doing law enforcement or military work that requires carrying a gun."[16]

Statutory Obligations of Police Officers

Although not technically a form of relief, it should be pointed out that most abuse prevention laws impose specific obligations on police officers to assist victims of domestic violence. An officer may be required to provide a victim with information about obtaining an order, to arrange or provide transportation to a hospital or shelter, to remain on the scene until the threat of immediate danger has passed, and to assist the victim to collect his or her belongings. In some states, the police may be able to seize a batterer's weapons when they have cause to believe that continued possession exposes the victim to the risk of serious injury. As discussed in the section entitled "Enforcement of Protective Orders," later in this chapter, the police also play a role in serving and enforcing protective orders.

Court Procedure: Obtaining Protective Orders

Due to the urgent nature of domestic violence cases, the court process for obtaining protective orders is simpler and quicker than it is in most other kinds of cases. Filing a petition does not require a lawyer, and many petitioners successfully obtain orders on their own. However, it can be very helpful to have an advocate present. Unanticipated issues can arise in the course of a hearing, particularly if minor children are involved, that an advocate can help sort out. It can also be very frightening and possibly dangerous for a victim to face an abuser in court, especially where the perpetrator has threatened to take revenge if a court action is filed. An advocate can provide much-needed support and help ensure that the victim is not pressured into abandoning the action. It should be noted that the scope of what an advocate is permitted to do varies from state to state, and sometimes from judge to judge within an individual state.

This section provides a general step-by-step overview of the process for obtaining a protective order. Of course, the particulars vary from state to state, and local rules should always be consulted.

▪ Obtaining a Protective Order

> ### OUTLINE OF STEPS FOR OBTAINING A PROTECTIVE ORDER
>
> 1. The party seeking the order files a complaint with a supporting affidavit. A filing fee is usually not required.
> 2. In most cases, the complaint is heard on an *ex parte* basis.
> 3. A temporary protective order is issued. Depending on the jurisdiction, the date for the second hearing may be set at this time.
> 4. Service is made on the defendant.
> 5. At the second hearing, the original order may be extended, modified, or vacated. If extended, a date for its expiration is usually established.
> 6. Prior to the expiration of the protective order, the plaintiff may return to court to seek an extension.

Ex Parte:
A hearing that is held without prior notice to the other side due to the urgent nature of the proceeding or the harm that such notice would cause

Temporary Order:
An order made during the pendency of a legal proceeding; temporary orders are superseded by the judgment

The court process for obtaining a protective order usually takes place in two distinct stages. First, the person seeking protection (the petitioner) goes to the appropriate court and files a complaint for protection from abuse (Exhibit 3.1). Many jurisdictions also require a supporting affidavit. As part of the filing process, most states allow the petitioner to request that his or her address be kept confidential. The case is generally heard right away on an *ex parte* basis, which means that notice is not given to the other side. If the petitioner shows an imminent risk of danger or that there will be an imminent risk once the other side knows the action has been filed, the judge can issue a **temporary order** without notice to the other side. Some statutes limit the relief that is available at this stage to restraining and eviction orders and postpone consideration of matters such as custody, support, and counseling until the second hearing. Some judges limit the relief they will grant at this stage even if not so restricted by the applicable statute, a practice that concerns many advocates.

Because abuse frequently takes place on weekends or in the evening when courts are closed, most states have a procedure in place for obtaining after-hour emergency orders. An emergency judge might be available on a 24-hour on-call basis, or an official, such as a magistrate, might be empowered to issue after-hour orders. These orders generally are good only until the next business day.

Service must be made on the other side (the respondent). This is usually accomplished by a police officer or a sheriff. As a general rule, service must be made in hand, although statutes often permit alternative means of service under specified circumstances, such as allowing the papers to be

Exhibit 3.1
Request for Protective Order

DV-100	**Request for Domestic Violence Restraining Order**

Clerk stamps date here when form is filed.

You must also complete Form CLETS-001, Confidential CLETS Information, and give it to the clerk when you file this Request.

① Name of Person Asking for Protection:

_____ Age: _____

Your lawyer in this case *(if you have one)*:

Name: _____ State Bar No.: _____

Firm Name: _____

Address *(If you have a lawyer for this case, give your lawyer's information. If you do not have a lawyer and want to keep your home address private, give a different mailing address instead. You do not have to give your telephone, fax, or e-mail.):*

Address: _____

City: _____ State: _____ Zip: _____

Telephone: _____ Fax: _____

E-Mail Address: _____

Fill in court name and street address:

Superior Court of California, County of

Court fills in case number when form is filed.

Case Number:

② Name of Person You Want Protection From:

_____

Description of person you want protection from:

Sex: ☐ M ☐ F   Height: _____ Weight: _____ Hair Color: _____ Eye Color: _____

Race: _____ Age: _____ Date of Birth: _____

Address *(if known)*: _____

City: _____ State: _____ Zip: _____

③ Do you want an order to protect family or household members? ☐ Yes ☐ No

If yes, list them:

Full name	Sex	Age	Lives with you?	Relationship to you
_____	_____	_____	☐ Yes ☐ No	_____
_____	_____	_____	☐ Yes ☐ No	_____
_____	_____	_____	☐ Yes ☐ No	_____

☐ *Check here if you need more space. Attach a sheet of paper and write "DV-100, Protected People" for a title.*

④ What is your relationship to the person in ② ? *(Check all that apply):*

a. ☐ We are now married or registered domestic partners.
b. ☐ We used to be married or registered domestic partners.
c. ☐ We live together.
d. ☐ We used to live together.
e. ☐ We are related by blood, marriage, or adoption (specify relationship): _____
f. ☐ We are dating or used to date, or we are or used to be engaged to be married.
g. ☐ We are the parents together of a child or children under 18:

If you do not have one of these relationships, the court may not be able to consider your request. Read Form DV-500-INFO for help.

Child's Name: _____ Date of Birth: _____
Child's Name: _____ Date of Birth: _____
Child's Name: _____ Date of Birth: _____

☐ *Check here if you need more space. Attach a sheet of paper and write "DV-100, Protected People" for a title.*

h. ☐ We have signed a Voluntary Declaration of Paternity for our child or children. *(Attach a copy if you have one).*

This is not a Court Order.

Judicial Council of California, www.courts.ca.gov
Revised July 1, 2014, Mandatory Form
Family Code, § 6200 et seq.

Request for Domestic Violence Restraining Order
(Domestic Violence Prevention)

DV-100, Page 1 of 5
→

Exhibit 3.1 cont.

Case Number: _____

(5) Other Court Cases

a. Have you or any other person named in (3) been involved in another court case with the person in (2)?

☐ No ☐ Yes *If yes, check each kind of case and indicate where and when each was filed:*

Kind of Case	County or Tribe Where Filed	Year Filed	Case Number *(if known)*
☐ Divorce, Nullity, Legal Separation			
☐ Civil Harassment			
☐ Domestic Violence			
☐ Criminal			
☐ Juvenile, Dependency, Guardianship			
☐ Child Support			
☐ Parentage, Paternity			
☐ Other *(specify):*			

☐ *Check here if you need more space. Attach a sheet of paper and write "DV-100, Other Court Cases" for a title.*

b. Are there any domestic violence restraining/protective orders now (criminal, juvenile, family)?

☐ No ☐ Yes *If yes, attach a copy if you have one.*

Check the orders you want.

(6) ☐ Personal Conduct Orders

I ask the court to order the person in (2) not to do the following things to me or anyone listed in (3):

a. ☐ Harass, attack, strike, threaten, assault (sexually or otherwise), hit, follow, stalk, molest, destroy personal property, disturb the peace, keep under surveillance, impersonate (on the Internet, electronically or otherwise), or block movements

b. ☐ Contact, either directly or indirectly, in any way, including but not limited to, by telephone, mail or e-mail or other electronic means

The person in (2) will be ordered not to take any action to get the addresses or locations of any protected person unless the court finds good cause not to make the order.

(7) ☐ Stay-Away Order

a. I ask the court to order the person in (2) to stay at least _____ yards away from *(check all that apply):*

☐ Me   ☐ My vehicle
☐ My home   ☐ The child(ren)'s school or child care
☐ My job or workplace   ☐ Each person listed in (3)
☐ My school   ☐ Other *(specify):* _____

b. If the person listed in (2) is ordered to stay away from all the places listed above, will he or she still be able to get to his or her home, school, job, workplace, or vehicle? ☐ Yes ☐ No *(If no, explain):*

_____

(8) ☐ Move-Out Order

(If the person in (2) lives with you and you want that person to stay away from your home, you must ask for this move-out order.)

I ask the court to order the person in (2) to move out from and not return to *(address):*

_____

I have the right to live at the above address because (explain): _____

_____

This is not a Court Order.

Exhibit 3.1 cont.

Case Number: _____

⑨ Guns or Other Firearms or Ammunition

I believe the person in ② owns or possesses guns, firearms, or ammunition. ☐ Yes ☐ No ☐ I don't know

If the judge approves the order, the person in ② will be ordered not to own, possess, purchase, or receive a firearm or ammunition. The person will be ordered to sell to, or store with, a licensed gun dealer, or turn in to law enforcement, any guns or firearms that he or she owns or possesses.

⑩ ☐ Record Unlawful Communications

I ask for the right to record communications made to me by the person in ② that violate the judge's orders.

⑪ ☐ Care of Animals

I ask for the sole possession, care, and control of the animals listed below. I ask the court to order the person in ② to stay at least _____ yards away from and not take, sell, transfer, encumber, conceal, molest, attack, strike, threaten, harm, or otherwise dispose of the following animals: _____

_____

I ask for the animals to be with me because: _____

_____

⑫ ☐ Child Custody and Visitation

a. ☐ I do not have a child custody or visitation order and I want one.

b. ☐ I have a child custody or visitation order and I want it changed.

If you ask for orders, you must fill out and attach Form DV-105, Request for Child Custody and Visitation Orders.

You and the other parent may tell the court that you want to be legal parents of the children (use Form DV-180, Agreement and Judgment of Parentage).

⑬ ☐ Child Support *(Check all that apply):*

a. ☐ I do not have a child support order and I want one.

b. ☐ I have a child support order and I want it changed.

c. ☐ I now receive or have applied for TANF, Welfare, CalWORKS, or Medi-Cal.

If you ask for child support orders, you must fill out and attach Form FL-150, Income and Expense Declaration or Form FL-155, Financial Statement (Simplified).

⑭ ☐ Property Control

I ask the court to give ***only*** me temporary use, possession, and control of the property listed here:

_____

⑮ ☐ Debt Payment

I ask the court to order the person in ② to make these payments while the order is in effect:

☐ *Check here if you need more space. Attach a sheet of paper and write "DV-100, Debt Payment" for a title.*

Pay to: _____ For: _____ Amount: $ _____ Due date: _____

⑯ ☐ Property Restraint

I am married to or have a registered domestic partnership with the person in ②. I ask the judge to order that the person in ② not borrow against, sell, hide, or get rid of or destroy any possessions or property, except in the usual course of business or for necessities of life. I also ask the judge to order the person in ② to notify me of any new or big expenses and to explain them to the court.

This is not a Court Order.

Exhibit 3.1 cont.

Case Number: _____

17 ☐ **Spousal Support**

I am married to or have a registered domestic partnership with the person in ② and no spousal support order exists. I ask the court to order the person in ② to pay spousal support. *(You must complete, file, and serve Form FL-150, Income and Expense Declaration, before your hearing).*

18 ☐ **Insurance**

I ask the court to order the person in ② NOT to cash, borrow against, cancel, transfer, dispose of, or change the beneficiaries of any insurance or coverage held for the benefit of me or the person in ②, or our child(ren), for whom support may be ordered, or both.

19 ☐ **Lawyer's Fees and Costs**

I ask that the person in ② pay some or all of my lawyer's fees and costs.
You must complete, file, and serve Form FL-150, Income and Expense Declaration, before your hearing.

20 ☐ **Payments for Costs and Services**

I ask the court to order the person in ② to pay the following:
You can ask for lost earnings or your costs for services caused directly by the person in ② (damaged property, medical care, counseling, temporary housing, etc.). You must bring proof of these expenses to your hearing.

Pay to: _____ For: _____ Amount: $ _____

Pay to: _____ For: _____ Amount: $ _____

21 ☐ **Batterer Intervention Program**

I ask the court to order the person listed in ② to go to a 52-week batterer intervention program and show proof of completion to the court.

22 ☐ **Other Orders**

What other orders are you asking for? _____

_____

_____

☐ *Check here if you need more space. Attach a sheet of paper and write "DV-100, Other Orders" for a title.*

23 ☐ **Time for Service (Notice)**

The papers must be personally served on the person in ② at least five days before the hearing, unless the court orders a shorter time for service. If you want there to be fewer than five days between service and the hearing, explain why below. For help, read Form DV-200-INFO, "What Is Proof of Personal Service"?

_____

_____

_____

24 **No Fee to Serve (Notify) Restrained Person**

If you want the sheriff or marshal to serve (notify) the restrained person about the orders for free, ask the court clerk what you need to do.

25 **Court Hearing**

The court will schedule a hearing on your request. If the judge does not make the orders effective right away ("temporary restraining orders"), the judge may still make the orders after the hearing. If the judge does not make the orders effective right away, you can ask the court to cancel the hearing. Read Form DV-112, *Waiver of Hearing on Denied Request for Temporary Restraining Order*, for more information.

This is not a Court Order.

Exhibit 3.1 cont.

Case Number: _____

(26) Describe Abuse

Describe how the person in ② abused you. Abuse means to intentionally or recklessly cause or attempt to cause bodily injury to you; or to place you or another person in reasonable fear of imminent serious bodily injury; or to harass, attack, strike, threaten, assault (sexually or otherwise), hit, follow, stalk, molest, keep you under surveillance, impersonate (on the Internet, electronically or otherwise), batter, telephone, or contact you; or to disturb your peace; or to destroy your personal property. (For a complete definition, see Fam. Code, §§ 6203, 6320.)

a. Date of most recent abuse: _____

b. Who was there? _____

c. Describe how the person in ② abused you or your child(ren): _____

☐ *Check here if you need more space. Attach a sheet of paper and write "DV-100, Recent Abuse" for a title.*

d. Did the person in ② use or threaten to use a gun or any other weapon? ☐ No ☐ Yes *(If yes, describe):*

e. Describe any injuries: _____

f. Did the police come? ☐ No ☐ Yes
If yes, did they give you or the person in ② an Emergency Protective Order? ☐ Yes ☐ No ☐ I don't know *Attach a copy if you have one.*
The order protects ☐ you or ☐ the person in ②

g. **Has the person in ② abused you (or your child(ren)) other times?**
If yes, ☐ check here and use *Form DV-101*, Description of Abuse *or describe any previous abuse on an attached sheet of paper and write "DV-100, Previous Abuse" for a title.*

(27) Other Persons to Be Protected

The persons listed in item ③ need an order for protection because *(describe):* _____

(28) Number of pages attached to this form, if any: _____

I declare under penalty of perjury under the laws of the State of California that the information above is true and correct.

Date: _____

_____
Type or print your name

▶ _____
Sign your name

Date: _____

_____
Lawyer's name, if you have one

▶ _____
Lawyer's signature

This is not a Court Order.

Revised July 1, 2014   **Request for Domestic Violence Restraining Order** (Domestic Violence Prevention)   **DV-100**, Page 5 of 5

left at the last and usual address when attempts at personal service have failed. As a general rule, the *ex parte* orders are not considered to be in effect until service has been made. In addition to being given a copy of the complaint and any *ex parte* orders, the respondent must be informed of the right to be heard in court. In some states, a second hearing date is set at the *ex parte* hearing, usually for somewhere between 10 to 20 days later, and the initial orders are only good until then. In other states, the second hearing date is not set by the court but must be requested by the responding party, who has a right to be heard promptly. Here, the *ex parte* orders remain in effect until the second hearing is held; if a hearing is not requested, they remain in effect until a judicially selected or a statutory expiration date is reached.

The next stage is the second hearing, at which both parties are given the opportunity to present their version of what took place. After hearing the evidence, the judge can either extend or decline to extend the original orders for an additional period of time. The judge can also address any matters that may have been left unresolved at the *ex parte* stage, such as support. Most states allow orders to be extended for up to at least one year, although the trend is in favor of longer extension periods, and a few states do not impose any mandatory durational limits. (For an example of an abuse prevention order, see Exhibit 3.2.) Most states allow the petitioner to return to court to seek an extension before the orders issued at the second hearing expire. An extension generally can be granted based on a credible fear of renewed harm — acts of violence do not need to have been committed while the order was in effect.

Although the practice has drawn considerable criticism and has been prohibited in a number of jurisdictions, some judges are inclined to grant **mutual orders of protection** at the second hearing whereby each party is ordered to refrain from harming the other, despite the fact that only one party has requested relief. By suggesting that both persons are responsible for the violence, mutual orders fail to hold abusers accountable for their behavior. They can also create enforcement problems for police responding to a call for assistance because each party can claim that he or she is the protected one and that the other should be arrested. Additionally, a mutual order can adversely affect the petitioner in a subsequent custody or visitation dispute in which the court is directed to consider the existence of prior protective orders when making an award because both parties will appear to be equally responsible for the violence. (See the discussion later in this chapter regarding the Violence Against Women Act and mutual restraining orders.)

Where the responding party fails to appear at the second hearing, many courts will continue the order based on the evidence presented by the petitioner, and in some states, this result is mandated by statute. In other states, a bench warrant may be issued to secure the respondent's appearance. In some states, if the petitioner fails to appear, the action

Mutual Orders of Protection: Granted by some courts to both parties where only one party has sought court intervention

Exhibit 3.2
Abuse Prevention
Order

DV-110 **Temporary Restraining Order**	Clerk stamps date here when form is filed.

Person in ① must complete items ①, ②, and ③ only.

① Name of Protected Person:

_____

Your lawyer in this case *(if you have one):*

Name: _____ State Bar No.: _____

Firm Name: _____

Address *(If you have a lawyer for this case, give your lawyer's information. If you do not have a lawyer and want to keep your home address private, give a different mailing address instead. You do not have to give your telephone, fax, or e-mail.):*

Fill in court name and street address:

Superior Court of California, County of

Address: _____

City: _____ State: ____ Zip: _____

Telephone: _____ Fax: _____

E-mail Address: _____

Court fills in case number when form is filed.

Case Number:

② Name of Restrained Person:

_____

Description of restrained person:

Sex: ☐ M ☐ F   Height: _____   Weight: _____   Hair Color: _____   Eye Color: _____

Race: _____   Age: ____   Date of Birth: _____

Address *(if known):* _____

City: _____   State: _____   Zip: _____

Relationship to protected person: _____

③ ☐ Additional Protected Persons

In addition to the person named in ①, the following persons are protected by temporary orders as indicated in items ⑥ and ⑦ *(family or household members):*

Full name	Relationship to person in ①	Sex	Age

☐ *Check here if there are additional protected persons. List them on an attached sheet of paper and write, "DV-110, Additional Protected Persons" as a title.*

The court will complete the rest of this form.

④ Court Hearing

This order expires at the end of the hearing stated below:

Hearing Date: _____   Time: _____   ☐ a.m. ☐ p.m.

This is a Court Order.

Judicial Council of California, www.courts.ca.gov
Revised July 1, 2014, Mandatory Form
Family Code, § 6200 et seq.
Approved by DOJ

Temporary Restraining Order
(CLETS—TRO)
(Domestic Violence Prevention)

DV-110, Page 1 of 6
→

Exhibit 3.2 cont.

Case Number: _____

---

5 ☐ **Criminal Protective Order**

    a. ☐ A criminal protective order on Form CR-160, *Criminal Protective Order—Domestic Violence,* is in effect.
        Case Number: _____ County: _____ Expiration Date: _____

    b. ☐ No information has been provided to the judge about a criminal protective order.

To the person in ❷

The court has granted the temporary orders checked below. If you do not obey these orders, you can be arrested and charged with a crime. You may be sent to jail for up to one year, pay a fine of up to $1,000, or both.

6 **Personal Conduct Orders**   ☐ **Not requested**   ☐ **Denied until the hearing**   ☐ **Granted as follows:**

    a. You must **not** do the following things to the person in ① and ☐ persons in ③ :

       ☐ Harass, attack, strike, threaten, assault *(sexually or otherwise),* hit, follow, stalk, molest, destroy personal property, disturb the peace, keep under surveillance, impersonate *(on the Internet, electronically or otherwise),* or block movements

       ☐ Contact, either directly or indirectly, in any way, including but not limited to, by telephone, mail, e-mail or other electronic means

       ☐ Take any action, directly or through others, to obtain the addresses or locations of the persons in ① and ③. *(If this item is not checked, the court has found good cause not to make this order.)*

    b. Peaceful written contact through a lawyer or process server or another person for service of Form DV-120 *(Response to Request for Domestic Violence Restraining Order)* or other legal papers related to a court case is allowed and does not violate this order.

    c. ☐ Exceptions: Brief and peaceful contact with the person in ①, and peaceful contact with children in ③, as required for court-ordered visitation of children, is allowed unless a criminal protective order says otherwise.

7 **Stay-Away Order**   ☐ **Not requested**   ☐ **Denied until the hearing**   ☐ **Granted as follows:**

    a. You **must** stay at least *(specify):* _____ yards away from *(check all that apply):*

       ☐ The person in ①   ☐ School of person in ①
       ☐ The persons in ③   ☐ The children's school or child care
       ☐ Home of person in ①   ☐ Other *(specify):* _____
       ☐ The job or workplace of person in ①   _____
       ☐ Vehicle of person in ①   _____

    b. ☐ Exceptions: Brief and peaceful contact with the person in ①, and peaceful contact with children in ③, as required for court-ordered visitation of children, is allowed unless a criminal protective order says otherwise.

8 **Move-Out Order**   ☐ **Not requested**   ☐ **Denied until the hearing**   ☐ **Granted as follows:**

    You must take only personal clothing and belongings needed until the hearing and move out immediately from *(address):* _____

This is a Court Order.

Revised July 1, 2014   **Temporary Restraining Order**   DV-110, Page 2 of 6
                                (CLETS—TRO)   →
                        (Domestic Violence Prevention)

Exhibit 3.2 cont.

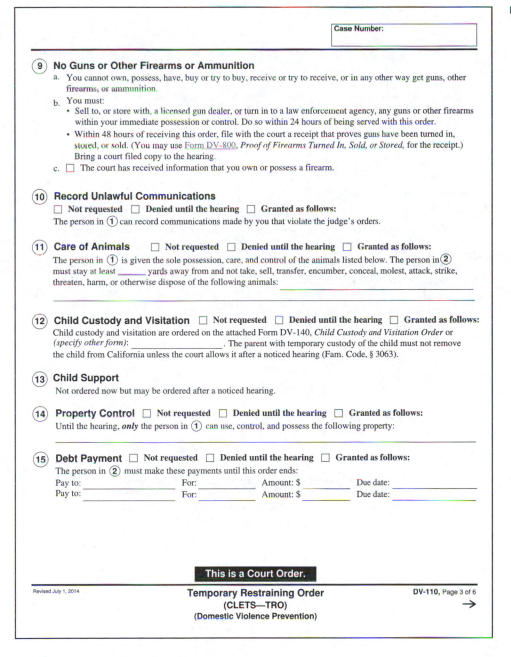

Case Number: _____

⑨ No Guns or Other Firearms or Ammunition

a. You cannot own, possess, have, buy or try to buy, receive or try to receive, or in any other way get guns, other firearms, or ammunition.

b. You must:
- Sell to, or store with, a licensed gun dealer, or turn in to a law enforcement agency, any guns or other firearms within your immediate possession or control. Do so within 24 hours of being served with this order.
- Within 48 hours of receiving this order, file with the court a receipt that proves guns have been turned in, stored, or sold. (You may use Form DV-800, *Proof of Firearms Turned In, Sold, or Stored,* for the receipt.) Bring a court filed copy to the hearing.

c. ☐ The court has received information that you own or possess a firearm.

⑩ Record Unlawful Communications
☐ **Not requested** ☐ **Denied until the hearing** ☐ **Granted as follows:**
The person in ① can record communications made by you that violate the judge's orders.

⑪ Care of Animals ☐ **Not requested** ☐ **Denied until the hearing** ☐ **Granted as follows:**
The person in ① is given the sole possession, care, and control of the animals listed below. The person in ② must stay at least _____ yards away from and not take, sell, transfer, encumber, conceal, molest, attack, strike, threaten, harm, or otherwise dispose of the following animals: _____
_____

⑫ Child Custody and Visitation ☐ **Not requested** ☐ **Denied until the hearing** ☐ **Granted as follows:**
Child custody and visitation are ordered on the attached Form DV-140, *Child Custody and Visitation Order* or *(specify other form)*: _____ . The parent with temporary custody of the child must not remove the child from California unless the court allows it after a noticed hearing (Fam. Code, § 3063).

⑬ Child Support
Not ordered now but may be ordered after a noticed hearing.

⑭ Property Control ☐ **Not requested** ☐ **Denied until the hearing** ☐ **Granted as follows:**
Until the hearing, *only* the person in ① can use, control, and possess the following property: _____
_____

⑮ Debt Payment ☐ **Not requested** ☐ **Denied until the hearing** ☐ **Granted as follows:**
The person in ② must make these payments until this order ends:
Pay to: _____ For: _____ Amount: $ _____ Due date: _____
Pay to: _____ For: _____ Amount: $ _____ Due date: _____

This is a Court Order.

Revised July 1, 2014

Temporary Restraining Order
(CLETS—TRO)
(Domestic Violence Prevention)

DV-110, Page 3 of 6
→

Exhibit 3.2 cont.

Case Number:

(16) Property Restraint ☐ Not requested ☐ Denied until the hearing ☐ Granted as follows:

If the people in ① and ② are married to each other or are registered domestic partners,

☐ the person in ① ☐ the person in ② must not transfer, borrow against, sell, hide, or get rid of or destroy any property, including animals, except in the usual course of business or for necessities of life. In addition, each person must notify the other of any new or big expenses and explain them to the court. *(The person in ② cannot contact the person in ① if the court has made a "no contact" order.)*

Peaceful written contact through a lawyer or a process server or other person for service of legal papers related to a court case is allowed and does not violate this order.

(17) Spousal Support

Not ordered now but may be ordered after a noticed hearing.

(18) Insurance

☐ The person in ① ☐ the person in ② is ordered NOT to cash, borrow against, cancel, transfer, dispose of, or change the beneficiaries of any insurance or coverage held for the benefit of the parties, or their child(ren), if any, for whom support may be ordered, or both.

(19) Lawyer's Fees and Costs

Not ordered now but may be ordered after a noticed hearing.

(20) Payments for Costs and Services

Not ordered now but may be ordered after a noticed hearing.

(21) Batterer Intervention Program

Not ordered now but may be ordered after a noticed hearing.

(22) Other Orders ☐ Not requested ☐ Denied until the hearing ☐ Granted as follows:

_____

_____

☐ *Check here if there are additional orders. List them on an attached sheet of paper and write "DV-110, Other Orders" as a title.*

(23) No Fee to Serve (Notify) Restrained Person

If the sheriff serves this order, he or she will do so for free.

Date: _____   _____

Judge (or Judicial Officer)

Warnings and Notices to the Restrained Person in ②

If You Do Not Obey This Order, You Can Be Arrested And Charged With a Crime.

• If you do not obey this order, you can go to jail or prison and/or pay a fine.

• It is a felony to take or hide a child in violation of this order.

• If you travel to another state or to tribal lands or make the protected person do so, with the intention of disobeying this order, you can be charged with a federal crime.

This is a Court Order.

Revised July 1, 2014

Temporary Restraining Order
(CLETS—TRO)
(Domestic Violence Prevention)

DV-110, Page 4 of 6

→

Exhibit 3.2 cont.

Case Number:

You Cannot Have Guns, Firearms, And/Or Ammunition.

You cannot own, have, possess, buy or try to buy, receive or try to receive, or otherwise get guns, other firearms, and/or ammunition while the order is in effect. If you do, you can go to jail and pay a $1,000 fine. You must sell to or store with a licensed gun dealer or turn in to a law enforcement agency any guns or other firearms that you have or control. The judge will ask you for proof that you did so. If you do not obey this order, you can be charged with a crime. Federal law says you cannot have guns or ammunition while the order is in effect.

Service of Order by Mail

If the judge makes a restraining order at the hearing, which has the same orders as in this form, you will get a copy of that order by mail at your last known address, which is written in ②. If this address is incorrect, or to find out if the orders were made permanent, contact the court.

Child Custody, Visitation, and Support

• **Child custody and visitation:** If you do not go to the hearing, the judge can make custody and visitation orders for your children without hearing from you.

• **Child support:** The judge can order child support based on the income of both parents. The judge can also have that support taken directly from a parent's paycheck. Child support can be a lot of money, and usually you have to pay until the child is age 18. File and serve a *Financial Statement (Simplified)* (Form FL-155) or an *Income and Expense Declaration* (Form FL-150) if you want the judge to have information about your finances. Otherwise, the court may make support orders without hearing from you.

• **Spousal support:** File and serve an *Income and Expense Declaration* (Form FL-150) so the judge will have information about your finances. Otherwise, the court may make support orders without hearing from you.

Instructions for Law Enforcement

This order is effective when made. It is enforceable by any law enforcement agency that has received the order, is shown a copy of the order, or has verified its existence on the California Law Enforcement Telecommunications System (CLETS). If the law enforcement agency has not received proof of service on the restrained person, and the restrained person was not present at the court hearing, the agency shall advise the restrained person of the terms of the order and then shall enforce it. Violations of this order are subject to criminal penalties.

Arrest Required if Order Is Violated

If an officer has probable cause to believe that the restrained person had notice of the order and has disobeyed the order, the officer must arrest the restrained person. (Penal Code, §§ 836(c)(1), 13701(b).) A violation of the order may be a violation of Penal Code section 166 or 273.6.

If the Protected Person Contacts the Restrained Person

Even if the protected person invites or consents to contact with the restrained person, the orders remain in effect and must be enforced. The protected person cannot be arrested for inviting or consenting to contact with the restrained person. The orders can be changed only by another court order. (Pen. Code, §13710(b).)

This is a Court Order.

Revised July 1, 2014

Temporary Restraining Order
(CLETS—TRO)
(Domestic Violence Prevention)

DV-110, Page 5 of 6

→

Exhibit 3.2 cont.

Case Number:

Conflicting Orders–Priorities for Enforcement

If more than one restraining order has been issued protecting the protected person from the restrained person, the orders must be enforced according to the following priorities (see Pen. Code, § 136.2, and Fam. Code, §§ 6383(h), 6405(b)):

1. *EPO:* If one of the orders is an *Emergency Protective Order* (Form EPO-001), and it is more restrictive than other restraining or protective orders, it has precedence in enforcement over all other orders.
2. *No-Contact Order:* If there is no EPO, a no-contact order that is included in a restraining or protective order has precedence in enforcement over any other restraining or protective order.
3. *Criminal Order:* If none of the orders includes a no-contact order, a domestic violence protective order issued in a criminal case takes precedence in enforcement over any conflicting civil court order. Any nonconflicting terms of the civil restraining order remain in effect and enforceable.
4. *Family, Juvenile, or Civil Order:* If more than one family, juvenile, or other civil restraining or protective order has been issued, the one that was issued last must be enforced.

Child Custody and Visitation

- The custody and visitation orders are on Form DV-140, items ③ and ④. They are sometimes also written on additional pages or referenced in DV-140 or other orders that are not part of the restraining order.
- **Forms DV-100 and DV-105 are not orders. Do not enforce them.**

Certificate of Compliance With VAWA

This temporary protective order meets all "full faith and credit" requirements of the Violence Against Women Act, 18 U.S.C. § 2265 (1994) (VAWA), upon notice of the restrained person. This court has jurisdiction over the parties and the subject matter; the restrained person has been or will be afforded notice and a timely opportunity to be heard as provided by the laws of this jurisdiction. **This order is valid and entitled to enforcement in each jurisdiction throughout the 50 states of the United States, the District of Columbia, all tribal lands, and all U.S. territories, commonwealths, and possessions and shall be enforced as if it were an order of that jurisdiction.**

(Clerk will fill out this part.)

—Clerk's Certificate—

Clerk's Certificate
[seal]

I certify that this *Temporary Restraining Order* is a true and correct copy of the original on file in the court.

Date: _____ Clerk, by _____ , Deputy

This is a Court Order.

may be automatically dismissed. Advocates for battered women have raised serious concerns about this approach because a victim's failure to appear at the second hearing may be the result of fear or intimidation, rather than the result of a voluntary decision not to proceed.

Enforcement of Protective Orders

If protective orders are to be worth more than the paper they are written on, effective enforcement is essential. Accordingly, although the orders themselves are civil in nature, violations can be prosecuted in the criminal justice system. Importantly, in most states, the act of violating an order is in and of itself a separate and independent crime. This is particularly valuable in situations where the violating behavior may not in and of itself be defined as an independent crime, such as where a party continually telephones the petitioner in violation of a no-contact order. However, most acts committed in violation of a protective order do constitute crimes (e.g., trespass, assault, battery, and false imprisonment), and the offending party can accordingly be prosecuted for any specific criminal acts, as well as for violating the order.

Until fairly recently, the criminal justice system did not take domestic abuse cases as seriously as other criminal matters, seeing them primarily as private family matters. Police officers were frequently reluctant to make arrests, and prosecutors often used their discretion to drop cases, especially if the victim was at all ambivalent about proceeding, without first inquiring whether the reluctance stemmed from fear or coercion. Advocates for battered women began to press for change, demanding that intimate assaults be taken as seriously as other kinds of violence and not treated as inconsequential private spats.

Responding to these concerns, most states have adopted mandatory arrest policies that require police officers to arrest a suspect, without having to first obtain a warrant, whenever there is probable cause to believe that an act of domestic violence has occurred, regardless of whether the officer witnessed the incident or not. By requiring arrest, these laws are intended to remove police discretion.

However, in a great disappointment to domestic violence advocates, in 2005, in the case of Gonzales v. Castle Rock, the U.S. Supreme Court held that a victim does not have a constitutionally protected right to police enforcement of a restraining order. In this case, Jessica Gonzales sued the local police department after they ignored her calls that her husband had taken the couple's three daughters in violation of a restraining order. Tragically, he ended up murdering the three girls. Although the police ignored Colorado's mandatory arrest law, the Court concluded that Ms. Gonzales did not have a recognized "property" interest in the restraining order because, despite the "seemingly mandatory legislative command," police apparently maintained some discretion over the arrest decision.[17]

It should be noted that the Supreme Court's ruling was not the end of the matter. Following her loss at the nation's highest court, Jessica Lenahan (formerly Jessica Gonzales) became the first domestic violence survivor from the United States to bring her case before the Inter-American Court on Human Rights (IACHR). In a landmark ruling, the IACHR held that the failure of the government to protect Jessica and her children constituted a violation of their human rights. In addition to recommending that Ms. Lenahan and her family receive "full reparations" for their loss, the IACHR also recommended that the United States "adopt multifaceted legislation at the federal and state levels, or to reform existing legislation making mandatory the enforcement of protection orders and other precautionary measures to protect women [and children in the context of domestic violence] from imminent acts of violence, and to create effective implementation mechanisms."[18]

Similarly, many states have adopted mandatory prosecution (or no-drop) policies that enable a prosecutor to pursue a domestic violence case even if the victim does not want to proceed. Some states maintain what is often referred to as a "soft-drop" approach, which means that there is no consequence to the victim if she chooses not to cooperate with the prosecution. In contrast, in states with a "hard-drop" approach, a victim may face contempt proceedings if she opts not to testify against her abuser.

Although the adoption of mandatory arrest and prosecution policies clearly signifies that domestic violence is being taken more seriously by the criminal justice system, this approach is nonetheless quite controversial. Supporters of a mandatory approach worry that the traumatic effects of abuse and the fear of reprisal can compromise the ability of victims to make appropriate decisions that maximize their well-being. They further worry that the "ongoing humiliation and assaults of personhood may encourage women to believe that they are partially responsible for their partner's violence which may compromise their ability to judge their own best interests."[19] So viewed, the benefit of a mandatory approach is that it permits the state to intervene in situations where a victim might not act in accordance with her own safety needs.

On the other hand, many advocates for battered women believe that mandatory policies deprive victims of the right to make decisions for themselves based upon a personal and individualized assessment of their own needs and safety concerns. Critics worry that divesting a woman of decisional authority will "perpetuate the disempowerment of the victim by sending a message that she is too helpless to survive without the controlling direction of a stronger person."[20] Another concern is that mandatory policies may actually endanger the people they were intended to protect, as anger over an arrest and prosecution may prompt an abuser to seek revenge against a victim, who, had she been given a choice, might have decided that it was too risky to seek the assistance of the criminal justice system.[21]

Supplementing the Enforcement Process: Criminal Anti-Stalking Laws

In 1990, California enacted the nation's first anti-stalking law following the murder of actress Rebecca Schaeffer, the star of a popular sitcom — *My Sister Sam* — by a fan who had pursued her for over two years. Since then, in recognition of the fact that stalking is a serious problem that potentially effects upward of 3 million people a year, all states have enacted criminal anti-stalking laws. Supplementing these laws, in 2006, Congress enacted the Interstate Stalking Punishment and Prevention Act, which makes it a federal crime to travel across state lines for the purpose of stalking someone.[22]

Although it was a celebrity murder that focused public attention on the dangers of stalking, about 85 percent of stalking victims are "ordinary" people with no "celebrity or public status."[23] Most victims are women, and the stalker is someone they know — most commonly a former intimate partner. Reinforcing the seriousness of the problem, studies indicate a close link between stalking and serious forms of abusive behavior, including violent assaults and murder.[24]

Stalking is generally defined as harassing or threatening behavior that an individual engages in on a repeated and often escalating basis that causes the victim to fear for his or her safety. It can include a variety of unwanted behaviors, such as following or spying on someone, repeatedly showing up uninvited at a person's home or work, making repeated phone calls, and repeatedly waiting in places for the victim (see the discussion later in this chapter regarding cyberstalking). Recognizing that behavior that may seem fairly innocent at the start frequently escalates in both frequency and severity and may result in serious physical harm or even death if not stopped, most statutes provide for the escalation of penalties for repeat violations. Additionally, in many states, an initial act of what is considered "aggravated" stalking, such as stalking in violation of a protective order and/or while armed with a weapon, will result in an enhanced penalty.

However, it is important to recognize that state laws vary quite a bit. For example, some jurisdictions require proof of a credible threat of bodily harm, while others treat the stalking itself as criminal behavior. By way of example, imagine a situation where every day when she leaves work, a woman's former boyfriend is standing at the exit staring at her. He then follows her a few blocks before vanishing into the crowd. On weekends, he is often waiting at the corner of her street and again follows her a few blocks. In states that require a "credible threat of bodily harm," his

Stalking:
The malicious, willful, and repeated tracking down and following of another person; stalking is often a precursor to acts of serious bodily harm

behavior may not be considered stalking. In contrast, in states where a "credible threat of bodily harm" is not a formal element of the crime, his behavior is likely to constitute stalking — in effect, the threat is regarded as implicit in his persistent course of conduct.

Some statutes also require proof that the stalker intended to induce fear in his victim. However, because it can be difficult to prove what a person's specific intent was, many states have made stalking a "general intent" crime. This means that intent to cause harm does not need to be established, only that the defendant intentionally engaged in a prohibited act.[25]

Cyberstalking

When stalking laws were first enacted in the 1990s, "few could have foreseen the current widespread use of e-mail, the Internet, chat rooms, websites, (GPS) cell phones, and tiny hand-held video and digital cameras to stalk."[26] Also unanticipated was that social networking sites, such as Facebook and MySpace, would provide stalkers with an easy way to track and monitor the whereabouts of their intended victims based on updating posts designed to keep family and friends abreast of current activities, or that spyware could be remotely installed on someone's computer as a way to gain access to "all of the victim's computer activities, including pass-words to e-mail and social networking sites."[27] Today, however, what is commonly referred to as "**cyberstalking**" is a significant problem that the law has only begun to catch up with. Like "offline" stalkers, most "online" stalkers "are motivated by a desire to control their victims,"[28] and they use a wide range of techniques to accomplish this:

> [A] cyberstalker may send repeated, threatening, or harassing mes-sages by the simple push of a button. More sophisticated cyberstalkers use programs to send messages at regular or random intervals without being physically present at the computer terminal. . . . In addition, a cyberstalker can dupe other Internet users into harassing or threatening a victim by, for example, posting a victim's name, telephone number, or e-mail addresses on a bulletin board or chat room.[29]

Although, like offline stalking, cyberstalking may place a victim in fear of his or her life and may lead to actual physical violence, law enforce-ment officials do not always take cyberstalking as seriously because it does not involve direct contact. Accordingly, the advice to a victim may simply be to turn off the computer. This advice, however, clearly fails to account for the potential seriousness of the offender's actions and the devastating impact they can have on a victim.

This lack of a serious response also fails to account for the fact that the cloak of anonymity offered by electronic means of communication may embolden a stalker who realizes that his true identity may be very hard

Cyberstalking:
The use of the Internet or other mode of electronic communication to threaten or harass someone

to track down. As explained by the U.S. Department of Justice in a report to Congress:

> Anonymity is a great advantage for the cyberstalker. Unknown to his victim, the perpetrator could be in another State, around the corner, or in the next cubicle at work. The perpetrator could be a former friend or lover, a total stranger met in a chat room, or simply a teenager playing a practical joke. A victim's inability to identify the source of the harassment or threats can be particularly ominous, and the view of anonymity might encourage the perpetrator to continue these acts.[30]

Although the technology has clearly outpaced the law, the law is beginning to catch up. A number of states have either enacted specific cyberstalking laws or amended their existing stalking laws to specifically include cyberstalking. In addition, the abovementioned Interstate Stalking Punishment and Prevention Act makes it a federal crime to use an "interactive computer service . . . to engage in a course of conduct that causes serious emotional distress" or that places a person in "reasonable fear of the death of, or serious injury to" himself or herself, an immediate family member, or his/her spouse or intimate partner.[31] However, these laws may not be comprehensive and may, for example, focus mainly on electronic communication and not include other technologies, such as video cameras and global positioning systems (GPS), that a stalker may use to track a victim's whereabouts. Moreover, regardless of the categories of coverage, if drafted with specificity, statutes may simply fail to keep abreast of the ever-increasing array of technologies that a stalker may use to harass or threaten a victim. With regard to states that have not taken specific steps to address cyberstalking, in some, existing definitions of stalking may be broad enough to encompass at least some types of cyberstalking, while in others, cyberstalking may fall outside the definitional boundaries of the applicable law. This is clearly an area of law that is rapidly developing as states continue to grapple with complex issues raised by the recent explosion in technologies.[32]

Specialized Domestic Violence Courts

As we have seen, intimate partner violence is a pervasive and multidimensional problem, and, in contrast to other types of family law matters, abuse prevention cases are both civil and criminal in nature. Adding to the complexity and potential fragmentation of the legal response, families may also be involved in separate proceedings, such as a divorce or custody action, in which domestic violence is a central consideration. These various court actions are rarely coordinated despite their overlapping issues. This lack of coordination is inefficient, and it can result in conflicting or inconsistent orders. But research points to a more serious consequence: that this "disjointed approach . . . has proven ineffective at stopping violence and protecting victims from repeated violence."[33] Even more chilling is the fact that violence may actually escalate after a victim has sought legal protection from abuse, and many domestic homicide victims had obtained a protective order prior to their death.[34]

Responding to this grim reality, many jurisdictions across the country have established specialized courts to solve the problems inherent in the traditionally fragmented approach to domestic violence cases. Although the models vary, most use a carefully coordinated approach to the handling of the civil and criminal components of these actions at its core. As one commentator observes,

> by making "domestic violence cases a top priority," many of these specialized court programs are able to "afford the victim a supportive and rapid procedural response to her complaint." Through the use of trained court personnel and cooperating victim advocates, these specialized domestic violence courts are able to inform a victim about the court process, both in criminal and in civil protection order cases. This assistance in negotiating the legal system is particularly helpful for pro se civil litigants who, without such help, may have previously been at risk of failing to recognize available remedies or social services available to them in the community.[35]

Another important advantage is that civil and criminal jurisdiction may be combined in a single court, thus enabling this court to both issue protective orders and prosecute criminal violations. Other innovations include the use of specially trained domestic violence clerks who can assist victims in navigating the court system, and, in some jurisdictions, the assignment of the case to a single judge who assumes responsibility for all of the related legal matters.

The Federal Response to Domestic Violence: The Violence Against Women Act

Violence Against Women Act (VAWA):
A federal law providing protection to victims of domestic violence, and funding for anti-violence programs

In 1994, Congress enacted the Violence Against Women Act (VAWA) as part of a national effort to combat intimate partner violence against women.[36] In addition to establishing federal protections and remedies for abuse victims, VAWA provides grants to states to enable them to better meet the needs of women who are the victims of domestic violence; funding is used to train police officers, support community anti-violence initiatives, provide victims with legal advocacy services, and assist victims with immigration matters. VAWA also established a national domestic violence hotline to provide 24-hour emergency assistance for abuse victims.

In recent years, VAWA funding has increased for services directed at targeted populations who face unique challenges or experience a disproportionately high rate of abuse. For example, based on the congressional finding that "youth, under the age of 18, account for 67 percent of all sexual assault victimizations reported to law enforcement officials,"[37] grants are provided to organizations, including schools, juvenile courts, and community groups, for the implementation of specialized programs designed to educate youth and enhance both the safety of victims and the accountability of perpetrators.

Similarly, based on findings indicating that American Indian and Alaska Native women suffer from a higher rate of intimate partner violence than any other population of women, VAWA now funds a range of efforts designed to enhance the understanding of and response to violence against native women. One important addition has been the establishment of a Deputy Director of Tribal Affairs within the federal Office on Violence Against Women who is charged with ensuring that a "portion of tribal set-aside funds" from any VAWA grant is used to enhance the "response of Indian Tribal governments to address domestic violence, sexual assault, dating violence, and stalking."[38]

Colleges and universities have also been placed under a growing obligation to report domestic violence, dating violence, and stalking beyond the crime categories that they are already obligated to report under the Clery Act — a federal statute that requires the reporting of crimes on and around college campuses.[39] They are also now required to adopt a variety of policies and procedures that are designed to enhance the safety of students.

Although a detailed discussion of VAWA is beyond the scope of this text, three of the Act's provisions are particularly important:

The Criminalization of Interstate Domestic Violence. Under VAWA, it is a federal crime to cross a state line to violate a protective order. It is also a crime to cross a state line in order to injure, intimidate, or stalk an intimate partner. VAWA also makes cyberstalking a federal crime. By making these acts federal crimes, VAWA makes it easier to prosecute abusers who pursue their partners across a state line.

The Extension of Full Faith and Credit to Abuse Prevention Orders. VAWA fills a significant enforcement gap by requiring states to give full faith and credit to protective orders from other states that meet the basic requirements of the Act — including that the court had jurisdiction over the parties and provided the defendant with reasonable notice and an opportunity to be heard — and to enforce these orders as if they were issued by a court in that state. Prior to VAWA, states often did not recognize protective orders from other states and required domestic violence victims who had left their home states to obtain new orders. Under VAWA, states must now also give full faith and credit to custody, visitation, and support provisions that are included in protective orders.

Protections for Battered Immigrant Women. VAWA recognizes that battered immigrant women are a vulnerable population. The fear of deportation or the dependence on a spouse for obtaining lawful permanent resident status may prevent immigrant women from seeking protection from or filing criminal charges against an abuser. VAWA therefore permits a battered immigrant to self-petition for lawful permanent resident status, which frees her from reliance on an abusive spouse to obtain this status and also offers her expanded opportunities to petition for relief from deportation proceedings.

If you are assisting a battered woman who is an immigrant, a variety of other protections may be available to her under VAWA and other related laws. Knowledge of these laws and of immigration law (which is a complex and highly specialized field) is essential for anyone working with immigrant women to ensure that their rights are fully protected and that no action is taken that jeopardizes their immigration status. Family law practitioners would be well advised to consult with an immigration expert in these situations.

Working with Victims of Domestic Violence

Although there is no easy formula for how to work with victims of partner violence, the following considerations will contribute to effective and supportive interactions with clients who have been abused:

- Victims often feel a tremendous sense of shame and may be reluctant to acknowledge the violence in their lives. Listen carefully for clues that may suggest an abusive relationship — for example, a woman who says "Well, I don't get out much; my husband doesn't approve of my friends." Inquire further in a sensitive manner. You might, for example, respond to such statements with the following questions: "Why doesn't your husband approve of your friends?" and "What might happen if you went out with someone he doesn't approve of?" With a client who is not quite ready to open up, these questions work more effectively than more direct questions such as, "So, is your husband abusive?"
- Trust the client's assessment of the danger; too often, professionals minimize the potential risks that victims face.
- Depending on the allocation of responsibilities in your office, you or the attorney for whom you work should fully inform clients about the abuse prevention laws in your state. If your office does not assist clients in obtaining protective orders, then provide referrals.
- Understand that it can be very difficult for persons to extricate themselves from an abusive relationship. For example, a client may have no money and be unable to find housing that she can afford. She may fear greater harm if she leaves. She may fear community or family

disapproval, or she may worry about taking the children away from their father. It is not your job to criticize her for failing to leave or take action. She should know that your services are available if and when she does decide to leave or seek a court order.

- Make certain that you have information available regarding local shelters, hotline numbers, and battered women's support groups. These are invaluable resources. Many shelters, hospitals, and police departments have developed materials on "safety plans" that help domestic violence victims think through how best to extricate themselves from a dangerous situation. You should also make these available.
- If you are assisting an abuse victim who is an immigrant to this country, you should be aware that certain protections may be available under the federal Violence Against Women Act. In this situation, it may be appropriate for the client to also meet with an immigration law specialist (see the discussion on VAWA earlier in this chapter).

Chapter Summary

Domestic violence is a serious problem among intimate partners, including those who are in dating relationships. All states have abuse prevention laws that enable domestic violence victims to obtain civil orders of protection. In some states, the statutes are broad and cover most intimate and family relationships; in other states, the scope of coverage is narrower, and many individuals—for example, someone being abused by a dating partner or a former cohabiting partner—may not be able to obtain protection. A few states also expressly exclude same-sex couples from the reach of their statutes. Protection can be obtained from a wide range of abusive behaviors, including physical abuse, attempted physical abuse, sexual assaults, and threats of harm and harassment. Many types of relief can be included in a protective order, such as ordering the respondent to refrain from further acts of abuse, to vacate the premises, to avoid any contact with the petitioner, and to relinquish any firearms. In most jurisdictions, the courts can also make temporary support and custody awards. A recent trend is to include provisions for the protection of pets.

A protective order is usually obtained in two stages. First, the petitioner appears before the court in an *ex parte* proceeding at which temporary relief may be ordered. The other party is then served with the order and informed of the right to be heard. At the second hearing, both parties are given the opportunity to present their version of events. The judge may either extend or decline to extend the *ex parte* order. Specialized domestic violence courts that provide integrated legal and social services are a recent innovation designed to eliminate the disjointed approach to domestic abuse cases.

Effective enforcement procedures are essential to ensure the safety of abuse victims, and much effort has been devoted to increasing the responsiveness of the criminal justice system, including the adoption of mandatory arrest and prosecution policies. These policies are quite controversial. Some experts believe that the policies play a critical role in enhancing victim safety, while others believe that they disempower victims and put them at risk of retaliatory violence. In many states, the violation of a protection order is an independent crime. All states now have anti-stalking laws that criminalize qualifying harassing or threatening behavior, and many now also treat cyberstalking, which is a rapidly growing problem, as a crime.

At the federal level, VAWA has increased protections for domestic violence victims by criminalizing interstate acts of violence and requiring states to give full faith and credit to protective orders. The Act also provides relief to battered immigrants, such as by allowing them to self-petition for lawful permanent resident status, thus avoiding reliance on the batterer and expanding anti-deportation protections.

Key Terms

Domestic Violence
Domestic Abuse
Intimate Partner
  Violence
Abuse Prevention
  Laws

Protective Order
Harassment Order
Restraining Order
Vacate Order
Stay-Away Order
No-Contact Order

Batterer Intervention
  Program
Ex Parte
Temporary Order
Mutual Orders of
  Protection

Stalking
Cyberstalking
Violence Against
  Women Act
  (VAWA)

Review Questions

1. Historically, what position did the law take with respect to domestic violence?
2. In brief, what is a civil order of protection?
3. What kinds of relationships would qualify for a protective order in an inclusive state?
4. What kinds of qualifications might a statute place on someone who is in a dating relationship?
5. What approaches do states take with respect to same-sex couples?
6. What kinds of abusive behavior are covered by most abuse prevention laws?
7. In what ways might an abuse protection order provide for the safety of a pet?
8. What kinds of relief are generally available under an abuse prevention law?
9. Why are gun relinquishment orders important to the safety of victims? What protections are provided by federal law?
10. What kinds of obligations do police officers have toward victims of domestic violence under an abuse prevention law?
11. Explain the two-step process for obtaining a protective order.
12. How are protective orders enforced?
13. How do mandatory arrest policies work?
14. What about mandatory prosecution policies?
15. What is stalking?
16. What is cyberstalking?
17. What are the nature and function of specialized domestic violence courts?
18. What are some of the key provisions of VAWA?

Discussion Questions

1. Many people wonder why battered women do not simply walk away from a relationship after the first incident of abuse. Why do you think this might not be an easy step for someone to take?
2. Do you think someone who is in a dating relationship should be allowed to seek protection under abuse prevention laws?
3. Do you think that mandatory arrest and prosecution policies make sense? Why or why not?

Assignments

1. Find the abuse prevention act for your state and determine the following:
   - What courts are these cases heard in?
   - Who can petition the court for relief?
   - Are dating partners eligible? If so, are there any qualifications?
   - Is a person in a same-sex relationship eligible to seek relief under the statute?
   - What kinds of protection are available?
2. Using the abuse prevention act located for question 1, trace the court procedure from start to finish. Make sure to include all relevant time frames.
3. Assume that you are doing an internship as a legal advocate at a local battered women's shelter. They have asked you to develop a brochure that sets out the basic elements of your state's abuse prevention law and explains the court process so women coming to the shelter will know what their legal rights are. The key here is to make sure the brochure is complete, accurate, and comprehensible to the layperson.

Endnotes

1. Please note that although much of the language in this chapter is cast in gender-neutral terms, gender-specific terminology is also used because most perpetrators of intimate partner violence are male and most victims are women.

2. R. Emerson Dobash and Russell Dobash, Violence Against Wives 35 (1979) (citing Not in God's Image: Women in History (Julia O'Faolain and Lauro Martines, eds., 1974)).

3. Joyner v. Joyner, 59 N.C. 324, 325 (1862).

4. Shannon Catalano, Intimate Partner Violence (2012), U.S. Department of Justice, Office of Justice Programs, Bureau of Justice Statistics, http://www.bjs.gov/content/pub/ascii/ipv9310.txt (accessed Apr. 4, 2014).

5. See Devon M. Largo, Refining the Meaning and Application of "Dating Relationship" Language in Domestic Violence Statutes, 60 Vand. L. Rev. 939, 954 (2007).

6. For further detail, see Lisa Vollendork Martin, What's Love Got to Do with It: Securing Access to Justice for Teens, 61 Cath. U. L. Rev. 457 (2012).

7. Catherine F. Klein and Leslye E. Orloff, Providing Legal Protection for Battered Women: An Analysis of State Statutes and Case Law, 21 Hofstra L. Rev. 859 (1993).

8. See Margaret E. Johnson, Redefining Harm, Reimagining Remedies, and Reclaiming Domestic Violence Law, 42 U.C. Davis L. Rev. 1107 (2009).

9. Sarah Lorraine Solon, Tenth Annual Review of Gender and Sexuality Law, Criminal Law Chapter: Domestic Violence, 10 Geo. J. Gender & L. 369, 422 (2009). This trend has been aided by the fact that almost all states have abrogated the doctrine of interspousal immunity that historically barred suits between spouses.

10. For detail, see id. at 420-423.

11. For detail, see Margreta Velluci, Restraining the (Real) Beast: Protective Orders and Other Statutory Enactments to Protect the Animal Victims of Domestic Violence in Rhode Island, 16 Roger Williams U. L. Rev. 224 (2011). For specific state statutory provisions, see Animal and Legal and Historical Center, http://www.animallaw.info/articles/ovusdomestcviolencelaws.htm (accessed July 26, 2012).

12. John Hopkins University, Center for Gun Policy and Research, Fact Sheet, "Firearms and Intimate Partner Violence," http://www.jhsph.edu/research/centers-and-institutes/johns-hopkins-center-for-gun-policy-and-research/publications (accessed Oct. 6, 2012).

13. Id.

14. This law is codified at 18 U.S.C. §922(g)(8). This provision contains an exception for certain government employees, such as police officers and military personnel, who are required to carry a weapon as part of their official duties.

15. This law is codified at 18 U.S.C. §924(g)(9). For further detail, see Lisa D. May, The Backfiring of the Domestic Violence Firearm Bans, 14 Colum. J. Gender & L. 1 (2005); Deborah Epstein, Margaret E. Bell, and Lisa A. Goodman, Transforming Aggressive Prosecution Policies: Prioritizing Victims' Long-Term Safety in the Prosecution of Domestic Violence Cases, 11 Am. U. J. Gender Soc.

Poly. & L. 465 (2003); and Darren Mitchell and Susan B. Carbon, Firearms and Domestic Violence: A Primer for Judges, 39 Ct. Rev. 32 (2002).

16. Allen Rostron, Protecting Gun Rights and Improving Gun Control After District of Columbia v. Heller, 13 Lewis & Clark L. Rev. 383, 406 (2009). Questions have been raised about the continued validity of the Lautenberg amendment following the Supreme Court's decision in the case of District of Columbia v. Heller, 554 U.S. 570 (2008), in which the Court held that the second amendment provides some protection to an individual's right to bear arms for nonmilitary purposes. See id. for detail.

17. Gonzales v. Castle Rock, 545 U.S. 748 (2005).

18. Jessica Lenahan (Gonzales) v. United States, Report No. 80/11 (2011), p. 53. For further developments in the matter, see https://www.aclu.org/womens-rights/us-fails-adequately-comply-domestic-violence-recommendations-issued-inter-american-com.

19. Donna Coker, Criminal Control and Feminist Law Reform in Domestic Violence Law: A Critical Review, 4 Buff. L. Rev. 801, 823-826 (2001).

20. Erin L. Han, Mandatory Arrest and No-Drop Policies: Victim Empowerment in Domestic Violence Cases, 23 B.C. Third World L.J. 159, 176 (2003).

21. See, e.g., Deborah Epstein, Margaret E. Bell, and Lisa A. Goodman, Transforming Aggressive Prosecution Policies: Prioritizing Victims' Long-Term Safety in the Prosecution of Domestic Violence Cases, 11 Am. U. J. Gender Soc. Poly. & L. 465 (2003).

22. 18 U.S.C.S. §2261A(1) (2012). For a compilation of federal and state stalking laws, see http://www.victimsofcrime.org/our-programs/stalking-resource-center (accessed July 26, 2012).

23. Naomi Harlin Goodmo, Cyberstalking, A New Crime: Evaluating the Effectiveness of Current State and Federal Laws, 72 Mo. L. Rev. 125, 129 (2007).

24. Stalking Fact Sheet, Stalking Resource Center, The National Center for Victims of Crime, http://www.victimsofcrime.org/our-programs/stalking-resource-center (accessed May 27, 2014).

25. Strengthening Anti-Stalking Statutes, Legal Series Bulletin #1. http://www.ncjrs.gov/App/Publications/alphaList.aspx?alpha=S (accessed July 25, 2012).

26. Stalking Technology Outpaces State Laws, The National Center for Victims of Crime, http://www.victimsofcrime.org/docs/src/stalking-technology-outpaces-state-laws17A308005D0C.pdf?sfvrsn=2 (accessed April 24, 2015).

27. See, Laurie L. Baughman, Friend Request or Foe? Confirming the Misuses of Internet and Social Networking Sites by Domestic Violence Perpetrators, 19 Widener L. J. 933, 942-943, (2010).

28. U.S. Department of Justice, Office of Justice Programs, Violence Against Women Office, Stalking and Domestic Violence, Report to Congress, p. 2 (2001), available at http://www.ncjrs.gov/pdffiles1/ojp/186157.pdf (accessed April 24, 2015).

29. Id.

30. *Id*. at 2-3. *See also* Ashley N.B. Beagle, Modern Stalking Laws: A Survey of State Anti-Stalking Statutes Considering Modern Mediums and Constitutional Challenges, 14 Chap. L. Rev. 457 (2011), and Baughman, *supra* note 27.

31. 18 U.S.C.S. sec. 2261A (2)(b) (2012).

32. For a discussion of some of the first amendment concerns raised by these laws, *see* Timothy L. Allsup, United States v. Cassidy: The Federal Interstate Stalking Statute and Freedom of Speech, 13 N.C. J.L. & Tech. On. 227 (2012), and Sarah Jameson, Cyberharassment: Striking a Balance Between Free Speech and Privacy, 17 CommLaw Conspectus 231 (2008).

33. Judge Lowell D. Castleton et al., Ada County Family Violence Court: Shaping the Means to Better the Result, 39 Fam. L.Q. 27, 31 (2005).

34. Betsy Tsai, The Trend Toward Specialized Domestic Violence Courts: Improvements on an Effective Innovation, 68 Fordham L. Rev. 1285, 1292 (2000).

35. Jennifer Thompson, Who's Afraid of Judicial Activism? Reconceptualizing a Traditional Paradigm in the Context of Specialized Domestic Violence Courts, 56 Me. L. Rev. 407, 428 (2004), citing Tsai, *supra* note 34, at 1298.

36. Violence Against Women Act, Pub. L. No. 103-322, 108 Stat. 1902 (1994). VAWA was enacted as Title IV of the Violent Crime Control and Enforcement Act of 1974, Pub. L. No. 103-322, 108 Stat. 1796 (1994). The Act has since been updated several times. For purposes of this discussion, no distinction will be made successive versions of the Act.

37. As quoted in Leila Abolfazli, Violence Against Women Act, 7 Geo. J. Gender & L. 863, 880 (2006).

38. The Violence Against Women and Department of Justice Reauthorization Act of 2005. The National Task Force to End Sexual and Domestic Violence Against Women. nnedv.org/downloads/Policy/VAWA2005Summary.pdf (accessed May 27, 2014).

39. For further details, *see* http://clerycenter.org/ (accessed May 27, 2014).

Chapter Four

The Law of Divorce, Annulment, and Legal Separation

Put simply, **divorce** is the legal dissolution of a marital relationship. Marriage creates a legal bond; divorce severs it. For the divorcing couple, however, divorce is not this simple; the process is multidimensional, with profound emotional, spiritual, economic, and legal consequences. Lives are profoundly reshaped—often in unanticipated ways. For some, divorce brings tremendous relief and a welcome opportunity to build a better life; for others, it brings loneliness or new relationships that recycle the difficulties of the past.

This chapter focuses on the substantive law of divorce. As you read the chapter, and as you work with people going through a divorce, it is important to be aware that the applicable legal principles are not mere abstractions but touch the core of people's lives. Accordingly, divorce law should not be thought of in isolation from its human context. (For a discussion on working with emotionally distraught clients, see Chapter 10 on the divorce process.)

Divorce:
The legal dissolution of a marital relationship, such that the parties are no longer spouses

Historical Overview

Throughout history, many societies practiced divorce by mutual consent of the parties. This was true in what was to become England and much of western Europe until sometime into the tenth or eleventh century, when marriage came under the authority of the Catholic Church. As the Church gained in influence, a cohesive theology emerged, and a systematic body of canon law, including laws regulating marriage, was developed. According to the teachings of the Church, marriage was a sacrament that conferred grace on a couple and was a spiritual instrument of salvation. The relationship between a husband and a wife was thought to

Indissoluble:
The belief that the legal relationship between a spouses is permanent and can never be terminated

Marital Fault:
Acts of wrongdoing by one spouse toward the other that serve as the basis of a fault divorce

mirror the loving bond between Christ and His Church, and the bond was similarly regarded as **indissoluble**. As a result, divorce was prohibited.

In the early 1500s, the Protestant Reformation challenged many of the Catholic Church's teachings, including those related to marriage. According to Reformation thinkers, marriage was not a sacrament — it was of this world and carried no promise of spiritual redemption. Having divested marriage of its holy and redemptive status, Protestants accepted the necessity of divorce in cases involving grievous marital sins committed in violation of Christian principles.[1]

Reflecting the fact that many of the colonial settlers in the Americas were Protestants, divorce was permitted from the outset in many regions of the English colonies. It should, however, be noted that slaves did not have formal access to divorce in any locale, due mainly to the fact that the colonists refused to honor the validity of marriages between enslaved persons. Although divorce was regarded as a civil matter, divorce grounds were rooted in Christian notions of sin. Cast as a remedy for an innocent spouse against a grievous wrongdoer, the dissolution of a marriage required proof of serious **marital fault**, such as adultery.

Following independence from England, attitudes toward divorce became a bit more relaxed as revolutionary ferment found its way into the domestic sphere. Leaders such as Thomas Jefferson transposed arguments about individual rights to liberty and happiness from the struggle against England to the marital context. Divorce was thus cast as a means to oust tyrannical husbands and ensure that women were not trapped in domestic regimes that denied them their humanity. Changing expectations about the marital relationship also contributed to a greater acceptance of divorce. With industrialization, production moved out of the home, and the family no longer stood at the center of economic activity. As a result, the significance of marriage as an economic arrangement diminished, and spouses increasingly looked to each other for love and companionship. As they came to expect more from one another, the risk of disappointment also increased, as marriage did not always provide the parties with what they were looking for, and divorce was increasingly accepted as a necessary safety valve for spouses who were trapped in failed marriages.[2]

Despite these changes, until the no-fault divorce reform movement of the 1970s, divorce remained firmly linked to grievous marital wrongdoing and was only available to innocent spouses who could prove fault in accordance with the available grounds in their jurisdiction (but see the discussion of collusive divorce later in this chapter). By retaining the link between divorce and fault, divorce law supported the permanency of marriage by strictly limiting the permissible grounds for marital exits while also acknowledging that some spouses transgressed the boundaries of acceptable marital conduct.

Fault Divorce: Common Grounds and Defenses

During the final quarter of the last century, this country underwent a no-fault divorce "revolution." As a result, **fault divorce** is no longer as common as it once was, and, as discussed later in this chapter, is actually not an option in all jurisdictions. (No-fault divorce is covered in the next section.) However, it is still important to have a basic understanding of the major fault grounds and the primary defenses to charges of marital misconduct. As always, you need to check the specifics of your state's laws because other statutory options may be available. (See Chapters 7 and 8 for a discussion of the role that fault plays in determining spousal awards and the division of property.)

Fault Divorce:
A divorce that is premised on the marital fault of one spouse

Divorce Grounds

Adultery

Historically, adultery has been regarded as the most serious marital wrong and has been the most widely accepted ground for divorce. **Adultery** is generally defined as a voluntary act of sexual intercourse by a married person with someone other than his or her spouse. In the past, the law did not treat a husband's extramarital relations as seriously as a wife's transgressions. In many states, a woman could not obtain a divorce for adultery unless she could also establish aggravating circumstances, such as cruelty or that her husband had engaged in a course of adulterous conduct, whereas a man had to show only that his wife had committed a single adulterous act. Although no longer legally true today, some experts believe that social attitudes have not necessarily changed, and that many people continue to regard adultery by a woman, especially if she is a mother, as a greater wrong than when committed by a man.

Adultery:
Voluntary sexual intercourse between a married person and someone who is not his or her spouse

Because there are usually no eyewitnesses, a claim of adultery, when disputed, is generally established by circumstantial evidence. A party must show that his or her spouse had both the opportunity and the disposition or inclination to commit adultery. Relevant evidence might include love letters, public displays of affection, and frequent visits to a home or hotel, or the introduction of venereal disease into the marriage.

Recently, several courts have addressed the question of whether adultery is limited to acts of sexual intercourse between a man and a woman, or whether it can be defined to include sexual relations between a married person and someone of the same sex. Most courts that have considered this issue have concluded that adultery is not limited to heterosexual intercourse. As one court explained: "We view appellant's definition of adultery as unduly narrow and overly dependent upon the term sexual intercourse.... [E]xplicit extra-marital sexual activity constitutes adultery regardless of whether it is of a homosexual or heterosexual character."[3] However, in 2003, the New Hampshire Supreme Court reached the opposite conclusion. Relying on both the dictionary meaning of *adultery* and nineteenth-century case law, the court held that the "concept of adultery was premised upon a specific act. To include in that concept other acts of a sexual nature, whether between heterosexuals or homosexuals, would change beyond recognition this well established ground for divorce."[4] The dissenting justices argued that the majority was closing its eyes to "the sexual realities of our world" and that a more realistic definition of adultery would include all "extra marital intimate sexual activity with another, regardless of the specific intimate sexual acts performed, the marital status, or the gender of the third party."[5]

Desertion/Abandonment

Desertion:
Involves the voluntary, nonconsensual departure of one spouse without justification for a period of time defined by statute

Desertion (or abandonment) has long been accepted as an appropriate ground for divorce. Prior to no-fault divorce, desertion was particularly important in states that did not recognize cruelty or construed it narrowly (see the section "Cruelty," later in this chapter). As a general rule, desertion requires a departure from the marital residence. Some courts have held that the refusal to have a sexual relationship with one's spouse satisfies the separation requirement even if the parties remain in the marital home; however, withdrawal from other aspects of the marital relationship is unlikely to be considered desertion.

In most jurisdictions, a spouse must prove the following elements to establish desertion:

1. There has been a voluntary separation;
2. for the statutory period;
3. with the intent not to return;
4. without consent; and
5. without justification.

For the separation to qualify, the departing spouse must leave of his or her own will. An involuntary departure, such as where a person is drafted, jailed, or committed to a mental hospital, is not desertion. The separation must exist continuously for the statutory time period. Interruptions by, for example, a good-faith offer of reconciliation or even a single act of sexual intercourse may stop the time from running. As a general rule, the calculation of time begins again if there is a second departure—the time periods cannot be added together.

It is not desertion if the "stay-at-home" spouse consents to the departure because desertion by its very nature is a nonconsensual act. If the departure is justified, such as when a spouse flees physical abuse, it is also not classified as desertion. In fact, the spouse who has caused the departure through his or her misconduct may be considered the deserting spouse based on the doctrine of **constructive desertion**, which imputes the act of desertion to the spouse responsible for the other's departure.[6]

Constructive Desertion: Imputes the act of desertion to the spouse responsible for the other's departure

Cruelty

In most states, **cruelty** was not initially included as a ground for divorce, but by the late 1800s, most divorce statutes had been amended to add it as a ground. It soon became the most commonly used ground. Statutes employ a variety of terms such as "extreme cruelty," "cruel and inhuman treatment," and "indignities," but the meaning is generally the same. Initially, borrowing from ecclesiastical law, cruelty was narrowly defined to include only repeated acts of severe physical abuse that inflicted bodily harm. The concept has gradually expanded and in most states, it now includes acts of mental as well as physical cruelty, although some jurisdictions require that the mental cruelty result in some kind of physical symptoms. Proof that the symptoms abated or improved after the parties separated may also be required. The thinking here is that by requiring objective evidence of physical impairment, trivial or false claims of cruelty will be weeded out. However, many courts accept fairly general and unsubstantiated statements about loss of sleep, changes in appetite, and increased anxiety as proof of physical impairment.[7]

Cruelty: Mistreatment of a relatively serious nature; generally can include either physical or emotional wrongdoing

Defenses

When marital fault is alleged, the defendant-spouse can raise legal defenses to absolve himself or herself of marital wrongdoing. If successful, the divorce cannot be granted on the basis of the alleged fault. However, because most divorce actions are ultimately settled, these defenses are of little practical significance. Moreover, because of the availability of no-fault divorce, when cases are contested, the dispute almost always involves matters of custody, support, and the like, rather than the grounds for the divorce itself. Nonetheless, some familiarity with the major defenses is important, as a defendant-spouse may need to raise a defense in responding to a fault complaint. (See Chapter 10 on the divorce process.)

Connivance

The essence of the defense of **connivance** is consent. This defense has primarily been used in adultery cases in which the defendant-spouse seeks to prove the party seeking the divorce consented to the adultery, such as by helping to arrange the liaison. In some states, a more passive course of action, such as a spouse's not actively seeking to prevent a known affair, constitutes connivance.

Connivance: A divorce defense, the essence of which is that the plaintiff consented to the wrongdoing on which his or her complaint for divorce is based

Condonation

Condonation:
A divorce defense, the essence of which is that the plaintiff has forgiven the acts of marital misconduct upon which his or her complaint for divorce is based

The essence of the defense of **condonation** is forgiveness. If a spouse forgives his or her partner's marital misconduct, this misconduct can no longer be the basis of a divorce action; condonation restores the marital innocence of the erring spouse. In some states, if a spouse reengages in wrongful activity, the condonation may be canceled and the original divorce grounds revived.

States differ as to what constitutes forgiveness. In some states, engaging in sexual relations after the plaintiff has learned of the misconduct is by itself condonation; here, the plaintiff's state of mind is irrelevant. In other states, the plaintiff's state of mind is key; the plaintiff must actually forgive the defendant—forgiveness will not be inferred from resumed intimacy.

Recrimination

Recrimination:
A divorce defense that prevents a divorce from being granted on the basis that both parties are guilty of marital misconduct

The defense of **recrimination** has been subject to much criticism and has been abolished in many jurisdictions. Here, a defendant-spouse, rather than seeking to defeat a divorce by minimizing the wrongfulness of his or her conduct, seeks to defeat it by showing that the plaintiff-spouse, rather than being an innocent victim, is also guilty of marital wrongdoing. When mutual wrongdoing is established, neither spouse is entitled to a divorce, and the couple must remain married even though each has treated the other badly. Although seemingly illogical, this defense is rooted in the view of divorce as a remedy for the innocent; accordingly, when both spouses are guilty of marital transgressions, neither qualifies as the innocent victim entitled to relief. In some states, the harshness of this result has been modified by the doctrine of **comparative rectitude**, which allows a court to grant a divorce if the plaintiff-spouse's wrongdoing is adjudged to be less serious than the defendant's.

Comparative Rectitude:
Ameliorates the harsh effects of the traditional divorce defense of recrimination by allowing a divorce when one party's marital fault is regarded as less serious than the other party's

Collusion

Collusion:
An agreement by a couple to obtain a divorce in avoidance of the fault principle that requires a guilty and an innocent spouse

Collusion involves an agreement by a couple to obtain a divorce and the deliberate crafting of a case for presentation to the court. Collusion can occur in several ways. The parties could agree that one spouse would actually commit a marital wrong, such as adultery, in order to provide grounds for divorce (this would also be considered connivance). More likely, the parties would agree to fabricate a marital wrong, exaggerate the extent of their discontent with one another, or fail to present a valid defense. This ground runs counter to the basic assumptions of the fault system, which conceptualizes divorce as an adversarial process. The reality is that although collusion is generally classified as a defense, it is unlikely to be raised by either party because it would prevent the granting of the divorce that the parties were attempting to set up.

No-Fault Divorce

No-Fault Divorce:
Divorce that is based on the breakdown of the marital relationship rather than on the marital fault of one spouse

During the 1960s, there was a groundswell of support for divorce reform. Critics of the fault system argued that it was outmoded and ineffectual and that the time had come to give couples the option of divorcing without having to prove marital wrongdoing. They pointed to the practice of collusive divorce, by which parties who wanted out of their marriage would, in direct contravention of the fault requirement that an innocent spouse prove marital wrongdoing, agree to divorce and then carefully stage the process, as an indication that the fault model had run its course.

An important critique of the fault system was that it increased the anger and hostility between divorcing spouses by forcing them into an adversarial posture that destroyed any possibility of reconciliation or an amicable settlement. Reformers hoped that by eliminating fault, the divorce process would become less adversarial and accordingly less destructive to the parties and their children. Fault divorce was further criticized as being out of keeping with the contemporary understanding of marital relationships. Reformers argued that the messy reality of people's marriages did not conform to the fault model, which naively assumed that all marital breakups involved a good spouse and a bad spouse and that this determination could be made simply by identifying who had committed the marital wrong. To reformers, it had become apparent that the named ground was often a symptom of marital distress rather than the actual cause of the breakup. For example, an affair, rather than being the singular "bad" act that brought a marriage to an end, might instead be a response to a complete withdrawal of affection on the part of the other spouse, thus making it unfair to characterize the affair as the only marital transgression.

In keeping with the trend toward greater individual autonomy and privacy within the domestic realm, reformers further argued that the right of an unhappy spouse to leave a marriage should not be subordinated to the state's interest in family preservation, and that individuals should have greater control over when and why to leave a marriage. In seeking to shift the balance from the historic interest of the state in family preservation toward the right of an unhappy spouse to leave a failed marriage, some reformers were also influenced by the feminist movement's emphasis on the right of women to leave marriages that compromised their emotional and/or physical integrity.

No-Fault Laws

Beginning with California in 1970, no-fault reform swept the country. Within 15 years, the legal landscape had been radically altered. When California reformed its law, it essentially opted to abolish all fault grounds and replace them with a single no-fault standard. A significant number of states followed California's lead and now have only no-fault grounds.

A majority of states, however, chose to maintain their existing fault grounds and add no-fault provisions, thus creating a dual system of divorce.

No-Fault Grounds

**Marital Breakdown/
Irreconcilable Differences:**
A no-fault divorce ground, the essence of which is that the parties are no longer compatible and there is no hope of reconciliation

Living Separate and Apart:
Requires the parties to have lived apart for a statutory period of time, with the separation serving as proof of marital breakdown

There are two primary no-fault grounds: **marital breakdown** and **living separate and apart**, with the former being the most common. A few states have combined these grounds and require proof of both a marital breakdown and a separation. Although both grounds will be discussed in greater detail next, keep in mind that many states have unique requirements, making familiarity with the laws of your jurisdiction essential.

Marital Breakdown. Marital breakdown is the principal no-fault ground. Statutes use a variety of terms to express this essential concept—such as "irreconcilable differences" or the "irretrievable" or "irremediable breakdown" of the marriage. Whichever term is used, the emphasis is on the failed state of the marital relationship rather than on the conduct of the spouses.

At least in theory, the judge at the divorce hearing is supposed to conduct a searching inquiry into whether the marriage is in fact broken and beyond hope of repair. (See Chapter 10 on the divorce process.) Factors relevant to this determination include the following:

- the degree to which the parties are unable to relate to one another;
- the extent of any differences between them;
- prior efforts to resolve their marital difficulties;
- whether there is any hope of reconciliation.

Many states specifically bar evidence of fault; in other states, such evidence is not considered relevant, except perhaps to help establish the extent of the breakdown.

No-fault hearings were not intended to be mere rubber stamps of the parties' decision, and judges in most states have considerable discretion to decide whether a marriage is truly over. In fact, some reformers hoped to give judges more freedom to deny a divorce if they believed there was any hope of reconciliation than they had under the fault system, where proof of fault mandated the granting of the divorce. Accordingly, in some states, a judge can stay the proceedings until the parties have sought counseling if the judge is not convinced that the marriage is over.

In reality, however, it appears that searching inquiries into whether a marriage is really over are rare. Couples are generally taken at their word that the marriage is beyond repair, and a few states have eliminated the requirement of a hearing if there are no collateral issues to resolve.

Many states do not require both parties to agree that the marriage is over before a no-fault divorce can be granted. This raises the possibility that a spouse could seek to block the divorce by expressing his or her continued love and belief that the marriage was still intact or not beyond repair; but most judges will grant a divorce in this situation on the basis that a viable partnership does not exist where each spouse has such a radically different view of the relationship. When faced with this situation, a judge, where allowed to do so, might stay the proceedings and order the couple into counseling.

Living Separate and Apart. The other major no-fault ground is that the parties have lived separate and apart for a statutory period of time. Time periods range from about 18 months to three years, with most falling somewhere in between. The underlying assumption is that the separation itself is proof of marital breakdown, and judicial inquiry into the relationship's demise is not required. The term "separate and apart" has generally been construed to require separate residences, but some courts have granted a divorce when a couple remained under the same roof but had essentially ceased all interaction for the requisite time period.

Some courts impose an intent requirement and will not qualify the separation even if it lasts for the statutory period unless the parties intended for it to be a permanent one. Thus, if a separation begins as a temporary one, the statutory period will not start to run unless and until the parties decide to make the separation permanent. Some states also require that the separation be voluntary on the part of both parties. Accordingly, if the parties are living apart because of desertion, flight from abuse, or over the objection of one spouse, the separation is not voluntary and will not qualify the parties for a divorce. Similarly, a separation caused by involuntary circumstances such as the draft, hospitalization, or incarceration would not be a valid ground for divorce. Also, when one spouse is mentally incompetent, a separation initiated by the other spouse will not generally be regarded as voluntary if the non-initiating spouse lacks the ability to comprehend what is going on and to give his or her consent. In a few states, the separation need be voluntary only on the part of one spouse.

Where voluntariness is required, a separation that begins involuntarily can be converted into a voluntary one if the parties agree that they wish to live apart. The running of the statutory period is calculated from the time the parties reached this agreement rather than from the time of the initial separation. Many jurisdictions, however, do not impose a voluntariness requirement; accordingly, virtually any separation for the statutory time period can ripen into a divorce action.

The No-Fault Divorce Debate

No-fault divorce has come under increasing criticism from individuals and groups who believe that it is undermining the institution of marriage. Critics contend that it has contributed to a "divorce culture" that emphasizes the pursuit of individual happiness and fulfillment over commitment to one's spouse and children. According to this view, rather than accepting that all marriages have their ebbs and flows and that it takes effort to sustain intimacy, no-fault divorce encourages spouses to walk out the door in pursuit of their own goals. No-fault divorce is thus blamed for cheapening the meaning of connection and permanence with its seductive promise of an easy way out.

Critics further contend that children are the primary victims of this trend toward loosened marital ties. They point to both the economic and psychological dislocation that often follows divorce, and criticize parents for placing their own needs over the needs of their children. Although generally not opposed to divorce that is truly fault based, they criticize adults whom they see as placing their own need for fulfillment over their children's need for stability and sustained connections.

In response to these concerns, a variety of reform measures that aim to make marital dissolution more difficult have been introduced with varying degrees of success. By increasing the barriers to divorce, it is hoped that spouses will be more inclined to work out their differences rather than opting for no-fault's promise of an "easy" escape from commitment. Some measures seek to eliminate no-fault as a ground for divorce altogether; others seek to limit its availability to couples who do not have minor children, and still others seek to impose lengthy waiting periods. Another approach is to require **mutual consent**, particularly if there are minor children, thus eliminating the option of "unilateral" no-fault divorce.

Mutual Consent:
The idea that a no-fault divorce should require the agreement of both spouses

Seeking to prevent divorce by strengthening marriage at the front end, a handful of states have passed laws to encourage couples to participate in premarital counseling. By way of an incentive, participants are typically offered a discount on the marriage license fee. Another possible approach is to set a longer waiting period for the issuance of a marriage license, which can then be waived for couples who have gone through premarital counseling.

Although research on the effectiveness of this approach is limited, some studies suggest that participation in premarital counseling may help to weed out poorly matched couples before they actually tie the knot, and it may also improve the communication skills of those who do marry, although the impact on the actual divorce rate is, as of yet, unclear. Moreover, because premarital counseling laws are far less restrictive of individual autonomy and choice than other divorce reform measures, they have generated less opposition (as discussed later) from those do not believe that the state should seek to compel unhappy couples to remain together for the benefit of their children or for the good of society.

Covenant Marriage:
Law that emphasizes the permanency of marriage and limits the availability of divorce

Covenant marriage is a particularly controversial approach that seeks to both strengthen marriage at the front end and make divorce more difficult to obtain. Louisiana passed the nation's first covenant marriage law in 1997. Since then, although covenant marriage bills have been considered in many states, only Arizona and Arkansas have also enacted such a measure into law. Nonetheless, this approach, which seeks to "restore the institution of marriage" by offering, to "those who belong to a religious community or those who adhere to a traditional morality, a safe haven from the post-modern dominant culture," remains a particularly attractive option to marriage traditionalists.[8]

Covenant marriage laws give couples who are contemplating marriage a choice—they can either opt for "regular" marriage or choose to enter into a "covenant" marriage. As a general matter, prospective spouses who opt for a covenant marriage agree to undergo premarital counseling and to return to counseling if necessary in order to keep their marriage on track. Perhaps most significantly, they agree in advance that they will not seek a no-fault divorce. By eliminating this option, they commit themselves at the outset of their marriage to divorcing only if there has been a complete breach of the marital commitment.

On the other hand, those who support the continued availability of unrestricted no-fault divorce challenge the view that it is responsible for altering our understanding of marital commitment. Pointing to the widespread practice of collusive divorce, they argue that no-fault divorce responded to rather than initiated changes that had already taken place in society's understanding of marriage. In support of this view, no-fault supporters point out that divorce rates began to rise before no-fault reform owing to a number of factors, including increased social acceptance of divorce, the Vietnam War (studies consistently show that divorce rates increase during times of war), the women's rights movement, and changing economic conditions.[9] Accordingly, supporters argue that eliminating no-fault divorce is a misguided strategy that will not accomplish its intended goal of significantly reducing the rate of divorce.

Supporters of no-fault divorce also recognize that divorce can be difficult on children, but they draw attention to the harms of growing up in a household that is rife with conflict. Again challenging the critics' understanding of causality, they point out that many of the emotional and psychological harms that are attributed to divorce may be due to long-standing problems in the family. Accordingly, they argue that efforts to compel parents to remain together may exacerbate rather than alleviate childhood distress. Moreover, no-fault supporters point out that the impact of divorce can be mitigated by carefully structured custody and visitation plans to account for the needs of the children and by support awards that are sufficient to offset the potential economic disruption of divorce.

No-fault supporters fear that tightening up on divorce laws by imposing measures such as waiting periods or limiting its availability to couples without children will recreate many of the problems of the past, including the practice of collusive divorce and trapping women in abusive marriages. Interestingly, Barbara Defoe Whitehead, a self-described critic of contemporary divorce practices, also raises concerns about the impact that the elimination of no-fault would have on battered women:

> Some marriages will be preserved that probably should end, including those that involve physical abuse and violence. Unfortunately, fault is likely to be most successful in deterring socially isolated and timorous women, often battered wives, from seeking divorce. It would be a cruel irony indeed if a pro-marriage policy unintentionally became a pro-bad-marriage policy.[10]

Whitehead also points to another possible unintended consequence of reform — that restricting the availability of no-fault divorce may deter people from marrying in the first place. She argues that based on life experience and cultural messages about the high rates of marital failure, young adults are already apprehensive about marital commitments. If they then hear how hard it is to get divorced, they may "interpret legal restrictions on divorce as yet another reason to avoid marriage."[11]

When it comes to covenant marriage, in addition to objecting that it infuses a biblical conception of marriage into state law, thus breaching the required boundary between church and state, critics argue is that it is impossible to predict the future, and committing one's self in advance to a particular course of action may work to a spouse's detriment. Thus, for example, if a husband turns out to be abusive, by entering into a covenant marriage, a woman has committed herself to participating in counseling with him, when the best and safest course of action may be for her to disengage from the relationship as quickly as possible. Critics have also raised concerns about the costs associated with counseling and about the inefficacy of counseling when parties are acting out of legal compulsion rather than a genuine desire to work on their problems.[12]

▪ The Law of Annulment

Annulment:
A decree establishing that spouses were never actually married because an impediment existed at the time the marriage was celebrated

Marriages can also be "terminated" by the granting of an **annulment**. Although annulments are rare, it is nonetheless important to have a basic understanding of the law in this area. A client who comes to your office may want an annulment for religious reasons, or a client may be confused about the law, believing, for example, that an annulment is the only way to end a short-term or unconsummated marriage.

As you read this section, keep in mind that we are speaking only about the civil annulment process. A number of religious bodies also grant annulments in accordance with their own internal principles and procedures.

Distinguished from Divorce

An annulment is a retroactive declaration that no valid marriage ever existed between the parties. The modern annulment action emerged out of ecclesiastical practice. Unlike divorce, the procedure was consistent with the religious belief in the indissolubility of the marital relationship because an annulment establishes that the parties were never validly married.

Divorce is premised on the existence of a valid marriage. It operates to dissolve the legal bond between spouses based on problems that arose during the course of the marriage. It operates prospectively to terminate the bond from the date of the divorce forward. In contrast, an annulment works retrospectively to invalidate the marital bond based on a defect that existed at the time the marriage was celebrated—it is a statement that because of this defect, the marriage was flawed from its inception. Accordingly, an annulment cannot be granted for a problem that arises after a marriage is celebrated because a valid marriage would have been established, and annulment speaks to marital invalidity. Thus, although common, it is technically incorrect to speak of an annulment as terminating a marriage because it is a declaration that the parties were never in fact married.

Grounds

Grounds for annulment vary from state to state. Most of the grounds can be grouped into two categories: (1) those involving the lack of capacity or intent and (2) those involving breaches of state marital restriction laws.

This distinction has important practical significance. Some defects make a marriage **void** from its inception, while others make it **voidable**. In general, a marriage contracted in violation of state marital laws is considered void from its inception (however, see the discussion on the next page regarding marital restrictions). This means that a decree of annulment is not required to invalidate the marriage—the marriage is regarded as having never taken place. However, a party may prefer to obtain a decree of annulment in order to eliminate any confusion about his or her marital status.

In contrast, a marriage with the defect of **lack of capacity** or intent is generally considered voidable rather than void. A voidable marriage is considered valid until and unless it is invalidated by a decree of annulment. As a general rule, the annulment petition can be filed only by the "innocent" spouse—the one not responsible for the defect. The annulment may be denied if the spouse seeking the annulment knew about the defect at the time of celebration or ratified the marriage by cohabitation after learning of it. Prior knowledge and ratification are not defenses if the marriage is void.

Void:
A marriage that is without any legal effect from its inception; does not require a decree of annulment to invalidate it

Voidable:
A marriage that is considered valid unless and until it is declared invalid by a decree of annulment

Lack of Capacity:
Lack of ability of a party to enter into legally enforceable agreements

Marital Restriction Laws

An annulment can be granted if a marriage is contracted in violation of a marital restriction law. Specific grounds include bigamy, incest, and being under the age of capacity (see the section entitled "Marital Age" in Chapter 1). Incestuous and bigamous marriages are void and cannot be ratified by cohabitation or consent. In contrast, a marriage that is contracted when one or both parties are under age is generally voidable, and continued cohabitation beyond the age of consent will ratify the marriage.

Lack of Capacity or Intent

An annulment may also be granted if one party lacked the capacity or the intent to contract a real marriage due to fraud, duress, mental incapacity, insanity, and, possibly, incurable impotence. Of these, considerations of fraud probably come up the most. To warrant an annulment, the fraud must go to the "essentials" of the marriage. This concept has traditionally been limited to the sexual and procreative aspects of marriage, such as concealing a pregnancy by another man, misrepresenting an intent to consummate the marriage, or misrepresenting an intent to have children where no such intent exists. Some jurisdictions have expanded the concept of fraud to include other critical aspects of the marital relationship, such as religious beliefs — for example, where one party pretends to be deeply religious in order to entice the other into marriage.

A spouse may be able to defeat an annulment action by showing that the other spouse has ratified the marriage. For instance, using the example about religious misrepresentation, if the deceived partner remains in the marriage after learning about the deception, she or he will probably be deemed to have ratified the marriage and would not be entitled to an annulment. Similarly, a court might find that the passage of years has mitigated the impact of the defect because the parties would have had the time to establish an independent relationship.

Consequences of an Annulment Decree

As a matter of logic, if an annulment decree undoes a marriage back to the date of celebration, then any children born to the couple would be "illegitimate"; additionally, no marital rights to support or property would accrue. Although this was the common law approach, this is no longer the case in most states.

Children

In keeping with the modern legal approach to children of unmarried parents (see Chapter 12), children of an annulled marriage are no longer considered illegitimate. Accordingly, the law treats these children similarly to children of divorcing parents when it comes to custody, visitation, and support determinations.

Spousal Support and the Division of Property

Because alleviating financial hardship is considered important enough to outweigh the risk that a party will have been required to support someone eventually determined not to be his or her spouse, many courts will award temporary support during the pendency of an annulment action. However, regardless of need, support will not usually be awarded to a spouse who is denying the validity of the marriage because these are regarded as mutually inconsistent claims. A number of states have enacted statutes allowing an award of permanent alimony in cases of need following an annulment, but some permit an award only if this spouse entered into the marriage with a good-faith belief in its validity. In authorizing support, these statutes eschew reliance on legal formalities and recognize that the declaration of invalidity does not mitigate the financial needs of an economically dependent partner. In the absence of express statutory authorization, a court might make an alimony-like award, such as it might do in a cohabitation case. With respect to property, many statutes expressly authorize the court to make a distribution of accumulated assets much as it would do in a divorce case (see Chapter 9).

Revival

Following an annulment, difficult questions may arise regarding the nature of third-party obligations when such obligations turn on the recipient's marital status. Using a hypothetical, two situations will be briefly discussed.

Let's assume that the marriage of Juan and Maria ended in divorce and that Juan was to pay support until such time as Maria remarried. Now assume that Maria remarries and Juan stops paying alimony based on the fact of her remarriage. What happens if Maria's second marriage is subsequently annulled? Because annulment effectively cancels out the second marriage, Maria could logically argue that there was no remarriage and that Juan's support obligation is subject to **revival**. Moreover, she could claim that he owes her money back to the date he stopped paying. Most courts would reject Maria's claim for support on the basis that Juan had a right to rely on the marriage as it appeared, as distinct from its technical, legal status, and his support obligation would not be revived.

However, when benefits such as Social Security are involved, courts are much more likely to revive payments upon an annulment. For example, if, before her second marriage, Juan had died and Maria was receiving Social Security benefits, these payments would cease upon her remarriage,

Revival:
The restoration of certain rights deriving from a prior marriage following the annulment of a subsequent marriage

but if this second marriage were annulled, most courts would revive the payments because the payor does not rely on the remarriage in the same way as a former spouse would when planning for the future.

◾ Legal Separation

The third remedy for an unhappy marriage is a **legal separation**, also known as a "judicial separation," a "limited divorce," and, historically speaking, a *divorce a mensa et thoro* (a divorce from board and bed).

The Nature of the Action

A legal separation is a judicial decree formally permitting (or, perhaps more accurately, requiring) spouses to live apart. In some states, a separation can be granted for an unlimited period of time; in others, there are durational limits. Grounds are generally similar to those found in fault-based divorce laws, although some statutes simply give a judge the discretion to decide if sufficient cause for a separation exists. The no-fault concept has not permeated this action, perhaps because, unlike with a divorce, a couple can always agree to separate without a court decree.

A legal separation does not terminate the marital relationship. Accordingly, it does not free the parties to remarry. As part of its decree, a court can determine custody and award both child and spousal support. In some states, a division of property also may be ordered; in others, the distribution of property is prohibited unless and until the parties actually divorce. One might wonder why an unhappy spouse would file for a legal separation rather than for a divorce. One reason might be religious beliefs that do not permit divorce because the marital bond is considered indissoluble but would allow a separation because this does not dissolve the marriage. A variety of personal and emotional reasons also might influence the decision to seek a separation rather than a divorce. An individual wishing to live apart from his or her spouse may not be ready to file for divorce but might need the protection of court orders — if, for example, he or she fears that the other spouse might disappear with the children — or the financial support that the court could award. A spouse also might hope to send a wake-up call to his or her partner.

A number of states provide for the conversion of a separation into a divorce after the passage of a specified period of time. Where conversion is not allowed, filing for a separation and then filing for divorce (should a divorce eventually be desired) entails a significant duplication of efforts; therefore, a client's reasons for wanting to start with a legal separation rather than initiating divorce proceedings should be carefully explored.

For instance, if the client knows that the marriage is over but isn't quite ready emotionally to implement the decision, it is worth exploring whether it makes sense to wait to initiate legal proceedings until he or she is ready to proceed with the divorce.

Distinguished from an Action for Separate Maintenance

Upon separation, a party might file a complaint for **separate mainte-nance**. Although similar to an action for a legal separation, the essence of a complaint for separate maintenance is a claim for support. Thus, the focus is on the plaintiff's need for support rather than on the reason for the parties' separation. The decree usually does not involve findings on the reason for separation, nor does it specifically authorize the parties to live apart, although reconciliation generally terminates the support obligation. Also, in most states, the court cannot order a division of property or deter-mine custody as part of a separate maintenance action.

Separate Maintenance: Similar to a legal separation, but here the essence of the action is a request for support

Chapter Summary

Divorce is a legal action that dissolves the marital bond. Our divorce laws are rooted in the Protestant concept of marital sin. Historically, divorce law was premised on marital fault, and a divorce could be granted only to an innocent spouse based on marital wrongdoing. Many couples, however, evaded the law's strictness through the practice of collusive divorce. Beginning in the 1960s, concerns about collusion and the adversarial nature of the fault system led to no-fault reform. Some states eliminated fault grounds altogether and enacted pure no-fault systems. Others added no-fault grounds as an option. The principal no-fault grounds are marital breakdown and living separate and apart for a statutorily prescribed time period.

No-fault laws have been the subject of considerable debate, and there has been a recent backlash against them. Many proposals have been suggested to make divorce more difficult to obtain, especially when a married couple has children. Covenant marriage is a key example of such an effort. A couple entering into a covenant marriage must seek premarital and pre-divorce counseling and waive the right to seek a no-fault divorce. However, concerns have been voiced about these efforts, including that they blur the line between church and state and may entrap spouses in marriages that are abusive or otherwise destructive.

An annulment is a declaration that no valid marriage ever existed between the parties due to an impediment that was present at the time of celebration. Annulments are usually based on a lack of capacity or intent, or a violation of a marital restriction law. Some defects, such as a prior existing marriage, render a marriage void from its inception, while others, such as the lack of capacity, make a marriage voidable.

A legal separation is a decree that the parties have good cause for living apart. It does not terminate the marital relationship, and the parties cannot remarry. It is distinguishable from an action for separate maintenance, which focuses on support rather than on the reason for the underlying separation.

Key Terms

Divorce	Connivance	Marital Breakdown/	Void
Indissoluble	Condonation	Irreconcilable	Voidable
Marital Fault	Recrimination	Differences	Lack of Capacity
Fault Divorce	Comparative	Living Separate and	Revival
Adultery	Rectitude	Apart	Legal Separation
Desertion	Collusion	Mutual Consent	Separate
Constructive Desertion	No-Fault	Covenant Marriage	Maintenance
Cruelty	Divorce	Annulment	

Review Questions

1. What were the Catholic Church's views on marriage?
2. How did the Protestant view of marriage differ from that of the Catholic Church? What impact did this have on divorce law?
3. What are the key fault grounds? What are the requirements for each one?
4. What views do courts hold on the question of whether adultery can be defined to include extramarital same-sex relationships?
5. What are the key divorce defenses? What is the essence of each one?
6. What criticism did the no-fault reformers level at fault-based divorce?

7. What is the difference between a pure no-fault and a dual system?
8. Explain the no-fault ground of marital breakdown.
9. What kind of judicial inquiry is usually conducted in these hearings? How does this differ from the vision of some reformers?
10. Explain the no-fault ground of living separate and apart.
11. What concerns have been raised about the availability of no-fault divorce? What reform measures have been proposed?
12. What concerns have supporters of no-fault divorce raised about present efforts to reform or eliminate no-fault divorce?
13. What is covenant marriage? What do its supporters hope to accomplish?
14. What are some of the criticisms of covenant marriage?
15. What is an annulment, and how does it differ from a divorce?
16. What is the difference between a void marriage and one that is voidable?
17. What is a legal separation? How does an action for separate maintenance differ from a legal separation?

Discussion Questions

1. Many people believe that no-fault divorce makes divorce too easy and has caused people to lose respect for the institution of marriage. Do you think this is true? Why or why not? Does the law of divorce influence your own thoughts about marriage?
2. With no-fault divorce, a spouse usually can obtain a divorce because he or she no longer loves the other spouse. Should this be permitted over the objection of a spouse who claims to still be madly in love and committed to working out the relationship? What should the court do in this situation? Should the presence of minor children be taken into account in resolving this question?
3. Apart from the needs of children, do you think the state has a legitimate interest in encouraging marital permanency through its divorce laws? If so, how should the state's interest be balanced with the interests and needs of the parties to a marriage?

Assignments

1. Locate your state's divorce law and determine the following:
   - Are fault grounds still used, or is your state a "pure" no-fault jurisdiction?
   - If yes, what grounds are available? What defenses are available?
   - What no-fault ground(s) is (or are) available in your state?
   - What must a party show to qualify for a no-fault divorce?

   Having reviewed the statute, identify and describe any recent changes, if any, that have been enacted that are designed to slow down the divorce process (such as waiting periods or counseling requirements) or limit divorce options (such as limiting no-fault divorce to couples without children).
2. A client has come to the office where you work as a paralegal. She is unhappy in her marriage but does not know what she wants to do. The attorney you work for has asked you to draft a letter explaining her legal options. At this point, you do not have all the facts, but, based on a brief interview, you know the following:
   - She thinks that her husband never loved her and that he married her solely to make his family happy.
   - They have been married for three years, during which time, based on his wishes, they have

lived totally separate lives, although they have had sexual intercourse on occasion.

In your letter, you should explain the general differences between divorce, annulment, and legal separation and discuss the specific requirements of the laws in your state.

3. Assume that you are a law clerk for a family court judge who has recently taken a divorce case under advisement because it raises a new issue of law in your jurisdiction. The wife filed

for divorce on the grounds of adultery because her husband has engaged in an intimate relationship with another man. The husband denies that this is adultery, asserting that the concept only covers heterosexual intercourse. The judge has asked you to locate cases from other jurisdictions that have addressed this issue and write an interoffice memorandum in which you first analyze the case law and then set out your thoughts as to how she should rule in this case.

Endnotes

1. *See* John Witte, Jr., The Reformation of Marriage Law in Martin Luther's Germany: Its Significance Then and Now, 4 J.L. & Religion 295 (Summer 1986).

2. Glenda Riley, Divorce: An American Tradition 53-84 (1991).

3. RGM v. DGM, 410 S.E.2d 564, 566-567 (S.C. 1991).

4. In re Blanchflower, 150 N.H. 226, 230, 834 A.2d 1010, 1013 (2003).

5. *Id.* at 1014 (dissenting opinion of Justices Brock and Broderick citing S.B. v. S.J.B., 609 A.2d 124, 126 (N.J. Super. Ct. Ch. Div. 1992)). For further discussion, *see* Peter Nicolas, The Lavender Letter: Applying the Laws of Adultery to Same-Sex Couples and Same-Sex Conduct, 63 Fla. L. Rev. 97 (2011).

6. Homer H. Clark, Jr., The Law of Domestic Relations in the United States 503-506 (Hornbook Series student ed., 1988).

7. *Id.* at 506-509.

8. Katherine Shaw Spaht, The Last One Hundred Years: The Incredible Retreat of Law from the Regulation of Marriage, 63 La. L. Rev. 243, 261 (2003).

9. Donna S. Hershkowitz and Drew R. Liebert, The Direction of Divorce Reform in California: From Fault to No-Fault . . . and Back Again? Counsel Assembly Judiciary Committee, California State Legislature, http://www.assembly.ca.gov (click on Committee Directory, and then click on Committee on Judiciary, and then click on Hearing Reports). *See also* Stephen Bahr, Social Science Research on Family Dissolution: What It Shows and How It Might Be of

Interest to Family Law Reformers, 4 J.L. Fam. Stud. 5, 8 (2002).

10. Maggie Gallagher and Barbara Defoe Whitehead, End No-Fault Divorce? FirstThings: The Journal of Religion and Public Life, August/September (1997) http://www.firstthings.com/article/2008/09/001-end-no-fault-divorce (accessed Oct. 7, 2012).

11. *Id.*

12. Much has been written on both sides of the divorce reform debate, including the following works: Kimberly Diane White, Covenant Marriage: An Unnecessary Second Attempt at Fault-Based Divorce, 61 Ala. L. Rev. 869 (2010); Peter Nash Swisher, Marriage and Some Troubling Issues with No-Fault Divorce, 17 Regent U. L. Rev. 243 (2004/2005); Nicholas H. Wolfinger, The Next Blessings of No-Fault Divorce, 4 Whittier J. Child & Fam. Advoc. 407 (2005); Katherine Shaw Spaht, A Proposal: Legal Re-Regulation of the Content of Marriage, 18 Notre Dame J.L. Ethics & Pub. Poly. 243 (2004); Justin Wolfers and Betsey Stevenson, Bargaining in the Shadow of the Law: Divorce Laws and Family Distress 19 (Stanford Law and Economics Olin Working Paper No. 273; Stanford Law School, Public Law Working Paper No. 73, December 2003), http://ssrn.com/abstract3478162; Allen M. Parkman, Reforming Divorce Reform, 41 Santa Clara L. Rev. 379 (2001); James Hubie DiFonzo, Customized Marriage, 75 Ind. L. Rev. 875 (2000); Robert M. Gordon, Note, The Limits of Limits on Divorce, 107 Yale L.J. 1435 (1998).

Chapter Five

Child Custody

In cases involving child **custody** and **visitation** disputes between divorcing parents, judges face the daunting task of allocating rights and responsibilities between two parents who are likely to have very different perceptions of the arrangement that would be best for their children. Judges often have to make agonizingly difficult choices that have profound and lasting consequences for the parents and their children. Increasingly, judges are also being called on to resolve custody and/or visitation disputes between a child's legal parent and a "third party," most commonly a co-parent, stepparent, or grandparent.[1] These cases raise complex questions about how we define parenthood and the nature of the associated relational interests.

When it comes to disputes between parents, courts generally rely on the "best interest of the child" standard to resolve the conflict. This standard is gender neutral and enables a judge to tailor a decision to meet the specific needs of the children in any given family. On the flip side, the flexibility of the standard means that outcomes can be unpredictable and possibly subjective, thus infusing the determination process with a sense of indeterminacy. When the dispute involves a "third party," there is far less certainty about the appropriate standard, as the best interest approach assumes that both parties stand in an equal legal relationship to the children in question, which, as we will see, is not the case in the third-party context. Before considering the contemporary legal framework for resolving custody disputes, we begin with a historical overview.

Custody:
The care of and responsibility for a child

Visitation:
The time that a noncustodial parent spends with his or her child

Historical Overview

During the colonial era in America, the family was extremely hierarchical in nature, and each member had a defined place in its internal structure. The husband/father was the "governor" of the household, and his wife and children occupied well-defined subordinate positions, subject to his unquestioned authority and control. A father had complete command over the education, training, and discipline of his children. He also owned his children's labor — a valuable right in an agrarian society where the world of work and home were essentially one and the same. In turn, a father was charged with the responsibility of supporting his children and preparing them, particularly his sons, for passage into the world. In sharp contrast, a mother was "entitled to no power, but only reverence and respect."[2]

Paternal Preference: The common law doctrine that vested fathers with the absolute right to care and custody of their children

Custodial rights were understood in property terms: "Custody law held children to be dependent, subordinate beings, assets of estates in which fathers had a vested right."[3] During his lifetime, a father could assign the care and custody of his children to a third party regardless of the wishes of the children's mother, and he could do the same upon his death through his will. Upon family dissolution, the **paternal preference** rule gave fathers a near-absolute right to custody.

In the late eighteenth century, the patriarchal family structure began to break down as the nation moved from an agrarian to an industrial society. As production moved from the family farm into the factory, the world of work became increasingly identified with men and the world of home with women. Children, who had been seen both as economically valuable assets and as needing a father's stern corrective influence, began to be seen more as innocent beings in need of protection and nurture, and mothers replaced fathers as "the most powerful agent in developing a child's character."[4]

Tender Years Presumption: The traditional custodial assumption that children of a young age should be raised by their mothers

Gradually, the favored legal status of fathers gave way to a clear maternal preference. By the end of the nineteenth century, the common law doctrine of paternal rights had been displaced by the **tender years presumption**, which embodied the belief that children, particularly young children, belonged with their mothers. This presumption was expressly incorporated into some statutes, while others authorized the court to award custody to either parent, sometimes specifying that the controlling factor should be in the best interest of the child. However, through judicial decisions, the term "**best interest**" became virtually synonymous with maternal custody, at least with respect to young children. As a result, maternal custody became the norm until the latter part of the twentieth century.

Best Interest: The predominant legal standard for resolving custody disputes between parents; a child-centered standard, focusing on the needs of the child rather than on the rights of the parents

By the 1970s, as fixed notions about proper roles for men and women began to break down, the tender years presumption lost favor. By 1990, virtually all states had eliminated the explicit use of the tender years presumption in favor of a gender-neutral best interest standard. Formally uncoupled from gender determinants, the best interest of the child standard is supposed to ensure that each case is resolved on its own merits, with neither parent being given an advantage based on assumptions about gender.

If parents reach an agreement regarding custody and visitation, a judge will review the terms at the divorce hearing (see Chapter 10) to determine whether they promote the best interest of the children. In most states, the judge conducting this review is not required to defer to the wishes of the parents as embodied in their agreement; rather, the agreement is simply viewed as expressive of their preferences and is only one of many factors in the assessment of best interest. Based, however, on the belief that parents are in a better position than the court to know what is best for their children, some states have begun to give more weight to their custodial preferences, by, for example, adopting a presumption that, without clear evidence to the contrary, the agreed-upon terms are in the best interest of the children.

The Modern Best Interest Test

Formulating the Test

The best interest test requires an analysis of a child's needs and an assessment of which parent can best meet those needs. It is intended to be a flexible, child-centered approach that allows a judge to take a child's individual circumstances into account when making a custody determination. The inherent flexibility of this approach allows an individualized consideration of all relevant factors. On the flip side, the best interest standard has been criticized for being too vague and indeterminate, which means that judges have room to import their personal views into custody determinations, making results unpredictable and possibly idiosyncratic.

Some states have attempted to address this concern by adopting guidelines enumerating specific factors that a judge must consider in making a custody decision. The Michigan statute given here is a good example of this multifaceted approach. In determining custody, according to the statute a judge must consider and enter findings of fact on each of the following:

> "[B]est interests of the child" means the sum total of the following factors to be considered, evaluated, and determined by the court:
> a. The love, affection, and other emotional ties existing between the parties and the child.
> b. The capacity and disposition of the parties involved to give the child love, affection, and guidance and to continue the education and raising of the child in his or her religion or creed, if any.
> c. The capacity and disposition of the parties involved to provide the child with food, clothing, medical care or other remedial care recognized and permitted under the laws of this state in place of medical care, and other material needs.

  d. The length of time the child has lived in a stable, satisfactory environment, and the desirability of maintaining continuity.

  e. The permanence, as a family unit, of the existing or proposed custodial home or homes.

  f. The moral fitness of the parties involved.

  g. The mental and physical health of the parties involved.

  h. The home, school, and community record of the child.

  i. The reasonable preference of the child, if the court considers the child to be of sufficient age to express preference.

  j. The willingness and ability of each of the parties to facilitate and encourage a close and continuing parent-child relationship between the child and the other parent or the child and the parents.

  k. Domestic violence, regardless of whether the violence was directed against or witnessed by the child.

  l. Any other factor considered by the court to be relevant to a particular child custody dispute.[5]

Although statutes like this generally require a judge to consider each enumerated factor, they typically do not require judges to prioritize them or give them equal weight. Accordingly, a judge generally has the discretion to assign the weight to each factor that he or she believes it merits based on either the circumstances of the case or individual beliefs about what considerations are most important. For example, one judge might regard the preference of the child as the primary consideration, while another might attach little weight to it. Moreover, the factors do not lend themselves to precise definitions. For example, what does the term "satisfactory environment" mean? One judge might emphasize the emotional environment of a parent's home, while another might consider more tangible qualities, such as dwelling size. In short, although these statutes set out the framework within which custody determinations are to be made, judges nonetheless retain considerable decisional discretion based on the weight and meaning they assign to the individual statutory factors.

Applying the Test

In this section, we will look more closely at some of the factors that judges tend to emphasize in custody determinations. These include:

- the parent-child bond;
- past caretaking;
- time availability;
- stability of the environment;
- preference of the child; and
- domestic violence.

The Parent-Child Bond

Important to any custody determination is the attempt to evaluate the strength and integrity of the bond that each parent has with his or her children. In some cases, such as where one parent is abusive or disengaged from the family, this task is easy. However, given that most parents have a deep attachment to their children, this assessment can be difficult and may require a multifaceted approach in which a judge weighs a variety of considerations, such as (1) the amount of time each parent spends with the children, (2) the quality and the appropriateness of the interactions, (3) the degree of emotional engagement, and (4) whom the child relies on for emotional and other kinds of essential support.

Past Caretaking

Past caretaking has always been an important consideration in custody determinations. Responding to concerns about the vagueness of the best interest standards, some states now give greater weight to considerations of the caretaking role of each parent during the marriage and favor the primary caretaker. Some states have accomplished this by statute, while others leave it to judicial discretion. (See also the discussion of the primary caretaker presumption and the American Law Institute's (ALI) approximation rule in the section entitled "Critiques of and Alternative Approaches to the Best Interest Standard.")

Primary Caretaker: The parent who has been primarily responsible for the day-to-day care and nurture of a child

A number of distinct, mutually supportive rationales support reliance on past caretaking as a critical factor in the decisional matrix. First, there is general agreement among experts that a child usually develops the strongest psychological bond with the parent who has been most involved with his or her daily care (i.e., the primary caretaker) and that preservation of this relationship is essential to a child's healthy development. This attachment theory "suggests that a strong, caring parent-child dyad leads to a strong secure attachment [and an emotionally secure child]. This same theory posits that if the care provided is unsupportive or unpredictable, then insecurity is manifested."[6] However, some commentators worry that the attachment theory is too simplistic and does not fully account for the complexity of human relations.

Predictability is another major reason that past caretaking has become an increasingly important consideration in custody determinations. Predictability is important for two distinct reasons. First is the belief that reliance on past caretaking will reduce some of the inherent uncertainty about how a child will be cared for following a divorce. A parent's prior commitment to providing primary care is seen as a reasonably reliable predictor of how he or she will respond to the child's needs in the future, whereas determining how a parent who has not been intimately involved with caretaking will respond is far more speculative. Accordingly, reliance on past caretaking patterns provides a protective buffer for children, carrying forward familiar rhythms and interactions.

A second, more recent consideration is that because past caretaking is a more objective criterion than other custody variables, reliance upon it makes custody outcomes more predictable. In turn, this predictability enables couples to enter into custody negotiations with a clearer sense of what they would be likely to gain or lose by going to court. This is particularly important for women because studies have shown that mothers are likely to give up some economic benefits in order to secure custody of their children. If results were more predictable, going to court would be less of a risk, and there would be less need to sacrifice financial entitlements for custodial security.[7] (See the discussion of the primary caretaker presumption later in this chapter.)

In addition to the psychological bond and predictability rationales, reliance on past caretaking accords with the overall trend in favor of the private ordering of family relationships. By looking at the arrangements that the parties agreed on for the care of their children, greater weight is being given to what they believe (or, perhaps, more accurately, believed) makes sense for their family rather than to what a judge believes is best.

Time Availability

The time that a parent has available to devote to his or her children is another important consideration. This is a sensible concern that tends to favor the parent with a less demanding work schedule who has more flexibility to respond to the needs—both routine and unanticipated—of the children. It is likely that this parent is the one who has provided most of the past caretaking and thus has a primary attachment to the children.

Stability of Environment

Children generally have a need for stability and continuity in the wake of divorce's dislocation. Accordingly, judges often give considerable weight to a parent's ability to maintain a stable home environment. The emphasis on stability may lead a judge to look with disfavor on a parent who has moved around a lot. This can be problematic where the frequency of moves is attributable to the economic strain occasioned by the marital breakup. In order to avoid penalizing a parent in this situation, it is important for judges to consider a number of factors, including intangible ones such as continuity of care, when assessing the stability of a child's environment.

Preference of the Child

Given that the undisputed focus of a best interest inquiry is the child, an important consideration is how much weight should be given to a child's stated preference. This is a difficult question that has generated considerable controversy.

Historically, the custodial preferences of children carried little, if any, weight. This disregard of children's views reflected the traditional understanding of children as lacking an independent legal identity. However, this understanding of children has changed over time, and especially as they reach their teen years, children are now regarded as distinct legal persons with some degree of autonomy and say about their lives, including post-divorce custodial arrangements.

Today, all states allow for consideration of a child's wishes. Generally, there are no fixed rules about minimum qualifying ages, and many states require that a child's wishes be seriously considered once she or he reaches a certain age, usually 12 or 14. A few states give a child over the age of 14 the right to choose the parent with whom he or she wishes to live, and his or her choice will be disregarded only if that parent is deemed unfit. Even where not specified by statute or judicial decision, most lawyers believe there is no point in litigating a case where a child over the age of 14 has a clear preference, as a court will almost always respect his or her wishes.

Although chronological age is an important factor in determining whether a child's views will be elicited, and if elicited, what weight they will be given, it is not the only consideration. A judge might also look to the child's maturity, including his or her decision-making ability, and the articulated reasons for any expressed preference. Family circumstances, such as whether there is a history of violence or whether a child blames one parent for ending the marriage, may also be taken into account in assessing the reliability of the child's views.

The Debate over the Appropriate Role of Children.   Some experts believe that it is too stressful for children to be brought into a custody dispute. Of concern here is that children often have complex, shifting views regarding the nature of their relationship with each parent and, by being drawn into the conflict, they may feel as if the weight of the world has been placed on their shoulders. Given that children often blame themselves for their parents' divorce, the fear is that participation will intensify their distress.

Another concern is that a child's stated preference may be shaped by considerations unrelated to best interest, such as fear of reprisal or worry about upsetting a parent perceived as sensitive. A child may also be subject to the undue influence of a parent or may choose a distant, disapproving parent as a way of winning that parent's love. A child may also identify with the parent who she or he perceives as being more powerful in order to avoid feeling powerless or like a "loser." This is of particular concern in cases involving domestic violence because a child may seek to avoid identification with the victim, who is perceived as weak and vulnerable, in order to enhance his or her own sense of security. This tendency may be more pronounced in boys, especially as they approach adolescence. A child also may be angry at the parent who initiated the divorce and may blame that parent for destroying the family. This anger, which may not be articulated, may influence the child to choose the "innocent" parent in order to get back at the other.

A further consideration is that judges, who usually are not experts in child psychology, will not be able to unearth these complex and often deeply buried motivations and may thus give too much weight to "surface" explanations. Although the use of experts can be helpful, their presence does not necessarily solve the problem. The complexity of a situation may not be fully revealed within the necessary time frame for making a decision, and experts often reach conflicting conclusions, thus still leaving a judge with the job of sorting through competing understandings of a situation.

On the other hand, experts who believe the child's preference should be seriously considered argue that children are entitled to a say in a proceeding with such significant implications for their lives and that to do otherwise is paternalistic and demonstrates a lack of respect for the ability of children to participate in important decisions. They fear that if a child is not listened to, his or her true needs might never surface, since parents, although professing concern for the child, are often seeking to vindicate their own rights and fulfill their own needs. Custody battles may become a fight for supremacy between the parents, with the child as a shadow player. Parents may thus distort (deliberately or not) the wishes of the child to suit their own position.

Although recognizing the difficulties inherent in sorting through the motivational factors, those who favor eliciting the views of children believe that judges are capable of sifting through layers of meaning. They suggest that understanding the views of a child is no more challenging than sorting through other kinds of conflicting evidence, and that making sense of the entangled strands of a family's situation is the essence of the judicial function in a custody case.

Drawing on social science research, some experts have shifted the focus away from casting children as *decision makers* to focus on the importance of incorporating them as *participants* in the decisional process. According to these studies, children who are excluded from the process "complain about feeling isolated and lonely during the divorce process, and many older youngsters express anger and frustration about being left out."[8] Providing children with a structured mechanism for giving voice to both their feelings and possible arrangements can counteract these feelings, but inclusion must be more than a symbolic gesture. Children are entitled to expect that "both their parents and the professionals involved will listen with respect to their comments. When parents indicate that they do not value and respect their children's thinking, feelings, worries, and needs, it is unlikely to be helpful, and may create cynicism and anger."[9] There are a number of ways to involve children in the proceedings, including having the judge interview them in chambers and using a third-party professional — such as a guardian ad litem, mental health expert, mediator, or some combination thereof — who can engage the child in a meaningful discussion of what is going on and what the various options might be, without putting him or her in the difficult position of having to choose between parents.[10]

Domestic Violence

Traditionally, courts did not consider interspousal violence — as distinct from physical abuse of the child — relevant to the determination of best interest. Spousal abuse was seen as connected to the marital relationship, with little or no spillover effect into the parent-child arena. However, new understandings of the dynamics of abuse have led to important changes in the law, and whether through judicial decision or legislative enactment, courts in most states are now required to take spousal violence into account when making custody determinations. This shift reflects the reality that, even if not themselves direct victims of violence, many children are exposed to acts of parental violence, and that the exposure itself may have enduring negative consequences. Accordingly, in contrast to the historic disassociation of spousal abuse from the well-being of children, the contemporary approach embodies the view that "the perpetrator of violence against any family member engages in unacceptable behavior that violates his . . . obligations as a parent."[11]

According to the research, somewhere between 70 and 87 percent of children in homes where domestic abuse is present have witnessed violence against their mothers.[12] This exposure can have a significant adverse impact on children. According to one early study, "Children who witness violence between their parents . . . are no less victimized than children who are direct victims of abuse. All our findings show that children from violent homes retain searing memories of violence between their parents."[13] Since then, researchers have confirmed that this victimization has serious emotional and developmental implications. Children exposed to domestic violence are at greater risk of engaging in aggressive and destructive "externally" directed behaviors, such as bullying and assaultive conduct. They also suffer from "internally" directed problems, including depression and anxiety, and they may suffer from post-traumatic stress disorder.[14] Other negative outcomes include cognitive and behavioral delays, which can affect a child's functioning in school and ability to develop friendships.

Another serious concern is that children who are exposed to battering are at greater risk of both becoming abusers and being abused themselves in intimate relationships. According to one study, about one-half of the children who had witnessed violence between their parents experienced violence in their own adult intimate relationships, the boys as abusers and the girls generally as victims.[15]

Also highly relevant is the fact that spousal abuse does not necessarily end upon separation and divorce; in fact, "it is well documented that separation can serve as a catalyst for increased violence" and that "escalated abuse by the batterer as a response to actual or perceived separation is so common that experts have coined the phrase 'separation assault' to describe it."[16] Accordingly, an abusive parent's right of access to the children may need to be limited in order to safeguard the well-being of the abused parent. In turn, paying attention to the safety of the custodial parent has multiple implications for the well-being of children. Not only will this vigilance shield children from continuing exposure to violence, and the associated risk of harm, the reduced threat of violence may well enhance the ability of a caretaker parent to focus on the needs of her children.

Custody statutes generally take one of two approaches with respect to domestic violence. The majority of statutes direct judges to take domestic violence into account as one of the factors that must be weighed when determining custody, with a few statutes directing judges to weigh it more heavily than other considerations. The other approach is to create a rebuttable presumption against awarding sole or joint custody to a parent who has been the perpetrator of domestic violence. To rebut the presumption, a spouse might, for example, seek to show that he has successfully completed a batterer's treatment program and no longer engages in violent behavior.

Parental Lifestyle and Life Circumstances

In determining best interest, it is not uncommon for a parent to argue that some aspect of the other parent's lifestyle or life circumstances will have a detrimental impact on the children and/or to also claim that, conversely, he or she is better positioned to meet the needs of the children based on his or her own life circumstances. These kinds of arguments raise the question as to what weight, if any, a judge should give to a parent's lifestyle or life circumstances when determining best interest, especially if these considerations place the parent outside what can loosely be referred to as the "mainstream." Are these matters of morality relevant? Is it appropriate for a judge to base decisions on his or her own views about what constitutes a proper environment for a child? Should a judge be allowed to reflect popular community views—for example, that children should be raised by heterosexual parents?

Judges are not supposed to make custody decisions based on their own subjective sense of what is right for a child, or on their assessment of community standards, as these determinations would embody a judge's own personal view of the world and would result in highly idiosyncratic and unpredictable outcomes. To prevent this kind of subjective decision making, the basic rule is that there must be a direct **nexus** (or connection) between the parental attribute in question and the well-being of the child. This approach is intended to limit judicial discretion and keep the child's needs at the center of the decision-making process. However, it is worth considering whether it is realistic to think that judges can completely disregard their own views when deciding the cases that come before them.

Nexus:
Connection

Considerations of Race and Culture

In the landmark case of Palmore v. Sidoti in 1984,[17] the U.S. Supreme Court reversed a Florida trial court decision transferring custody of a young girl from her mother to her father because the mother, who was white, married a black man subsequent to the parties' divorce. In transferring custody, the trial court focused on the possibility that the child would suffer from the stigma of living in a racially mixed household, especially once she began school. In reversing the decision, the Supreme Court made clear that social prejudice should not determine custody outcomes and that the equal protection clause prohibits giving effect to personal bias through the medium of custody adjudications. Moreover, the Court made clear that harm to a child cannot be assumed even though racial prejudice may subject him or her to "a variety of pressures and stresses not present if the child were living with parents of the same racial or ethnic origin."[18]

Although unambivalent in condemning custody decisions premised on racial prejudice, the *Palmore* decision has not been interpreted to mean that race is *never* a permissible consideration in custody determinations. For example, in the case of Gambla v. Woodson, an Illinois appeals court held in a custody dispute involving a biracial child that, although it would have been inappropriate for the trial court to have awarded custody to the mother "solely because she is African-American," it was not in error for having taken into account the fact that she could provide her daughter with a "breadth of cultural knowledge and experience" that the father could not offer her, and was therefore in a better position to prepare her daughter for existing "as a biracial woman in a society that is sometimes hostile to such individuals."[19]

Paralleling this result, the custody statutes in a few states expressly identify a child's cultural background as one of the factors that is to be taken into account when assessing which parent is in a better position to meet the child's needs. In addition, in states where culture is not included as an express statutory factor, some courts have woven a consideration of a child's cultural needs into other statutory criteria for assessing best interest. Thus, for example, in evaluating the importance of maintaining a child's ongoing connection with the community in which he or she lives, a court might include a consideration of the extent to which that community offers the child an opportunity to "interact with others who share his or her heritage."[20]

Sexual Activity: Heterosexual

Another important question is what weight, if any, should a judge give to the sexual behavior of a parent seeking custody of a minor child? The majority view is that sexual behavior by itself or the fact that a parent is living with a partner she or he is not married to is not relevant unless a detrimental effect on the child or the parent-child relationship is clearly established. In requiring proof of a nexus between the behavior of the parent and the well-being of the child, harm to the child is not to be presumed from the fact that the parent is engaged in a nonmarital relationship, as this would be tantamount to a moral pronouncement embodying the judge's subjective views rather than an assessment of the parent's actual ability to care for the child. Rather, such conduct is relevant only where detriment can be shown—for example, where sexual activity occurs in front of the children or where the parent leaves the children on their own in order to pursue a relationship.

Sexual Orientation: Gay and Lesbian Parents

Although the unquestioned majority approach is that a parent's involvement in a heterosexual dating or cohabiting relationship will not impact his or her ability to obtain or maintain custody absent a clear showing that this involvement somehow harms the child, the law's approach has been more varied when it comes to gay and lesbian parents. For years, the dominant approach was to presume, without requiring proof of harm, that it was bad for a child to be raised by such a parent. This is frequently referred to as the **per se approach**, in which harm is assumed to flow from the parent's conduct without requiring proof of actual detriment based on concerns such as that homosexuality is immoral and unnatural and that children must be protected from its influence or that children will be stigmatized.

Per Se Approach:
The idea that some behaviors are so inherently harmful that they should be the basis for denying custody to a parent without proof of actual harm

However, a growing number of states have rejected the per se approach in favor of the nexus standard. Requiring a "sexual orientation-neutral" lens, judges may no longer treat gay and lesbian parents differently from parents who are in a heterosexual dating or cohabiting relationship. Accordingly, a parent cannot be denied custody based on a presumption of harm; rather, as when a parent seeking custody is in a heterosexual relationship, actual detriment to the child from the relationship must be proved before it can be factored into the custody outcome. In adopting the nexus approach, states have been influenced by the weight of social science studies that have concluded "that the family environments provided by lesbian and gay parents are as likely as those provided by heterosexual parents to foster and promote children's psychological well-being."[21]

Although not common, another approach falls somewhere between the nexus and the per se approaches. In this intermediate approach, the status of being a gay man or a lesbian is not in and of itself deemed harmful, as it would be under a per se approach; rather, the focus is on associated conduct. Under this approach, a court might award a gay or lesbian parent custody but impose certain behavioral limitations. For example, a parent might have to agree, as a condition to receiving or keeping custody, that she or he will not engage in any displays of affection in front of the children or participate in any gay-identified activities. One might ask whether this approach is simply a twist on the per se rule, as it requires a parent to forgo any meaningful expressions of intimacy and personal identity in order to qualify for custody.

It will be interesting to see what impact the Court's decision in the marriage equality case of Obergefell v. Hodges has on the law in those jurisdictions that employ either the per se approach or impose limits on a parent's conduct as a condition of custody. Importantly, in this regard, one of the important pillars of the decision was that marriage safeguards the interests of children with same-sex parents by, among other reasons, enabling children to "'understand the integrity and closeness of their own family and its concord with other families in their community and in their daily lives.'"[22]

Religion

The issue of religion usually comes up in custody disputes in one of two ways. A parent may claim that he or she can best meet the religious needs of the child and should therefore be awarded custody. Alternatively, a parent may claim that the religion of the other parent is detrimental to the child or goes against the child's established identity, and that this should therefore disqualify that parent from custodial consideration. In the first situation, religion is presented as a positive, qualifying factor; in the second, it is presented as a negative, disqualifying one.[23]

In evaluating these claims, a court becomes involved in a delicate and sensitive task, as it must respect the first amendment rights of both parents. This amendment (which is applied to the states through the due process clause of the fourteenth amendment) prevents state interference with an individual's freedom of religion and undue state involvement with religion (e.g., expressing a preference for one religion over another). Absent a compelling interest, a state must remain neutral and uninvolved where religion is concerned.

Where a parent raises religion as a qualifying factor, it cannot be the sole custodial determinant because the judge would be expressing a preference for the religion of one parent over the religion of the other or over the lack of religious involvement. Moreover, the court would be giving preferential weight to religion, saying, in effect, that it is the most important aspect of a child's upbringing. However, where religion is an established part of a child's life, a court may be able to take a child's actual religious needs into account when determining which parent is best able to provide stability and continuity of care. Thus, for example, if a child regularly attends religious services and educational classes, the court might look at which parent has been actively involved with these activities, much as it would evaluate parental involvement in other areas of the child's life. In effect, it is evaluating which parent will best be able to meet the ongoing needs of the child, without making a value judgment about the kind of religious upbringing a child should have.

Where religion is raised as a disqualifying factor, the parent often belongs to a religion that is considered outside of the mainstream by the parent seeking custody. Typically, the nonmember parent argues that the other's religious beliefs or practices pose a threat of harm to the child's emotional, physical, or psychological well-being. For example, a common concern is that a child will be isolated from his or her peers by restrictions that prohibit certain activities, such as participation in school celebrations, watching television, or associating with nonmembers. The parent seeking custody may also fear that the child will be alienated from him or her if the religion of the other parent teaches that, as a nonbeliever, he or she is evil and will suffer eternal consequences.

Most courts employ a nexus approach in these cases. A parent must show actual harm before the other parent's religious practices are considered relevant. At least in theory, this avoids the risk that a court will make value judgments about a parent's religion. Other courts employ a somewhat less exacting standard and may disqualify a parent if his or her religious beliefs and practices are shown to pose a substantial or reasonable likelihood of harm. Even under this lower standard, however, general assertions about potential isolation or confusion from being raised in a "different" environment should not be given legal effect.

Under the risk of harm standard, a number of cases have dealt with the difficult question of how to evaluate the potential risk when the parent seeking custody belongs to a religion that prohibits certain medical practices, such as blood transfusions. Some courts have held that where there is no evidence of medical need, the risk is too speculative to justify a denial of custody on that ground alone. For example, in the 1995 case of Garrett v. Garrett, the Nebraska Court of Appeals stated with respect to the award of custody to a mother who was a practicing Jehovah's Witness:

> [I]n order for Jeanne's religion to constitute a ground for awarding custody to Larry, we must be able to determine from the record that the Jehovah's Witness religion as practiced by Jeanne constitutes an immediate and substantial threat to the minor children's temporal well-being. . . .
>
> As evidence of an immediate and substantial threat to the minor children, Larry makes reference to the fact that even in the case of a

medical emergency, Jeanne would refuse to consent to any of the children's receiving a blood transfusion. . . .

No evidence was presented showing that any of the minor children were prone to accidents or plagued with any sort of an affliction that might necessitate a blood transfusion in the near future. We cannot decide this case based on some hypothetical future accident or illness which might necessitate such treatment.[24]

On the other hand, some courts have found that such a belief, in and of itself, poses a substantial risk of harm and do not require specific proof that a child is actually in need of a religiously prohibited medical procedure.

Critiques of and Alternative Approaches to the Best Interest Standard

The best interest standard has been subject to serious criticisms. Two notable concerns are that it lends itself to gender-biased decisions, and that its flexible nature lends itself to unpredictable and idiosyncratic results.

Although the best interest standard is gender neutral on its face, concerns continue to be raised that judges import gender bias into their custody decisions. Fathers' rights groups argue that fathers are often less valued as parents than mothers and that judges often assume that men cannot be primary caretakers. They thus argue that despite gender-neutral laws, the concept of best interest remains linked to beliefs about the natural superiority of maternal nurturing and caretaking abilities.

On the other hand, many women's groups argue that when fathers seek custody, they are often favored by judges, especially when a mother works outside the home, as women are held to a higher parenting standard than men. Accordingly, an employed mother may be regarded as unsatisfied with her role as mother and as being more concerned with gratifying her own needs than caring for her children. Exacerbating this problem, they note that fathers may get "extra credit" for the time they spend with their children, as this contribution is seen as "special" — as being over and above what is expected of them as men. This double standard thus penalizes mothers for time spent away from their children while unduly rewarding fathers for time spent with them.

The other key critique of the best interest standard is its unpredictability. On the positive side, unpredictability is a function of the standard's flexibility, which permits a judge to tailor results to the circumstances of an individual case. This can be very helpful given the complexity and variability of family relationships. On the other hand, as suggested earlier, it also means that judges have considerable room to make decisions that reflect their personal views of what is best for a child.

Consider the following situation. A couple has two children in grade school and live in a middle-class suburb. The father is employed full time and the mother is a stay-at-home parent. Both parents are kind and loving, but the children's primary attachment is to the mother. Both parents want sole custody. If the father is awarded custody, he will be able to remain in the home and to offer the children the presumed advantages of a middle-class lifestyle, including keeping the children in the school they presently attend. If the mother is awarded custody, she will need to move to a less expensive community where the schools are not as good because, even with child support and possible part-time employment, she will not be able to afford the home they live in.

What is the likely outcome? Does the best interest standard compel one result over the other? The answer is hard to predict because the outcome depends on whether the judge regards continuity of caretaking or continuity of home, school, and community as more important. Given the flexibility of the standard, and the corresponding decisional discretion of judges, either outcome could be justified as serving the children's best interest.

The indeterminacy of the best interest standard has significant implications for the settlement process (see Chapter 10). If the outcome cannot be predicted with some degree of certainty, then it means that custody negotiations are taking place in the absence of a transparent decisional framework, thus making it difficult for the parties to assess what they stand to gain or lose as they consider various proposals. In significant part, this problem has given rise to the formulation of two alternative standards that seek to make custody outcomes more predictable. In this section, we consider these critiques and look at the two alternative standards: the **primary caretaker presumption** and the ALI's "approximation" rule.

Primary Caretaker Presumption:
A legal rule that gives preference to the primary caretaker parent in the event of a custody dispute

The Primary Caretaker Presumption

Emerging out of dissatisfaction with the vagaries of the best interest standard, a number of states have considered adopting a custodial presumption in favor of the parent who has been the primary caretaker. Under this standard, primary caretaking would be the sole determinant of best interest.

In 1981, in the leading case of Garska v. McCoy, West Virginia became the first state to adopt the primary caretaker standard (although it has since moved to the ALI's approximation rule). In adopting this standard, the *Garska* court focused on the harm caused to the primary care parent by the unpredictability of the best interest test:

> The loss of children is a terrifying specter to concerned and loving parents; however, it is particularly terrifying to the primary caretaker parent, who, by virtue of the caretaking function, was closest to the child before the divorce. . . . Our experience instructs us that uncertainty about the outcome of custody disputes leads to the irresistible temptation to trade the custody of the child in return for lower alimony and child support payment.[25]

In anchoring custody outcomes to a fixed standard, the court was thus seeking to prevent custody from being used as a bargaining weapon to extract economic concessions from the primary caretaker parent in order to ensure a favorable custody result.

This presumption has been praised for its recognition of the undervalued job of parenting and the importance of the bond between children and their primary caregivers. It has also been praised for introducing certainty into the process and protecting the often vulnerable economic status of primary caretaking parents. However, the presumption has also been criticized for being overly mechanistic and failing to account for the complexity of parent-child relationships. Fathers' rights groups have attacked the presumption for being gender biased, asserting that it is a thinly disguised effort to reintroduce the tender years presumption to the detriment of fathers.[26] Others disagree, noting that if a father is the primary caregiver, the presumption will favor him. Moreover, it is noted that although more mothers than fathers might end up with custody under the presumption, this would reflect the actuality of how families allocate caretaking responsibilities rather than generalized assumptions about gender-appropriate roles.

It has also been argued that the presumption can work against women as well. Although a stay-at-home mom, or one who is employed on a very part-time basis, would clearly be identified as the primary caretaker, the concern is that a judge may not recognize that a woman who works full time may nonetheless still be the primary caregiver. The judge may assume that the world of work and home are incompatible, thus rendering invisible a woman's continued domestic and caretaking responsibilities.

Despite the considerable interest and discussion that the primary caretaker presumption has generated, states have not rushed to adopt it. Nonetheless, it has contributed to ongoing discussions and efforts to reformulate the best interest standard, including the ALI's approximation rule.

The American Law Institute's Approximation Rule

In 2002, after more than a decade of research, the prestigious American Law Institute published the *Principles of the Law of Family Dissolution: Analysis and Recommendations* in order to bring "conceptual clarification and improved adaptation to social needs" to the dissolution process.[27] With respect to custody, the principles recommend shifting from the best interest standard to a more objective "approximation" standard that would allocate custodial responsibilities between divorcing parents in rough proportion to the amount of time each parent spent engaged in caretaking responsibilities during the marriage. In short, the post-divorce parenting arrangement would *approximate* their pre-divorce arrangement.

Proponents of the approximation approach argue that it injects a strong measure of predictability into what is currently a highly unpredictable process. With the result more predictable, proponents argue that primary caretakers will be less likely to bargain away economic rights in order to secure custody, thus promoting outcomes that are related to the needs of children rather than to the bargaining positions of the parties. They also argue that this approach would provide children with greater stability and continuity of care because, to the extent possible, their parents would continue to play the same role in their lives that they did prior to the divorce. In short, children would be buffered from some of the radical reconfiguring of the parent-child relationship that so often accompanies a divorce.

However, some important concerns have also been raised about the approximation rule. First, some commentators worry that it is too deferential to parents and not sufficiently child-centered. What if, for example, past caretaking arrangements were adopted to meet the needs of the parents rather than to provide optimal care for the children? What if other ways of allocating custodial responsibilities would be better for the children? However, reflecting what is believed to be the rule's overly mechanistic approach to determining custody, these kinds of considerations would not be relevant. Another important question is whether it is overly optimistic to assume that arrangements that worked when the parents presumably got along with one another will continue to work in the aftermath of dissolution when parental cooperation and goodwill is apt to be at a minimum.

Additionally, as with the primary caretaker presumption, the argument is made that this approach is simply an effort to sneak the tender years presumption back into custody determinations. However, once again, proponents argue that if mothers end up with more custodial time as a result of the approximation rule, this outcome reflects the reality of existing caretaking arrangements that the parties themselves decided upon, rather than suggesting a built-in gender bias in favor of women.[28]

Custody and Visitation Arrangements

Resolution of a custody case becomes even more complex when one takes the variety of custodial and visitation arrangements that are available into account. Traditionally, custody was essentially a unitary concept — one parent, usually the mother, was responsible for raising the child and making all significant decisions affecting the child's life, and the other parent simply visited.

However, beginning in the 1970s, the wisdom of allocating parental roles along such lines was questioned, and joint custody emerged as an approach that would enable children to maintain an ongoing relationship with both parents following a divorce. By 1990, most jurisdictions had amended their custody laws to include joint custody as an option, and some created a presumption that joint custody is in the best interest of the child, although some of these laws have since been repealed. In this section, we focus on the actual working out of custody and visitation arrangements.

Physical and Legal Custody Distinguished

For the sake of clarity, the terms "physical custody" and "legal custody" will initially be defined in reference to one parent, but as will become apparent, either can be shared. Also, you should be aware that there has been some movement away from the traditional terminology, in part to reflect the current emphasis on cooperative post-divorce parenting. Thus, for example, the ALI Principles use the term "custodial responsibility" instead of "physical custody," and the term "decision-making responsibility" for "legal custody." Also, physical custody is now sometimes referred to as "residential custody."

Physical custody refers to where a child lives. A parent with physical custody maintains a primary residence for the child and is generally responsible for the child's daily care. With physical custody comes the authority to make all of the day-to-day decisions that arise in the course of caring for a child.

Legal custody refers to decision-making authority. Whereas physical custody incorporates the right to make routine decisions, legal custody gives a parent the right to make major decisions affecting the health, welfare, and education of a child, such as whether a child should go to private school or begin mental health counseling. As a general rule, major decisions are distinguished from day-to-day decisions by their importance and their nonrepetitive nature, although, as discussed in the following section, this distinction is often easier to state than to apply.

Physical Custody:
Refers to where a child lives; a parent with physical custody usually maintains a home for the child and is responsible for the child's day-to-day care; can be either sole or joint

Legal Custody:
Confers on a parent the authority to make major decisions related to his or her child's life; can be sole or joint

Sole and Joint Custody Distinguished

The term "sole custody" refers to the vesting of custodial rights in one parent; either legal or physical custody can be sole. With an award of *sole physical custody*, the child lives with one parent and that parent has primary caretaking responsibility. With an award of *sole legal custody*, one parent has the authority to make all of the major decisions affecting the child. Where both custodies are vested in one parent, the other parent will generally have visitation rights without significant parenting responsibilities.

Joint custody refers to the sharing of rights and responsibilities; both legal and physical custody can be allocated on a joint basis. *Joint legal custody* denotes the sharing of decision-making authority, and *joint physical custody* denotes the sharing of the day-to-day responsibility for raising a child.

Sole Custody:
The vesting of custodial rights in one parent

Joint Custody:
The sharing of parental rights and responsibilities

A Closer Look at Shared Custody Arrangements

Two shared custody arrangements are most likely: A couple may share both physical and legal custody, or one party may have sole physical custody and share legal custody with the other parent. It is also theoretically possible for a couple to share physical custody, with sole legal custody assigned to one parent, but it is hard to envision many situations where a parent who is responsible for the daily care of a child would not want major decision-making authority or would be deemed incapable of handling it.

Where parents share legal custody, neither one is supposed to make a major decision affecting the child without the participation and consent of the other parent, absent emergency circumstances. Where parents disagree, no action can be taken until a resolution is reached. This can have serious implications for the well-being of a child, where, for example, parents disagree about whether the child needs to be evaluated by a therapist. Ultimately, these disputes may have to be submitted to a court for resolution.

In situations where one parent has sole physical custody with shared legal custody, the distinction between major and day-to-day decisions can become critical. Some decisions are easy to characterize: Enrollment in a private school, elective surgery, or mental health counseling are clearly major issues. The choice between blue socks or green or whether to attend a friend's birthday party are clearly of the daily variety. But what about ear piercing? Or violin versus tuba lessons? Or a significant change in hairstyle? These decisions are harder to characterize and can lead to tremendous conflict over who has the right to make such decisions.

Where parents share physical custody, both are responsible, though not always equally, for the day-to-day care of the child. Here, many arrangements are possible. A child could spend roughly equal amounts of time with each parent, rotating between the households according to a fixed schedule that allocates time on a daily, weekly, monthly, or even yearly basis. Each parent would maintain a home for the child, who would in effect have two principal places of residence. It is also possible for the sharing to be less equal. A child might have one primary residence but spend a significant amount of time with the other parent, who would remain much more directly and consistently involved in the child's life than the traditional visiting parent.

The Joint Custody Controversy

The joint custody trend began in the 1980s based on a number of considerations. First, a number of studies indicated that fathers tended to drift out of their children's lives following a divorce, causing children to feel a sense of abandonment and rejection. Rather than blaming fathers for not caring about their children, joint custody proponents saw this disengagement as stemming from the awkwardness and insignificance of being cast in a visitor's role and hoped that, given a more meaningful place in their children's lives, fathers would remain more connected to them. Second, an emerging fathers' rights movement was seeking to combat what they perceived as anti-male bias in the family courts, and joint custody became a central demand as a way of wresting custodial control from women. Third, corresponding to the no-fault goal of making divorce a less adversarial process, it was hoped that joint custody would encourage parents to stop fighting over their children and to work out a cooperative arrangement where neither emerged the victor.

Although it has become more commonplace, joint custody remains a contentious issue. Most experts agree that where parents freely choose joint custody and are committed to making it work, it can be a positive arrangement because it gives a child meaningful contact with both parents. However, making it work can be extremely difficult. Parents need to be able to set aside their anger and disappointment in the other as a spouse and respect him or her as a parent. In short, they must have the ability to distinguish between their spousal and their parenting roles. Even where parents are able to work things out between them, concerns have been raised that joint custody may overburden children, as it requires them to negotiate life in two different households.

The far more contentious issue is whether courts should be able to impose joint custody where one parent objects to it. According to fathers' rights proponents, it is essential for courts to have this authority in order to counteract the bias they believe exists against fathers in the divorce courts. They argue that if joint custody were allowed only where it was agreed upon, mothers could routinely defeat the claims of fathers by objecting to joint custody. Fathers' rights groups thus have lobbied for laws that create a presumption in favor of shared custody; the groups also have brought class action lawsuits based on the argument that state laws that do not ensure each parent an equal share of parenting time violate parents' fundamental right to the care and custody of their children. Although these legal challenges generally have not been successful, with courts finding that the best interest of children trumps a parent's asserted right to equal custodial time, many states have amended their custody laws to include a preference or presumption in favor of joint custody.

However, serious doubts have been raised about the wisdom of giving courts the authority to compel joint custody over the objection of a parent, particularly in high-conflict families, especially when there has been a history of domestic violence. A major concern is that the frequent interaction that joint custody demands may keep alive spousal animosity and conflict and thereby interfere with the parents' ability to disengage from the marriage. Perpetuating spousal animosity is likely to have a spillover effect on the children, who may experience serious mental health issues as a result of continuing exposure to parental anger and arguments.[29] Based on growing evidence that imposing joint custody on recalcitrant and noncooperative parents can have negative effects on children, and that "the bulk of newly divorced spouses cannot remain as positively involved with each other on an everyday basis as joint physical custody requires, [and] that the presumption is causing more litigation to already crowded dockets," states have begun to move away from joint custody presumptions in favor of making joint custody one of the options to consider when determining the best interest of children.[30]

Legal Status of the Noncustodial Parent

Noncustodial Parent:
A parent who has been divested of both legal and physical custody, but is still a legal parent with enforceable rights, such as visitation

At the opposite end of the custodial spectrum from a shared physical and legal custody arrangement is one in which both custodies are vested in a single parent, and the other is a **noncustodial parent**. As discussed next, this parent is usually granted visitation rights; however, before considering visitation, it is important to understand this parent's legal status.

Loss of custody in the context of a divorce action does not sever the parent-child relationship; a mother or father who does not have either legal or physical custody of a child is still that child's parent. (The termination of parental rights is covered in Chapter 13.) The retention of one's legal status as a parent has the following important ramifications:

1. Because custodial determinations are not permanent, a noncustodial parent may always seek to modify the existing arrangement and thus may acquire custodial rights at some point in the future; in contrast, a termination of parental rights results in a permanent severance of the parent-child relationship.
2. Noncustodial parents retain a number of important rights. These include visitation rights; the right of access to school, medical, and other records; and the right to make medical decisions in the event of an emergency or the unavailability of the custodial parent.
3. In addition to these rights, a noncustodial parent remains subject to a support obligation.
4. With the legal relationship intact, benefits and statutory rights that depend on the existence of a parent-child relationship will most likely not be lost. For example, if a noncustodial parent dies without a will, the child will be entitled to a share of the estate under a state's intestacy laws. However, entitlements that depend on proof of actual dependency may be denied.

Thus, although loss of custody may be a devastating event in a mother or father's life, she or he is still a parent. This may seem like a legal abstraction to a noncustodial parent, who may no longer feel like a parent;

however, the legal relationship carries with it a bundle of rights and an ongoing support obligation.

Visitation Rights

The general assumption is that following a divorce, it is in a child's best interest to have continued contact with both parents. Accordingly, in virtually all cases, a noncustodial parent (referring here to a parent without physical custody) will be granted visitation rights. Because this parent plays a less significant role in the life of a child than the custodial parent does, courts generally use a lower standard for deciding about visitation than they do for deciding about custody. Accordingly, a parent who may not be capable of providing the day-to-day care and nurture that a child needs will, in most cases, be considered capable of spending some meaningful time with the child on a regular basis.

However, as discussed in more detail next, if continued contact is deemed to pose a risk of emotional or physical harm to a child, visitation rights will be denied or subject to limitations.

The Visitation Schedule

As the following discussion makes clear, working out a viable visitation schedule, including determining the appropriate nomenclature, involves the careful consideration of multiple factors.

Amount of Time and Frequency of Visits. Because there is so much variability in visitation arrangements, it is hard to state with any certainty how much time the "average" visiting parent spends with his or her children. However, the unquestioned trend is to increase visitation time and frequency well beyond the traditional four hours on Sunday afternoon, which gave dad just enough time to take the kids to the zoo and out for a quick dinner.

Setting aside, for the moment, those cases in which visitation may pose a threat to a child's physical or emotional well-being, visitation rights are now seen as providing the noncustodial parent with the opportunity to remain an integral part of his or her child's life as opposed to simply being the "fun" parent. When the parents live close to one another, the noncustodial parent may be able to see the child on a regular basis, which can provide a sense of continuity and familiarity. The schedule may well include some overnight time and some extended time during school and summer vacations. When the parents do not live near each other, visitation will, of course, be less frequent, and it will be harder for the noncustodial parent to remain connected to the rhythms of a child's daily life. This may be offset somewhat by extended visitation time over the summer and school vacations.

Setting the Parameters. Visitation arrangements, as set out in a court order, separation agreement, or parenting plan, can be open-ended, spelled out in elaborate detail, or somewhere in between. An open-ended arrangement generally provides for a right of reasonable or liberal visitation and leaves the details up to the parties. This kind of arrangement usually works best if the parties have been separated for a while and have informally worked out and implemented a mutually satisfactory schedule. Because an open-ended agreement requires frequent communication, it is not likely to succeed if the parties are angry and hostile or have not been successful at working out an informal arrangement. The constant negotiations necessitated by an open-ended schedule may serve to keep the anger between the parties alive longer and prevent them from settling into a reasonably calm visitation pattern, to the clear detriment of the children. A visitation arrangement can be spelled out with great specificity, detailing precisely when each and every visit is to occur and who is responsible for transporting the children to and from the visits. A visitation schedule for summer and school vacations and holidays also may be detailed. Specific guidelines for when a parent may deviate from the schedule may be included as well. (See Chapter 10 for an example of a separation agreement with a very specific visitation schedule.)

A middle-ground approach is to provide a fairly set schedule, with a proviso that this does not represent the full extent of the visiting parent's rights and that he or she may also visit at other mutually agreed-upon times. This minimizes the negotiations inherent in a completely open-ended arrangement but also builds in a degree of flexibility that may benefit both parents—especially if it is written to accommodate both of their needs.

Parents often do not anticipate how emotionally difficult the visitation process can be for both them and the child, especially around holidays and when a former partner begins to date. Accordingly, at least in the initial period following a divorce, a good argument can be made that most parents do better with a specific visitation plan that minimizes the need for constant negotiations. Frequently, after the initial emotional intensity has dissipated, parents are better able to be more flexible in responding to the needs of the other parent.

The Boundary Between Shared Physical Custody and Sole Custody with Visitation Rights. The formal boundary between sole custody with visitation rights and joint physical custody cannot always be fixed with precision, although some states have set a minimum amount of time that a parent must spend with a child for the arrangement to qualify as shared custody. For example, the following arrangement could, absent specific statutory criteria, be characterized either way: A child lives with his mother during the week and spends every weekend—from Friday at 6 P.M. until

Sunday evening — with his father. He also has dinner with his father every Wednesday night.

In negotiating an agreement, many attorneys try to avoid using these terms because they carry a lot of emotional baggage. For example, if parents have negotiated an arrangement in which the children are to be with the mother 70 percent of the time and with the father 30 percent, the mother may object to calling this shared physical custody because it obscures the fact that she has the children most of the time. On the other hand, the father might object to his time being identified as visitation because this can suggest minimal involvement. Accordingly, alternative terms such as "primary care parent" and "secondary care parent" can be substituted, or the agreement may refer to shared parenting responsibilities, with each parent having custody when the children are with him or her, regardless of how the total time is allocated.

When Unrestricted Visitation Is Not in a Child's Best Interest

Despite the priority that the law gives to preserving the relationship between a child and the noncustodial parent, there are situations in which continued contact is considered not to be in a child's best interest, such as where it would place a child at risk of emotional or physical harm. Another possibility is that visitation would be allowed but would be subject to restrictions, such as that visits be supervised by a third party. The parent might also be required to be in therapy and/or attend some kind of parenting class.

Restrictions on visitation may also be imposed where a history of domestic violence places the custodial parent at risk even if the child has not been a direct victim of the abuse. Here, restrictions are generally aimed at limiting contact between the parents, such as that the child is dropped off and picked up at a neutral location (for instance, an agency that provides custody exchange services) at a timed interval so there is no contact between the parents.

Frequently, a parent who has been denied visitation rights or who has restricted visitation will return to court seeking unrestricted access to his or her child. In response, a judge must determine if the child (or the custodial parent) is still at risk of harm. If visits are being allowed for the first time, a judge is likely to impose some restrictions. Judges vary in their approach to requests for the lifting of existing restrictions. Some judges are reluctant to modify restrictions on the ground that the risk of potential harm outweighs the potential benefit of allowing visitation to occur in a more natural, unstructured way. Other judges take the view that if a parent has complied with the requirements of the initial restrictions, he or she is entitled to a second chance to reestablish a relationship with his or her child that is not dependent on the involvement of third parties.

Parenting Plans, Parenting Coordinators, and Parent Education Programs

Although, as noted previously, the trend has shifted away from joint custody presumptions in favor of making joint custody an option, this shift does not signal a return to the traditional "zoo daddy" model, in which fathers typically had a few hours of fun with their children on Sunday afternoons and an occasional holiday, with no expectation of a sustained and meaningful role in their children's lives. Rather, as we have seen, the preferred approach today is to create a structure that enables both parents to maintain meaningful ties with their children. Although studies indicate that children fare better when they sustain a quality post-dissolution relationship with both parents, the research also makes clear that continued parental conflict and hostility, which can be exacerbated by frequent contact, has a deleterious impact on children. Accordingly, to minimize post-divorce animosity and enhance the ability of parents to coordinate caring for their children, parenting plans and parenting education programs have become increasingly popular legal options.

A growing number of states now require parents to develop and submit a "parenting plan" to the court for approval if custody is to be shared, and a few states require the submission of a plan in all cases involving minor children. In other states, judges have the option of requiring the submission of a plan in any case where they deem it appropriate to do so. A **parenting plan** is a written agreement in which the parents detail how they intend to care for their children following a divorce. Designed to minimize hostility and foster cooperative parenting, parenting plans generally must cover all aspects of child rearing, including how time between the two households is to be divided, how responsibilities are to be allocated, and how decisions are to be made and disputes resolved. Depending on the state, other matters, such as relocation and child support, may also be addressed. In some states, parents may be required to participate in mediation if they cannot agree upon the terms of a plan.

Paralleling the criticisms of joint custody with which these plans are often associated, serious concerns have been raised about the appropriateness of requiring parenting plans in cases involving domestic violence or where there is parental hostility. Accordingly, exemptions or special protections have been incorporated into many of these laws to cover situations where the kind of cooperative parenting envisioned by parenting plans is either not safe or not feasible.

A more recent innovation, particularly in high-conflict divorces, is the appointment of parenting coordinators who are tasked with the responsibility of helping parties to successfully implement their parenting plan. A number of states have specifically enacted parenting coordinator provisions, while others rely upon "existing statutes that allow for 'mediators'

Parenting Plan:
A written agreement in which the parents detail how they intend to care for their children following a divorce

or 'special masters' as a basis for appointing parenting coordinators," and in the absence of any such statutory authority, it is arguable that "the discretion given to judges to fashion orders in the best interest of . . . children, could be extended . . . to order [parents] to cooperate with a parenting coordinator."[31]

Although the scope of their authority varies from state to state, parenting coordinators typically focus on helping parents to develop strategies for resolving conflicts that arise around custody. However, as a general rule, they do not have the authority to alter the parameters of the parenting plan or to change the allocation of custodial rights and responsibilities between the parents. In some states, parenting coordinators are able to make certain decisions when the parents are unable to resolve a conflict that arises over a day-to-day parenting issue, but these decisions are generally subject to court review. Parenting coordinators may also have the authority to made recommendations to the court.[32]

A related trend is the enactment of laws setting up parenting education programs for divorcing parents. Depending on the state or the circumstances of the family, these programs may be mandatory or offered on a voluntary basis, and, like parenting plans, they are intended to facilitate the transition to post-divorce parenting. These programs are designed to educate "parents about the potential effects of their behavior and attitudes on their children."[33] The hope is that, once they gain such awareness, parents will modulate negative behaviors so that they can respond more effectively to the needs of their children.

Again, important concerns have been raised about parent education programs where there has been a history of domestic violence. In states where participation is mandatory, judges are usually allowed to waive the attendance requirement for good cause, such as where necessary to protect a party from the risk of abuse. Other options have also been suggested that would enable a victim of domestic violence to attend a parent education class while also protecting her safety, such as by having the parents attend class on different nights or in different locations.[34]

A more recent innovation is for courts to offer educational programs for the children of divorcing parents to help them understand and cope with the changes in their lives. Children are usually grouped according to age, and the curriculum is adapted to the development needs of the targeted age. Although these programs are usually offered on a voluntary basis, they may be required in some jurisdictions. For instance, under local court rules in Kentucky, children in many parts of the state are required to attend the children's component of the state's Divorce Education program. That portion of the overall program is designed to "provide a sense of security, awareness, and understanding as a beginning point for children learning to cope with dual parenting in separate households." Children in grades 1 through 5 attend Kids' Time, and those in grades 6 through 8 attend Tweens' Time.[35]

INTERVIEW CHECKLIST

Following is a list of the kinds of information you will need to learn about in cases where custody or visitation (or both) may be an issue. As discussed in greater detail in Chapter 10, it often takes a while for a client to feel comfortable enough to speak openly about the intimate details of his or her life. Thus, absent an emergency situation where an immediate custody decision must be made, all of the following information does not need to be obtained at the initial interview. In fact, you are likely to obtain a more accurate and complete picture if you do not push for all this information up front. Accordingly, the checklist shown here should not mechanistically be converted into a set of interview questions. Also keep in mind that parents, regardless of their particular situations, are likely to be worried and anxious about their future relationship with their children; you need to be sensitive to the volatility of child-related issues. Remember, too, that information about the other parent coming from your client is likely to be different from the information the other parent provides to his or her own attorney.

1. What is the nature of the relationship each parent has with the child?
2. How have responsibilities been allocated between the parents over time? More specifically:
   - Who makes the child-care arrangements?
   - Who transports the child to and from child care or school?
   - Who arranges the child's activities?
   - Who stays home with the child when he or she is sick?
   - Who supervises homework?
   - Who helps the child get off to child care or school in the morning (e.g., getting breakfast, clothing)?
   - Who is responsible for bathing the children and putting them to bed?
   - Who makes the child-related purchases?
   - Who attends school meetings (including parent-teacher conferences)?
3. How much time does each parent have available to be with the child?
4. What is each parent's approach to discipline (including any potential concerns about abuse)?
5. What activities does each parent enjoy with the child?
6. How does each parent intend to make post-divorce adjustments in his or her schedule to accommodate the changed family structure?
7. What are each parent's strengths and weaknesses?
8. Does either parent have a history of alcohol or drug abuse?
9. Does either parent have a history of mental health problems?
10. What are the available support systems, such as friends and relatives, of each parent?
11. What are each parent's commitments, in addition to work?

Post-Divorce Custody and Visitation Disputes

Following a divorce, disputes often arise regarding custody or visitation arrangements — or both — and a parent may return to court seeking to either enforce or change existing arrangements. The former is accomplished through a **complaint for contempt** and the latter through a **complaint for modification**; as a general rule, a complaint for modification must be based upon an unforeseen change in circumstances that alters the existing arrangement so that it is no longer in the best interest of the child. Courts have continuing jurisdiction over these disputes until children reach the age of majority and are no longer subject to the custodial authority of their parents. Rather than returning to court, parents also may seek to resolve these disputes through mediation or arbitration; in fact, their separation agreement may require them to try to resolve their dispute through one of these methods before they can seek court relief. (For details on the procedural aspects of this paragraph, see Chapter 10.)

These post-divorce actions can be a double-edged sword. On the one hand, in order to make certain that a child is protected from harm and that his or her needs are being met, courts must have the authority to hear and resolve post-divorce disputes. On the other hand, this creates the possibility that parents who are engaged in an acrimonious dispute for control of a child will continuously return to court, claiming that the child is not being cared for properly. Because courts have a duty to ensure that custodial arrangements do not pose a risk of harm to a child, a court must assess the situation, even where it appears that in bringing the action, the parent was motivated by hostility rather than a genuine concern for the child. Next, we consider three common categories of post-divorce disputes, and the emerging debate over "virtual visitation."

Complaint for Contempt: A parent's return to court following a divorce, to enforce existing arrangements about custody or visitation after a dispute

Complaint for Modification: A parent's return to court following a divorce to change existing arrangements about custody or visitation after a dispute

Disputes About Custody

Following a divorce, parents often express concern about the custodial arrangements and seek to change them. Thus, for example, in a situation of shared legal custody, it may turn out that the parents cannot make decisions without a protracted struggle, and the parent with physical custody feels that this is interfering with his or her ability to meet the needs of the child. Or where parents share physical custody of a child who is now a teenager, the parent who lives in the town where the child attends school may seek sole custody because the teen resents having to spend sustained time away from his or her primary group of friends. Or a parent may realize that the other parent, who had been sober for an extended period at the time of the parties' divorce, has relapsed and is again abusing alcohol and is thus not able to care for the child properly.

In these examples, the desired modifications are based both on a genuine concern for the well-being of the child and on a change in circumstance that makes the existing arrangement unworkable. Of course, the other parent may not see the situation in the same way, and she or he may vehemently oppose the requested change. Some requests for modification, however, are not based on a concern for the child but stem from continued hostility toward the other parent. Thus, for example, a parent may resent the fact that his or her former spouse is cohabiting with a new partner and may seek to have that parent's custodial rights revoked, claiming that the partner is a bad influence on the child. Note that although this is clearly a change in circumstances, there must also be an adverse impact on the child. It is not always easy for the court to sort out what is going on, and modification actions that stem from parental hostility often become bitter and protracted as old antagonisms resurface.

Disputes About Visitation

As with custody, bitter fights may occur around visitation. The visiting parent may assert that the custodial parent refuses to let him or her see the child, while the custodial parent may assert that he or she always gets the child ready and the other parent never shows up. These disputes are difficult to resolve. Often, there is not much a court can do other than admonish the parties to comply with the terms of the visitation arrangement. If, however, the custodial parent is truly interfering with the visiting parent's ability to see the child by, for example, consistently not being at home when the visiting parent is supposed to pick up the child, the visiting parent can bring a contempt action; the ultimate sanction for interference with visitation rights would be a transfer of custody to the other parent. If, on the other hand, the custodial parent has good cause for limiting access, such as when the visiting parent has shown up intoxicated to pick up the child or there is a consistent failure of the visiting parent to adhere to the schedule, the custodial parent may be able to bring a modification action to curtail or restructure the existing arrangement. Unfortunately, there is no real remedy for a custodial parent who wishes to compel the other parent to exercise his or her visitation rights. A parent cannot be forced to visit when he or she chooses not to.

Relocation Disputes

Relocation Disputes: A disagreement arising during or after a divorce in which the custodial parent seeks to move to another state with the children, and the noncustodial parent seeks to prevent the move

Following a divorce, most states do not permit a custodial parent to move out of state with the child without first obtaining the consent of the other parent or the court. As might be expected, **relocation disputes** are fraught with bitterness. A custodial parent is likely to resent the potential limitation on the ability to seek a better life, especially in light of the fact that a visiting parent can move about freely without having to secure anyone's consent, and the noncustodial parent is likely to resent the potential loss of access to the child.

States take a variety of approaches to relocation cases, but the recent trend has been to favor the right of the custodial parent to relocate with the children. Generally, the parent must show that the move is motivated by good faith—such as by a job opportunity or the desire to move closer to extended family, rather than by a desire to interfere with the rights of the noncustodial parent—and is in the child's best interest.[36]

Under this approach, the concept of best interest is usually broadened to take the needs of the custodial parent into account, based on the view that the child and custodial parent are interdependent and a move that benefits the parent, by, for example, locating him or her closer to extended family, will inure to the benefit of the child. As explained in one of the first cases to adopt this expanded view of best interest:

> [t]he children, after the parents' divorce or separation, belong to a different family unit than they did when the parents lived together. The new family unit consists only of the children and the custodial parent, and what is advantageous to that unit as a whole, to each of its members individually and to the way they relate to each other and function together is obviously in the best interests of the children. It is in the context of what is best for that family unit that the precise nature and terms of visitation and changes in visitation by the noncustodial parent must be considered.[37]

The relationship between the child and the noncustodial parent is certainly not an irrelevant consideration in jurisdictions favoring the custodial parents in relocation disputes. However, given that the primary focus is on the importance of continuity of care within the custodial household and what is needed to make that family function effectively, the fact that visitation will occur on a less regular basis is generally not enough to prevent a move. It may be enough to defeat the move, however, when considered with other factors, such as when the move is not prompted by reasons calculated to benefit the custodial household but by, for example, a desire to change scenery.

States that favor the custodial parent generally approach the issue differently where the parents share physical custody. Here, the child has two distinct post-divorce households, and his or her best interest is not so clearly identified with one parent as it is when one parent has sole custody. In this situation, a court might decide that preserving the status quo is in the child's best interest and deny the relocation request. Another possible approach would be to modify or terminate the existing custody order, and make a de novo determination of the child's best interest, which would incorporate a determination about relocation.

The other approach is to give more weight to the interests of the noncustodial parent in preserving his or her relationship with the child. Accordingly, the custodial parent most likely will be required to prove more than simply good faith and best interest. In terms of his or her motivation for moving, he or she may need to establish that the move is compelled by "extraordinary reasons." In terms of its impact on the child, the parent may need to show that it offers a "real advantage," although the meaning of this term is not entirely clear. At a minimum, the parent may need to prove that the child would gain a tangible benefit that is not available in the home state. Under this approach, courts generally do not take an expanded view of best interest and will thus not assume, without supporting evidence, that changes for the better in the custodial parent's life naturally benefit the child.

Recently, the trend favoring the custodial parent in relocation disputes has been questioned by some commentators who argue that this approach simply assumes that a child's well-being is tied to the custodial parent and fails to account for the actual experiences of the child. Thus, for example, one recent study suggests that children might be adversely impacted when they move more than an hour's drive from the noncustodial parent, while others suggest that relocation outcomes might vary based upon a complex array of factors, such as the age of the children, how soon the move follows the time of separation, and the nature and frequency of contact the children and the noncustodial parent have before the move.[38] Such research could well influence the future direction of relocation cases.

Virtual Visitation

In 2001, in the case of McCoy v. McCoy, after finding that the custodial mother had a good-faith reason for relocating to California, a New Jersey court concluded that in assessing whether the existing visitation arrangement could be restructured to "accommodate and preserve the relationship that the child had with her father," the trial court had failed to give adequate weight to the mother's "suggested use of the Internet to enhance visitation." Characterizing her proposal as "both creative and innovative," the appeals court concluded that if the "actual" proposed visitation arrangement was inadequate, the judge should have considered this supplemental means of communication. In what is generally considered to be a groundbreaking approach, the court stressed that technology could be used to ensure "continued development" of the child's relationship with her father, while also preserving the mother's right to move.[39]

Today the concept of **virtual visitation**, which refers to the use of "email, instant messaging, webcams, and other internet tools to provide regular contact between a noncustodial parent and his or her child,"[40] is no

Virtual Visitation: The use of electronic communication tools as a supplemental way for a child and a noncustodial parent to connect

longer regarded as groundbreaking, and many courts routinely consider the availability of virtual means of communication when deciding relocation cases. Taking this trend a step further, in an effort to enhance the post-divorce relationship between a child and the noncustodial parent, some judges now include virtual visitation provisions in cases that do not involve an out-of-state move.

When fashioning virtual visitation orders, the growing tendency is for courts to be quite specific about what kind of technology is to be used, who is to pay for it, and when and under what conditions it is to take place. In this regard, the most valuable communications tools are generally considered to be those, such as webcams and Skype, that make real-time communication possible, thus enabling a parent to be present, albeit virtually rather than physically, in his or her child's life. However, as some commentators have noted, not all judges are fully versed in the wide range of available technologies, and their orders may thus not take full advantage of cutting-edge modalities.

In general, courts do not appear to be factoring the possibility of virtual communication into the relocation decision itself as a threshold matter; custodial parents are thus still expected to establish a legally sufficient reason for the proposed move. Accordingly, in *McCoy*, for example, it was only after the mother had shown, to the court's satisfaction, that the move was prompted by the prospect of a better job and a better climate for her daughter, who suffered from asthma, that it considered the possibility of using virtual visitation to supplement the father's actual time with his daughter. In short, it does not appear that courts are relying on the availability of virtual visitation to short-circuit the relocation decision itself.

Concerns, however, have been raised that judges may begin to rely on the availability of this technology in making the underlying relocation decision itself. Here, it would not simply be a way to supplement other avenues of communication once an independent decision had been made, but it would be a factor in the decisional matrix, to be weighed along with other considerations, such as the reason for the move and the best interest of the child. This raises profound questions about the nature of human interaction and how meaningful relationships are maintained with people who are not in physical proximity. Must connection occur in person for it to count as meaningful contact? Can one really "interact" virtually? What is lost when technological connections replace physical contact? What does it mean for human relationships when spatial proximity is no longer needed for real-time communication? These and other related questions will only become more pressing in the coming years as the distance between virtual and actual reality continues to diminish.

Finally, several states have enacted virtual visitation statutes, and a number of other states are considering such measures. Generally speaking, these legislative enactments are aimed at ensuring greater uniformity and consistency within any given jurisdiction with respect to the circumstances under which virtual visitation can be ordered and how such orders are to be structured. Thus, for example, a statute may spell out that virtual visitation orders are meant to supplement in-person contact, not to serve as a substitute for it. In addition, these laws may also be able to address the growing concern of some commentators that in cases involving a history of domestic violence, the use of "electronic communication may give the abusive ex-spouse the ability to invade the privacy of his or her former spouse."[41] Particularly worrisome is that it may be used to ferret out that parent's whereabouts in situations where safety needs dictate the nondisclosure of location.

The Custodial and Visitation Rights of "Nonparents"

Up to this point, the focus of this chapter has been on custody and visitation disputes between divorcing parents. In these disputes, the rights of each party, at least in a formal legal sense, are deemed to be equal. Each is entitled to try to establish that an award of custody to him or her would further the best interest of the child. In this section, we turn to a consideration of custody and visitation disputes between parents and "nonparents"—namely, grandparents, stepparents, and co-parents, although, as we will see, the term "nonparent" is problematic in the co-parent context, as it assumes the lack of parental status, which is often the controversial issue.

Before considering these disputes, it will be helpful to review four fundamental principles that have guided the law's traditional understanding of the parent-child relationship:

1. Parenthood is achieved solely through biology or adoption.[42]
2. Parents have a fundamental right to direct the upbringing of their children, including deciding who will have access to them.
3. A child can have only one legally recognized mother and one legally recognized father, for a sum total of two different-sex parents.
4. In a dispute between a parent and a "nonparent," there is an automatic preference in favor of the parent based on the assumption that he or she is best able to meet the child's needs absent extraordinary circumstances.

In accordance with these principles, these disputes are treated differently from those between two divorcing parents. Although the approaches vary from jurisdiction to jurisdiction, the basic rule is that as a nonparent, this party must establish something more than best interest in order to maintain an ongoing relationship with a child in the face of opposition from a parent. She or he may need to prove that the parent is unfit before being able to assert her or his own rights to see the child, or that severing the relationship between the child and the party would cause demonstrable harm to the child. In some instances, a "nonparent" may even be denied standing (this concept is discussed next) to assert a claim in the first instance.

Grandparents

At common law, grandparents had no legal right of access to their grandchildren. This approach began to change in the 1960s, and today, all states have statutes that, to varying degrees, permit grandparents to seek visitation rights. Some states have enacted specific grandparent visitation statutes, while others include grandparents within a broader third-party visitation statute. This shift reflects the growing awareness of the importance of providing children with continued access to essential relationships in order to help buffer the dislocation of divorce. Closely related, they also acknowledge how important the bond between a grandparent and child can be.[43]

In looking at grandparent visitation statutes, it is helpful to ask two questions: (1) Under what circumstances may a grandparent seek visitation rights? and (2) What substantive standard will be used to resolve the dispute? The first question is often characterized as a matter of **standing**, which is a jurisdictional concept that requires a person to have a sufficient stake in the outcome of a controversy in order to be allowed to maintain a legal action. If a party lacks standing, his or her action is dismissed. Most statutes require that there be some kind of family disruption, such as divorce or parental death, in order for a grandparent to have standing. In other states, the statutes give grandparents a more general right to seek visitation without specifying the circumstances under which a petition can be filed. However, based on considerations of family privacy, many courts will not allow a petition to go forward where the family is "intact" and require some kind of disruption or proof of parental unfitness as a prerequisite to the maintenance of an action.

Once it is determined that a grandparent has standing to seek visitation rights, the next consideration is the standard to be used for resolving the dispute. Some states have adopted a best interest standard (see, however, the discussion of the *Troxel* case next), although judges generally require proof of something more than simply that the child would enjoy a continued relationship with the grandparent. Other states have adopted a higher burden of proof, most frequently by requiring the grandparent(s) to establish that the denial of visitation rights would harm the child.

Standing:
A jurisdictional concept requiring a person to have a sufficient stake in the outcome of a controversy in order to maintain a legal action

As grandparents began turning to the courts to gain access to their grandchildren after contact had been denied or limited by a son or daughter (or by a daughter- or son-in-law), some parents responded by challenging the constitutionality of the grandparent visitation laws, arguing that such laws were an unwarranted intrusion into the realm of family privacy. Initially, courts tended to uphold the validity of the statutes, finding that any intrusion into a fit parent's right to direct the upbringing of his or her children was offset by the benefit to the child of a continued relationship with his or her grandparent. As expressed by the Kentucky Supreme Court in the case of King v. King, these early decisions tended to sentimentalize the grandparent-grandchild relationship:

> If a grandparent is physically, mentally and morally fit, then a grandchild will ordinarily benefit from contact with the grand-parent. . . . Each benefits from contact with the other. The child can learn respect, a sense of responsibility and love. The grandparent can be invigorated by exposure to youth, can gain an insight into our changing society, and can avoid the loneliness which is so often a part of an aging parent's life.[44]

In 1993, however, starting with the decision of Tennessee Supreme Court in the case of Hawk v. Hawk, courts began to give greater consideration to the rights of parents to decide who should have access to their children:

> . . . Bill and Sue Hawk argue that grandparent visitation is a "compelling state interest" that warrants use of the state's parens patriae power to impose visitation in "best interests of the children." . . . We find, however, that without a substantial danger of harm to the child, a court may not constitutionally impose its own subjective notions of the "best interests of the child" when an intact, nuclear family with fit, married parents is involved.
>
> The requirement of harm is the sole protection that parents have against pervasive state interference in the parenting process.[45]

In 2000, the U.S. Supreme Court, in the case of Troxel v. Granville, entered the fray. Under consideration in this case was the state of Washington's open-ended statute that gave "any person" the right to petition the court for visitation rights at "any time" based on the best interest of the child. This case involved an unmarried couple with two children. After the relationship ended, the father moved in with his parents. He saw his children on a regular basis, with the visits often taking place at his parents' home. About two years after the separation, the father committed suicide. The grandparents continued to visit with the children. The mother then decided to limit the visits, and the grandparents sued for increased access to their granddaughters.

The Court found that the statute was invalid *as applied* to the facts of the case before it. Of primary concern was the "sweeping breadth" of the statute, which effectively allowed a judge to substitute his or her views regarding visitation for the views of a fit parent:

> Once . . . the matter is placed before a judge, a parent's decision that visitation would not be in the child's best interest is accorded no deference. . . . Instead, the Washington statute places the best-interest determination solely in the hands of the judge. Should the judge disagree with the parent's estimation of the child's best interests, the judge's view necessarily prevails. Thus, in practical effect, in the State of Washington a court can disregard and overturn any decision by a fit custodial parent concerning visitation whenever a third party affected by the decision files a visitation petition, based solely on the judge's determination of the child's best interests.[46]

In deciding this case, the Court made clear that it was not declaring as a matter of constitutional principle that all third-party visitation laws are an impermissible encroachment on the rights of parents, or that harm must be established before allowing visitation over the wishes of a parent. Instead, the Court held only that, at a minimum, some "special weight" must be given to the stated preference of a fit parent—a result that has led to various interpretations. Some courts have read *Troxel* broadly to require almost complete deference to parents as long as they are fit; others have read it more narrowly—to, for example, place a burden on grandparents to show that something more than the child's best interest is needed in order to override the wishes of a fit parent.[47]

Stepparents

Traditionally, if a second marriage ends in divorce, a **stepparent** (the spouse of a child's parent) has not been entitled to visitation or custody on the theory that the stepparent's status derives from the marriage and thus lasts only as long as the marriage does. This result would, of course, be different if the stepparent had adopted the child because adoption creates a permanent parent-child relationship that is not dependent on the continued existence of the marriage. However, compelled by the awareness that stepparents often play a critical role in the lives of children, particularly when the noncustodial parent is uninvolved, the law has begun to give stepparents greater rights upon marital dissolution.

Some states have statutes that specifically allow a stepparent to seek visitation, and possibly also custodial, rights following a divorce. In other states, in the absence of a statute, courts have used a number of theories to extend parental-like rights to stepparents at the time of marital dissolution. For instance, a Michigan court extended parental status based on the

Stepparent:
The legal relationship of a new spouse to the children of a prior marriage

Equitable Parenthood:
A doctrine used to extend parenting rights to a stepparent when there is a developed, consensual relationship with the child, and he or she wishes to assume the rights and responsibilities of parenthood

concept of **equitable parenthood** and permitted a stepparent to be treated as a parent where:

> (1) the husband and child mutually acknowledge a relationship as father and child, or the mother of the child has cooperated in the development of such a relationship over a time prior to the filing of the complaint for divorce, (2) the husband desires to have the rights afforded to a parent, and (3) the husband is willing to take on the responsibility of paying child support.[48]

In Loco Parentis:
Common law doctrine conferring parental rights and responsibilities on someone who voluntarily assumes a parenting role

Other courts have extended rights to stepparents based on the doctrine of *in loco parentis*.[49] Here, parental rights (and obligations, such as the duty to pay child support) may be extended to someone who has assumed the role of a parent over an extended period of time through the provision of sustained nurturance and support. To be *in loco parentis*, a stepparent must intend to participate in a child's life as a parent—a casual relationship will not give rise to this status. Although this doctrine has been used to extend a stepparent-child relationship beyond the end of a marriage of the stepparent to the child's parent, a limitation is that the relationship can be terminated at will by the stepparent (or the child), thus bringing the legal bond with its corresponding rights and duties to an end. (See the discussion next of the *in loco parentis* doctrine in the context of co-parent custody/visitation cases.)

In jurisdictions where stepparents can pursue post-dissolution claims, the approach tends to be more liberal where visitation, as distinct from custody, is at issue. Where there is a meaningful connection between a stepparent and child, a court may recognize the importance of continuing this bond beyond the marriage and allow visitation based on a best interest standard. Following *Troxel*, some courts may be inclined to require more than proof of best interest, while others see a distinction between a grandparent and someone who has been in an actual parental role. Where custody is at issue, the traditional preference in favor of biological parents means that considerably more weight will be given to the expressed views of the legal parent. To prevail, a stepparent may need to establish unfitness or the presence of "extraordinary circumstances" that would merit depriving the biological parent of custody.

Co-Parents

Like heterosexual couples, many same-sex couples decide that they wish to share in the joys of raising a child together—for the purpose of our discussion, we will assume a lesbian couple, as most of the major reported cases to date have involved co-mothers.[50] Accordingly, based on their mutual intent to share in the raising of a child, one woman is either inseminated or adopts a child (see Chapter 13 regarding co-parent adoption). Although both women may regard the child as equally theirs, and the child may likewise regard both women as his or her mother, the law has not generally seen it this way. Despite the intent of the parties and their actual parenting arrangements, only the parent with the actual biological or adoptive connection to the child has traditionally been regarded as a legal parent, thus relegating the co-parent to the status of "legal stranger" to the child.

Co-Parent: A parent who shares the raising of a child with his or her partner in the absence of a formally recognized parent-child relationship

However, the law has begun to change in response to cases brought by co-parents who have sought to establish their right to maintain an ongoing relationship with the child they helped to raise when their relationship with the legal parent ends. Seeking to be recognized as legal parents, co-parents have used a number of legal theories, such as those discussed previously in relationship to stepparents, to advance their claims. Regardless of which approach is used, at the heart of these cases is the desire to be recognized as a parent based on shared intent and the reality of her parental relationship with the child. Although, as discussed next, a growing number of jurisdictions have responded favorably to these claims, others have not been sympathetic and continue to regard a co-mother as a legal stranger based on her lack of a biological or adoptive connection to the child. Here, great weight is given to traditional understandings of parenthood and the right of exclusivity that this status confers.

Where denied parental status, a co-mother is then essentially treated as a third party. In jurisdictions where third-party standing is limited to a defined class of persons, such as grandparents and stepparents, she most likely will not be able to assert the right to an ongoing relationship with the child, regardless of the weight and nature of the bond between them. Typically relying on the constitutional principle that legal parents have a fundamental interest in the "care, custody, and protection" of their child,[51] which encompasses the right to determine who has access to the child based upon the presumption that a fit parent will make decisions that promote his or her child's best interest, the court in these cases never even reaches the question of what impact the severing of the bond with the co-parent will have on the child.

In jurisdictions where standing is conferred on a broader group of persons — such as all persons with a significant relationship with a child — a co-parent may be able to assert her claim, although it is also possible that a court would refuse to recognize the relationship as significant. If the party is able to meet this jurisdictional threshold, the dispute would still be characterized as one between a parent and a nonparent, and the parental preference would be triggered. Accordingly, unlike a divorcing mother and father, the parties would not begin on equal footing, and the co-parent would need to show something more than best interest to overcome the preference, such as that the child would suffer actual harm from the severing of the relationship, which is clearly a more difficult standard to meet.

However, over the course of the past 15 or so years, a small but growing number of jurisdictions have moved beyond this formalistic conception of what it means to be a family and have used a number of different legal theories to extend parental status and rights to co-parents.

De Facto Parent Status

De Facto Parent:
An individual who has no biological relation to a child, but who has functioned as a family member; must show that he or she resided with the child and shared caretaking responsibilities with the consent and cooperation of the legal parent

In 1996, in the landmark case of Holzman v. Knott, the Supreme Court of Wisconsin became the first court to expressly extend **de facto parent** status to a lesbian co-parent.[52] Since then, a number of other states have followed suit. In *Holzman*, a lesbian couple decided to have and rear a child together. Following the termination of the relationship, Holzman sought visitation rights when her former partner, the child's biological mother, refused to allow her to see the child. Rejecting the assertion that a biological parent has a constitutionally protected right "to determine who shall visit her child," the court concluded that a party with a "parent-like" relationship with a child that has been disrupted by the termination of that relationship has standing to seek visitation (note that this case did not involve custody). To determine if there is a parent-like relationship, a party must be able to establish the following elements:

1. The legal parent consented to and fostered the relationship.
2. She resided with the child in the same household.
3. She assumed the responsibilities of parenthood.
4. She was in the parental role long enough to establish meaningful connection with the child.[53]

Since *Holzman*, courts adopting this approach have stressed the importance of a couple's mutual decision to have and raise a child together. Thus, for example, in a subsequent case from Massachusetts, the parties sent out joint birth announcements; embodied their parenting intent in a range of legal documents, including a co-parenting agreement; gave the child both of their last names; and fully shared parenting responsibilities.[54]

This element of mutual consent ensures that this status is not one that a court can impose on a legal parent. As explained by the New Jersey Supreme Court:

> This opinion should not be viewed as an incursion on the general right of a fit legal parent to raise his or her child without outside interference. What we have addressed here is . . . the volitional choice of a legal parent to cede a measure of a parental authority to a third party. . . . In such circumstances the legal parent has created a family with the third party and the child, and has invited the third party into the otherwise inviolable realm of family privacy.[55]

This requirement also responds to the concern raised by some that a nanny or babysitter could somehow end up as a de facto parent simply by participating in the life of a child. Further responding to this concern, some courts have stressed that the caretaking functions must be performed "for reasons primarily other than financial compensation."[56]

Once recognized as a de facto parent, a party is no longer a "legal stranger." However, the question still remains as to whether a de facto parent stands on equal footing with her former partner, much as a divorcing husband and wife would. For instance, the New Jersey Supreme Court stated that "[o]nce a third party has been determined to be a psychological parent to a child, under the previously described standards, he or she stands in *parity* with the legal parent." The court went on to emphasize, however, that "parity" does not require equality of treatment, and that because "... in the search for self-knowledge, the child's interest in his or her roots will emerge," if "the evidence concerning the child's best interests (as between a legal parent and psychological parent) is in equipoise," custody should be awarded to the legal parent.[57] In contrast, in a more recent co-parent custody case, the Supreme Court of Washington made clear that once a party is found to be a de facto parent, he or she is in "legal parity" with the other parent, which places them in "equivalent parental positions."[58]

Presuming Maternity Based Upon State Parentage Laws

As will be discussed in Chapter 11, most states have a parentage statute that recognizes a husband who consents to the insemination of his wife as the legal father of the resulting child and cuts off any potential rights in the sperm donor. In keeping with the recommended approach of the Uniform Parentage Act (UPA), a number of states extend this same recognition to an unmarried man who consents to the insemination of his partner with the "intent to be the father of the child."[59]

By logical extension, a few courts have looked to the UPA's statement that "[p]rovisions of this [Act] relating to determination of paternity apply to determinations of maternity"[60] to reach the same result in cases involving two women. For example, in the case of Elisa B. v. Emily B., the California court concluded that under the UPA, as adopted by California, just as a similarly situated man would be the presumed legal father, a woman who consents to the insemination of her partner, and then receives the child into her home and openly holds the child out as her own, is the presumed legal mother of that child. Likewise, a New Jersey court ruled that the state's sperm donor law, which treats a husband who consents to his wife's insemination as the child's legal father, was equally available to committed same-sex partners, thus allowing the names of both women to be placed on their child's birth certificate as her legal parents.[61]

Presuming Parenthood Based Upon Marriage

Marriage also offers another likely pathway to legal parenthood for a co-parent. More specifically, the wife of a woman who bears a child during the marriage should be regarded as a presumed parent in conformity with the long-standing common law presumption of paternity that treats the husband as the legal father of any child who is born into the marriage. (See Chapter 9 regarding this common law presumption.) The parallel application of the marital presumption means that a spouse would not have to prove that she is a de facto parent in order to maintain a relationship with the child in the event of a divorce or separation; rather, this status and the correlative rights would flow from the existence of marriage (or civil union) itself.

Chapter Summary

Historically, fathers had an absolute right to the custody of their children. With industrialization, the rights of fathers yielded to the tender years presumption, which assumed that mothers were the best caretakers of young children. Now, virtually all statutes use a best interest of the child standard. In theory, this is a child-centered, gender-neutral approach to resolving custody disputes. Judges are directed to evaluate each case on its individual merits, focusing on the needs of the child rather than the rights of the parents. Where parental conduct or lifestyle is at issue, most jurisdictions employ the nexus approach and require proof of harm. However, this standard has been criticized for its lack of predictability and objective criteria.

Custody has both a legal and a physical component; either may be awarded on a sole or a joint basis. Although there has been an increased focus on shared custody, this approach has been subject to criticism, especially in cases involving a history of domestic violence. A noncustodial parent is presumptively entitled to visitation unless there is a risk of harm to the child. To facilitate post-divorce parenting, there has been an increased focus on parenting plans and parenting education.

Custody and visitation disputes have increasingly involved claims by "third parties," most notably grandparents, stepparents, and co-parents. Where grandparents are concerned, all states have statutorily modified the common law rule of nonaccess and permit visitation under certain circumstances, and a number of states also now recognize post-divorce claims of stepparents seeking to maintain an ongoing relationship with the child of their former spouse. A small but growing number of states have extended formal recognition to co-parents under a number of different legal theories including parental presumptions. Now that marital equality is a national reality, co-parents may well be deemed parents under the long standing common law marital presumption rule.

Key Terms

Custody	Nexus	Noncustodial Parent	Virtual Visitation
Visitation	Per Se Approach	Parenting Plan	Standing
Paternal Preference	Primary Caretaker	Complaint for	Stepparent
Tender Years	Presumption	Contempt	Equitable
Presumption	Physical Custody	Complaint for	Parenthood
Best Interest	Legal Custody	Modification	*In Loco Parentis*
Primary	Sole Custody	Relocation	Co-Parent
Caretaker	Joint Custody	Disputes	De Facto Parent

Review Questions

1. What were the rights of fathers at common law?
2. When and why did mothers become the preferred custodial parent?
3. What is the best interest standard?
4. What factors is a judge likely to consider when determining best interest?
5. What criticisms are commonly made about the best interest standard?
6. What are the pros and cons of basing a custody decision on the stated preference of a child?
7. What impact does witnessing spousal abuse have on children? For what other reasons do courts take interspousal violence into account when deciding custody?
8. What did the Supreme Court say in Palmore v. Sidoti about the role of race in custody disputes?

9. Post-*Palmore*, can race and culture ever be taken into account when deciding custody? Explain.

10. Explain the difference between the nexus and the per se harm approaches to resolving custody disputes where parental lifestyle is an issue.

11. How do courts approach custody cases in which one parent is involved in a heterosexual relationship? In a same-sex relationship?

12. How do courts generally approach the issue of religion when it is raised as a positive factor? As a negative factor?

13. Explain the primary caretaker presumption. How does it respond to the concerns about the best interest standard?

14. Explain the ALI approximation rule. How does it respond to the concerns about the best interest standard?

15. What is the difference between physical and legal custody? Between sole and joint custody?

16. What concerns have been raised about joint custody? Under what circumstances is it most likely to be successful?

17. What is the legal status of a noncustodial parent?

18. Why will courts generally grant visitation rights to a parent who might not be an appropriate custodial parent?

19. What are the general approaches to structuring visitation?

20. What kinds of restrictions might a court impose on a visiting parent?

21. Discuss the intended functions of parenting plans and parent education programs.

22. What role might a parenting coordinator play in a divorce case?

23. What are the two basic approaches that states take with respect to post-divorce relocation disputes?

24. How have courts taken the possibility of "virtual visitation" into account when faced with relocation decisions?

25. What concerns are raised by virtual visitation orders in cases where there has been a history of domestic violence?

26. What is meant by the term "natural parent preference"?

27. What was the common law status of grandparents in relationship to their grandchildren?

28. Under what circumstances do most grandparent visitation statutes permit a grandparent to seek visitation rights? Why did the Supreme Court invalidate the state of Washington's grandparent visitation statute?

29. Explain the concept of "standing."

30. What is the traditional legal status of stepparents? How has this begun to change?

31. What approach has the law typically taken with regard to the parenting rights of a lesbian co-parent?

32. Explain the concept of de facto parent. What considerations does a court take into account when deciding whether someone qualifies as a de facto parent? Why is the element of consent so important?

33. What other theories might a co-parent rely on to establish her parenting rights?

Discussion Questions

1. In determining custody, what weight do you think "moral" considerations should have? Do you think it is possible for judges to set aside their own views of morality when making decisions about custody?

2. What role do you think considerations of a child's cultural/racial heritage should play in a custody dispute? What are the potential benefits of giving weight to this factor? What are the potential risks?

3. Would you allow a grandparent to have visitation rights with a grandchild over the objections of the parent(s)? Does your answer depend on whether the family is intact or has been disrupted by death or divorce?

4. Many fathers' rights organizations have argued that unless a court can order joint custody even where one parent is opposed, men will never be treated fairly. What do you think of this position?

5. Assuming that a relocation decision is made in good faith, do you think the court should give greater weight to the desire of the custodial parent to move or to the noncustodial parent's wish to maintain the existing visitation arrangement? What factors would you weigh?

6. Assuming mutual consent between the parties, do you think a same-sex co-parent should be treated as a legal parent? Why or why not?

Assignments

1. Locate the custody provisions of your state's divorce statute and answer the following questions:
   - Have any specific guidelines for determining best interest been adopted by statute or judicial decision?
   - Based on the guidelines or key court decisions, what factors are to be considered when determining custody?
   - Is domestic violence a factor to be considered? If so, how?
   - Is joint custody a permissible option? If yes, is there a presumption in favor of joint custody? Can it be ordered over the objection of a parent?

2. Assume that you are working in a law firm, and the supervising partner has asked for your assistance in a custody relocation dispute in which your firm is representing the father. The father is seeking to prevent his former wife, who is the custodial parent, and children from moving out of state to another state that is about 350 miles away. Assume that the children are ages 5 and 7, that the father visits with them regularly and has a good relationship with both daughters, and that money is not a significant concern. The attorney has asked you to prepare an in-house legal memorandum in which you analyze the relevant statutory section, if any, and controlling case law on this issue.

3. Develop a detailed client intake questionnaire for use in all cases where custody or visitation might be an issue. Think carefully about all of the information you would want to know about your client and his or her spouse.

4. The attorney you work for has asked you to prepare the first draft of a parenting plan for a divorce case she is working on. She represents the wife and is concerned that the parties will not be able to effectively carry out the joint custody arrangement that they want. She would like the plan to be as detailed as possible. At a minimum, it should cover the allocation of time and responsibilities, how decisions are to be made, and a process for resolving any disputes that come up. Given her concerns, she would like the plan to be drafted with particular care so that it facilitates the intended custodial arrangement. The following are the relevant facts:
   - The parties have agreed to share physical and legal custody of their daughter, Melinda, age 4.
   - Both parents work full time, although the mother's schedule is more flexible, and she tends to work shorter hours than the father; however, she travels about once a month.
   - The parties want to try to make this arrangement work, but communication is tense and has gotten worse since the father has begun living with his new girlfriend.
   - The parties live in the same town.
   - The mother worries that the father is too strict and rigid in relationship to Melinda, and the father worries that the mother is too permissive and sets no rules.

   (Note: If the courts in your state have a standard parenting plan form, you should use this form for the assignment.)

Endnotes

1. As discussed later in this chapter, the term "third party" is not accurate as applied to co-parents.

2. William Blackstone, Commentaries on the Laws of England 372-373 (19th London ed. 1857).

3. Michael Grossberg, Governing the Hearth: Law and the Family in Nineteenth Century America 235 (1985). Although rarely mentioned in works discussing the nature of paternal authority, it is important to recognize that fathers who were slaves did not have this kind of authority over their children; slave owners had complete control over the lives of their slaves without regard for their family relationships.

4. Elizabeth Pleck, Domestic Tyranny: The Making of American Social Policy from Colonial Times to the Present 39 (1987).

5. Mich. Comp. Laws §722.23 (2009).

6. Robert F. Kelly and Shawn L. Ward, Allocating Custodial Responsibilities at Divorce: Social Science Research and the American Law Institute's Approximation Rule, 40 Fam. Ct. Rev. 350, 356, 358 (2002).

7. See Margaret F. Brinig, Feminism and Child Custody Under Chapter Two of the American Law Institute's Principles of the Law of Family Dissolution, 8 Duke J. Gender L. & Poly. 301, 308-309 (2001).

8. Joan B. Kelly, Psychological and Legal Interventions for Parents and Children in Custody and Access Disputes: Current Research and Practice, 10 Va. J. Soc. Poly. & L. 129, 150 (2003). According to Kelly, these feelings are also attributed to parents' failure to "talk with their children about even the most elementary and relevant aspects of the separation or divorce." Id. See also Barbara A. Atwood, Hearing Children's Voices in Custody Litigation: An Empirical Survey and Suggestions of Reform, 45 Ariz. L. Rev. 629 (2003).

9. Kelly, supra note 8, at 154.

10. Id. at 152-161.

11. Elizabeth Scott, Parental Autonomy and Children's Welfare, 11 Wm. & Mary Bill Rts. J. 1071, 1093 (2003).

12. See N. Zoe Hilton, Battered Women's Concerns About Their Children Witnessing Wife Assault, 7 J. Interspousal Violence 1 (1990).

13. Judith S. Wallerstein and Sandra Blakeslee, Second Chances—Men, Women, and Children a Decade After Divorce 113-121 (1989).

14. Hon. Donna J. Hitchens and Patricia Van Horn, Courts Responding to Domestic Violence; The Court's Role in Supporting and Protecting Children Exposed to Domestic Violence, 6 J. Center for Fam. Child. & Cts. 31 (2005). This article contains an excellent review of the relevant literature. See also Peter G. Jaffee et al., Custody Disputes Involving Allegations of Domestic Violence: Toward a Differentiated Approach to Parenting Plans, 46 Fam. Ct. Rev. 500 (2008).

15. Wallerstein and Blakeslee, supra note 13, at 110-121.

16. Cynthia Grover Hastings, Letting Down Their Guard: What Guardians Ad Litem Should Know About Domestic Violence in Child Custody Disputes, 24 B.C. Third World L.J. 283, 301-302 (2004).

17. Palmore v. Sidoti, 466 U.S. 429 (1984).

18. Id. at 433.

19. Gambla v. Woodson, 367 Ill. App. 3d 441, 853 N.E.2d 847, 863, 869-871 (2006), appeal denied by Gambla v. Woodson, 222 Ill. 2d 571, 861 N.E.2d 654 (2006), cert. denied, 2007 U.S. LEXIS 10286 (U.S. Oct. 1, 2007).

20. See Cynthia R. Mabry, The Browning of America—Multicultural and Bicultural Families in Conflict—Making Culture a Customary Factor in Child Custody Disputes, 16 Wash. & Lee J. Civ. Rts. & Soc. Just. 413, 422 (2010).

21. Serena Lambert, Gay and Lesbian Families: What We Know and Where to Go from Here, 13 The Family Journal: Counseling and Therapy for Couples and Families, 43, 49 (2005). For a comprehensive discussion of these studies, see Abie Goldberg, Lesbian and Gay Parents and Their Children: Research on the Family Life Cycle (APA 2009). For an alternative perspective on the research, see Lynn D. Wardle, Considering the Impacts on Children and Society of "Lesbigay" Parenting, 23 Quinnipiac L. Rev. 541 (2004).

22. Obergefell v. Hodges, 576 U.S. at____(2015) quoting U.S. v. Windsor, (slip op., at 23). In short, it may be difficult for states to treat same-sex parents differently in light of the respect shown by the Court for their parental rights and abilities.

23. This discussion draws on the following articles: Carol Wah, Restrictions on Religious Training and Exposure in Child Custody and Visitation Orders: Do They Protect or Harm the Child, 45 J. Church & St. 14 (2003); Carol Wah, Religion in Child Custody and Visitation Cases: Presenting the Advantage of Religious Participation, 28 Fam. L.Q. 269 (1994); Note, The Establishment Clause and Religion in Child Custody Disputes: Factoring Religion into the Best Interest Equation, 82 Mich. L. Rev. 1702 (1984); Collin R. Magnum, Exclusive Reliance on Best Interest May Be Unconstitutional: Religion as a Factor in Child Custody Cases, 15 Creighton L. Rev. (1982).

24. Garrett v. Garrett, 527 N.W.2d 213, 221-222 (Neb. Ct. App. 1995).

25. 167 W. Va. 59, 278 S.E.2d 357 (1981).

26. See Ronald K. Henry, "Primary Caretaker": Is It a Ruse? 17 Fam. Advoc. 53 (1994).

27. ALI Press Release, May 15, 2002, http://www .ali.org/ali_old/pr051502.htm (accessed April 24, 2015).

28. The following articles discuss the ALI's approximation rule from a variety of perspectives: Richard A. Warshak, Parenting by the Clock: The Best-Interest-of-the-Child Standard, Judicial Discretion, and the American Law Institute's "Approximation Rule," 41 U. Balt. L. Rev. 83 (2011); Katherine T. Bartlett, U.S. Custody Law and Trends in the Context of the ALI Principles of the Law of Family Dissolution, 10 Va. J. Soc. Poly. & L. 5, 17-18 (2002); Margaret F. Brinig, Feminism and Child Custody Under Chapter Two of the American Law Institute's Principles of the Law of Family Dissolution, 8 Duke J. Gender L. & Poly. 301 (2001); Robert F. Kelly and Shawn L. Ward, Allocating Custodial Responsibility at Divorce: Social Science Research and the American Law Institute's Approximation Rule, 40 Fam. Ct. Rev. 350 (2002).

29. For a discussion of some of these concerns, see Christy M. Buchanan and Parissa L. Jahromi, The Best

Interests of the Child: A Psychological Perspective on Shared Custody Arrangements, 43 Wake Forest L. Rev. 419 (2009); Judith S. Wallerstein and Janet R. Johnston, Children of Divorce, Recent Findings Regarding Long-Term Effects and Recent Studies of Joint and Sole Custody, 11 Pediatrics in Rev. 197 (1990).

30. Margaret F. Bring, Extending Default Rules Beyond Purely Economic Relationships: Penalty Defaults in Family Law: The Case of Child Custody, 33 Fla. St. U. L. Rev. 779, 782 (2006).

31. Marlene Eskind Moses with Beth A. Townsend, Parenting Coordinators: The Good, The Bad and the Ugly, 48 Tenn. B.J. 24, 25 (2012).

32. *See generally id.*, as well as "Understanding the Parenting Coordination Process," http://www.afccnet .org/ResourceCenter/ResourcesforFamilies/ProductID/10 (accessed July 29, 2012).

33. Joan Kelly, Psychological and Legal Interventions for Parents and Children in Custody and Access Disputes: Current Research and Practice, 10 Va. J. Soc. Poly. & L. 129, 135 (2002). *See also* Susan L. Pollet and Melissa Lombreglia, A Nationwide Survey of Mandatory Parent Education, 46 Fam. Ct. Rev. 375 (2008).

34. Victoria L. Lutz and Cara E. Grady, Models of Collaboration in Family Law: Domestic Violence and Parent Education: Necessary Measures and Logistics to Maximize the Safety of Victims of Domestic Violence Attending Parent Education Programs, 42 Fam. Ct. Rev. 363 (2004).

35. For a description of Kentucky's Divorce Education programs, *see* http://courts.ky.gov/courtprograms/divorceeducation/Pages/default.aspx (accessed April 24, 2015).

36. *See generally* Lucy S. McGough, Starting Over: The Heuristics of Family Relocation Decision Making, 77 St. John's L. Rev. 291 (2003); Charles P. Kindregan, Family Interests in Competition: Relocation and Visitation, 36 Suffolk U. L. Rev. 31 (2002); Edwin J. Terry, Relocation: Moving Forward or Moving Backward?, 31 Tex. Tech L. Rev. 983 (2000).

37. D'Onofrio v. D'Onofrio, 144 N.J. Super. 27, 365 A.2d 27, 29-30 (Ch. Div. 1976), *aff'd*, 144 N.J. Super. 352, 365 A.2d 716 (App. Div. 1976).

38. For a discussion of some of this research, *see* Kenneth Waldron, A Review of Social Science Research on Post Divorce Relocation, 19 J. Am. Acad. Matrimonial Law. 337 (2005); Eric G. Mart and Rachel M. Bedard, Child Custody and Post-Divorce Relocation in the Light of Braver et al., 31 Vt. B.J. & L. Digest 47 (2005).

39. McCoy v. McCoy, 336 N.J. Super. 172, 764 A.2d 449 (App. Div. 2001).

40. David Welsh, Virtual Parents: How Virtual Visitation Legislation Is Shaping the Future of Custody Law, 11 J.L. Fam. Stud. 215 (2008).

41. *See* Jim Mackay, Virtual Parenting, Government Technology (2006), http://www.govtech/com/gt/100099 (accessed July 29, 2012). *See also* Welsh, *supra* note 39.

42. As discussed in Chapter 11, the common law presumption of paternity under which all children born to a married woman are presumed to be offspring of the marriage even if they were conceived as a result of an extramarital affair is a long-standing exception to this rule, as it allows for fatherhood by presumption. As also discussed in

Chapter 11, the rules for establishment of paternity when a child is conceived through donor insemination are a further exception to the basic rule that parenthood is accomplished by adoption or biology.

The operative principle—that legal parenthood is a function of biology or adoption—also has been challenged by the practice of assisted reproduction, such as surrogate motherhood. For further information, *see* Helene S. Shapo, Assisted Reproduction and the Law: Disharmony on a Divisive Social Issue, 100 Nw. U. L. Rev. 465 (2006); David D. Meyer, Parenthood in a Time of Transition: Tensions Between Legal, Biological, and Social Conceptions of Parenthood, 54 Am. J. Comp. L. 125 (2006); Sanja Zgonjanin, What Does It Take to Be a (Lesbian) Parent? On Intent and Genetics, 16 Hastings Women's L.J. 251 (2005).

43. *See* Patricia S. Fernandez, Grandparent Access: A Model Statute, 6 Yale L. & Poly. Rev. 109 (1988).

44. 828 S.W.2d 630, 632-633 (Ky. 1992).

45. 855 S.W. 2d 573, 580-583 (Tenn. 1993 (internal citations omitted).

46. Troxel v. Granville, 530 U.S. 57, 64 (2000).

47. For a discussion of post-*Troxel* decisions, *see* Joan Catherine Bohl, That "Thorny" Issue, California Grandparent Visitation Law in the Wake of Troxel v. Granville, 36 Golden Gate U. L. Rev. 121 (2006); Kristine L. Roberts, Troxel v. Granville and the Courts' Reluctance to Declare Grandparent Visitation Statutes Unconstitutional, 41 Fam. Ct. Rev. 14 (2003).

48. Atkinson v. Atkinson, 160 Mich. App. 601, 608-609, 408 N.W.2d 516, 519 (1987).

49. For a discussion of this approach, *see* Bryce Levine, Divorce and the Modern Family: Providing In Loco Parentis Stepparents Standing to Sue for Custody of Their Stepchildren in a Dissolution Proceeding, 25 Hofstra L. Rev. 315 (1996).

50. We will also assume that the sperm donor is unknown and thus cannot assert any claims to the child. In this regard, it should be noted that although the principles discussed in this section would apply equally to a gay male couple, their situation might be complicated somewhat if a surrogate mother was involved, as she might be able to assert her own claims to the child.

51. *Troxel, supra* note 45, at 65.

52. Holzman v. Knott, 193 Wis. 2d 649, 533 N.W.2d 419 (1995), *cert. denied*, 516 U.S. 976 (1995).

53. *Id.* at 436-437.

54. E.N.O. v. L.M.M., 429 Mass. 824, 711 N.E.2d 886, *cert. denied*, 528 U.S. 1005 (1999).

55. V.C. v. M.J.B., 163 N.J. 200, 748 A.2d 539 (2000).

56. *E.N.O., supra* note 53, at 891, n.6.

57. *V.C., supra* note 54, at 554-555.

58. Carvin v. Britain (In re Parentage of L.B.), 155 Wash. 2d 679, 122 P.3d 151, 178 (2005), *cert. denied*, 547 U.S. 1143 (2006).

59. UPA, Article 7, §703 (as amended 2002).

60. UPA, Article 1, §106 (2001).

61. The California case is Elisa B. v. Emily B, 117 P.3d 660 (Cal. 2005), and the New Jersey case is In re Parentage of the Child of Kimberly Robinson, 383 N.J. Super. 165, 890 A.2d 1036 (2005).

Chapter Six

Child Support

As we have seen so far, family law is primarily a matter of state concern. However, this changes when we come to child support, an arena in which the federal government plays an important role.

Between 1970 and 1981, the number of people in female-headed families living below the poverty level increased significantly, and the term "feminization of poverty" was coined to underscore the fact that households made up of women and children were sliding into poverty. Underlying the concern about poverty was an increased awareness of the difference in post-divorce standards of living between men and women with children. Studies consistently showed that the financial well-being of men improved following a divorce, while that of women and children deteriorated; for instance, one study found a 17 percent increase in standard of living for men compared to a 29 percent decline for women and children.[1]

At the federal level, there was a growing awareness that many women and children were being forced to turn to public assistance because they were not receiving the child support they were entitled to. (At the time, assistance was available through the Aid to Families with Dependent Children (AFDC) program, which was more commonly referred to as "welfare." Since the welfare reform act of 1996, assistance has been provided through the Transitional Aid to Needy Families (TANF) program.)

This sobering picture prompted the federal government to enter the child support field. In 1974, hoping to force absent parents to become financially responsible and thereby reduce federal welfare expenditures, Congress passed the Child Support Enforcement and Establishment of Paternity Act of 1974, which added Title IV-D to the Social Security Act. As explained by Margaret Heckler, then secretary of the U.S. Department of Health and Human Services, in favor of this increased federal role: "Children deserve to be supported by both parents. For the sake of America's children, we must put an end to what has become a national disgrace. Our new federal

Child Support:
The duty of financial support owed by a noncustodial parent to his or her minor children and to children over the age of majority in limited situations, such as in cases of disability

Title IV-D:
Law that amends the Social Security Act to establish a cooperative federal-state program for the obtaining and enforcement of child support orders

149

legislation will help States obtain support orders quickly and pursue them vigorously."[2] This new law required states to develop comprehensive child support programs to help custodial parents obtain and enforce child support awards. Since 1974, Congress has amended Title IV-D multiple times and passed other child support legislation intended to strengthen the ability of both states and tribes and tribal organizations to establish and collect child support awards in a timely and efficient manner.[3]

Administrative Framework for the Establishment and Enforcement of Child Support Orders

The Federal Office of Child Support Enforcement

The Child Support Enforcement and Establishment of Paternity Act of 1974 established the federal Office of Child Support Enforcement (OCSE). The OCSE is located within the Administration for Children and Families (ACF) in the U.S. Department of Health and Human Services (HHS). OCSE is the national oversight agency with responsibility for helping states to develop, manage, and run their child support programs effectively and in accordance with federal law.[4] More recently, the OCSE inaugurated a Tribal IV-D program, which provides direct funding to Indian tribes and tribal organizations for the administration of comprehensive tribal IV-D child support programs.

In addition, the OCSE is responsible for operating the Federal Parent Locator Service (FPLS). The FPLS "is an assembly of systems operated by OCSE to assist states in locating noncustodial parents, putative fathers, and custodial parties for the establishment of paternity and child support obligations, as well as the enforcement and modification of orders for child support, custody, and visitation. It also identifies support orders or support cases involving the same parties in different States."[5]

At the State Level: The IV-D Agency

The 1974 Act required each state to develop a comprehensive child support program and to designate a single state agency — often referred to as a **IV-D agency** — to administer the program. IV-D agencies must provide the following five basic services to custodial parents:

IV-D Agency:
Administrates the Title IV-D program

- assistance in locating absent parents;
- establishment of child support awards;
- periodic review of awards;
- enforcement of support awards; and
- where necessary, the establishment of paternity.

Before looking at these components of the child support system, we will look at how custodial parents access the services of a IV-D agency. As will become clear, the process differs depending on whether or not the parent is a recipient of public assistance through TANF, the federal block grant program that provides time-limited support to poor families.[6]

Eligibility for IV-D Services

A custodial parent who applies for TANF benefits is automatically referred to a IV-D agency for child support services. In order to receive benefits, she must agree to assign her right to child support to the state. She must also agree to cooperate with the state in its effort to obtain support unless she can establish good cause for noncooperation, such as the fear of abuse.[7] With the assignment, the noncustodial parent's support obligation runs to the state rather than to the custodial parent.

Once support is collected on behalf of a family receiving public assistance, federal law provides the state with several distribution options. A state can keep all of the collected funds in order to reimburse itself (and the federal government) for assistance payments made to the family. It can choose to "pass through" all of the collected funds to the family, or it can pass through a portion of the funds and retain the balance for reimbursement purposes. Although advocates for low-income families have encouraged states to adopt a "family-first" approach and pass through all of the collected support in order to help lift children out of poverty, few states have adopted this approach. Most either retain all of the collected funds, or pass through a limited amount, typically $50 or $100, to the family.[8] If a state does pass through collected funds, it typically disregards this amount when determining the family's continued eligibility for public assistance.

IV-D agencies also must provide child support assistance to families who are not applying for or receiving public assistance. Today, in contrast to the early years of the IV-D program, most of the families who receive child support services are not on public assistance, although many are former welfare recipients.[9] This represents a shift "from an emphasis on recouping federal funds to the current mission of ensuring the support and care of America's children, without regard to receipt of government assistance."[10] A parent in this category must complete an application requesting IV-D services and may be charged a nominal fee. Because public funds are not involved, the use of a IV-D agency is optional, and there is no assignment of support rights or a cooperation requirement, and all collected support payments go directly to the custodial parent. (Private child support agencies are discussed later in this chapter.)

Locating Absent Parents

A major barrier to obtaining and enforcing child support orders is that many noncustodial parents cannot be located, and some try to conceal their identity to avoid paying child support. To address this problem, the 1974 Act established the Federal Parent Locator Service (FPLS), which is operated by the OCSE, and required each state IV-D agency to establish its own **parent locator service.**

Parent Locator Service:
A federal or state agency that is responsible for locating absent parents in order to establish or enforce a child support award

If a custodial parent does not know where the other parent is, he or she can request assistance from the state parent locator service. The locator service will check the records of other state agencies, such as the registry of motor vehicles or department of revenue, to see if it can locate the absent parent; credit-reporting agencies are also an important source of information. The locator service must also search the State Case Registry, a database with information regarding all state support cases, and the State Directory of New Hires, a database containing information submitted by employers containing information about all new hires, to determine if there is a match. If the parent cannot be located within the state, and there is cause to believe the parent is in another state, the parent locator service in the second state must initiate a search as described here.

If the parent still cannot be located, the state locator service can ask the FPLS to assist in the search. Requests for federal assistance must come from a IV-D agency; individuals cannot file a direct request for federal assistance. Information needed to track down a parent can be obtained from both internal and external data sources. Internal to the FPLS is the Federal Case Registry of Child Support Orders (FCR), a comprehensive database containing information on all U.S. child support cases, and the National Directory of New Hires, a database including information about all new hires nationwide and persons who have applied for unemployment. Additionally, the FPLS can conduct an external search through the databases of other federal agencies, such as the Internal Revenue Service (IRS) or the Social Security Administration. (See the section entitled "Enforcing the Child Support Obligation," later in this chapter, for more information on these databases.)

Although the increased focus on the centralization and exchange of information facilitates the child support collection process, it also raises concerns about the privacy rights of individual family members. Of particular concern is the need to "ensure that the databases are secure enough so that abusers are unable to penetrate their safeguards to locate abused women and children."[11] Accordingly, federal law contains multiple safeguards to protect against the unauthorized use or disclosure of confidential information gathered by IV-D agencies. Additional layers of protection are required in cases involving domestic violence, such as the inclusion of a domestic violence indicator or flag on an at-risk individual's file to restrict disclosure of any information that might jeopardize that person's safety.

Child Support Guidelines

To address the problem of inadequate and inconsistent awards, federal law requires each state to adopt child support guidelines. The guidelines must provide specific numeric criteria for the computation of support awards, and calculations must result in a presumptively correct support amount. Deviations from the guideline amount are permitted, but only where justifiable based on the circumstances of the case. Some guidelines include specific factors for a decision maker to consider when determining if a deviation is warranted, while other guidelines are general.

Guidelines are controlling with respect to both temporary and "permanent" child support awards.[12] The guidelines also control in cases in which the parents reach agreement on the support amount; to guard against the risk that a parent might bargain away support rights in exchange for something else of value (most commonly custody), any deviation must be justified to the court or reviewing agency. To assist in the computation of support amounts, many states have developed a standardized support worksheet. In preparing a case, a paralegal may be asked to complete a support worksheet, so it is important for you to have a complete and accurate understanding of how the guidelines work in your jurisdiction. Exhibit 6.1, a child support worksheet from the state of New Jersey, is included as a sample to give you a sense of what a worksheet looks like.

Child Support Guidelines: Mandated by federal law, guidelines employing numeric criteria used to calculate the amount of child support to be paid by the noncustodial parent

Support Worksheet: A worksheet that is tied to child support guidelines and is used in calculating a support award

Guideline Formulas

Although federal law requires states to adopt child support guidelines, it left the job of developing the actual guidelines up to the states. In developing their guidelines, most states have used either a percentage-of-income or an income-shares approach. A few states use a hybrid approach, which is often referred to as the "Melson formula" after Judge Elwood F. Melson, Jr., of the Delaware Family Court.

Percentage of Income

The percentage-of-income (or fixed-percentage) approach sets the support amount as a fixed percentage of the noncustodial parent's income. Usually, the only relevant variable is the number of children in the household, although some states permit consideration of other factors, such as shared custody arrangements. Thus, for example, the support percentage might be set at 25 percent of the noncustodial parent's income for one child, at 30 percent for two children, and at 34 percent for three children.

Exhibit 6.1
Child Support
Worksheet

Appendix IX-D

Child Support Guidelines - Shared Parenting Worksheet

Case Name:		v.			County:
Plaintiff			*Defendant*		Docket #:
PPR is the: ☐ Plaintiff ☐ Defendant					Number of Children:

All amounts must be weekly	Parent of Primary Residence (PPR)	Parent of Alternate Residence (PAR)	Combined
1. Gross Taxable Income	$	$	
1a. Mandatory Retirement Contributions (non-taxable)	-$	-$	
1b. Alimony Paid (Current and/or Past Relationships)	-$	-$	
1c. Alimony Received (Current and/or Past Relationships)	+$	+$	
2. Adjusted Gross Taxable Income ((L1-L1a-L1b)+L1c)	$	$	
2a. Federal, State and Local Income Tax Withholding	-$	-$	
2b. Prior Child Support Orders (Past Relationships)	-$	-$	
2c. Mandatory Union Dues	-$	-$	
2d. Other Dependent Deduction (from L14 of a separate worksheet)	-$	-$	
3. Net Taxable Income (L2-L2a-L2b-L2c-L2d)	$	$	
4. Non-Taxable Income (source: _____)	+$	+$	
5. Government (Non-Means Tested) Benefits for the Child	+$	+$	
6. Net Income (L3+L4+L5)	$	$	$
7. Each Parent's Share of Income (L6 Each Parent ÷ L6 Combined)	0._____	0._____	1.00
8. Basic Child Support Amount (from Appendix IX-F Schedules)			$
9. Number of Overnights with Each Parent			
10. Each Parent's Share of Overnights with the Child (L9 for Parent ÷ L9 Combined)	0._____	0._____	1.00
If PAR time sharing is less than the equivalent of two overnights per week (28%), use Sole Parenting Worksheet.			
11. PAR Shared Parenting Fixed Expenses (L8 x PAR L10 x 0.38 x 2)			+$
12. Shared Parenting Basic Child Support Amount (L8 + L11)			$
13. Each Parent's Share of SP Basic Child Support Amount (L7xL12)	$	$	
14. PAR Shared Parenting Variable Expenses (PAR L10 x L8 x 0.37)		-$	
15. PAR Adjusted SP Basic Child Support Amount (PAR L13 – L11 – L14)		$	
16. Net Work Related Child Care (from Appendix IX-E Worksheet)			+$
17. Child's Share of Health Insurance Premium			+$
18. Unreimbursed Health Care Expenses over $250 per child per year			+$
19. Court-Approved Extraordinary Expenses			+$
20. Total Supplemental Expenses (L16+L17+L18+L19)			$
21. PAR's Share of Total Supplemental Expenses (PAR L7 x L20)		$	
22. Government Benefits for the Child Based on Contribution of PAR		$	
23. PAR Net Work-Related Child Care PAID		$	
Continued on Page 2			

Form Revised to Be Effective September 1, 2013, CN: 10727 (Court Rule Appendix IX-D)

Exhibit 6.1 cont.

Appendix IX-D

Child Support Guidelines - Shared Parenting Worksheet

All amounts must be weekly	PPR	PAR	Combined
24. PAR Health Insurance Premium for the Child PAID		$	
25. PAR Unreimbursed Health Care Expenses >$250/child/year) PAID		$	
26. PAR Court-Approved Extraordinary Expenses PAID		$	
27. PAR Total Supplemental Expenses PAID (L22+ L23 + L24 + L25 + L26)		$	
28. PAR Net Supplemental Expenses (L21 – L27)		$	
29. PAR Net Child Support Obligation (L15 + L28)		$	
If neither parent is requesting the other dependent deduction, go to line 33.			
30. Line 29 PAR CS Obligation WITH Other Dependent Deduction		$	
31. Line 29 PAR CS Obligation WITHOUT Other Dependent Deduction		$	
32. Adjusted PAR Child Support Obligation ((L30 + L31) ÷ 2)		$	
33. Self-Support Reserve Test: (L6 - L29 or L32 for PAR; L6 – L13 for PPR)	$	$	
If L33 for PAR is greater than 105% of the federal poverty guideline for one person (*pg*) or L33 for the PPR is less than the *pg*, enter the L29 or L32 amount on the PAR L35. If PAR L33 is less than the *pg* and PPR's L33 is greater than the *pg*, go to L34. If L29 or L32 is negative, see App. IX-B for instructions.			
34. Maximum CS Obligation (Obligor Parent's L6 net income – 105% of the poverty guideline for one person). Enter result here and on Line 35.	$	$	
35. Child Support Order (negative L29 or L32 denotes PPR Obligation)	$	$	
If the PAR is the Obligor, Continue on Line 36			
36. PPR Household Income Test (L6 PPR net income from all sources + net income of other household members + L35 order). If less than the PPR household income threshold (see App. IX-A, ¶14(c)), the *Sole Parenting Worksheet* should be used.	$		

Comments, Rebuttals, and Justification for Deviations

1. This child support order for this case ☐ was ☐ was not based on the child support guidelines award.

2. If different from the child support guidelines award (Line 35), enter amount ordered:

3. The child support guidelines were not used or the guidelines award was adjusted because:

4. The following extraordinary expenses were added to the basic support obligation on Line 19:

5. PPR Taxes:	☐ App IX-H	☐ Circ E	☐ Other	#Allowances:	Marital:
PAR Taxes:	☐ App IX-H	☐ Circ E	☐ Other	#Allowances:	Marital:

Prepared By:	Title:	Date:

Form Revised to Be Effective September 1, 2013, CN: 10727 (Court Rule Appendix IX-D)

The advantage of this model is its simplicity. However, by not building in consideration of multiple factors, the results may be inequitable. For example, a custodial parent who is employed part time or at home with young children would get the same amount of support as a custodial parent who is employed at a well-paying job.

Income Shares

The income-shares approach is premised on the assumption that children are entitled to receive the same share of parental income that they would have had the family stayed together. To arrive at the support amount, the income of both parents is combined and a basic support obligation computed. This obligation is then allocated between the parents in proportion to income, with the noncustodial parent paying his or her share in support payments and the custodial parent assumed to be paying his or her share in direct expenditures on the children.

Critics of this approach argue that it falls short in two ways that are particularly applicable in sole custody cases. First, it ignores the fact that following a divorce, the expenses of the custodial parent generally increase because he or she now must pay for services — such as baby-sitting, household cleaning, and repairs — to compensate for losing the contribution that the other parent would have made to the household. Second, it discounts the large noneconomic contribution that the custodial parent makes to the well-being of the children.

The Melson Formula

Under this approach, a noncustodial parent is first permitted to keep a minimum level of income for his or her essential needs. This is referred to as a "self-support reserve." Then, until the basic needs of the children are met, the parent cannot retain income above this minimum level; it must be allocated to child support. Once these needs are provided for, a percentage of the remaining parental income is allocated to increasing the basic support amount, thus enabling the children to benefit from a higher standard of living.

Determining What Income Is Subject to the Child Support Obligation

In developing their guidelines, states, in addition to determining which basic approach to use, also had to decide what income would be subject to the support obligation. This determination entails two distinct considerations: (1) How is income to be defined? and (2) What support base will be used?

Defining Income

Most guidelines define "income" broadly. All states include earned employment income in their definition, although treatment of sporadic income, such as income from occasional odd jobs or overtime, varies. In some states, sporadic income is excluded. In other states, it is averaged over time and added to regular earnings.

Most guidelines also recognize the concept of imputed (or **attributed**) income. Here, a parent who is voluntarily unemployed or underemployed is treated as if he or she has income commensurate with his or her earning capacity, and support is calculated based on this amount rather than on actual earnings. By attributing income to a parent and setting the support amount accordingly, a parent must find suitable employment or face sanctions for nonsupport. In some states, if a noncustodial parent remarries or cohabits and voluntarily stops working in reliance on the new partner's income, a portion of the household income will be attributed to that parent. In states where the income of the custodial parent is factored into the support equation, income may also be attributed to this parent where he or she is voluntarily underemployed or unemployed. However, most courts will not impute income if a parent has reduced his or her earnings due to child-related responsibilities, at least not until the child reaches a certain age — commonly age 6.

Imputed/Attributed Income: The attribution of income to a party who is deliberately underemployed or unemployed, based on earning capacity, for the purpose of establishing the amount of his or her support obligation

The ability to attribute income is important in situations where a parent deliberately reduces earnings in order to avoid a support obligation. However, what if a parent has reasons other than the avoidance of support for reducing his or her income? For example, take the situation of an attorney who after years of working in a major firm decides that she is burned out and wants to open a small practice, with a resulting loss of income. Should she be permitted to drastically reduce support payments? Is this fair to the children? On the other hand, is it fair to force a parent to remain in a particular career track by maintaining a support obligation based on earning potential?

Some states, either through guidelines or judicial decision, also permit income to be imputed to assets a party owns, such as jewelry or antiques, even if they are not income earning. The rationale for such a policy "is to discourage spouses from placing all of their assets into non-income yielding forms and thus shielding all of their assets from consideration in support."[13]

The definition of *income* almost always includes investment earnings, rents, profit shares, dividends, annuities, and governmental benefits, such as Social Security retirement and unemployment benefits. Some states also include the value of non-income-producing assets — such as jewelry, antiques, and undeveloped real estate — within the meaning of the term "income."

Setting the Income Base

In addition to defining income, the relevant income base must be determined. Here, states have three basic choices: Support can be calculated based on gross income, adjusted gross income, or net income.

Gross Income Base.   A gross income base is used by many states. In this approach, the gross income of the support obligor is used as the base for determining the support amount. The advantage of this approach is its simplicity and the fact that income cannot be manipulated because no deductions are taken before the support amount is calculated. On the other hand, gross income may not be an accurate measure of the income that is actually available to the support obligor.

Adjusted Gross Income Base.   Other states use an adjusted gross income base. To arrive at this amount, federal and state tax obligations, including Social Security, are deducted from gross earnings; nonvoluntary payroll withholdings, such as union dues and retirement payments, as well as prior support obligations, also are usually deducted. Support is then based on this adjusted amount. Many believe that this is the fairest approach, as it is a more accurate measure of the obligor's available income, although it does not permit the same kind of discretionary deductions that are allowable under the net income approach.

Net Income Base.   Still other states use a net income base, which allows for further deductions than the adjusted gross income base. Gross income is reduced, for example, by voluntary payroll withholdings and job-related expenses before the support amount is calculated. The drawback of this approach is that it can be manipulated to show a reduced income, thus limiting the support base. On the other hand, it may be the most accurate indicator of actual available income.

Consideration of Specific Factors

Most child support guidelines include a number of factors that are to be taken into account when calculating the support amount. Others fix a basic amount varied only by a limited number of factors, such as the number of children, and then identify factors that will justify a deviation from the presumptive amount. These factors are relevant in determining both the initial amount and whether a modification is warranted. Commonly considered factors include:

- income of the custodial parent;
- income of a new partner;
- income/resources of the child;

- multiple families;
- extraordinary expenses;
- health insurance; and
- custody and visitation arrangements.

Income of the Custodial Parent

With the exception of states using the percentage-of-income approach, most guidelines take the income of the custodial parent into account. Under the income-shares approach, the income of both parents is combined to establish a basic support obligation. This amount is then allocated in proportion to income, and the noncustodial parent contributes his or her share in support payments. Another approach is to base the initial support calculation on the noncustodial parent's income and then reduce it to account for the custodial parent's income. States generally use a percentage reduction formula, rather than a dollar-for-dollar offset, as this could significantly reduce the amount of support available to the children. In some states, the custodial parent's income is disregarded until it reaches a threshold amount, and then only income above this threshold is considered.

Income of a New Partner

If either parent remarries or cohabits with a new partner, the question often arises as to how this partner income should be treated. As a general rule, this person has no direct support obligation to the children. Accordingly, few, if any, guidelines require inclusion of this income, and some specifically exclude it from consideration. However, because it may free up parental income, some states permit consideration of partner income as a basis for deviating from the presumptive guideline amount.

Income/Resources of the Child

Situations may arise where a minor child has independent resources; for example, he or she may receive governmental benefits, have income from a part-time job, or be the beneficiary of a trust or an inheritance. Most states do not build this into their support formulas or treat this as income to the custodial parent. Again, however, this income may be considered in determining if a deviation from guidelines is appropriate.

Multiple Families

Almost 75 percent of people who are divorced remarry, and many then have children with their new spouses.[14] Cases involving multiple families raise difficult questions about how (often scarce) resources can be fairly allocated between two households.

A thorny question is whether a noncustodial parent should be allowed to reduce support to his or her first family upon establishing a new household, especially if he or she has additional children with this new partner. The traditional guideline approach puts "first families first" and does not permit reductions based on obligations to a subsequent family. The children from the first family are said to have a preexisting, and hence superior, claim to the income, which the parent should have considered before starting a second family. However, based on the recognition that this approach may shortchange the children in the second family, who have no control over their place in the birth order, some states do permit support adjustments to account for obligations to subsequently born children. In some of these jurisdictions, the presence of subsequent children can be used as a "shield" to defend against a request for an upward modification but not as a "sword" to request a downward modification.

Given the high failure rate of second marriages, another difficult issue is how support payments to a second family are to be calculated if this relationship also dissolves. If a parent is already paying child support under a court order to a prior family, most guidelines permit him or her to deduct this amount from income before the support order for the second family is calculated. This arguably favors the first family, as the income base available to them is larger; however, it is generally thought fair to protect this family's standard of living from fluctuations based on changes in the noncustodial parent's life over which the family has no control.[15]

Extraordinary Expenses

Guidelines are generally based on the assumption that the custodial parent is responsible for the ordinary costs of raising a child. A trickier question is whether she or he is also responsible for extraordinary expenses, or whether these should be dealt with separately. The term "**extraordinary expense**" has been defined as "any large, discrete, legitimate child-rearing expense that varies greatly from family to family or from child to child," as distinct from "ordinary expenses," which tend to be "relatively small, predictable, and fairly consistent in families of the same size and income level."[16] This issue most often arises with respect to medical, child-care, and educational expenses; as far as medical expenses are concerned, some guidelines specify that unreimbursed medical expenses in excess of an identified dollar amount per occurrence or calendar year are considered extraordinary expenses, while other guidelines identify the qualifying kinds of expenditures.

States use a number of approaches when dealing with extraordinary expenses, and within a particular state, the approach may vary depending on the category of expense. One common approach is to treat extraordinary expenses as an "add-on" to the basic support amount. The expense is

Extraordinary Expense: Any large, discrete, expenditure that does not recur on a regular basis, as distinct from the day-to-day expenses of raising a child

prorated between the parents based on their income, and the noncustodial parent's share is added to the support amount. Another possibility is to permit deviations from the guideline amount to account for extraordinary expenses. For example, a judge might be permitted to increase the basic support amount if the custodial parent were faced with significant medical bills. This deviation would most likely be temporary in nature, and the guideline amount would be reinstated once the custodial parent was no longer facing these expenditures.

Health Insurance

Under federal law, state child support guidelines must address how parents will provide for the health care needs of their children through either health insurance coverage or cash medical support. Strengthening this mandate, all child support orders obtained through a state IV-D agency must include a medical support provision, and the agency must petition the court or administrative authority to include private health insurance coverage in the support order if it is available through one or both parents. If ordered, an employer-sponsored group health plan must provide coverage to the children named by the court (or a qualified administrative agency), in what is known as a **qualified medical child support order** (QMCSO).[17]

Qualified Medical Child Support Order (QMCSO): A court order requiring that a child be covered by the noncustodial parent's group health insurance plan

With respect to the cost of coverage, some state guidelines allow the noncustodial parent to deduct the amount of the premium that is attributable to family coverage from gross income before calculating the support amount. Correspondingly, if the custodial parent is providing the insurance, a portion of the premium amount may be added to the basic support obligation. Another approach is to prorate the cost of the insurance between the parents based on their proportion of the total income, and then add the obligor's share to the support payments. Still other state guidelines consider the provision of health insurance as a ground for deviating from the presumptive support amount.

Custody and Visitation Arrangements

Support guidelines are generally based on the assumption that one parent has physical custody and the other has visitation rights, and visitation-related expenditures do not usually impact the support calculation. However, guidelines may permit adjustments to account for situations where a parent either spends a significant amount of time with a child or, conversely, hardly sees the child at all. Some guidelines spell out what time allocation will trigger a support reduction, such as where the child spends more than a specified percentage of time or more than a certain number of overnights with the noncustodial parent, while other guidelines leave it to the decision maker to determine when a reduction is warranted.

The amount of the reduction is usually left to the decision maker, although limits may be placed on his or her discretion. Some judges take a cautious approach to these reductions based on the recognition that increased visitation does not necessarily result in substantial savings in child-related expenditures, as the custodial parent usually remains responsible for them. Although less frequently addressed by guidelines, nonvisitation also may be the basis for an upward revision of support, as the custodial parent is assuming responsibility for visitation-associated expenses that the guidelines implicitly allocated to the noncustodial parent.

Turning to custodial arrangements, it is often assumed that joint physical custody and split custody (where at least one child lives with each parent) will cancel the support obligation because both parents are providing for the children on an equal basis. This assumption, however, is not accurate.

First, although an arrangement may be identified as joint custody, the time allocation between the two households may not be equal. Second, even where it is equal, one parent, typically the primary caregiver during the marriage, often continues to assume greater parenting responsibilities, including making most of the purchases for the child. Thus, although both parents maintain a home for the child, the cost of raising the child is not borne equally. Another concern is that eliminating the support award will put the lower-income parent in a worse financial situation than that parent would have been in had he or she maintained sole custody and received the guideline amount. In this regard, experts note that a disparity in the standard of living between parental households is especially confusing for a child in a joint custody situation, since both residences are the child's home.

Accordingly, although most guidelines permit consideration of these custodial arrangements in determining the support amount, they do not automatically trigger its elimination. One approach that is used is to compute a support obligation for each parent as if he or she had sole custody, offset the amounts, and order the parent with the greater obligation to pay the net amount to the other. Of course, support may be eliminated where parents earn close to the same amount and really share responsibility for raising the children.

Financial Disclosure

Financial Affidavit:
A document that discloses income and assets, which parties must complete in family court proceedings where property or support is at issue

As this discussion makes clear, a proper child support order cannot be calculated unless all relevant information has been disclosed. Accordingly, most, if not all, states require each party to make full financial disclosure to the other, usually by completing and filing a **financial affidavit**. Some also require the filing of supporting documents, such as tax returns and wage stubs. Additionally, in an effort to encourage attorneys to monitor and prevent the filing of fraudulent or inaccurate financial affidavits, some states require the affidavit to be signed by the lawyer as well as by the party submitting it. Exhibit 6.2 is a sample financial affidavit.

Despite their usefulness, affidavits often do not provide a complete financial picture. The form itself may not call for full disclosure. Also, affidavits provide a snapshot of a party's current financial situation but do not give a picture of his or her financial situation over time; for instance, an affidavit probably would not reveal a reduction in income or a transfer of assets or income that took place before the affidavit was completed. In many states that require parties to update affidavits as a divorce proceeds, subsequent changes may be revealed. Accordingly, a party may need to engage in other *discovery* — the process by which a party obtains information from the other side — to gain a more complete picture of the other side's financial situation. This step is critical because the failure to obtain complete and accurate information will result in an inaccurate assessment of a parent's financial situation and thus an incorrect support calculation.

Paralegals often play a critical role in this process. It may be your job to assist the client in completing the financial affidavit. These forms can be confusing. For example, a party who is asked to itemize expenditures on a weekly basis may be inclined to ignore expenditures that are made on a less regular basis, such as for clothing. You can help a client figure out what he or she spends on clothing over the course of a year, accounting for seasonal fluctuations, in order to arrive at an average weekly clothing amount.

If formal discovery is required, you may be involved in drafting documents and organizing the responses, including the supporting materials such as tax returns and bank statements that are often requested. You may also be responsible for helping your office's client respond to requests from the other side, which again may require you to sort through and organize financial data. (For more detail on discovery, see Chapter 10.)

Enforcing the Child Support Obligation

In addition to addressing the problem of inadequate and inconsistent awards, federal child support laws also address the endemic problem of nonpayment by support obligors, which has resulted in a national support arrearage totaling more than $1 billion. Seeking to rectify this, an elaborate network of interconnected databases has been created for the collection and exchange of child support–related information (discussed earlier in this chapter in the section entitled "Locating Absent Parents").[18]

Exhibit 6.2
Financial
Disclosure
Affidavit

IN THE CIRCUIT COURT OF THE NINETEENTH JUDICIAL CIRCUIT
LAKE COUNTY, ILLINOIS

IN RE: The ☐ Marriage of: ☐ Custody of: ☐ Support of:

```
                                      )
                                      )
                                      )
_____ )
                          Petitioner  )
        and                           )   No. _____
                                      )
                                      )
_____ )
                          Respondent  )
```

FINANCIAL AFFIDAVIT 11.02

Affiant, _____, having been duly sworn, upon oath, states

that the information contained herein is true and correct as of _____, 20_____

Name:	Telephone No: (847)
Address:	Petitioner Date of Birth: _____ (mmddyyyy)
	Respondent Date of Birth: _____ (mmddyyyy)
Date of Marriage: _____ (mmddyyyy)	Date of Dissolution of Marriage: (if applicable) _____ (mmddyyyy)

Minor and/or Dependent Children of this Marriage:

Name	Date of Birth (mmddyyyy)	Currently Living With

(Attach additional page(s) as needed)

Current Employer:	Address:
Self Employment:	Address:
Other Employment:	Address:

☐ Check if unemployed

Number of Paychecks per year: *(Please Check box)* ☐ 12   ☐ 24   ☐ 26   ☐ 52   ☐ Other _____

Number of Exemptions claimed: _____

Number of Dependents claimed: _____

Gross Income from all sources last year: _____

Gross income from all sources this year through _____: $ _____
                                                          Date

Exhibit 6.2 cont.

STATEMENT OF INCOME
Gross Monthly Income

Salary/Wages/Base Pay	$
Overtime/Commission	$
Bonus	$
Draw	$
Pension and Retirement Benefits	$
Annuity	$
Interest income	$
Dividend income	$
Trust income	$
Social Security	$
Unemployment benefits	$
Disability payment	$
Worker's Compensation	$
Public Aid/Food Stamps	$
Investment income	$
Rental income	$
Business income (including non-taxable distributions)	$
Partnership income	$
Royalty income	$
Fellowship/stipends	$
Other income (specify): _____	$
TOTAL GROSS MONTHLY INCOME:	$ $

Additional Cash Flow (Monthly)

Spousal support received (specify)	$
☐ Pursuant to a prior judgment or order in another case	$
☐ Pursuant to a prior judgment or order in this case	$
☐ Voluntarily paid in this case	$
Child Support received (specify)	$
☐ Pursuant to a prior judgment or order in another case	$
☐ Pursuant to a prior judgment or order in this case	$
☐ Voluntarily paid in this case	$
Total additional cash flow:	$ $

Required Monthly Deductions

Federal Tax (based on _____ exemptions)	$
State Tax (based on _____ exemptions)	$
FICA (or Social Security equivalent)	$
Medicare Tax	$
Mandatory retirement contributions required by law or as condition of employment	$
Union Dues (Name of Union: _____)	$
Health/hospitalization Premiums	$
Prior obligation(s) of support actually paid pursuant to Court order	$
Other (specify):	$
TOTAL REQUIRED DEDUCTIONS FROM INCOME:	$ $

NET MONTHLY INCOME:	$ $

Exhibit 6.2 cont.

STATEMENT OF MONTHLY LIVING EXPENSES

1. Household

a. Mortgage or rent (specify):	$	
b. Home equity loan payment	$	
c. Real estate taxes, assessments	$	
d. Homeowners or renters insurance	$	
e. Heat/fuel	$	
f. Electricity	$	
g. Telephone (include long distance)	$	
h. Water and Sewer	$	
i. Refuse removal	$	
j. Laundry/dry cleaning	$	
k. Maid/cleaning service	$	
l. Furniture and appliance repair/replacement	$	
m. Lawn and garden care/snow removal	$	
n. Food (groceries, household supplies, etc.)	$	
o. Liquor, beer, wine, etc.	$	
p. Other (specify):	$	
SUBTOTAL HOUSEHOLD EXPENSES:	$	$

2. Transportation

a. Fuel	$	
b. Repairs/maintenance	$	
c. Insurance/license/city stickers	$	
d. Payments/replacement	$	
e. Other (specify):	$	
SUBTOTAL TRANSPORTATION EXPENSES:	$	$

3. Personal

a. Clothing	$	
b. Grooming	$	
c. Medical (after insurance proceeds/reimbursement)		
(1) Doctor	$	
(2) Dentist	$	
(3) Optical	$	
(4) Medication	$	
d. Insurance		
(1) Life – Term/Whole (**specify**)	$	
(2) Medical/Hospitalization	$	
(3) Dental/Optical	$	
e. Other (specify)	$	
SUBTOTAL PERSONAL EXPENSES:	$	$

4. Miscellaneous:

a. Clubs/social obligations/entertainment	$	
b. Newspapers, magazines, books	$	
c. Gifts	$	
d. Donations, church or religious affiliations	$	
e. Vacations	$	
f. Other (specify)	$	
SUBTOTAL MISCELLANEOUS EXPENSES	$	$

171-12 FD33 (R01/06)

Exhibit 6.2 cont.

5. Expenses of Minor and/or Dependent Children of this Marriage:

a. Clothing	$	
b. Grooming	$	
c. Education		
(1) Tuition	$	
(2) Books/Fees	$	
(3) Lunches	$	
(4) Transportation	$	
(5) Medication	$	
d. Medical (after insurance proceeds/reimbursement)		
(1) Doctor	$	
(2) Dentist	$	
(3) Optical	$	
(4) Medication	$	
e. Allowance	$	
f. Child care/After-school care	$	
g. Sitters	$	
h. Lesson and supplies	$	
i. Clubs/Summer Camps	$	
j. Vacation	$	
k. Entertainment	$	
l. Other (specify)	$	
SUBTOTAL CHILDREN'S EXPENSES:	$	$
TOTAL MONTHLY LIVING EXPENSES:	$	$

STATEMENT OF LIABILITIES

CREDITOR'S NAME	PAYMENT FOR	BALANCE DUE	MONTHLY PAYMENT
		$	$
		$	$
		$	$
		$	$
		$	$
		$	$
		$	$
		$	$
		$	$
		$	$
		$	$
		$	$
		$	$
		$	$
		$	$
		$	$
		$	$
		$	$
		$	$
		$	$
		$	$
	TOTAL LIABILITIES	$	
	TOTAL MONTHLY DEBT SERVICE		$

(Attach additional page(s) as needed)

171-12 FD33 (R01/06)

Exhibit 6.2 cont.

STATEMENT OF ASSETS

Valuation Date: _____ (mmddyyyy)

Marital Residence and Other Real Estate:

	Market Value	Debt
1. Marital Residence at:	$	$
2.	$	$
3.	$	$
4.	$	$
TOTAL REAL ESTATE	$	$

Cars & Other Personal Property:

	Market Value	Debt
1.	$	$
2.	$	$
3.	$	$
4.	$	$
5.	$	$
6.	$	$
TOTAL CARS & OTHER PERSONAL PROPERTY	$	$

Businesses:

	Market Value	Debt
1. Business Interest -	$	$
2.	$	$
3.	$	$
4.	$	$
5.	$	$
6.	$	$
TOTAL BUSINESSES	$	$

Financial Assets (Cash or Cash Equivalents):

	Market Value	
1. Savings or interest-bearing accounts	$	
2. Checking Accounts	$	
3. Certificates of Deposit	$	
4. Money Market Accounts	$	
5. Cash	$	
6. Other (specify):	$	
7. Other (specify):	$	
TOTAL CASH OR CASH EQUIVALENTS:	$	$

Retirement & Deferred Compensation:

	Market Value	
1. Retirement:	$	
2.	$	
3.	$	
4.	$	
TOTAL RETIREMENT & DEFERRED COMPENSATION	$	$

Investment Accounts and Securities:

	Market Value	
1. Stocks	$	
2. Bonds	$	
3. Tax exempt securities	$	
4. Other (specify):	$	
5. Other (specify):	$	
6. Other (specify):	$	
TOTAL INVESTMENT ACCOUNTS AND SECURITIES	$	$

Exhibit 6.2 cont.

RECAP OF INCOME AND EXPENSES:

Net Monthly Income (+)	$
Total Monthly Living Expenses (-)	$
Less Monthly Debt Service (-)	$
Total Income Available per Month (=)	$

STATEMENT OF HEALTH INSURANCE COVERAGE

Currently effective health insurance coverage? ☐ Yes ☐ No

Name of insurance carrier: _____

Policy of Group No.: _____

Type of insurance: ☐ Medical   ☐ Dental   ☐ Optical

Deductible: Per individual: $_____   Per family: $_____

Persons covered: ☐ Self   ☐ Spouse   ☐ Dependents

Type of policy: ☐ HMO   ☐ PPO   ☐ Full indemnity

Provided by: ☐ Employer   ☐ Private Policy   ☐ Other Group

Monthly costs: ☐ Paid by Employer   ☐ Paid by employee:

$	for dependents
$	for self

VERIFICATION

The foregoing Financial Affidavit has been carefully read by the undersigned who states under oath, under penalties as provided by law pursuant to 735 ILCS 5/109, that this affidavit includes all of his/her income and expenses, he/she has knowledge of the matters stated and he/she certifies that the statements set forth in this Affidavit are true and correct, except as to matters specifically stated to be on information and belief, and as to such matters the undersigned certifies as aforesaid that he/she believes same to be true.

_____   _____
Signature of Petitioner   Signature of Respondent

_____   _____
Typed or Printed Name of Petitioner   Typed or Printed Name of Respondent

Date signed: _____   Date signed: _____

Federal law requires states to adopt specific support enforcement methods. Going beyond these requirements, many states have adopted additional enforcement mechanisms such as lottery-winning intercepts or the use of the Denver boot, "a steel, fifty-pound clamp that is attached to an automobile tire, effectively immobilizing the vehicle by preventing it from being driven until the offender responds to the legal system," which in this context would mean satisfaction of the support debt.[19] Supplementing support collection efforts at the state level, the Federal Office of Child Support Enforcement administers a federal offset program.

After considering key enforcement mechanisms, we turn to the enforcement process in interstate cases, followed by a discussion of the contested entry of private collection agencies into the child support arena. We conclude this section by looking at the continued availability of traditional state law remedies for the enforcement of child support orders.

Support Enforcement at the State Level

Income Withholding

Wage Withholding:
An order directing a support obligor's employer to take support payments directly out of that party's paycheck

Under federal law, all child support orders must include a **wage (or income) withholding** provision that enables support payments to be directly deducted from a noncustodial parent's paycheck, in much the same way as taxes are withheld. Income also can be withheld from other forms of periodic payments, such as those received from a pension plan or government benefits. Where benefits are concerned, the general rule is that they must be a form of remuneration for employment, such as Social Security or unemployment benefits; needs-based benefits, such as Supplemental Security Income (SSI) payments, are not subject to withholding.[20] This is unquestionably one of the most effective means of ensuring that support is paid.

Arrearage:
Money that is overdue or unpaid; in this context, an outstanding support obligation

All child support orders must include a wage withholding provision that is to take place immediately, which means that a party does not have to wait for an **arrearage**—an overdue or unpaid amount—to accrue in order for the withholding to take effect. There are only two exceptions to immediate withholding: (1) when good cause to suspend it is established and (2) when the parties enter into a written agreement providing an alternative arrangement.

If the withholding is suspended, it must take effect once an arrearage equal to the support payable for a month has accrued. The noncustodial parent is entitled to notice that withholding is to commence. He or she may challenge the effectuation of the withholding, but may raise only mistakes of fact, such as a miscalculation of the arrearage. The validity of the underlying order cannot be challenged.

Employers are responsible for withholding the designated amount. An employer who fails to withhold child support will be responsible for the amount of support that should have been withheld. Also, fines can be levied against an employer who takes adverse action against an employee because of the withholding.

One problem has been that withholding does not keep up with a parent's job changes if the parent does not provide the information necessary to effectuate the withholding with his or her new employer. The new data-matching process addresses this problem. Information in the State or National Directory of New Hires can be matched with information in the Federal or State Case Registry, which enables the state to contact the new employer and direct it to begin withholding wages in accordance with the existing support order.

Liens

Under federal law, states must now have a law that creates a lien against the personal and real property of the noncustodial parent in the amount of unpaid support. A lien is a nonpossessory interest in property that operates as a cloud against title, and would prevent the noncustodial parent from selling, transferring, or borrowing against the property until the arrearage is paid.

Lien:
A nonpossessory interest in the property of another that operates as a cloud against title

The following passage from the Office of Child Support Enforcement's manual, *Essentials for Attorneys in Child Support Enforcement*, provides an excellent description of how liens operate:

> A lien is often referred to as a "slumbering" interest that allows the noncustodial parent to retain possession of the property, but which prevents transfer of clear title of affected property either directly (by prohibiting the recording agency from issuing a new title or deed) or indirectly (by providing that all subsequent interests in the property will be subject to the lien). The latter method is most common. It works because subsequent potential purchasers and lenders receive notice of the ... lien ... [and] react to this ... by requiring the noncustodial parent to satisfy the lien, or to obtain a release from the custodial parent, before proceeding with the transfer or loan.[21]

Under federal law, the lien must arise as a matter of law, which means that it happens automatically, without any required action on the part of the custodial parent. However, under state law, the custodial parent may need to take certain steps to "perfect" the lien, such as recording a copy of the support order in the appropriate office or registry of public records, in order for it to have priority over other liens.

Credit Reporting

Under federal law, IV-D agencies must report to **credit-reporting** agencies the name of any parent whose support arrearage has reached a specific dollar amount. Before the report is made, the parent must be given notice and an opportunity to correct any inaccurate information. Although reporting does not result in an immediate transfer of income to the custodial parent, it is hoped that the threat of a negative credit report will serve as an inducement to support obligors who might otherwise be tempted to avoid paying child support.

Licenses

Federal law also requires states to adopt procedures by which they can withhold, suspend, or restrict an individual's professional or occupational license, driver's license, or recreational/sporting licenses due to the nonpayment of support. As with credit reporting, these sanctions do not directly transfer money to the custodial parent. Rather, it is hoped that the threat of losing or having restrictions placed on one's license will operate as a strong deterrent to the nonpayment of support.

The Federal Offset Program

The Federal Offset Program assists states to enforce child support obligations through a variety of remedies including the Federal Tax Refund Offset and the Passport Denial Program. These are administered by OCSE in tandem with other federal (and state child support) agencies.

Federal Tax Offset

Acting in tandem with the two federal agencies, the IRS and the Financial Management Service (a bureau of the U.S. Department of the Treasury), the OCSE can intercept a federal tax refund owed to a noncustodial parent and use the funds to pay a past-due child support obligation. This remedy is available only in cases that are being handled through a state IV-D agency. In other words, a custodial parent acting on his or her own cannot request that delinquent support payments be collected through a tax intercept.

The noncustodial parent is entitled to receive a pre-offset notice that explains the process, including how to challenge the offset. Available arguments to challenge are limited. The parent can argue that no support is owed, that the arrearage calculation is incorrect, or that the refund is owed to his or her new spouse and therefore is not subject to the intercept, but the validity of the underlying order itself cannot be challenged.

The Passport Denial Program

Following certification by a state that a noncustodial parent owes at least $2,500 in back child support, the OCSE can submit that parent's name to the Department of State (DOS), which will then refuse to issue him or her a passport. If the parent already has a passport, DOS will revoke it or otherwise restrict its use. A parent is not automatically released from the Passport Denial Program when the support arrearage drops below $2,500, as it is up to each state to determine the terms of release, with some requiring that the full arrearage be paid first. As with the tax intercept, this process can be initiated only by a state IV-D agency.

Interstate Cases

About one-third of child support cases involve parents who live in different states. These cases have been the bane of the child support system. The process of obtaining and enforcing support orders across state lines has been notoriously difficult due to the lack of coordination between states, the lack of access to information, and the low priority given to these cases.[22] To improve this system, the IV-D agency in each state must have a Central Registry that coordinates interstate cases. States also are required to give interstate cases the same priority that they give to cases involving their own residents. Additionally, two fairly recent federal laws, the Uniform Interstate Family Support Act (UIFSA) and the Full Faith and Credit for Child Support Orders Act (FFCCSOA), address some of these concerns and are intended to streamline the interstate process.

The Uniform Interstate Family Support Act (UIFSA) and the Full Faith and Credit for Child Support Orders Act (FFCCSOA)

In 1996, the welfare reform act (i.e., the Personal Responsibility and Work Opportunity Reconciliation Act) required states to adopt and implement UIFSA by 1998 in order to remain eligible for federal child support funds.[23] A primary purpose of UIFSA is to avoid the proliferation of competing orders as family members move to different states, with the resulting confusion regarding validity and enforceability. Under UIFSA, there should be only one valid support order at any given time, which must be enforced in all states according to its original terms.[24]

The Initial Support Order. UIFSA allows a custodial parent to seek the initial child support order in his or her home state, so long as the state can assert personal jurisdiction over the noncustodial parent through its "long-arm" provisions (see Chapter 9), or in the state of the noncustodial parent. In the latter case, the custodial parent initiates the action in his or her home state, and the IV-D agency then sends it on to the IV-D agency in the respondent's state, in what is referred to as a "two-state" proceeding.

Enforcing the Order.   Once there is a support order, it can be enforced in any state where the noncustodial parent or his or her assets are located. This is usually done through the IV-D agencies in the appropriate states. However, an important innovation is "direct income withholding," by which an IV-D agency, or the custodial parent himself or herself, sends the income withholding order directly to the noncustodial parent's employer. Assuming that the order is "regular on its face," the employer must honor the order, as if it had been issued by a court in the employer's home state, and withhold wages as directed.

Of critical importance, the issuing state retains exclusive jurisdiction to modify the order so long as either parent or the child remains in that state.[25] By vesting continuing authority in the issuing state, UIFSA avoids the potential confusion of multiple orders. Only when all parties have left the issuing state will modification jurisdiction shift to a new state. Further strengthening this "one-order" system, FFCCSOA[26] requires states to give "full faith and credit" to properly issued orders from other states, thus also limiting the ability of states to modify orders from other states.

Enforcement by Private Child Support Collection Agencies

Over the course of the past 10 or 15 years, a new player has entered the child support enforcement field to help custodial parents collect child support that is owed to them — the for-profit child support collection agency. Such an agency promises to fill the existing gap in enforcement services that IV-D agencies seem unable to fix. Many in the child support field argue that this is an idea whose time has come — that we need to face the reality that despite considerable progress, IV-D agencies are not able to handle the high volume of existing support cases:

> [T]he government child support enforcement program simply cannot meet the needs of all families needing child support service.
>
> The most recent data (FY 2000) provided by the federal Office of Child Support Enforcement shows that the national Title IV-D program made collections in only 41.6 [percent] of the 17.4 million cases in its caseload. . . .
>
> The troubling situation is not likely to change, no matter how effectively the state Title IV-D agencies use the vast information and enforcement resources available to them. The amounts of obligated, but uncollected support will continue to mount at a rate beyond the ability of the program ever to collect.[27]

Some have argued that if we are to solve the current support crises, these private agencies (as well as the private bar) need enhanced power and increased resources. To this end, a variety of legislative proposals have been introduced that would give these private entities access to the databases, the parent locator resources, and the enforcement tools, such as tax refund intercepts, of the IV-D agencies.

Yet many in the field are wary of these agencies and do not want to encourage their proliferation or their access to governmental databases and enforcement tools. Serious concerns have been raised about some of these agencies' business practices, particularly the fees they charge, which can be as high as 50 percent of the collected support, thus diverting funds intended for the support of children. Moreover, these fees often are demanded even if the money is ultimately collected and disbursed by the IV-D agencies.[28] Other criticized practices include contracts that are almost impossible to cancel, harassment of the support obligor, threats of arrest without proper authority, and the collection of fees from current, rather than past, support as required.[29]

Other concerns focus on the risks of providing access to governmental databases and enforcement tools. It is argued that access to information may lead to breaches of privacy or to the potential misuse of highly confidential information and that increasing the tools at the disposal of these agencies may exacerbate existing questionable trade practices. Again, this raises particular concerns about the safety of domestic violence victims.

Enforcement Under State Law Procedures

In addition to the remedies discussed previously, a support award can be enforced through traditional state remedies, such as a **criminal nonsupport** or a **contempt proceeding**. These remedies can be pursued by an individual or by a IV-D agency on behalf of a custodial parent who is receiving its services.

Criminal Nonsupport

Most, if not all, states make the failure to support minor children a crime. Generally, nonsupport is classified as a misdemeanor. As in all criminal proceedings, the goal is punishment of the offender and vindication of the public interest. However, most states will suspend the sentence if the defendant agrees to pay support, which accomplishes the civil goal of providing support to the children. If the payment is not made following the suspension, the sentence will be reimposed.

For a conviction, the failure to support must be willful. The state has the burden of proving willfulness by establishing that the defendant had

Criminal Nonsupport:
The willful failure to pay child support when one has the ability to do so

Contempt Proceeding:
A proceeding against a party who is in violation of a court order

the ability to provide support and deliberately failed to do so. Some states also require proof that the nonsupport left the children in "destitute or necessitous" circumstances. In these states, support from the custodial parent or a third party that keeps the children out of poverty may bar a conviction. The defendant is entitled to the procedural protections that apply in all criminal cases, including the privilege against self-incrimination. This may make proof of ability to pay difficult because the defendant cannot be forced to testify or to disclose adverse information through discovery.

For these reasons, criminal nonsupport actions generally are not the remedy of choice. However, they can be useful where the failure to pay support is flagrant or where the obligor is self-employed, thus precluding wage withholding. The willful failure to pay a past-due support obligation on behalf of a child in another state is now a federal crime. In addition, under the Deadbeat Parents Punishment Act of 1998, it is a felony to travel interstate (or internationally) in order to avoid an unpaid support order that meets specified durational and amount requirements.[30]

Contempt

A contempt action can be brought where an obligor fails to comply with a court order of support. Contempt actions can be either civil or criminal in nature. A contempt action is usually not the remedy of choice, but it can be a useful supplemental remedy, especially where a parent is self-employed and thus not amenable to a wage withholding.

Civil Contempt.   The purpose of a civil contempt proceeding is to secure compliance with the support order, and a jail sentence may be imposed for this purpose. In most states, the obligor must have the present ability to pay the ordered support amount in order to be found in civil contempt. If found in contempt, the obligor must be given the opportunity to avoid jail or, if jailed, to secure release by purging the contempt, usually by satisfying the terms of the underlying order.

Criminal Contempt.   The purpose of a criminal contempt proceeding is to punish the support obligor for violating the court's order. In contrast to civil contempt, if a jail sentence is imposed, its purpose is to punish the violation rather than to secure compliance with the order. Unlike in a civil contempt, an obligor cannot purchase his or her freedom by complying with the order. Accordingly, present ability to pay is not a required element; instead, the state must prove ability to pay during the time of noncompliance. As with criminal nonsupport, the procedural protections generally available to defendants in criminal cases are available here.

Modification and Adjustment of Support Awards

Once a child support amount has been established, subsequent events may occur that warrant a change in the amount. Where this occurs, a parent may seek a **modification** of the support order. Additionally, states must implement a **review and adjustment procedure** for all support cases enforced through the IV-D agency.

Modification:
The alteration of an existing order based on a change in circumstances

Review and Adjustment Procedure:
The periodic assessment and potential revision of a child support order by a IV-D agency

Modification Based on Changed Circumstances

Child support orders are not generally considered final judgments and are subject to modification. However, modification actions are not designed to give parents a second bite at the apple; that is, issues that have already been determined are not supposed to be relitigated.

In a "traditional" modification action, the petitioner must show that there has been a **change in circumstances** that justifies an upward or downward revision of the support amount. Most, if not all, states also require that the change was not foreseeable at the time the order was entered. Support amounts agreed on by the parties in a separation agreement are subject to modification, as the right to adequate support belongs to the child and cannot be bargained away by a parent. However, some courts give considerable weight to parties' agreements and impose a greater burden on the petitioner to prove that a modification is warranted.

Change in Circumstances:
A future event that arguably makes an existing order unfair and serves as the basis for a request for modification

Either party can seek a modification. Typically, a custodial parent who is seeking an upward revision looks to changes such as increased needs of the children, an increase in the other parent's income, remarriage of the noncustodial parent, or a decrease in his or her own income. Typically, a noncustodial parent who is seeking a downward revision looks to changes such as a decrease in his or her own income, responsibility for a second family, an increase in the custodial parent's income, remarriage of the custodial parent, or employment of the child.

A contentious question is whether a noncustodial parent can seek a reduction in support payments if the custodial parent is interfering with his or her visitation rights. The majority view is that visitation and support issues are independent variables and should not be linked. Exceptions to this policy of nonlinkage may occur in extreme situations — for example, where a parent falsifies employment information to avoid paying support or a custodial parent hides a child to prevent visitation from taking place.

In addition to the traditional change in circumstances standard, most states' guidelines, in accordance with federal regulations, include a modification provision authorizing a change in the amount of support "when there is a threshold difference between the current support amount and the presumptive guideline amount." This difference is usually expressed either as a dollar or a percentage of the support amount.[31]

The fact that support orders can be modified has historically caused considerable confusion in the interstate arena because states have readily modified orders of other states, resulting in multiple and potentially conflicting orders. However, FFCCSOA addresses this problem by vesting exclusive and continuing jurisdiction over the order in the issuing state so long as the child or any other party continues to reside there; as long as this condition is met, other states are precluded from modifying the order.

The Review and Adjustment Procedure

In addition to modification based on changed circumstances, parents have a right under federal law to have their support orders reviewed every three years (or earlier if a state elects a shorter review cycle). Where the state's child support guidelines or changes in the cost of living justify a modification, a support order will be adjusted either upward or downward to account for the changes.[32]

Duration of the Parental Support Obligation

In general, a parent has an obligation to support his or her child until the child reaches 18 — the age of majority. In certain situations, however, the support obligation may be terminated before majority or extended beyond it. These durational issues are generally controlled by state law.

Termination of Support Prior to Majority

Support can be terminated prior to majority only under very limited circumstances, such as emancipation of the minor, death of the parent paying support, or the termination of parental rights. A custodial parent does not generally have the authority to agree to a termination of support because, again, the right of support belongs to the child, not to the parent.

Emancipation

Emancipation:
The point at which a child is no longer considered a dependent of his or her parents

Emancipation extinguishes the reciprocal rights and obligations that exist between a parent and child and releases the child from the authority and control of his or her parents. Many states recognize a common law doctrine of emancipation under which certain acts, most notably marriage and entry into the armed services, are regarded as creating a status that is incompatible with parental control and thus serve to emancipate the minor. In some states, a child who is living on his or her own and is self-supporting may also be considered emancipated. Some states have a statutory emancipation procedure that permits a child, or possibly a parent, to file a court petition seeking a declaration of emancipation.

Once a child is emancipated, the support obligation will in all likelihood terminate because the child is now considered able to care for himself or herself. However, where emancipation occurs through a court proceeding, a court might decide to only partially emancipate a minor, such as for the limited purpose of consenting to medical procedures, and continue the support obligation.

Parental Death

At common law, the death of a parent terminated the support obligation. This responsibility did not pass to the decedent's estate, but the estate was liable for arrearages that had accrued prior to death. Many states now have statutes that authorize a court to hold the parent's estate responsible for continued support payments unless the parties otherwise agreed in a separation agreement.

In the absence of a specific statute or separation agreement, many judges believe that they lack the authority to order post-death support, as this would upset the estate plan of the decedent, who has a legal right to disinherit his or her children. According to this view, ordering such support would give greater rights to children of divorced parents compared to children of still-married parents. Other judges take a different view of the matter and may continue support following the death of the noncustodial parent. These judges give greater weight to providing for children than to protecting the stability of estate plans and the expectations of beneficiaries. This approach also recognizes that a noncustodial parent may be more likely to disinherit his or her children, thus creating a greater need for a remedy.

Adoption/Termination of Parental Rights

Where parental rights are extinguished through adoption or an involuntary termination proceeding, the parental support obligation is likewise extinguished. The only issue is identifying *when* the obligation ceases. The general rule is that this occurs upon the actual cessation of the parent-child relationship rather than upon the consent to the adoption.

Extension of Support Beyond Majority

The Adult Student

With the age of majority now set at 18 in most states, the question often arises as to whether an adult child has a right to continued support if he or she is still in high school or wishes to attend college. Most, if not all, states provide for the continuation of support until a child completes high school, even if he or she turns 18 prior to graduation. In short, emancipation for child support purposes is deemed to be the later of these two occurrences. However, the picture is far less clear when it comes to post-minority support for a child who wishes to attend college.

The question as to whether a parent can be required to pay child support or to contribute to the educational expenses of an adult child has become increasingly pressing given that in today's advanced economy, a college degree (or other type of postsecondary education) is generally regarded as necessary to ensure some measure of financial autonomy and stability. Of particular concern in this regard is the fact that children of divorced parents are significantly less likely than children of still-married parents to receive financial help from one or both parents for college.[33] Capturing this imbalance, one commentator writes that

> parents of intact families achieve extraordinary wealth transfer by providing higher education for their children. This transfer exists almost entirely outside of the traditional child support system. As a result, the equality principle on which child support is based fails to accommodate children of non-intact families in receiving higher education.[34]

To remedy this inequity, the author suggests that the federal child support laws should be amended to require "states, when establishing their guidelines, to provide for some level of post-secondary support absent any agreement between the parents."[35] However, this proposal raises the counter equity argument that doing so would impose a *formal* duty on divorced parents that is not likewise imposed on parents who are married.

As for the approaches that states do take, a sizable minority of jurisdictions have enacted statutory provisions that permit a judge to order the continuation of child support up to a certain post-minority age, typically 21 or 22, if the child is a full-time student or regularly attending school. In some of these states, in addition to or in lieu of child support, a parent can be ordered to pay a share of the child's educational expenses. Where both types of payments are ordered, the child support amount is typically adjusted downward to account for the parent's contribution to the costs of his or her child's education.[36] Even if not expressly authorized by statute, most states will enforce an agreement between parents that obligates one or both of them to provide child support for a post-minority child who is attending college.

In the absence of a specific statute, courts generally take one of two approaches to the award of support for post-minority students. Many judges believe it is not fair to require divorced parents to pay for their children's college education, since, had the family remained together, the parents would have been free to decide whether to contribute to their children's college education, and the children would have no legal claim to such support.

Other courts take the position that education is a basic parental obligation and will order support in appropriate cases. These courts often point out that had the parents remained together, it can be assumed that they would have made a reasonable effort to finance their children's education and that divorce should not work a deprivation. They are also aware that if support is not ordered, the financial burden will most likely fall on the custodial parent.

In deciding whether to order support so a child may attend college, courts generally look at a number of factors, including the reasonable expectations of the child, academic interest and ability, and the parents' financial status. Courts may also try to determine whether the family would have provided a college education had the parents remained together. Unfortunately, these factors may work against a young person who is not from a middle-class family, as a judge may decide that a college education is not necessary or within reasonable expectations.

Mental and Physical Disabilities

Almost all states permit courts to continue support beyond age 18 where an adult child is mentally or physically disabled and is incapable of self-support. Some states require the disability to have begun during minority and will not require support if the child becomes disabled as an adult.

Tax Implications of Child Support Awards

There are two basic tax questions to consider with regard to the payment of child support:

- How are payments to be treated for tax purposes?
- What is the relationship between paying support and claiming the dependency exemption for the children?

Characterization of Child Support Payments

The basic rule is that child support payments are not considered income to the custodial parent and are not subject to taxation. Because payments are not includible in income to the recipient, the noncustodial parent is not entitled to deduct the amount of the payments from his or her income. In effect, payment of child support is a tax-neutral event.

This changes, however, if child support payments are lumped together with alimony payments so that a single support payment is made without designating how much is for alimony and how much for child support. This is commonly referred to as **unallocated support**. Where support is unallocated, the entire amount will be treated as alimony. Unlike child support, alimony is regarded as taxable income to the recipient and entitles the payor spouse to deduct the payments from his or her gross income.

Unallocated Support: Child and spousal support awards combined in a single support amount without designation

Given this potential tax benefit, a support obligor may be tempted to characterize the entire support amount as alimony. This could also benefit the support recipient because the tax savings realized by the obligor could be passed on, in whole or in part, as additional support payments. This would, of course, increase the recipient's taxable income but, if he or she is in a lower tax bracket, it could result in a net gain.

To deter parties from disguising child support payments as spousal support, the federal tax code now includes rules regarding the treatment of unallocated support payments. Where support is unallocated, reductions that are tied to a contingency relating to a child or to a time associated with such a contingency create a refutable presumption that the amount of the reduction was in fact child support, and it will be treated as such.

Child-related contingencies include reaching majority, marriage, and completing school. For example, if the wife is to receive $500 per month with no contingencies other than remarriage or death, the full amount will be considered alimony. But if the agreement calls for payments to be reduced to $200 per month at the child's eighteenth birthday, the IRS will recharacterize the amount of the reduction as child support. Moreover, if a creative attorney tries to avoid this rule and has the reduction occur two months before the child's birthday, the IRS will consider this as occurring at a time associated with a child-related contingency and will again presume that this amount is child support. The presumption can be rebutted by proof that the timing of the reduction was selected based on independent, nonchild-related considerations.

The Dependency Exemption and Child Tax Credit

The basic rule is that the custodial parent is entitled to claim the children as dependents for federal tax purposes. However, because the noncustodial parent is usually in a higher tax bracket, the dependency exemption may be worth more to this parent. Accordingly, as part of divorce negotiations, parties often negotiate over who will take the **dependency exemption**. If the custodial parent agrees that the noncustodial parent can claim the children, the custodial parent must effectuate this by signing a written release. The release can be made permanent or for a

Dependency Exemption: Deduction that a taxpayer can take from gross income for a person who is principally dependent on the taxpayer for support

temporary period. Parties may also agree to alternate years for claiming the exemption or to each claim the exemption for a different child.

Since 1997, decisions about which parent will claim the children as dependents have assumed an even greater importance because the parent who claims the child is now also entitled to a child tax credit. Unlike the dependency exemption, which permits an adjustment to gross income, the child tax credit gives a parent an actual credit against his or her tax liability.

Child Tax Credit: Credit against tax liability provided to parents; available to the parent with the dependency exemption

Chapter Summary

In 1974, Congress enacted the Child Support Enforcement and Establishment of Paternity Act, marking the entrance of the federal government into the child support arena. States must now have a comprehensive child support program in effect, which is administered by a single entity, known as an IV-D agency. Child support awards must be based on guidelines that use numeric criteria to arrive at a presumptive amount; deviations are permitted under limited circumstances. States must also have an array of enforcement mechanisms in place to help with the collection of child support. The most important of these is income withholding. To aid in the establishment and enforcement of child support, federal law has mandated the creation of an extensive interconnected set of databases, which permit the collection, sharing, and matching of information regarding child support cases.

Interstate cases have been the bane of the child support system. To address this situation, all states must now have a central registry for the coordination of interstate cases. Furthermore, all states have adopted UIFSA, which, by continuing modification jurisdiction in the issuing state for as long as a parent or child remains there, eliminates the problem of conflicting orders. Under FFCCSOA, all states must give full faith and credit to child support orders of other states.

A parent's support obligation generally lasts until a child reaches the age of majority (18), but under limited circumstances, it can be terminated earlier or extended beyond this point. Support orders can be modified based on a change in circumstances; they are also subject to a periodic review and adjustment process.

Child support payments are not considered income to the recipient, nor are they deductible by the payor. If folded into an unallocated support award, the entire amount will be treated as alimony unless reductions are tied to child-related contingencies. Unless released, the dependency exemption belongs to the custodial parent. The parent who takes the dependency exemption is also entitled to the child tax credit.

Key Terms

Child Support
Title IV-D
IV-D Agency
Parent Locator Service
Child Support
    Guidelines
Support Worksheet
Imputed/Attributed
    Income

Extraordinary
    Expense
Qualified Medical
    Child Support Order
    (QMCSO)
Financial Affidavit
Wage Withholding
Arrearage
Lien

Credit Reporting
Criminal
    Nonsupport
Contempt
    Proceeding
Modification
Review and
    Adjustment
    Procedure

Change in
    Circumstances
Emancipation
Unallocated
    Support
Dependency
    Exemption
Child Tax
    Credit

Review Questions

1. Why did the federal government decide to enter the child support field?
2. When was the federal OCSE established, and what is its function?
3. What is a IV-D agency, and what is its role in the child support field?
4. What must a custodial parent do when applying for public assistance? What is the nature of the parent's relationship with the IV-D system?
5. How does a custodial parent who is not on public assistance access the services of a IV-D agency?
6. What is a parent locator service?

7. Explain how child support guidelines work, making sure that you include an explanation of the concept of deviation.

8. Identify and explain the various guideline approaches.

9. How do states generally define income?

10. What is meant by imputed or attributed income, and when is this concept used?

11. Explain the terms "gross income," "adjusted gross income," and "net income" in the child support context.

12. How do guidelines typically treat the income of the custodial parent's new partner?

13. How do guidelines treat the income of a child?

14. Where a parent is ordered to pay support for a second family, how is his or her prior support order usually accounted for?

15. How do guidelines treat the situation where an obligor wants to pay less to his first family because he now has a second family with minor children?

16. Explain the concept of extraordinary expenses and how states treat them when determining support.

17. When might visitation arrangements trigger an adjustment in support?

18. Why do courts generally not terminate support where parents have joint custody? What approaches do courts take in these situations?

19. What kinds of databases exist at the state and federal level, and what roles do they play in the child support system? What concerns have been raised about them?

20. Explain how income withholding works. When can an income withholding be bypassed?

21. What is a lien, and what role does it have in the child support context?

22. What is the concept of a tax refund intercept?

23. What is the function of the central registry in an interstate case?

24. What is the overall purpose of UIFSA? What are its key provisions?

25. What does FFCCSOA require?

26. What role do private support collection agencies seek to fill? What arguments have been raised in favor of and against such an approach?

27. What is the goal of a criminal nonsupport case? How is the civil goal of supporting children accomplished?

28. Explain the difference between criminal and civil contempt.

29. Explain the two ways in which support orders can be changed.

30. What is the relationship between support and visitation?

31. What circumstances might trigger a termination of support prior to majority?

32. What circumstances might permit a continuation of support after majority?

33. What approaches do states take with respect to post-minority support for children who are attending school?

34. As a general matter, what tax impact does child support have?

35. Explain the tax rules regarding unallocated support awards.

36. Who is entitled to the dependency exemption? How can the other parent become entitled to it?

Discussion Questions

1. Despite all the legislative changes discussed in this chapter, serious concerns still exist regarding the inadequacy of support payments and noncompliance with support orders. Why do you think child support continues to be such a social problem? Given what you have learned about divorce, what dynamics do you think might be at work?

2. Let's take a hypothetical case: A couple divorces when their child is three years old. Mom has custody, and Dad moves out of state. For the first few years, Dad sees the child regularly, but now he has remarried and his visits are infrequent. He is now happily and actively participating in the raising of his two new children.

He wishes to reduce support to his first child because he feels resentful about providing for a child with whom he has no relationship, and money is tight in his new household. Do you think he should be permitted to do this? What do you base your opinion on? Does your answer change if Mom has interfered with his visits without good reason? Does your answer change if Mom left him because he was abusive? Should these kinds of issues influence support determinations?

3. Here's another hypothetical: Two parents divorce. Dad has custody of the two children, ages 2 and 4. He works half time. Mom is a corporate executive and hates her work. She earns a good salary and pays enough child support so that Dad and the children are reasonably comfortable. It is important to Dad that the children not be in full-time day care. Mom decides to leave her job and pursue her lifelong dream of being a freelance writer. Assume that Mom is acting in good faith; in other words, she is not making this job change for the purpose of avoiding child support. Do you think the court should impute income to her based on her earning capacity and use this figure for the calculation of support? How do you balance the equities in this situation? What factors would you weigh?

4. Should judges be able to order divorced parents to contribute to their children's college education?

5. Do you think private support collection agencies are a good idea? Do you think they benefit or harm children?

Assignments

1. Obtain a copy of your state's child support guidelines and answer the following questions:
   a. What approach is used?
   b. How is income of the custodial parent treated?
   c. How is income of the child treated?
   d. What happens when the obligor has a prior family? A subsequent family?
   e. How are extraordinary expenses treated?
   f. What other factors influence the amount?

2. Obtain a copy of the child support worksheet that is used in your state to calculate support awards. Using the worksheet and consulting the guidelines where necessary, calculate a support award based on the following facts:
   a. Mom has custody of the two children, ages 4 and 9.
   b. Her gross income is $22,000; her adjusted gross income is $18,700.
   c. She has yearly child-care expenses of $8,000.
   d. Dad's gross income is $46,000; his adjusted gross income is $39,000.
   e. He spends what would be considered a typical amount of time visiting with his children.
   f. Dad maintains a family health insurance policy that covers the children—the cost of this policy to him is $380 per month, and the cost of maintaining an individual policy would be $190 per month.
   g. The nine-year old child has severe learning disabilities, which require the hiring of special tutors—the monthly cost of this is $225.
   h. Neither parent has other children.

3. Determine whether your state has implemented any support enforcement tools that go beyond those that are required under federal law.

4. Develop a client intake questionnaire for use in cases where support is an issue. Make sure that you consult the guidelines so all relevant considerations are accounted for.

5. Assume that a client in your office is seeking a divorce from her husband, who left the state five years ago. Since that time, she has had no contact with him, but she does know where he is living. Locate UIFSA as adopted by your state and determine whether your state can exercise personal jurisdiction over him for purposes of entering a child support order. Now, do the same but with the following change. Assume that the client and her husband never lived together in your state, but that she moved here following their separation. However, the husband makes periodic visits to see the child. Under this set of facts, can your state obtain personal jurisdiction over him? Explain your answer.

Endnotes

1. Joseph I. Lieberman, Child Support in America: Practical Advice for Negotiating and Collecting a Fair Settlement 14 (1988).

2. U.S. Dept. of Health and Human Services, Child Support: An Agenda for Action (1984). The citation for Title IV-D is Pub. L. No. 93-647 (1974) (codified as amended at 42 U.S.C. sec. 651-652).

3. No systematic attempt will be made to match developments with a particular legislative enactment. For your reference, some of the more significant amendments to date include the Child Support Enforcement Amendments of 1984, Pub. L. No. 98-378, 98 Stat. 1305 (42 U.S.C. §667); the Family Support Act of 1988, Pub. L. No. 100-485, 102 Stat. 2343 (codified in scattered sections of 42 U.S.C.); the Child Support Recovery Act of 1992, Pub. L. No. 102-521, 106 Stat. 3403 (codified as amended at 18 U.S.C. §228 and scattered sections of 42 U.S.C.); the Personal Responsibility and Work Opportunity Reconciliation Act of 1996, Pub. L. No. 104-193, 110 Stat. 105 (42 U.S.C. §§601 et seq.); and the Deficit Reduction Act of 2005, Pub. L. No. 109-171, 120 Stat. 4.

It should also be noted that this chapter does not address the complex issue of *who* may be liable for child support in the context of "nontraditional" family structures. This issue is touched on in Chapter 11. For further information, the following articles are a good starting point: Leslie Joan Harris, The Basis for Legal Parentage and the Clash Between Custody and Child Support, 42 Ind. L. Rev. 611 (2009); Laura W. Morgan, Child Support Fifty Years Later, 42 Fam. L.Q. 365 (2008); Katherine K. Baker, Bionormativity and the Construction of Parenthood, 42 Ga. L. Rev. 649 (2008); M. Scott Serfozo, Sperm Donor Child Support Obligations: How Courts and Legislatures Should Weigh the Interests of Donor, Donee, and Child, 77 U. Cin. L. Rev. 715 (2008); Jennifer L. Rosato, Children of Same-Sex Parents Deserve the Security Blanket of the Parentage Presumption, 44 Fam. Ct. Rev. 74 (2006); Sara R. David, Turning Parental Rights into Parental Obligations — Holding Same-Sex, Non-Biological Parents Responsible for Child Support, 31 New Eng. L. Rev. 921 (2005).

4. A state that does not comply with federal law risks losing a percentage of its federal funding for the administration of its child support program.

5. http://www.acf.hhs.gov/programs/cse/newhire/library/brochures/fpls/fpls.htm.

6. As noted previously, in 1996 Congress replaced AFDC with the TANF program. Designed, at least in theory, to move people off public assistance, among other differences, TANF includes a lifetime cap on the number of months that a person may receive benefits. For further discussion, *see* generally the relevant publications on the Center for Law and Social Policy's website: http://www.clasp.org (accessed Nov. 14, 2012).

7. For a detailed discussion of safety concerns raised by the child support collection process, *see* Ali Stieglitz and Amy Johnson, Final Report: Making Child Support Safe: Coordinating Child Support and Public Assistance Agencies in Their Response to Domestic Violence (2001), available at http://www.acf.hhs.gov/programs/cse/pubs/reports/mpr 8548300/index.html; and Susan Notar and Vicki Turetsky, Models for Safe Child Support Enforcement, 8 Am. U. J. Gender Soc. Poly. & L. 657 (2000).

8. For further detail, including a discussion of how collected support is to be allocated once a family is no longer receiving TANF benefits, *see* Paul Legler and Vicki Turetsky, More Child Support Dollars to Kids: Using New State Flexibility in Child Support Pass-Through and Distribution Rules to Benefit Government and Families, (2006), Center for Law and Social Policy, www.clasp.org/admin/site/publications/files/0305.pdf. Regarding each state's approach, *see* Michelle Vinson and Vicki Turetsky, State Child Support Pass-Through Policies, www.clasp.org/admin/site/publications/files/PassThroughFinal061209.pdf (accessed Jan. 19, 2010).

Please note that a detailed discussion about the complex relationship between the child support and the public assistance systems is beyond the scope of this text. If you are working with clients who are applying for or receiving public assistance, you must become familiar with the interplay between them. This is particularly important if your client is a victim of domestic violence, as the initiation of a child support action can trigger or escalate abuse or possibly lead to the disclosure of a victim's whereabouts. It may also trigger a retaliatory custody or visitation action. The abovementioned Center for Law and Social Policy website is an excellent place to start your inquiry.

9. Vicki Turetsky, What If All the Money Came Home? Welfare Cost Recovery in the Child Support Program, 43 Fam. Ct. Rev. 402 (2005).

10. Office of Child Support Enforcement, Essentials for Attorneys in Child Support Enforcement, ch. 3 (3d ed., 2002) (*Essentials*), http://www.acf.hhs.gov/programs/cse/pubs/2002/reports/essentials/ (accessed Jan. 22, 2010).

11. Susan Notar and Vicki Turetsky, Models for Safe Child Support Enforcement, 8 Am. U. J. Gender Soc. Poly. & L. 657, 698 (2000).

12. The word "permanent" does not mean "forever," as support awards are modifiable. Rather, the term "permanent support" is used to distinguish awards that are entered at the time of divorce from those that are entered during the pendency of the case and are thus interim in nature.

13. Laura W. Morgan, Imputing Income to Non-Income and Low-Income Earning Assets, 17 Am. J. Fam. L. 191 (2004).

14. Essentials, *supra* note 10, ch. 9. Although questions about multiple families usually arise in the course of a modification proceeding, the topic will be discussed here in keeping with the organizational format of many guidelines. For an excellent discussion of this topic, *see* Marianne Takas, U.S. Dept. of Health and Human Services, The Treatment of Multiple Family Cases Under State Child Support Guidelines (1991).

15. For further discussion, *see* Adrienne Jennings Lockie, Multiple Families, Multiple Goals, Multiple Failures: The Need for "Limited Equalization" as a Theory of Child Support, 32 Harv. J.L. & Gender 109 (2009).

16. Sally F. Goldfarb, Child Support Guidelines: A Model for Fair Allocation of Child Care, Medical and Educational Expenses, 21 Fam. L.Q. 325, 331 (1987).

17. For details, *see* Compliance Guide for Qualified Medical Child Support Orders, http://www.acf.hhs.gov/programs/cse/pubs/2003/guides/dept_labor_qmcso.html (accessed Jan. 19, 2010).

18. Office of Child Support Enforcement FY 2006 Annual Report to Congress, http://www.acf.hhs.gov/programs/cse/pubs/2009/reports/annual_report/ (accessed Jan. 19, 2010).

19. Drew A. Swank, Das Boot! A National Survey of Booting Programs' Impact on Child Support Compliance, 4 J.L. Fam. Stud. 265, 268 (2002).

20. Essentials, *supra* note 10, ch. 10.

21. *Id.* at p. 9.

22. Interstate Child Support Remedies (Margaret Campbell Haynes with Diane G. Dodson eds., 1989).

23. http://www.ncsea.org/wp-content/uploads/2012/02/UIFSA_2001.pdf (accessed April 24, 2015).

24. Our focus is on interstate cases. Other complex jurisdictional issues are raised by cases in which one parent is living in another country. For recent developments, *see* Michael J. Peters, International Child Support: The United States Striving Towards a Better Solution, 15 New Eng. J. Intl. & Comp. L. 91 (2009).

25. The 2001 revisions also permit parties to consent to continuing jurisdiction in this state, even if everyone has moved away.

26. FFCCSOA can be found at 28 U.S.C. §1738B (2001). For an excellent overview of interstate issues, *see* Patricia Hatamyer, Interstate Establishment, Enforcement, and Modification of Child Support Orders, 25 Okla. City U. L. Rev. 511 (2000).

27. Laura W. Morgan, Private Attorney Access to Child Support Enforcement Tools: Recommendations of the Interstate Commission, 16 Am. J. Fam. L. 169 (2002).

28. Drew A. Swank, Note from the Field: Child Support, Private Enforcement Companies, and the Law, 2002 Army Law. 57, 58.

29. *Id.*

30. Child Support Recovery Act, *as amended by* "Deadbeat Parents Act," Pub. L. No. 105-187 §2, 112 Stat. 618 (1998) (codified at 118 U.S.C. §228).

31. Essentials, *supra* note 10, ch. 11.

32. In light of the fact that the review and adjustment process has been somewhat cumbersome, the federal Office of Child Support Enforcement has set up a collaborative federal-state initiative to help states automate the process. *See* Automated Systems for Child Support Enhancement: A Guide for Enhancing Review and Adjustment Automation, U.S. Department of Health and Human Services, Administration for Children and Families, Office for Child Support Enforcement, July 2006, http://www.acf.dhhs.gov/programs/cse.

33. Monica Hof Wallace, A Federal Referendum: Extending Child Support for Higher Education, 58 Kan. L. Rev. 665 (2010).

34. *Id.* at 667.

35. *Id.* at 686.

36. These determinations can be quite complex and variable. For a detailed discussion, *see* Madeline Marzno-Lesnevish and Scott Adam Laterra, Child Support and College: What Is the Correct Result? 23 J. Am. Acad. Matrimonial Law. 335 (2009).

Chapter Seven

Spousal Support

At the time of divorce, one spouse may be required to provide financial support to the other. This support, traditionally known as "**alimony**," from the Latin *alimonia*, meaning "nourishment" or "sustenance," is now also commonly referred to as "maintenance" or "**spousal support**." As we will see, no-fault divorce reform triggered a major restructuring of the traditional support model that was closely linked to marital fault and grounded in a vision of permanent female economic dependence.

Alimony/Spousal Support: A monetary amount paid to one spouse by the other for support pending or after legal separation or divorce

Historical Overview

Historically, alimony was considered an extension of the husband's marital duty to support his wife, who upon marriage lost most of her property rights and control over her earnings. Alimony was awarded only to "innocent" wives; if a wife was the "guilty" party, the right was lost.

In awarding alimony, courts came to explain it in terms of the role it played in a fault-based divorce system. It became the measure of damages paid to an injured wife to compensate her for the loss occasioned by her wrongdoing husband, much like damages in a tort or breach of contract action.[1] Spousal awards typically did not have any durational limits (see the section later in this chapter entitled "Different Approaches to Structuring Spousal Support"), and reflecting the gendered nature of the obligation, as a general rule, divorcing wives could not be ordered to pay alimony, as they had no underlying support obligation to their husbands.

With no-fault reform, the traditional legal framing of divorce as a necessary evil justifiable only in cases of grievous marital wrongdoing gave way to a greater acceptance of divorce as a solution for unhappy marriages. The elimination of fault as an essential precondition for the granting of a divorce led many to reconceptualize marriage as a partnership, which, as in the business world, is terminable by either party based on dissatisfaction with the undertaking. In keeping with the partnership model, the desirability of allowing each partner to make a **clean break** from the marriage has become an increasingly common way of conceptualizing the post-divorce obligations of the former spouses. In short, as with the dissolution of a business relationship, continuing obligations deriving from the failed marital relationship are to be kept to a minimum (of course, this principle is not applicable so far as minor children are concerned).

As discussed in this chapter, the declining role of fault and the corresponding emergence of the partnership model of marriage prompted a profound reconceptualization of the traditional support model, as follows:

- **Prioritization of Property Division over Spousal Support**
  - Many states now emphasize property division as the preferred way to adjust the post-divorce economic rights of the parties. As the division of property is a final, unmodifiable event (see Chapter 8), it is thought to more closely correspond with the emerging partnership model of marriage than does an award of spousal support. As in a business, the assets of the failed enterprise are distributed, leaving the former partners free to pursue other endeavors unencumbered by the past.
- **Shifting the Focus from Moral to Economic Considerations**
  - Support is no longer awarded as a way to compensate an injured wife for the marital wrongdoings of her husband. Largely uncoupled from fault, support is now tied to economic considerations and, in a blame-free manner, is intended to respond to financial needs arising out of the marital relationship.
- **Degendering the Support Obligation**
  - The support obligation has also been uncoupled from its origins as a male-only responsibility. The U.S. Supreme Court has held that gender-specific alimony laws are unconstitutional because they carry the "inherent risk of reinforcing stereotypes about the 'proper place' of women and their need for special protection."[2] In theory, spousal support is now a gender-neutral concept and is no longer premised on an assumption that married women, as a class, are financially dependent and incapable of self-support. In practice, however, few men (at least in heterosexual unions) meet the economic criteria for a support award.
- **Shifting from an Assumption of Female Economic Dependence to an Assumption of Economic Self-Sufficiency**
  - Following no-fault reform, the idea of permanent alimony awards fell out of favor. Seen as embodying outmoded assumptions regarding female economic dependence and requiring ongoing entanglement, a clear trend developed in favor of

short-term support awards intended to help a spouse acquire the skills needed to become self-supporting. (See the discussion of rehabilitative alimony next.) In sharp contrast to the past, this shift embodied the assumption that all married women, regardless of the role they played during the marriage, should be self-supporting either at the time of divorce or following a brief transitional period. It thus corresponded with both the changing role of women and the partnership model of marriage, which minimizes the ongoing responsibility of a former spouse.

Although this gender-neutral clean-break approach has an appealing simplicity, it has been subject to significant criticism. Of primary concern, critics argue that because many heterosexual marriages embody a gendered division of labor, with the husband's career assuming primary importance even where the wife works outside the home, the assumption that a division of assets will permit both parties to begin life anew with an equal capacity for economic self-sufficiency is erroneous, particularly in households with minor children. It is argued that this marital division of labor has serious and long-lasting implications that endure well beyond the end of the marital relationship. In families in which wives devote considerable effort to the domestic realm, they will generally leave the marriage with a diminished earning capacity. In contrast, a husband who has been far less encumbered by household and child-related responsibilities is likely to exit the marriage with an enhanced earning capacity. By failing to recognize and account for this differential, a woman's domestic contribution — which enhances family life during the marital relationship — hinders her ability to create a secure postmarital life.

Economic Self-Sufficiency: The idea that after a divorce, both spouses should become self-supporting as quickly as possible

Proposing a very different approach, critics of this trend thus argue that alimony needs to be reformulated to eliminate the disadvantage that flows from this marital allocation of work and family responsibilities. In support of their position, they argue that since the economic consequences of marriage continue beyond its duration, so must the financial obligations, so that a primary wage earner does not disproportionately gain from the marital allocation of labor.[3]

Support Determinations

Whether adopted by statute or by judicial decision, most states now use a multifactored approach to determine if spousal support should be awarded in a specific case, and if so, the amount to be awarded. Although, much as in custody cases, judges are usually required to consider all of the enumerated factors, they similarly also usually have the discretion to give each factor the weight they believe it merits in light of the particular circumstances of the case. Again, as with custody, this gives judges the flexibility to consider the unique circumstances of a divorcing couple's situation, but it also makes it difficult to predict the circumstances under which alimony will be awarded. In this section, we first look at the kinds of factors that courts weigh in deciding about spousal support. Reflecting the concerns about the unpredictability and uncertainty of this approach, we then look at some of the reform proposals that are currently being considered, followed by a discussion of the basic ways that support awards can be structured.

Factors to Be Considered

In most states, judges are required to consider a variety of factors when deciding if a spouse should be provided with support. These factors often include the following:

- financial need;
- earning potential;
- age;
- duration of the marriage;
- physical and mental health;
- income and financial resources;
- the marital standard of living; and
- contribution to the marriage.

Additionally, although greatly diminished in importance and eliminated from consideration in a number of jurisdictions, many states still include marital fault as one of the factors that must be considered, and it continues to operate as a complete bar to a spousal support award in a handful of states. Where it is identified as a factor to be considered, marital wrongdoing is generally balanced against other factors, such as need. Also, even in states where marital fault in the traditional sense of the word is not identified as a factor, economic fault may be a permissible consideration. Thus, for example, in assessing the husband's need for support, the court might give weight to the fact that the wife had squandered the family fortune on her lover, thus placing the husband in an economically vulnerable position.

It should also be noted that "contribution to the marriage" is not limited to financial considerations but is generally intended to account for a spouse's nonmonetary contributions to a marriage in the domestic realm. This allows for the recognition that a spouse may have a diminished capacity for self-support because of a primary commitment to the home and/or child rearing.

The general rule is that a judge must consider all of the enumerated factors but can assign them whatever weight he or she believes is appropriate in light of the circumstances of each case. This provides a consistent framework for evaluating cases while giving a judge the freedom to attach different weights to different combinations of factors based on a couple's particular situation. However, need tends to be the most important across-the-board factor, and many of the other factors often are tied to need. Thus, for example, a spouse's need may be more acute because of age, health, or a diminished earning capacity, as these considerations often build off one another in a cumulative way.

To get a clearer picture of how this works, let's look at how a judge might weigh different factors based on the individual circumstances of a case. For example, in a case involving a disabled spouse, a judge might give significant weight to considerations of health and need and little or no weight to the fact that the spouses were married only for a short period of time. However, in another short-term marriage case, the same judge might give considerable weight to this factor and decide that the brevity of the relationship precludes a support order. In yet another short-term marriage situation where one party — let's say a husband in his early 60s — gave up a good job to move across country to join his new spouse and has been unable to find work, the same judge might again discount duration in favor of the combined weight of need, age, earning potential, and, possibly, contribution, with respect to the sacrifice that he made so the couple could be together.

Searching for Greater Certainty: Alimony Guidelines

As indicated by this discussion, an important advantage of the flexibility that is built into this multifactored approach is that judges can make individualized determinations that fit the facts of each case, rather than having to squeeze everyone into a one-size-fits-all support package. As we have seen, in determining if alimony is to be awarded, the duration of the marriage might be a critical consideration in one case and an insignificant one in another.

However, the flexibility of this approach is also problematic and has been the source of much critical commentary. At the heart of these concerns is the inherent lack of consistency and predictability. According to one study, this uncertainty may dissuade economically dependent spouses from even seeking support based on the "reluctance to expend money on litigation costs without the likelihood of any beneficial result."[4] Moreover, as we saw in the child custody context, lack of certainty can make it very difficult for parties to negotiate a settlement. Without a coherent framework, it is difficult to assess the value of a negotiated exchange if one does not know what one is giving up or gaining in the exchange process.

As we have seen, when it comes to child support, the historic vagaries of the law have given way to child support guidelines that employ specific numeric criteria resulting in predictable support amounts. Accordingly, whether the case is litigated or settled, parties participate in the process with a fairly stable sense of the likely support amount.

Seeking this same kind of predictability, some family law experts have recommended a similar approach to spousal support. The use of clear guidelines and numeric criteria would, they argue, remove the guesswork from the process and allow parties to negotiate their differences based on a clear understanding of what a court is likely to do. To this end, a few states and a number of counties have recently adopted a guidelines approach to spousal support awards, and this may be a slowly growing trend.

One critical difference is that child support guidelines do not need to address the question of whether the support should be awarded in the first place. Instead, as required by federal law, they can simply be structured to provide a computational framework that yields a "presumptively correct support amount." In contrast, given that there is not parallel entitlement to spousal support, guidelines may also need to address the issue of whether support is due at all, and if so, for what purpose it is being paid, and how accordingly it is to be structured (see the next section, "Different Approaches to Structuring Spousal Support"). As a result, it is clearly more difficult to develop spousal support guidelines that readily yield a "presumptively correct support amount" as these multiple determinations often shade into one another.

In addition to this complexity, in some jurisdictions, guidelines are used only for the purpose of determining temporary spousal support awards, and they thus do not control the ultimate outcome, which remains indeterminate. Furthermore, guidelines may be developed for the purpose of providing parties with a starting point for negotiations, rather than being structured to provide a presumptively correct support amount, which once again leads to less predictability than is the case with regard to child support.[5]

Different Approaches to Structuring Spousal Support

As developed in this section, support can be structured in a variety of ways to accomplish different objectives. Each approach has its own rules regarding the modification and termination of the support award.

Permanent Alimony

Permanent Alimony:
An ongoing support award to a spouse who is unlikely to become economically self-sufficient

"Permanent" alimony is probably what most people think of when they think of alimony, but since no-fault reform, it has been somewhat eclipsed by rehabilitative support (discussed next). The primary purpose of **permanent alimony** is to provide financial assistance to the spouse in an economically weaker position. It is payable in regular intervals on an ongoing basis. Permanent alimony can also serve a compensatory purpose. A spouse (almost always the wife) who restricts her participation in the paid labor force to care for her family experiences a loss of earning capacity over the course of the marriage. At the same time, the earning capacity of her spouse is enhanced, as he is freed up to focus on his labor market participation. Although this may be a mutually beneficial arrangement during the marriage, the spouses stand on very different footing upon divorce — in effect, there has been a transfer in earning ability from one spouse to the other. Alimony payments may be used to offset this result and compensate a spouse for the **opportunity cost** of having invested a significant portion of her time in the domestic realm to the detriment of her earning ability. Unlike that of rehabilitative support, the goal of permanent alimony is not to help a spouse achieve economic self-sufficiency, and there is no duty to use the money for this purpose. Accordingly, a defining aspect of a permanent support award is that it is not subject to a fixed time limitation but is continuous.

Opportunity Cost: The loss of earning potential attributable to the lack of a sustained relationship with the labor force, often due to a spouse's primary investment in the domestic realm

Although permanent alimony is not subject to durational limits, *permanent* does not necessarily mean "forever." The term is used to distinguish support awarded at the time of divorce from support awarded during the pendency of the divorce action — known as **alimony pendente lite**, or temporary alimony — which is intended to assist a spouse during this interim period. Thus, although not subject to preestablished durational limits, permanent alimony is subject to reduction or termination based on a **change in circumstances**, with the near universal rule being that remarriage of the recipient spouse or the death of either one terminates the obligation. (See the section later in this chapter entitled "Post-Divorce Modification and Termination of Support.")

Alimony Pendente Lite: Temporary support paid to one spouse by the other during the pendency of a divorce

Change in Circumstances: A future event that arguably makes an existing order unfair and serves as the basis for a request for modification

Lump-Sum Support

Although not a frequently used option, many states authorize the award of a **lump-sum support** payment, sometimes referred to as **alimony in gross**. Unlike permanent alimony, this involves the payment of a sum certain. It is generally paid in a single installment, although it can also be made payable in periodic installments until the full amount of the order is reached. Once ordered, most states agree that the recipient acquires a vested right to the entire amount, thus making it nonmodifiable based on a change in circumstances, including remarriage of the recipient. This remains true even where the lump sum is payable in installments. If the payor dies before the full amount is paid, the balance is chargeable to his or her estate; likewise, if the recipient dies before receiving payment in full, the balance due can be collected by his or her estate. Accordingly, along the lines of the old adage "a bird in the hand is worth two in the bush," a recipient may prefer to accept a potentially smaller but definite

Lump-Sum Support/ Alimony in Gross: A support award of a specific amount of money, usually payable in a single installment, although it can also be made payable in periodic installments until the full amount of the order is reached

lump-sum payment instead of running the risk that periodic payments will not always be made.

Rehabilitative Support

Rehabilitative Support/Transitional Support:
Time-limited support intended to enable a spouse to obtain the education or training necessary to become economically self-sufficient

As noted previously, following no-fault reform, **rehabilitative support,** often called "**transitional support,**" became the preferred approach in many jurisdictions. Rehabilitative support is awarded on a time-limited basis for the purpose of enabling an economically dependent spouse to obtain the education or training necessary to become financially self-sufficient.

To establish the durational limit, a court will try to predict how long it will take for a spouse to become self-sufficient and then set this as the date for the expiration of the obligation; in some states, maximum time limits are set by statute. In some states, courts may retain jurisdiction and extend the time limit if a spouse can show that despite a good-faith effort, he or she has not been able to achieve the degree of self-sufficiency contemplated at the time of the award. Many jurisdictions, however, do not permit extensions even where a spouse is not yet self-sufficient despite a good-faith effort. Here, rather than focusing on the economic situation of the spouse seeking to achieve self-sufficiency, the courts prioritize the expectancy interest of the payor spouse and his or her wish to plan for the future, unencumbered by unexpected obligations from a previous marriage.

Although there is general agreement that the goal of rehabilitative support is self-sufficiency, there is disagreement about what this means. A few states take a bare-bones approach and consider a person self-sufficient if, at the end of the rehabilitative period, he or she is not dependent on public assistance. Other courts, particularly in situations involving a long-term marriage, define self-sufficiency by reference to the marital standard of living. Here, the goal is met when a spouse is able to obtain employment that would enable him or her to approximate the prior marital standard of living.

Rehabilitative support took hold quickly during the period of no-fault reform, as it represented a break from the traditional alimony model that was associated with outmoded assumptions about fault and the economic incapacity of divorced women. Its underlying objectives were commendable and consistent with the new approach to restructuring family obligations following divorce. Rehabilitative support sets out to accomplish the following goals:

- to enable previously economically dependent spouses to develop their earning potential and realize true independence;
- to enable spouses to make a clean break and begin life anew on equal footing in keeping with the partnership view of marriage; and
- to release spouses from ongoing financial obligations derived from a failed relationship.

Beginning in the mid-1980s, however, a countertrend emerged. Appellate judges began to set aside rehabilitative awards, denouncing them as an abuse of judicial discretion. One judge went so far as to label them a "male-oriented, sexist approach."[6] These reversals have generally come in cases of long-term marriages where a woman has forgone labor market participation or has moved in and out of the workplace based on the needs of her family. According to the courts, the goal of economic self-sufficiency is illusory in these situations because a woman who has been family-centered will not be able to recapture her lost earning potential, and a rehabilitative award would leave the spouses with a gross disparity in earning capacity—a result that undervalues her contribution to the marriage.

Accordingly, trial courts have become a bit more circumspect, particularly in cases involving long-term marriages where responsibilities have been allocated along traditional gender lines. Rather than assuming that a rehabilitative award is appropriate, a court might instead place a burden on the party seeking to limit support to show how the other spouse will be able to achieve meaningful financial independence within the proposed time frames. This may require evidence about available educational programs and labor market conditions in the spouse's area of interest that indicate a likelihood of employment at a decent wage.

The Professional Degree Cases

Although the permanent, lump-sum, and rehabilitative approaches to spousal support are relatively easy to characterize, there has been considerable confusion regarding what to do in cases where one spouse supports the other through a professional degree program, thus greatly increasing the degree-holding spouse's future earning capacity, but the marriage ends before these gains are realized to the benefit of the supporting spouse. In this section, we consider the various options.

One possible option would be to treat the degree as marital property and subject it to division along with the other marital assets. However, the overwhelming majority of jurisdictions have rejected this approach, deciding that a degree, or the enhanced earning capacity it represents, does not fit within the meaning of the term "property," based on a variety of considerations including the difficulty of valuing a degree, that its acquisition requires substantial personal effort and sacrifice, and that it is personal to the holder and cannot be sold, transferred, or left to future generations. (See Chapter 8 for property-related concepts.)

Instead, courts have typically adopted one of two general approaches to support in this situation (although other approaches are certainly possible). The first approach is to simply consider the degree as one of the factors that must be weighed in determining if support should be awarded.

This is a flexible option that enables a court to emphasize different considerations. Thus, one court might give greater weight to the contribution and sacrifice of the supporting spouse, while another might focus on the enhanced earning capacity of the degree-holding spouse relative to the stagnant or possibly even diminished earning capacity of the supporting spouse.

Reimbursement Alimony: A support award intended to reimburse a spouse for contributions to the professional education of the other spouse; may also compensate for the loss of future income

Another accepted approach is to fashion a **reimbursement alimony** award. The Supreme Court of New Jersey is generally credited with developing this concept in the 1982 case of Mahoney v. Mahoney, in which the husband left the marriage soon after earning an advanced degree with the wife's dedicated support:

> In this case, the supporting spouse made financial contributions towards her husband's professional education with the expectation that both parties would enjoy material benefits flowing from the professional license or degree. It is therefore patently unfair that the supporting spouse be denied the mutually anticipated benefit while the supported spouse keeps not only the degree, but also all of the financial and material rewards flowing from it. . . .
>
> . . . Also, the wife has presumably made personal financial sacrifices, resulting in a reduced or lowered standard of living. Additionally, her husband, by pursuing preparations for a future career, has forgone gainful employment and financial contributions to the marriage. . . . She has postponed, as it were, present consumption and a higher standard of living, for the future prospect of greater support and material benefits. . . . The unredressed sacrifices . . . coupled with the unfairness attendant upon the defeat of the supporting spouse's shared expectation of future advantages, further justify a remedial award.[7]

In fashioning the award, the court held that the supporting spouse was entitled to be reimbursed for all financial contributions made to the training of the other spouse, including "household expenses, educational costs, school travel expenses, and any other contribution used by the supported spouse in obtaining his or her degree or license."[8] Through reimbursement, courts can thus adjust this imbalance by returning the contribution to the spouse who will not participate in the anticipated benefits because of divorce. Consistent with their focus on dashed expectations, courts have generally disallowed reimbursement where the marriage continued for a reasonable period of time after the degree was obtained on the theory that the supporting spouse would have realized his or her expectation during the marriage.

Some courts have broadened the concept of reimbursement alimony beyond simply providing recompense for actual expenditures to include "lost opportunity costs," such as forgone income while the degree-holding spouse was enrolled in school and possibly also for forgone educational opportunities. Alternatively, some courts have instead provided rehabilitative support so the non-degree-holding spouse could also obtain further education.

An important critique of the reimbursement approach is that it only repays a spouse's initial investment in the career of the other and does not provide the spouse with any return on the investment through giving him or her a share of the increased earnings attributable to the enhanced earning capacity. Simply put: "[T]his approach treats the supporting spouse as a lender, not as an investor in the asset."[9]

Medical Insurance

The issue of continued medical coverage frequently arises with considerable urgency at the time of divorce because one spouse, typically the primary wage earner, may have a group policy through his or her employer that provides family coverage. Many states now have laws that authorize the court to order a spouse to continue to provide health insurance coverage for his or her former spouse, at least during the time that a support order is in effect.

In addition, although there is no federal law comparable to state statutory provisions requiring the continued provision of health insurance, divorced spouses may be entitled to post-divorce coverage under COBRA (short for the Consolidated Omnibus Budget Reconciliation Act), which was passed by Congress in 1986. Under COBRA, employers with more than 20 employees must provide the spouse of a divorcing employee with a temporary extension of group health coverage if a timely request is made. However, the covered spouse is responsible for the entire amount of the premium since COBRA does not hold the employer or the employed spouse responsible for the cost of the continued coverage.[10]

Post-Divorce Modification and Termination of Support

The General Concept

Following a divorce, as with custody or child support, either party may seek to revise the spousal support amount by filing a complaint for modification. Some states have enacted specific modification statutes that set out the basic requirements for these post-divorce actions, while in others, the requirements have been established by judicial decisions. In either event, the basic principles discussed next are fairly stable; however, as always, the precise procedural and substantive details vary from state to state.

Modification:
The alteration of an existing order based on a change in circumstances

This action is usually filed in the court that entered the original support order, which has continuing jurisdiction over the matter. If a support order is not entered at the time of divorce, a court may lose jurisdiction; accordingly, to protect against this, some courts will order payment of a nominal support amount, such as a dollar per month. This preserves its jurisdiction should the need for support arise in the future. The complaint for modification must be based on a change in circumstances that makes the original order unfair. States use different yardsticks to measure unfairness. Some employ a strict unconscionability standard, while others employ a more relaxed standard. Again, the general rule is that the change must have been unforeseeable. Accordingly, a future job change that was known about at the time of the original order cannot generally be the basis for a modification, as this should have been accounted for in the original order. Similarly, most jurisdictions will not base a modification upon inflation or cost-of-living increases in the obligor's salary, as these events are foreseeable and could have been addressed.

In addition to being unforeseeable, courts may require that the change be involuntary. Accordingly, an obligor who seeks to reduce payments because she has left the corporate world to become an artist will probably not be successful. Likewise, a support recipient who relocates to a luxury apartment complex and then seeks an upward revision based on the increased rent is not likely to succeed.

Modifiability and Termination of "Permanent" Support

Remarriage, cohabitation, and a change in financial circumstances are the most common reasons for a modification action. Each is discussed next.

Remarriage

In most states, the statutory rule is that an award of "permanent" support automatically terminates upon the remarriage of the recipient spouse. In some of these jurisdictions, termination occurs immediately upon remarriage without the need for any kind of court action, while in others, the support obligor must file a modification petition, which almost certainly will be granted. The principle underlying the termination rule is that the recipient's new spouse has a support obligation, and a person is not entitled to be supported by both a spouse and a former spouse at the same time.

The basic rule — that remarriage terminates the spousal support obligation — has also been firmly established by judicial decisions in states that do not have a statutory termination provision through judicial decision. Although some of these jurisdictions follow the automatic termination approach, others are more flexible. A few treat remarriage as simply a factor to be considered in determining whether a change in circumstances justifies a modification, although the more common approach is to presume termination, absent a showing of extraordinary circumstances. The concept of "extraordinary" is typically defined narrowly, and the burden of proof is placed upon the alimony recipient, rather than, as is usually the case, on the person seeking the modification.

This termination rule raises difficult questions about what should happen if a spouse who is receiving rehabilitative support remarries during the rehabilitative period. From a recipient's perspective, the remarriage may be irrelevant, as he or she is seeking to regain economic independence. However, from the payor's perspective, it may seem unfair to continue paying support in a situation where the former spouse is remarried and now has access to other sources of income. It should thus come as no surprise that jurisdictions approach this issue differently, with some giving greater weight to the recipient's interest in completing the education that he or she embarked on, while others are more focused on shifting responsibility to the new spouse.

The general rule is that remarriage by the paying spouse does not entitle him or her to a downward revision of support. Courts generally focus on the voluntary aspect of the act and the inequity to the former spouse. However, remarriage combined with other circumstances, such as the birth of children, may support a downward revision. Conversely, if the payor spouse remarries someone with substantial income or assets, the question may arise as to whether the recipient spouse can rely on this as a change in circumstances warranting an upward adjustment. While it is clear that the recipient has no direct claim on the new spouse's income, some courts may be willing to consider a modification based on the fact that this money may liberate some of the former spouse's income.

Cohabitation

Whereas remarriage almost always terminates alimony, the result is less certain where a recipient cohabits with a new partner because, unlike marriage, cohabitation does not impose a legal duty of support. The majority approach is to focus on whether cohabitation has resulted in an improvement in the recipient's financial situation — and only where it has done so will support be reduced or terminated. Some states impose an initial threshold requirement: The party seeking to reduce or terminate support must show that the relationship is not merely fleeting but instead rises to a certain level of intensity and commitment. Only when this has been shown will the court consider the cohabiting party's financial situation. A few states employ a rebuttable presumption that cohabitation automatically improves a party's financial situation. This presumption shifts the burden of proof to the cohabiting spouse to show that his or her financial situation has not improved as a result of the relationship.

Change in Financial Circumstances

Parties frequently seek to modify support based on a change in the financial circumstances of one or both of them. As noted previously, a court will generally not modify due to foreseeable changes such as an annual cost-of-living salary increase. On the other hand, an increase in salary based on an unexpected promotion may warrant an upward revision of support. However, many jurisdictions will not modify based on this type of event alone and instead also require proof of an increased financial need on the part of the recipient spouse. A mutual change in circumstances is generally required, on the theory that the recipient spouse does not have an automatic right to share in this gain because it is unrelated to the marital enterprise. In response, the recipient spouse might argue that she is entitled to a share in this increase to compensate for the fact that the original order did not provide her with adequate income, but it was all that the payor spouse could afford at the time. Here, the modification would serve a compensatory purpose. If the recipient spouse's financial circumstances improve, a downward revision is generally allowed.

Modifiability of Specific Types of Support

Even where a change in circumstances can be established, spousal support awards other than permanent alimony are generally considered nonmodifiable.

Lump-Sum Support

The majority rule is that a lump-sum award is not modifiable or terminable by death or remarriage. The support recipient is deemed to have acquired a vested right to the full amount, even if it is payable in installments.

Rehabilitative Support

The rules regarding modifiability of rehabilitative support are more complex. Because this award is for a designated purpose, most courts — absent extraordinary circumstances — will not modify it for reasons unrelated to the original purpose of the award. For example, whereas a change in circumstance such as a job promotion might warrant an increase in permanent alimony, it would not warrant an increase in rehabilitative support, as this is incidental to the goal of helping the support recipient achieve economic self-sufficiency.

Some courts will not modify a rehabilitative award to extend the durational limit or increase the support amount even where the request is directly related to the goal of achieving economic self-sufficiency. Although this may be fair where the party has not taken reasonable steps to obtain education or training, it can be a harsh result where the person has made a good-faith effort but the original time estimate was inadequate, or where she or he has encountered unanticipated obstacles such as illness or the loss of affordable child care.

Reimbursement Alimony

The general rule is that reimbursement alimony is not modifiable or terminable by the death of either party or the remarriage of the recipient spouse. This is a logical result because the award is not based on present financial circumstances, but rather is designed to repay a spouse for past expenditures. Accordingly, post-divorce changes in circumstances are irrelevant. However, it is hard to imagine a court refusing to make some adjustment, perhaps in the nature of a temporary suspension of payments, in a case of genuine hardship, such as serious illness.

Agreement of the Parties to Prohibit Modification

Sometimes parties include a clause in a separation agreement stating that neither will seek to modify the support award in the future. Such a clause often is insisted upon by the supporting spouse, who wants to limit his or her obligation. Some jurisdictions may refuse to honor such a clause on public policy grounds, especially if enforcement would force a spouse into public assistance. Here, the duty to pay support is regarded as having a public dimension that cannot be abrogated by a private agreement.

▪ Enforcement of Support Awards

As is often the case with child support orders, once spousal support has been ordered, the risk of nonpayment is substantial, and the recipient may need to take action to enforce the order.

Contempt

In most states, the primary enforcement mechanism is an action for contempt. As with child support, the contempt action can be either civil or criminal in nature (see Chapter 6). Most likely, an obligor will not

Contempt:
A proceeding against a party who is in violation of a court order

be found in contempt if the inability to pay existed at the time the support payments were due. A more complicated question, which jurisdictions are split on, is whether present inability to pay is a valid defense where the defendant had the ability to pay at the time that payments were due.

If a defendant is found to be in civil contempt, the court will order him or her to pay the overdue amount, and a payment schedule is usually established. To compel payment, the court may impose a jail sentence, but, in keeping with the remedial purpose of a civil contempt action, the defendant must be given the opportunity to purge the contempt by paying the arrearage and thus avoid jail. The right to purge oneself of the contempt is ongoing, and the jail sentence is imposed for an indefinite time terminable upon payment of the arrearage. Where there is a present inability to pay (and this is not considered a valid defense), a jail sentence will generally not be imposed because the obligor does not have the means to purge the contempt. In contrast, a sentence in a criminal contempt case is imposed for a fixed period of time because the purpose is punitive, and the defendant cannot shorten it by purging the contempt.

Other Enforcement Measures

In seeking to enforce a spousal support award, a recipient who also has a child support order in place may be able to obtain enforcement assistance from the state's IV-D agency, and many of the same collection tools, such as wage withholding and tax refund intercepts, are available to secure spousal support payments (see Chapter 6). Additionally, many states, in implementing the enforcement procedures required under federal law for child support, extended their availability to spousal support recipients who choose not to go through the IV-D agency or are not eligible for IV-D agency support because they do not also have a child support order in place.

As with child support, spousal support awards can be enforced across state lines under the Uniform Interstate Family Support Act (UIFSA). However, child support collection is the priority of the interstate system and dominates enforcement efforts.

■ Bankruptcy and the Support Obligation

Bankruptcy:
The filing of a court action in which a party seeks to be discharged from responsibility for paying his or her debts

Filing for **bankruptcy** provides an individual who is overwhelmed by debt with the opportunity to discharge qualified debts, thus enabling him or her to make a "fresh start." What then happens if the individual seeking to be relieved of his or her debts has existing financial obligations to a spouse or child stemming from a divorce or separation? Until recently, the Bankruptcy Code prevented the discharge of debts that were in the nature of "alimony, maintenance, or support." The Code allowed, however, the discharge of debts that were in the nature of a property settlement, such as payments being made to a former spouse to effectuate the debtor's buyout of the equity in the marital home (see Chapter 8), unless the payor former spouse could establish some kind of hardship or inability to pay. However, the distinction between support and property distribution was eliminated by the Bankruptcy Abuse Prevention and Consumer Protection Act of 2005 in the context of some personal bankruptcy filings.[11]

Tax Consequences

As developed in this section, unlike child support, spousal support payments have tax implications for both the payor and the recipient spouse.

The Basic Rule of Includibility/Deductibility

The basic tax rule is that spousal support payments are considered income to the recipient and are includible in his or her taxable income; correspondingly, the payor is entitled to a deduction from gross income for spousal support payments he or she has made.[12] To qualify as alimony, payments must be in cash or a cash equivalent, must cease at the death of the recipient, and must be required under a divorce or separation instrument, and the parties may not live in the same household at the time payments are made. If parties wish to avoid this rule of includibility/deductibility, they may specifically state that payments that would otherwise qualify as alimony are not includible in the income of the recipient nor deductible by the payor. In effect, this means that for tax purposes, the payments are no longer considered to be alimony.

The basic rule of includibility/deductibility is straightforward; however, under the following two circumstances, the tax consequences may be other than what the parties intended.

Unallocated Payments

Where both spousal support and child support are to be paid, it may be better financially for the parties if the payments are characterized as spousal support. This gives the payor a deduction for the entire amount, and the tax savings may be then used to increase the amount of support payments. Although this increases the recipient's taxable income, he or she may nonetheless realize a net gain.

If a separation agreement provides a support amount without designating how much is for spousal support and how much is for child support, the entire amount will be treated as spousal support. However, as mentioned in Chapter 6, if the agreement provides reductions in support based on child-related contingencies (such as reaching age 18, getting married, or establishing a separate residence) or at a time that is "clearly associated" with a child-related contingency, a rebuttable presumption arises that the amount of the reduction was in the nature of child, rather than spousal, support. The presumption may be rebutted upon proof that the reduction is attributable to a valid nonchild-related reason. Even if the agreement does not specifically mention the contingency, the Internal Revenue Service may treat a reduction as child-related if it finds that it occurred at a time associated with such a contingency, unless again the parties can establish a valid nonchild-related explanation for the reduction.

Reclassification can have significant tax repercussions, especially for the obligor. If payments are reclassified, it means that the obligor has been taking a deduction that he or she is not entitled to, since child support, unlike alimony, is not deductible from gross income.

Recapture of Excess Payments

As discussed in Chapter 8, payments made from one spouse to the other as part of a property settlement are neither deductible from the income of the payor spouse nor includible in the income of the recipient spouse. For example, if an agreement calls for a husband to buy out his wife's interest in the marital residence by paying her $300 a month over three years, these payments are "tax neutral." However, over the years, divorcing couples have often attempted to disguise these payments as alimony, thus allowing the payor to deduct them from gross income.

Recapture:
The recomputation of a support obligor's gross income to include amounts that had been improperly deducted as spousal support payments, and the readjustment of his or her tax obligation

To deter parties from doing this, the Tax Code now includes "alimony **recapture** provisions." These provisions are triggered when parties engage in the "excess front loading" of support payments in the first years following a divorce. These front-loaded payments serve as a red flag that the parties may be attempting to disguise payments that are in the nature of a property settlement as support payments.

The recapture rules focus on payments that are made in the first three years following divorce. This time frame was chosen because property settlements are usually paid within a relatively short period of time. Excess front loading of alimony is deemed to occur when payments in year one significantly exceed the average payments in years two and three, and there is more than a $15,000 decrease in payments between years two and three. The excess or disguised payments must then be included in the gross income of the payor, as he or she is deemed to have taken an unwarranted deduction. This amount is thus "recaptured" for tax purposes. The recipient becomes entitled to a corresponding deduction.

Chapter Summary

Prior to no-fault reform, marriage embodied a clearer notion of permanent commitment and obligation. Upon divorce, if the husband were at fault, the wife had a claim to continued support. After no-fault reform, marriage was often analogized to a partnership, with divorce as the vehicle for making a clean break from the past. In keeping with this partnership model of marriage, property distribution became the preferred approach to adjusting economic rights between spouses. The clean-break approach has been criticized for failing to account for economic disparities between spouses that frequently result from the marital division of labor.

In deciding whether to provide spousal support, judges usually consider multiple factors, with need as a central determinant. In most jurisdictions, fault is no longer a central consideration, and it may not play any role in the support determination; however, marital misconduct continues to operate as a bar to a support award in a few states. This approach promotes flexibility, as judges may assign whatever weight they deem appropriate to individual factors based on the facts of a case; however, such flexibility also contributes to a lack of predictability and coherence. Consequently, a few jurisdictions have implemented numeric guidelines for the computation of amounts, much as in the child support arena, and the American Law Institute (ALI) recommends shifting to a compensatory focus.

Following no-fault reform, "permanent" alimony fell out of favor, and rehabilitative support, with its emphasis on helping a spouse to become economically self-sufficient, became the preferred approach. However, some courts have reevaluated the appropriateness of rehabilitative support in cases involving long-term marriages where a spouse has little chance of becoming economically self-sufficient. In addition to permanent and rehabilitative support, courts may award lump-sum alimony. Additionally, in professional degree cases, some courts may award reimbursement alimony.

"Permanent" support awards are subject to modification based on changed circumstances and are terminable upon remarriage, death, and (possibly) cohabitation. Some states permit the modification of a rehabilitative award if, despite a good-faith effort, the recipient has not become self-sufficient. Lump-sum payments are generally not modifiable.

The most common enforcement mechanism for failure to pay spousal support is a contempt action. Other enforcement mechanisms—such as wage withholding—are also now available following the expansion of available procedures in the child support arena.

Support payments are not dischargeable in bankruptcy. With respect to taxation, the basic rule is that support payments are includible in the income of the recipient and deductible by the payor, although parties may choose to opt out of this rule. Unallocated payments will be treated as alimony unless reductions correspond to child-related contingencies. Care also must be taken to avoid recapture rules, which may be triggered when property settlement payments are characterized as alimony.

Key Terms

Alimony	Permanent Alimony	Lump-Sum Support/	Reimbursement
Spousal	Opportunity Cost	Alimony in Gross	Alimony
Support	Alimony Pendente	Rehabilitative	Modification
Clean Break	Lite	Support	Contempt
Economic Self-	Change in	Transitional	Bankruptcy
Sufficiency	Circumstances	Support	Recapture

Review Questions

1. Historically, what was the relationship between marital fault and alimony?
2. Describe the key way in which the support obligation was reformulated following no-fault reform.
3. What criticisms have been raised regarding the clean-break approach to spousal support awards?
4. What kinds of factors do courts consider when making an alimony determination?
5. What are the advantages of the multifactored approach to support determinations? What are the potential problems?
6. Why have some jurisdictions begun to consider adopting spousal support guidelines?
7. What is permanent alimony? What functions does it serve? Why is permanent alimony not really permanent?
8. What is lump-sum alimony?
9. What is rehabilitative alimony? What functions does it serve?
10. Why have some appeals courts begun to reverse awards of rehabilitative support?
11. What are the two common approaches that courts take with respect to fashioning a support award when one spouse earns a professional degree prior to a divorce?
12. What is the basic rule regarding modification of a permanent support award?
13. Why is an increase in the cost of living generally not an appropriate ground for a modification?
14. What are the rules regarding remarriage and termination of support?
15. What are the rules regarding cohabitation and termination of support?
16. What are the rules regarding modification of lump-sum alimony? Rehabilitative alimony? Reimbursement alimony?
17. In a civil contempt action, what right does a defendant have if a jail sentence is imposed?
18. What is the principal defense in a contempt action?
19. What are the rules regarding the dischargeability of family support obligations in a bankruptcy proceeding?
20. What are the basic rules regarding the taxation of spousal support awards?
21. Explain what happens if reductions in unallocated support payments are tied to child-related contingencies.
22. Explain the concept of recapture.

Discussion Questions

1. If a husband and wife mutually agree that the wife will devote most of her energy to caring for the couple's home and rearing their children, should she be "compensated" for this through a spousal support award if the couple divorces? What kinds of considerations do you think are important here?
2. Despite the gender neutrality of spousal support laws, many people express discomfort at the thought of alimony being awarded to men. Why do you think this is? What is your reaction?
3. Some would argue that we have gone too far in eliminating fault as a consideration in support awards. What role do you think fault should play, if any?

Assignments

1. Locate the statutory provisions that govern the award of spousal support for your state and determine the following:
   - What factors, if any, are enumerated for court consideration?
   - Can marital fault be considered? If yes, under what conditions?
   - Do any of the sections specify what kinds of support can be awarded? If so, identify the

available support approaches and describe their statutory features.

2. The attorney you are working for does not do much family law and has asked you to help her figure out whether her client, Mary Smith, is likely to be awarded spousal support—and if so, what kind and in what amount. At this point, you do not have all the necessary information about the case, but she wants you to provide her with a reasonable range of options. To do this, you should examine the cases in your jurisdiction and write her an interoffice memo. Try to identify what additional information will be needed in order to determine what, if anything, the client is likely to receive in spousal support.

The following are the facts as they are presently known: Mary Smith was married to her husband for eight years. They have two minor children, ages 6 and 8. Ms. Smith is a paralegal with an associate's degree in paralegal studies. She has worked half time since the birth of her first child. She presently earns $18,000 per year. Her husband, David Smith, is the director of personnel at a large company. He earns $140,000 per year. You can assume that Ms. Smith will have primary physical custody of the children.

3. Following a lengthy trial, a client of the office you work for was denied spousal support. The attorney on the case is thinking about filing an appeal and has asked you to provide some initial research assessing whether you think the judge made an error of law. He thinks his client is certainly entitled to rehabilitative support and possibly to permanent support. Here are the facts: Tom (your office's client) and his wife, Melanie, were married for eight years. Melanie was a corporate executive and worked extremely long hours. The couple has no children. They agreed that because Melanie earned so much money, Tom would not work outside the home, but would maintain their house, pursue his various interests in the arts and music, and serve as a volunteer for various charitable enterprises. In year three of their marriage, Melanie obtained her Ph.D. in business administration; she had begun work on this degree the year before the couple married. Tom has an associate's degree in commercial art, although he has never pursued this line of work. In year five, Tom was diagnosed with multiple sclerosis; so far, the disease has been mild, with no impact on his level of functioning.

After locating the cases that you think are relevant, write an informal in-house memorandum to the attorney on the case, in which you discuss whether you think the client is entitled to support and why. Be sure to discuss and cite all relevant cases.

Endnotes

1. *See* Mary O'Connell, Alimony After No-Fault: A Practice in Search of a Theory, 23 New Eng. L. Rev. 437 (1988).

2. Orr v. Orr, 440 U.S. 268, 288 (1978) (citing United Jewish Orgs. v. Carey, 430 U.S. 144, 173-174 (1977)).

3. For a discussion of various reform proposals, *see* Alicia Brokars Kelly, Actualizing Intimate Partnership Theory, 50 Fam. Ct. Rev. 258 (2012); Alicia Brokars Kelly, Rehabilitating Partnership Marriage as a Theory of Wealth Distribution at Divorce: In Recognition of a Shared Life, 19 Wis. L.J. 141 (2004); Robert Kirkman Collins, The Theory of Marital Residues: Applying an Income Adjustment Calculus to the Enigma of Alimony, 24 Harv. Women's L.J. 23, 50 (2001); June Carbone, Income Sharing Redefining the Family in Terms of Community, 31 Hous. L. Rev. 359 (1994).

4. Mary Kay Kisthardt, Rethinking Alimony: The AAML's Considerations for Calculating Alimony, Spousal Support, or Maintenance, 21 Am. Acad. Matrimonial Law. 61 (2008).

5. *See generally* Marie Gordon, Spousal Support Guidelines and the American Experience: Moving Beyond Discretion, 19 Can. J. Fam. L. 247 (2002); June Carbone, The Futility of Coherence: The ALI's *Principles of the Law of Family Dissolution*, Compensatory Spousal Payments, 43 J.L. & Fam. Stud. 43 (2002).

6. Avirett v. Avirett, 187 N.J. Super. 380, 383, 454 A.2d 917, 919 (Ch. Div. 1982) (overruled on other grounds). For discussion of this trend, *see* Joan M. Krauskopf, Rehabilitative Alimony: Uses and Abuses of Limited Duration Alimony, 21 Fam. L.Q. 579 (1988).

7. Mahoney v. Mahoney, 91 N.J. 488, 453 A.2d 527, 534-535 (1982).

8. *Id.* at 534.

9. *See* Alicia Brokars Kelly, The Marital Partnership Pretense and Career Assets: The Ascendancy of Self over the Marital Community, 81 B.U. L. Rev. 59, 107 (2001).

10. COBRA, Pub. L. No. 99-272, 100 Stat. 82 (29 U.S.C. §§1161 et seq.) (1986). For additional detail, *see* Elizabeth L. Bennett and John W. Goldsborough, Guaranteeing Medical Insurance Coverage After Separation and Divorce, 28 Fam. L.Q. 305 (1994).

11. This section is intended to be a brief, simple introduction to the relationship between support obligations and bankruptcy law. This area of the law, however, is quite complex. For further detail, *see* Daniel A. Austin, For Debtor or Worse: Discharge of Marital Debt Obligations Under the Federal Bankruptcy Abuse Prevention and Consumer Protection Act of 2005, 51 Wayne L. Rev. 1369 (2005).

12. The spousal support rules can be found in §71 of the Internal Revenue Service Code, 26 U.S.C. §71 (2012). Please be aware that these rules are complex and are presented here in a simplified manner. For a discussion of key concepts, *see* Joanne Ross Wilder, Divorce and Taxes: Fifty Years of Changes, 24 J. Am. Acad. Matrimonial Law. 489 (2012); Stacia Gawronski, Spousal Support Under the Federal Tax Code, 20 J. Contemp. Legal Issues 63 (2011/2012).

Chapter Eight

Division of Marital Property

This chapter focuses on the division of **marital property** at divorce. As discussed in the last chapter, since no-fault reform, the trend has been to treat the division of property as the primary economic event between divorcing spouses. The rationale for this development is that a division of property, as distinct from an award of alimony, is more in keeping with the modern partnership view of marriage, which seeks to allow both spouses to make a clean break from the past, unencumbered by the failed relationship. In theory, the partnership is fully dissolved after the distribution, leaving the parties free to reconstruct their lives without ongoing financial obligations or entanglements.

Accordingly, in some jurisdictions, spousal support is now an option only where the court determines there is insufficient property to provide for the needs of both spouses. However, as discussed in the previous chapter, this approach has drawn increasing criticism for failing to recognize that a division of property may not account for the fact that spouses may exit from a marriage with very different earning capacities based, at least in part, on the marital allocation of work and family commitments.

Marital Property: Assets acquired during a marriage as a result of marital efforts or funds, which are subject to division at divorce

Overview of the Two Marital Property Systems

Although the differences have become less pronounced over time, two marital property systems exist in this country. In this section, we compare the community property and the common law approaches to marital property.

The Community Property Approach

The majority of states looked to English common law when devising rules regarding marital property rights, but eight states, based on patterns of colonial influence and territorial acquisition, looked to Spanish or French civil law and adopted their community property approach. These states are Arizona, California, Idaho, Louisiana, Nevada, New Mexico, Texas, and Washington.[1]

Unlike English common law, civil law did not consider the husband and wife to be a single person. Rather, marriage was considered a partnership of two individuals, and married women accordingly retained the right to own property, although historically, husbands were given the right of exclusive management and control over marital assets. Based on this understanding of marriage as a partnership, the **community property** approach assumes that each spouse acts for the benefit of the marital unit rather than for his or her own individual gain. The contribution of each spouse to the marriage, including domestic and child-rearing contributions, is recognized, entitling each spouse to share in the financial gains of the marriage. This is accomplished by giving both parties an immediate, vested interest in one-half of the property acquired during the marriage through the efforts of either spouse or the expenditure of marital funds.

Upon divorce, this community property is subject to division based on a theory of co-ownership without regard to financial contribution, and responsibility for the debt is likewise allocated between the parties. Although most community property states initially divided property on an equal basis, many now use an equitable division standard, which (as developed later in this chapter) allows a court to make an unequal distribution based on considerations of fairness.[2]

Property that is not acquired through the expenditure of marital efforts or funds is considered separate property and belongs to the acquiring spouse rather than to the community. Neither spouse acquires rights in the other's separate property because it stands apart from the marital enterprise. Typically, separate property includes assets brought into the marriage, gifts and inheritances acquired by one spouse during the marriage, and property acquired in exchange for separate property. At divorce, each spouse takes his or her separate property, although in a few states, courts may have limited authority to transfer separate property in cases of extreme hardship.

Community Property: A system of property ownership between husband and wife in which each spouse has a vested one-half ownership interest in all marital property, regardless of title

The Common Law Approach

As discussed in Chapter 1, the common law vision of the marital relationship assumed the loss of a wife's legal identity. She lost the right to own personal property or control any real property to which she had title. The common law approach to marital property rights flowed directly from this understanding of the marital relationship. Here, there was no community — there was simply the husband who owned all of the property except for his wife's realty, which he controlled. Accordingly, there was no notion of a marital enterprise representing the cumulative efforts of both spouses.

Even as married women gradually acquired property rights through the passage of the Married Women's Property Acts, the concept of marital community did not take hold in the common law states. Instead, traditional common law property concepts, which extolled the virtues of individual rights, were extended to married women.[3] Property was his or hers depending on who supplied the purchase funds — which in reality meant that it was mostly his. In contrast to the community property states, the nonfinancial contributions of a homemaker spouse did not give rise to ownership rights.

Until fairly recently, at the time of divorce, common law states generally divided property according to **title**. This meant that the spouse who owned an asset was entitled to it at divorce. Mitigating the potential harshness of this approach, a number of courts developed the *special equity* rule, under which a spouse who had made a financial contribution to property titled in the name of the other could be granted an equitable interest in the asset, thus entitling her or him to a share at divorce. Some courts expanded this rule to provide rights based on the nonfinancial contributions of a homemaker spouse. Begun as an exception, this rule helped pave the way for the shift from a title-based approach to the division of marital property to the equitable distribution rules now in effect in all common law states.

Title:
The right of exclusive ownership and control of an asset

Equitable Distribution

No-fault divorce also helped to usher in changes in the rules of property distribution. All common law states now divide marital property according to **equitable distribution** principles rather than title. Influenced by the sharing principles long recognized in community property states, the equitable distribution approach acknowledges that the accumulation of marital assets derives from the efforts of both spouses. Accordingly, at divorce, a spouse's nonfinancial contributions to the well-being of a household will give rise to an enforceable property interest in accumulated assets.

Equitable Distribution:
The division of property at divorce based principally on considerations of fairness and contribution rather than title

Following the community property approach, the majority of equitable distribution jurisdictions classify property at divorce as either marital or separate. This is often referred to as the **dual property** approach because a formal distinction is made between the two categories of assets. The distributive authority of the courts is restricted to the marital estate, although a few states have created a limited exception to this rule and permit distribution of separate property in cases of hardship. The classifying principle is essentially the same as in the community property states. Property acquired during the marriage through the efforts of either spouse or the

Dual Property:
States that distinguish between marital property and separate property for distribution purposes

Separate Property:
Property that belongs to the acquiring spouse and is not subject to distribution at divorce

All-Property:
States that allow a couple's accumulated assets to be distributed at divorce without a formal distinction between separate property and marital property

expenditure of marital funds is considered marital because it derives from the contribution that each person is credited with making to the partnership. **Separate property** is that which is unrelated to this joint undertaking and generally includes property owned prior to marriage, gifts, inheritances, and property acquired in exchange for separate property.

In contrast to the dual property approach, a minority of states have adopted what is known as an **"all-property"** approach. Here, no formal distinction is made between separate and marital property, and courts are empowered to distribute all assets, regardless of when and how they were acquired. This is sometimes referred to as the "hotchpot of assets" approach. It should be noted, however, that the informal practice among attorneys in all-property states when negotiating a settlement may be to disregard property that would be considered separate in a community or dual property state, or to allocate it separately from the balance of the marital estate in order to give greater weight to its "separate" identity.

With the adoption of equitable distribution laws, the difference between common law and community property states has become less pronounced, although the all-property approach is exclusively identified with common law states. Accordingly, this chapter will focus on general legal concepts and will not distinguish between the two approaches unless relevant; however, you should bear in mind that regardless of which approach is followed, each state has its own rules and standards.

The Property Distribution Process

The process of dividing property between divorcing spouses can be broken down into four steps:

1. *Defining property.* A preliminary issue in some cases is whether a particular asset falls within the definition of the term "property"; if it falls outside the definition, the asset is not subject to distribution.
2. *Classification.* Except in all-property states, property must be classified as either marital or separate.[5]
3. *Valuation.* The value of each asset must be determined.
4. *Distribution.* The assets must be allocated in accordance with the applicable legal standard.

Before we look at these four steps, a few general points should be considered. First, in many cases, especially where the parties have few assets, the division of property is relatively simple, and couples often figure this out themselves without involving their attorneys or applying formal legal principles. A couple may simply divide their belongings based on need or preference. Of course, an attorney should ensure that a client understands that without a more formal process, there is no way of knowing whether the client is getting the share of assets that he or she may legally be entitled to.

Second, when couples do fight about property, the fight is often rooted in the emotional undertow of divorce. An object may be treasured for its sentimental meaning, or it may have tremendous symbolic importance for one or both parties. For example, if your client is fighting fiercely for the old brown sofa, it may have become the symbolic locus of his or her anger and he or she may not really care about the sofa itself. Alternatively, the client may believe it is worth fighting for based on its sentimental worth—perhaps it was the couple's first purchase, thus standing as a reminder of happier times. If you are involved in helping to resolve a property dispute, it is important to be aware of these potential dynamics so you can help a client sort out what is going on; that way, needless time, money, and emotional energy is not spent pursuing an object for the wrong reason.

Third, when a property dispute does involve legal considerations, such as classification or valuation, the governing rules are often complex and variable; for example, there are multiple approaches to valuing a closely held corporation, which differ from the multiple approaches to valuing pension plans or commodity futures. Expert witnesses are often required to resolve the complex legal and accounting issues.

Defining Property

Most cases do not involve definitional questions. During the marriage, couples accumulate items such as furniture, jewelry, cars, and household goods, which are so clearly property that this definitional step is bypassed without any thought to the matter. However, there are times when it is not clear whether a particular item, such as the goodwill of a professional practice or an unvested pension, is in fact property.

Since the enactment of equitable distribution laws and increased emphasis on the division of property, these definitional questions have assumed increasing importance, and this is an ever developing and expanding area of the law. When working on a case, you must carefully consider all possible property interests. This means there is much room for creative legal thinking. Who knows? Given the right opportunity, you may "discover" a new form of property!

The Tangible/Intangible Distinction

Traditionally, property was defined as a tangible item over which an individual could exercise absolute dominion and control. **Tangible property** is easy to identify, as it is what we normally think of as property—it has a physical presence and can be touched, seen, and transferred from one person to another.

Tangible Property: Property with a physical presence, which is capable of being felt and seen

Intangible Assets:
Property that lacks a physical presence and cannot be ascertained by the senses

Over time, the definition of property has expanded. Moving beyond physical presence, property is now usually described in relational terms as the "bundle of rights" a person has in something. In essence, the concept has been "dephysicalized,"[4] and thus, **intangible assets** — assets that lack a physical presence and cannot be ascertained by the senses — may well come within the concept of property. Intangible assets often involve the right to something, such as the future right to participate in a pension plan or, as evidenced by a stock certificate, the right to participate in the management of a corporation and receive a proportional share of earnings. Common examples of intangible assets include the goodwill of a business, a legal claim, stocks, bonds, and pension plans.

Few property distribution statutes provide a definition of the term "property," so courts have had to struggle with the concept. Some jurisdictions are expansive and consider a broad array of intangibles to be property. Other jurisdictions are more restrictive and tend to exclude intangibles that lack traditional property attributes. Accordingly, if an intangible asset cannot easily be transferred to another person, is difficult to value, and cannot be owned jointly, a court in a restrictive jurisdiction is likely to determine that it is not property. Thus, for example, in comparing a professional degree (see Chapter 7) with a car, one can see how such a court might refuse to consider it property. Unlike the car, the degree cannot be transferred or left to someone as an inheritance, its worth is much harder to determine, and it cannot be jointly owned. Underlying these distinctions — and potentially significant to the courts — is that many of these intangibles, such as a degree or goodwill, seem personally connected to the efforts of the holder.

Most definitional battles focus on whether or not an intangible interest should be treated as property. The outcome can have significant consequences for the economic future of the divorcing spouses because intangibles, such as a pension or the goodwill of a business, may be very valuable. Before looking at these definitional disputes more closely, however, we turn to a question that has recently received considerable attention: At the time of divorce, how should disputes over the family pet be resolved? Should a pet be treated as an item of property or as a member of the household?

Divorce and the Family Pet

Based on established legal doctrine, pets are generally considered to be the "personal property" of their "owners." Accordingly, upon divorce, the determination of a pet's future is controlled by property distribution principles. Thus, for example, a court might award a dog to a spouse who came into a marriage with the pet based on the classification principle that the dog is a separate asset, rather than to the spouse who had been the pet's primary caretaker over the course of the marriage. In effect, this "pet as property" approach means that the fate of the family dog or cat will be resolved by reference to the same principles that govern the distribution of the household furniture or a couple's automobiles.

Over the past 15 or so years, this approach has increasingly been challenged by a number of legal scholars, animal rights activists, and litigants seeking to maintain their post-dissolution relationship with a pet, who have argued that conflicts between divorcing spouses over a pet should be treated as akin to a custody dispute rather than as a disagreement over the allocation of marital assets, and that a best interest standard should be employed. This changed standard would honor the reality that unlike a chair, animals are living beings who are both loyal and loving and, like children, are dependent upon adults to provide for their basic needs. Moreover, as with a child, the loss of relationship cannot be redressed by providing a spouse with an offsetting asset to compensate him or her for the deprivation caused by award of the pet to the other spouse.[5]

However, courts and legislatures have not generally been receptive to these arguments, and pets generally continue to be treated as property in the marital dissolution context. For example, in a 1995 Florida divorce case, the appeals court concluded that the trial court had erred in awarding custody of the couple's dog to the husband with visitation rights to the wife because under Florida law, a dog is personal property and "[t]here is no authority which provides for a trial court to grant custody or visitation pertaining to personal property."[6] The court further stated that, as a policy matter, "[d]eterminations as to custody and visitation lead to continuing enforcement and supervision problems (as evidenced by the proceedings in the instant case). Our courts are overwhelmed with the supervision of custody, visitation, and support matters related to the protection of our children. We cannot undertake the same responsibility as to animals."[7] Taking this a step further, a Pennsylvania appeals court refused to enforce an agreement between a couple regarding the allocation of custodial and visitation rights between divorcing spouses, stating:

> In seeking "shared custody" and a "visitation" arrangement, Appellant appears to treat Barney, a dog, as a child. Despite the status owners bestow on their pets, Pennsylvania law considers dogs to be personal property. . . . Appellant, however, overlooks the fact that any terms set forth in the Agreement are void to the extent that they attempt to award custodial visitation with or shared custody of personal property. . . . As the trial court aptly noted, Appellant is seeking an arrangement analogous, in law, to a visitation schedule for a table or a lamp.[8]

Although courts have continued to resist treating disputes between divorcing spouses over a family pet as akin to a child custody dispute, animal lovers can take heart in the fact that some judges have quietly begun to pay attention to the post-dissolution needs of family pets within the "pet as property" paradigm. A recent Virginia divorce case provides an excellent example of this hybrid approach. At trial, although each party introduced relevant evidence under the state's equitable distribution law to establish his or her superior claim to the dog, which included a dispute over whether the dog should be classified as a marital asset, or, as argued by the wife, as a separate asset based upon her claim that the dog had been a gift to her from her husband, they also testified to the fact that "they loved the dog and they considered her to be a family member," and each "presented evidence that they had a strong bond with the dog."[9]

Following the court's decision to award the dog to the wife under the state's equitable distribution statute, with an offsetting financial award to the husband so he could acquire a dog "of like kind," the husband filed an appeal arguing that the court had erred by failing to "consider that the dog is not an inanimate object, but rather a living sentient being," and by refusing to use the "best interest standard." Although the appeals court rejected the husband's argument that the dispute should have been resolved by reference to a best interest rather than an equitable distribution standard, it approvingly pointed out that in making its allocation decision, the trial court "noted that a dog has a unique 'intrinsic value' because the parties care for the dog and have a 'significant interest' in the dog," and that it did "not in any way want to minimize the significance of a pet in a person's life." Accordingly, the lower court had properly taken into account "the unique circumstances presented by determining the equitable distribution of the dog," and made sure that she would be provided with a "stable and caring environment."[10]

Unvested Pensions and Accrued Leave Time: Are They Property?

In this section, we look at two intangible assets that have posed definitional difficulties for the courts — unvested pensions and accrued vacation and sick leave time. These assets have been selected because they raise recurring issues that are central to the definitional process. Before proceeding, it should be noted that sometimes the question we are considering here — whether an intangible asset is property or not — is framed as an inquiry into whether the asset should be considered a separate rather than a marital asset because of its special characteristics, such as that it is personal to the holder and nontransferable. Regardless of which approach is used, the relevant considerations are quite similar.

Pensions:
Deferred compensation payable at retirement

Unvested Pensions. **Pensions** are an important job-related benefit. They are a form of deferred compensation: An employee earns the right to the benefit in the present, but realization of the benefit is deferred until retirement or some other future date after the employee has left his or her job. Some pension plans are funded solely by employer contributions; others are funded solely by employee contributions; and some are funded by a combination of employer and employee contributions.

An individual's interest in his or her pension is either vested or unvested.[11] When rights are vested, an employee does not forfeit retirement benefits when he or she leaves the place of employment prior to retirement. Vesting usually occurs after an employee has worked for an employer for a specified number of years. In contrast, if an employee who is not vested leaves the job, he or she forfeits the retirement benefits. The right to retirement benefits is thus contingent on continued employment through the vesting period.

The clear trend is to recognize both vested and unvested pensions as a property interest. However, there has been considerable debate over unvested pensions, and some jurisdictions continue to regard them as an expectancy interest rather than as a form of property because the right to benefits is contingent upon continued employment through the vesting period, which may or may not take place. In general, an expectancy is not considered a form of property because of its uncertain, conditional nature.

Other jurisdictions give greater weight to a spouse's interest in an unvested pension because, although presently uncertain, the right to benefits will become legally enforceable upon the happening of a future contingency — fulfillment of the time requirement. This greater certainty serves to distinguish an interest in an unvested pension from a true expectancy, such as the hope of being named a beneficiary in a will, which is completely speculative, and supports treating unvested pensions as property.

In defining unvested pensions as property, many jurisdictions have been influenced by equitable considerations. A pension is often a couple's most valuable asset, and exclusion based on a technical distinction would downgrade the contribution of a homemaker spouse to the marital enterprise because, although both partners contributed to the marriage, only the employed spouse would enjoy retirement benefits. Another fairness consideration is that the right, although contingent, is acquired during the marriage. (See the discussion regarding distribution of pensions later in this chapter.)

Accrued Vacation and Sick Leave Time.   Many employers permit their employees to accumulate unused sick and vacation time. Upon retirement, an employee may be paid the value of this accrued time. The question has arisen in a number of cases as to whether this accrued time is a marital asset, capable of valuation and division upon divorce. Although the courts that have considered this issue are divided, the majority approach is toward inclusion.

In seeking to determine whether accrued leave time is an asset, many courts have framed it as a question of whether this time is an alternative form of wages, and thus not property, or more akin to deferred compensation, such as a pension, and thus includible as property. In a Kentucky Court of Appeals decision, the court concluded that accrued leave time was "less tangible, more difficult to value, and more personal than pension and retirement benefits," and therefore should not be classified as property.[12]

The court found the reasoning of an earlier decision from Maryland to be persuasive:

> We just are not persuaded that accrued holiday and vacation entitlement is the same as a pension or retirement benefit, a form of deferred compensation; since it replaces wages on days when the worker does not work, it is really only an alternative form of wages. . . . It need not be liquidated by the payment of cash; it may be, and often is, dissipated when the person entitled to do so takes vacation or holiday time. Thus, it is far from as tangible as, and much more difficult to value, not to mention and more personal than pension and retirement benefits.[13]

In contrast, the New Mexico appeals court found that the value of accumulated hours comes within the definition of marital property, much like other employee benefits:

> The essence of leave is that it is a benefit of employment and . . . it has independent value. If taken during marriage, leave time devoted to vacation or to recovery from illness benefits the community. If not taken, leave that accumulates will be available to benefit the community in the future. If the community ends, the accumulated leave attaches to the employee. Unless some equitable distribution is made or the asset is divided upon dissolution of marriage, the employees take the full community asset.[14]

Unlike other courts that have considered this issue, the New Mexico court was more concerned with fairness than with deciding if accrued time is more like wages or more like deferred compensation. The court went on to state that there was no policy reason why the husband should exit the marriage with the full value of the accumulated leave time, given that it resulted from marital effort. Thus, as we saw previously with respect to unvested pensions, considerations of fairness may influence the definitional process.

Classification of Property

The classification of property as marital or separate is a crucial step in both common law dual property and community property states because it determines the pool of assets that is subject to division (although, in a few states, courts can reach even separate property in cases of hardship). In theory, classification is not relevant in all-property states; however, in practice, classification principles may influence how attorneys, and possibly judges, approach the distribution of property.

Defining Marital and Separate Property

In most states, marital and separate property are defined in relationship to one another: One is what the other is not. Frequently, a statute will define marital property as all property acquired during the marriage, except for that which is considered separate. Separate property is then specifically defined, and almost always includes property owned at the time of marriage, gifts, inheritances, and items received in exchange for separate property. Some statutes also identify specific assets, such as appreciation on separate property, unvested pensions, and professional licenses, as coming within the definition of separate property. Again, the rationale underlying the distinction between marital and separate property is that marital accumulations derive from the overall contribution of both spouses to the marriage, regardless of which spouse actually paid for any particular item, whereas separate assets do not derive from the marital efforts of either spouse and thus stand apart from the marriage. However, as discussed later in this chapter in the section entitled "Transmutation," the initial characterization of an asset may change over time. Classification also can be influenced by presumptions, and in most states, it is presumed that all property owned by the spouse at the time of divorce is marital. This places the burden of proof on the party who is claiming that a particular asset is separate property, and he or she must produce sufficient evidence to rebut the presumption, or the asset will be considered marital and subject to division.

The Significance of Timing

A central characteristic of marital property is that it is acquired during the marriage. As a general rule, **premarital acquisitions**, property that a spouse comes into the marriage with, remain his or her separate property. This distinction usually is straightforward, but a few situations require elaboration.

Premarital Acquisitions: Property owned by a spouse prior to marriage

Determining the Time of Acquisition. If a person purchases an asset, such as a car, before getting married and then makes payments on it after the marriage, is the car a premarital or a marital acquisition? One approach known as the **inception of title rule** fixes the time of acquisition at the time of initial purchase because this is when title or the right to title is obtained. Once set, the characterization cannot be changed, and postmarital contributions have no impact on the classification. Here, property is a unitary concept and value cannot be apportioned between the marital and the separate estates, although the nonowner spouse might be entitled to some reimbursement for his or her contribution.

Inception of Title Rule: A rule fixing title at the time an asset is acquired

Source of Funds Rule:
An approach that ties the time of acquisition of an asset to the contribution of funds and also permits the dual characterization of an asset as both marital and separate in proportion to contribution

Most jurisdictions have rejected this approach as too formalistic and incompatible with sharing principles because it focuses on title to the exclusion of contribution. The preferred approach to determining the time of acquisition is the **source of funds rule**. Here, acquisition is seen as a dynamic process that unfolds over time as payment is made; one might say that each payment effectuates a partial acquisition. Accordingly, an asset can be both marital and separate, and its value apportioned between the two estates in proportion to contribution.

A brief example will demonstrate the difference between these approaches. Let's say that in 2001, Nekeisha purchases an oil painting for $12,000. She pays $8,000 in cash and takes out a loan to pay the balance.

One month later, she marries Victor, and payments on the loan are made from their newly established joint checking account. In year three, the loan is paid off. Unfortunately, in year four, the couple divorces.

Under the inception of title rule, the entire value of the painting would be the separate property of Nekeisha because she acquired title or the right to title before the marriage, although Victor may be entitled to reimbursement. Under the source of funds rule, the value of the painting would be apportioned between Nekeisha's separate estate and the marital estate in the amounts of $8,000 and $4,000 respectively, thus adding to the total worth of marital assets. (Note that this example assumed the painting did not increase in value during the marriage. Appreciation raises other issues, which are discussed later in this chapter.)

Property Acquired in Contemplation of Marriage or During Cohabitation. Usually, there is no doubt that property owned by a person at the time of marriage is separate. However, sometimes purchases may be made in contemplation of marriage. In this situation, some jurisdictions have stretched statutory categories and will treat this property as marital based on the parties' intent to use it as such. Here, intent displaces the timing of acquisition as the controlling factor.

A related question is how property acquired during a period of premarital cohabitation will be treated. Reluctant to treat cohabitation as the legal equivalent of marriage, most courts do not consider assets acquired during a period of cohabitation as marital. However, if, during cohabitation, property is purchased in contemplation of marriage, it might come within this rule and be treated as marital based on the parties' intent rather than on the fact of cohabitation.

Fixing a Cutoff Point for Marital Acquisitions. Timing questions that can influence classification also arise at the other end of the relationship—specifically, at what point in the dissolution process will acquired assets no longer be considered marital? Strictly speaking, a husband and wife remain legally married until a final decree of divorce is entered; thus, property that is acquired up until this moment in time is technically marital. However, motivated by practical and policy considerations, most jurisdictions use an earlier cutoff point, after which time property that is acquired is no longer considered marital despite the continuation of the legal relationship.

To signal the effective end of the marital partnership, most state statutes fix the cutoff point at the date of legal separation, the initiation of a permanent separation, or the filing of a dissolution action, although a few states leave it to the discretion of the judge. Although utilizing different moments in time, each of these approaches reflects the underlying view that once spouses have gone their separate ways, the theoretical justification for pooling based on mutual contribution and effort no longer exists. It should be noted that practical problems can arise where the cutoff point is the date of permanent separation. Frequently, a separation that is intended to be permanent is followed by a series of contacts, some or all of which may rise to the level of reconciliation. This makes it difficult to fix the date of separation, particularly if the spouses disagree about the meaning and impact of these postseparation contacts, which makes it difficult to classify property accumulated during these intervals of parting and coming together.

Looking Beyond Definitions: The Complexities of Classification

Although the distinction between marital and separate property is easy to state, applying it can be difficult. This section discusses some situations that present difficult classification issues.

Gifts.   As a general matter, a **gift** is a voluntary transfer of property made with donative intent, meaning that the gift-giver (donor) simply wishes to give the recipient something without requiring anything in exchange. For a gift to be effective, the transfer must be complete — the donor must fully relinquish all vestiges of ownership and control.

In the divorce context, a gift is generally classified as separate property, as it is not acquired through the effort of either spouse. Sometimes, however, a transfer that appears to be a gift is really not, such as when the donor, rather than being motivated by donative intent, is providing compensation for past or future services. Community property jurisdictions have long distinguished between gifts made with true donative intent and those that are really a form of compensation, treating the latter as marital property because the acquisition is tied to the recipient's efforts. This distinction is now also made in some common law dual property jurisdictions.

For example, assume that Bob and Karen are married. One day, Karen's great-aunt Ernestine gives her a beautiful oil painting that is

Gift:
A voluntary transfer of property made with donative intent; to be effective, the transfer must be complete — the donor must fully relinquish all vestiges of ownership and control

worth a lot of money. At first glance, classification appears obvious: The painting is a gift to Karen and is thus her separate property. However, what happens if the next time Bob and Karen visit Ernestine, she mentions that she gave the painting to Karen as a way of thanking her for taking such good care of her during her last illness? Now, if the couple were to divorce, Bob could argue that the painting should be classified as marital property because it was not given to Karen as a gift but as a form of compensation, and thus was acquired through the expenditure of marital efforts.

What if instead of being from a third party, the gift is from one spouse to another? Should these be treated in the same manner? What if the gift was purchased from marital funds — should the source of contribution or the nature of the exchange control the classification?

In some states, interspousal gifts have been exempted from the general characterization of gifts as separate property by either statute or judicial decision, with some of these states limiting the exclusion to gifts that were purchased with marital funds. The underlying rationale here is that unlike third-party gifts, interspousal gifts derive from partnership efforts. In contrast, other jurisdictions focus on the gift aspect of the transaction, rather than on the source of funds. These courts treat completed interspousal gifts in the same manner as third-party gifts, even where purchased with marital funds.

Appreciation of Separate Property. Difficult classification issues can arise in situations where separate property has increased in value over the course of the marriage. One approach is to tie the classification of the **appreciation** to the classification of the underlying asset. This means that if the asset is characterized as separate, any appreciation in value — even if it occurred during the marriage — will also be classified as separate. This approach is similar to the previously discussed inception of title rule that fixes ownership at the time of acquisition.

Appreciation:
The increase in value of an asset

Let's return to Nekeisha and the oil painting that she purchased for $12,000 one month before her marriage to Victor. If the painting increased in value during the marriage, under this approach, the entire increase would be classified as separate based on the classification of the underlying asset. Note that any reimbursement due Victor would not capture the value of this increase.

As with the inception of title rule, most jurisdictions have rejected this approach as too rigid and not in keeping with contemporary sharing principles. The preferred approach is to classify appreciation based on the reason for the increase. If the increase is unrelated to spousal efforts and is due to causes such as inflation or market conditions, it is usually considered the separate property of the spouse who owns the asset. This kind of increase is often referred to as *passive appreciation*. If instead the gain is due to the investment of marital funds or efforts, it is usually considered marital. This kind of increase is often referred to as *active appreciation*. If the gain is attributable to both passive and active forces, it can be apportioned between the separate and marital estates.[15]

Property Received in Exchange for Separate Property.   What happens if a spouse exchanges or sells separate property during the marriage? Most jurisdictions treat property that is received in exchange for separate property as separate: The exchange is regarded as an alteration in the form of the asset, which leaves its underlying separate nature intact.

Generally, based on the presumption that all property owned at the time of divorce is marital, the party seeking to segregate an asset from the marital estate has the burden of proving its separate identity. Where exchanged property is involved, segregation requires **tracing** the asset directly back to a separate source. Tracing can be simple, such as where one painting has been exchanged for another, or it can be complex, such as where there have been successive exchanges or where funds from an account containing separate and marital funds have been used. If the tracing fails, and the separate identity of the asset cannot be established, it will be treated as marital. As discussed next, this result is transmutation by commingling.[16]

Tracing:
The process by which a party seeks to establish the separate identity of an asset owned at the time of divorce so that it is not subject to distribution

The Nature of the Asset.   Classification difficulties also may be triggered by specific types of property. As noted previously, these inquiries are sometimes framed as definitional questions and sometimes as classification ones. Personal injury awards are a good example of an interest that poses difficult classification issues, as well as presenting an underlying definitional question. Similar issues are raised when other damages awards, such as disability or workers' compensation benefits, are involved.[17]

Assuming, for the sake of discussion, that we are in a jurisdiction that considers a personal injury award to be property, the traditional approach was to classify the entire award as marital if it was acquired during the marriage. However, this is now a minority approach, and the clear classification trend is to divide the award into component parts and allocate them between the separate and marital estates in accordance with general classification principles. Using this approach, most states will classify the portion of the award attributable to lost wages and medical expenses as marital property because it compensates for economic loss incurred during the marriage.[18] The portion of the award attributable to the pain and suffering of the injured spouse is then classified as separate property because it is so intimately connected to the injured spouse that it is deemed to exist apart from the marriage. If the award also compensates the injured person for future economic losses, this portion of the award usually would be classified as separate because the other spouse has no recognized interest in these future rights.

Transmutation

Our final classification topic is transmutation. **Transmutation** refers to a postacquisition change in an asset's classification from separate to marital or from marital to separate, although almost all transmutation cases involve the reclassification of separate assets. Transmutation can occur in four ways: (1) by agreement, (2) by joint titling, (3) by commingling, and (4) by use.

Transmutation by Agreement. The simplest way that transmutation can occur is where the parties agree to recharacterize property. Statutes in many community property states and a few common law jurisdictions specifically authorize this result, although the term "transmutation" is usually not used. In the absence of express authority, most courts will uphold an agreement between spouses to recharacterize property. The agreement may need to be in writing and conform to whatever requirements the particular jurisdiction imposes on marital agreements.

Transmutation by Joint Titling. Property may be transmuted if a spouse places separate property or property purchased with separate funds in joint name — for example, where one spouse purchases a car with inherited funds and then takes title in both names. In most jurisdictions, joint titling triggers a rebuttable presumption that the separate asset has transmuted into a marital one because the titling demonstrates an intent to bestow a benefit on the marital estate. To rebut the presumption, a spouse may be able to show that the intent of joint titling was not to confer a benefit upon the marital estate but instead was done for estate planning purposes or to satisfy the requirements of a lender or because of pressure from his or her spouse. If the presumption is rebutted, the property will not transmute but rather will retain its original characterization as separate property.

Transmutation by Commingling. The most common way for property to transmute is by commingling. When separate property has been mixed with marital property, it will be treated as marital unless the party wishing to segregate the asset can establish its separate identity. Here, the failure of a party to keep assets separate may be regarded as evidence of an intent to benefit the marital estate. The party wishing to claim an asset as separate must be able to "uncommingle" the mass of property. As with exchanged property, this is done by tracing. If the separate identity of the asset cannot be established with sufficient certainty, the tracing fails and the property is deemed to have transmuted by commingling.

Transmutation by Use. A few jurisdictions allow transmutation by use. For example, if a spouse permits the other to use his or her separately owned car on a regular basis, this use could transmute the car into a marital asset. This approach has been both praised for promoting sharing principles and criticized as an encroachment on individual property rights that effectively punishes a spouse for his or her generosity.[19] Depending on the situation, the same result might also be accomplished by reference to the commingling doctrine.

Valuation

Before property can be divided between spouses, marital assets need to be valued. Valuation involves determining the worth of the assets so that an appropriate distribution can be effectuated. Where an equitable as distinct from an equal distribution standard is used, separate assets also may need to be valued, as the value and nature of this estate may influence the allocation of marital property. For example, if one spouse has considerable separate assets, it may be fair to give the other spouse a greater share of the marital estate (see the section entitled "Distribution" later in this chapter). As a practical matter where property issues are resolved by agreement rather than at trial, parties often divide up their belongings without having them valued, as **valuation** can be both expensive and time consuming. Of course, this means that there is no real way of knowing whether the settlement is fair, especially if potentially valuable assets are involved. In this situation, attorneys usually include a provision in the separation agreement in which the parties acknowledge that they have knowingly and willingly dispensed with a valuation and have divided their property without full knowledge of its worth.

Valuation:
The determination of what an asset is worth, most commonly by ascertaining its fair market value; usually done by an expert

When property issues are resolved at trial, it can be a reversible error for the court to divide property without first determining value. Although valuation may be framed as the court's responsibility, in many jurisdictions, a party who fails to present evidence of value is deemed to have waived his or her right of appeal on this issue.

Valuation Methods

Few statutes specify how assets should be valued, and a wide range of approaches are generally acceptable. When a trial court is presented with competing valuation methods, it has relative freedom to select among the approaches or to combine them to arrive at its own value.

A common valuation approach is to determine an asset's fair market value. **Fair market value** is generally described as the price that a willing buyer would pay to a willing seller where neither party is under any compulsion to buy or sell. Establishing this price requires detailed knowledge of the asset, as well as the specific market conditions that would influence transferability. Although common, the fair market value approach is far

Fair Market Value:
The price that a willing buyer would pay to a willing seller when neither party is under compulsion to buy or sell

from universal and would not be appropriate where, for example, a closely held corporation or a pension is involved, as neither has a readily determinable market value.[20]

The Role of Experts

The valuation of assets is generally outside the expertise of lawyers and requires the use of experts. As a general rule, there is no such thing as an all-purpose valuation expert. Instead, an expert must be carefully selected based on his or her specialized knowledge. For example, an accountant may be the most appropriate person to value a professional corporation but would not be the best choice where a rare stamp collection is involved; this would require the services of a rare stamp appraiser. Where real estate is involved, a real estate broker or appraiser would be appropriate, but if the present value of a pension needs to be determined, the services of an actuary would be required, as this entails an assessment of how future risks affect the value of the employee spouse's interest.

Clearly, in any single case, the valuation process may require more than one expert. This can greatly increase the time and expense of a divorce proceeding and can significantly disadvantage the spouse with less income, who may lose the battle of the experts. To address this problem, some courts, upon request, may order one spouse to pay the costs of the other's experts or may appoint its own expert and order one party to pay all or most of the costs. The expense and time involved in hiring experts may encourage couples to settle rather than litigate; alternatively, it may encourage the financially more secure spouse to litigate vigorously in order to outdo the other.

Time of Valuation

An important valuation issue is when value should be determined. Possible dates include time of (1) separation, (2) trial, or (3) entry of the decree of dissolution. Traditionally, most jurisdictions selected a single valuation time and used it in all cases. However, the trend is toward greater flexibility, with a preference for determining value as close to the date of distribution as possible. However, most courts will readily depart from this approach where required by considerations of fairness. For example, if after separation one party dissipates assets, the court may use the date of separation for valuation purposes. This date might also be used if an asset has appreciated in value based on the postseparation efforts of one spouse.

Distribution

After property has been classified as marital or separate and valued, the actual distribution must be effectuated. This final step is the focus of this section.

The Standard for Division: Equal or Equitable?

When dividing property, the majority of states use an *equitable distribution standard*, which directs courts to divide the property in a manner that is described as fair, just, or equitable. A minority of states, made up mainly of community property jurisdictions, use an *equal distribution standard*. These courts must divide marital property equally between the spouses — although a few states permit deviations based on equitable considerations, such as where one spouse has no other resources and is otherwise likely to end up on public assistance. A few states use a *hybrid approach*. Here, property is to be divided equitably, but there is a rebuttable presumption that equitable is in fact equal. Accordingly, a party seeking a greater share of the assets would have the burden of proving why this is fair under the particular circumstances.

With the exception of the hybrid states, appellate courts in jurisdictions using an equitable distribution standard have generally made clear that it is inappropriate for trial courts to rely on fixed formulas or presumptions. However, it is generally acceptable for a court to use a 50-50 split as its starting point, so long as this does not result in an overly mechanistic approach to the allocation of assets. Nonetheless, as a practical matter, some judges and lawyers seem to assume that "equitable" means "equal," thus implicitly placing a burden on the party seeking a greater share of the assets to justify why this division is appropriate.

A frequent concern raised by commentators who have examined the economic impact of divorce on women is that a division that appears equal or equitable on its face may have a very different value to each spouse based on differences in earning capacity, as the spouse with higher earnings can more readily replace items that were lost in the distribution.[21] This problem may be exacerbated if the low-earning spouse also has custody of the children, as the custodial parent often has increased household needs. Moreover, as we have seen, these considerations are often linked, because a spouse with greater domestic responsibilities frequently has a diminished earning capacity. One suggested solution is for courts to look beyond ensuring that the distribution appears equitable or equal solely at the time of divorce, and to assess the relative impact of the distribution on each spouse over time in light of earning potential and domestic arrangements as well. When this suggests a diverging value, the allocation could be adjusted to ensure greater fairness over time.

Consideration of Specific Factors

Most states with an equitable distribution standard have a statute that enumerates the factors that must be considered in determining how property is to be allocated. Some statutes are general in their approach, while others are detailed. Frequently, the factors that must be considered are the same as those that must be considered in making a spousal support award.

The following section from a New Jersey statute is a good example of a fairly detailed approach to what must be taken into account when determining the distribution of property:

> In making an equitable distribution of property, the court shall consider, but not be limited to, the following factors:
> a. The duration of the marriage or civil union;
> b. The age and physical and emotional health of the parties;
> c. The income or property brought to the marriage or civil union by each party;
> d. The standard of living established during the marriage or civil union;
> e. Any written agreement made by the parties before or during the marriage or civil union concerning an arrangement of property distribution;
> f. The economic circumstances of each party at the time the division of property becomes effective;
> g. The income and earning capacity of each party, including educational background, training, employment skills, work experience, length of absence from the job market, custodial responsibilities for children, and the time and expense necessary to acquire sufficient education or training to enable the party to become self-supporting at a standard of living reasonably comparable to that enjoyed during the marriage or civil union;
> h. The contribution by each party to the education, training, or earning power of the other;
> i. The contribution of each party to the acquisition, dissipation, preservation, depreciation, or appreciation in the amount or value of the marital property, or the property acquired during the civil union as well as the contribution of a party as a homemaker;
> j. The tax consequences of the proposed distribution to each party;
> k. The present value of the property;
> l. The need of a parent who has physical custody of a child to own or occupy the marital residence or residence shared by the partners in a civil union couple and to use or own the household effects;
> m. The debts and liabilities of the parties;
> n. The need for creation, now or in the future, of a trust fund to secure reasonably foreseeable medical or educational costs for a spouse, partner in a civil union couple or children;
> o. The extent to which a party deferred achieving their career goals; and
> p. Any other factors which the court may deem relevant.[22]

As we have seen in other contexts, most statutes set out the factors that must be considered in dividing property, but do not require that equal weight be given to each one. Accordingly, judges are free to weigh the factors as deemed appropriate in light of the circumstances of the individual case. This approach maximizes the flexibility and discretion of the court and is generally considered to be consistent with the goal of achieving a fair result, but, as we have seen, the potential downside of this flexibility is that it can lead to inconsistent results.

In some jurisdictions, judges must make detailed findings of fact showing the consideration given each statutory factor. In others, a more general statement in support of the result is acceptable. In states using an equal distribution standard or presumption, findings of fact are usually required only when the judge departs from the norm and makes an unequal distribution.

Effectuating the Distribution

There are many ways that property can be divided between the parties. The simplest and most common way to distribute property is for each spouse to take possession of a designated portion of the assets. For example, the wife might get the living room furniture and the husband the dining room furniture; the wife the computer and the husband the home stereo system; each might get one-half of the linens, the towels, the kitchen items, and so on until everything is distributed.

If a couple has a significant asset—such as a business, a valuable collection, or (as discussed in greater detail next) a house or pension—with no other comparable assets, a number of options are possible. Probably the simplest alternative is to award one spouse the major asset and give the other a greater share of the remaining assets. However, this may not always be feasible because the remaining property is often not of sufficient offsetting value. Another option is for the asset to be sold and the proceeds divided. Or one spouse could retain the asset and buy out the other's marital interest in it. Where a buyout occurs, a lump-sum payment (where feasible) is generally preferable to installment payments because it provides a clean break and minimizes the risk of nonperformance.

The Marital Residence.   Many property disputes center on the marital residence, most likely due to the convergence of financial, emotional, and practical considerations. In the event of a dispute, a court may consider the desirability of enabling the children to remain in their home because this provides them with some stability at a time of tremendous change. In fact, some property distribution statutes expressly include this as a factor for judicial consideration. [See, e.g., paragraph (l) of the New Jersey statute shown previously.] Dispositional options for the marital residence include the following:

1. Sell the house and divide the proceeds.
2. One spouse keeps the house, buying out the other spouse or exchanging offsetting assets.

3. Keep the house in joint name, with one spouse having the right of exclusive use and occupancy until a future dispositional date.

If neither spouse wishes to retain the house, it can be sold and the proceeds divided equally or in accordance with the overall distribution formula. In some cases, a sale may be the ultimate result because no other option is feasible.

If the parties agree in principle that one spouse can retain the house, the question becomes how this can be accomplished. Often the simplest solution is to give the other spouse an asset or assets of roughly equal value; sometimes a pension will be used as the offsetting asset. Frequently, however, there will not be enough resources to do this, since a house is often the most valuable asset a couple owns. Another option is for the acquiring spouse to buy out the interest of the other spouse. To do this, the acquiring spouse usually takes out a home equity loan or refinances the existing loan. Again, this may not be feasible because he or she may not qualify for the loan or have the ability to make the loan payments.

If neither of these options is feasible, another possibility is to keep the property in joint name and give one spouse the right of exclusive use and occupancy until a designated time in the future, such as the emancipation of the youngest child or the remarriage of the occupying spouse. Upon the earliest of these to occur, the occupying spouse would be required to effectuate a buyout of the other spouse's interest or to sell the house and allocate the proceeds according to a preexisting formula. The nonoccupying spouse is often given the right of first refusal.

The advantage of this approach is that it enables a spouse to remain in the home, which may be particularly important where children are involved, without having to either give up a share of other assets or go into debt. But there is also a significant drawback: The property continues to be owned by two people with enough relational difficulties that they cannot live together. For this arrangement to have any hope of working, it is best that all necessary details be spelled out in the court's order or in the parties' separation agreement. It may also be advisable for the court to retain jurisdiction in case problems arise after the divorce. Some of the issues that need to be addressed are the following: Who pays for repairs? Who pays for improvements that increase the value of the house? How are these expenses accounted for upon sale? What if the occupying spouse neglects the house and its value declines? How are sale proceeds to be allocated? How is appreciation accounted for? Even when these details are worked out with care, the emotional risk factor involved in this approach remains a wild card.

Pensions.   The distribution of pensions raises complex issues. This section provides a basic overview of the two principal ways that pensions can be divided.[23]

The Present Value Approach.   One approach is to determine the present value of the pension and then assign the nonemployee spouse an offsetting share of property. The primary advantage of this approach is that the matter is resolved at the time of divorce and is not left hanging until some future date. However, it also presents some potential disadvantages. First, it is often difficult and costly to determine the present value of a pension plan because it is not payable until some time in the future and a number of contingencies — such as the salary of the employee spouse — can influence its value or affect whether it is payable at all. Second, there may not be enough offsetting property; even where there is, the nonemployee spouse gets the offsetting property immediately, while the employee spouse must wait until a future date to enjoy his or her share of the distribution. Additionally, if the plan is not vested, the employee spouse bears the risk of not receiving a full share of the distribution; however, she or he has some control over this, as a voluntary job change can be postponed until after the pension has vested. Accordingly, this approach is not generally used if a plan is unvested or the employee spouse is years away from retirement.

The "If, As, and When" Approach.   The other approach is to award the nonemployee spouse a share of pension funds "if, as, and when" the employee spouse receives them. Typically, at the time of divorce, the court uses a formula for allocating the future payments between the spouses; however, it is also possible that a court might instead opt to reserve jurisdiction over the matter and defer the determination of the nonemployee's share until the pension actually matures and is thus payable. In determining the percentage amount, most states use a "marital fraction" formula that calculates the nonemployee's share based on the ratio that the years of the marriage bear to the total number of years of employment at the time of distribution.

The primary advantages of this distribution method are that it avoids the need to determine the present value of the plan; an offsetting award is not required; and the risk of nonreceipt is not born solely by the employee spouse because the nonemployee spouse receives his or her share "if, as, and when" the employee spouse does. If the employee leaves before his or her pension vests, neither spouse gains or loses in a differential fashion. However, a potential disadvantage to the nonemployee spouse is the fact that the other spouse has control over this eventuality and thus has the ability to defeat the interest of the nonemployee spouse. This could give the employee spouse the upper hand in the event of postmarital disagreements, as he or she could threaten to quit work if the other spouse did not capitulate to his or her demands.

Where the pension funds are actually reached, distribution is usually made pursuant to a **Qualified Domestic Relations Order** (QDRO), which

Qualified Domestic Relations Order:
A court order that allows the distribution of pension benefits to a nonemployee spouse

is served on the administrator of the pension. A QDRO is a judgment or decree of a state court that enables the nonemployee spouse to receive all or part of the benefits that are payable to the employee spouse. A QDRO must be carefully drafted so it satisfies the legal requirements of the Employee Retirement Income Security Act (ERISA), as modified by the Retirement Equity Act of 1984 (REA), and contains all of the necessary information, such as the formulas used to determine the amounts of payment, how payments are to be made, and when payments will begin and end.[24]

Tax Consequences of a Property Distribution

For federal tax purposes, property transfers between spouses either during a marriage or after a marriage ends that are incidental to a divorce are not taxable events.[25] To understand the significance of this rule, it is helpful to step outside the divorce context for a moment. Assume that A purchases a painting for $10,000 and five years later sells it to B for $20,000. Upon the sale, A has realized a gain of $10,000, which is subject to taxation. However, if A were married to B, and this transfer were made during the marriage or incident to a divorce, A would not realize any taxable gain even if A receives an asset worth $20,000 in exchange for the painting.

Cost Basis:
The cost of an asset, used to calculate the amount of appreciation from the time of purchase

Let us now analyze the transfer from B's perspective. Where A and B are strangers, and B purchases the painting for $20,000, B acquires what is referred to as a **cost basis** in the painting of $20,000. If B subsequently transfers the property, his gain will be computed using this basis as the starting point. Accordingly, if he sells the painting for $35,000, he will realize a gain of $15,000 ($35,000 – $20,000). However, if A and B are spouses, and the transfer is incident to a divorce, the tax consequences for B are quite different. Here, B acquires A's basis of $10,000 — it is literally carried over from A to B (as it would be in the case of a gift). Now, if B sells the painting for $35,000, he will realize a gain of $25,000 ($35,000 – $10,000).

Clearly, this rule affects the actual value of a property transfer because the recipient of appreciated property may eventually be accountable for a significant gain. These potential tax consequences must be taken into account when effectuating a division; otherwise, parties may not actually receive the value that they believe they have agreed to.

Chapter Summary

Historically, at the time of divorce, courts in common law states had limited distributive authority — property followed title. In contrast, courts in community property states had the authority to divide all assets acquired through the expenditure of marital efforts or funds. With the passage of equitable distribution laws, common law jurisdictions have moved closer to the community property model. Tracking this shift, most states, including all community property states, distinguish between separate and marital property and permit distribution of all community assets. A distinct minority of common law states, however, do not make this distinction, and courts are thus empowered to distribute all property owned by a couple at the time of divorce.

A division of property entails four critical steps: (1) a determination whether the asset in question is in fact "property"; (2) the classification of property as either marital or separate (this step is not required in all-property states because the courts in these jurisdictions can reach both separate and marital property); (3) the value of each asset must be determined; and (4) the assets must be allocated in accordance with the applicable legal standard, with states employing either an equitable or an equal division rule.

The transfer of property incident to a divorce does not result in a taxable gain or loss to the transferring spouse; however, the recipient acquires a carry-over basis in the transferred asset that may result in a significant gain at the time of a future transfer.

Key Terms

Marital Property	All-Property	Inception of Title Rule	Valuation
Community Property	Tangible Property	Source of Funds Rule	Fair Market
Title	Intangible Assets	Gift	Value
Equitable Distribution	Pensions	Appreciation	Qualified Domestic
Dual Property	Premarital	Tracing	Relations Order
Separate Property	Acquisitions	Transmutation	Cost Basis

Review Questions

1. Following no-fault reform, why did property distribution become the preferred way to address the economic interests and needs of divorcing spouses?
2. Describe the partnership view of marriage that underlies the community property approach to the division of marital assets.
3. Prior to the passage of equitable distribution laws, how did common law states divide property? What was the special equity rule?
4. What is a dual property state? What is an all-property state?
5. What steps are involved in the division of property?
6. What is the difference between tangible and intangible property?
7. How does the law characterize family pets? What implications does this have for divorce cases? What new approach have some suggested the law should take?
8. What is the difference between a vested and an unvested pension?
9. Why do some states exclude unvested pensions from their definition of property?
10. Why is classification a critical step in dual property and community property states, but not in all-property states?
11. How is marital property generally defined?
12. What is generally included within the definition of separate property?
13. Why is it important to determine when property is acquired?

14. What is the inception of title rule? The source of funds rule?
15. How might property acquired in contemplation of marriage be classified? Why? What about property acquired during premarital cohabitation? Why?
16. What cutoff dates are commonly used for determining when property will no longer be considered marital?
17. What is a gift? When might a gift be classified as marital rather than separate?
18. What is the difference between passive and active appreciation? Why is this difference important with respect to the appreciation of separate property?
19. What happens to the classification of separate property that is exchanged for other property during the marriage?
20. Explain the concept of tracing.
21. How are personal injury awards classified?
22. What is transmutation? Explain the four different ways by which property can transmute.
23. Why is valuation important?
24. What is meant by the term "fair market value"?
25. At what point in the process is property usually valued?
26. What is the difference between an equal and an equitable distribution standard?
27. How do courts decide what is equitable? What factors are generally considered important?
28. What are basic ways a distribution can be effectuated?
29. Describe the dispositional options for the marital residence.
30. What are the two different approaches to distribution of a pension? What are the relative advantages and disadvantages of each approach?
31. What is a QDRO?
32. What are the basic tax consequences of a property distribution?

Discussion Questions

1. Let's assume that Mr. Jones worked hard at a small company to provide for his family. He never particularly enjoyed his work but took his financial obligations to his family seriously. His wife, Ms. Jones, happily stayed home and raised the children and took care of the house.

    Assume that the Joneses are getting divorced after 15 years of marriage. During this time, Mr. Jones contributed to his pension plan at work, and he is fully vested. Should this asset be subject to division? Is it fair to Mr. Jones to divide this employment asset, which is based on his workplace efforts? Explain your position.

2. Some commentators have argued that what is equal or equitable should be determined, at least in part, by looking at future results. Viewed from this perspective, a division that appears equal or fair on its face may reveal itself as less valuable to a more economically vulnerable spouse who cannot readily replace lost assets.

    In dividing property, should the court seek to ensure that the resulting impact of the award is equal or fair, even if this would require making disproportionate allocations?

3. Assume that for most of an eight-year marriage, the husband has been very depressed. As a result, he has bounced from job to job, with frequent periods of unemployment, and has contributed little by way of caring for the house and the children. The wife has held down a steady job and has done most of the home care and child care.

    There is no question that their contributions are grossly unequal. How should this affect the property division? Does it make any difference if the wife knew about the husband's depression before the marriage? Does it make any difference if, instead of being depressed, the husband was an alcoholic? Drug dependent? Physically ill? Lazy?

4. In the divorce context, do you think the law should treat pets as personal property and distribute them like other assets, or would it be preferable if they were regarded more like children and decisions were made based on the best interest of the pet?

Assignments

1. Locate the property distribution statute for your state and try to answer the following questions based on the statutory language. Note that all questions will not be relevant in all jurisdictions.
   a. Are you in a community property or an equitable jurisdiction state?
   b. Does your state use a dual property or an all-property approach?
   c. How is marital/community property defined? How is separate property defined?
   d. Are there any statutory presumptions?
   e. Is there a cutoff date for the acquisition of marital property?
   f. What factors must a court consider when making a distribution?

2. Review the relevant cases in your jurisdiction to determine what factors the courts seem to think are the most important when allocating property. Write a memo analyzing your findings.

3. Interview an attorney or a paralegal who works in the family law field. Ask him or her about the following:
   - In what proportion is property usually divided between the spouses?
   - Under what circumstances does this vary?
   - What factors do lawyers and judges seem to think are the most important?
   - How are the nonfinancial contributions of spouses with regard to domestic responsibilities viewed? Are they respected as much as financial contributions?

4. The attorney you work for has asked you to draft him a memorandum setting out the options in the following situation: His client, Ms. Perez, is getting divorced from Mr. Rivera. The parties have two small children, and Ms. Perez will have physical custody. The couple owns a small house. Ms. Perez wishes to remain there while the children are young. In theory, Mr. Rivera has no problem with this, but he is not going to let her do this without receiving what he is entitled to. The house is worth about $150,000, and there is an outstanding mortgage of $120,000. Mr. Rivera has a vested pension plan, but its value has not yet been determined.

   What are all of the possible ways that a settlement could be structured? Set out the advantages and disadvantages of each possible option.

   As part of the memo, he also wants you to draft some preliminary separation agreement language that gives Ms. Perez the right of exclusive use and occupancy of the residence. You should cover as many contingencies as you can.

5. Draft a comprehensive checklist that can be used when working on cases to ensure that all property has been considered.

6. The attorney you work for has asked you to look into how appreciation of premarital property is handled in your state. Her client, Rita Small, came into the marriage with a summer home and a rare stamp collection. Both assets appreciated in value during the course of the marriage. Although she does not yet have accurate or complete information about the increases in value, you can assume that the increase in the value of the stamp collection is attributable to market forces and the increase in the value of the house is attributable to market forces, as well as to improvements that were made by the husband. Write an in-house memorandum explaining how the appreciation will be classified. Be sure to consider whether your jurisdiction treats passive and active appreciation differently.

7. The judge you work for has asked you to do some research in preparation for a divorce case that includes a dispute over a much-loved family dog. She wants you to do the following:
   a. Determine if there are any statutes in your state that are relevant to determining the legal status of pets.
   b. Determine if there are any cases in your state that would have bearing on this matter — do not limit yourself to divorce cases.
   c. Locate and read at least three articles on the topic, and provide the judge with a summary of the different arguments that are presented in terms of how pets should be treated in a divorce case.

Endnotes

1. Wisconsin also is now generally regarded as a community property state due to statutory changes initiated in 1986.

2. *See generally* Scott Greene, Comparison of the Community Property Aspects of the Community Property and Common-Law Marital Property Systems and Their Relative Compatibility with the Current View of the Marriage Relationship and the Rights of Women, 13 Creighton L. Rev. 71, 88 (1979); Judith T. Younger, Marital Regimes: A Story of Compromise and Demoralization, Together with Criticism and Suggestions for Reform, 67 Cornell L. Rev. 45 (1981).

3. *See* Younger, *supra* note 2, at 61-64.

4. This word, coined by Willard H. DaSilva, conveys wonderfully the shift in the meaning of the word "property." Willard H. DaSilva, Property Subject to Equitable Distribution, *in* Valuation and Distribution of Marital Property (John P. McCahey ed., 1985).

5. *See generally* Elizabeth Paek, Fido Seeks Full Membership in the Family: Dismantling the Property Classification of Companion Animals by Statute, 25 Hawaii L. Rev. 481, 489 (2003), and Rebecca Huss, Separation, Custody and Estate Planning Issues Relating to Companion Animals, 74 U. Colo. L. Rev. 181, 198-199 (2003). *See also* David Favre, Living Property: A New Status for Animals Within the Legal System, 93 Marq. L. Rev. 1021 (2010); Tabby T. McLain, Adapting the Child's Best Interest Model to Custody Determinations of Companion Animals, 6 J. Animal L. 151 (2010); Christopher D. Seps, Treating Pets as Persons in Tort and Custody Disputes, 2010 U. Ill. L. Rev. 1339.

6. Bennett v. Bennett, 650 So. 2d 109, 111 (Fla. Dist. Ct. App. 1995).

7. *Id.*

8. Desanctis v. Pritchard, 803 A.2d 230, 233 (Pa. Super. Ct. 2002).

9. Whitmore v. Whitmore, 2011 Va. App. LEXIS 57 (unpublished opinion).

10. *Id.*

11. Note that the concept of vesting applies only to the employer's contribution; an employee is always vested with respect to his or her own contribution.

For a good discussion of pension plans, *see* Mary E. O'Connell, On the Fringe: Rethinking the Link Between Wages and Benefits, 67 Tul. L. Rev. 1421 (1993); Susan J. Prather, Characterization, Valuation, and Distribution of Pensions at Divorce, 15 J. Am. Acad. Matrimonial Law. 443 (1998).

12. Bratcher v. Bratcher, 26 S.W.3d 797, 801 (Ky. Ct. App. 2000).

13. *Id.* (citing Thomasian v. Thomasian, 556 A.2d 675, 681 (Md. Ct. Spec. App. 1989)) (internal citations omitted).

14. Arnold v. Arnold, Opinion No. 2003-NMCA-114 (N.M. Ct. App. 2003), http://pub.bna.com/fl/22765.htm.

15. *See generally* Joan M. Krauskopf, Classifying Marital and Separate Property: Combinations and Increase in Value of Separate Property, 89 W. Va. L. Rev. 996, 997 (1987). For discussion of specialized rules developed by some states regarding appreciation, *see* Suzanne Reynolds, Increases in Separate Property and the Evolving Marital Partnership, 24 Wake Forest L. Rev. 239, 291-299 (1989).

16. For a detailed analysis of the complexities of tracing, *see* Thomas J. Oldham, Tracing, Commingling, and Transmutation, 23 Fam. L.Q. 219 (1989).

17. *See* Aloysius A. Leopold, "Loss of Earning Capacity" Benefits in the Community Property Jurisdiction — How Do You Figure? 30 St. Mary's L.J. 367 (1999).

18. For a review of different approaches to the classification of the loss of earning capacity benefits, *see id.* at 385-397.

19. *See* Krauskopf, *supra* note 15, at 1008. For a discussion of this and other related considerations in relationship to the marital home, *see* Brett R. Turner, Unlikely Partners: The Marital Home and the Concept of Separate Property, 20 J. Am. Acad. Matrimonial Law. 69 (206). On transmutation generally, *see* Oldham, *supra* note 16, ch. 11.

20. For detail on valuation approaches, *see* The Handbook for Divorce Valuations (Robert E. Kleeman, Jr., et al. eds., 1999).

21. *See* Joan Williams, Do Wives Own Half? Winning for Wives After *Wendt*, 32 Conn. L. Rev. 249 (2000).

22. N.J. Rev. Stat. Sec. 2A:34-231.

23. This discussion is very general in nature. It does not address valuation issues, the different kinds of private pensions, or the connection between the two. Nor does it include consideration of Social Security benefits. For further information, *see* Stanley W. Welsh and Frank J. Hargrave, Social Security Benefits at Divorce: Avoiding Federal Preemption to Allow Equitable Division of Property at Divorce, 20 J. Am. Acad. Matrimonial Law. 285 (2007); Dylan A. Wilde, Obtaining an Equitable Distribution of Retirement Plans in a Divorce Action, 49 S.D. L. Rev. 141 (2003); Elizabeth Barker Brandt, Valuation, Allocation, and Distribution of Retirement Plans at Divorce: Where Are We?, 35 Fam. L.Q. 237 (2001). The following two articles focus on the timely issue of the distribution of military retirement benefits: Patricia K. Hinshaw, Navigating the Uniformed Services Former Spouses' Protection Act, 19 S.C. Law. 32 (2008), and Michael T. Flannery, Military Disability Election and the Distribution of Marital Property Upon Divorce, 56 Cath. U. L. Rev. 297 (2007).

24. Prior to the Retirement Equity Act (REA), pension funds could not be reached in a divorce because of ERISA's general anti-assignment rule, prohibiting the transfer of an employee's pension funds to a third party. The rules governing distribution of pension funds are complex and must be followed with great care in order for the QDRO to be effective. *See* Dodi Walker Gross, How to Ensure That a QDRO Qualifies Under the Detailed Tax and ERISA Requirements, 81 J. Taxn. 346 (1994).

25. I.R.C. §1041. *See generally* Craig D. Bell, Need-to-Know Divorce Tax Law for Legal Assistance Officers, 177 Mil. L. Rev. 213 (2003).

Chapter Nine

Jurisdiction

This chapter focuses on **jurisdiction**, which, stated broadly, refers to the authority of a court to hear and resolve cases. The question of jurisdiction must be carefully considered before a legal action is begun because lack of jurisdiction affects the availability and validity of court orders.

Jurisdiction:
The authority of a court to hear and resolve a case before it

Overview of Subject Matter and Personal Jurisdiction

Before looking at the jurisdictional issues that arise in divorce actions, it is important that you understand the basic concepts of subject matter jurisdiction and personal jurisdiction.

Subject Matter Jurisdiction

Subject matter jurisdiction refers to the authority of a court to hear a particular type of dispute. The subject matter jurisdiction of a court is generally established by statute. Some courts, such as a housing court or a juvenile court, are granted limited subject matter jurisdiction and can hear only certain kinds of cases. Other courts, such as a district court, are granted general subject matter jurisdiction and can hear a wide array of criminal and civil matters. In most states, exclusive subject matter jurisdiction over divorce actions—including all collateral issues such as support, property, and custody—is vested in a specialized court commonly known as *family court* or *family and probate court*.

In contrast to personal jurisdiction, which a party can voluntarily assent to (as discussed next), parties cannot confer subject matter jurisdiction on a court, and judgment that is rendered by a court that lacks subject matter jurisdiction is void.

Subject Matter Jurisdiction:
The authority of a court to hear a particular kind of case

Personal Jurisdiction

Personal Jurisdiction:
The authority of a court over a defendant

Personal jurisdiction refers to a court's ability to exercise authority over a defendant. The exercise of jurisdiction must conform to the requirements of the due process clause of the fourteenth amendment, which prohibits a state from "depriving any person of life, liberty, or property" without providing fair procedures, such as notice and the opportunity to be heard. The requirement of procedural fairness has also been interpreted to mean that a state may not exercise authority over a defendant who lacks a sufficient relationship with that state. Accordingly, considerations of personal jurisdiction are significant in cases involving parties who live in different states. To ensure that the court has personal jurisdiction over the defendant, the plaintiff can always file the action in the state where the defendant lives, but this is more expensive, time consuming, and inconvenient.

Consistent with the due process clause, states can acquire personal jurisdiction over a defendant based on domicile, minimum contacts, consent, or presence:

Domicile:
A person's permanent home; the place to which the person intends to return when away

1. *Domicile.* States have personal jurisdiction over all persons who are domiciled within its borders. Domicile means that the state is someone's permanent home — the place they leave from and return to. It is important to be aware of the distinction between "domicile" and "residence." A person may have several places of residence, such as a college dorm or one's family home, but only one domicile (one's permanent home).[1]

Minimum Contacts:
Enables a state to assert personal jurisdiction over a nonresident when he or she has a sufficiently developed relationship with that state

Long-Arm Statutes:
Spells out when a state may assert personal jurisdiction over a nonresident

2. *Minimum contacts.* A state may exercise personal jurisdiction over a nonresident defendant who has sufficient **minimum contacts** with the state such that it is not unfair to require him or her to return to the state and respond to a lawsuit there.

To implement this minimum contacts rule, most states have enacted what are known as **long-arm statutes**. These statutes generally specify the kinds of contacts that will give rise to personal jurisdiction and typically include the following contacts: transacting business within the state, owning property within the state, or committing a tortious act within the state. A few states have elected not to enumerate the qualifying contacts but instead employ statutory language to the effect that the state will permit the exercise of jurisdiction to the fullest extent possible under the due process clause.

A number of states have also enacted special long-arm provisions for use in family law cases. Here, the assertion of jurisdiction is often premised on the fact that the state was the marital domicile for a period of time preceding the filing of the divorce action. Other provisions are framed more broadly and tie the exercise of jurisdiction to the maintenance of an ongoing relationship with a person located in that state or to the payment of support; however, these contacts must be of a sufficient nature to satisfy the fairness requirements of the due process clause. Additionally, all states have enacted the Uniform Interstate Family Support Act (UIFSA), which contains a broad, long-arm provision for the assertion of jurisdiction over nonresident defendants in support matters.

3. *Consent.* A nonresident may consent to jurisdiction and thereby agree to submit himself or herself to the authority of the court.

4. *Presence.* A state can exercise personal jurisdiction over a nonresident who is physically present and personally served with a summons within that state.

Jurisdiction and the Divorce Action

Turning to the divorce action, jurisdictional concepts are best understood if examined in relationship to specific aspects of the proceeding, as different considerations come into play at different points in the process. Specifically, we will look at the jurisdictional standards that govern the dissolution of the marital relationship, the award of support, the distribution of property, and the determination of custody.

It thus goes without saying that in the course of your work as a paralegal, you must always be attuned to jurisdictional considerations and any relevant time periods within which jurisdiction must be asserted. If you are responsible for interviewing clients, it is essential that you inquire into the location of all parties, as this can have critical consequences for your client.

Does the Court Have Jurisdiction to Dissolve a Marriage?

Having just set out the importance of personal jurisdiction, we immediately bump up against the well-worn maxim that for every rule, there is an exception. In this instance, divorce provides the exception because in most, if not all, states, a court can dissolve a marriage even if it does not have personal jurisdiction over the defendant, if the plaintiff is domiciled in that state.

Thus, when it comes to divorce, it is the plaintiff's relationship with the "forum" state (the state in which the action is filed) that matters. The rationale for this domicile rule is captured by the following passage from a 1942 U.S. Supreme Court decision:

> Each state as a sovereign has a rightful and legitimate concern in the marital status of persons domiciled within its borders. The marriage

relation creates problems of large social importance. Protection of offspring, property interests, and the enforcement of marital responsibilities are but a few of the commanding problems in the field of domestic relations with which the state must deal. Thus it is plain that each state . . . can alter within its own borders the marriage status of the spouse domiciled there, even though the other spouse is absent.[2]

According to this reasoning, a relationship with the defendant is not necessary because states have an overriding interest in the marital status of persons living within their borders.[3]

If a spouse is not actually domiciled in a state but has gone there for the purpose of obtaining a divorce, the defendant-spouse may be able to attack the validity of the divorce judgment for lack of jurisdiction. This right is generally limited to a spouse who did not receive notice of the action and therefore did not have an opportunity to raise jurisdictional objections during the divorce proceeding.

Until recently, same-sex couples faced a unique access barrier to divorce in many of the states that restricted marriage to heterosexual couples. If a married same-sex couple was living in a marriage equality state at the time of divorce, then so long as the plaintiff was domiciled in that state, she or he would have access to the courts on the same basis as a heterosexual couple. However, if the plaintiff (or the couple) had moved to a state that did not recognize same-sex marriages in another state, the courts would most likely have refused to assume jurisdiction over the divorce, even if the domiciliary requirement had been met, based on the logic that to do so would have been tantamount to recognizing the marriage in violation of the state ban. However, this perplexing problem has been resolved by the Supreme Court's decision in Obergefell v. Hodges, as marriages between same-sex partners are a legal reality across the nation, thus eliminating this access barrier.

Does the Court Have Jurisdiction to Award Support?

As discussed previously, jurisdiction to dissolve a marriage is based on domicile—personal jurisdiction over the defendant is not required. However, the jurisdictional rule is different where spousal and child support is involved; a state must have personal jurisdiction over a defendant in order to adjudicate support rights. Accordingly, it is possible that a state would have the authority to dissolve a marriage but lack the authority to enter a support award. This is sometimes referred to as a **divisible divorce**.

This, however, is where long-arm statutes come into play. These statutes permit a state to assert its authority over a nonresident within

Divisible Divorce:
A divorce in which the court has jurisdiction to dissolve the marriage based on a party's domicile but cannot resolve support and property matters because it lacks personal jurisdiction over the defendant

the fairness requirements of the due process clause, and many states authorize the assertion of long-arm jurisdiction over a nonresident when that state had been the marital domicile of the parties. Often, this is a time-limited option, and personal jurisdiction will continue for only a fixed period of time, perhaps for a year or two, after the individual has left the state. Once this time period has run, the state loses its ability to assert personal jurisdiction over the defendant unless there are other independent qualifying bases.

In addition to state long-arm statutes, the UIFSA, which was discussed at length in Chapter 6, contains a long-arm provision that a state can use to acquire personal jurisdiction over a nonresident defendant to establish a spousal or child support order. Moreover, under the Act, this state will retain continuing exclusive jurisdiction to modify the order so long as the support obligor, the support obligee, or the child for whose benefit support is being paid continues to live in that state. In addition, in states that have adopted the 2001 amended version of UIFSA, the parties may consent to continued jurisdiction in this state even if everyone has moved out. UIFSA sets out the following eight grounds for the exercise of personal jurisdiction over a nonresident defendant:

1. The defendant is personally served within the state.
2. The defendant consents to jurisdiction.
3. The defendant at one time resided with the child in the state.
4. The defendant resided in the state at one time and provided "prenatal expenses or support for the child."
5. The child lives in a state as a result of the parent's "acts or directives."
6. The defendant "engaged in sexual intercourse in the state" that may have led to the child's conception.
7. The defendant "asserted paternity in the putative father registry."
8. Where there is any other basis for the state's exercise of jurisdiction.[4]

All of these jurisdictional grounds are available in child support cases, but only grounds one, two, and eight are available for the assertion of personal jurisdiction over a nonresident in spousal support cases.

Does the Court Have Jurisdiction to Divide Property?

The jurisdictional rules regarding property distribution are more complex than they are with respect to support and will be set out as a series of general principles:

1. As a foundational matter, jurisdiction is not premised upon domicile, as it is for the divorce itself.
2. If the court has personal jurisdiction over the defendant, it may effectuate a division of all property located within its borders.

In Rem Jurisdiction:
The authority of a court to resolve a case based on the presence of property within its borders

3. Even if a court lacks personal jurisdiction over a defendant, it may be able to effectuate a division of property based on its authority over property located within its borders. This is known as **in rem jurisdiction.** As a general rule, to satisfy due process requirements, in rem jurisdiction requires a connection between the underlying cause of action and the claims to the property—a connection that would be satisfied in the divorce context. (Some commentators have questioned the fairness of this rule, and we thus may see a gradual shift to a minimum contacts rule—as always, you should check the status of your state's jurisdictional requirements when it comes to dividing property in a divorce with a nonresident defendant.)

4. Even if it has personal jurisdiction over the defendant, a court cannot directly affect title to property that is located outside the state. However, it may be able to accomplish this result indirectly by ordering the defendant to convey title to the property. In short, based on its authority over the defendant, a court can require him or her to take actions that affect how the property is held, even though the court is unable to affect title directly.

Does the Court Have Jurisdiction to Determine Custody?

Traditionally, most states exercised jurisdiction over child custody matters based on the physical presence of the child within its borders. Although this rule usually meant that the court that granted the divorce had jurisdiction over the initial custody determination, it also served to encourage a dissatisfied spouse to remove his or her children to a new state in order to relitigate the issue in hope of a more favorable outcome. In addition to encouraging parental removals, this approach often resulted in conflicting decrees, creating an enforcement nightmare.

In 1968, prompted by this jurisdictional morass, the National Conference of Commissioners on Uniform State Laws (NCCUSL) approved the Uniform Child Custody Jurisdiction Act (UCCJA) in the hope that consistent jurisdictional standards would deter the removal or kidnapping of children, eliminate interstate jurisdictional competition, and prevent states from relitigating custody decisions from other states. All states have since adopted the UCCJA, although some states have modified the uniform provisions. In 1980, in the face of continued parental removals and interstate jurisdictional conflicts, Congress passed the Parental Kidnapping Prevention Act (PKPA)[5] to close some of the gaps left open by the UCCJA. In 1997, in light of ongoing jurisdictional complexities and inconsistencies, the NCCUSL adopted the Uniform Child Custody Jurisdiction and Enforcement Act (UCCJEA), which revises the UCCJA.[6] At present, the UCCJEA has been adopted in all states except Massachusetts. Where adopted, it replaces the UCCJA.

Interstate custody cases are among the most complex in the family law field and contain many traps for the unaware. This section will provide you with a basic overview of key jurisdictional rules; however, you should be aware that the Acts contain many other important rules, such as those pertaining to notice and disclosure, that are not addressed here. Moreover, the discussion does not cover the array of differences and potential conflicts among the three Acts, nor does it discuss other laws that might come into play in an interstate custody case, such as the full faith and credit provisions of the Violence Against Women Act (VAWA).[7] In light of these complexities, it is very important that when conducting a client interview, you elicit detailed information about the present and past locations of both parties and the children, as this can have important jurisdictional implications.

Jurisdictional Requirements Under the UCCJA and the UCCJEA

In this section, we consider the four jurisdictional bases for **initial custody determination** under the UCCJA and the UCCJEA: (1) home state, (2) significant connection, (3) emergency, and (4) last resort. We then look at when a state may assume modification jurisdiction under these Acts and the full faith and credit requirement of PKPA.[8] An important consideration underlying these Acts is that in contrast to the traditional approach, the mere physical presence of a child in a state is not sufficient to confer jurisdiction; in fact, with the exception of emergency jurisdiction, the physical presence of a child, although preferred, is not an essential prerequisite to a state's assumption of jurisdiction.

Initial Custody Determination:
The first custody decision in a case, as distinct from subsequent modifications

Initial Custody Determinations

Home State Jurisdiction.   A state that is or has been the child's home may assert **home state jurisdiction** over a custody dispute. A *home state* is the state in which a child has lived for six continuous months or, if younger than six months, has lived in from birth. Temporary absences from the state do not stop the running of the clock but are included in the time computation.

A state may exercise jurisdiction if it is the child's home state at the commencement of the custody proceeding, or if it was the child's home state within six months prior to the commencement of the proceeding. Once a state acquires "home state" status, it can retain that status for six months after the departure of the child so long as a parent or a parent substitute remains in that state.

Home State Jurisdiction:
Enables a state to assert jurisdiction over a custody dispute based on the fact that the child lives or had lived in that state for the six months prior to the initiation of the action, or for the child's lifetime

Significant Connection Jurisdiction.   A state may exercise **significant connection jurisdiction** in situations where it has a significant connection with the child and at least one contestant, and substantial evidence

Significant Connection Jurisdiction:
Permits a court to assert jurisdiction over a custody dispute based on the fact that a child and at least one contestant has a meaningful relationship with that state, and relevant evidence is available there; available under PKPA only when no state qualifies as the home state

is available in that state that is relevant to the merits of the custody determination.

Comparing the Relationship Between Home State and Significant Connection Jurisdictions in the UCCJA and the UCCJEA. Home state and significant connection jurisdictions are the most important jurisdictional bases. However, because the UCCJA does not expressly prioritize between them, it is possible for two states to claim jurisdiction at the same time. For example, let's assume that a couple who has been living in state Y separates. Dad moves to state X with the couple's daughter, who is 10 years old, and Mom remains in state Y. Eight months later, Dad files for divorce and seeks custody of the child. At this point, state Y has lost home state status, and state X has become the child's home state because she has lived there for the six months prior to the filing of the action. However, because the child has spent most of her life in state Y, it is possible that Y could claim significant connection jurisdiction. The UCCJEA closes this loophole (as does PKPA, which is discussed later in this chapter) by prioritizing home state jurisdiction. Under the UCCJEA, a state may exercise significant connection jurisdiction only where there is no home state, or the home state declines jurisdiction. Thus, in this example, state Y could not claim significant connection jurisdiction because X is now the home state, unless state X declines to hear the case.[9]

Emergency Jurisdiction: Permits a court to assert jurisdiction over a custody dispute when a child is physically present in the state and has been abandoned or needs immediate protection from abuse or neglect

Emergency Jurisdiction. A state may exercise emergency jurisdiction where the child is physically present in the state and has been abandoned or needs emergency protection from abuse or neglect. Although the child must be physically present, the endangerment need not have occurred within that state. Courts are generally cautious when proceeding under this section and will generally assume emergency jurisdiction only in "extraordinary circumstances." Also, most courts will assume emergency jurisdiction only on a temporary basis to stabilize the situation and will then refer the case back to the state with either home state or significant connection jurisdiction.

Comparing Emergency Jurisdiction in the UCCJA and the UCCJEA in Domestic Violence Cases. Although the UCCJA's emergency jurisdiction provision references harm to children, it is silent when it comes to spousal abuse. Accordingly, most courts have declined to exercise emergency jurisdiction in situations where a parent has fled to escape abuse in the absence of direct harm to the child, even though (as discussed in Chapter 6) bearing witness to violence can be devastating to children. Some states, however, either by statute or judicial decision, do take violence against a parent into account, such as where "one parent has been assaulted or terrorized by an intimate partner in the child's presence."[10] In contrast, under the UCCJEA, emergency jurisdiction has been broadened to include situations in which it is necessary in an emergency "to protect the child because the child, or a sibling or parent of the child, is subjected to or threatened with mistreatment or abuse."[11]

Last Resort Jurisdiction. Last, and in this case least, a state that does not meet the requirements of any other section may assume jurisdiction if no other state has or is willing to assume it, and it is in the best interest of the child for the state to do so. This **last resort jurisdiction** is subsidiary in nature to the others, and is rarely invoked. An example of when it might be used is when a child has moved around so frequently that no state qualifies as the home state or has a significant connection to the child.

Last Resort Jurisdiction: Enables a state to assert jurisdiction over a custody dispute when no other state has or is willing to assume jurisdiction, and it is in the best interest of the child to do so

Modification Jurisdiction

An important goal of the UCCJA was to limit the ability of states to modify custody determinations of other states to prevent the proliferation of potentially conflicting orders. Accordingly, under the Act, a state could modify the custody order of another state only if it appeared that the decree state no longer had jurisdiction and the new state could assert jurisdiction in accordance with the UCCJA.[12] This means that the initial decree state should have exclusive **modification jurisdiction**, sometimes referred to as **continuing jurisdiction**, until such time as it no longer can satisfy the jurisdictional requirements of the UCCJA.

Modification Jurisdiction: The authority of a court to modify a custody or support decree

Continuing Jurisdiction: The continuation of the initial decree state's authority to modify a decree to the exclusion of other states

However, as with initial determination jurisdiction, it is possible that two states could simultaneously assert modification jurisdiction. For example, let's say that state A makes an initial determination giving custody to Mom, with visitation rights to Dad. Mom then moves to state B with the child, but the child visits Dad regularly in state A. What happens if Dad files a modification action in state A ten months after Mom's departure? At this point in time, home state status has shifted to state B, but state A still has a connection to the child and one parent and could thus claim significant connection jurisdiction. But if Mom then filed a modification action in state B, that court could decide that A's connection is not significant enough to retain authority over the case and that modification jurisdiction had shifted to state B, the child's present home state.

As with the exercise of initial custody jurisdiction, the UCCJEA has addressed this problem (as does PKPA) by providing for continuing, exclusive modification jurisdiction in the initial state (subject to the emergency jurisdiction exception) until one of two determinations are made: (1) the initial state determines that it no longer has jurisdiction because it lacks a significant connection to the case and substantial evidence is no longer available there, or (2) it is established that neither the child nor either parent still lives there.[13] Returning to our example, under the UCCJEA, state B could not modify the initial order based on its status as the home state unless state A first determined that it no longer had a significant connection to the case. Given the facts, this is unlikely, as the dad still lives there, the child left the state only ten months earlier, and the child still visits there on a regular basis.

Declining Jurisdiction

In addition to determining when a state may properly assume jurisdiction over a custody dispute, the UCCJA and the UCCJEA also encourage states to decline jurisdiction under certain circumstances. Based on the doctrine of *forum non conveniens*, states are encouraged to decline jurisdiction if it is an inconvenient forum and another state is in a better position to hear the case. Further, based on the "clean hands" doctrine, states are urged to refuse jurisdiction where the petitioner has engaged in wrongful conduct, such as improperly removing a child from the home state. However, a parent who has fled a state with a child for good cause, such as to escape from violence, should not be penalized by this provision. Although not explicit in the UCCJA, the UCCJEA makes clear that so long as the emergency jurisdiction requirements are met, a state may not decline jurisdiction based on the conduct of the petitioner.[14]

Jurisdictional Requirements of PKPA

As we have seen, the UCCJA did not resolve the problem of interstate jurisdictional conflicts. Accordingly, in 1980, Congress enacted the PKPA, which requires states to give full faith and credit to custody decrees of other states if they conform to PKPA's jurisdictional requirements. Thus, states must enforce and cannot modify conforming decrees from other states unless certain conditions (discussed next) are met. Like the UCCJA and the UCCJEA, PKPA has four jurisdictional bases: home state, significant connection, emergency, and last resort. However, as with the UCCJEA, PKPA prioritizes home state jurisdiction. Accordingly, for a decree to be enforceable under PKPA, it can assume significant connection jurisdiction only if no other state qualifies as the home state; the two are not alternative jurisdictional bases. If a state does assume jurisdiction based on its connection with the case where another state qualifies as the home state, the decree will not be entitled to interstate recognition in other states. PKPA also vests exclusive, continuing jurisdiction in the initial state so long as a parent or the child remains there, and the state has jurisdiction under its own laws. So long as this state has jurisdiction, no other state may modify its decree. Modification jurisdiction shifts only when everyone has moved away from the decree state (or it declines jurisdiction) and another state can satisfy PKPA's jurisdictional requirement.

To understand how PKPA interacts with the UCCJA, let's return to our modification fact pattern. As set out previously, Mom received custody in state A and then moved to state B with the child, while Dad remained in state A. Under the UCCJA, it is almost certain that at some point, modification jurisdiction would shift to state B as either the new home state or the significant connection state. However, under PKPA, state A has continuing jurisdiction so long as Dad continues to live there. This means that if state B modified the decree, it would not be entitled to interstate recognition even though the requirements of the UCCJA were met. Again, given that the UCCJEA also vests continuing, exclusive jurisdiction in the home state, this problem is not likely to arise under the UCCJEA.

In sum, the hope is that PKPA (and now also the UCCJEA), by giving priority to the home state and vesting continuing jurisdiction in a single state, will eliminate the final vestiges of interstate competition in the custody arena. However, due to the complex legal and factual nature of these cases, true interstate harmony is unlikely in the foreseeable future.

International Child Abduction

In addition to the complex jurisdictional issues that are raised by custody disputes involving two or more states, the process of globalization with the corresponding increase in transnational migration makes it more likely that disputes over children will be played out on the global stage. In this regard, many countries have been particularly concerned about the importance of establishing common legal standards for the handling of cases in which a parent is charged with the wrongful removal of a child to another country, as the return process has historically been quite haphazard. Accordingly, in 1980, the Hague Conference on Private International Law (an intergovernmental organization whose primary purpose is "to work for the progressive unification of the rules of private international law") approved a multilateral treaty, known as the Hague Convention on the Civil Aspects of International Child Abduction. The Abduction Convention "seeks to protect children from the harmful effects of abduction and retention across international boundaries by providing a procedure to bring about their prompt return."[15]

Similar to PKPA and the UCCJEA, the Abduction Convention seeks to deter parents from removing a child to another jurisdiction with the hope of obtaining a more favorable custody outcome. To this end, for the purpose of determining custody, jurisdictional priority is vested in the country that is a child's "habitual residence"—a concept that is doctrinally similar to that of home state jurisdiction.

Accordingly, in brief, if a parent removes a child to another country in violation of the "left-behind" parent's custodial rights, the "left-behind" parent can file a legal action seeking the return of the child. If the court determines that the child was removed from a country that is his or her place of "habitual residence," it can order the prompt return of the child unless the parent who took the child can justify the removal based on the limited exceptions provided in the Convention, such as that the "left-behind" parent consented to the removal, or that the child "objects to being returned and has attained an age and degree of maturity at which it is appropriate to take account of its views." A parent may also seek to establish that "there is a grave risk that his or her return would expose the child to physical or psychological harm or otherwise place the child in an intolerable situation."[16]

It is important to be aware that a hearing held pursuant to the Abduction Convention is intended to address the narrow question of whether the removal was wrongful and thus whether the child should be returned home. Under the terms of the Convention, the court making this determination is precluded from deciding the merits of the custody case unless it determines that the removal was not wrongful and that the child may remain in that country.

Chapter Summary

Broadly stated, *jurisdiction* refers to the authority of a court to hear a case and render a binding decree. More specifically, *subject matter jurisdiction* refers to the authority of a court to hear specific types of cases, while *personal jurisdiction* refers to a court's authority over a defendant. Personal jurisdiction can be based on domicile, minimum contacts, consent, or physical presence. Long-arm statutes allow states to assert personal jurisdiction over nonresident defendants who have sufficient minimum contacts with the forum state. The assertion of personal jurisdiction must satisfy the fairness requirement of the due process clause.

Jurisdiction to dissolve the marriage is usually based on domicile; personal jurisdiction over the defendant is not required. However, a court cannot order a defendant to pay support if it does not have personal jurisdiction over him or her. Personal jurisdiction may be asserted over a nonresident through the long-arm provisions of UIFSA or a state jurisdictional statute. Where property is concerned, a distribution can be effectuated based either on personal jurisdiction over the defendant or on the court's in rem authority over property located within its borders.

Jurisdiction over child custody disputes is determined by the UCCJA, the UCCJEA, and PKPA. These Acts respond to the earlier "physical presence" rule, which encouraged parental abductions and created enforcement nightmares. These Acts establish four jurisdictional bases for when a state may assert jurisdiction over a custody dispute: home state, significant connection, emergency, and last resort. The UCCJA does not prioritize among these bases; thus, it is possible for two states to claim authority over a case at the same time; however, both PKPA and the UCCJEA prioritize home state jurisdiction. The UCCJEA and PKPA vest continuing exclusive jurisdiction in the home state until certain conditions are met; PKPA also requires states to give full faith and credit to conforming custody decrees from other states. In the global arena, the Hague Convention on the Civil Aspects of International Child Abduction likewise seeks to deter the wrongful removal of children and to ensure their prompt return to their place of "habitual residence," absent extenuating circumstances.

Key Terms

Jurisdiction	Long-Arm Statutes	Home State	Last Resort
Subject Matter	Divisible Divorce	Jurisdiction	Jurisdiction
Jurisdiction	In Rem	Significant	Modification
Personal Jurisdiction	Jurisdiction	Connection	Jurisdiction
Domicile	Initial Custody	Jurisdiction	Continuing
Minimum Contacts	Determinations	Emergency Jurisdiction	Jurisdiction

Review Questions

1. Broadly defined, what is jurisdiction?
2. What is subject matter jurisdiction?
3. Explain the concept of personal jurisdiction. What are the ways in which a court can obtain personal jurisdiction over a defendant?
4. What is a long-arm statute?
5. What is the jurisdictional basis for dissolving a marriage?
6. What criticisms have been raised about this approach?
7. What step might a spouse in a same-sex marriage have to take in order to file a divorce if he or she lives in a state that does not recognize the marriage?
8. Explain the jurisdictional role of UIFSA in support cases.

9. What is meant by the term "divisible divorce"?
10. Explain the jurisdictional concepts that are relevant to the distribution of property.
11. Traditionally, what has been the basis for the exercise of jurisdiction over a child custody dispute? What problems did this create?
12. What is the UCCJA? The UCCJEA? PKPA? Why were these laws enacted?
13. What is a home state? When may a state assert home state jurisdiction?
14. What is significant connection jurisdiction?
15. Explain how two states could assert initial jurisdiction at the same time under the UCCJA.
16. What is emergency jurisdiction?
17. What is last resort jurisdiction?
18. What provision does the UCCJEA make for domestic violence victims?
19. Under what circumstances does the UCCJEA encourage states to decline jurisdiction?
20. Under PKPA, when must a state enforce the decree of another state?
21. Under PKPA, what is the relationship of home state and significant connection jurisdiction? What would be the result if a state asserted significant connection jurisdiction when another state qualified as the home state?
22. Under PKPA, when can a state modify the decree of another state?
23. Under PKPA, at what point does the continuing jurisdiction of the decree state terminate?
24. What would be the result if a new state modified a decree where the decree state had continuing jurisdiction?
25. What is the Hague Convention on the Civil Aspects of International Child Abduction?
26. Pursuant to the Convention, on what grounds can a parent try to justify the removal of a child from his or her place of "habitual residence"?

Discussion Questions

1. PKPA's continuing jurisdiction rule has been criticized as favoring stability over the needs of children because it can vest exclusive jurisdiction in a state that has lost any meaningful relationship with the child. Do you think the Act has gone too far? Should a state with no present connection with a child have modification jurisdiction? How do you accommodate the goals of flexibility and predictability?

2. Do you think the emergency jurisdiction provision of the UCCJEA might encourage parents to flee with children in the absence of a genuine emergency situation in order to try to gain an advantage in a custody dispute? Is there another way to protect the needs of victims of violence?

Assignments

1. Using the appropriate digest, find all the cases from your state that involve an interstate custody dispute. Now choose two of the cases and analyze how the court made its decision. In the course of your analysis, refer back to the UCCJA or the UCCJEA and make sure that you both understand and discuss all provisions relevant to the court's analysis in each case.
2. Locate UIFSA as adopted by your state. Now, locate any additional long-arm statutes that can be used in support cases in your state. Review the circumstances under which long-arm jurisdiction can be asserted and determine if they add anything to the UIFSA grounds.
3. Assume that a client has come to your firm's office seeking a divorce. All you know at this point is that she and her husband and their children have moved frequently over the past five years, and she has recently moved to your state with the children. In preparation for the interview, an attorney in your office has asked you to develop some questions in advance so that all facts bearing on jurisdiction will be covered. In developing the questions, make sure that you think about all aspects of the case.

Endnotes

1. Although many statutes use the term "residence," virtually all courts have interpreted this to mean "domicile." Rhonda Wasserman, Divorce and Domicile: Time to Sever the Note, 39 Wm. & Mary L. Rev. 1, 23 (1997).

2. Williams v. North Carolina, 317 U.S. 287, 298-299 (1942).

3. Some commentators have suggested that this domicile rule is out of keeping with the modern jurisdictional emphasis on the relationship of the defendant to the adjudicating state and recommend that a minimum contacts standard be used in divorce cases, as it is in other civil actions. However, an important concern is that such a shift could prevent domestic violence victims from being able to file for divorce in a state to which they have fled to escape abuse because the minimum contacts requirement would not be satisfied unless the defendant happened to have a qualifying relationship with that state. Accordingly, the victim would be forced to return to her prior home state (or if the defendant had moved, to his new home state) in order to file a divorce.

4. UIFSA §201(1)-(8) (2001). The text of this Act can be found at http://www.law.upenn.edu/bll/ulc/ulc_frame.htm and clicking on the link to the Uniform Interstate Family Support Act, Final Act 2001 (accessed Oct. 11, 2004).

5. 28 U.S.C. §1738A (1994).

6. The texts of the UCCJA and the UCCJEA can be found on the University of Pennsylvania Law School's website, which is the official site for the NCCUSL. The address is http://www.law.upenn.edu/bll/ulc/ulc.htm.

The following articles provide more detail and a comparative discussion of the UCCJA and the UCCJEA. See Deborah M. Goelman, Shelter from the Storm: Using Jurisdictional Statutes to Protect Victims of Domestic Violence After the Violence Against Women Act of 2000, 13 Colum. J. Gender & L. 101 (2004) (this article also discusses PKPA); Joan Zorza, The UCCJEA: What Is It and How Does It Affect Battered Women in Child-Custody Disputes? 27 Fordham Urb. L.J. 909 (2000); Russell M. Coombs, Child Custody and Visitation by Non-parents Under the New Uniform Child Custody Jurisdiction and Enforcement Act: A Rerun of Seize-and-Run, 16 J. Am. Acad. Matrimonial Law. 1 (1999); Kelly Gaines Stoner, The Uniform Child Custody Jurisdiction and Enforcement Act (UCCJEA) — A Metamorphosis of the Uniform Child Custody Jurisdiction Act (UCCJA), 75 N.D. L. Rev. 301 (1999) (briefly discusses jurisdictional issues with respect to custody orders issued by Indian tribal courts); Patricia M. Hoff, The ABC's of the UCCJEA: Interstate Child Custody Practices Under the New Act, 32 Fam.

L.Q. 267 (1998). The following texts provide a thorough comparison of PKPA and the UCCJA. See Linda M. DeMelis, Interstate Child Custody and the Parental Kidnapping Prevention Act: The Continuing Search for a National Standard, 45 Hastings L.J. 1329 (1994); Ann B. Goldstein, The Tragedy of the Interstate Child: A Critical Reexamination of the Uniform Child Custody Act and the Parental Kidnapping Prevention Act, 25 U.C. Davis L. Rev. 845 (1992); Russell M. Coombs, Interstate Child Custody: Jurisdiction, Recognition, and Enforcement, 66 Minn. L. Rev. 711 (1982).

7. You should be aware that other laws come into play if the child who is the subject of the custody dispute is a Native American or if the conflict involves more than one country. In the former situation, reference must also be made to the Indian Child Welfare Act of 1978, 25 U.S.C. §§1901 et seq., the Indian Civil Rights Act of 1968, 25 U.S.C. §§1301 et seq., and the appropriate Tribal Code. Other laws also may come into play. International custody disputes are discussed in the final section of this chapter.

Although the focus here is on custody disputes that arise in the context of divorce actions, the UCCJA, UCCJEA, and PKPA pertain to a range of child custody disputes, including, for example, guardianship proceedings and child placement disputes.

8. See UCCJEA §201, available at http://www.uniformlaws.org/ (accessed Oct. 7, 2012).

9. UCCJEA §201.

10. Goelman, supra note 7, at 122-123.

11. UCCJEA §204(a).

12. Id. §14.

13. UCCJEA §201.2.

14. Id. §208(a).

15. http://www.hcch.net/ (accessed Aug. 14, 2012). For further detail, see Noah L. Browne, Relevance and Fairness: Protecting the Rights of Domestic Violence Victims and Left-Behind Fathers Under the Hague Convention on International Child Abduction, 60 Duke L.J. 1193 (2011), and Merle H. Weiner, Half-Truths, Mistakes, and Embarrassments: The United States Goes to the Fifth Meeting of the Special Commission to Review the Operation of the Hague Convention on the Civil Aspects of International Child Abduction, 2008 Utah L. Rev. 221.

16. Article 13, Hague Convention on the Civil Aspects of International Child Abduction, http://www.hcch.net/ (accessed Aug. 14, 2012). This latter exception is most commonly invoked by women who have fled to another country in order to escape an abusive partner.

Chapter Ten

The Divorce Process

In this chapter, we look at how a divorce case makes its way through the legal system. We begin with the initial client interview and move through each successive stage of the process, from the filing of the action through postjudgment procedures. As we progress, we look at the role that paralegals play in the preparation of a case and at the skills they need. We also look at some important ethical considerations.

The Initial Client Interview

We begin with the initial client interview. At this meeting, detailed information about the client's situation is obtained; of equal importance, the interview establishes the foundation for the office's relationship with the client. One important goal is to develop a sense of mutual trust and purpose between the interviewer and the client.

Good interviews do not just happen; they require sensitivity and skill. Unfortunately, many legal professionals do not give much thought to client interviewing, perhaps because it does not appear to require specialized legal skills and knowledge. However, a poorly conducted interview can have long-term repercussions. A client who leaves a law office feeling disrespected or unheard may not develop the trust and confidence essential to a good working relationship. As a result, he or she may be reluctant to fully disclose all relevant information, particularly if it is of a sensitive or potentially damaging nature.

It is important to be attuned to the role that culture plays in the communication process, as the failure to do so can lead to misunderstandings with potentially serious consequences. In a powerful example of this dynamic, sociolinguist Diane Eades describes how differences in cultural approaches to seeking information played a major role in the conviction of an Australian Aboriginal woman for killing her abusive husband. Using standard interviewing techniques, which are based on the assumption that direct questions are the best way to elicit information, the woman's attorneys had been unsuccessful in eliciting her story, which included a horrific history of violence, from her. As Eades explains, when "Aboriginal people want to find out what they consider to be significant or . . . personal information, they do not use direct questions. . . . People volunteer some of their own information, hinting about what they are trying to find out. Information is sought out as part of a two-way exchange."[1] Moreover, personal information is not generally shared in the absence of a developed, trusting relationship. Called in as a sociolinguistic expert in the appeal, Eades concluded that it would have been extremely difficult for the defendant to share highly personal information in the context of a formal interview with a stranger. This is a dramatic example of the failure of cultural sensitivity, but it is an important reminder of how cultural differences (as well as other differences, including class and educational backgrounds) can lead to communication difficulties between clients and legal professionals.

Another important consideration in conducting effective interviews is understanding the emotional impact of divorce. Clients going through a divorce frequently enter a law office with intense feelings and emotional needs that cannot be ignored. Before we look at the interview process, we briefly consider the emotional framework within which divorce interviews often take place.

The Emotional Context

The breakup of a marriage can wreak emotional havoc in a person's life. Profound feelings of jealousy, anger, hopelessness, and despair are often unleashed. The process of divorce has been described as the emotional opposite of falling in love, generating powerful feelings of hate and rage rather than of intense pleasure.[2] A person going through a divorce may feel as if he or she has failed in a central aspect of life, and thus may be struggling with acute feelings of worthlessness. He or she is likely to go through many emotional stages: "Divorce is best conceptualized as a series of transitional life experiences rather than a single discrete event. Therefore, . . . the impact of divorce on family members will vary with the point in the transition process."[3]

Many of the clients you interview are thus likely to be experiencing overwhelming and constantly shifting emotions. This can make your task difficult, but it is important to remain sensitive to what the client may be going through. If clients are going to trust you, they need to feel that their well-being matters. The failure to acknowledge a client's emotional needs can also interfere with his or her ability to move on to other topics, whereas the acknowledgment of these feelings can facilitate this process.

Providing emotional support is particularly important in the divorce context where, as noted previously, individuals often experience a diminished sense of self-worth. Moreover, divorce often disrupts a person's social support system. Friends and family may disapprove of the marital split, feel loyalty to the other spouse, be uncomfortable with the intensity of feeling, or fear that "another person's divorce will illuminate the cracks in their own relationships."[4]

However, as important as providing support is, you also need to be aware of the limitations of your role. Your job is not to help the client analyze or resolve his or her feelings, although the client may on some level expect you to do this. You are not the client's friend or therapist, and you should be careful not to take on these roles. You should be attuned to when a referral to a mental health professional might be appropriate. Before bringing up the possibility of a referral with a client, be sure that you know what the policy of your office is. It may be that this responsibility is entrusted to the supervising attorney.

Conducting the Client Interview

The Role of the Paralegal

In many offices, paralegals are responsible for conducting the initial interview. In other offices, attorneys conduct them, while in others, the two work as a team. Also, within a single office, the practice might vary based on the nature, sensitivity, and complexity of the case. Regardless of who conducts the interview, it is important, if possible, that the client meet both the attorney and paralegal who will be working on the case. This personalizes the process and helps establish rapport and trust.

Ethical Considerations

When working with clients, it is important to be aware of the ethical rules that define the parameters of the professional relationship.[5] Interviews and all other contact must conform to ethical requirements. Accordingly, before focusing on the client interview, we consider the ethical framework within which paralegals operate. We then focus on the rules regarding the unauthorized practice of law and client confidentiality because these bear most directly on the paralegal-client relationship.

The Ethical Framework

All states have a code of ethics that is binding on attorneys. These codes are not directly binding on paralegals, but paralegals are expected to adhere to them, and noncompliance may result in a disciplinary action against the attorney for whom the paralegal works. These codes are promulgated by the highest court in each state, and most are modeled after the American Bar Association's (ABA) Model Rules of Professional Conduct.

The codes contain disciplinary sanctions for ethical violations. The most serious sanction is disbarment. In many states, the code of ethics has been supplemented by statutes that impose civil or criminal penalties for certain unethical acts, such as the unauthorized practice of law.

Many states now have guidelines in place to assist attorneys in working effectively with paralegals, and some states specifically require that "attorneys take affirmative steps to educate legal assistants about the attorney's ethical obligations and to ensure their compliance."[6]

The two major national paralegal organizations, the National Federation of Paralegal Associations and the National Association of Legal Assistants, both have promulgated ethical codes that are binding on paralegals, as have some local and regional paralegal associations. Sanctions, including removal from membership, may be imposed for ethical violations. These codes do not carry the same weight as those for attorneys do, both because they are not court-promulgated and because paralegals are not presently state licensed and thus cannot be barred from practice as can an attorney.[7]

Also relevant when considering standards of conduct is the fact that, like attorneys, paralegals can be sued for malpractice. Although malpractice actions extend well beyond ethical breaches, the failure to conform to expected standards of behavior can play a role in these suits.

Specific Practices

The Unauthorized Practice of Law. All states limit the practice of law to licensed attorneys, but determining what is meant by the term "practice of law" is not always easy. Certain conduct, such as signing court pleadings, conducting depositions, or representing a client in court, are considered to be the practice of law. But even here, there are some exceptions. For example, some states allow paralegals to appear in court for an attorney on uncontested matters, and many allow paralegals to serve as advocates in domestic violence cases. Paralegals also are allowed to represent clients before many state and federal administrative agencies.[8]

The giving of legal advice is also regarded as the practice of law; however, the definition of this term is imprecise. At a minimum, it includes independently advising a client about her or his legal rights, a potential course of action, and the predicting of legal outcomes. Thus, it is clear that advising a client as to what kind of divorce should be filed is the giving of legal advice—but what about explaining basic statutory options such as the difference between a fault and a no-fault divorce? Some would classify this as legal information, which a paralegal could disseminate, while others would classify it as advice. Although a paralegal cannot provide legal advice independently, he or she can serve as a conduit between the attorney and client, so long as it is made clear to the client that the advice is from the attorney and not from the paralegal.

Maintaining the appropriate boundaries can be difficult. Clients are often vulnerable and without reliable support, and may implore you to tell them what to do. This can be hard to resist. It is flattering, and you are likely to be moved by the client's situation and want very much to help. But no matter how difficult, it is important to work within the existing ethical framework and not be pulled into doing more than is appropriate.

Client Confidentiality.   In working with clients, you must always be aware of your ethical responsibility to maintain strict client **confidentiality**. The duty to maintain client confidences is at the heart of the attorney-client relationship and is also binding on paralegals. Without the assurance of confidentiality, a client may be reluctant to provide all of the information that is needed to thoroughly prepare a case, especially if it is of a sensitive, embarrassing, or potentially damaging nature. The client may worry that it will be disclosed to the opposing side or to other third parties. Accordingly, clients should be told at the outset of the interview that their communications with the office are strictly confidential. If you sense a client is struggling with whether to tell you something, it can be helpful to remind him or her that disclosures are confidential.

You should also be aware that there may be limited exceptions to the confidentiality rule, such as where a client discloses that he or she is planning to commit a serious crime or where there is good cause to believe that the client is harming his or her children. Depending on the situation and the state you are in, disclosure may be discretionary or it may be required, such as where a child protective law requires all persons who believe a child is being abused or neglected to file a report with a state's child protective agency (see Chapter 13). A decision to disclose should never be made lightly, as it is a clear exception to the overriding duty to maintain client confidentiality. As a paralegal, you should never act on your own in this regard. You should review the situation with the supervising attorney who may well be the one who is ultimately responsible for the disclosure decision.

Confidentiality:
An ethical rule prohibiting attorneys and persons working with them from disclosing client information, except under limited circumstances

Developing Good Listening Skills

The manner in which you listen to clients is vital because it signals whether you are simply going through the motions or are really paying attention to what is being said. If a client senses that you are engaged, he or she is likely to open up more because people are generally more comfortable when they sense their listener is responsive to what they are saying.

Nonverbal Communication. In thinking about how you listen to someone, it is important to recognize that much is communicated nonverbally. Direct eye contact signals that you are present and engaged. It also enables you to pick up nonverbal clues from the client that might otherwise be missed.

Likewise, your body position is important. Leaning forward toward the client indicates involvement. A somewhat relaxed posture tends to reduce the distance between the interviewer and interviewee. In contrast, leaning back in a chair with legs up on a desk can signal a lack of focused attention and involvement. This position also can be intimidating to a client because it tends to enhance the status of the interviewer.[9]

Active Listening:
An engaged way of listening, involving reflection back of informational and emotional content

Active Listening. Through a technique known as **active listening**, you can let a client know that you are really hearing what is being said. Active listening involves the use of verbal responses that reflect back to the client the informational or emotional content of what has been said.

With respect to the reflection of informational content, you should occasionally repeat back to the client some of the key information he or she has given you. This makes it clear that you have heard what has been said and have not been daydreaming about the upcoming weekend. It also helps ensure the accuracy of your information gathering because it gives the client the opportunity to correct any misunderstandings.

This should not become a mechanical process, and you should not break the flow of the story. A good time to reflect back is when the client has come to a logical break in the narrative. Be careful, however, that you do not begin to sound like a parrot, mindlessly repeating back what it has heard.

With respect to the reflection of emotional content, you should occasionally respond to what the client says she or he is going through on an emotional level. This acknowledges that you are aware of the client's emotional needs and that it is acceptable for him or her to express them. Although it may be tempting to share your personal experiences as a way of showing the client that you can understand what he or she is going through, these kinds of disclosures should be avoided. Although it is important to be supportive, you should never lose track of the fact that this is a professional relationship.

To illustrate the technique of active listening, let's assume that you are interviewing a client named Carl Johnson and that you are beginning the narrative phase of the interview. (See the discussion on the narrative phase next.) You have asked him, "Why don't you tell me something about your marriage?" and he has responded as follows:

> Well, my wife and I have been married for 15 years. We met in college—she was my first true love, and has remained my only love

during all these years. We have had a few rocky patches. My mother died right after our daughter was born. I became depressed. I had been very close to both my parents and had already lost my dad.

My wife felt I withdrew from her and the baby. I denied it at the time, but in retrospect, I realize she was right. In any event, I thought we had a loving marriage.

Well, a few years ago, my wife seemed more remote. She lost interest in sex and, well, things just seemed different. At first I attributed it to the pressure we were under. My business had gone under, I was looking for work, we had our daughter, my wife was working full time, and I was still struggling with depression.

We were also threatened with foreclosure proceedings, although we were able to save the house by borrowing money from her parents. Since then, they haven't let me forget that if I had been a proper husband, able to hold down a decent job, my family would not have been in that predicament. I also think they blame me for the fact that their daughter works so hard, but they don't understand that she loves her job.

Anyway, I gradually began to get suspicious that something else was going on. My wife began to have more night meetings, a few times when I answered the phone the person at the other end hung up — all the classic signs. For a while she denied that anything was going on, but finally, about a month ago she admitted that she had been seeing someone in her office. I asked her to break it off, but she said she couldn't promise to do that and needed some time to work things out. Well, that was it. I was and still am totally destroyed. It's embarrassing to admit, but she is the only woman I have ever had sex with. As far as I am concerned, the marriage is over.

This is probably a logical point to interject briefly. To reflect the emotional content, you might simply say something like: "I can see why you are devastated. This must be a very difficult time for you." You want to avoid statements like, "I know what you are going through, I remember what it was like when my husband walked out on me." This may seem obvious, but, in the intensity of the moment, the temptation to support a client in this manner can be hard to resist.

To reflect the informational content, you might say something like:

I'd like to take a minute to make sure I understand what you have just told me; please let me know if anything I say is inaccurate.

You and your wife have been married for 15 years, and despite a few rough times, you would characterize your relationship as solid. You have one child.

You've struggled with depression, particularly after the death of your mother. Recently, your wife has acknowledged she is having an affair and is not sure what she wants to do. As a result, you have decided your marriage is over.

The Interview Itself: A Three-Stage Approach

It is useful to think of the interview as having the following three distinct stages:

1. *Opening stage*: establishes the parameters of the interview and creates an atmosphere of trust
2. *Information-gathering stage*: elicits the client's basic story (narrative phase) and fills in the key details with questions (focused phase)
3. *Wrapping up or disengaging phase*: concludes the interview

This three-stage approach should not be followed mechanistically. Each person you interview is unique, and you need to accommodate a range of expressive styles. Some clients may respond only to focused questions, while others, at least initially, will be so overwhelmed that they will not respond to focused questions. They may need to tell you their story over and over in their own manner and sequence. This human dimension is the great challenge that no book can fully prepare you for.

In the following sections, we will look at each stage of the interview process, using the interview with Mr. Johnson to demonstrate various points. The model presented here assumes that a preprinted form is not being used for anything more than obtaining the basic factual information needed to complete a divorce complaint — such as the place and date of the marriage, the date last lived together, and the names and birthdates of the marital children — although some offices do use forms to obtain comprehensive client information.

Stage 1: Establishing the Parameters and Creating an Atmosphere of Trust.   When a client first comes to a law office, it is important to realize that he or she is probably nervous. Engaging in some preliminary chit-chat can help put a client at ease. For example, you might inquire whether he or she found the office without difficulty, whether it is still snowing, or the like. It is also a nice gesture to offer a cup of coffee or tea.

At the beginning, you should explain who you are and what role you will play. Let's assume that Mr. Johnson has just entered your office. To begin the interview, you might say something like the following:

> Hi, Mr. Johnson, my name is Elaine Chin. I am the family law paralegal who will be working on your case with Attorney Jane Martin. I am going to be interviewing you today. Afterward, Attorney Martin and I will meet to review the information and begin preparing your case. If Ms. Martin returns from court before we are finished with the interview, I will introduce you to her.

You should then inform the client that everything he or she tells you will be held in strict confidence, and explain what will take place during the interview. Following is an example of what this might sound like:

> Mr. Johnson, I am going to begin by asking you some very basic questions so I'm sure to get all the information that is asked for on the court forms. I will use our standard questionnaire for this.
>
> Afterward, I'll ask you to tell me about your situation and what you are thinking about doing at this stage. During the course of the interview, I will take some notes so I'm sure to remember everything you tell me.
>
> Also, you should know that everything you tell me is strictly confidential within this office. You do not need to worry that somehow your wife or her attorney will find out about what you tell us.
>
> Once I have a complete picture of your situation, we'll be through for the day. But, before you go, I'll tell you what you can expect and what you need to begin doing, such as collecting necessary papers.
>
> Do you have any questions before we begin?

At this point, the client knows who you are, what to expect, and that communications are confidential. This establishes a solid foundation for the interview itself.

Stage 2: Obtaining Information.   Where possible, it is best to gather information in two phases. In the first phase, the client should be encouraged to tell his or her story. In the second phase, the interviewer can complete the inquiry by asking focused questions. This is sometimes referred to as a "funneling" process because the questions begin broadly and then gradually become narrower.

Eliciting the Client Narrative.   In the first phase of information gathering, the emphasis is on having the client tell his or her story. This is done by asking open-ended questions that elicit a narrative rather than a focused response. In using open-ended questions, the interviewer loses some control over the process because the client shapes the telling of the story. However, this approach respects the fact that it is the client's problem and acknowledges that "the client is an important, essential resource in the information gathering process."[10] Open-ended questions can be either general or topic-specific. By asking topic-specific questions, the interviewer focuses the field of inquiry while still calling for a narrative response.

By way of example, let's return to Mr. Johnson. As set out previously, the initial question to him was, "Why don't you tell me something about your marriage?" and in answering, he mentioned he has a child. A logical follow-up question might be, "Why don't you tell me about your child?"

This question is topic-specific but is still open-ended because it asks for a narrative response. Let's assume that he gives the following answer:

> Well, Sara is our only child. She's seven and is in the second grade. She's a terrific kid, I know all parents say that, but she really is special. She does real well in school, has a lot of friends, and loves sports.
>
> Lately, though, she seems to be having a bit of a hard time. I've tried to talk to her about it, but sometimes she just doesn't seem to want to talk much to me. My wife says it's because I didn't bond with her as a baby, but I think she's going through something now, maybe with all this marriage stuff. I'm sure it's nothing serious.
>
> Her last report card was real good, but her teacher says that Sara has been kind of withdrawn at school. I am very worried about how she'll react to the divorce. I guess she's kind of a sensitive kid.

As he completes talking about his daughter, you could direct him to other topic areas by asking similar questions, such as, "You mentioned earlier that a few years ago your wife started seeming remote. Why don't you describe this period to me?"

It is during this narrative phase that the technique of active listening is particularly important. If possible, it is best to take a minimum of notes during this phase because note taking can interfere with your ability to remain focused and engaged.

Focusing in: Following up with Closed-Inquiry Questions. After the narrative phase, you should proceed with more focused questions to elicit more complete information. At this point, you will probably want to take detailed notes. As you shift to the closed-inquiry phase, you gain greater control over the process; however, where possible, your inquiry should be informed by and responsive to what the client tells you.

To begin this phase, you might say something like this to the client:

> Mr. Johnson, you've given me a good picture of your situation. Now, what I would like to do is go back over what you have told me and ask you some specific questions so I am sure my information is complete. Also, I will now be taking notes so I have a good record of what you tell me.

You can then go back over the information in a focused manner. Here is what some follow-up questions to Mr. Johnson about his daughter might sound like:

Q: You used the word "special" in describing your daughter. Why don't you tell me what you mean by that?

A: Well, like I said, she does well in school, has a lot of friends, and loves sports. But, I guess beyond that, she is just a very kind and thoughtful child. She seems to have a sensitivity beyond her years. She understands a lot about the world, and really wants to help people.

Q: Does she understand what is happening at home?

A: To some extent. We've told her that Mommy and Daddy don't love each other anymore and that Daddy will be moving to a new home, but that I still love her very much. I don't think she really understands why I've been sleeping in the guest room or why Mommy and Daddy aren't speaking to each other much.

Q: Why don't you tell me more about your relationship with Sara?

A: As I said, I was somewhat depressed when she was first born, and maybe I wasn't really that involved with her care, but I think I've made up for that in the past five or so years. During this time, I've been very involved in her care.

Q: Can you describe your caretaking role?

A: Well, sometimes I bring her to school in the morning, but I usually have to be at the office pretty early and I try to pick her up from her after-school program a few times a week. I share putting her to bed at night, and on weekends I try to do a special activity with her — just the two of us.

Q: How would you characterize the division of child-care responsibilities between you and your wife?

A: Well, I think it's pretty equal. I'm a pretty involved dad — I mean maybe it's not fifty-fifty, but I'm not one of those dads who doesn't even know the names of his child's friends.

Q: At some point, I'll probably want to get more detail on the caretaking arrangements, but let me ask you a few other things first. You mentioned that your daughter has been having a hard time and hasn't wanted to speak with you about what's going on. Can you elaborate on this?

A: Let me start with our relationship. We've been pretty close. I don't spend as much time with her as I would like, but when we're together we have a lot of fun. Sometimes I get impatient with her, and then I feel badly. I guess she usually confides more in her mother; I try not to get jealous, but sometimes I feel left out. I can't express my feelings as well as my wife can — we didn't do any of that in my family, and maybe it's a male thing also — so maybe Sara feels somewhat closer with her mom. But I love my daughter and would do anything for her.

Q: Who does your daughter turn to for comfort when she is sick or doesn't feel well?

A: Both of us, but my wife is usually the one to stay home with her when she is sick. Her job is more flexible than mine is, and when I was self-employed, I couldn't afford to take the time off. Also, sometimes, I think my wife overindulges her, and keeps her home if she just has a sniffle. I don't think it's good to treat kids like babies. . . . With respect to what Sara has been going through, she's been kind of moody and withdrawn. I don't know if it's in response to what has been going on at home, or if it's just one of those things that kids go through.

Q: Have you consulted anyone about this?

A: No—it hasn't seemed like that big a deal. But, maybe with the divorce, we should have her talk to someone. I don't really know.

Here, the interviewer is clearly trying to elicit specific information, but the questions flow from the client's answers, and there is a nice sense of give and take. This is not always possible. Where the client is less focused, the interviewer cannot be as responsive and will need to impose more of a structure in order to obtain the necessary information. Also, in reviewing these questions, you should note the constant pattern of moving from broader to narrower questions; this funneling process is also valuable within this closed-inquiry phase.

Stage 3: Wrapping up the Interview. Once you have obtained the necessary information, it is time to wrap up the interview. At this point, you need to tell the client what will happen next and explain what he or she needs to do, if anything. You should remind the client to feel free to call you with any questions.

To conclude the interview, you might say something like this:

Mr. Johnson, I think I have gotten all of the information that I need today. Let me explain what will happen next. I will write up the results of our interview and will go over them with Attorney Martin. She will evaluate your options, and we will then set up a meeting so she can go over things with you in detail. At that time, she will also review our office's fee structure and if you wish to proceed, she will work out a fee agreement with you.

In the meantime, I am going to give you a financial statement to fill out. I'll give you some written instructions, but feel free to call me if you have any questions. It would be very helpful if you could complete this before our next meeting.

I will call you by the end of the week to set up the next meeting. But please don't hesitate to call me if anything at all comes up before then. You can also call Attorney Martin directly, but it is likely easier to reach me because she is often in court. You should also be aware that as a paralegal, I cannot give you legal advice. I can answer some questions for you, but others I will need to convey to Ms. Martin, and then she can call you back or I can communicate her response to you.

▪ The Divorce Action: Initial Steps and Discovery

In this and subsequent sections, we trace the stages of a divorce case from the drafting of the complaint through postjudgment procedures. This discussion is intended to give you an overview of this process, but it is important to recognize that each state has its own procedural rules. In some states, these rules are found in the code of civil procedure, which applies generally to all civil actions[11]; other states have specialized rules of domestic procedure; and other states use a combination of general and specialized procedural rules. When working on a case, it is essential that the applicable rules be ascertained and followed so that a client's rights are safeguarded.

Please note a couple of points about terminology. First, this chapter uses the terms "complaint," "plaintiff," and "defendant," but other terms such as "petition," "petitioner," and "respondent" (respectively) may be used in some states. Also, in most instances where a phrase such as "the plaintiff files the complaint" or "the defendant must answer in a timely fashion" is used, the task is actually performed by that party's attorney. The language denotes which side is responsible for the task, not the allocation of responsibility between a party and his or her attorney.

The Initial Steps

The following steps in the divorce process will be discussed in this section:

1. Drafting/filing the complaint
2. Service of process
3. Defendant's response

The Complaint

The first official step in the divorce process is the filing of the **complaint** (or **petition**); until the complaint is filed, the court has no authority over the parties. Divorce complaints tend to be fairly straightforward, and, in many states, preprinted forms are available from the court. (See Exhibit 10.1 for an example of a preprinted petition from the state of Connecticut.) Despite this relative simplicity, the complaint is a crucial document that must be drafted with care because it frames the plaintiff's case to both the court and the defendant.

Complaint/Petition:
In a civil case, the pleading filed by the plaintiff to initiate a lawsuit; includes factual allegations, a statement of legal claims against the defendant, and a request for relief

The Functions of a Complaint. Like any other complaint, the divorce complaint serves a number of purposes. It identifies the parties to the action and, through a recitation of the parties' addresses and the

Exhibit 10.1
Divorce Complaint

DIVORCE COMPLAINT
(DISSOLUTION OF MARRIAGE)
JD-FM-159 Rev. 8-13
C.G.S. §§ 46b-40, 46b-56c, 46b-84,
P.B. § 25-2, et seq.

STATE OF CONNECTICUT
SUPERIOR COURT
www.jud.ct.gov

CROSS COMPLAINT CODE ONLY
CRSCMP

ADA NOTICE
The Judicial Branch of the State of Connecticut complies with the Americans with Disabilities Act (ADA). If you need a reasonable accommodation in accordance with the ADA, contact a court clerk or an ADA contact person listed at *www.jud.ct.gov/ADA*.

☐ **Complaint:** Complete this form. Attach a completed Summons (JD-FM-3) and Notice of Automatic Court Orders (JD-FM-158).
☐ **Amended Complaint.**
☐ **Cross Complaint:** Complete this form and attach to the Answer (JD-FM-160) unless it is already filed.

Judicial District of	At *(Town)*	Return date *(Month, day, year)*	Docket number

Plaintiff's name *(Last, First, Middle Initial)*	Defendant's name *(Last, First, Middle Initial)*

1. Plaintiff's birth name *(If different from above)*	2. Defendant's birth name *(If different from above)*

3. a. Date of marriage	3. b. Date of civil union that merged into marriage by subsequent ceremony or by operation of law	4. Town and State, or Country where marriage took place

5. *("X" all that apply)*
☐ The *("X" one)* ☐ plaintiff ☐ defendant   has lived in Connecticut for at least 12 months immediately before the filing of this divorce complaint or before the divorce will become final.
☐ The *("X" one)* ☐ plaintiff ☐ defendant   lived in Connecticut at the time of the marriage, moved away, and then returned to Connecticut, planning to live here permanently.
☐ The marriage broke down after the *("X" one)* ☐ plaintiff   ☐ defendant   moved to Connecticut.

6. A divorce is being sought because: *("X" all that apply)*
☐ This marriage has broken down irretrievably.
☐ Other *(must be reason(s) listed in section 46b-40(c) of the Connecticut General Statutes)*:

_____

_____

"X" and complete all that apply for items 6-13. Attach additional sheets if needed.
7. ☐ No children were born to either the plaintiff or defendant after the date of this marriage.
8. ☐ There are no children of this marriage under the age of 23.
9. ☐ The following children are either: (a) the biological and/or adoptive children of both of the parties, or (b) have been born to one of the parties on or after the date of the marriage and are claimed to be children of the marriage. *(List only children who have not yet reached the age of 23.)*

Name of child *(First, Middle Initial, Last)*	Date of birth *(Month, day, year)*

10. ☐ The following children were born on or after the date of the marriage to the *("X" all that apply)*
☐ plaintiff   ☐ defendant and are not children of the other party to this marriage.
(List only children who have not yet reached the age of 23.)

Name of child *(First, Middle Initial, Last)*	Date of birth *(Month, day, year)*

(Continued...)

Exhibit 10.1 cont.

11. If there is a court order regarding custody or support for any child listed above, name the child(ren) below and specify the person or agency awarded custody or ordered to pay support:

Child's name	Name of person or agency awarded custody	Name of person ordered to pay support
Child's name	Name of person or agency awarded custody	Name of person ordered to pay support
Child's name	Name of person or agency awarded custody	Name of person ordered to pay support

12. The ("X" all that apply) ☐ plaintiff ☐ defendant or any of the child(ren) listed above have received from the State of Connecticut:
   ☐ financial support ("X" one) ☐ Yes ☐ No ☐ Do not know
   ☐ HUSKY Health Insurance ("X" one) ☐ Yes ☐ No ☐ Do not know

   If yes, **you must** send a copy of the Summons, Complaint, Notice of Automatic Court Orders and any other documents filed with this Complaint to the Assistant Attorney General, 55 Elm Street, Hartford, CT 06106, and file the Certification of Notice (JD-FM-175) with the court clerk.

13. ☐ The ("X" all that apply) ☐ plaintiff ☐ defendant is pregnant with a child due to be born on _____.
   The other parent of this unborn child is the ☐ plaintiff or ☐ defendant ☐ unknown   (date)
   ☐ not the plaintiff ☐ not the defendant.

14. The ("X" all that apply) ☐ plaintiff ☐ defendant or any of the child(ren) listed above has received financial support from a city or town in Connecticut. ("X" one) ☐ Yes (State city or town: _____)
   ☐ No ☐ Do not know. If yes, send a copy of the Summons, Complaint, Notice of Automatic Court Orders and any other documents filed with this Complaint to the City Clerk of the town providing assistance and file the Certification of Notice (JD-FM-175) with the court clerk.

The Court is asked to order: ("X" all that apply)

☐ A divorce (dissolution of marriage).

☐ A fair division of property and debts.

☐ Alimony.

☐ Child Support.

☐ An order regarding the post-majority educational support of the child(ren).

☐ Name change to: _____

And anything else the Court deems fair.

Regarding Parental Decisionmaking Responsibility:
☐ Sole custody.
☐ Joint legal custody.
☐ A parenting responsibility plan which includes a plan for the parental decisionmaking regarding the minor child(ren).
   AND
Regarding Physical Custody:
☐ Primary residence with: _____
☐ Visitation.
☐ A parenting responsibility plan which includes a plan for the schedule of physical care of the minor child(ren).

Signature	Print name of person signing	Date signed
Address		Juris number (If applicable)	Telephone (Area code first)

- **If this is a Complaint, attach a copy of the Automatic Court Orders before serving a copy on the Defendant.**

- **If this is an Amended Complaint or a Cross Complaint, you must mail or deliver a copy to anyone who has filed an appearance and you must complete the certification below.**

Certification

I certify that a copy of this document was mailed or delivered electronically or non-electronically on (date) _____ to all attorneys and self-represented parties of record and that written consent for electronic delivery was received from all attorneys and self-represented parties receiving electronic delivery.

Name and address of each party and attorney that copy was mailed or delivered to*

*If necessary, attach additional sheet or sheets with name and address which the copy was mailed or delivered to.

Signed (Signature of filer) ▶	Print or type name of person signing	Date signed
Mailing address (Number, street, town, state and zip code)		Telephone number

JD-FM-159 (Back) Rev. 8-13

length of time that the plaintiff has lived in the state, establishes whether the court is the proper one with respect to both jurisdiction (see Chapter 9) and venue (see the discussion on the next page).

The complaint also sets out the facts that underlie the action. At a minimum, these would include the following basic allegations:

- when and where the parties were married;
- the names and birthdates of any children of the marriagel;
- the location where the parties last lived together; and
- the date and cause of marital separation.

Beyond this, states vary with respect to how much factual detail is required, but at a minimum, the complaint must include sufficient information to establish the basis for the divorce. For instance, if a plaintiff filed a divorce for cruel and abusive treatment, in some states it would be sufficient to state that the defendant treated him or her in a cruel and abusive manner on a particular occasion or occasions; while in other jurisdictions, greater detail about the acts constituting the cruel and abusive behavior would need to be set out.

Request/Prayer for Relief: The portion of a complaint in which the plaintiff sets out the relief that he or she is seeking from the court

The complaint also includes a **request for relief** (sometimes known as a **prayer for relief**), in which the plaintiff sets out the relief that he or she is seeking. In addition to asking the court to dissolve the marriage, the plaintiff sets out what she or he is seeking with respect to collateral matters such as custody, support, and the division of property. These are usually stated in general terms; for example, the plaintiff may request a reasonable amount of support or a fair and equitable division of property. However, local rules or customs might call for greater detail. States' rules differ with respect to whether a plaintiff can ask for something at trial that was not requested in the complaint. Some states strictly limit a plaintiff to the relief requested in the complaint, while others are more liberal. To avoid potential problems, many complaints are drafted to include a catchall phrase, asking the court to award any and all further relief that is deemed fair and equitable.

Amending the Complaint. After filing, a plaintiff may wish to change something on the complaint. For example, a plaintiff who files a fault divorce may subsequently agree to amend to a no-fault divorce. In most states, a plaintiff is permitted to amend the complaint within a specified time period, such as before the defendant files the answer, without seeking permission from the court or the defendant. After this time, the plaintiff must seek the permission of either the defendant or the court. Most courts are fairly liberal in allowing amendments unless the rights of the defendant would be prejudiced.

Joint Petitions. In some states, spouses may have the option of filing a no-fault petition for divorce jointly. Here, the parties are considered co-petitioners; neither is the plaintiff or the defendant. Joint petitions may entail special procedures or requirements. For example, in Massachusetts, parties who file a **joint petition** also must file an affidavit of irretrievable breakdown of the marriage, attesting to the fact that the marriage is over. A signed separation agreement also must be filed at this time or shortly thereafter. In California, couples without children who have been married a short time and have few assets may be eligible to file a Joint Petition for Summary Dissolution, which enables them to get divorced without a court hearing. (See Exhibit 10.2 for a sample joint petition and supporting affidavit.)

Joint Petition:
A pleading filed in a no-fault divorce action by co-petitioners to initiate the divorce

Filing the Complaint

Once the complaint is drafted, it is filed in the appropriate court together with any other required documents, such as a certified copy of the parties' marriage certificate. Before the complaint and any accompanying documents are accepted for filing, they are usually reviewed by a clerk to ensure that everything is in order. Upon acceptance, the case is assigned a **docket number**, which is then used on all subsequent case documents. In most states, filing can be done either in person or by mail. The advantage of filing in person is that any problems with the paperwork can be taken care of at the time. Also, as this responsibility is frequently delegated to paralegals, it provides a good opportunity to become familiar with the courts and court personnel.

Docket Number:
The number assigned to each case by the court; used for organizational and reference purposes and included on all papers filed in a case

Venue. Venue is a geographical concept that determines the specific court in which an action must be filed. Thus, for example, once it is ascertained that the probate and family court has subject matter jurisdiction over divorce actions, venue rules would tell you which probate and family court the action should be filed in. As a general rule, an action is filed where either the plaintiff or the defendant lives or where the cause of action arose. In divorce cases, other factors, such as where the parties last lived together as spouses, may be relevant to determining venue.

Venue:
A geographical concept designating which locale an action is to be filed in

Filing Fees and Fee Waivers. Most states charge a **filing fee** for the entry of a civil action. Filing fees are imposed to help defray administrative costs and possibly to deter frivolous actions. This fee, together with the related costs of service of process, can impose a serious financial hardship on low-income persons. So that these costs do not impose a barrier to court access, states must allow low-income divorce plaintiffs to seek a waiver of the filing fee. Plaintiffs also may be able to request that the state pay for costs related to the service of process and, less commonly, for those related to discovery (e.g., the hiring of a stenographer for a deposition). Although ensuring access to the court, the waiver of these fees does not, of course, resolve the greater problem of obtaining access to affordable legal representation. (See Exhibit 10.3 for Application for Indigent Status.)

Filing Fee:
The administrative fee charged by a court for the filing of an action

Exhibit 10.2
Joint Petition and Affidavit

Commonwealth of Massachusetts
The Trial Court

_____ **Division**   **Probate and Family Court Department**   **Docket No.** _____

JOINT PETITION FOR DIVORCE PURSUANT TO G.L. c. 208, § 1 A

_____ and _____
            Petitioner A   Petitioner B

_____   _____
          (Street address)   (Street address)

_____   _____
   (City/Town)   (State)   (Zip)   (City/Town)   (State)   (Zip)

1. Petitioners were lawfully married at _____

   on _____ and last lived together at _____

   on _____

2. The minor or dependent child(ren) of this marriage is/are:

   _____   _____
    (Name of child and date of birth)   (Name of child and date of birth)

   _____   _____
    (Name of child and date of birth)   (Name of child and date of birth)

3. Petitioners certify that no previous action for divorce, annulment or affirmation of marriage, separate support, desertion, living apart for justifiable cause, or custody of child(ren) has been brought by either against the other except: _____

   _____

   _____

4. On or about _____ , an irretrievable breakdown of the marriage under G.L. c. 208, § 1A occurred and continues to exist.

5. Wherefore, the petitioners request that the Court:

   ☐ grant a divorce on the ground of irretrievable breakdown

   ☐ approve the notarized separation agreement executed by the parties

   ☐ incorporate and merge the agreement executed by the parties

   ☐ incorporate but not merge said agreement, which shall survive and remain as an independent contract

   ☐ allow petitioner A to resume the former name of _____

   ☐ allow petitioner B to resume the former name of _____

   ☐ _____

   Date _____

_____   _____
(Signature of attorney or petitioner A, if pro se)   (Signature of attorney or petitioner B, if pro se)

_____   _____
          (Print name)   (Print name)

_____   _____
         (Street address)   (Street address)

_____   _____
   (City/Town)   (State)   (Zip)   (City/Town)   (State)   (Zip)

Tel. No. _____   Tel. No. _____

B.B.O. # _____   B.B.O. # _____

CJ-D 101A (9/07)   C.G.F

Exhibit 10.3
Application for Indigent Status

IN THE CIRCUIT/COUNTY COURT OF THE ----------------- JUDICIAL CIRCUIT
IN AND FOR ---------------- COUNTY, FLORIDA

CASE NO._____

Plaintiff/Petitioner or In the Interest Of

vs.

Defendant//Respondent

APPLICATION FOR DETERMINATION OF CIVIL INDIGENT STATUS

Notice to Applicant: If you qualify for civil indigence you must enroll in the clerk's office payment plan and pay a one-time administrative fee of $25.00. This fee shall not be charged for Dependency or Chapter 39 Termination of Parental Rights actions.

1. I have _____ **dependents.** *(Include only those persons you list on your U.S. Income tax return.)*
   Are you Married? Yes No Does your Spouse Work?...Yes No Annual Spouse Income? $_____

2. **I have a net income of** $_____ paid weekly every two weeks semi-monthly monthly yearly other _____

*(Net income is your total income including salary, wages, bonuses, commissions, allowances, overtime, tips and similar payments, **minus** deductions required by law and other court-ordered payments such as child support.)*

3. **I have other income** paid weekly every two weeks semi-monthly monthly yearly other _____.
(Circle "Yes" and fill in the amount if you have this kind of income, otherwise circle "No")

Second Job...Yes $ _____ No	Veterans' benefits..Yes $ _____ No	
Social Security benefits	Workers compensation..Yes $ _____ No	
For you..............................Yes $ _____ No	Income from absent family members ....Yes $ _____ No	
For child(ren) ....Yes $ _____ No	Stocks/bonds...Yes $ _____ No	
Unemployment compensation ....Yes $ _____ No	Rental income..Yes $ _____ No	
Union payments ....Yes $ _____ No	Dividends or interest...Yes $ _____ No	
Retirement/pensions.............................Yes $ _____ No	Other kinds of income not on the list...............Yes $ _____ No	
Trusts ....Yes $ _____ No	Gifts ....Yes $ _____ No	

I understand that I will be required to make payments for fees and costs to the clerk in accordance with §57.082(5), Florida Statutes, as provided by law, although I may agree to pay more if I choose to do so.

4. **I have other assets:** *(Circle "yes" and fill in the value of the property, otherwise circle "No")*

Cash ....Yes $ _____ No	Savings account ....Yes $ _____ No
Bank account(s) ....Yes $ _____ No	Stocks/bonds ....Yes $ _____ No
Certificates of deposit or	Homestead Real Property*.....................................Yes $ _____ No
money market accounts.........................Yes $ _____ No	Motor Vehicle*...Yes $ _____ No
Boats* ....Yes $ _____ No	Non-homestead real property/real estate* ....Yes $ _____ No

*show loans on these assets in paragraph 5

Check one: I DO DO NOT expect to receive more assets in the near future. The asset is_____.

5. **I have total liabilities and debts of** $_____ as follows: Motor Vehicle $_____, Home $_____, Other Real Property $_____, Child Support paid direct $_____, Credit Cards $_____, Medical Bills $_____, Cost of medicines (monthly) $_____,
Other $_____.

6. **I have a private lawyer in this case**............ Yes No

A person who knowingly provides false information to the clerk or the court in seeking a determination of indigent status under s. 57.082, F.S. commits a misdemeanor of the first degree, punishable as provided in s.775.082, F.S. or s. 775.083, F.S. **I attest that the information I have provided on this application is true and accurate to the best of my knowledge.**

Signed this _____ day of _____, 20____.

_____   _____
Date of Birth   Driver's License or ID Number

_____
Signature of Applicant for Indigent Status
Print Full Legal Name _____
Phone Number: _____

_____
Address, P O Address, Street, City, State, Zip Code

CLERK'S DETERMINATION

Based on the information in this Application, I have determined the applicant to be ( ) Indigent ( ) Not Indigent, according to s. 57.082, F.S.
Dated this _____ day of _____, 20____.

Clerk of the Circuit Court by _____

This form was completed with the assistance of: _____
Clerk/Deputy Clerk/Other authorized person.

APPLICANTS FOUND NOT TO BE INDIGENT MAY SEEK REVIEW BY A JUDGE BY ASKING FOR A HEARING TIME.
THERE IS NO FEE FOR THIS REVIEW.
Sign here if you want the judge to review the clerk's decision _____

Accompanying Documents. Other documents may need to be filed with the complaint. The requirements vary from state to state and may vary within a state depending on the nature of the divorce action. For example, as noted previously, in Massachusetts, an affidavit of irretrievable breakdown must accompany a joint petition or the petition will not be accepted for filing. The most common requirement is that the complaint be accompanied by a certified copy of the parties' marriage certificate; if the marriage took place in a foreign country, a qualified translation of the certificate may also need to be filed. Also, if there are minor children, an affidavit, or like document, may need to be filed disclosing any prior or pending custody actions involving the children.

Service of Process

After the complaint is filed, it must be served on the defendant so that he or she is provided with notice of the action. The right to notice is grounded in the due process clause, which, as discussed in Chapter 9, requires states to provide individuals with procedural rights.

Summons:
Informs the defendant of the action and that he or she is required to respond within a certain period of time or risk entry of a default judgment

Service of Process:
Delivery of a summons and complaint to a defendant; provides notice of the action and informs the defendant that a default judgment may be entered unless an answer is filed within a specified time

The Summons. Upon the filing of the complaint, the court issues a summons to the plaintiff (see Exhibit 10.4). A **summons** is a document that informs the defendant that he or she has been sued and that the failure to respond within a certain time period may result in a default judgment. The plaintiff is responsible for completing the summons and serving it on the defendant with a copy of the complaint. This is referred to as **service of process.**

Methods of Making Service. Service must be made in strict accordance with the applicable rules of procedure. Improper service may result in dismissal of the action. Although procedural requirements vary from state to state, making familiarity with local rules critical, some general principles can be identified. In discussing service, it is useful to distinguish between resident and nonresident defendants.

Personal Service:
Delivery of the summons and complaint by hand to the defendant

Serving a Resident Defendant. The most common method of service is by personal service of the papers on the defendant or, where allowed, by leaving them at his or her usual place of residence. In the latter situation, most states require that the papers be left with a competent adult. Traditionally, most states have required that **personal service** be made by a sheriff, a marshal, or other person specially designated to serve process, but the modern trend is to allow personal service to be made by any disinterested person over the age of 18.

Most states also allow service to be made by mail. Here, the summons and complaint are mailed to the defendant, usually by certified mail requesting acknowledgment of receipt. For the service to be considered

Exhibit 10.4
Summons

IN THE CIRCUIT COURT OF THE _____ JUDICIAL CIRCUIT,
IN AND FOR _____ COUNTY, FLORIDA

Case No.: _____
Division: _____

_____,
Petitioner,

and

_____,
Respondent.

SUMMONS: PERSONAL SERVICE ON AN INDIVIDUAL

TO/PARA/A: {enter other party's full legal name} _____,
{address (including city and state)/location for service} _____.

IMPORTANT

A lawsuit has been filed against you. You have **20 calendar days** after this summons is served on you to file a written response to the attached complaint/petition with the clerk of this circuit court, located at: {street address} _____.
A phone call will not protect you. Your written response, including the case number given above and the names of the parties, must be **filed** if you want the Court to hear your side of the case.

If you do not file your written response on time, you may lose the case, and your wages, money, and property may be taken thereafter without further warning from the Court. There are other legal requirements. You may want to call an attorney right away. If you do not know an attorney, you may call an attorney referral service or a legal aid office (listed in the phone book).

If you choose to file a written response yourself, at the same time you file your written response to the Court, you must also serve a copy of your written response on the party serving this summons at:

{Name and address of party serving summons} _____

_____.

If the party serving summons has designated e-mail address(es) for service or is represented by an attorney, you may designate e-mail address(es) for service by or on you. Service must be in accordance with Florida Rule of Judicial Administration 2.516.

Copies of all court documents in this case, including orders, are available at the Clerk of the Circuit Court's office. You may review these documents, upon request.

Florida Family Law Rules of Procedure Form 12.910(a), Summons: Personal Service on an Individual (09/12)

Exhibit 10.4 cont.

You must keep the Clerk of the Circuit Court's office notified of your current address. (You may file Designation of Current Mailing and E-mail Address, Florida Supreme Court Approved Family Law Form 12.915.) Future papers in this lawsuit will be served at the address on record at the clerk's office.

WARNING: Rule 12.285, Florida Family Law Rules of Procedure, requires certain automatic disclosure of documents and information. Failure to comply can result in sanctions, including dismissal or striking of pleadings.

THE STATE OF FLORIDA
TO EACH SHERIFF OF THE STATE: You are commanded to serve this summons and a copy of the complaint in this lawsuit on the above-named person.

DATED: _____

CLERK OF THE CIRCUIT COURT

(SEAL)

By: _____
Deputy Clerk

Florida Family Law Rules of Procedure Form 12.910(a), Summons: Personal Service on an Individual (09/12)

good, the defendant must sign and return the acknowledgment card, which is returned to the plaintiff by the postal service. This can be a simple and inexpensive way to obtain service, but if the defendant does not acknowledge service, it does not qualify as personal service.

If the defendant is "of parts unknown" or is avoiding service, most states permit service to be made by publication and mailing. Service by this method usually involves two discrete steps. First, the summons is published in a newspaper for a specific number of weeks; second, the plaintiff sends a copy of the summons and complaint to the defendant at his or her last known usual place of residence. Again, this would be sent by certified mail with acknowledgment requested so the plaintiff would know whether it was actually received.

Service by publication and mailing is often referred to as **constructive service** because — unless the defendant signs the acknowledgment card — there is no way of knowing whether he or she received notice of the action. This has potentially serious ramifications because it most likely means that even if the jurisdictional requirements are met, the court will not be able to assert personal jurisdiction over the defendant (see Chapter 9).

Constructive Service: Service of a summons and complaint on a defendant in a manner other than by delivering it to him or her in person, usually by publication, mailing, or both

In some states, the plaintiff may be able to avoid the potential difficulties of trying to obtain service on the defendant by arranging for the defendant to accept service of the complaint. If the defendant is cooperative, the plaintiff can simply provide him or her with a copy of the complaint and the original summons, which the defendant signs to acknowledge **acceptance of service**.

If the plaintiff's attorney arranges for the acceptance of service and the defendant is unrepresented, he or she must be careful not to provide the defendant with any legal advice about the divorce and should encourage the defendant to seek representation. Of course, this applies to paralegals as well.

Acceptance of Service: Assent by a defendant to being presented with the summons and complaint, and the defendant's willing acknowledgment of the receipt of the same

Serving an Out-of-State Defendant. Most states authorize service to be made on a nonresident by the same methods that are available for serving residents or by any manner authorized by the defendant's home state. There are practical difficulties in serving a nonresident; however, where the state can exercise personal jurisdiction over the defendant, it is important to make the effort to actually serve the defendant because, as mentioned previously, it is usually a necessary precondition to the court's ability to exercise personal jurisdiction over the defendant where the jurisdictional requirements of the long-arm statute are otherwise satisfied.

Return of Service. The person who serves the defendant must certify when, where, and how service was made. This is usually done on the back of the original summons under the heading "Proof of Service" (see Exhibit 10.5). The summons is then filed in court. This is known as the

Exhibit 10.5
Proof of
Service

INSTRUCTIONS FOR FLORIDA SUPREME COURT APPROVED FAMILY LAW FORM 12.914, CERTIFICATE OF SERVICE

When should this form be used?

After the petition has been properly served (through either a **personal service** or **constructive service**), both parties **must** send copies of all additional documents or papers they **file** with the clerk to the other **party** or his or her attorney, if he or she has one. Each time you file a document, you must certify that you provided the other party with a copy. Many of the Florida Family Law Forms already have a place above the signature line for this certification. It looks like this:

> I certify that a copy of this document was [√ **one** only] ( ) mailed ( ) faxed and mailed ( )
> hand-delivered to the person(s) listed below on *[date]* _____.
>
> **Other party or his/her attorney:**
> Name: _____
> Address: _____
> City, State, Zip: _____
> Fax Number: _____

If a form you are filing has a certificate, you do not need to file a separate **Certificate of Service**, ✎☐ Florida Supreme Court Approved Family Law Form 12.914. However, **each time** you file a document that does not have a certificate like the one above, you must file a **Certificate of Service**, ✎☐ Florida Supreme Court Approved Family Law Form 12.914, and send a copy of the document to the other party. This includes letters to the **judge**.

This form should be typed or printed in black ink. After completing this form (giving the name of each form, document, or paper filed), you should sign the form before a **notary public** or **deputy clerk**. You should file the original with the **clerk of the circuit court** in the county where your case was filed and keep a copy for your records.

The copy you are providing to the other party must be mailed (postmarked) or delivered to the opposing party or his or her attorney on the same day indicated on the certificate of service.

Where can I look for more information?

Before proceeding, you should read "General Information for Self-Represented Litigants" found at the beginning of these forms. For more information, see rule 1.080, Florida Rules of Civil Procedure and rule 12.080, Florida Family Law Rules of Procedure.

Special notes...

Remember, a person who is NOT an attorney is called a nonlawyer. If a nonlawyer helps you fill out these forms, that person must give you a copy of **Disclosure from Nonlawyer,** ✎☐ Florida Family Law Rules of Procedure Form 12.900 (a), before he or she helps you. A nonlawyer helping you fill out these forms also **must** put his or her name, address, and telephone number on the bottom of the last page of every form he or she helps you complete.

Instructions for Florida Supreme Court Approved Family Law Form 12.914, Certificate of Service (9/00)

Exhibit 10.5 cont.

IN THE CIRCUIT COURT OF THE _____ JUDICIAL CIRCUIT,
IN AND FOR _____ COUNTY, FLORIDA

Case No.: _____
Division: _____

_____,
Petitioner,

and

_____,
Respondent.

CERTIFICATE OF SERVICE

I certify that a copy of {name of document(s)} _____
_____
was [√ **one** only] ( ) mailed ( ) faxed and mailed ( ) hand delivered to the person listed below on
{date} _____.

Other party or his/her attorney:
Name: _____
Address: _____
City, State, Zip: _____
Fax Number: _____

_____
Signature of Party
Printed Name: _____
Address: _____
City, State, Zip: _____
Telephone Number: _____
Fax Number: _____

**IF A NONLAWYER HELPED YOU FILL OUT THIS FORM, HE/SHE MUST FILL IN THE
BLANKS BELOW:** [✍ fill in **all** blanks]
I, {full legal name and trade name of nonlawyer} _____,
a nonlawyer, located at {street} _____, {city} _____,
{state} _____, {phone} _____, helped {name} _____,
who is the [√ **one** only] ____ petitioner **or** ____ respondent, fill out this form.

Florida Supreme Court Approved Family Law Form 12.914, Certificate of Service (9/00)

Return of Service:
The acknowledgment to the court by the person serving the defendant that service was made

return of service. Depending on the method of service used, additional papers may need to be filed for the return of service to be complete. For example, if service was by publication, the pages from the newspaper usually must be submitted to the court.

The Defendant's Response

Answer:
The pleading filed by a defendant in response to a plaintiff's complaint, in which he or she seeks to avoid liability

Once the defendant is served, he or she is allowed a certain time period within which to file a response to the complaint; this responsive document is the **answer** (see Exhibit 10.6). This response period is usually significantly longer when service is made by publication.

What happens if a defendant fails to respond? In the typical civil action, a defendant who fails to answer in a timely manner is in default. This has two consequences: (1) the plaintiff is relieved of the obligation of providing the defendant with notice about subsequent case proceedings, and (2) the plaintiff may seek to have a judgment entered in his or her favor without a hearing on the merits. This is known as a **default judgment**.

Default Judgment:
A judgment entered against a defendant who fails to respond to a complaint or otherwise defend the action

The practice is somewhat different in the divorce context. Because of the importance of the rights at stake, courts tend to be reluctant to consider a divorce defendant in default and will generally not do so where the defendant has made any effort to preserve his or her rights. Even where the defendant has not responded at all, courts may not consider a divorce defendant to be in default. Accordingly, the plaintiff will not be relieved of the obligation of providing the defendant with notice of all related case proceedings and the court will not enter a judgment by default without a hearing.

As a result of the more relaxed rules about defaults in the divorce context, the local practice custom may be to forgo the filing of an answer. However, this failure may serve to preclude the defendant from contesting matters raised by the plaintiff or from seeking certain kinds of relief. Accordingly, given the unpredictable nature of divorce litigation, the better practice is to file an answer in all cases to ensure that a client's rights are safeguarded.

The Component Parts of an Answer

Admissions/Denials

In the first portion of an answer, the defendant responds to the factual allegations in the complaint by either admitting or denying them. For example, a defendant might deny the validity of the parties' marriage, that a child named on the complaint was in fact born of the marriage, or that the plaintiff is entitled to the requested relief. Denials thus serve to delineate areas of potential controversy. If the defendant lacks knowledge about an allegation, the defendant can state that he or she is without

Exhibit 10.6
Answer

FL-120

ATTORNEY OR PARTY WITHOUT ATTORNEY *(Name, State Bar number, and address):*	*FOR COURT USE ONLY*

TELEPHONE NO.:   FAX NO.:
E-MAIL ADDRESS:
ATTORNEY FOR *(Name)*:

SUPERIOR COURT OF CALIFORNIA, COUNTY OF
    STREET ADDRESS:
    MAILING ADDRESS:
    CITY AND ZIP CODE:
    BRANCH NAME:

PETITIONER:

RESPONDENT:

RESPONSE ☐ **AND REQUEST FOR** ☐ **AMENDED**	CASE NUMBER:
☐ **Dissolution (Divorce) of:** ☐ Marriage ☐ Domestic Partnership	
☐ **Legal Separation of:** ☐ Marriage ☐ Domestic Partnership	
☐ **Nullity of:** ☐ Marriage ☐ Domestic Partnership	

1. **LEGAL RELATIONSHIP** *(check all that apply):*
   a. ☐ We are married.
   b. ☐ We are domestic partners and our domestic partnership was established in California.
   c. ☐ We are domestic partners and our domestic partnership was NOT established in California.

2. **RESIDENCE REQUIREMENTS** *(check all that apply):*
   a. ☐ Petitioner ☐ Respondent   has been a resident of this state for at least six months and of this county for at least three months immediately preceding the filing of this *Petition. (For a divorce, at least one person in the legal relationship described in items 1a and 1c must comply with this requirement.)*
   b. ☐ We are the same sex and were married in California but are not residents of California. Neither of us lives in a state or nation that will dissolve the marriage. This case is filed in the county in which we married.
       Petitioner's residence *(state or nation):*   Respondent's residence *(state or nation):*
   c. ☐ Our domestic partnership was established in California. Neither of us has to be a resident or have a domicile in California to dissolve our partnership here.

3. **STATISTICAL FACTS**
   a. ☐ (1) Date of marriage *(specify):*   (2) Date of separation *(specify):*
       (3) Time from date of marriage to date of separation *(specify):*   Years   Months
   b. ☐ (1) Registration date of domestic partnership with the California Secretary of State or other state equivalent *(specify below):*
       (2) Date of separation *(specify):*
       (3) Time from date of registration of domestic partnership to date of separation *(specify):*   Years   Months

4. **MINOR CHILDREN** *(children born before (or born or adopted during) the marriage or domestic partnership):*
   a. ☐ There are no minor children.
   b. ☐ The minor children are:

Child's name	Birthdate	Age	Sex

       (1) ☐ continued on Attachment 4b.
       (2) ☐ a child who is not yet born.
   c. If there are minor children of Petitioner and Respondent, a completed *Declaration Under Uniform Child Custody Jurisdiction and Enforcement Act (UCCJEA)* (form FL-105) must be attached.
   d. ☐ Petitioner and Respondent signed a voluntary declaration of paternity. A copy ☐ is ☐ is not   attached.

Page 1 of 3

Form Adopted for Mandatory Use
Judicial Council of California
FL-120 [Rev. January 1, 2015]
RESPONSE—MARRIAGE/DOMESTIC PARTNERSHIP
(Family Law)
Family Code, § 2020
www.courts.ca.gov

Exhibit 10.6 cont.

PETITIONER:	CASE NUMBER:
RESPONDENT:	

Respondent requests that the court make the following orders:

5. **LEGAL GROUNDS** (Family Code sections 2200–2210; 2310–2312)
   a. ☐ **Respondent contends** that the parties never legally married or registered a domestic partnership.
   b. ☐ **Respondent denies** the grounds set forth in item 5 of the petition.
   c. ☐ **Respondent requests**
      (1) ☐ divorce ☐ legal separation of the marriage or domestic partnership based on
         (a) ☐ irreconcilable differences. (b) ☐ permanent legal incapacity to make decisions.
      (2) ☐ nullity of void marriage or domestic partnership based on
         (a) ☐ incest. (b) ☐ bigamy.
      (3) ☐ nullity of voidable marriage or domestic partnership based on
         (a) ☐ respondent's age at time of registration of domestic partnership or marriage. (d) ☐ fraud.
         (b) ☐ prior existing marriage or domestic partnership. (e) ☐ force.
         (c) ☐ unsound mind. (f) ☐ physical incapacity.

6. **CHILD CUSTODY AND VISITATION (PARENTING TIME)**

		Petitioner	Respondent	Joint	Other
a.	Legal custody of children to..	☐	☐	☐	☐
b.	Physical custody of children to...	☐	☐	☐	☐
c.	Child visitation (parenting time) be granted to	☐	☐		☐

   As requested in: ☐ form FL-311 ☐ form FL-312 ☐ form FL-341(C)
      ☐ form FL-341(D) ☐ form FL-341(E) ☐ Attachment 6c(1)
   d. ☐ Determine the parentage of children born to Petitioner and Respondent before the marriage or domestic partnership.

7. **CHILD SUPPORT**
   a. If there are minor children born to or adopted by Petitioner and Respondent before or during this marriage or domestic partnership, the court will make orders for the support of the children upon request and submission of financial forms by the requesting party.
   b. An earnings assignment may be issued without further notice.
   c. Any party required to pay support must pay interest on overdue amounts at the "legal" rate, which is currently 10 percent.
   d. ☐ Other (specify):

8. **SPOUSAL OR DOMESTIC PARTNER SUPPORT**
   a. ☐ Spousal or domestic partner support payable to ☐ Petitioner ☐ Respondent
   b. ☐ Terminate (end) the court's ability to award support to ☐ Petitioner ☐ Respondent
   c. ☐ Reserve for future determination the issue of support payable to ☐ Petitioner ☐ Respondent
   d. ☐ Other (specify):

9. **SEPARATE PROPERTY**
   a. ☐ There are no such assets or debts that I know of to be confirmed by the court.
   b. ☐ Confirm as separate property the assets and debts in ☐ Property Declaration (form FL-160) ☐ Attachment 9b
      ☐ the following list.
      Item   Confirm to

FL-120 [Rev. January 1, 2015]

RESPONSE—MARRIAGE/DOMESTIC PARTNERSHIP
(Family Law)

Page 2 of 3

Exhibit 10.6 cont.

PETITIONER:	CASE NUMBER:
RESPONDENT:	

10. COMMUNITY AND QUASI-COMMUNITY PROPERTY

a. ☐ There are no such assets or debts that I know of to be divided by the court.

b. ☐ Determine rights to community and quasi-community assets and debts. All such assets and debts are listed
    ☐ in *Property Declaration* (form FL-160) ☐ in Attachment 10b.
    ☐ as follows *(specify)*:

11. OTHER REQUESTS

a. ☐ Attorney's fees and costs payable by ☐ Petitioner ☐ Respondent

b ☐ Respondent's former name be restored to *(specify)*:

c. ☐ Other *(specify)*:

☐ Continued on Attachment 11c.

I declare under penalty of perjury under the laws of the State of California that the foregoing is true and correct.

Date:

_____
(TYPE OR PRINT NAME)

▶ _____
(SIGNATURE OF RESPONDENT)

Date:

_____
(TYPE OR PRINT NAME)

▶ _____
(SIGNATURE OF ATTORNEY FOR RESPONDENT)

NOTICE: You may redact (black out) social security numbers from any written material filed with the court in this case other than a form used to collect child, spousal or partner support.

NOTICE—CANCELLATION OF RIGHTS: Dissolution or legal separation may automatically cancel the rights of a domestic partner or spouse under the other domestic partner's or spouse's will, trust, retirement plan, power of attorney, pay-on-death bank account, survivorship rights to any property owned in joint tenancy, and any other similar thing. It does not automatically cancel the right of a domestic partner or spouse as beneficiary of the other partner's or spouse's life insurance policy. You should review these matters, as well as any credit cards, other credit accounts, insurance polices, retirement plans, and credit reports, to determine whether they should be changed or whether you should take any other actions. Some changes may require the agreement of your partner or spouse or a court order.

The original response must be filed in the court with proof of service of a copy on Petitioner.

FL-120 [Rev. January 1, 2015] **RESPONSE—MARRIAGE/DOMESTIC PARTNERSHIP** Page 3 of 3
(Family Law)

sufficient information to either admit or deny the matter. If the defendant fails to respond to an allegation, it is usually treated as an admission of that fact.

Affirmative Defenses

Affirmative Defense:
A response to an allegation in a complaint in which the defendant seeks to establish that the plaintiff is not entitled to recover on his or her claim

In an **affirmative defense**, a defendant seeks to establish that the plaintiff is not entitled to prevail even if his or her allegations are established. Thus, for example, a defendant might assert that by continued cohabitation, the plaintiff forgave the defendant's marital trespasses. Since no-fault divorce, however, as discussed in Chapter 4, affirmative defenses are far less significant. Because it is virtually impossible for one spouse to prevent the other from obtaining a divorce, parties are much less likely to fight about the legal significance of marital fault.

Counterclaims

Counterclaim:
A claim made by the defendant against the plaintiff

A defendant can also assert claims for relief against the plaintiff in his or her answer by way of a **counterclaim**. Where a counterclaim is asserted, roles are reversed: The defendant functions as a plaintiff, and the plaintiff functions as a defendant and has a right to respond to the counterclaim.

In a divorce case, a defendant might counterclaim for a divorce from the plaintiff and set out the relief he or she is seeking, such as custody of the children or a spousal support award. Depending on local rules, a defendant might also be able to set out claims for relief even if he or she is not actually counterclaiming for divorce.

Motion to Dismiss:
A request to the court that it dismiss the plaintiff's case for lack of jurisdiction, improper service, or the plaintiff's failure to state a valid claim entitling him or her to relief

The Motion to Dismiss.   A defendant may also respond to a complaint by filing a **motion to dismiss** the divorce action. Common grounds for seeking a dismissal are lack of jurisdiction, inadequate service, or improper venue. If the action is dismissed, the defendant does not need to file an answer. If the motion is denied, the defendant will need to answer, although the time period for responding will be extended. Of course, the plaintiff will most likely refile, making sure to correct the error that led to the dismissal.

Discovery

Discovery:
The process by which each side is able to acquire information from the other side in advance of trial

Discovery is a pretrial process for obtaining information from the other side. Most states have modeled their discovery rules after the federal discovery rules contained in the Federal Rules of Civil Procedure, so these rules will serve as the basis for our discussion. Of course, the rules of your state should always be consulted when working on a case.

General Purpose

Discovery serves a number of important purposes, including the following:

1. It facilitates trial preparation because both parties can use the obtained information to help develop their respective cases.
2. It reduces the possibility of surprise during trial since information is obtained in advance.
3. It enables both sides to assess the relative strengths and weaknesses of the case and can thus facilitate the settlement process.

Despite these benefits, there is a potentially troubling aspect to discovery. Given how open-ended the process is, it is possible for the spouse with greater resources to "out-discover" the other. This can push the spouse with fewer resources into a premature and potentially disadvantageous settlement. It can also result in different levels of trial preparedness. Either outcome may be the result of a well-crafted strategy or simply a byproduct of thorough preparation. Although courts can impose some limitations, they generally will not interfere with discovery absent egregious behavior.

Scope of Discovery

In most states, the permissible scope of discovery is broad. In keeping with the federal standard, discovery can be had of any unprivileged matter that is *relevant* to the case. The information sought does not need to be admissible at trial so long as it is "reasonably calculated to lead to the discovery of admissible evidence."[12] State rules may or may not define what is considered *privileged* and beyond the scope of discovery. In most states, communications between an attorney and client, a doctor and patient, and a priest and penitent are privileged; communications between spouses and between a psychotherapist and patient may also be considered privileged. Additionally, states generally recognize the privilege against self-incrimination. Many states now also recognize a privilege based on rights of privacy; thus certain very personal information may be off limits. However, the parameters of this privilege are not always clear, and a party may be deemed to have waived it if she or he has put a particular matter in issue.

In the divorce context, an enormous range of information is commonly sought through the discovery process. For instance, where property or support is at issue, discovery will focus on the other party's financial situation. He or she will be asked for detailed information about income, expenditures, assets, and liabilities in accordance with the applicable statutory factors. For example, a stay-at-home spouse might be asked to detail all of the nonfinancial contributions he or she has made to the marriage by way of household and child-care responsibilities. Where conduct is a permissible factor, a spouse might be asked to detail all of his or her "bad acts." Where custody is at issue, a party may be asked to provide detailed information about his or her relationship with the children, including caretaking functions performed. Discovery can also be used to explore potential areas of concern. A party may be asked about whether he or she has ever struck the child or used drugs or alcohol in the child's presence. Pertinent information can also be discovered from other persons with knowledge about the child, such as neighbors, teachers, and therapists.

Discovery Methods

There are five basic methods of discovery:

1. Depositions
2. Interrogatories
3. Request for production of documents and electronically stored information
4. Request for a physical or mental examination
5. Request for admissions

In any given case, a single method may be used, or more than one may be used in combination with one another. Before considering these different methods, it is important to be aware that some cases are completed without any or with only a minimum of discovery. This may be because the case is simple or is uncontested. It also may be because the parties have the information they need in order to proceed. Cost may also be an important consideration, which, as noted earlier, can be particularly problematic if the weight of this concern falls more heavily on one spouse than the other.

Paralegals often play a major role in the discovery process. Thus, the discussion of each method of discovery includes the responsibilities that a paralegal might be asked to assume. Although not the focus of our discussion, keep in mind that paralegals also often play a significant role in coordinating the logistical aspects of discovery, such as arranging deposition dates. Of course, each office is different, and in any workplace, you will need to establish exactly what is expected of you. Also, in setting out these responsibilities, it is assumed that the paralegal's work is subject to an attorney's direction and review.

Deposition:
A method of discovery in which the oral testimony of a witness is obtained through questions that are answered under oath

Deponent:
The person whose deposition is being taken

Depositions. One common method of discovery is the **deposition**. A deposition can be taken of a party or any potential witness, including an expert witness such as a real estate appraiser or a psychiatrist. If the **deponent** is a party, the deposition can be taken upon sending the party a notice naming the date, time, and location of the deposition and listing any documents that he or she should bring. If the deponent is a nonparty witness, his or her presence must be secured by a **subpoena**; if the nonparty witness is to bring documents, he or she must be served with a **subpoena duces tecum**, which specifically designates the documents to be produced.

At the deposition, the deponent is placed under oath and is questioned by the attorney taking the deposition. The other attorney is in the role of "defending the deposition" and may also ask questions. Usually, these questions are limited to clearing up confusion or eliciting information that the deponent forgot to provide.

A court reporter or certified shorthand reporter is usually present at a deposition. He or she records the proceeding and prepares a verbatim transcript. Due to the cost involved, some states may permit depositions to be audiotaped or videotaped. Where this is done, all of the procedural requirements must be carefully adhered to so the validity of the deposition is not subject to challenge.

The primary advantages of depositions are their flexibility and spontaneity. Although most attorneys prepare their witnesses in advance, it is virtually impossible to anticipate and prepare for all possible questions. Even when prepared, the witness must answer the questions on his or her own; unlike answering interrogatories, the defending attorney cannot help craft the answers. Additionally, the deponent's answers can be immediately followed up with additional questions, and the attorney conducting the deposition can pursue a line of inquiry to its logical conclusion. This spontaneous interchange can lead to valuable information. An additional benefit is that witness credibility can be assessed and a determination made about how well he or she is likely to do in court.

The primary disadvantages of depositions are that they are expensive and time consuming. To minimize these burdens, an attorney might choose to wait to do depositions until he or she has established a baseline of information through the use of interrogatories and requests for documents, and then use the depositions to focus on matters already determined to be significant.

Subpoena: A writ commanding a witness to appear at a particular time and place to give testimony

Subpoena Duces Tecum: A writ commanding a witness to produce books, papers, or other items, usually at a deposition or trial

The Role of the Paralegal

Taking Depositions

If your office is taking the depositions:

- Determine who should be deposed.
- Prepare the notice of intent to take deposition if a party deponent; prepare the summons or the summons duces tecum if a nonparty deponent.
- Organize the information that will be useful in preparing the deposition questions, such as financial documents, bank statements already in your possession, and school records.

- Draft the deposition questions.
- Listen carefully at the deposition and take detailed notes. Provide the attorney with possible additional questions that you think will be useful. Also, help to evaluate the witnesses' credibility — be prepared to discuss how well you think each witness will do in court.
- Review any documents that have been brought to the deposition to ensure that the production request has been fully complied with.
- After the depositions, carefully review the transcript of the deposition and prepare a summary in accordance with your office's summary procedure.

If your office is defending the deposition:

- Develop questions that you anticipate the other side will ask and conduct a mock deposition.
- Organize the documents that your witness is asked to bring. If the attorney is objecting to a production request, draft a motion for a protective order.
- At the deposition, listen carefully and suggest questions that the defending attorney might want to ask the deponent to clarify responses or elicit missing information. Also, evaluate the witness's credibility — be prepared to discuss how well you think the witness will do in court.
- Obtain a copy of the deposition transcript and review it with the witness for accuracy. Correct any mistakes in accordance with local rules.
- Prepare a summary of the deposition transcript in accordance with your office's summary procedures.

Interrogatories:
A discovery method involving written questions to a party, which must be answered under oath

Interrogatories. Interrogatories are written questions that must be answered in writing within a certain time period, usually 30 days. Unlike depositions, interrogatories can only be served on parties — they cannot be served on nonparty witnesses. Interrogatories are answered under oath, and in many states, the respondent has a duty to supplement answers if additional information becomes available.

Many states limit the number of questions that can be asked, although courts usually have the authority to allow additional questions. Attorneys can also agree to allow additional questions, and some have been known to employ creative numbering techniques in an effort to squeeze in as many questions as possible! Some states have developed standard interrogatory forms for use in appropriate circumstances.

In responding to interrogatories, a party must base his or her answers on all available information. Unlike a deposition, a party cannot respond based solely on what he or she knows personally but instead has an obligation to consult resources in his or her custody or control. For example, if a husband is asked about how much money he spent on clothing in the past five years, he would be obligated to review relevant financial records, such as canceled checks and credit card statements, whereas no such obligation would exist if this question were asked during a deposition. As a result of this duty to investigate, interrogatory answers may be more complete than answers given in a deposition; however, this method lacks the spontaneity and flexibility that characterize the deposition process.

When interrogatories are received by an office, the usual approach is to have the client provide the requested information to the legal team, which then drafts the responses. Clearly, although honesty is required, good drafting skills can help to shape the answers in a light most favorable to the client. Even if follow-up interrogatories are generated by the answers, the second round of responses are again subject to scrutiny. There is no opportunity for the open-ended give-and-take that characterizes the deposition process.

The Role of the Paralegal

Interrogatories

If your office is preparing the interrogatories:

- Analyze what information is needed from the other side.
- Draft the interrogatory questions.
- When the answers are returned, review them carefully to determine if all requested information has been provided. If not, discuss strategies and then draft a letter to the other side seeking supplemental information or draft a motion to compel.
- Summarize the responses and determine what information still needs to be obtained.

If your office is responding to the interrogatories:

- Enter the return date on your office's tickler system, and keep track of it.
- Remind the attorney to contact the other side if additional time is needed; if necessary, prepare a motion requesting additional time.
- Determine if any questions are objectionable and should not be answered; if necessary, prepare a motion for a protective order.
- Contact the client immediately and provide him or her with a copy of the interrogatories and instructions for preparing a response.
- Meet with the client and review the information and relevant documentation.
- Draft answers. When complete, have client come in to review, make appropriate adjustments, and obtain the client's signature.
- Make sure that, if required by state law, the client understands the obligation to supplement answers.

Request for Production of
Documents:
A discovery method in
which a party can obtain
documents from the other
side that are needed to
prepare the case

Request for Production of Documents and Electronically Stored Information.   As part of the discovery process, a party may seek to review documents in the possession or under the control of the other side. To access the documents, a party serves a **request for production of documents** that details what is to be made available for inspection. The term "document" is usually defined in the request, and liberal, all-encompassing definitions are the norm. The request also specifies the time, place, and manner of production. Commonly, production is made at the office of the requesting attorney. The requesting party then has the right to make copies of the documents that he or she wishes to retain. A party may also enter onto land or other property in the possession or control of the other side for the purpose of inspection, although court permission may be needed for this. This is not done routinely in divorce cases, but it could be important where, for example, the value of a professional practice or a closely held corporation is at issue.

In a divorce case, parties often make very liberal use of the production process, especially when seeking financial information. Among other things, a spouse may be asked to produce all of his or her pay stubs, canceled checks, credit card and bank statements, receipts for purchases over a specified amount, and loan payments over a specific time period, which could well be the length of the marriage. Clearly, these requests can be burdensome to the party who must locate the requested documents — as well as to the person (most commonly a paralegal) who must review them!

Interesting issues arise when one spouse requests access to books and records from a professional practice. Access to these documents may be necessary for property distribution purposes in order to establish the value and the nature of the spouse's interest in the practice. The request may be objected to, however, where production could compromise confidentiality through disclosure of information about clients, patients, or work associates. In this situation, a judge is likely to order production but structure it in such a way that confidentiality is preserved by, for example, ordering the deletion of names and identifying information.

In addition to requesting documents, discovery can now be had of electronically stored information (ESI), which includes "emails, voicemails, instant messages, text messages, documents and spreadsheets, file fragments, digital images, and video."[13] Although e-discovery has become increasingly important in the digital era, the process requires a certain amount of technological sophistication and may thus present certain stumbling blocks for the unwary practitioner.

For example, documents frequently contain "invisible" information known as "metadata," which is generally defined as "data hidden in documents that is generated during the course of creating and editing such documents. It may include fragments of data from files that were previously deleted, overwritten, or worked on simultaneously."[14] Although hidden, this "data about data" is, in fact, retrievable. Accordingly, when an attorney produces electronic files pursuant to a discovery request, he or she may inadvertently be providing the other attorney with confidential or privileged information that he or she is unaware is embedded in the produced materials, in potential breach of the duty to maintain client confidentiality. In terms of the ethical obligation of the recipient, a number of states have concluded that the "receiving attorney has an ethical duty not to review the information" in accordance with a "strong public policy . . . against an attorney engaging in conduct that would amount to an unjustified intrusion into the opposing counsel's attorney-client relationship."[15] However, the law is clearly evolving in this arena, and as one commentator suggests, to avoid potential ethical breaches "an attorney should be charged with an active duty to stay current on technological advances in document transmission to best understand the potential risks and best methods of transmitting information to opposing parties."[16]

In a similar vein, the fact that one has deleted a document does not actually mean that it has been erased from the hard drive; accordingly, "the chances are good that unless the user has used software to erase or wipe the hard drive, significant amounts of deleted data or bits and pieces of deleted data will remain," that can be retrieved by forensic software.[17] Accordingly, if access is given to the actual computer, which may be necessary for the purpose of authenticating the requested electronic data, as with metadata, an attorney may likewise inadvertently be providing the opposing counsel with far more information than he or she realizes if unaware that deleted files are not necessarily vanquished from the computer's memory, thus again potentially compromising client confidentiality.

Although the e-discovery process is clearly not without its difficulties, a spouse who seeks to gain access to the other party's electronically stored information outside of the formal discovery process may well find that not only is the evidence inadmissible, but that he or she has committed a crime under federal and state laws that are designed to protect an individual's right of privacy in the digital realm by prohibiting both the interception of electronic communications and unauthorized access to such communications. In the divorce context, the question of what constitutes "unauthorized" use can be particularly murky, given that spouses may both use the same computer. For example, in the case of Byrne v. Byrne, the husband had a laptop from work that he allowed his children to do their homework on. The wife brought the computer to her attorney because she believed it contained important financial information in its memory. Rejecting the husband's claim that her actions were improper, the court likened the memory of a family computer to a file cabinet, and ruled that in the same manner that the wife "would have access to the contents of a file cabinet left in the marital residence . . . she should have access to the contents of the computer."[18] However, the result may well have been different if, for example, the computer had not been characterized by the court as a family computer, or if the wife had gained access to password-protected information. It is important to keep in mind that this is a rapidly evolving area of the law, and the legal standards for what constitutes unauthorized access to electronically stored information tends to be both highly fact-sensitive and variable from state to state.

The Role of the Paralegal

Requesting the Production of Documents

If your office is requesting the documents:

- Determine what documents are needed.
- Draft the request with the requisite specificity so that you get what is needed without being flooded with extraneous documents.
- When the documents are received, match them against the request to ensure it has been compiled with. If information is missing or objected to, develop a strategy for obtaining it—draft a letter to the other side requesting the information or draft a motion to compel for court.
- Determine what documents are needed and make copies of them. In the event of uncertainty, err on the side of copying more than is needed rather than less.
- Organize and label the documents so they are immediately accessible.

If your office is responding to a request for documents:

- Upon receiving the request for production, immediately contact the client and set up a time to review the request with him or her. Make sure that the client understands the time frame.
- Keep track of the production deadline. If it cannot be met, remind the attorney to contact the other side to arrange an extension; if necessary, draft a motion for an extension of time.
- Determine if any of the requests are objectionable.
- When the documents are provided by the client, review them to see if the request has been complied with and if any documents should be held back based on privilege.
- Organize the documents for production, indicating any objections, and note all instances where documents are unavailable.

Comment: Please note that the same basic tasks are applicable in the context of e-discovery; however, given the complexities of the process, the role of the paralegal should be carefully spelled out by the supervising attorney so as to avoid the kinds of problems discussed here, or the myriad of other difficulties that can arise when seeking access to or responding to requests for electronically stored information.

Request for a Physical or Mental Examination. If a party's mental or physical condition is at issue, such as in a contested custody case, the other side may request that he or she submit to a mental or physical examination. Given the inherently invasive nature of this request, court permission usually must be obtained before a party can be required to submit to such an exam. Courts generally will approve such a request upon proof of "good cause."

Request for a Physical or Mental Examination: A discovery method in which a party asks the court to order the other side to submit to a medical or mental evaluation

---

The Role of the Paralegal

Physical and Mental Examinations

If your office is requesting the examination:

- Draft the motion asking for court permission and, if necessary, draft an accompanying memorandum or affidavit to support the request.
- If in accordance with local practice, develop a short list of proposed examiners for presentation to the court.
- Review the report and, if needed, prepare a summary. If incomplete, prepare a list of possible follow-up questions to ask the examiner.

If your office is responding to the request for an examination:

- If the request is contested, prepare a memorandum or affidavit setting out the grounds for opposition to the request.
- If in accordance with local practice, prepare a short list of proposed examiners for presentation to the court.
- If the request is allowed, help prepare the client for what to expect.
- View the report and, if needed, prepare a summary.

Request for Admissions. The final discovery device is the **request for admissions,** in which one side asks the other party to admit to specific legal or factual allegations, to the authenticity of documents, or to the qualifications of an expert witness. Thus, for example, the husband might be asked to admit to the fact that he is taking medication for depression, or that he has twice been married and divorced, or that all documents relating to his business are authentic. This is done primarily to simplify the issues for trial because once something has been admitted to, it does not need to be proved. The request for admission thus differs from other discovery devices because it is used to confirm rather than to obtain information.

In responding to a request for admission, a party can either admit or deny an allegation, state that he or she is without sufficient information to

Request for Admissions: A discovery method in which a party asks the other side to admit to the truth of certain facts or to the authenticity of certain documents

admit or deny, or object to the propriety of the request. However, before responding that he or she is without sufficient information, a party has a duty to conduct a limited inquiry into the matter. In most states, a party has 30 days in which to reply to a request for admission.

The Role of the Paralegal

Requests for Admissions

If your office is making the request:

- Determine which documents are likely to be introduced at trial, and what factual or legal assertions may possibly be reduced to an admission.
- Draft the request for admission.
- Review the response, and prepare a summary of what has been admitted to. If the response is incomplete or objections made, draft a letter to the other side or prepare a motion to compel.

If your office is responding to the request:

- Promptly review the document and set up a time to meet with the client. Make sure the client knows about the time limit for responding.
- Keep track of the time limit, and remind the attorney to contact the other side if it cannot be complied with; if necessary, draft a motion for an extension of time.
- Carefully prepare a response, making sure that each and every request is properly addressed.[19]

Discovery Difficulties

In most cases, discovery proceeds without too many wrinkles; however, occasionally problems do arise that may require court intervention. Following is a brief discussion about the ways in which the court may be pulled into the discovery process.

Limiting Discovery. A party who believes that discovery has become excessive may seek to limit it by bringing a motion for a **protective order**. A protective order can also be sought when irrelevant or privileged information is requested, but the more common response in this situation is to object to the request. In evaluating the motion, the court looks to determine if the discovery request would produce "annoyance, embarrassment, oppression, or undue burden or expense."[20] If the answer is yes, the court

Protective Order:
A court order to shield the victim from harm; although civil in nature, violation of these orders is a criminal offense in many states

may impose limits even if the information is otherwise discoverable. Courts tend, however, to hold the moving party to a fairly high standard and do not impose limitations lightly.

A party who is concerned about discovery can also file a motion requesting that the court convene a **discovery conference**; in most states, a discovery conference can also be initiated by a judge. At the conference, the court may develop a discovery plan, which typically clarifies the issues for discovery, the methods by which it will proceed, and a time frame for the completion of each phase.

Discovery Conference: A meeting at which the court develops a plan for how discovery will proceed in a case

The Motion to Compel and the Imposition of Sanctions. Where discovery requests are not complied with, attorneys usually try to resolve the matter informally. If this fails, a party can file a **motion to compel**, asking the court to order a response and, possibly, to impose the cost of bringing the motion on the noncomplying party.

Motion to Compel: A request to the court that it order the other side to comply with a discovery request

Where the motion is allowed, the noncomplying party is then under court order to respond according to the terms and conditions set by the court. Thereafter, the failure to respond will subject this party to sanctions. Possible sanctions include imposing costs, treating certain matters in contention as established, preventing the sanctioned party from introducing certain evidence, and in extreme cases, entering a default judgment or a dismissal of the action. In some jurisdictions, a judge may have the discretion to impose sanctions without having first entered a motion to compel.

The Middle Phase: Moving Toward Resolution or Trial

In addition to discovery, other important events take place between the time of filing of the divorce and the divorce hearing. During this time, the parties generally seek to resolve outstanding issues and protect their respective interests. If matters are resolved, the parties will reduce their agreement to writing and proceed to a relatively simple, uncontested divorce hearing. If matters remain unresolved, they will proceed to trial. This discussion assumes that both parties are participating in the process. If the defendant cannot be located or refuses to participate, an uncontested hearing will eventually be held, but it will be uncontested due to lack of participation—rather than because of agreement.

In this section, we look at what takes place during this middle phase of the divorce process. We begin by looking at court motion practice, followed by a discussion of other dispute resolution mechanisms (specifically, negotiation, mediation, and arbitration). We then discuss separation agreements, taking a close look at a sample agreement.

Although this chapter treats each of these topics separately, you should be aware that in the unfolding of an actual divorce case, parties may utilize some or all approaches in various combinations and in various sequences in the process. For example, in one case, a party might first seek temporary orders and then enter into negotiations; in another, the parties might work out an informal interim agreement and then proceed directly to a settlement conference, or they might then turn to the court for temporary orders if an impasse is reached and then resume negotiations. Another couple might reach their final agreement through mediation before the divorce is even filed. In short, there is no prescribed pattern, and the flow of this phase is determined by the circumstances of the individual case.

Motions for Temporary Relief

Overview of Motion Practice

During the pendency of a divorce action, issues may arise that require immediate attention. In this situation, either side can file a motion asking the court to enter an order resolving the matter. Any order entered in response to the motion is temporary and will eventually be superseded by the divorce judgment. The fact that the relief is temporary does not lessen its importance; significant rights may be at stake. Moreover, **temporary orders** frequently shape the final result. As a basic rule, a court's ruling on a motion cannot be appealed because the right of appeal generally attaches to final judgments. However, this rule is not absolute. Thus, for example, a ruling on a motion that would bring a case to an end, such as where a court allows a motion to dismiss, can usually be appealed. Depending on the applicable rules of procedure, appeals may be allowed in other limited situations as well, such as where particularly significant interests are at stake.

Temporary Order:
An order made during the pendency of a legal proceeding; temporary orders are superseded by the judgment

Preparation and Service. Motions are prepared in writing and served on the other party, together with notice as to when and where the motion is to be heard. (For an exception to the advance notice requirements, see the next section, "*Ex Parte* Relief.") Service requirements are usually less formal than at the complaint stage. Most commonly, service is made by the attorney for the moving party, either in hand or by mail, within the requisite number of days, as determined by the applicable rules of procedure, before the motion is scheduled to be heard.

Frequently, a party will submit an affidavit to the court in support of the motion. An **affidavit** is a first-person, sworn statement that, in this instance, sets out the underlying facts showing why the moving party is entitled to the requested relief. A motion may also be accompanied by a

Affidavit:
A factual statement that is signed under the penalties of perjury; often submitted to a court in support of a motion

legal memorandum that provides legal support for the moving party's position. The opposing party may also submit an affidavit or a legal memorandum (or both) to show why the requested relief should be denied. In some jurisdictions, either or both of these documents may be required.

Ex Parte **Relief.** In certain situations, a party may be harmed if he or she gives the other side advance notice of the motion and hearing date. For example, let's say that a father is threatening to take the children out of the country and the mother wants to get a court order prohibiting him from doing this. If she gives him advance notice, he might disappear before the hearing takes place. In this situation, the court could hear her motion on an *ex parte* basis, meaning without notice, enter an order, and then provide the father with the opportunity to come to court and present his side of the story. Other examples of when *ex parte* relief may be appropriate include situations where a party is seeking protection from abuse or seeking to prevent a spouse from dissipating marital assets, as again, advance notice could trigger the very result the party is trying to avoid.

Ex Parte:
A hearing that is held without prior notice to the other side due to the urgent nature of the proceeding or the harm that such notice would cause

Grounded in considerations of procedural fairness, as required by the due process clause, most courts will grant *ex parte* relief only if the moving party can show that giving notice poses a substantial risk of harm. In deciding whether to allow the requested relief, a court must balance the right of an individual to be heard before his or her interests are affected with the need to protect the moving party from the risk of injury or loss. Only where the risk is substantial will it outweigh the procedural rights of the other side. If an order is entered, notice will be provided and the other side will have an opportunity to be heard within a short period of time following the *ex parte* hearing.

Presentation to the Court. Following service, the motion is presented to the court. The procedure for scheduling motions varies from state to state, and within a state may vary from court to court. If you are responsible for scheduling a motion, you should always call the particular court to find out how to get the motion heard.

In some states, the hearing on a motion is conducted like a mini-trial. The rules of evidence are in effect, and the parties take the witness stand and give testimony in response to questions by counsel. In most states, however, the presentation is less formal. The parties are not sworn in as witnesses; instead, they stand before the judge with their attorneys, who present and oppose the motion through oral argument. The parties may then be asked some questions by the judge. Here, formal rules of evidence or procedure are not in effect. After hearing the matter, the judge can enter an order on the spot or can take the matter under advisement. A judge is likely to postpone making the decision when the issue is especially complex or controverted. In some states, judges may be able to make decisions based solely on written submissions, thus eliminating the need for a hearing.

Diversion to Court Conciliation or Mediation Services. In some states, the parties must sit down with a court worker to see if they can resolve matters before the motion can be heard by the judge. Typically, this worker is from the court's family service office or a court-based mediation program. In some states, an exception to the diversion requirement will be made in cases where there is a history of domestic violence. This exception is based on the recognition that it can be unfair and potentially unsafe to require a victim of violence to mediate with an abusive spouse.

If an agreement is reached through this process, it is reduced to writing and presented to the judge for approval. If approved, it becomes the temporary order of the court. If agreement is not reached, the motion is then argued before the judge. In many states, the court worker participates in this court hearing. He or she may report back to the judge on what took place during their session and make recommendations. In other states, the meeting with the court worker is considered confidential, and the worker thus does not participate in the motion session.

While this diversion to a court-based mediation or conciliation program can help couples reach mutually satisfactory agreements, a number of concerns, including the following, have been raised about this process:

1. Especially where they are unrepresented, parties, in locales that do not protect these communications, may not realize that what they tell the court worker is not confidential and will be reported back to the judge.
2. Court workers may pressure the parties to settle, and the failure by a party to agree to a settlement proposal may result in an unfavorable report or recommendation to the court.
3. This process is inappropriate where there has been domestic violence because it requires a victim to sit down, in a spirit of cooperation and conciliation, with someone who has been abusive. In this regard, it should be noted that some diversion programs have a domestic violence exemption.

Specific Divorce Motions

Motion practice in the divorce context is extremely varied. Many motions, such as those for temporary custody or support, are fairly standard, but much creativity can be used to fashion motions to deal with specific problems. For example, let's say that a couple has temporary joint legal custody of their daughter, and the mother has physical custody. The mother gives the daughter a haircut that substantially alters the length and style of her hair. The father objects to her having done this without his consent, and seeks to prevent it from recurring. He could design a motion to address this situation with a caption such as: "Motion to Prevent Wife from Altering Daughter's Hair Without the Husband's Prior Consent." Many attorneys enjoy this creative aspect of family law practice, while it drives others to distraction, particularly when they are on the receiving end of a highly original motion.

Following is a brief description of some of the commonly filed motions, followed by a sample motion and supporting affidavit.

Motion for Temporary Custody and Visitation. After a divorce is filed, many couples work out an informal, temporary arrangement regarding the children. Where this is not possible, one party will usually file a motion asking the court to award him or her temporary custody. After a hearing, the court will enter an order for custody and visitation, which will then be in effect until the divorce judgment is entered unless problems arise and a change is sought via another motion.

The importance of a temporary arrangement—whether through agreement or by a court order—should not be underestimated. Because courts are reluctant to disrupt children once they are settled into a satisfactory routine, temporary arrangements often ripen into permanent ones. The longer the interim stage, the more likely it is that the parent with temporary custody will end up as the custodial parent.

Temporary custody orders are also important where there is any risk that one parent might flee with the children. If an order is in place, a parent who interferes with the custodial or visitation rights of the other parent can be held in contempt of court. Moreover, a temporary custody order may be a necessary prerequisite to the initiation of parental kidnapping charges in the event a parent disappears with the children. Accordingly, even where parties are able to work things out informally, a temporary custody order may be prudent.

Motion for the Appointment of an Investigator or Evaluator. Where custody is contested, a party may ask to have someone appointed to perform a custody evaluation or investigation. An investigation is usually done by a **guardian ad litem**. Typically, a guardian ad litem interviews the parents and other involved adults, such as teachers and neighbors, and spends time with the children. He or she may also visit the homes of both parents. The guardian ad litem then files a written report with the court containing his or her recommendations about custodial and visitation arrangements.

Guardian ad Litem:
A person who is appointed by a court to conduct a custody investigation; may also refer to a person appointed to provide legal representation to a child

In some cases, such as where there are concerns about the mental or emotional well-being of a parent or child, it may make more sense to have an evaluation done by a mental health professional. Here, the evaluation most likely would consist of a series of interviews and observations. Typically, each parent and each child is interviewed separately, and the children are observed alone and with each parent. Again, a written report and recommendations are filed with the court.

In either situation, the parties are entitled to a copy of the report and to an opportunity to question the guardian ad litem or the evaluator in court. This right is important because these reports tend to carry a lot of weight with judges, and parties must be given the chance to question the findings where they disagree with them.

Motion for Temporary Support.

During the pendency of a divorce, a party may be in immediate need of child or spousal support and unable to wait until a permanent financial arrangement is in place. Accordingly, all states permit an interim award of child support and most permit an interim award of spousal support. Again, because this interim order often ripens into the permanent one, it is vital that all supporting financial documentation be carefully prepared and presented to the court.

Motion for Payment of Fees and Costs.

As a general rule, each party is responsible for paying his or her own attorney's fees. However, in most states, a spouse who lacks the resources to secure ongoing representation can ask the court to order the other spouse to pay his or her fees. This request can be made at trial or during the pendency of the action.

In evaluating the request, the court will compare the financial status of both parties. Where there is a significant disparity, the court may award fees. However, there is no right to a fee award, and the decision is generally within the sound discretion of the trial judge. In many states, judges tend to award fees only in cases of extreme hardship.

Motions Relating to the Protection of Assets.

A frequent concern during the pendency of a divorce is that a party will dissipate marital assets. To protect against this, the other spouse can seek a variety of protective court orders.

A party can ask the court to issue a restraining order enjoining the other spouse from disposing of or encumbering the asset in question. He or she can also ask the court to attach property, which serves to put the world on notice that the asset is subject to an unresolved claim and makes the asset difficult to sell. The court can also freeze assets that belong to a spouse but are under the control of a third party, such as a bank. Here, the order would command the bank not to allow the spouse to withdraw or transfer funds. These motions need to be drafted with particular care, as they may need to satisfy the technical requirements of nondivorce statutes that govern interests in property.

As mentioned earlier, if a party has a well-grounded fear that upon receiving notice of a motion to protect assets, his or her spouse is likely to dispose of the assets in question, he or she can appear before the court on an *ex parte* basis. If the court agrees that the danger is real, it will secure the asset first and then provide the other side with notice and the opportunity to be heard.

Motion for Protection from Abuse. During the pendency of the divorce, most states allow either party to seek protection from abuse by way of a motion. A spouse can ask that the other party be ordered to leave him or her alone and, if they are still living together, that the abusive spouse be vacated from the marital premises. In most states, this approach is not exclusive; a divorcing spouse may bring a motion within the framework of the divorce, file a separate petition under the state's abuse protection act, or both. However, these approaches may yield different results. The order entered in response to a divorce motion may have less clout than one entered pursuant to the state's abuse prevention law; the former is less likely to be criminally enforceable and it may not enhance the arrest powers of the police (see Chapter 3). Of course, these differences should be assessed before action is taken, so the most appropriate course can be pursued.

Sample Motion and Supporting Affidavit

Exhibit 10.7 is a sample motion for temporary custody with a supporting affidavit. The body of the motion contains the following three parts:

1. The relief desired
2. Supporting reasons
3. A prayer for relief

As a general rule, motions are written in simple, straightforward language so the judge, who in all likelihood has countless motions before him or her, can quickly determine what is being requested.

The Role of the Paralegal

As with discovery, paralegals play an important and varied role in motion practice. Paralegals may be responsible for drafting the necessary court papers—such as the motion, supporting affidavit, and legal memorandum. Drafting the affidavit requires careful interviewing of the affiant to get his or her story, putting it into a cohesive, first-person narrative, and reviewing it with the affiant for accuracy. Preparation of the memorandum requires good research and writing skills, as the appropriate legal authority must be identified and presented in a persuasive manner.

Paralegals can also play a vital role in preparing for the court hearing. Supporting documents such as financial statements may need to be

304 Chapter 10 The Divorce Process

Exhibit 10.7
Motion for
Temporary
Custody and
Supporting
Affidavit

STATE OF ANYWHERE

Middlesex County

Family Court,
Civil No. 2245

JERRY FREEMAN,
    Plaintiff

v.

CARRIE GREEN,
    Defendant

PLAINTIFF'S MOTION FOR TEMPORARY CUSTODY

NOW COMES the plaintiff in the above-captioned action and asks that this Honorable Court award him temporary physical and legal custody of the party's minor daughter, Melissa, age seven years old.

In support of his Motion, Plaintiff states as follows, and also incorporates by reference, the attached Affidavit, which more fully sets out the facts in support of his request:

1. That the plaintiff has been the primary caretaker of Melissa for the past three years. Before this time, the parties shared child-care responsibilities on a more or less equal basis.

2. That over the past three years, as a result of depression and increased alcohol consumption, the wife has provided little attention or care to Melissa, and has been emotionally abusive toward her.

3. That the wife moved out of the family home approximately six months ago, and since then has had infrequent and irregular contact with Melissa.

4. That the best interest of Melissa would be served by awarding temporary legal and physical custody to the father so that continuity of care and nurturing is maintained.

WHEREFORE, the Plaintiff requests that this Honorable Court grant this Motion and award him temporary custody of Melissa.

Respectfully Submitted,
Jerry Freeman
By his Attorney

_____

Ellen Jones
Jones & Hernandez
11 Court Street
Freeport, Any State 02167

Exhibit 10.7 cont.

STATE OF ANYWHERE

Middlesex County

JERRY FREEMAN,

      Plaintiff

v.

CARRIE GREEN,
      Defendant

Family Court,
Civil No. 2245

AFFIDAVIT OF PLAINTIFF IN
SUPPORT OF HIS MOTION FOR
TEMPORARY CUSTODY

I, Jerry Freeman, do depose and say:

1. I am married to the defendant Carrie Green, and I filed a divorce complaint with this Court on April 18, 2015.

2. We have one child. Her name is Melissa and she was born on March 15, 2008.

3. During the first four years of Melissa's life, my wife and I shared child-care responsibilities, although Carrie was the primary caretaker of Melissa during her first six months. After this time, we both fully participated in all aspects of Melissa's life, including making child-care arrangements for her while we were at work.

4. Three years ago, Carrie lost both of her parents in a tragic accident. As a result, she became depressed and began to drink heavily. She has refused to get any help for either the depression or the drinking.

5. Since then, our family life has been torn apart. Carrie has been unable to hold down a job and has essentially withdrawn from the family. She has been unable to care for Melissa in any predictable manner. For example, she forgot to pick Melissa up from her after-school program on several occasions due to the fact that she was drinking. Needless to say, this was extremely upsetting for Melissa. After this occurred several times, I took over the responsibility for picking up Melissa. I also took her to school, except on those rare occasions when Carrie was able to get out of bed on time to take her.

6. Although she has not been physically abusive, Carrie has become emotionally abusive, especially when she has been drinking. She yells at Melissa for no reason, and also belittles her. But even more upsetting to Melissa has been her mother's withdrawal of love and affection.

Exhibit 10.7 cont.

7. I feel that I tried desperately to help my wife, but nothing worked, and about six months ago, she moved out.

8. During all of this time, I have been the primary caretaker of Melissa in addition to working full-time. I may not be a perfect parent, but I provide her with love and stability. I also am able to take care of all her daily needs.

9. Melissa and I are attempting to rebuild a life. She is in counseling to try to resolve some of her pain and confusion. On a few occasions, in order to help Melissa, the counselor has arranged to have all of us attend a family counseling session. Carrie has failed to attend all but one of these sessions. The one time she showed up she was intoxicated, and the counselor had to ask her to leave.

10. I fully believe that it is in Melissa's best interest that I be awarded sole custody and I am fully prepared to continue as her primary caretaker.

Signed under pains and penalties of perjury, this 20th day of June, 2015.

_____

Jerry Freeman

gathered, and clients need to be prepared so they can respond to questions from counsel or the judge. Some attorneys also like to have the paralegal who is working on the case accompany him or her to court. In court, the paralegal can perform a variety of important tasks. For instance, she or he can continue to prepare the client, offer the client emotional support, assist in the preparation of an updated financial statement if requested by the court, or assist the attorney in handling the flow of paperwork. In some jurisdictions, paralegals are allowed to present uncontested motions to the court.

Alternative Approaches to Dispute Resolution

Ultimately, the overwhelming majority of divorce cases are settled before trial, most commonly through the process of negotiation. In recent years, increasing numbers of divorcing couples also have used two alternative approaches to resolving their differences: mediation and, although far less common, arbitration. In this section, we compare these three dispute resolution approaches. Please note that the discussion is general in nature and does not address the more formal principles and theories of each approach. We also consider two new approaches to the practice of law — the provision of "unbundled" legal services and the collaborative law model.

Negotiation

Through **negotiation**, each attorney acts on behalf of his or her client to see if a settlement can be reached. In contrast to mediation and arbitration, no neutral third party is involved.

Negotiations can take place on the telephone, but it is also common for one side to contact the other at some point in the divorce process to see if a settlement conference can be arranged. This conference can be either two-way, involving just the attorneys, or four-way, involving the attorneys as well as the clients. A four-way conference is generally more productive because the clients can play an active role in initiating and responding to settlement proposals. However, in some situations, such as where there is tremendous animosity between the parties or there is a history of abuse, it may make more sense to have the attorneys meet, at least initially, without the clients present.

Ideally, each attorney will have met with his or her client before the conference to explore what the client wants and where he or she is willing to compromise. The attorney should also help the client to anticipate what the other side is likely to request so he or she can think about possible responses. If this advance work is done, both attorneys will begin the negotiations with a good understanding of their clients' positions.

At the conference, ground rules are usually established. An important consideration is whether each issue will be negotiated separately until impasse or agreement or whether everything will be placed on the table at the same time. The advantage of the former approach is that it minimizes the possibility of inappropriate linkage of issues; for example, the husband offering to give the wife sole custody if she drops her request for spousal support. If the parties decide to negotiate each issue separately, any agreement reached on a single issue is usually not considered final until all other issues have been resolved. By conditioning finality of each issue on reaching a comprehensive settlement, the parties do not risk the loss of potential bargaining chips. For example, if the parties agree on a division of property, a spouse could reopen this matter if unable to get what he or she wants with respect to spousal support. Thus, a husband might back away from his agreement to allow a wife to remain in the home if, later in the negotiations, she insists on spousal support.

Once the basic framework is established, one side will open with its offer. This offer rarely represents the party's bottom line because this would leave no room for the give-and-take that characterizes the negotiation process. However, if the proposal is too outrageous, the party may not appear to be negotiating in good faith, which can jeopardize the integrity of the process. When the other side responds, they too will leave room for concessions but again should avoid unreasonable counterproposals.

Negotiation:
The process through which attorneys seek to resolve a case outside court; often done at a settlement conference at which the clients are present

As the negotiations proceed, it is common for each party to confer privately with his or her attorney. At this time, responses and new proposals can be formulated. These meetings can also serve as valuable cooling-off periods because these conferences tend to get heated.

The negotiating session can conclude in a number of ways. One party may unilaterally declare it over and may even storm out, perhaps because of frustration with the process or as a deliberate "bullying" tactic designed to exact concessions. The parties may also mutually recognize that they can go no further. At this point, they may decide that the case should be marked for trial or that they should reconvene at a future date and give settlement another chance.

If the negotiations end in agreement, one side usually offers to prepare an initial draft of a separation agreement and then send it to the other side for review. This is possible even where the parties have not ironed out all of the details; here, one side offers to see if they can work out the missing details in a mutually satisfactory manner. Although drafting the agreement is time-consuming and potentially more expensive for the client, it is usually advantageous to be the drafter because once something is in writing, it seems to acquire a presumptive validity, and suggesting changes has a bit of an uphill quality to it.

Although paralegals do not, as a rule, participate in the negotiations themselves, they can serve a number of very useful functions at a settlement conference. Because the paralegal is not directly involved in the negotiations, he or she may be able to make observations that the attorney is too engaged to notice, such as subtle shifts in tone of voice or body language that may indicate that the other side is altering its position. An attending paralegal who is able to take in the whole process may also be in a good position to help formulate proposals and counterproposals. Note taking can also make an important contribution; good notes can lay the foundation for a subsequent settlement agreement and are essential if disputes arise over what was agreed on. Before the conference, the paralegal can, of course, play a crucial role in helping to prepare the client for what is often a nerve-wracking experience.

Mediation

Mediation:
A nonadversarial approach to dispute resolution in which a neutral third party helps parties reach a mutually satisfactory resolution to a conflict

Mediation is a nonadversarial approach to dispute resolution. It has become a popular option for divorcing couples who wish to resolve their differences without going to trial. Through mediation, a neutral third party—the mediator—helps couples reach their own agreement. The mediator is not an advocate for either side but rather guides the parties through the process of reaching agreement by helping them to identify important issues, consider options, and structure a realistic settlement.

Divorce mediators come from a range of professional backgrounds,[21] although most are either mental health professionals or attorneys. Mediators may work in interdisciplinary teams. Thus, for example, a social worker and an attorney might work together, as each brings a distinct but complementary body of knowledge and set of skills to the process.

Proponents of this approach believe that a primary advantage of mediation is that it stresses cooperation and encourages parties to work out long-term solutions that make sense for them. As a client-centered process, it stresses individual responsibility for decision making, and by not abdicating responsibility to judges or lawyers, participants gain a sense of control over their future. Moreover, it is hoped that by stressing cooperation and communication, mediation will give couples the tools they will need to resolve future disputes, thus promoting greater postdivorce stability and satisfaction.

However, in light of the fact that mediation emphasizes conciliation and cooperation, many experts in the field believe that the process is not appropriate in cases with a history of domestic violence. Accordingly, some mediators screen out these couples as unsuitable for mediation—while others have adopted specific protocols, such as separate interviews, in an effort to ensure a safe process and fair results.[22]

Turning briefly to the process (keep in mind that this overview is general in nature and that there is no single approach to mediation), during the initial session, the mediator explains the process, including the nature of his or her role, the responsibilities of the participants, and the applicable ground rules, such as those relating to confidentiality. If the mediation is to continue, a contract to mediate, which sets out the operative framework, is usually signed by the couple and the mediator.

Formal discovery is not available in mediation, and the mediator has no authority to compel disclosure. Accordingly, in signing the mediation agreement, the parties typically commit to full disclosure and to provide copies of documents that would ordinarily be requested in the course of discovery, such as tax returns, bank statements, and asset inventories. If during the course of mediation, the mediator suspects that a party is concealing assets, he or she can break off mediation and refuse to resume unless the parties confer with counsel. However, some mediators believe this would be overstepping their bounds, reasoning that the parties assumed this risk when they consented to mediation.[23]

After everyone is satisfied that all relevant information has been provided, the mediator helps the parties identify what they see as the various options and assists them in expanding the range of acceptable alternatives. The mediator often plays an active role in this stage in the process. Once the range of acceptable options have been identified, the parties are faced with the task of sorting through the possibilities, and the mediator generally steps back so that the parties themselves can reach the agreement, although he or she may play a critical facilitative role.

Once a settlement is reached, the mediator usually drafts an agreement embodying the parties' understanding. Most, if not all, mediators will strongly encourage each person to review the agreement with his or her lawyer before signing it.[24] The mediated agreement may be redrafted into a formal separation agreement, which includes the standard separation agreement provisions, or it may serve as the document presented to the court for approval at the divorce hearing.

People working in the family law field have responded to the increased use of divorce mediation with both enthusiasm and trepidation. According to enthusiasts, a primary advantage of mediation is that it stresses cooperation and encourages parties to work out long-term solutions that make sense for them. As a client-centered process, it stresses individual responsibility for decision making, and by not abdicating responsibility to judges or lawyers, participants gain a sense of control over their future. Moreover, it is hoped that by stressing cooperation and communication, mediation will give couples the tools they will need to resolve future disputes, thus promoting greater post-divorce stability and satisfaction.

Despite these potential benefits, many persons who work with battered women, including some mediators, have raised serious concerns about the appropriateness of mediation where violence is a factor. Of primary concern is that mediation emphasizes conciliation and cooperation, which assumes a degree of mutual respect and equality of status that is not present in violent relationships. Accordingly, some mediators screen out cases with a history of domestic violence as inappropriate for mediation — while others have adopted specific protocols, such as separate interviews, in an effort to ensure a safe process and fair results.

Arbitration

Arbitration:
A dispute resolution mechanism whereby parties agree to submit their disagreement to a neutral decision maker; usually binding, subject to a limited right of court review

Long identified with labor, commercial, and international disputes, **arbitration** has not traditionally been used by divorcing couples to reach a settlement agreement. Where utilized in the divorce context, it has typically been pursuant to a clause in a separation agreement in which the parties agree to submit certain postdivorce disputes to arbitration. However, there has been a notable increase in the use of predivorce arbitration as an alternative to litigation, and a number of states now have specific statutes that govern the use of arbitration in family law cases.

Arbitration is similar to the judicial process in that the parties present their case to a neutral, third-party decision maker (or panel of decision makers), but the process is considerably more flexible, and the parties retain a greater degree of control than they have in court. A dispute can be submitted to arbitration only if the parties so agree; one side cannot force the other to arbitrate unless specifically required by prior agreement. The arbitrator's authority derives from the parties' agreement — the arbitrator cannot make decisions about matters not directly entrusted to him or her by the parties.

As a general rule, there is a presumption in favor of the validity of the arbitral award, and courts will typically only modify or vacate an award under limited circumstances, such as where there has been fraud or bias, or where the arbitrator exceeded the scope of his or her authority. However, many courts review arbitral decisions more carefully when they are made in the family law context, especially when the rights of children are at stake, and some courts will not enforce provisions relating to custody and visitation.

The Collaborative Law Model

In addition to these three established dispute resolution alternatives, the collaborative law model has surged in popularity in the divorce context, and a number of states have enacted collaborative law statutes to guide the practice. The hallmark of this approach is that the parties and their lawyers commit in advance to settling the case. Reinforcing the centrality of this commitment, the attorneys in a collaborative divorce agree in advance to disqualify themselves from representing their clients in court should the process break down before all issues are fully resolved. Accordingly, if a trial becomes necessary, each party will have to hire a new attorney, which is likely to add both time and cost as the new attorney will need to be brought up to speed on the details of the case.

Collaborative Law: An approach to the practice of law that stresses cooperation and the avoidance of litigation

The collaborative divorce process bears some resemblance to both mediation and negotiation. Like mediation, the focus is on helping the parties work through their differences in a nonconfrontational manner. The parties also are encouraged to speak directly to one another in the course of the settlement process. However, in contrast to mediation, no neutral third party guides the process; rather, each spouse is represented by his or her own attorney. Individual representation aligns the collaborative law with the negotiation process that typically accompanies a divorce; however, in contrast, in addition to the emphasis on cooperation, the threat that a party will break off negotiations in favor of litigation if the party does not get what he or she wants is considerably less, as the party would have to hire a new lawyer to represent him or her in court. Thus, there is a built-in incentive to settle the case. Collaborative divorce also can be characterized as a type of unbundled legal services (see the discussion that follows), as an attorney is hired for the bounded purpose of settling the case, agreeing in advance not to take the matter to court should the settlement process break down.

Proponents of this approach stress that the four-way commitment to settlement fosters a creative and engaged problem-solving ethos as distinct from the typically bitter, winner-take-all approach of the traditional adversarial model of lawyering. They also stress the benefit to clients of being at the center of the process. Not surprisingly, however, the practice also has its detractors. Of particular concern is that the disqualification requirement may potentially put an attorney in breach of the ethical requirement that he or she zealously represent the interests of his or her client, as those interests may well necessitate taking the case to court in the event the settlement process breaks down. Another concern is that rather than being empowering, clients may experience the emphasis on settlement as coercive, since they know that if the process fails, they will need to retain new counsel.[25]

Unbundled Legal Services

Although not quite an alternative mode of dispute resolution, an innovative approach to the practice of law that has been gaining popularity in the family law arena also merits attention. In what is referred to as "unbundled" legal services, or limited task representation, an attorney agrees to provide a client with limited assistance from a menu of options instead of providing him or her with comprehensive representation. Unbundled services include the giving of legal advice, coaching on how to handle a case, assistance with drafting pleadings (a practice that is also referred to as *ghostwriting*), and perhaps, less typically, representation in court.[26]

Unbundled Legal Services: An attorney agrees to provide a client with limited assistance from a menu of options instead of providing the client with comprehensive representation

Clearly cost-effective, this approach has been praised as a way to provide legal assistance to low- and middle-income litigants who lack the resources to retain a lawyer for full-service representation—and who therefore would otherwise try to navigate the legal system on their own. This approach has also been commended for giving individuals greater choice and flexibility by "dissolv[ing] the all-or-nothing model of lawyering and creat[ing] an opportunity to access the expertise of a lawyer only when the client determines that one is needed most."[27]

However, some commentators have raised the important concern that a client may not fully understand the allocation of responsibilities between himself or herself and the lawyer, particularly if the case turns out to be more complex or contested than originally anticipated, which is not uncommon in the divorce arena. Supporters of the unbundled approach stress that potential confusion can be avoided through the drafting of clear contracts for services; nonetheless, the concern remains that a party who is confronting the emotional strain of divorce may not have a clear understanding of an agreement for limited assistance, and therefore may nonetheless come to expect more from the attorney, especially if the case becomes more involved or hotly contested than originally anticipated.

Reaching Resolution: The Separation Agreement

As discussed in the previous section, divorce cases may proceed along many different pathways, but the vast majority of cases are ultimately settled before trial. Where the parties are able to resolve all outstanding issues, their understanding is embodied in a **separation agreement**. The usual process is for one side to offer to draft an initial agreement, which is then reviewed by the other side. Comments are made, and the agreement usually goes through several revisions before the parties sign it. Once the agreement is executed, the case is considered uncontested, and a simple divorce hearing rather than a trial on the merits can be scheduled. (See the section entitled "The Uncontested Case," later in this chapter.)

Separation Agreement: A contract between divorcing spouses in which they set out the terms of their agreement relative to all collateral matters

Technically, a separation agreement is a contract in which the parties structure their postdivorce rights and responsibilities. However, because of the state's interest in the marital relationship, separation agreements are not treated like ordinary contracts. In most states, they are subject to careful review at the divorce hearing, and a judge can set aside an agreement or any provisions that he or she determines to be unfair or to have been agreed on without adequate disclosure.

Drafting the Agreement

In drafting agreements, most offices rely to some extent on standard forms. For routine clauses, such as those regarding waivers, severability, and the governing law, this usually presents no problem, although each provision should nonetheless be reviewed to make certain it is appropriate in the particular case. (See the sample separation agreement starting on page 317.) Beyond routine clauses, great care must be taken to tailor the separation agreement to the case at hand. Each situation should be carefully reviewed and the agreement drafted with all of the particulars in mind. Unfortunately, this is not always done, and the drafting process can be reduced to a filling in of names and dates on a standardized form. This is unfair to clients because it minimizes the importance of this document that, especially where children are involved, regulates critical aspects of a couple's postdivorce lives for many years into the future.

The Role of the Paralegal

An important part of your work as a paralegal may be to assist in the drafting of separation agreements. Before you begin drafting, it is essential that you have a clear understanding of what has been decided on so the agreement is both complete and accurate. Despite the care with which you approach the task, issues sometimes do not become apparent until the drafting is under way. For example, as you are drafting the visitation provisions, you may realize that in the complexity of the arrangements, the parties neglected to spell out arrangements for the children's birthdays. It can be helpful to the attorney handling the case if you keep track of all possible omissions and bring them to the attorney's attention. It can also be useful for you to draft the missing provisions, but you must make it clear that these are proposed as distinct from agreed-upon provisions.

After the attorney reviews the agreement, he or she may go over it with the client or ask you to do so before mailing it to the other side. Reviewing the agreement with the client ensures that it accurately reflects what your client believes he or she has settled on. In the event that your client changes his or her mind about anything — not an infrequent occurrence — it is better to know about it before the agreement is sent to the other side.

If your office is reviewing rather than drafting an agreement, you may be asked to assist in this process. The agreement should be read carefully to make sure that it conforms with what has been decided on. After reviewing it, you should draft a memorandum to the attorney in charge of the case, setting out any potential discrepancies. Also, during your review, you may notice issues that have not been addressed; these should be noted in your memo, making clear that to the best of your knowledge, these are omissions as distinct from inaccuracies. Most offices will also have the client review the agreement to ensure that it conforms with his or her understanding of what was agreed upon. Again, in the event your client has changed his or her mind about anything, it is always better to know about it before the other side is told that the agreement as drafted looks fine.

Sample Separation Agreement and Comments

The sample separation agreement (Exhibit 10.8), with its explanatory comments, will give you an understanding of how to construct a well-drafted agreement. Keep in mind that this agreement covers one couple's situation; it is not universal in its reach and does not contain all possible provisions.

▪ The Divorce Hearing

Once the parties have worked out their differences and reduced their agreement to writing, or it has become clear that a settlement is not possible, a **divorce hearing** is requested. Where the parties have reached an agreement, an uncontested hearing is requested; where they have not reached agreement, the request would be for a contested hearing, more commonly referred to as a *trial*. Most courts retain separate scheduling calendars for contested and uncontested cases. Uncontested hearings are brief and easily scheduled, whereas contested cases usually must be pre-tried, and the trial itself can easily last a week or longer.

Divorce Hearing:
The court hearing at which a marriage is dissolved and collateral issues resolved; results in a divorce judgment

Exhibit 10.8
Separation
Agreement

SEPARATION AGREEMENT BY AND BETWEEN
MARIE SMITH AND DAVID SMITH

This Separation Agreement is entered into this 10th day of May 2014, by David Smith (the "husband" or the "father") and Marie Smith (the "wife" or the "mother"). All of the references to "parties" shall be to the husband and wife.

Statement of Facts

1. The parties were married at Chicago, Illinois, on July 6th, 2006, and last lived together at 129 Cherry Lane in Newtowne, Any State, on or about September 15, 2013.

2. Two children were born to the marriage. John was born on October 17, 2009, and Carla was born on May 11, 2007. All of the references to "children" shall be to John and Carla.

3. The husband and wife have separated, they are living apart, and the wife has filed a Complaint for Divorce on the grounds of irretrievable breakdown of the marriage in the Any County Probate and Family Court.

The husband and wife desire by this Agreement to confirm their separation and to settle between themselves all of the questions pertaining to their respective property and estate rights, spousal support, care and custody of their children, and all other rights and obligations arising from their marital relationship that should be settled in view of the pending Complaint for Divorce.

NOW THEREFORE, in consideration of the foregoing and of the mutual covenants and agreements hereinafter contained, the parties mutually agree as follows:

Comment:

These introductory clauses, sometimes referred to as "recitals," set out basic factual information about the parties. If the divorce has not been filed at the time the agreement is signed, language should be included to make clear that the subsequent filing of the divorce will not affect the validity of the agreement.

Most commonly the parties are referred to as "husband" and "wife." To avoid confusion, it is best not to refer to them as the plaintiff and defendant, since in a future action the designations could be reversed. Some agreements refer to the parties by their first names. This imparts a friendlier, less formal tone, and may not be appropriate in many cases.

The "NOW THEREFORE," clause sets out that the agreement is supported by consideration in that both parties are relinquishing certain rights in exchange for promises from the other.

Exhibit 10.8 cont.

Article One — Custody and Visitation

A. CUSTODY

The wife shall have physical custody of the children subject to the husband's right of visitation. Her home shall be their primary residence, and subject to the below exception for when the children are with the husband, the wife shall be responsible for making the day-to-day decisions regarding the children. However, when the children are with their father, he may make the day-to-day decisions necessary in order for him to care for them.

The parties shall have joint legal custody of the children and shall make all major decisions regarding the children together. Major decisions include, but are not limited to, decisions about education, medical care, mental health treatment, camps, and significant after-school activities, such as participation in Little League baseball.

In the event of a medical emergency, either parent may act without obtaining the prior consent of the other parent if consent cannot be secured in a timely fashion. The other parent shall be notified of the emergency at the first possible moment.

Comment:

It is always a good idea to define the custodial terms used in the agreement. If the applicable statute contains a definition, this language can be incorporated into the agreement.

As can be gleaned from the above clause, a fertile ground for postdivorce disputes is whether a certain decision is major or minor. This, of course, is relevant to the allocation of decision-making authority between the parties. One approach to this potential problem is to include a list identifying possible areas of future decision making as either major or minor, but it is virtually impossible to anticipate all contingencies.

B. VISITATION

The parties agree that the husband may spend time with the children in accordance with the following schedule:

1. The father shall pick both children up from school on Wednesdays and return them to the mother's house by 7:30 P.M. It is understood that he will usually pick them up from their extended day program by 5:00 P.M., but he may pick them up anytime following the end of their regular school day. If the children have homework, he will make sure it is completed before he returns them to the mother's house.

2. So that the father can enjoy separate time with each child, he shall pick John up on Tuesdays, and Carla up on Thursdays in accordance with the arrangement described in paragraph 1 above. The inability of one child to visit in a given week due to illness or other commitments will not affect the father's right to spend separate time with the other child. Also, the parties agree to try to arrange another visit to replace the missed one; if this is not practical, the father will forgo the visit for that week.

Exhibit 10.8 cont.

3. The arrangement described above in paragraphs 1 and 2 shall continue during the summer without alteration, except during designated vacation times, and the father will pick the children up from whatever activity they are enrolled in instead of from school.

4. The arrangement described above in paragraphs 1 and 2 shall be suspended during Christmas, February, and spring vacations. The children will spend February vacation with their father, and he shall be responsible for arranging for child care while he is at work. The children shall remain with their mother for Christmas and spring vacations, but the father agrees to take two days off during each of these weeks, excluding Christmas, New Year's Day, or any other legal holiday that falls during either week, in order to be with the children. These days may be consecutive, and the children can sleep at the father's house on the intervening night.

5. The children will visit with their father every Saturday. On alternate weeks, they may sleep at his house on Saturday night. He will pick them up from their mother's at 9:00 A.M. on Saturday. If it is not an overnight week, he will return them on Saturday at 5:00 P.M. If it is an overnight week, he shall return them by 11:00 A.M. on Sunday.

6. In addition to the above, the parties agree to the following with respect to the summer and holidays:

   (1) Every summer, each parent may spend an uninterrupted two weeks with the children. In selecting vacation weeks, the parties will confer so that vacation schedules can be coordinated with the children's summer activities. Each agrees to provide the other with information about where they will be during this vacation time, and will provide a telephone number and allow the other reasonable telephone access to the children.

   (2) With respect to holidays, time shall be allocated in accordance with the below schedule. The parties agree that this schedule supersedes the regular visitation schedule.

       (i) The children shall be with the mother on Mother's Day and her birthday.

       (ii) The children shall be with the father on Father's Day and his birthday. The children may stay over at the father's house on both of these occasions.

       (iii) The children shall be with the father on the first two nights of Passover and on the first and last nights of Hanukkah. The children may stay over at the father's house on these occasions. The parties further agree that at the request of the father, the children may visit with him on any other major Jewish holiday. However, these will not be overnight visits.

       (iv) The children shall be with the mother on Christmas Eve and Christmas Day and on Easter.

       (v) The children shall be with their mother on Halloween. However, the parties agree that the father may come to the mother's home before the children go out trick-or-treating so he can see them in their costumes.

Exhibit 10.8 cont.

(vi) The parties will rotate Thanksgiving Day on a yearly basis. The children shall be with their mother in 2014, their father in 2015, and shall continue to alternate yearly. The parent who does not have the children on Thanksgiving Day may spend that Friday with them.

(vii) The parties will rotate spending New Year's Eve and New Year's Day with the children. In 2014, the children shall spend New Year's Eve with their father and New Year's Day with their mother, and shall alternate on a yearly basis.

(viii) With respect to the children's birthdays, the parties agree that they both shall have the right to spend time with the children on their birthdays. At present, the parties believe they can work out the details on their own. If this does not work, they agree to consult with their attorneys to develop a more structured arrangement.

(ix) The parties agree that there will be no special schedule for the rest of the holidays, and the regular schedule will be followed on these occasions.

7. The parties recognize that from time to time something may come up that requires an adjustment in this visitation schedule. For example, the mother occasionally has meetings on Monday evenings; when this occurs, she shall notify the father, and he shall make every effort to arrange his schedule so he can visit with the children on Monday instead of Wednesday. The parties agree they will make every effort to accommodate reasonable requests of the other parent. If such adjustment results in a loss of visitation time by the father, the parties will try to make up this time.

Comment:

This is a very detailed visitation arrangement. Many agreements do not include this level of detail, and some simply provide for the right of reasonable visitation. However, unless the parties get along well, detail can be crucial to the success of visitation arrangements. Parents often underestimate how painful the coordination of custody and visitation arrangements can be, and how easily things can fall apart. A set schedule reduces the amount of negotiation that must take place, and thus reduces the potential for conflict, although, as this agreement does, parties can certainly include language that permits schedule changes based on mutual agreement.

Moreover, even where parents are reasonably friendly, holidays can trigger strong emotional reactions. Without a structure in place, parents may be unable to work out arrangements that permit both of them to spend holiday time with the children. As any family law attorney can attest to, the holiday season is likely to be one of their busiest and most stressful times of year.

Another matter that suggests caution when contemplating an unstructured visitation clause is the new relationship factor. Parents often fail to anticipate how painful it can be when their former spouse begins dating, especially if a relationship becomes serious. At this juncture, even parents who have been flexible and accommodating may find themselves caught up in conflict about arrangements. Mom might be less willing to let the

Exhibit 10.8 cont.

children go to Dad's house when she suspects his new romantic interest is present, and Dad might seek increased time with the children to keep them away from Mom's new romantic interest. In short, parental jealousy and hurt may result in a distortion of previous arrangements.

This agreement makes a clear distinction between physical custody and visitation rights — there is no doubt that the children live with their mother and visit with their father. However, there may be situations where this distinction is blurred. For example, let's assume that at the four-way settlement conference, Mom asks for sole physical custody, and Dad asks for joint physical custody, but, in fact they have similar views about how much time the children should spend with each parent and that the allocation is essentially sole physical custody with liberal visitation rights. But what if Dad objects to being characterized as a visiting parent because it connotes a lack of involvement? Here, creative drafting might save the agreement. Instead of using the terms "sole physical custody" and "visiting parent," Mom could be identified as the primary caretaker parent with her home as the children's primary residence, and Dad could be identified as the secondary care parent. Sometimes when parents are fighting about how they are to be identified, rather than how time is actually to be spent with the children, these kinds of creative compromises can prevent negotiations from collapsing (see Chapter 5).

C. PARENTAL COOPERATION

Each party agrees to foster a feeling of affection between the children and the other party, and each agrees not to do anything to estrange the children from the other party or to hamper the free and natural development of either child's love and respect for the other party. The parties agree not to discuss the other's personal life with the children.

Comment:

Although it is fairly standard to include a parental cooperation clause, these clauses are probably not enforceable. It is unlikely that a court would hold someone in contempt for failing to foster a feeling of affection for the other parent, although a court might alter custody or visitation arrangements if one parent was actively seeking to alienate the children from the other.

D. RIGHT OF EACH PARENT TO FULL MEDICAL AND SCHOOL INFORMATION

Each parent is entitled access to the health and educational records of the children to the extent permitted by law. Neither parent shall interfere with the other parent's right of access.

Comment:

Language to this effect is pretty standard in most separation agreements. However, when abuse is an issue, access may need to be restricted in order to protect the safety of a spouse or child. Where a right of access to records is provided by statute, a parent may need some kind of court order in order to limit the rights of the other parent.

Exhibit 10.8 cont.

Article Two — Child Support

A. BASE AMOUNT AND APPLICABILITY OF THE GUIDELINES

1. The husband shall pay to the wife the sum of $175.00 per week for the support of the children in accordance with the Child Support Guidelines ("Guidelines"). The parties agree that the payments shall be by wage assignment, and the husband agrees to promptly notify the court of any changes in his employment and to complete any necessary paperwork so delays will not be occasioned by the change. He shall also maintain group health insurance for the benefit of the children until they reach the age of 23.

2. The parties agree to review the support amount on a yearly basis to determine if it remains in conformity with the Guidelines, and to exchange all documentation necessary for completion of this review no later than ten days before the review date.

   If the amount no longer conforms with the Guidelines, it shall be adjusted so that it is in conformity. If the parties cannot reach agreement, they will consult with their attorneys, who shall attempt to reach agreement. Any adjustment shall be reduced to writing as a modification of this agreement, and presented to the court for approval. If the parties acting alone or with the assistance of counsel cannot reach agreement, either party can petition the court for a modification.

   In addition to the above, the parties agree to the following support obligations. In no event shall payments made pursuant to this paragraph affect the husband's weekly support obligation.

   (a) The wife shall be responsible for the first $500.00 of uninsured medical expenses for each child in each calendar year. As used in this paragraph, the term "uninsured medical expenses" shall include, but not be limited to, any deductibles and co-payments, dental expenses, and the cost of mental health therapy, so long as both parties have consented to the particular course of therapeutic treatment. Once this amount is reached, the husband will pay half of the uninsured expenses for that child or both children if the limit is reached for both.

   (b) The parties agree that the children are entitled to a postsecondary education, and that they both will contribute to this education in proportion to their taxable income. The parties further agree that at a minimum, their contribution should enable each child to attend a four-year state university, and that contributions should cover the cost of applications and tests, tuition, fees, room and board, and books. The parents' obligation to make educational contributions shall terminate upon the child's reaching his or her 23rd birthday, or upon graduation, whichever occurs first.

3. Upon emancipation of John, the husband's support obligation shall be adjusted downward so it conforms with the guideline amount for one child.

   Upon emancipation of Carla, the husband's support obligation shall cease, subject to his obligations set out above in paragraph 2(b).

   For purposes of this agreement, emancipation shall be defined as:

   (a) the child's achieving the age of 18, graduation from high school, or marriage, whichever is later.

Exhibit 10.8 cont.

Comment:

In addition to establishing the support amount, it is useful to build in a review process tied to the guidelines. Some agreements also contain language defining what constitutes a change in circumstances that would warrant a modification. This can eliminate an area of possible contention, although again, it is virtually impossible to cover all possible contingencies.

Note that with respect to college education, the agreement does not bind the parents to a specific dollar amount. Instead, it provides for proportional contributions and establishes a minimal level of commitment. Often parents are reluctant to commit themselves to paying for college in an agreement. However, without such a commitment, it can be difficult to get the noncustodial parent to contribute, especially if over the years he or she has become less involved with the children, and in many states, the court has no statutory authority to order contribution in the absence of an agreement. Where parents have sufficient income, the option of setting up an educational trust whereby parents are obligated to set aside money on a yearly basis should be explored.

Article Three — Spousal Support

The husband acknowledges that he is fully self-supporting, and he hereby waives any right he may have to seek past, present, or future alimony from the wife.

The wife acknowledges that she is fully self-supporting, and she hereby waives any right she may have to seek past, present, or future alimony from the husband.

Comment:

Here, each spouse is waiving the right to seek alimony from the other. Sometimes, based on the assumption that only the wife might seek alimony, attorneys fail to make these waiver provisions reciprocal, but if the true intent is that neither party shall have a claim, reciprocal waivers are appropriate.

It is important to be aware that some judges will not accept a clause calling for a permanent waiver of support rights. Even where such a waiver is accepted, a court might later override it on public policy grounds if support becomes necessary to prevent a former spouse from going on public assistance.

If spousal support is to be paid, the precise nature and extent of the obligation should be spelled out. For example, if the husband is to make rehabilitative alimony payments, the agreement should define the circumstances under which the obligation can be extended, such as where the wife has been unable to complete her course of training due to no fault of her own.

Also, as discussed in Chapter 8, alimony payments are normally deductible by the payor spouse and includible in the income of the payee spouse. If the parties wish to alter this so that the payments are neither deductible nor includible, they can do so, but the agreement must specifically set out their intent.

Exhibit 10.8 cont.

Last, in this case, each party is employed and has health insurance. If one spouse has been covered on the other's plan, language regarding continued coverage should be included, unless other arrangements for coverage have been made.

Article Four — Life Insurance

Until the youngest child has reached the age of 23, the husband shall pay for and maintain in full force and effect a life insurance policy on his life having death benefits of no less than $600,000, and he shall name the wife as beneficiary. If the husband dies while the policy is in effect, the wife shall use the funds for the benefit of the children.

Until the youngest child has reached the age of 23, the wife shall pay for and maintain in full force and effect a life insurance policy on her life having death benefits of no less than $400,000, and she shall name the husband as beneficiary. If the wife dies while the policy is in effect, the husband shall use the funds for the benefit of the children.

Comment:

It is common to require a support obligor to maintain life insurance for the duration of the support obligation. In the event of death, the insurance would serve as a support replacement. If the custodial parent is also employed, it makes sense to have him or her maintain insurance as well.

In this agreement, the other spouse is named as the beneficiary. This is the simplest way to set things up, but it requires a degree of trust that many parties do not have in one another. Another option is to name the children as direct beneficiaries, but if they are young, this is impractical. Also, where proceeds are left to minors, many states require that management of the funds be placed under court control, which can be inconvenient. Alternatively, the money could be left to the children in trust, with the surviving spouse or a third party named as trustee. This would place the spouse under a formal legal obligation to spend the money on behalf of the children; there is thus greater accountability than if he or she is simply named as the beneficiary with a contractual obligation to use the money for the children.

Article Five — Real Property

1. The parties presently own as tenants by the entirety a house and land located at 129 Cherry Lane, Newtowne ("house").

2. The parties agree that the fair market value of the house is $260,000, as determined by the appraisal done by Best Real Estate Company on April 15, 2014. The parties have placed the house on the market at this price and have listed it with Best Real Estate Company.

3. The parties agree that they will both fully cooperate with all matters related to the sale, including the execution of all necessary documents.

Exhibit 10.8 cont.

4. Until the house is sold, the wife shall have the right of exclusive use and occupancy and agrees to maintain the house in its present condition. The husband agrees that the wife is entitled to be reimbursed for all expenses related to maintaining the house, including the cost of a weekly cleaning so the house is presentable during this sale period. The wife shall make the monthly mortgage payments to Evergreen Mortgage Company, including principal, interest, and the tax escrow. The husband shall be responsible for paying the water and sewer bills and the homeowner's insurance.

5. Upon sale, after the payment of the mortgage, the broker's commission, and all related costs, the wife shall be reimbursed for all expenditures during the sale period related to maintaining the house; thereafter, sale proceeds shall be divided equally between the parties.

6. If the house is not sold by July 15, 2014, the parties agree to reconsider the asking price. If they cannot agree on a new price, they agree to be bound by the price recommendation of Best Real Estate Company. This process shall be repeated every three months until the house is sold.

Comment:

As discussed in Chapter 9, there are many ways to dispose of real estate in a divorce. Here, the sale option was most likely selected because neither spouse could buy out the interest of the other and there were no significant offsetting assets that could be used to lower the buyout price. Another option would have been to give the wife, as the custodial parent, the right of use and occupancy until some future date, but, as discussed in Chapter 8, the downside of this arrangement is that it keeps the parties enmeshed and frequently leads to unanticipated problems. Here, the parties must continue to interact, but only until the house is sold. If the parties are uncooperative, additional safeguards might be included relative to this time period, such as specifying what happens if the wife does not maintain the property or if a party fails to make a required payment.

Article Six — Personal Property

The parties state that they have divided all of their personal property to their mutual satisfaction. Hereafter, each shall own, have, and enjoy all items of personal property of every kind now or hereafter acquired free of any claim or right of the other with full power to dispose of the same as fully and effectively, in all respects and for all purposes, as if he or she were unmarried.

Comment:

It is generally advisable for the parties to divide their assets before the agreement is executed, as this avoids potential enforcement problems. If this is not feasible, the details of any postexecution transfer should be spelled out.

Exhibit 10.8 cont.

Article Seven—Debts

1. The wife agrees that she will be solely responsible for payment of the following debts:

    (a) MasterCard (joint account)

    Account number: 66793021

    Amount due: $1,500

    (b) Sears (wife's account)

    Account number: 3390

    Amount due: $479.56

    (c) Evergreen Mortgage Company

    Account number: 73796

    Amount due: $140,000

2. The husband agrees that he will be solely responsible for payment of the following debts:

    (a) American Express (joint account)

    Account number: 440902881

    Amount due: $5,600

    (b) Student Loan Service (husband's student loan)

    Account number: 4490

    Amount due: $4,500

3. Each party represents and warrants to the other that exclusive of the debts identified in this agreement he or she has not incurred any obligations for which the other shall or may be liable. If either party is called upon to pay an obligation that the other is responsible for, the responsible party shall indemnify and hold the other harmless therefrom, including attorney's fees and related expenses. Each, or the estate of each, promises to notify the other if any claim is made against him or her or his or her estate as a result of any debt charge or liability incurred by the other, and to give the other an opportunity to defend against the claim.

Comment:

It is important to recognize that although parties may spell out who is responsible for payment of joint debts, their arrangement is not binding on creditors, as they are not parties to the agreement. Accordingly, notwithstanding the agreement, each party remains obligated to joint creditors. It is extremely important that this be pointed out to clients; otherwise, they may not be getting what they think they agreed to.

As in the above provision, an indemnification clause should always be included whereby each spouse agrees to reimburse the other if called upon to pay a debt allocated to the other. However, this clause may be of limited utility because the nonpayment probably stems from a lack of funds.

Exhibit 10.8 cont.

Article Eight — General Provisions

General Comment:

In all states, boilerplate provisions such as those that follow are routinely included in agreements. However, they should not be included without review because adjustments may need to be made in individual circumstances.

A. SEPARATION

The husband and wife shall continue to live apart. Each shall be free from interference, molestation, or restraint by the other. Neither shall seek to force the other to live with him or her, or to otherwise interfere with the other's personal liberty.

Comment:

Despite the language establishing that neither party shall molest or restrain the other, this clause does not take the place of a protective order and should not be relied on as a substitute for one. In most states, it is not placed on record with the police and is not criminally enforceable.

B. GENERAL RELEASE

Each party releases and forever discharges the other from all causes of action, claims, rights, or demands whatsoever, at law or in equity, he or she ever had or now has or can hereafter have against the other, by reason of any matter, cause, or thing from the beginning of the world to the date of this Agreement, except any causes of action for divorce and except further that nothing contained in this Article shall release or discharge either party from such party's covenants, promises, agreements, representations, warranties, or other undertakings or obligations as contained in this Agreement.

Comment:

As drafted, this is a very broad release. Each spouse is giving up all rights against the other except for filing for divorce and securing rights pursuant to the agreement. This should be carefully explained to the client, as there may be situations where such a broad waiver is not appropriate.

C. WAIVER OF ESTATE CLAIM

Except as otherwise provided in this Agreement, each party waives, releases, and relinquishes any and all rights that he or she may now have in the property of the other (such as the right of election, dower, curtesy, and inheritance) and all rights he or she may now have or hereafter acquire under the laws of this state or any other jurisdiction:

a. To share, as a result of the marital relationship, in the other party's property or estate upon the latter's death; or

b. To act as executor or administrator of the other's estate, or to participate in the administration thereof.

Exhibit 10.8 cont.

This Agreement shall and does constitute a mutual waiver by the parties of their respective rights of election to take against each other's last will and testament now or hereafter in force under the laws of any jurisdiction.

It is the intention of the parties that their respective estates shall be administered and distributed in all respects as though no marriage had been solemnized between them. The consideration for each party's waiver and release is the other party's reciprocal waiver and release.[42]

Comment:

The primary importance of this clause is to protect each spouse's estate in the event of death before divorce. It serves to shift the statutory consequences of divorce, which is a divestiture of estate rights based on marital status, to the time the agreement is executed.

D. ENTIRE UNDERSTANDING

The husband and wife have incorporated into this Agreement their entire understanding. No oral statement or prior written matter, extrinsic to this Agreement, shall have any force or effect.

Comment:

This relatively simple clause is important because it prevents either party from enforcing any side agreements. For example, let's say that the wife promises the husband that he can have a certain painting in her possession, but this promise is not reflected in the agreement. After execution, the husband cannot enforce this promise because it is not included in this agreement.

E. VOLUNTARY EXECUTION

The husband and wife acknowledge that they are entering into this Agreement freely and voluntarily and that they have each obtained independent legal advice; that they have ascertained all the relevant facts and circumstances; that they understand their legal rights; that each is satisfied that he or she has received full disclosure as to the other's finances, assets, income, expectancies, and other economic matters; and that they clearly understand and assent to all of the provisions of this Agreement.

F. MODIFICATION

Any modification of this Agreement shall be in writing and shall be duly signed and acknowledged by each party in the same manner as this Agreement. No oral representation or statement shall constitute an amendment, waiver, or modification of the terms of this agreement.

Comment:

This language requiring that all modifications be in writing precludes either party's establishing new rights based on oral representations.

Exhibit 10.8 cont.

G. WAIVER

A waiver by either party of any provision of this Agreement shall not prevent or stop such party from enforcing such provision in the future. The failure of either party to insist upon the strict performance of any of the terms and provisions of this Agreement by the other party shall not be a waiver or relinquishment of such term or provision; the same shall continue in full force and effect.

Comment:

This language should be read in conjunction with paragraph F. Here, it is made clear that failure to insist on performance of any term will not modify the agreement and is not a waiver of that party's right to subsequently insist on strict performance. For example, if the wife agreed to take a reduced amount of child support for a few weeks because the husband was having financial difficulties, this would not modify the original agreement and at any point, she could again insist on full payment.

H. CONSENT TO JURISDICTION

The parties acknowledge that this Agreement is to be construed and governed by the laws of *State X*. Both parties consent to the continuing jurisdiction of this State in any subsequent action to modify or enforce this Agreement.

Comment:

Generally, the term "continuing jurisdiction" as used here is understood to refer to jurisdiction over the persons of both parties and is not intended to deal with jurisdiction over subsequent custody disputes.

I. AGREEMENT TO MEDIATE

In the event a dispute arises between the parties concerning any of the terms or provisions of this Agreement, which they are unable to resolve on their own or with the assistance of their attorneys, they agree that before filing any action in court, they will try to resolve the dispute through mediation at the Family Mediation Service or other similar agency. However, nothing in this paragraph shall prevent the wife from going directly to court or pursuing any other legal remedy if the husband defaults on any of his financial obligations under this Agreement.

J. SEVERABILITY

If any provision of this Agreement shall be held invalid or unlawful by any court of competent jurisdiction, the remainder of this Agreement shall nevertheless remain valid and enforceable according to its terms.

Comment:

This clause protects the validity of the agreement in the event any provision is found to be invalid or illegal. A clause found to be invalid or illegal would thus be dropped from the agreement without affecting any other clause.

Exhibit 10.8 cont.

K. ARTICLE HEADINGS — NO EFFECT

The headings at the beginning of each article of this Agreement and the titles of the same are included for reference purposes only. They are not terms or conditions of this Agreement.

L. EXECUTION IN COUNTERPART

This Agreement may be executed in two or more counterparts, each of which shall be deemed as original.

M. INCORPORATION AND MERGER WITH SPOUSAL SUPPORT EXCEPTION

At any hearing on the Divorce Complaint, a copy of this Agreement shall be submitted to the court and shall be incorporated and, subject to the below exception, merged into the judgment of divorce and shall not retain any independent legal significance. However, Article Three shall not be merged into the judgment of divorce, but instead shall survive and retain its independent legal significance.

Comment:

At the divorce hearing, the parties' separation agreement is presented to the court for approval. If it is approved, the court incorporates the agreement into the divorce judgment. In effect, through the process of incorporation, the agreement becomes an enforceable order of the court.

Beyond this, the agreement either merges with the court decree and loses any significance as an independent contract, or it survives the incorporation and retains its significance as an independent contract. Whether the agreement merges or survives has important future consequences. If the agreement merges, it ceases to exist as a separate document and is fully modifiable and enforceable, as the court's own judgment would be. If the agreement survives, it continues to exist as a contract. This makes modification more difficult because choosing survival over merger usually indicates that the parties intended for the agreement to be permanent. Moreover, if the agreement survives, it is, at least in theory, an independent contract, which may still be enforceable as such.

Frequently, as in the present agreement, some provisions merge, and others survive the incorporation. Here, as is commonly done, the spousal support provisions survive, making modification much more difficult.

Signed this 10th day of May 2014.

_____   _____
David Smith   Marie Smith

Exhibit 10.8 cont.

STATE OF X

Then personally appeared the above-named David Smith and acknowledged the foregoing instrument to be his free act and deed for the purposes therein set forth before me.

_____
Notary Public
My Commission Expires: _____

STATE OF X

Then personally appeared the above-named Marie Smith and acknowledged the foregoing instrument to be her free act and deed for the purposes therein set forth before me.

_____
Notary Public
My Commission Expires: _____

The Uncontested Case

In most jurisdictions, the uncontested hearing is a relatively simple matter and may last only for five or ten minutes. The typical hearing occurs in two phases: First is the dissolution phase, and second is the separation agreement review phase. Our focus is on cases that are uncontested because the parties have reached an agreement, but a case can also be uncontested because the defendant fails to appear. In the latter situation, the plaintiff must comply with the requirements of the Soldiers and Sailors Relief Act of 1940, which protects members of the military from default judgments.[29] The plaintiff must attest to the fact that the defendant's non-appearance is not because he or she is serving in the military. If uncertain, the plaintiff may need to determine this before the divorce can proceed.

Dissolving the Marriage

During the marital dissolution phase, the plaintiff must establish that the parties have a validly contracted marriage and that the divorce grounds set forth in the complaint actually exist. Where a joint petition has been filed, either or both of the parties would testify to these matters. Establishing grounds is usually little more than a formality, but the court must be satisfied that the requisite elements are present. Also, keep in mind that "uncontested" is not synonymous with "no-fault." Parties can reach agreement regardless of the underlying grounds; thus, one could have an uncontested divorce that is premised on cruel and abusive treatment. However, once agreement is reached, the plaintiff frequently amends the complaint from fault to no-fault grounds.

Generally, the plaintiff's attorney or the judge will ask the plaintiff a series of questions to elicit the necessary information. Since the case is uncontested, there is no cross-examination. Usually the defendant does not testify; however, in a no-fault case, the judge may ask the defendant if he or she agrees with the plaintiff that the marriage is truly over.

Approving the Separation Agreement

In the second phase of the typical no-fault hearing, the judge reviews the separation agreement. If it is accepted, the judge will approve it for **incorporation** into the divorce judgment, and the agreement will either **survive** or **merge** in accordance with its terms (see paragraph M of the sample separation agreement).

In some states, the primary focus of the review is on procedural fairness. The judge will inquire into whether the parties entered into the agreement freely and voluntarily and whether they understand it. Even where the focus is on procedural rather than substantive fairness, the judge will usually check to see if the child support amount conforms to the guidelines, and if not, will evaluate whether the deviation is justifiable; some judges will also review spousal support arrangements. In other states, there is an additional focus on substantive fairness, and a judge will scrutinize the agreement in its entirety. In some states, judges will reject a term only if it is unconscionable; in others, judges may reject a term that is unfair or significantly favors one side over the other.

Where the judge believes the agreement is unfair, he or she will usually give the parties a chance to correct the problems and resubmit it for approval. If the necessary changes are minor, they can usually be made on the spot, and the hearing can proceed to completion. However, if the unfairness permeates the agreement, such as where one spouse was forced into signing it, the hearing will probably be suspended until the agreement is reworked or the case recast as a contested one.

Assuming the separation agreement is approved, the judge will enter the **divorce judgment**. The judgment both dissolves the marriage and incorporates the separation agreement, making it an enforceable order of the court. The timing of the entry of judgment varies from state to state. In some states, the judgment enters at the conclusion of the hearing; in others,

Incorporation:
Upon approval of a separation agreement, the inclusion of its terms into the divorce judgment such that those terms become part of the judgment

Survival:
The incorporation of a separation agreement into the divorce judgment but the retention of its significance as an independent agreement

Merger:
When a separation agreement, once approved by the court, loses its separate identity and thereafter exists only as part of the court's judgment

Divorce Judgment:
The court decree that dissolves the marriage

it does not enter until a certain amount of time has elapsed. In some states, the initial judgment is in the form of a **decree** *nisi*. This is an interim judgment, which automatically ripens into a final one unless the parties seek to revoke it. This interim judgment gives the parties a chance to be absolutely certain that they do not wish to reconcile.

Decree *Nisi*:
A provisional judgment of divorce that automatically ripens into the final divorce decree absent a challenge or decision by the parties to vacate the divorce

The Contested Case

When a divorce case is contested, a trial, rather than a simple hearing, becomes necessary. It is important to keep in mind that when a case is contested, it is almost never because the parties are fighting the divorce grounds; most cases are contested because the parties cannot reach agreement on one or more of the collateral issues, such as support or custody.

The Pretrial Conference

In most jurisdictions, a case cannot proceed to trial until there has been a **pretrial conference** with a judge. This conference generally serves two primary purposes. First, it may be used to explore settlement. In some instances, a judge may actively encourage settlement by indicating the likely outcome if the case were to go to trial. Second, it can be used to simplify matters for trial. The judge can help the parties identify the issues in dispute, and uncontested matters can then be admitted. Additionally, documents can be authenticated and witness lists established.

Pretrial Conference:
A meeting held by a judge with counsel prior to trial, mainly to streamline issues and determine the possibility of settlement

In preparation for this conference, each party must submit a **pretrial statement**. This document provides the judge with information about the parties and the procedural history of the case. Each party identifies the facts and issues in dispute and his or her position relative to the matters in contention.

Pretrial Statement:
A memorandum prepared by each side in advance of a pretrial conference; a key purpose is the delineation of issues still in contention

The Trial

Throughout this chapter, references have been made to the fact that procedural rules tend to be applied in a more relaxed fashion in the divorce context. However, once a divorce is at the trial stage, this is no longer true; a divorce trial proceeds much like any other civil trial, except it is not tried before a jury. The rules of evidence are in effect, and all testimony and submissions must conform to these rules. Each side has the opportunity to present an opening and closing statement, introduce evidence, call witnesses, and cross-examine the other side's witnesses, and the entire proceeding is recorded by a court stenographer.[30]

Following the trial, the judge reviews all of the evidence and makes a decision on the merits. The divorce decree is then entered, which both dissolves the marriage and contains the court's order regarding the issues before it. As in uncontested cases, the judgment may enter as a decree *nisi*.

In many jurisdictions, the order must contain detailed findings of fact and conclusions of law. These details can be crucial because this order, much like a separation agreement, structures the postmarital relationship between the parties.

Trial Preparation and the Role of the Paralegal

Trial Notebook:
A binder containing everything needed to present a case in court

Trials require intensive preparation, and paralegals are often involved in this process.[31] They may be responsible for setting up the **trial notebook**, which is a binder containing everything needed to present the case in court, such as pleadings and motions, witness lists, deposition summaries, and a description of all exhibits. Paralegals may also be responsible for gathering and organizing all potential exhibits and assisting with witness preparation, including preparation of the client. This is an important task, which usually includes the following steps:

1. Reviewing all relevant information with the client to ensure that it is complete and accurate.
2. Reviewing the direct examination questions — the questions that each side asks of its witnesses — with each witness so he or she knows what to expect at trial. Although witnesses cannot be told what to say, they can be helped with how to present their answers to the court so they are delivered in the most effective or, depending on the circumstances, least damaging manner.
3. Reviewing with the client and other witnesses what the other side is likely to ask of them during cross-examination and explaining how best to respond to these questions, which are usually designed to undermine credibility.

▪ Postdivorce Proceedings

Motion for a New Trial:
A posttrial request that the court set aside the judgment and order a new trial because of prejudicial errors during the trial

A case is not necessarily over once a judgment has been entered. A party who is dissatisfied with the result can file a posttrial motion for relief or an appeal. Further on down the line, either party can file a modification action (if there has been a change in circumstances) or a contempt action (if the other side has violated an order).

Posttrial Motions

Motion for Relief from Judgment:
A posttrial request that the court vacate or modify its judgment, usually because of an error, unfairness, or newly discovered evidence

The two most common posttrial motions are the **motion for a new trial** and a **motion for relief from judgment**, although other motions may be available in some jurisdictions. In permitting these forms of relief, most states have looked to the cognate provisions of the Federal Rules of Civil Procedure and have adopted similar, if not identical, rules.[32]

Motion for a New Trial

After judgment has been entered, the losing party can bring a motion asking the court to set aside the judgment and order a new trial. The essential basis for this motion is that prejudicial errors were made during the course of trial that affected the outcome. The motion is usually presented to the judge who presided over the trial. It must be brought within a short time after entry of judgment, usually within ten days.

Motion for Relief from Judgment

Most states also allow a party to seek relief from judgment for a variety of reasons, including, but not limited to, mistake, inadvertence, excusable neglect, fraud, newly discovered evidence, or for "any other reason justifying relief from judgment."[33] A party usually has longer to file this motion than a motion for a new trial. Under the Federal Rules of Civil Procedure, a party must file the motion within a "reasonable time," which in most instances is not later than a year after judgment was entered. The year time limit does not apply if the underlying reason for the motion falls into the catchall category.

The motion for relief from judgment is generally regarded as a request for extraordinary relief and will be granted only in exceptional circumstances. For example, when a party seeks to set aside a judgment for newly discovered evidence, the party must show that even with due diligence, it could not have been discovered either during the trial or within the period for bringing a motion for a new trial, and that it would likely have led to a different outcome. Where allowed, the court may vacate and modify its judgment or order a retrial.

Appeals

Overview of Appellate Practice

The losing party can **appeal** from the court's final judgment, or that portion of the judgment that is adverse to him or her. The general rule is that a party can appeal only from a final judgment. For appeal purposes, a decree *nisi* is considered the final judgment—and if a party waits until the *nisi* decree ripens into a final decree, the appeal is likely to be untimely. Usually, the appeal goes from the trial court to the intermediate **appellate court** but, in states without an intermediate-level court, the appeal goes directly to the state's supreme court. The decision of an intermediate court can usually be appealed to the supreme court.

An appeal is not a retrial. The appellate court reviews what took place at the trial level to determine if any errors were made that might have affected the outcome of the case. This review is based on the record, and

Appeal:
Resort to an appellate court for review of a lower-court decision; usually involves questions of law rather than of fact

Appellate Court:
A court with jurisdiction to review lower-court decisions

new evidence cannot be introduced. In reviewing for errors, the court is primarily concerned with errors of law. Findings of fact cannot be upset unless the court determines that they are unsupported by the evidence. The appeals court cannot substitute its view of what took place for the findings of the trial judge, who actually sees and hears the witnesses and is in the best position to evaluate their credibility.

The appeals court can affirm or reverse the decision of the trial court, or remand the case for a new trial. A remand is likely if additional information is needed, such as if the court improperly excluded evidence or allowed evidence that should have been excluded, as either may have altered the outcome of the case.

Appellate Procedure

Each state has its own rules governing the particulars of appellate procedure. These rules tend to be very detailed and contain multiple time limits that must be met at each step of the process to preserve the right of review. Nonetheless, some basic steps common to most, if not all, states can be identified.

An appeal is commenced by the filing of a notice of appeal. This notice is usually filed in the court that heard the case. After it is commenced, the record on appeal must be prepared. Typically, the appealing party (appellant) is responsible for designating those portions of the trial court materials that he or she wishes to include in the record. In addition to pleadings and documents, the record includes the transcript of the proceedings or relevant portions of it. The appellant is responsible for contacting the stenographer and making arrangements to have the transcript prepared and filed. If the appellant does not need to have all of the documents or the entire transcript included in the record, the appellant must inform the other side (appellee) what he or she has designated for inclusion, and the appellee then has the right to cross-designate documents or portions of the transcript for inclusion. The actual assembly of the record is done by a trial court clerk. Once it is assembled, the case is docketed with the appeals court.

The parties then submit briefs to the court. The appellant submits the first brief within a certain amount of time after docketing, and the appellee then has a specified number of days after this within which to file his or her brief. The appellant can then file a reply brief responding to the points made in the appellee's brief. After the briefs are submitted, the court can decide the case based on the written submissions alone, or it can schedule oral arguments, which give the attorneys a chance to argue the case before the court. Many states impose strict limits on the time allotted for oral argument.

The Role of the Paralegal

A paralegal may be asked to oversee the appeals process. This is a daunting task that requires making sure that each step is taken at the right time and that all rules are complied with. There is very little give here — an omitted detail or a missed deadline can lead to the dismissal of the appeal. Another important role that a paralegal can play is in researching and writing the appellate brief. These briefs are painstaking to write. They require fine-tuned analytical skills and must conform to all of the particulars governing the submission of appellate briefs; accordingly, this task is usually assigned only to senior paralegals.

The Complaint for Modification

Modification of judgments has been discussed at various points in this book. Here, some general points are made, and this action is distinguished from other postjudgment procedures.

The basis for a modification action is that circumstances have changed since the entry of the divorce order, making enforcement of certain provisions unfair. A modification is thus different from the postjudgment remedies discussed here because it does not challenge the validity of the order as originally entered; rather, it focuses on subsequent events that have since made it unworkable. Accordingly, a modification action can be filed in a case that was initially settled by the parties.

In principle, a modification is considered a continuation of the original action. In some jurisdictions, it is initiated by the filing of a motion, while in others, a new complaint must be filed and served (see Exhibit 10.9). As with the divorce, a court can enter temporary orders during the pendency of the modification proceeding, and the resulting judgment is itself subject to modification if there is a subsequent change in circumstances. Unlike other postjudgment remedies, there are generally no time limits within which a party may file a modification complaint.

The Complaint for Contempt

Contempt actions also have been discussed at various points throughout the book; the primary purpose of this section is to contrast this action with other postjudgment remedies.

A contempt action is brought to enforce an existing order where a party is in noncompliance. Like a modification action, a complaint for contempt can be brought following a case that was settled by the parties (see Exhibit 10.10). The action, by seeking enforcement, affirms the ongoing validity of the existing order. It is not uncommon for a defendant in a contempt hearing to argue that as entered, the underlying order is unfair

Exhibit 10.9
Motion for
Modification

Form Number 2

STATE OF INDIANA   )   IN THE _____ SUPERIOR/CIRCUIT COURT
) SS:
COUNTY OF _____   )   CASE NO. _____

IN RE THE _____ OF: _____

_____

Petitioner,

and

_____

Respondent.

VERIFIED PETITION FOR MODIFICATION OF CHILD SUPPORT

Comes now _____, pro se, and hereby files a Verified Petition for

Modification of Child Support, and states as follows:

1.   That parties have _____ minor child (ren), namely:

     NAME   DATE OF BIRTH

     _____   _____

     _____   _____

     _____   _____

     _____   _____

2.   On _____, this Court ordered that _____ pay child support to

_____ in the weekly amount of $_____ to the above named child(ren) effective on _____.

3.   Since that time, there has been a change in circumstances, so substantial and continuing as to make the terms of the current support order unreasonable for the following reasons: _____
_____
_____
_____.

4.   Child support should be modified to reflect the substantial change in circumstances as outlined above.

5.   A hearing should be set to determine if child support should be changed.

WHEREFORE, _____ requests that this Court set this matter for hearing, and upon hearing, modify the existing child support as is appropriate, and order all other further relief that is just and proper in the premises.

I affirm under the penalties of perjury that the foregoing representations are true.

_____
Signature

_____
Print your name

Exhibit 10.9 cont.

Mailing address

Town, State and Zip Code

Telephone number, with area code

CERTIFICATE OF SERVICE

I hereby certify that I sent a copy of this Petition by first class mail to the opposing attorney, or the opposing party if the opposing party is not represented by an attorney, on _____.

Signature

Print your name

---

or that circumstances have changed, which makes its current enforcement unfair. Given the range of available corrective procedures, courts are not very sympathetic to these arguments. Most judges will inform a contempt defendant that if he or she wishes to challenge the order, he or she must take the appropriate steps to do so and that until that time, the plaintiff has a right to rely on the order as it exists.

Exhibit 10.10
Complaint for Contempt

IN THE FAMILY COURT OF _____ COUNTY, WEST VIRGINIA

In Re:
The Marriage / Children of: Civil Action No. _____

_____, and   _____.
Petitioner   Respondent

_____   _____

_____   _____
Address   Address

_____   _____
Daytime phone   Daytime phone

PETITION FOR CONTEMPT

1.   Your name: _____. List any other name(s) you were known by during this case. _____

Your current address: _____

2.   Name of the person you want the court to hold in contempt: _____

Address: _____

Daytime telephone number: _____ Social Security number: _____

3. Your Reasons for Making this Contempt Petition

___A. Failure to Make Payments of Money

____ I believe the person I want the court to hold in contempt has failed to make court ordered payments of:

____ Child support

____ Spousal support

____ Separate maintenance

____ Equitable distribution

____ Medical support

____ Other (List, and be specific.) _____

You must attach a copy of the order requiring these payments.

List the due dates and amounts for all payments that have not been made.

_____

_____

SCA-FC-251 (12/01)   Contempt Petition   Page 1 of 3

Exhibit 10.10 cont.

_____

_____

_____

List the total amount due and unpaid on the date you sign this petition: $_____.

___**B.** Failure to Obey Court Ordered Parenting Plan

___ I believe the person I want the court to hold in contempt has failed to abide by the terms and conditions of a court ordered Parenting Plan. For each instance you believe the person has failed to abide by the Parenting Plan, you must list the date, and explain *specifically* how the person failed to abide by the plan; and you MUST attach a copy of the Parenting Plan.

_____

_____

_____

_____

_____

_____

___**C.** Failure to Obey *Other* Terms, Conditions, or Requirements of a Court Order

___ I believe the person I want the court to hold in contempt has failed to abide by the terms, conditions, or requirements of a court order in some way other than those listed in items A. and B. above. For each instance you believe the person has failed to abide by the terms, conditions, or requirements of an order, you must list the date, and explain *specifically* how the person failed to abide by the order; and you MUST attach a copy of the order.

_____

_____

_____

_____

_____

_____

4. I have attached to this Petition documents I believe prove the person I have named has failed to obey a court order. The documents I have attached are:

_____

_____

_____

Exhibit 10.10 cont.

For the reasons stated above, I request that the Court issue a Notice of Contempt Hearing / Rule to Show Cause setting a hearing to determine if the person named in this Petition should be held in Contempt of Court.

_____   _____
Your Signature / Petitioner   Date

VERIFICATION of CONTEMPT PETITION

I, _____, after making an oath or affirmation to tell the truth, say that the facts I have stated in this Contempt Petition are true of my personal knowledge; and if I have set forth matters upon information given to me by others, I believe that information to be true.

_____   _____
Signature   Date

This Verification was sworn to or affirmed before me on the _____ day of _____,
200___.

_____
Notary Public / Other Official

My commission expires:_____.

Chapter Summary

Good case preparation begins with a well-organized client interview. At this interview, essential information is obtained and a foundation of trust is established. Active listening and respect for the client's emotional concerns are important in establishing an effective relationship.

The first formal step in a divorce case is the filing of the complaint (or a joint petition). The complaint and summons are then served on the defendant, who must answer within a certain period of time. In theory, failure to respond will result in a default judgment, but most courts are reluctant to default a defendant in a divorce case. Once the case has been initiated, both sides usually engage in the process of discovery, which is used to acquire information about the other side in order to help prepare for trial, structure the settlement, or both.

Frequently, during the period between filing and the final hearing, motions for temporary orders will be filed asking the court to provide interim relief. The general rule is that advance notice must be given to the other side; however, *ex parte* relief may be allowed where such notice poses a substantial risk of harm. Notice and an opportunity to be heard must subsequently be provided. Common motions include those for support, custody, the protection of assets, and protection from abuse.

Most parties wish to settle their case and avoid a trial on the merits. The most common approach to dispute resolution is negotiation, where each attorney acts in a representational capacity and seeks to obtain the best possible settlement for his or her client. Another approach, which is growing in popularity, is mediation. Here, a neutral third party assists the parties to reach agreement on their own. Arbitration is another alternative, but it is not used frequently in divorce cases. Here, the dispute is presented to a decision maker who renders a binding decision. The process is more flexible than a court hearing, and the parties retain a greater degree of control. Another alternative model is collaborative divorce where the parties and their attorneys agree in advance that the lawyers will not take the case to court should the process break down. Although not an alternative dispute resolution procedure, unbundled legal services allows clients to select the legal services that they wish to hire a lawyer for from a menu of specific options.

Once the parties reach an agreement, they reduce their understanding to a written separation agreement. This agreement is comprehensive and must be drafted carefully because it governs the postdivorce relationship between the parties. With the execution of the agreement, the case becomes uncontested, and a relatively simple hearing can be scheduled at which the marriage is dissolved and the agreement reviewed and approved by the court.

If the parties cannot reach resolution, the case is contested and a trial on the merits is scheduled. Here, a judge resolves the dispute and enters an order reflecting his or her decision. The losing party can challenge this decision by way of motion or appeal. Further down the line, parties may seek to modify or enforce the existing order by filing a modification or contempt action.

Key Terms

Confidentiality	Docket Number	Constructive Service	Counterclaim
Active Listening	Venue	Acceptance of Service	Motion to Dismiss
Complaint/Petition	Filing Fee	Return of Service	Discovery
Request for Relief/	Summons	Answer	Deposition
Prayer	Service of Process	Default Judgment	Deponent
Joint Petition	Personal Service	Affirmative Defense	Subpoena

Subpoena Duces Tecum	Protective Order	Arbitration	Decree *Nisi*
Interrogatories	Discovery Conference	Collaborative Law	Pretrial Conference
Request for Production of Documents	Motion to Compel	Unbundled Legal Services	Pretrial Statement
Request for a Physical or Mental Examination	Temporary Order	Separation Agreement	Trial Notebook
	Affidavit	Divorce Hearing	Motion for a New Trial
	Ex Parte	Incorporation	Motion for Relief from Judgment
Request for Admissions	Guardian ad Litem	Survival	Appeal
	Negotiation	Merger	Appellate Court
	Mediation	Divorce Judgment	

Review Questions

1. Why is it important to pay attention to cultural differences when interviewing a client?
2. Why is it important to acknowledge how a client is feeling at the initial interview?
3. What does the term "unauthorized practice of law" mean, and how does it limit your relationship with a client?
4. Why is maintaining client confidentiality so important?
5. What is meant by the term "active listening"?
6. What are the three stages of a client interview?
7. What are the benefits of asking open-ended questions during an interview?
8. What is the funneling process?
9. What purposes are served by the divorce complaint?
10. What are the basic component parts of a divorce complaint?
11. What are the possible consequences of failing to include something in a complaint?
12. What is a joint petition?
13. Explain what is meant by the term "venue."
14. What is a summons?
15. What is meant by the term "service of process"?
16. Why is it important to try to personally serve a defendant?
17. What are the ways in which service can be accomplished?
18. What is "return of service"?
19. What happens if a divorce defendant does not respond to the complaint in a timely fashion? How is this different from other civil actions?
20. What are the component parts of an answer?
21. Why is it generally advisable to file an answer?
22. What is a motion to dismiss, and when might a defendant file one?
23. What is the purpose of discovery?
24. Describe the five available discovery procedures.
25. What is "metadata"?
26. What potential "traps for the unwary" need to be kept in mind when responding to a request for electronically stored information?
27. Describe some of the key ways in which paralegals can assist with discovery.
28. What is a protective order, and when may a party seek one?
29. What can a party do when the other side fails to respond to discovery requests?
30. What is a motion? Why would a party file one?
31. When would a party file a motion *ex parte*?
32. What happens to temporary orders once a divorce judgment is entered?
33. Can a temporary order be appealed? Why or why not?
34. What is an affidavit?
35. Describe each of the three dispute resolution approaches, and explain the key differences among them.
36. What is a collaborative divorce? How is it similar to and different from other alternative dispute resolution approaches?
37. Explain what is meant by the term "unbundled legal services."
38. What is a separation agreement?
39. What are the benefits of spelling out the custody and visitation arrangements?

40. What are the most common ways for real estate to be disposed of?
41. With respect to the allocation of joint debts, why might a spouse be called on to pay a debt allocated to the other party in a separation agreement?
42. What are meant by the terms "incorporation," "merger," and "survival as an independent contract" as used in separation agreements?
43. What takes place at an uncontested hearing?
44. What does a judge look at when reviewing an agreement for procedural fairness? For substantive fairness?
45. How does a trial in a contested case differ from an uncontested hearing?
46. What purpose is served by a pretrial conference?
47. What is a motion for a new trial?
48. What is a motion for relief from judgment?
49. What is the primary focus of an appeals court when reviewing a lower court decision?
50. Outline the steps involved in bringing an appeal.
51. How do modification and contempt actions differ from other postjudgment procedures?

Discussion Questions

1. Assume that you are conducting an initial client interview with a client who is involved in a custody dispute with her husband, and that you become fairly certain that the client is lying to you. What do you think you should do at this stage of the process? Do you confront the client? Do you ignore your concerns? Are there any techniques you might use for eliciting the truth? Is it your responsibility to elicit the truth?

   Assume that you continue working with this client and, despite your concern, you have established a good relationship with her. One day, she comes into your office and tells you that she has been lying to you and that she is a drug addict and is frequently high when she is with her children.

   What do you do at this point? In thinking about it, assume that you are the only paralegal in a busy office and that although you could ask to be taken off the case, this would make matters difficult for the supervising attorney.

2. Assume that you are a family law paralegal in a large law firm. One day, a close friend of yours who is paralegal in another division of the firm asks if she can speak to you privately. She has recently initiated divorce proceedings against her husband, and she is unsure about whether or not she is being well represented by her attorney. She asks you if you will review the case file for her and let her know what you think about how her attorney is handling the case. She also informs you that she has come to you rather than to one of the firm's family law attorneys because she does not want her personal life to get back to her supervising attorneys. How should you handle this request? What ethical issues are raised by this scenario?

3. Do you think mediation is appropriate in cases involving domestic violence? What about cases not involving violence, but where there is a significant power imbalance between the spouses?

Assignments

1. Draft the custody provisions of a separation agreement in accordance with the following instructions:

   To: Polly Paralegal
   From: Anita Attorney
   Re: Ramirez divorce

   As you know, we represent Ms. Ramirez in her current divorce action. I just completed a round of settlement negotiations, and I would like you to try to draft the custody and visitation provisions of the separation agreement. Following are the things you need to know in order to do this:
   a. The parties have one child, a daughter named Lucinda, age 8.
   b. Both parents work outside the home, with the mother working about 35 hours per week and the father working about 50.

c. Both parents have a good relationship with Lucinda, although Mom is clearly the primary parent.

d. Ms. Ramirez and her husband, Mr. Lewis, cannot stand each other, although they think they can handle joint legal custody.

e. The real issue is physical custody. We have more or less reached agreement as to when each parent will spend time with Lucinda, but we are stuck regarding how to define the arrangement. Dad is adamant that he not be called the "visiting parent," and Mom is adamant that the arrangement not be called "joint physical custody."

f. Your job is to try to come up with a creative solution! At this point, just worry about the regular weekly schedule; we will deal with holidays, etc., later.

g. Here are the agreed-on time allocations: (1) Lucinda will stay at Mom's house during the school week, with the exception of Wednesday nights, when Dad will pick her up and she will stay with him. (2) Every other week, Lucinda will stay with Dad from 10:00 A.M. on Saturday until school-time on Monday, and he will take her to school. On the other weekends he will spend Saturdays from 10:00 A.M. until 8:00 P.M. with her.

h. As you can see, Mom has the bulk of time, and there is no doubt in anyone's mind that she will do most of the general parenting stuff, such as schedule doctor's appointments, buy clothes, etc., but it's also clear that Dad has some real time with her. So, good luck with the drafting.

2. This assignment requires you to go to your local family court. Observe at least two different types of court procedures, such as a motion session and part of a trial, and then write a paper detailing what you have observed. In your paper, you should do the following:

a. Identify all participants in the proceeding, including court personnel, making sure that you use the correct titles.

b. Identify the nature of the proceeding, such as a motion for temporary support.

c. Identify what each side was trying to accomplish and how they were seeking to do this.

d. Discuss what was most effective, and discuss any weaknesses you identified in either side's presentation of their case.

3. With respect to motion practice in your area, determine the following:
a. how motions are served
b. what the time requirements for service are
c. how motions are marked up
d. when, if ever, accompanying affidavits are required
e. whether parties are ever diverted to some kind of settlement process, and if so, under what circumstances

4. Assume that you are working in an office and a divorce client has just frantically called to inform the attorney handling the case that her husband has just threatened to take the kids out of the country so she will never receive custody of them. The attorney has asked you to draft an *ex parte* motion with a supporting affidavit seeking to prevent the father from doing this. Draft these documents in accordance with the governing standards in your jurisdiction.

5. Your office is representing the husband in a divorce case. The parties have three children and are involved in a bitter custody dispute. The husband strongly suspects that the wife has begun dating a local drug dealer and may have begun using drugs herself. He also worries that she is neglecting the children. The children live with their mom but see their dad fairly regularly. Their ages are 2, 4, and 5. The mom is not employed outside the home. The attorney you work for has asked you to draft a set of interrogatories relevant to custody. He wants useful information but would like to proceed with tact so things do not blow up. He would also like the interrogatories to inquire into the wife's financial situation, as child and spousal support are likely to become contested.

6. The attorney you work for has just received a request for the production of electronically stored information. He is not very computer savvy and recognizes that there are potential

pitfalls he should be aware of. He has asked you to prepare an interoffice memo that explains some of the complexities of this process so he does not inadvertently compromise client confidentiality or make other mistakes. You should use the text as your starting point, but you should also find two law journal articles that go into greater depth regarding some of the potential pitfalls of responding to requests for ESI, and incorporate this information into your memo.

Endnotes

1. Diane Eades, Lawyer-Client Communication: "'I Don't Think the Lawyers Were Communicating with Me': Misunderstanding Cultural Differences in Communicative Style," 52 Emory L.J. 1109, 1118 (2003). This discussion about cultural differences in communication is based on Eades's outstanding article that should be required reading for anyone engaged in client interviewing. It should be pointed out that the defendant's conviction was reversed on appeal, at least in part due to the author's testimony. The article also provides a fascinating description of how the appeal came about.

In addition to the Eades article and those cited in notes 11 and 12, *see* the following for thoughtful approaches to the client interview: Robert Dinerstein et al., Connection, Capacity, and Morality in Lawyer-Client Relationships: Dialogues and Commentary, 10 Clinical L. Rev. 755 (2004); V. Pualani Enos and Lois H. Kanter, Problem Solving in Clinical Education: Who's Listening? Introducing Students to Client-Centered, Client-Empowering, and Multidisciplinary Problem-Solving in a Clinical Setting, 9 Clinical L. Rev. 83 (2003); Laurel E. Fletcher and Harvey M. Weinstein, Problem Solving in Clinical Education: When Students Lose Perspective: Clinical Supervision and the Management of Empathy, 9 Clinical L. Rev. 135 (2002).

2. *See* Judith S. Wallerstein and Sandra Blakeslee, Second Chances—Men, Women, and Children a Decade After Divorce: Who Wins, Who Loses—and Why 6 (1990).

3. Mavis E. Hetherington and Kathleen A. Camara, Families in Transition: The Process of Dissolution and Reconstitution, *in* The Review of Child Development Research 406 (Ross Park ed., 1984).

4. Wallerstein and Blakeslee, *supra* note 2, at 8.

5. This section on ethics draws heavily from Therese A. Cannon's book Ethics and Professional Responsibility for Legal Assistants (6th ed., 2011). This book is written for both students and working paralegals and is an invaluable guide to legal ethics. For more detail on the topics covered in this section, as well as other ethical considerations, please refer to this book.

6. *Id.* at 28.

7. However, a number of states are actively considering licensing paralegals, and some states, such as California, have enacted laws regulating the paralegal profession. *See* http://apps.americanbar.org/legalservices/paralegals/update/cacannon.html (accessed Oct. 8, 2012). For more on the regulation and certification of paralegals, you can visit the websites of the two major national paralegal organizations at http://www.paralegal.org and http://www.nala.org (accessed Oct. 8, 2012).

8. In addition to Cannon, *supra* note 5, ch. 3, *see also* Debra Levy Martinelli, Are You Riding a Fine Line? Learn to Identify and Avoid Issues Involving the Unauthorized Practice of Law, 15 Utah B.J. 18 (2002); Marilu Peterson, Do You UPL?, 15 Utah B.J. 44 (2002).

9. *See* Robert M. Bastress and Joseph D. Harbaugh, Interviewing, Counseling, and Negotiating: Skills for Effective Representation (1990).

10. *See* Don Peters, You Can't Always Get What You Want: Organizing Matrimonial Interviews to Get What You Need, 26 Cal. W. L. Rev. 256, 268 (1990).

11. For a good basic book on civil procedure, *see* Joseph W. Glannon, Examples and Explanations: Civil Procedure (5th ed., 2011).

12. Fed. R. Civ. P. 26(b)(1). In addition to the protection of privileged materials, an attorney's work product (e.g., notes) is generally not subject to discovery.

13. Gaetano Ferro et al., Electronically Stored Information: What Matrimonial Lawyers and Computer Forensics Need to Know, 23 J. Am. Acad. Matrimonial Law. 1, 2 (2010). *See also* Rachel K. Alexander, E-Discovery Practice, Theory and Precedent: Finding the Right Pond, Lure, and Lines Without Going on a Fishing Expedition, 56 S.D. L. Rev. 25 (2011).

14. Mathew Robertson, Why Invisible Electronic Data Is Relevant in Today's Legal Arena, 23 J. Am. Acad. Matrimonial Law. 199, 202 (2011), quoting NYSBA, Formal Op. 782.

15. *Id.* at 208.

16. *Id.* at 209.

17. Ferro et al., *supra* note 13, at 32-35.

18. Byrne v. Byrne, 650 N.Y.S.2d 499, 501 (1996).

19. For more detail, *see* Peggy N. Kerley, Joanne Banker Hames, Paul Sukys, Civil Litigation (7th ed., 2012).

20. Fed. R. Civ. P. 26(c).

21. At present most states do not have formal training and licensing requirements for mediators, although a number of professional organizations have developed practice standards.

22. *See generally* Lydia Belzer, Domestic Abuse and Divorce Mediation: Suggestions for a Safer Process, 5 Loy. J. Pub. Int. L. 37 (2002); Sarah Krieger, The Dangers of Mediation in Domestic Violence Cases, 8 Cardozo Women's L.J. 235 (2002); Penelope E. Bryan, Killing Us Softly: Divorce Mediation and the Politics of Power, 40 Buff. L. Rev. 441 (1992); Peter Salem and Kristin Koeffler, When Domestic Abuse Is an Issue, 14 Fam. Advoc. 34 (1992).

23. I wish to thank my colleague, Professor David Matz, Professor in the Conflict Resolution, Global Governance and

Human Security Department at the University of Massachusetts, Boston, for sharing many of his thoughtful insights into this and other complexities inherent in the mediation process. For a critical look at some of the complexities posed by mediation, *see* Marsha B. Freeman, Divorce Mediation: Sweeping Conflicts Under the Rug, Time to Clean House, 780 U. Det. Mercy L. Rev. 67 (2000).

24. For an interesting argument that this review comes too late in the process to be meaningful, *see* Kevin M. Mazza, Divorce Mediation: Perhaps Not the Remedy It Was Once Considered, 14 Fam. Advoc. 40 (1992).

25. Regarding some of the complexities presented by the collaborative model, *see* Christopher M. Fairman, Growing Pains: Changes in Collaborative Law and the Challenge of Legal Ethics, 30 Campbell L. Rev. 237 (2008); Larry R. Spain, Collaborative Law: A Critical Reflection on Whether a Collaborative Orientation Can Be Ethically Incorporated into the Practice of Law, 56 Baylor L. Rev. 141 (2004); Dafna Lavi, Can the Leopard Change His Spots?! Reflections on the "Collaborative Law" Revolution and Collaborative Advocacy, 13 Cardozo J. Conflict Resol. 61, 107-108 (2011).

26. For further detail, *see* The Changing Face of Legal Practice: Twenty-Six Recommendations for the Baltimore Conference: A National Conference on "Unbundled" Legal Services, 40 Fam. Ct. Rev. 26 (2002); *see also* the American Bar Association's Pro Se/Unbundling Resource Center, http://www.americanbar.org/groups/delivery_legal_ services/resources.html (accessed Oct. 8, 2012).

27. Jessica S. Steinberg, In Pursuit of Justice? Case Outcomes and the Delivery of Unbundled Legal Services, 18 Geo. J. on Poverty L. & Poly. 453, 464 (2011).

28. This language is taken from Stephen W. Schlissel, Separation Agreements and Marital Contracts 617-618 (1986).

29. 50 U.S.C. §520.

30. A detailed look at the trial process is beyond the scope of this book and is likely to be covered in other courses.

31. A number of good books discuss the skills that paralegals need to develop if they are to effectively assist with case preparation. For example, *see* Peggy N. Kerley, Joanne Banker Hames, Paul Sukys, Civil Litigation (7th ed., 2012).

32. Fed. R. Civ. P. 59 & 60(b).

33. Fed. R. Civ. P. 60(b).

Chapter Eleven

Determining Paternity

Historically, the legal relationship between parent and child was determined by the marital status of the parents. Simply put, children were considered "**legitimate**" if born to married parents and "**illegitimate**" if born to unwed parents. Gradually, the law has moved away from strict reliance on marital status as the legal determinant of the parent-child relationship, and the traditional distinction between children of married parents and those of unmarried parents has been virtually eliminated. However, some differences remain; most notably, unwed fathers do not always have the same rights and status that both unwed mothers and married fathers have.

Legitimate:
Refers to a child born to married parents

Illegitimate:
An outdated term for a child born to unmarried parents

We begin this chapter by tracing the evolution of the legal status of children of unmarried parents. We then consider the constitutional rights of unwed fathers, followed by a discussion of paternity establishment and a look at the relatively new topic of paternity disestablishment. We conclude with a discussion about sperm donation and paternal rights. With the exception of the discussion on sperm donors, the focus of this chapter is on heterosexual couples because this is the context within which the law related to paternity has developed. For a discussion regarding the children of unmarried same-sex couples, see Chapter 5.

Historical Overview

According to traditional English common law, a child of unmarried parents was considered a "filius nullius"—a child of no one, a bastard. "Bastardy" rules were designed to deter sexual promiscuity, reinforce the institution of marriage, and protect family lineage by ensuring that a father's property, name, and status passed to his legitimate sons in an orderly manner.[1] However, from very early on, some children were saved from the harsh consequences of the bastardy rules by the common

Presumption of Paternity:
The legal assumption that the father of a child born to a married woman is the women's husband.

law **presumption of paternity**. Based on this presumption, all children born to a married woman were considered offspring of the marriage, even if they were the result of an extramarital relationship. Rebuttal was difficult, and at times it could be accomplished only by proof of the husband's impotence or his extended absence from England.

Although the laws in this country initially adopted the English common law approach, reforms were gradually adopted over the course of the nineteenth century that softened the harshness of its exclusionary focus. A central reform was the extension of legal recognition to the mother-child unit. No longer a child of no one, nonmarital children were became formally recognized as the children of their mothers; as a result, mothers were entitled to custody and obligated to provide support. A second significant reform was the gradual rejection of the harsh common law rule that a child's status was fixed permanently at birth, and beginning with Virginia in 1823, most states amended their laws to allow for **legitimation**, where parents married each other after the birth of a child.

Legitimation:
The process of altering the status of a child born to unmarried parents so that he or she is the legal equivalent of a child born to married parents

Constitutional Developments

Although the abovementioned reforms mitigated some of the harsh common law rules, children of unmarried parents remained a distinct legal category of persons well into the next century. Referred to as "bastards" or "illegitimates," they suffered a variety of legal disabilities, particularly in relationship to their fathers. For example, they were frequently excluded as beneficiaries under statutory benefit programs, such as workers' compensation; they lacked inheritance rights under state intestacy laws; and they were denied standing in wrongful death actions for the loss of a parent. Additionally, unwed fathers had few legal rights in relationship to their children. Beginning in the 1960s, a number of lawsuits were brought challenging this differential treatment of children of unmarried parents and the denial of rights to unwed fathers. In the following sections, we will look at the U.S. Supreme Court's response to these challenges.

The Equal Protection Challenge to Differential Treatment

Equal Protection Clause:
A clause in the fourteenth amendment to the U.S. Constitution that prevents states from imposing arbitrary and discriminatory legislative classifications

In 1968, in the landmark case of Levy v. Louisiana, the Supreme Court held that the state of Louisiana had violated the **equal protection clause** by denying children the right to recover for the death of their mother under the state's wrongful death law because of their "illegitimate" status. As explained by the Court:

> Legitimacy or illegitimacy of birth has no relation to the nature of the wrong allegedly inflicted on the mother. These children, though

illegitimate, were dependent on her; she cared for them and nurtured them; they were indeed hers in the biological and spiritual sense; in her death they suffered wrong in the sense that any dependent would.[2]

The Court thus recognized that the significance of the parent-child relationship does not depend on the marital status of the parents, and further, that children should not be discriminated against based on parental conduct over which they had no control.

Since *Levy*, the Court has decided a number of cases involving similar equal protection challenges to laws that discriminated against children born to unmarried parents by, for example, denying or limiting their ability to obtain statutory benefits or to inherit under state intestacy laws. Unfortunately, these decisions are not always clear and consistent with one another; nonetheless, some general principles do emerge from them.[3]

First, a court must carefully review any law that classifies children based on the marital status of their parents. Central to this review, the court must evaluate the reason for the statutory classification. If its purpose is to deter nonmarital sexual relations or promote the state's interest in marriage, the classification is invalid because these goals do not justify the discriminatory treatment of children. Children may not be disadvantaged based on circumstances over which they have no control. Moreover, states may not deprive children of benefits based on the assumption that there can be no meaningful parent-child relationship outside the marital family unit.

Second, although a law may not discriminate against children of unmarried parents in order to promote marriage or regulate sexual behavior, all legal distinctions between children of unmarried parents and children of married parents are not necessarily unconstitutional. Most important, if a distinction is carefully drawn for the purpose of preventing fraudulent claims, it is likely to withstand constitutional scrutiny. For example, although a state may not deprive nonmarital children of paternal inheritance rights under its intestacy statute in order to encourage marriage, it probably can condition these rights upon a prior adjudication of paternity in order to prevent fraudulent claims. Thus, a state may be able to exclude a child from receiving a statutory share of benefits where the father-child relationship had not been formally established prior to the father's death.

The Legal Status of the Unwed Father

As developed in the previous discussion, the differential treatment of children of unmarried parents is impermissible for the purpose of discouraging nonmarital sexual relations or promoting marriage. Let's now look at the issue from a different perspective: What if it is the unwed father, rather than the child, who is singled out for differential treatment? Should the law treat him in the same manner that it treats an unwed mother or a married father, or does he occupy a distinct legal position in relationship to his child? Are cases involving the interests of unwed fathers the flip side of cases involving children, or are different considerations at stake? To consider these questions, we turn to a series of landmark U.S. Supreme Court cases focusing on the rights of unwed fathers. These cases give us a different lens through which to view the unfolding and uncertain legal construction of nonmarital family relations.

Challenging the Exclusion of Unwed Fathers: Stanley v. Illinois

In 1972, in the case of Stanley v. Illinois,[4] the Supreme Court considered whether it was unconstitutional for a state to presume that all unwed fathers were unfit parents. Peter and Joan Stanley had lived together on an intermittent basis for 18 years. During this time, they had three children. When Joan Stanley died, the state of Illinois initiated a dependency proceeding. The children were declared wards of the state for lack of a surviving parent and placed in the care of a court-appointed guardian. Peter Stanley was not provided with an opportunity to challenge the removal of his children because the state of Illinois presumed that all unwed fathers were unfit to raise their children. In contrast, married parents and unwed mothers could not be deprived of their children without a hearing on the issue of fitness.

Stanley challenged the presumption of unfitness, which effectively severed his tie with his children without inquiry into their actual circumstances, and argued that, like other parents, he was entitled to a hearing on the question of fitness. Although acknowledging, as argued by the state, that most unwed fathers may in fact be "unsuitable and neglectful" parents, the Court nonetheless agreed with Stanley that he could not be deprived of custody without a hearing. In supporting Stanley's claim, the Court recognized the potential for meaningful relationships between unwed fathers and their children and made clear that paternal rights do not merit protection only when developed within a marital family unit.

Following *Stanley*, it appeared as if the Court might be moving in the direction of eliminating all distinctions between unwed fathers and other parents. However, the Court did not make clear why it was protecting Stanley's rights. Would a mere biological connection to these children have entitled him to a hearing, or was he entitled because he had both "sired and raised" them?

What Makes an Unwed Father a Father?

After *Stanley*, a number of unwed fathers brought lawsuits challenging state laws that permitted the adoption of nonmarital children based solely on the consent of the mother. Building on *Stanley*, they argued (1) that an unwed father has a constitutionally protected liberty interest in maintaining a parental relationship with his child that cannot be abrogated without his consent absent proof of unfitness; and (2) that differential treatment of unwed fathers and unwed mothers violates the equal protection clause.

In responding to these challenges, the Court answered the question left open in *Stanley*. In the 1983 case of Lehr v. Robertson, the Court clarified that the rights of unwed fathers do not spring into being based solely on the biological link between father and child. According to the Court, the significance of the biological connection is that it provides a father with the unique opportunity to develop a relationship with his offspring. If he grasps that opportunity and assumes some responsibility for the child, he may be entitled to some of the benefits and rights that attach to the parent-child relationship; however, if he fails to grasp this opportunity, he cannot claim a constitutionally protected right to participate in the adoption decision.[5] (Note: We return to the adoption rights of unmarried fathers in Chapter 13.) In short, outside the marital context, biology alone does not a father make. Instead, a man must act like a father to be legally recognized as one, and thus be entitled to an equal say regarding adoption. This "biology-plus" approach drew harsh criticism from the dissent, who argued that the biological tie itself merits protection because it is the nature rather than the weight of the interest that is important.

In short, the legal treatment of unmarried fathers differs from the treatment of unmarried mothers, as women are not required to demonstrate that they have "grasped the opportunity" provided by the biological relationship in order to be legally recognized as a mother. For women, the parental relationship is thought to flow directly from the fact that she "carries and bears" the child. Here, biology is central—while men must become fathers, women are mothers. For men, biology provides the opportunity to become a legally recognized father; for women, motherhood is embedded in biology.[6] An unmarried father is also treated differently from a married father, who, because of marriage, is presumed to have a developed relationship with his children.

Unfortunately, the matter is a bit more complex than it has been presented so far. In 1989, the Court rendered a very important decision, which appears to limit the scope of the biology-plus approach—at least where it bumps up against the presumption of paternity. We now turn to the case of Michael H. v. Gerald D.

The Biology-Plus Approach Confronts the Presumption of Paternity

The following facts will set the stage for our analysis of the Court's decision in Michael H. v. Gerald D. (*Michael H.*).[7] In 1981, a girl named

Victoria was born to a woman named Carol. At the time, Carol was married to Gerald, who was listed as the father on the birth certificate. However, subsequent blood tests showed a 98.7 percent probability that a man named Michael was actually Victoria's father. During Victoria's early years, three men moved in and out of her life. At times, Victoria, Carol, and Gerald made up a household; at other times, Victoria, Carol, and Michael made up a household. (We'll ignore the third man, Scott, who for our purposes is irrelevant, as he did not seek to assert paternal rights.)

To secure his relationship with Victoria, Michael filed a paternity action seeking formal legal recognition as her father. Not surprisingly, Gerald opposed his quest for recognition, arguing that under California law, he was Victoria's presumed father based on his marriage to Carol and that Michael lacked standing to assert paternal rights. In response, Michael argued that the presumption was unconstitutional because it deprived him of his interest in maintaining a relationship with his daughter. Drawing on the unwed father cases, Michael argued that since he satisfied both prongs of the *Lehr* test — biological fatherhood plus a developed relationship — he was entitled to recognition as Victoria's father. Having grasped the opportunity afforded him by his biological connection to Victoria, he maintained that California could not bar his assertion of paternal rights based on the marital presumption.

Although there was little doubt that Michael met the biology-plus standard, the Court chose to focus its attention elsewhere. Zooming in on the adulterous relationship between Michael and Carol, the Court determined that the bond between Michael and Victoria was not deserving of recognition because it did not take root within the sanctity of a "unitary family." The Court thus concluded that when faced with a choice between an "adulterous natural father" and a marital father who parents within "the integrity of the traditional family unit," the Constitution does not compel recognition of the "irregular" relationship over one that conforms to traditional standards.[8]

In a biting dissent, it was argued that the unwed father cases had nothing to do with protecting "unitary families" and everything to do with protecting unwed fathers who, like Michael, had developed a relationship with their children. From the dissenter's perspective, the relevant inquiry should have been whether the "relationship under consideration is sufficiently substantial to qualify as a liberty interest under our prior cases," without reference to the constellation of household arrangements.[9] In short, according to the dissent, the goal of protecting the marital unit does not justify overriding the interests of a biological father who seeks to maintain a relationship with his child.

According to the *Michael H.* decision, the federal constitution does not require states to provide unwed fathers with the opportunity to challenge the marital presumption; however, they are not prohibited from doing so.

Accordingly, a number of states permit unwed fathers to challenge the presumption and assert their own claim to fatherhood, although many of these states impose a threshold requirement that a father must meet before he can proceed. Typically, he may be required to show that rebuttal of the presumption would be in the child's best interest, that he has a substantial relationship with the child, or both. A few states do not impose these limitations and permit a challenge in almost all situations; here, the interests of unwed fathers may be given heightened protection under the state constitution.

▪ Establishing Paternity

When parents are unmarried, paternity must be established in order for a man to be recognized as the legal father of a child. The two primary approaches to establishing paternity are **adjudication** and **acknowledgment**. In some instances, as we have seen, it may also be established by presumption, such as when a child is born to a married woman.

In 1973, when Congress entered the child support arena, it also sought to upgrade state procedures for paternity establishment so that more support awards could be established for the benefit of children of unmarried parents. Accordingly, the aptly named Child Support Enforcement and Establishment of Paternity Act (discussed in detail in Chapter 6) directed states to conform their paternity laws to the new federal requirements or risk loss of federal funding. These federal requirements (which have since been strengthened by subsequent federal laws) apply to both the adjudication and the acknowledgment of paternity.

Adjudication of Paternity: Paternity determined through a court action

Acknowledgment of Paternity: Paternity established voluntarily, through the completion of a notarized paternity affidavit

The Adjudication of Paternity

The modern-day paternity action evolved from the colonial era bastardy proceeding, which was criminal in nature and intended to punish the "fornicator." The goal of punishing sexual misconduct has dropped by the historical wayside, and today, paternity actions (see Exhibit 11.1) are brought to identify a man as the legal father of a child based on his biological connection.

Most paternity actions are initiated by mothers or a IV-D agency (recall from Chapter 6 that in order to receive Temporary Assistance to Needy Families/TANF benefits, a mother must assign her child support rights to the state and cooperate in establishing paternity, unless she can show good cause for noncooperation) so that the child can receive support, as well as other potential benefits that flow from an established parent-child relationship. Although far less common, men may also initiate paternity proceedings in order to secure custody and visitation rights. Here, in a

F. C. A. §§ 522, 523   Form 5-1
S.S.L. §111-g   (Paternity Petition)
[**NOTE**: Personal Information Form 4-5/5-1-d,   10/2012
containing social security numbers of parties and
dependents, must be filed with this Petition]

FAMILY COURT OF THE STATE OF NEW YORK
COUNTY OF
....

In the Matter of a Paternity Proceeding   Docket No.

                                    Petitioner,   PATERNITY
                                                                 PETITION
         -against-   (Individual)

                                    Respondent

....

TO THE FAMILY COURT:

   The undersigned Petitioner respectfully alleges that:

   1. [check applicable box(es)]:
   ❏ I am the [check one]: ❏ birth mother of ❏ pregnant with   the child who is the subject of
this petition and am submitting this petition to request an order declaring Respondent to be the
father of the child.
   ❏ I am the father of the child who is the subject of this petition and am submitting this
petition to request an order declaring me to be the father of the child.
   ❏ Upon information and belief, I may be the father of the above-named child and am
submitting this petition to request an order determining the paternity of the child.

   2. a. I reside at [specify]:[1]

      b. Respondent resides at [specify]:[2]

---

   [1] Unless ordered confidential pursuant to Family Court Act § 154-b because disclosure would
pose an unreasonable risk to the health or safety of the petitioner: *see* forms GF-21 and 21a, available at
www.nycourts.gov.

   [2] Unless ordered confidential pursuant to Family Court Act § 154-b, because disclosure would
pose an unreasonable risk to the health or safety of the respondent: *see* forms GF-21 and 21a, available at
www.courts.gov.

Exhibit 11.1 cont.

Form 5-1 page 2

3. I had sexual intercourse with the above-named Respondent during a period of time beginning on or about the _____ day of _____ , _____ , and ending on or about the _____ day of _____ , _____ .

4. [Check applicable box]:
    a. ☐ I OR ☐ Respondent gave birth to [specify name of child]: _____ , a ☐ male ☐ female child out of wedlock on [specify date]: _____

    b. ☐ I OR ☐ Respondent is now pregnant with a child who is likely to be born out of wedlock.

5. [Check box, if applicable; if not, SKIP to ¶6]: ☐ I am requesting an order for genetic testing to determine the paternity of the child.

6. Upon information and belief, at the time of conception of the child, the mother
    ☐ was not married.
    ☐ was married to [specify]: _____ , whose last known address is [specify]: _____

7. [Check applicable box(es), if any; if not, SKIP to ¶8]:
    ☐ I have acknowledged paternity: ☐ in writing ☐ by furnishing support.
    ☐ Respondent acknowledged paternity: ☐ in writing ☐ by furnishing support.

8. Upon information and belief, no individual has been adjudicated father of this child, either in this court, or any other court, including a Native-American court; and no individual has signed an Acknowledgment of Paternity admitting paternity for this child, (except) [specify]: _____

9. No previous application has been made to any court or judge for the relief herein requested (except [specify]: _____

10. [Check applicable box(es)]:
    ☐ I have made application for child support services with the local Department of Social Services).
    ☐ I am now requesting child support services by the filing of this Petition.[3]
    ☐ I have continued to receive child support services after the public assistance or care case has closed.

---

[3]Pursuant to Section 111-g of the Social Services Law, signing this petition is deemed to be an application for child support enforcement services.

Exhibit 11.1 cont.

Form 5-1 page 3

☐ I do not wish to make application for child support services.
☐ I am the non-custodial parent of the subject child.

11. Upon information and belief, the subject child ☐ is ☐ is not a Native American child who may be subject to the Indian Child Welfare Act of 1978 (25 U.S.C. §§ 1901-1963).

12. Pursuant to F.C.A §§ 545, upon the entry of an Order of Filiation, the Court shall, upon application of either party, enter an order of support for the subject child.

WHEREFORE, I am requesting that this Court issue a summons or warrant requiring the Respondent to show cause why the Court should not enter a declaration of paternity, an order of support and such other and further relief as may be appropriate under the circumstances.

NOTE: (1) A COURT ORDER OF SUPPORT RESULTING FROM A PROCEEDING COMMENCED BY THIS APPLICATION (PETITION) SHALL BE ADJUSTED BY THE APPLICATION OF A COST OF LIVING ADJUSTMENT AT THE DIRECTION OF THE SUPPORT COLLECTION UNIT NO EARLIER THAN TWENTY-FOUR MONTHS AFTER SUCH ORDER IS ISSUED, LAST MODIFIED OR LAST ADJUSTED, UPON THE REQUEST OF ANY PARTY TO THE ORDER OR PURSUANT TO PARAGRAPH (2) BELOW. SUCH COST OF LIVING ADJUSTMENT SHALL BE ON NOTICE TO BOTH PARTIES WHO, IF THEY OBJECT TO THE COST OF LIVING ADJUSTMENT, SHALL HAVE THE RIGHT TO BE HEARD BY THE COURT AND TO PRESENT EVIDENCE WHICH THE COURT WILL CONSIDER IN ADJUSTING THE CHILD SUPPORT ORDER IN ACCORDANCE WITH SECTION FOUR HUNDRED THIRTEEN OF THE FAMILY COURT ACT, KNOWN AS THE CHILD SUPPORT STANDARDS ACT.

(2) A PARTY SEEKING SUPPORT FOR ANY CHILD(REN) RECEIVING FAMILY ASSISTANCE SHALL HAVE A CHILD SUPPORT ORDER REVIEWED AND ADJUSTED AT THE DIRECTION OF THE SUPPORT COLLECTION UNIT NO EARLIER THAN TWENTY-FOUR MONTHS AFTER SUCH ORDER IS ISSUED, LAST MODIFIED OR LAST ADJUSTED BY THE SUPPORT COLLECTION UNIT, WITHOUT FURTHER APPLICATION BY ANY PARTY. ALL PARTIES WILL RECEIVE A COPY OF THE ADJUSTED ORDER.

(3) WHERE ANY PARTY FAILS TO PROVIDE, AND UPDATE UPON ANY CHANGE, THE SUPPORT COLLECTION UNIT WITH A CURRENT ADDRESS, AS REQUIRED BY SECTION FOUR HUNDRED FORTY-THREE OF THE FAMILY COURT ACT, TO WHICH AN ADJUSTED ORDER CAN BE SENT, THE SUPPORT OBLIGATION AMOUNT CONTAINED THEREIN SHALL BECOME DUE AND OWING ON THE DATE THE FIRST PAYMENT IS DUE UNDER THE

Exhibit 11.1 cont.

Form 5-1 page 4

TERMS OF THE ORDER OF SUPPORT WHICH WAS REVIEWED AND
ADJUSTED OCCURRING ON OR AFTER THE EFFECTIVE DATE OF THE
ADJUSTED ORDER, REGARDLESS OF WHETHER OR NOT THE PARTY HAS
RECEIVED A COPY OF THE ADJUSTED ORDER.

_____
Petitioner

_____
Print or type name

_____
Signature of Attorney, if any

_____
Attorney's Name (Print or Type)

_____
_____
Attorney's Address and Telephone Number

Dated: ,   .

VERIFICATION

STATE OF NEW YORK   )
                                      : ss.:
COUNTY OF   )

being duly sworn, says that (s)he is the Petitioner in the above-entitled proceeding and that the foregoing petition is true to (his)(her) own knowledge, except as to matters herein stated to be alleged on information and belief and as to those matters (s)he believes it to be true.

_____
Petitioner

Sworn to before me this
      day of   ,   .

_____
(Deputy) Clerk of the Court
      Notary Public

historical shift, the father seeks to affirm rather than to deny his paternity. However, as discussed previously, if the mother is married to someone else, the presumption of paternity may bar the action, or a man may first have to satisfy a threshold requirement, such as that he has a substantial relationship with the child.

Genetic Testing:
Performed when paternity is contested; can prove or disprove paternity with virtual certainty

When paternity is contested, states must, under federal law, have procedures in place that require the parties and the child to submit to **genetic testing** if requested by either party. If the case is being handled by the IV-D agency, the agency must pay for the testing; however, it is entitled to recoup the funds from the father if paternity is established. Unlike in years past, when testing required the drawing of blood and was unreliable, DNA-based identity testing today can be done through a cheek swab and can prove or disprove paternity with virtual certainty. Unless an objection is made, the tests must be admissible without foundation testimony or proof of authenticity.

Under federal law, states must have rules in place that create a rebuttable presumption of paternity if the tests indicate that the man is the father of the child within a threshold degree of probability. Once the presumption is triggered, the burden shifts to the man in question to prove nonpaternity by, for example, establishing "nonaccess" or that he is sterile. States also have the option of making the presumption conclusive, in which case it would operate like a court judgment and could be challenged only under very limited circumstances.

Voluntary Acknowledgment of Paternity

Paternity can also be established voluntarily. This approach has gained favor, and under federal law, all states must have a simple procedure in place that enables parents to acknowledge paternity by completing a notarized paternity affidavit (Exhibit 11.2). States must offer paternity establishment services at hospitals and at the state agency responsible for maintaining birth records. States may also offer paternity establishment services at other locations where children and parents receive services or care, such as at pediatricians' offices and Head Start programs.

Before signing the paternity acknowledgment form, a parent must be provided with information regarding the legal consequences of establishing paternity. Some states have developed separate materials for mothers and fathers in recognition of the different concerns that each may have regarding, for example, child support obligations and custody and visitation rights. Although most state materials emphasize the benefits of acknowledging paternity, some address the concerns that victims of violence may have and may recommend against signing if the mother fears for her own safety or the safety of the child.[10] Typically, the parties are told about the availability of genetic testing; such notification is not required,

ILLINOIS VOLUNTARY ACKNOWLEDGMENT OF PATERNITY

Instructions: PRINT in **BLACK** ink. Do not cross out words or make corrections or your form will be rejected. If you make a mistake, print a new form. Print 4 copies, sign each copy and have your witness sign and complete each copy. See additional instructions on the second page of this form.

Read carefully and complete all information before signing this form. Call the Child Support Customer Service Call Center at 1-800-447-4278 if you have questions. Questions about the birth certificate must be directed to the Illinois Department of Public Health, Division of Vital Records, at www.idph.state.il.us/vitalrecords or 217-782-6554.

Child's First Name		Middle Name		Last Name (same as on birth certificate)		Sex ☐ M ☐ F
Date of Birth (mm/dd/yy)		Place of Birth - Hospital Name		City/State/Zip		

Father's Name (first/middle/last)		Date of Birth (mm/dd/yy)	Place of Birth (city/state)	
Address		City/State/Zip	Social Security Number	

Mother's Name (first/middle/last)	Maiden Name	Date of Birth (mm/dd/yy)	Place of Birth (city/state)
Address		City/State/Zip	Social Security Number

Were you married to a man other than the biological father when this child was conceived and/or born? ☐ Yes ☐ No

If yes, a Denial of Paternity must also be completed by the mother and the husband/ex-husband to place the biological father's name on this child's birth certificate.

By signing, I:

1. Understand that this is a legal document. I understand that when the Voluntary Acknowledgment of Paternity (hereafter called VAP) is signed and witnessed, it is the same as a court order determining the legal relationship between a father and child.
2. Understand that if I am a minor, I have the right to sign and have this form witnessed without my guardian's permission. I understand that when the parents are minors, paternity is not conclusive until six months after the younger of the parents turns 18.
3. Understand that both parents have the right to all notices of any adoption proceedings.
4. Understand my responsibility to provide financial support for the child that may include child support and medical support starting from the child's birth until the child is at least 18 years old.
5. Understand that this VAP does not give custody or visitation to the father. However, this gives the father the right to ask the court for custody or visitation.
6. Understand that either the mother or father may withdraw the action by signing a Rescission of VAP. The Rescission must be signed and received by the Department within 60 days of signing the VAP or the date of a proceeding relating to the child, whichever occurs earlier.
7. Have read the instructions on the second page of this form, been provided an oral explanation about the VAP and understand my rights and responsibilities created and waived by signing this form. Oral explanations can be heard by calling 1-800-447-4278.

I UNDERSTAND THAT I CAN REQUEST A GENETIC TEST REGARDING THE CHILD'S PATERNITY. BY SIGNING THIS FORM I GIVE UP MY RIGHT TO A GENETIC TEST.

Father's Signature _____	Mother's Signature _____
Print Name of Father _____	Print Name of Mother _____
Witness' Signature _____	Witness' Signature _____
Print Name of Witness _____	Print Name of Witness _____
Witness Address _____	Witness Address _____
Witness' Telephone # _____	Witness' Telephone # _____
Date Parties Signed _____	Date Parties Signed _____

Send one copy to HFS/ACU, 110 W Lawrence, Springfield, IL 62704 if signed in hospital. Send two copies to HFS if signed outside hospital. One copy is for the mother and one copy is for the father.

For Official Use Only _____ Case # _____ Docket # _____ CP RIN _____ NCP RIN _____ Child RIN _____

HFS 3416B INTERNET (R-7-10)

Exhibit 11.2
Voluntary Acknowledgment of Paternity

however, thus creating the possibility that the acknowledged father, either knowingly or unknowingly, may not necessarily be the biological father. (See the section entitled "Paternity Disestablishment," next.)

The parties have a set window of time within which to rescind the acknowledgment and thereby disestablish paternity. Thereafter, if the acknowledgment is not rescinded, it operates as a legal finding of paternity and is entitled to full faith and credit in other states. However, a subsequent challenge may be permitted on the limited grounds of fraud, duress, or mistake of fact.

Following the Determination of Paternity

Once paternity is established, the formerly putative father is now the legal father of the child, with the rights and responsibilities that this status entails. He can be required to pay child support and can seek court-ordered custody and visitation rights.

If paternity is established in court, a child support order can usually be established at the same time. The fact that the parties are not married should not affect the support amount. So far as custody and visitation are concerned, if the court is one of limited jurisdiction without broad authority over family matters, the father may need to bring a separate action in family court. Moreover, unlike with child support, some states use different substantive standards where unmarried parents of children, as distinct from divorcing parents, are involved. Although the focus remains the best interest of the child, some states employ a rebuttable presumption that it is in the child's best interest to remain with the parent who has been the child's primary caretaker or with whom the child has lived continuously for a certain period of time. This standard often favors the mother, who, especially where parents are unmarried, is likely to be the primary care parent.

▪ Paternity Disestablishment

A controversial issue that courts are deeply divided on is whether a father should be permitted to "disestablish" his paternity — that is, to undo a determination that he is the child's biological father. In large part, the ready availability of reliable genetic testing has prompted this push for biological certainty, even if the quest threatens to disrupt a well-established father-child relationship.

Paternity Disestablishment: The undoing or revocation of a determination that a man is a child's legal father

Like joint custody, **paternity disestablishment** is closely identified with the fathers' rights movement, which as noted in Chapter 5, emerged in the 1970s to address a perceived anti-male bias in the family courts. In this context, the ability to disavow fatherhood is seen as necessary to vindicate the rights of men who have been "duped" by women, often with the aid of the legal system. Proponents of "paternity fraud reform" often compare the situation of fathers who learn that they are not a child's biological parent to a criminal who has been wrongly convicted, and argue that "just as DNA evidence has revolutionized criminal laws, it should . . . lead to a revolution in family law . . . in the sense that evidence admissible to 'convict' should also be available to 'exonerate.'"[11] However, "exoneration" in the family law domain does not simply undo a mistake; it also serves to dismantle an established parent-child relationship, with potentially devastating emotional consequences for a child. Disestablishment is also likely to have an adverse financial impact on a child, as termination of the legal parent-child relationship typically operates to terminate a man's duty to provide support, which, of course, is often a primary motivating consideration behind the quest to disestablish paternity. Another potentially troubling distinction is that rather than simply seeking to right a wrong, men seeking to disestablish paternity may well be motivated by "anger and a desire to strike back at ex-wives and girlfriends."[12]

Paternity disestablishment cases once again present important questions regarding the weight and meaning of fatherhood. Is it a genetic link that makes a man a father? Is it grasping the opportunity presented by a genetic link to develop a relationship with a child, or can fatherhood be achieved in the absence of a biological link by assuming the role of a father in a child's life? How should the competing interests of a father who wishes to disavow his misidentified status be balanced with the needs of the child? As noted in a leading monograph on the subject, other critical questions include the following:

> At what point should the truth about genetic parentage outweigh the consequences of leaving a child fatherless? Is a child better off knowing his/her genetic heritage or maintaining a relationship with his/her father and his family that provides both emotional and financial support? Should it matter who brings the action or should the rules be the same for men trying to disestablish paternity, women seeking to oust a father from the child's life, and third parties trying to assert their paternity of a child who already has a legal father?[13]

States have begun addressing the issue of when to allow paternity disestablishment through both statutory enactments and judicial decisions. For example, some states have passed laws allowing men who have been adjudicated fathers to reopen the court decision to disprove their paternity through the introduction of genetic evidence. In other states, either the mother or the father can seek judicial relief where paternity has been adjudicated or acknowledged. Courts have expressed a dizzying array of opinions on the matter. In part, this reflects differences in underlying fact patterns; however, it also reflects deeply divided views on how the competing interests should be accommodated. We turn now to two paternity disestablishment decisions that weigh the best interest of the child in the decisional calculus very differently.

Considering Best Interest: Conflicting Approaches

In the case of Paternity of Cheryl,[14] the Massachusetts Supreme Judicial Court (SJC) refused to permit an unmarried father to disestablish paternity. Briefly, the facts are as follows. Cheryl was born in 1993. Shortly thereafter, the parents, who were not married, signed a voluntary acknowledgment, which was entered as a court judgment. The father participated in Cheryl's life as a father, and she referred to him as "Daddy." When Cheryl was 6, the state's IV-D agency sought an increase in child support. Five days later, the father raised doubts about his paternity, and genetic tests revealed that he was not the girl's biological father. In rejecting his request to vacate the paternity judgment, the SJC focused on the impact this would have on Cheryl:

> Where a father challenges a paternity judgment, courts have pointed to the special needs of children that must be protected, noting that consideration of what is in a child's best interest will often weigh more heavily than the genetic link between parent and child. . . . [C]hildren benefit psychologically, socially, educationally and in other ways from stable and predictable parental relationships. . . . [W]here a father and child have a substantial parent-child relationship, an attempt to undo a determination of paternity is "potentially devastating to a child who has considered the man to be the father."[15]

In contrast to this child-centered focus, the Court of Appeals of Maryland in Langston v. Riffe[16] concluded that the best interest of the child has no place in a paternity disestablishment action. In this consolidated action, three men were seeking to set aside a paternity judgment based on new evidence indicating in each case that another man might be the child's biological father. At issue was whether, in seeking reconsideration of a paternity judgment, the fathers had an automatic statutory right to blood or genetic testing as they would at the time of paternity establishment or, as argued by the state on behalf of the mothers, whether in this context, the court must first consider the best interest of the children. In reviewing the legislative history, the court concluded that the "'best interests of the child' standard generally has no place in a proceeding to reconsider a paternity declaration. . . . To not allow testing now would violate . . . the Legislature's intent . . . to provide relief to putative fathers seeking review of potentially false paternity declarations entered against them."[17]

What Makes a Man a Father?

Underlying these decisions is the familiar struggle to arrive at an understanding of what makes a man a father. The two cases embody different understandings of the role that biology plays in determining fatherhood. By focusing on the developed relationship between Cheryl and her father, the SJC downgraded the importance of the biological link between a father and child in favor of relational considerations. However, it is possible that the court would have paid less attention to this connection if Cheryl's biological father had been standing in the wings, ready, willing, and able to assume a role in her life. In contrast, the Maryland court, in focusing on the vindication of the father's interest without regard to the impact of disestablishment on the children of these men, elevated the biological dimension of fatherhood over relational considerations.

Determining Paternity When the Genetic "Father" Is a Sperm Donor

In this section, we consider how questions of paternity are addressed in situations where conception has been accomplished through **donor insemination** rather than through sexual intercourse. The involvement of a donor adds another layer of complexity to the determination of legal parentage. Although, as discussed, the law is relatively settled with regard to heterosexual married couples who rely on donor insemination to have a child, it is in considerably more flux when it comes to lesbian couples and single women, thus injecting a greater element of unpredictability and variability from state to state.

Donor Insemination: The process by which a woman is inseminated with or inseminates herself with sperm contributed by a donor, who may be known or unknown

Sperm Donation and the Married Heterosexual Couple

Where a married woman and her husband are unable to conceive due to his infertility (or possibly the risk of transmitting a genetic disease), one possibility is for her to be inseminated with the sperm of another man. Here, although she is married, the child is actually the biological offspring of two persons who are not married to each other. Under these circumstances, who is entitled to legal recognition as the father?

The previously discussed presumption of paternity, which operates to identify a woman's husband as the legal father of all children born during the marriage, provides a partial answer. As we have seen, however, this common law presumption is not absolute and is generally rebuttable by proof of infertility. To address this situation the Uniform Parentage Act (UPA) makes it clear that the "donor is not a parent of a child conceived by assisted reproduction," and that the consenting husband is the presumed father.[18] Importantly, the updated 2002 UPA has dropped the marriage requirement. As a result, the cutoff provision will apply regardless of a woman's marital status, and her consenting male partner steps into the shoes of the presumed father. The UPA further provides that the absence of a signed consent form does not preclude a finding of paternity where the couple resided together during the first two years of the child's life and the father holds the child out as his own.

Even in the absence of a statute, a court is likely to hold that a consenting husband is the legal father. For instance, in the case of People v. Sorenson,[19] one of the earliest and still influential decisions on this issue, a husband who had consented to the insemination of his wife and had held himself out as the child's father argued upon divorce that he should not have to pay child support because the sperm donor, not he, was the child's legal father. In rejecting this position, the court stated:

> [W]here a reasonable man who because of his inability to procreate, actively participates and consents to his wife's artificial insemination in the hope that a child will be produced whom they will treat as their own, knows that such behavior carries with it the legal responsibilities of fatherhood. . . . One who consents to the production of a child cannot create a temporary relation to be assumed and disclaimed at will. . . . [I]t is safe to assume that without defendant's active participation and consent, the child would not have been procreated.[20]

Accordingly, the father's consent bound him to the child, and he was not permitted to disavow the relationship. Courts have similarly relied on the doctrine of equitable estoppel to reach the same result, finding that where a husband consents to the insemination of his wife and then treats the child as his own, he may be estopped from denying his paternity in order to avoid paying child support in the event of a separation or a divorce.

Sperm Donation: Lesbian Couples and Single Women

As we have just seen, when a married heterosexual couple relies on a sperm donor to conceive a child, a set of interlocking rules typically serves to identify a consenting husband (or possibly a husband who holds the child out as his own) as the legal father of the child. In effect, his actions serve as a substitute for sexual intercourse, thus obviating the usual requirement of a biological link as the prerequisite to a finding of legal parenthood. This is a fairly straightforward result, not unlike that reached by application of the common law marital presumption, which, as discussed, treats a man as the legal father of children born to his wife, irrespective of biology. Less clear, however, is the nature of the legal relationships when either a single woman or a lesbian couple uses donor sperm, as there is not a husband standing in the wings to be identified as the legal father.

The Legal Status of the Donor

A single woman or lesbian couple may decide to obtain sperm from a sperm bank. This essentially forestalls the possibility of a future legal conflict over the establishment of paternal rights, as most facilities promise the donors anonymity and maintain their records in such a way as to make the subsequent matching of sperm donor and birth mother difficult. Moreover, it is unlikely that the donor was motivated by the desire to become a parent but was instead prompted by a wish to earn extra money, or possibly by an altruistic wish to assist others who were unable to bear children on their own; thus, his participation cannot be read as a sign of intended parenthood.

However, it should be noted that there is a growing push for greater openness in the process, and many programs now provide sperm donors with an identity-release option that allows children conceived with their sperm to obtain certain information about their biological fathers when they reach adulthood. Moreover, in 2000, a California appeals court, in a case involving a genetically transmitted disease, concluded that the donor's right to preserve his anonymity was outweighed by the state's compelling interest in protecting the health and welfare of minor children, including those born by artificial insemination. Accordingly, the court ordered the disclosure of the donor's identity so that needed medical information could be obtained.[21] Although this perhaps signals a growing awareness that a blanket guarantee of anonymity may not be in the interest of children conceived through donor insemination, this is a far cry from extending paternal rights to men who donate their sperm to a sperm bank.[22]

Rather than relying on a sperm bank, a couple (or an individual) may prefer to use a known donor. This approach provides the recipient with more control over the process and a greater knowledge of the child's origins. It also allows for the possibility that the donor can play a continuing role in the child's life.[23] However, a potential downside of using a known donor is that the parties may not be able to control the legal outcome should a dispute arise. In the absence of a specific agreement between the parties regarding the intended role of the donor, the outcome may turn on whether there is a UPA-type statute that cuts off the parental rights of a gamete donor or does so in the absence of a written agreement to the contrary. If there is not such a statute, it is possible that a donor could be determined to be a child's legal father through a paternity proceeding brought either by the donor himself, in order to establish his right to maintain a relationship with the child, or by the mother, in order to secure child support.

In many cases, the respective parties do enter into an agreement embodying their intent. They may, for example, agree that the donor will relinquish all rights in exchange for a commitment from the mother not to seek child support. Alternatively, they may agree that the donor will have the right to participate in the child's life and correspondingly will contribute to the support of the child. The critical question, of course, is what happens if a party changes his or her mind, and a donor who previously agreed to relinquish his rights decides he wants a relationship with the child, or a woman who had agreed to let him participate in the child's life now wishes to cut off the relationship?

It is here that the law becomes particularly murky, as jurisdictions are divided over the enforceability of these agreements. Believing that it is in a child's best interest to have an identifiable legal father, some courts are unlikely to enforce these agreements if the result would be the severance of the relationship between the donor and the child. Also relevant here is the principle that parents cannot bargain away rights that ostensibly belong to the child. Of possible relevance here also is the view that contract law is not an appropriate vehicle for structuring family relationships, as it injects market principles into the privatized realm of domestic connections. In effect, this approach serves to privilege the donor's biological link to the child over the express intent of the parties, with some courts making clear that, absent proof of unfitness, they will not cut off the rights of a biological "parent," even if his initial intended status was simply that of a sperm donor.

Other courts have been willing to enforce these agreements, recognizing that to do otherwise would be to discourage this form of assisted reproduction. Moreover, as noted by the Supreme Court of Pennsylvania in 2007, in a decision upholding the enforceability of an agreement cutting off the rights of a donor, it would discourage women from seeking "sperm from a man she knows and admires . . . whose background, traits, and medical history are not shrouded in mystery" in favor of an unknown donor.[24] Contrary to this approach, here, the presence of a genetic link is not deemed of sufficient weight to override the clear intent of the parties that the donor not be regarded as a legal parent. (See the section entitled "Co-Parents" in Chapter 5 for a discussion regarding maternity presumptions, as the application of such a presumption may also affect the legal status of a sperm donor.)

Chapter Summary

Once considered children of no one, today laws that differentiate children based on the marital status of their parents are unconstitutional if the underlying purpose is deterrence of nonmarital sexual relations or the promotion of an idealized family type. However, laws that differentiate for the narrow purpose of preventing fraud are generally allowed.

The rights of unwed fathers have also been expanded. Although biology alone does not give a man a protected interest in maintaining a relationship with his child, his rights cannot be unilaterally terminated where he has sought to develop a relationship with his child. However, where the mother is married to another man, the presumption of paternity may preclude the unwed father from seeking paternal rights.

Paternity cannot simply be assumed. It must be established either through a court proceeding (i.e., adjudication) or a voluntary acknowledgment of paternity. To improve paternity establishment procedures, states must now comply with federal requirements or risk the loss of federal funds. A court must order genetic testing if requested by one party, and states must have rules that create a rebuttable presumption of paternity if the tests establish that the man is the father of the child within a threshold degree of probability. States must also have simplified procedures in place, such as the availability of paternity affidavits, for the voluntary acknowledgment of paternity.

A highly contested issue is whether a man should be allowed to disestablish paternity based on scientific evidence that he is not the biological father. States are divided on how to approach this issue. Some focus on the effect that disestablishment will have on the child and take best interest into account in determining whether a father can disavow his legal relationship with the child. Other states take the position that best interest is irrelevant, and the focus should be solely on the rights and status of the man who is contesting his paternal status.

Where conception is accomplished through sperm donation, the presumption of paternity and sperm donor laws generally operate to make the husband who consents to the insemination of his wife the legal father of the child despite the lack of a biological connection, and the rights of the sperm donor are terminated. In the case of a single woman or a lesbian couple who uses a sperm donor to conceive a child, the allocation of parental rights is more variable and may turn on the existence and enforceability of a contract between the parties.

Key Terms

Legitimate	Legitimation	Adjudication	Genetic Testing
Illegitimate	Equal	of Paternity	Paternity
Presumption of	Protection	Acknowledgment of	Disestablishment
Paternity	Clause	Paternity	Donor Insemination

Review Questions

1. What was the common law status of children of unmarried parents?
2. What is the presumption of paternity?
3. What underlying statutory purposes will invalidate a law that treats children of married parents and children of unmarried parents differently? What purpose will sustain differential treatment?
4. In the case of Stanley v. Illinois, how was the father treated differently from unwed mothers or married fathers? How did the Court respond to Stanley's challenge?
5. Based on the case of Lehr v. Robinson, when must an unwed father be given a voice in the adoption process?

6. Why did the dissent in *Lehr* disagree with the majority position? What did they think should be controlling?

7. Why was the biological father barred from pursuing his paternity claim in the case of Michael H. v. Gerald D.?

8. Explain current state approaches with respect to allowing a father to pursue a paternity claim where the mother is married to another man.

9. What is the significance of establishing paternity?

10. What are the two ways that paternity can be established?

11. What federal requirements are imposed on states in contested paternity actions?

12. What is a voluntary acknowledgment of paternity? What legal effect does an acknowledgment have?

13. What information must a state provide to persons who are thinking about acknowledging paternity?

14. What are the legal consequences of establishing paternity?

15. What does it mean to disestablish paternity? In what situations do these cases arise? What are the two basic approaches that courts use in these cases?

16. Where a married woman becomes pregnant through donor insemination with the consent of her husband, who is the legal father?

17. What is the likely outcome where a single woman or a lesbian couple uses an anonymous donor?

18. What are the possible outcomes when a single woman or a lesbian couple uses a known donor?

Discussion Questions

1. Thinking back to the case of Michael H. v. Gerald D., do you think the biological father should have been permitted to establish his paternal rights, or do you think the Court was right to bar his claim? What competing rights and interests are at stake here?

2. Assume that a man and woman who know each other casually have sexual intercourse one time. As a result, she becomes pregnant and decides to have the baby. Based on this fleeting moment of intimacy, is it fair that the father be responsible for 18 years of child support? What if he offers to pay for an abortion? What if he already has a family? What if the woman lied and said she was using birth control when she was not?

3. If a woman who is not married becomes pregnant, do you think she and the father should have equal rights with respect to the child? Is your thinking influenced by the circumstances? For example, does it matter if they were in a long-term serious relationship or if the

pregnancy resulted from a casual fling? Should the law take circumstances such as these into consideration?

4. Assume that, upon separation from his wife or partner, a man who has believed himself to be the father of the child he has been raising suddenly has doubts and wishes to have genetic testing done to determine if he is in fact the biological father. Do you think he should be allowed to do this and, if the tests show he is not the father, to disestablish paternity? What considerations do you think are important here?

5. Assume that a lesbian couple has chosen to use a known donor, and they enter into an agreement in which the donor agrees not to seek any parental rights or to see the child, and the women agree not to hold him responsible for child support. If he later changes his mind and wants to establish his paternity and see the child, should he be allowed to do so, or should he be held to his agreement?

Assignments

1. For your state, locate the applicable paternity statute (and custody statute, if separate) and determine the following:
   a. What court are the proceedings held in?
   b. With respect to the use of genetic tests, at what percentage of probability of paternity is a man presumed to be the father?
   c. Does your state employ a rebuttable or a conclusive presumption of paternity?
   d. What is the legal standard for determining custody? Are there any differences in the treatment of married and unmarried parents?
2. Go to the appropriate court or other local agency and obtain the form your state uses for voluntary paternity acknowledgments. If explanatory information is not contained on the form, make sure that you obtain any supplementary documents.

   Now, assume that your office has a client who is contemplating executing the acknowledgment. You have been asked to send him the relevant documents with a cover letter explaining the process and its significance. In writing the letter, assume that the client is young and has no familiarity with legal concepts.
3. Assume that your office is representing an unmarried woman who is planning to be inseminated with the sperm of a known donor. You have been asked to draft an agreement between the parties to memorialize their intent. They have agreed on the following:
   - The donor waives all potential parental rights.
   - The donee agrees not to pursue any child support or other claims.
   - The donor may see the child as a friend of the family but agrees not to disclose his true relationship to the child or to anyone else.
   - The child is to have no established relationship with the donor's extended family.

   After drafting the agreement, draft a cover letter to the client explaining the legal provisions contained in the agreement.

Endnotes

1. Michael Grossberg, Governing the Hearth—Law and the Family in Nineteenth-Century America 196-198 (1985).
2. Levy v. Louisiana, 391 U.S. 68, 72 (1968).
3. For further detail, *see* Laurence C. Nolan, "Unwed Children" and Their Parents Before the United States Supreme Court from *Levy* to *Michael H.*: Unlikely Participants in Constitutional Jurisprudence, 28 Cap. U. L. Rev. 1 (1999).
4. 405 U.S. 645 (1972).
5. Lehr v. Robinson, 463 U.S. 248, 262 (1983). *See also* Quillion v. Walcott, 434 U.S. 246 (1977) (challenge to Georgia law denying an unwed father the right to prevent the adoption of his child unless the child had been legitimated); Caban v. Mohammed, 441 U.S. 380 (1979) (challenge to New York law allowing adoption of a nonmarital child upon the consent of the mother only).
6. *See Lehr*, 463 U.S. at 260 n.16. *See also* Janet L. Dolgin, Just a Gene: Judicial Assumptions About Parenthood, 40 UCLA L. Rev. 637 (1993) (a fascinating analysis of the unwed father adoption cases in which the author argues that the Court is principally concerned with the relationship of the unwed father to the mother, and is more comfortable recognizing fathers where the bond with the child is effectuated through an established relationship with the mother).
7. 491 U.S. 110 (1989).
8. *Id.* at 130.
9. *Id.* at 142 (dissenting opinion of Justice Brennan with Justices Marshall and Blackmun).
10. For detail on these efforts, including concerns about the potential for coercion, *see* Paula Roberts, Paternity Establishment: An Issue for the 1990s, 26 Clearinghouse Rev. 1019 (1993). *See also* Paula Roberts, The Family Law Implications of the 1996 Welfare Legislation, 30 Clearinghouse Rev. 988 (1997).
11. Mary R. Anderlik and Mark A. Rothstein, DNA-Based Identity Testing and the Future of the Family: A Research Agenda, 28 Am. J.L. & Med. 215, 221 (2002). *See also* Melanie B. Jacobs, When Daddy Doesn't Want to Be Daddy Anymore: An Argument Against Paternity Fraud Cases, 16 Yale J.L. & Feminism 193 (2004).
12. Anderlik and Rothstein, *supra* note 11, at 221. *See also* Jacobs, *supra* note 11.
13. Paula Roberts, Truth and Consequences: Part I—Disestablishing the Paternity of Non-Marital Children 2 (2003). *See also* Parts II and III of this series, as well as the 2006 update, all of which can be found on the website of the Center for Law and Social Policy, http://www.clasp.org/ (accessed Oct. 7, 2012). As these articles make clear, this is a complex and rapidly changing area of the law, and the rules vary from state to state based on the interplay of number of considerations, including who is bringing the

action, whether the parties are married, and whether paternity has been adjudicated or acknowledged.

14. 434 Mass. 23, 746 N.E.2d 488 (Mass. 2001).

15. *Id.* at 496-497, quoting Hackley v. Hackley, 426 Mich. 582, 598 n.11, 395 N.W.2d 906 (1986).

16. 359 Md. 396, 754 A.2d 389 (Md. 2000).

17. *Id.* at 405, 428.

18. UPA, secs. 702-704 (Last Amended or Revised in 2002). http://www.uniformlaws.org/shared/docs/parentage/upa_final_2002.pdf (accessed March 13, 2015. As originally written, in order for these rules to apply, the insemination had to be done under the supervision of a licensed physician; however, the National Conference of Commissioners on Uniform State Laws (NCCUSL) dropped this requirement when it updated the UPA in 2000, although some state statutes may still contain the physician requirement. *See* Browne Lewis, Two Fathers, One Dad: Allocating the Parental Obligations Between the Men Involved in the Artificial Insemination Process, 13 Lewis & Clark L. Rev. 949 (2009).

19. 68 Cal. 2d 280, 437 P.2d 495 (Cal. 1968).

20. *Id.* at 499. Again, contrast this result with the result in the co-mother cases.

21. Johnson v. The Superior Court of Los Angeles County, 80 Cal. App. 4th 1050, 95 Cal. Rptr. 2d 864 (2000).

22. For a discussion of some of these issues, *see* Vanessa L. Pi, Regulating Sperm Donation: Why Requiring Exposed Donation Is Not the Answer, 16 Duke J. Gender L. & Poly. 379 (2009); Michelle Dennison, Revealing Your Sources: The Case of Non-anonymous Gamete Donation, 21 J.L. & Health (2007-2008); Ethics Committee of the American Society for Reproductive Medicine, American Society for Reproductive Medicine, Informing Offspring of Their Conception by Gamete Donation, 81 Fertility and Sterility 527 (2004).

23. For the purpose of the present discussion, assume that only the woman who bears the child has a biological link to that child. However, it is certainly possible that both women could have a biological connection, such as where sperm is donated to one woman by a relative of the other, or where the egg of one woman is fertilized outside of the body and implanted in the other, thus making one the "genetic" and the other the "gestational" mother.

24. Ferguson v. McKiernan, 596 Pa. 78, 940 A.2d 1236, 1247 (2007).

Chapter Twelve

Child Abuse and Neglect

In this chapter, we look at the difficult topic of child abuse and neglect. The enormity of the problem is overwhelming. Each year, countless parents inflict devastating injuries upon their children. The newspapers are filled with lurid stories of children who have been burned, beaten, suffocated, and locked in filthy apartments with no heat, food, or water.

In thinking about how the legal system should respond to these situations, one must confront the tension that exists between respecting family autonomy and protecting children from harm. Respect for family privacy is enshrined in our legal system. The due process clause of the fourteenth amendment protects the fundamental right of parents to the care and custody of their children based on the assumption that parents are in the best position to love and nurture their children. However, this right is not absolute, and at some point, the state may step in to shield children from maltreatment.[1]

Although it is clear that the protection of children is an important social goal, how do we determine the point at which parental claims of autonomy can be overridden? How do we define "bad" parenting, and how do we compare the impact of bad parenting with the impact of disruption and dislocation, which may also result in lasting harm? How do we respect the multiplicity of views about appropriate ways to parent without abdicating responsibility to children? And how do we respond to the fact that many parents who harm their children are themselves victims of violence or other traumas and may be struggling desperately to care for their children in a way that is not hurtful to them?

To help frame the discussion, I would like to share a troubling incident that I witnessed a number of years ago. I was ice-skating at an outdoor rink in what could generally be described as a middle-class community. Two parents were skating with their child who looked about ten years old. The child was miserable. He was cold, tired, and wanted to get off the ice. When the child would ask to leave the rink, the father would insist that he continue skating — that he must master the basics before sitting down. Eventually, he began stumbling from fatigue and begged to leave the ice, but the father would still not permit him to stop skating. The father did not raise his voice or strike the child, but it was clear that the child felt he had no choice but to continue. During this time, the mother must have been aware of what was going on, but she continued to skate as if all was fine.

At one point, I cast a hostile glance at the father, who told me to mind my own business. When I left, the child was still on the ice despite his exhaustion and abject misery. This scenario raises troubling questions about how we evaluate parental behavior. Was this abuse? Alternatively, was this possibly an effective parenting technique — teaching a child how to push beyond obstacles and strive for perfection? It also raises difficult questions about what response is called for. Should I have said something to the father? To the mother? Should I have reported the situation to the rink manager? To the state child protection agency? Would outside intervention have been helpful? Intrusive? Destructive? By whose standards are these determinations to be made?

Defining an appropriate social and legal response to child abuse and neglect is not a new task, and so we begin with a historical overview. We then consider the kinds of behaviors that may constitute abuse or neglect. Finally, we focus on how states respond to families where child abuse or neglect is suspected.

Historical Overview

In 1874, a New York charitable worker's attention was drawn to the plight of Mary Ellen Wilson, a ten-year old who was being brutalized by her foster mother, Mrs. Connolly. Not knowing where to turn, the worker appealed to the American Society for the Prevention of Cruelty to Animals (ASPCA), in the belief that the society had the authority to intercede on behalf of maltreated children as well as maltreated animals. Moved by Mary Ellen's plight, the ASPCA decided to help. Lacking an obvious legal approach, the ASPCA's attorney petitioned to have Mary Ellen brought before the court under the authority of an old English writ that permitted a magistrate to remove a person from the custody of another. In court, Mary Ellen recounted the horrors she had suffered, including being gashed on the face with a large pair of scissors and almost daily beatings. Mrs. Connolly was convicted of assault and battery, and Mary Ellen was committed to an orphanage and subsequently entrusted to a new family.[2]

Mary Ellen's case triggered a public outcry and generated an awareness that although many societies existed to help mistreated animals, none existed for child victims. Within a year of Mrs. Connolly's conviction, the ASPCA's attorney, who had helped Mary Ellen, founded the New York Society for the Prevention of Cruelty to Children (NYSPCC), the first organization dedicated to child cruelty work. Similar societies soon emerged in other cities and towns. In general, these child protection agencies regarded themselves as an arm of the police and were committed to seeing that existing laws were vigorously enforced. Agents could arrest offending parents, search homes for evidence of abuse or neglect, remove children, and initiate prosecutions. The focus of the agents was on the offending parent rather than on the child, and punishment rather than assistance was the likely result.

The societies reached the peak of their influence in the 1920s. The Depression brought a loss of funding and a shift in societal emphasis from concern about family violence to family economic survival. Protection of children from parental harm would not surface again as a significant social issue until the 1960s.[3]

The Child Protective System

In the late 1950s, child abuse was "rediscovered" as a social problem. Based mainly on advances in x-ray technology, doctors came to identify patterns of injuries in children that were inconsistent with parental explanations of accidental occurrences. Doctors were also faced with parents who disclaimed a history of past injuries, yet x-rays revealed old fractures in various stages of healing. In 1962, a major study entitled "The Battered Child Syndrome" was published that detailed the harms children suffer at the hands of their caretakers.[4] As with the case of Mary Ellen Wilson nearly a century earlier, this study triggered a public outcry and paved the way for a major reworking of abuse and neglect laws.

Within about five years after publication of "The Battered Child Syndrome," all states had enacted **abuse reporting laws**. Initially narrow in scope, these laws focused on physical abuse and generally imposed reporting requirements only on doctors. A variety of agencies—including the police, juvenile courts, and child protection agencies—were designated to receive reports, but, unfortunately, most of the reporting laws did not specify who was to assume responsibility once a report had been made. As a result, reports often fell into a void and were passed from agency to agency without any clear lines of accountability. This fragmentary approach resulted in the loss of vital information and a gross inattention to the children who had been identified as possible abuse victims.[5]

Frustrated by this fragmentation, reformers pushed for greater coordination of protective services, and in 1974, Congress responded by

Abuse Reporting Laws: Laws that establish a mechanism for the reporting of suspected cases of child abuse and/or neglect to a state protective agency

passing the Child Abuse Prevention and Treatment Act (CAPTA). Since 1974, CAPTA has been reauthorized and amended multiple times in order to refine and expand the scope of the law, and it remains at the center of the child protective system.[6]

Under CAPTA, states that developed a coordinated child protective system, in accordance with federal requirements, became eligible for federal funding. In response, all states revised their existing laws and centralized responsibility in a single **child protection agency**. These agencies now stand at the forefront of what is intended to be a coordinated system to protect children from harm by parents or other caretakers. They are charged with responsibility for receiving and investigating reports of abuse or neglect, providing services to families, taking children into emergency custody, and initiating court dependency and termination proceedings. In some states, protection agencies may also be obligated to refer certain cases, such as those in which a child has been raped, has suffered serious physical injury, or has died, to the district attorney's office for investigation of possible criminal charges.[7]

In most cases, a family comes to the attention of a child protection agency when a report of suspected abuse or neglect is filed. The reporting triggers a complex responsive process that, in extreme cases, may ultimately result in a termination of parental rights. This section provides a general overview of this process.

Child Protection Agency: Usually a state agency with responsibility for handling cases of child abuse and neglect

Defining Abuse and Neglect

CAPTA provides a foundational definition of **abuse** and **neglect** as follows:

- any recent act or failure to act on the part of a parent or caretaker which results in death, serious physical or emotional harm, sexual abuse or exploitation; or
- an act or failure which presents an imminent risk of serious harm.[8]

With these minimal definitions as the operative floor, states are responsible for developing their own definition of abuse and neglect. Some statutes provide broad definitions and speak generally about conduct that poses a threat to a child's well-being, while others provide considerable definitional detail regarding the behaviors that come within the scope of the law.

Determining which behaviors meet the statutory definitions of "abuse" and "neglect" is a powerful act, as it mediates the boundary between family autonomy and permissible intervention. Once parental behavior is defined as coming within the statute, the door is opened to ongoing state involvement. Accepting the premise that family autonomy is worth protecting, how do we decide when it must yield in order to

Abuse: Broadly speaking, abuse refers to the physical, sexual, or emotional harm of a child by a parent/caretaker

Neglect: Broadly speaking, the willful failure by a parent/caretaker to provide for a child's basic needs

protect children? What if one family's notion of acceptable punishment is a social worker's idea of abuse? What if the family's view is shaped by cultural values that differ from the social worker's? What if lack of food or inappropriate clothing is due to poverty rather than lack of parental concern? These are delicate questions that highlight the pervasive tension between the need to protect children and the privacy rights of families.[9]

Physical Abuse

Physical abuse is generally defined as conduct that causes physical injury or endangers the health of a child. This definition clearly leaves room for some physical "correction." For example, slapping a child's hand would not support a finding of abuse, but submerging the hand in boiling water would. Between these acts, however, lies a range of behaviors that are more difficult to categorize, and a determination whether a child is being abused may involve multiple factors such as the frequency of punishment and the state of mind of the parent. For example, a parent who occasionally spanks a child in accordance with his or her understanding of the appropriate boundaries of parental authority is not likely to be considered abusive, whereas a parent who frequently spanks a child, especially if an instrument is used, may well be considered abusive.

Physical abuse can be difficult to prove. Often there are no witnesses, and parents may be able to provide a plausible explanation for their child's injuries. For example, a cigarette burn on an arm may be the result of an intentional act or an accidental occurrence. Complicating matters in cases of intentional injuries, the victim may be too young or too afraid to tell anyone what really happened. If a case reaches court, testimony from persons such as doctors, social workers, and teachers who observed the condition of the child, as well as expert witness testimony on the battered child syndrome, can be helpful in establishing that injuries were intentionally inflicted rather than being accidental.

Sexual Abuse

Child sexual abuse encompasses a range of actions from inappropriate touching to penetration. Unlike sexual assaults by strangers, incest by a family member often begins with nonspecific sexualized touching and gradually evolves into more overt sexual acts. The child is usually sworn to secrecy and may be threatened with great harm if disclosure is made.

Because sexual abuse is cloaked in secrecy and obvious physical manifestations are often lacking, it can be difficult to detect. At some point, a child may reveal what has been happening or may inadvertently say something suggesting that abuse has occurred. Sexual abuse may also come to light when a child complains about physical problems such as vaginal soreness, when physical manifestations such as vaginal scarring or a venereal disease are noticed during a physical examination, or when an adult becomes concerned about unusual or developmentally inappropriate behavior.

Emotional Abuse and Neglect

Emotional abuse and emotional neglect are more recently recognized forms of child maltreatment, and many statutes now include them as distinct categories of behavior that can trigger state intervention. These terms are difficult to define, and many statutes refer generally to parental conduct that is causally linked to mental or emotional injuries in a child, such as depression, self-destructive impulses, acute anxiety, withdrawal, and uncontrollable aggression.

Emotional abuse frequently involves subjecting a child to intense and recurring anger or hostility. The child may constantly be belittled, scapegoated, threatened, insulted, and verbally assaulted. Prolonged isolation or acts such as locking a child in a closet can also constitute emotional abuse. *Emotional neglect* usually refers to the withdrawal of love and affection. The boundary between emotional abuse and neglect is often blurry, and both may be present simultaneously.

State intervention is rarely based solely on emotional maltreatment for a number of reasons: (1) it usually coexists with other kinds of abuse or neglect; (2) the symptoms identified with emotional harm are difficult to identify and tend to emerge gradually over time; (3) it is difficult to establish a causal link between the parent's conduct and the child's emotional suffering; and (4) it is difficult to determine the standard that parents should be held to. How do we decide what is good enough parenting and when a parent's failure to provide a secure, loving environment slides into destructive behavior? These determinations require tremendous sensitivity and respect for a diversity of parenting styles so that an idealized vision of the "good" parent is not imposed on nonconforming families.

Neglect

Neglect is the failure to provide for a child's basic needs. It is a broad concept that encompasses a range of acts, including the failure to provide food, the provision of unsanitary or unsafe housing, the failure to obtain adequate medical care and related services, lack of supervision, neglect of personal hygiene, and educational neglect.[10] According to congressional findings, more children suffer from neglect than from any other form of parental maltreatment; for instance, in 2010, 75 percent of the cases of child maltreatment that came to the attention of child protective services involved neglect.[11]

To support a finding of neglect, most states require some degree of parental willfulness; thus, a parent's inability to meet a child's needs because of poverty should not be considered neglect. Nonetheless, advocates for the poor have raised serious concerns about whether poverty is too readily equated with neglect, as the overt manifestations may be similar. Thus, for example, if a parent sends a young child to school without breakfast because the parent has spent the last of her or his income on heating, that is not neglect, whereas if a parent does so because she or he stays up late partying and cannot get out of bed in the morning, that may be considered neglectful. An additional concern is that if a child is removed from the home, a family's poverty may influence a social worker's decision not to return the child, particularly if the family lacks adequate shelter.[12]

Establishing neglect usually requires evidence that the child has been harmed or faces a risk of serious harm due to the deprivation. In making this determination, the frequency of the neglectful act may be relevant. An occasional parental slipup, such as occasionally sending a child to school without his or her lunch, is not neglect, whereas a consistent failure to provide a child with adequate clothing in the winter might be (unless this is due to poverty). Also, where the risk of injury is great, such as where a child is left alone in an apartment with exposed wires, a single incident may constitute neglect.

A parent may also be considered neglectful for the failure to protect a child in his or her care from abuse; most commonly, in these situations, the abuse is committed by the parent's partner or the other parent. It is not uncommon in these situations for the "passive" parent to also be a victim of abuse; in these cases, courts may be less likely to find that the parent was neglectful, based on the recognition that her ability to take action may be impaired by the abuse she is experiencing. Moreover, it would hold the wrong person accountable for the harms rendered to the family.

The Reporting of Suspected Abuse or Neglect

Most families come to the attention of a child protection agency following a report of suspected child abuse or neglect. Far less frequently, a parent who is struggling to care for his or her children will contact a protective agency directly for assistance.

The reporting laws in most states distinguish between mandatory and permissive reporters. **Mandatory reporters** are specifically designated by statute and are usually professionals who are likely to encounter children in the course of their work, such as dentists, social workers, therapists, teachers, and physicians. Mandatory reporters are legally obligated to

Mandatory Reporters: People who are legally obligated to report suspected cases of child abuse or neglect pursuant to an abuse-reporting law

report suspected instances of abuse or neglect and may be subject to criminal sanctions for the failure to do so, although prosecutions are rare. Generally, these statutes abrogate professional privileges so that a reporter can disclose information without violating any duty of confidentiality. Most, if not all, also protect a reporter from liability for making the report, so long as it was made in good faith.

Permissive Reporters: People who may report suspected cases of child abuse or neglect to a child protection agency but are not legally obligated to do so

Any person not specifically identified as a mandatory reporter is considered a permissive reporter. **Permissive reporters** can, but are not obligated to, report suspected cases of abuse or neglect. To encourage these reports, most states permit them to be made on an anonymous basis. Because permissive reporters have no duty to report, the failure to act will not result in sanctions. However, as discussed previously, parents may be legally responsible for failing to protect their children from harm inflicted by the other parent or caretaker. Accordingly, even where not required by statute, the duty to protect may effectively impose a reporting obligation on a parent.

Other states do not distinguish between mandatory and permissive reporters. In these states, a reporting duty is imposed on any person who has reasonable grounds to believe that a child is being harmed.

Reports are generally made directly to the child protection agency, although in some locales, the reporter may have the option of filing with the police. Also, in specific circumstances such as where a child has been killed, the reporter may be required to contact both the protective agency and another party, such as the police or the district attorney's office. As a rule, reports must be made immediately or as soon as practicable after the harm comes to the reporter's attention. Due to this timeliness requirement, reports are usually made by telephone and then followed up on in writing.

In the course of your work as a paralegal, you may face a situation where a client either tells you about abuse that is taking place or you become suspicious that his or her children are being abused or neglected. If this happens, you face the question of whether you must or should file a report. Attorneys and paralegals are almost never included in the list of mandated reporters, although they may be under a general duty to report in states that do not distinguish between mandatory and permissive reporters. Of course, even if not legally required, a report can always be made on a permissive basis. However, reporting raises difficult ethical questions regarding the duty to preserve client confidentiality, as most states do not abrogate the attorney-client privilege for this purpose. It is thus possible that reporting would breach the duty of confidentiality owed to a client. In short, regardless of any impulse you may have, under no circumstances should you take any action without consulting the attorney on the case, as he or she is most likely the appropriate person to make the decision about what should be done.

Screening and Investigation

When a report is received, it is either screened in for investigation or screened out (i.e., not accepted for investigation). Cases are screened out where

- the facts do not suggest abuse or neglect;
- the matter falls outside the agency's authority, such as when the perpetrator is not a parent or caretaker;
- there is not enough information to identify or locate the child in question;
- the report was made in bad faith; or
- the agency is already involved with the family.

If a case is screened in, a social worker will promptly conduct an investigation to determine if the allegations can be substantiated. The investigation typically includes a home visit so the investigator can speak with all involved parties and evaluate the child's living situation; where the parents refuse access, the investigator may need to enlist the assistance of the police, the courts, or both. Other persons, such as neighbors, teachers, and health care providers, may be interviewed as well. In an emergency situation, the investigation must be completed within a very short time period.

If the investigator cannot substantiate the allegations contained in the report, the case is closed, and no further action is taken, although voluntary services such as parenting classes or day-care referrals may be offered to the family. If, however, the investigator has reasonable cause to believe that the child is being abused or neglected, the case will remain open and under the authority of the protective agency.

If the social worker has cause to believe that a child is in immediate danger of serious harm, he or she may remove the child without a court order or prior notice to the parents. Emergency removal is supposed to be limited to situations where there is no other way to ensure a child's safety while the investigation is pending. Following removal, the agency must immediately initiate court proceedings. The parents are entitled to a hearing (usually within 72 hours of removal), at which time they can challenge the state's actions. The court may decide the removal was in error and return the child to the home, or it may decide to keep temporary custody in the agency.

Substantiated Cases: Federal Law and the "Reasonable Efforts" Requirement

If the allegations of abuse or neglect are substantiated, the child protection agency must, in most cases, make **"reasonable efforts"** to keep the

Reasonable Efforts: The efforts that a child protection agency must make to prevent removal of a child from his or her home, or toward reunification

Foster Care:
The taking in and caring for a child who is unable to live at home, usually because of parental abuse or neglect

family together before it can seek to remove a child from the home and place him or her in **foster care**. If a child is removed, the agency must again, in most cases, make a reasonable effort to reunite the child with his or her family.

The reasonable efforts requirement has been a cornerstone of the child protective system since the passage of the federal Adoption Assistance and Child Welfare Act of 1980 (CWA).[13] CWA was enacted in response to concerns that children who were removed from the homes ended up spending much of their youth adrift in the foster care system. By emphasizing **family preservation**, the Act sought to "replace the costly and disruptive out-of-home placements that had dominated child welfare practice with preventative and reunification programs."[14] Accordingly, a child protection agency could not remove children from their parents unless "reasonable efforts" had been made to keep the family together; if removal did become necessary, the rights of the parents could not be terminated until reasonable efforts had been made to reunify the family.

Family Preservation:
A child welfare approach that stresses the use of "reasonable efforts" to keep family together or reunify them following a child's removal

This required emphasis on family preservation soon came under increasing criticism for two primary reasons. First, it became apparent that some children were being left with or returned to abusive parents; notably, several high-profile cases focused public attention on the plight of children who had been killed by a parent following an agency decision to either leave a child with or return a child to his or her parents.[15] The second concern was the lack of permanency in children's lives, as many continued to spend extended periods of time in the foster care system while child protection agencies attempted to "rehabilitate" their parents, even in situations where family reunification was highly unlikely. Thus, although foster care was supposed to be a short-term intervention strategy, children were "languishing for years in a child welfare system that moved at a 'glacial pace.'"[16]

In 1997, in response to these mounting concerns, Congress passed the Adoption and Safe Families Act (ASFA),[17] which shifted the emphasis of the child protective system from family preservation to child safety. Although AFSA preserves the "reasonable efforts" requirement, it makes the "health and safety" of the child the paramount consideration in determining if the state has done enough to try and keep the family together. Closely related, to avoid having children languish in foster care while ongoing efforts are being made to "rehabilitate" the parents, the Act prioritizes the development of a permanent resolution to the family situation.

AFSA thus "fast-tracks" the permanency planning process so that children are either returned home or parental rights are terminated so the children can be freed for adoption within a much tighter time frame than previously was provided. As a result, parents now have considerably less time in which to try to remedy the difficulties that brought them into the child protective system in the first place, which, as noted later in this chapter, has raised serious concerns that AFSA unduly penalizes parents who may need more time to resolve an often complex myriad of problems, such as drug addiction and mental illness, that impair their ability to care for their children.[18]

Before looking at these rules in more detail, it should be noted that like CWA, AFSA is a federal funding law. This means that rather than directly imposing substantive requirements on states, AFSA instead establishes the standards that a state must comply with in order to receive federal funding for its child protective program; in short, if a state fails to comply with federal mandates, it is at risk of being sanctioned by way of a reduction in federal support. However, AFSA does leave some determinations to the discretion of a state. For example, although, as discussed next, states are subject to a "reasonable efforts" requirement, they are entitled to define for themselves what constitutes "reasonable efforts," which, of course, means that the definition is likely to vary from jurisdiction to jurisdiction.

Reasonable Efforts Prior to Removal

When allegations of abuse or neglect have been substantiated, under ASFA a state must make reasonable efforts to work with the family so the child can remain safely at home. However, because "reasonable efforts" under CWA was often understood to mean keeping a family together at all costs, reasonable efforts are no longer permitted to jeopardize a child's safety. Accordingly, in determining whether reasonable efforts have been made, a child's health and safety must be the dominant consideration. ASFA also identifies a number of exceptions to the reasonable efforts requirement, such as where a parent has "committed murder or voluntary manslaughter of another of his or her children (or aided in the commission of the same)" or has "subjected a child to aggravated circumstances," which may include torture, chronic abuse, or sexual abuse.[19]

To meet the "reasonable efforts" requirement, the protective agency (assuming no risk to the child) must offer supportive services to help parents care for their children more successfully. Services may include day care, parenting education classes, counseling, and respite care. A **service plan** outlining the services to be offered is usually developed. The service plan may also impose certain obligations on the parents; for example, they may be required to get the children to school on time or to attend Alcoholics Anonymous meetings on a regular basis. Plans must take the special needs of parents with disabilities into consideration and tailor services to meet those needs.

Although entry into a service plan is voluntary in the sense that a caseworker cannot force a family to accept services, an agency can initiate court proceedings against parents it considers noncooperative, thus subjecting them to the risk that their children will be removed and possibly

Service Plan:
A plan developed by a child protection agency in cases of substantiated abuse that sets out the services to be provided to the parents; may also impose certain obligations on the parents

their parental rights terminated. While the plan is in effect, the family is subject to ongoing monitoring and review until the agency decides either that the situation has improved and the case can be closed or that it has deteriorated and court intervention is necessary.

Removal of a Child

The Dependency Proceeding

At some point after the substantiation of abuse or neglect, the protection agency may decide that a child should be removed from his or her home and placed in foster care. In situations where the agency is not required to use reasonable efforts to keep the family together (as discussed previously), this decision follows on the heels of substantiation; otherwise, it is made at a point where the agency determines that despite having made such efforts, it appears that the child cannot remain safely at home.

Dependency Proceeding: A court process to determine if a child's parents lack the present ability to care for him or her; may result in a transfer of custody to the state

To remove the child, the agency files a court action, commonly referred to as a **dependency proceeding**, in which it seeks to have the child adjudicated as dependent or in need of care and protection.[20] Essentially, the state is asking the court to find that the parents are currently unable to care for their child and that alternative arrangements for the child must be made. If the court agrees that the parents cannot presently care for the child, the child is adjudicated as dependent. With this determination, custody is usually transferred to the agency, which then assumes primary responsibility for making decisions involving the child, and the child is placed in foster care.

The Reasonable Efforts Requirement

Following removal, the child protection agency must make reasonable efforts to reunite the family, subject to the exceptions that exempted the agency from having to make reasonable efforts to keep the family together in the first instance. Reasonableness is again determined in light of the child's health and safety needs. A reunification case plan—which usually includes services to help the parents address the problems that led to the removal in the first place—is developed. Unless contraindicated, a visitation plan is also usually developed. The hope here is that the preservation of family connections may increase the likelihood of reunification.

Permanency Hearing: A hearing to determine if a child who has been removed from the home due to abuse or neglect can safely return home or whether parental rights should be terminated and the child freed for adoption

Permanency Planning

In most cases, ASFA requires that a **permanency hearing** be held no later than 12 months after a child has entered into foster care, although states are free to set a shorter time frame for this hearing, and a number have done so. In addition to assessing both the safety and appropriateness of the child's placement and the services that are being offered to help the family work toward unification, the primary purpose of the hearing is to develop a "**permanency plan**," which includes a determination of whether the child can return home safely or whether the rights of the parents should be terminated so the child can be freed for adoption.[21] Under the plan, both options can be pursued concurrently so the child is not left hanging if the goal of reunification fails, as the state can only offer "time-limited" reunification services. Reinforcing AFSA's focus on time limits, a state is also required to initiate (or join) proceedings to terminate parental rights if a child has been in foster care for 15 of the previous 22 months unless the child is being cared for by a relative, the initiation of proceedings would not be in the child's best interest, or where the state has failed to provide services that would have enabled the child to return home safely.

This fast-tracking of cases, referred to by one scholar as a "fish or cut bait" approach,[22] may be the most significant change that ASFA has made to the child protective system. For example, under CWA, a hearing was also required whenever a child was in the foster care system; however, it was held later in the process, and served as more of a status review than the ultimate determinant of whether the child should go home or be freed for adoption. What this means is that parents now have significantly less time in which to "get their act together" before facing the possibility of the permanent loss of their child.[23]

To appreciate the significance of this change, it is important to understand what is at stake here. **Termination of parental rights** is a drastic measure because it permanently severs the parent-child relationship. Upon termination, the child is freed up for adoption and can thus be permanently incorporated into a new family. Because termination results in an irrevocable change in parental status, it must be based on clear and convincing proof of **parental unfitness**. Unlike in a custody dispute between two parents, a court cannot extinguish the rights of a parent because it believes the child would be better off with a different parent, as this would give the state enormous discretion to reconfigure familial relationships in pursuit of idealized arrangements.

As discussed, in moving away from the emphasis on family preservation, ASFA sought to protect children from being left with or sent back to abusive parents and to limit the amount of time that children spend languishing in the foster care system. Although these are admirable goals, important concerns have been raised that ASFA has gone too far the other way and does not provide well-intentioned parents with an adequate opportunity to resolve serious problems, such as a drug or alcohol addiction, that would then enable them to resume caring for their children. Specific concerns have also been raised that this approach penalizes parents who have been incarcerated by basing termination proceedings solely

Permanency Plan:
A plan that either calls for the return of a child home following removal for abuse or neglect or for the termination of parental rights

Reunification Services:
Services that a child protection agency provides to a family following the removal of a child for the purpose of enabling the child to return home

Termination of Parental Rights:
The permanent severance of the parent-child relationship based on parental unfitness

Parental Unfitness:
Parental abuse or neglect that is severe enough to warrant a termination of rights

upon the length of time of the parent-child separation without a separate inquiry into whether there have been independent acts of abuse or neglect that would themselves support a termination of parental rights.[24] Of course, on the other side, the argument is that the safety of children should not be subordinated to an idealized vision of family connection and integrity—that a child's need for stability and certainty cannot be endlessly subordinated to the perhaps-futile efforts of a parent to get his or her life on track.

Chapter Summary

Child abuse and neglect are not recent phenomena, but a systematic legal response to these problems did not emerge until the latter half of the twentieth century following medical evidence revealing the seriousness and scope of the problem. Following the enactment of the federal CAPTA in 1974, all states enacted abuse reporting laws and established a coordinated child protective system under the authority of a single state agency.

A family usually comes to the attention of a protective agency when a report of suspected abuse or neglect is filed. If, after an investigation, the allegations are substantiated, the family remains under the authority of the agency. Subject to limited exceptions, reasonable efforts must be made to prevent the need to remove the child from the home; reasonableness is determined in light of the child's

health and safety needs. If removal becomes necessary, a dependency proceeding is initiated, in which the state seeks a determination that the parents are presently unable to care for the child and that the child should be removed and placed in foster care. Following removal, reasonable efforts at reunification must be made, subject, again, to limited exceptions.

In most cases, a permanency hearing must be held within 12 months of the time that the child enters foster care to decide if the child can return home or whether the rights of the parents should be terminated. The termination of parental rights is the most drastic form of intervention because it permanently severs the parent-child relationship. Once parental rights have been terminated, the child can be adopted by another family.

Key Terms

Abuse Reporting Laws
Child Protection Agency
Abuse
Neglect
Mandatory Reporters
Permissive Reporters
Reasonable Efforts
Foster Care
Family Preservation
Service Plan
Dependency Proceeding
Permanency Plan
Reunification Services
Termination of Parental Rights
Parental Unfitness

Review Questions

1. Who was Mary Ellen Wilson, and how did her situation lead to the birth of societies for the prevention of cruelty to children? How did these societies aim to protect children?
2. What role did x-rays play in the rediscovery of child abuse in the 1960s?
3. Describe the first generation of reporting laws and explain their primary shortcoming.
4. How did the federal government first become involved in the child protection field?
5. Speaking generally, what is meant by the term "child protective system"? What role does a child protection agency play in this system?
6. What is the core meaning of physical abuse?
7. Why does sexual abuse often remain hidden?
8. What is emotional abuse and neglect?
9. What is neglect? Why is willfulness an important factor?
10. Explain the concept of failure to protect.
11. What is the relationship between the child protective system and partner abuse?
12. How do reporting laws work?
13. Explain the difference between a mandatory and a permissive reporter.
14. Why might a report of suspected abuse or neglect be screened out?

15. What happens after a case is screened in?
16. Explain the concept of reasonable efforts. When is this obligation triggered?
17. What is a dependency proceeding?
18. What is a permanency hearing? When must such a hearing be held?
19. Generally speaking, how did ASFA change the approach to cases of substantiated child abuse or neglect?
20. What does it mean to terminate parental rights? What must the state prove at a termination hearing?

Discussion Questions

1. Assume that the following report has been made regarding the Smith family: A neighbor knocked on the door of the Smith residence to see if anyone there had seen her missing cat. Upon being admitted to the home, she observed that the house was filthy. Garbage was piled all over, and rotten food was covering the counters. Both the mother and her four-year old child were dirty, although no symptoms of illness or injury were apparent. The neighbor departed after about five minutes and promptly called the state protective service agency to report what she had seen.

    Based on these facts, what do you think the agency should do? Is this neglect? Is intervention warranted? If so, what action is appropriate?
2. Do you think a parent should be held accountable for failing to protect his or her child from being abused by the other parent? What if the parent did not know what was going on? Does a parent have an obligation to know? If a parent has knowledge of the abuse, should he or she be obligated to report his or her partner to a protective agency?
3. Do you think parents who have been extremely abusive deserve a second chance at parenting?
4. The ASFA has shifted the focus away from family reunification in favor of fast-tracking permanency planning for children in the foster care system. As a result of this shift in emphasis, parents may have less time to address the problems that brought the family into the protective system in the first place. Do you think this shift makes sense in order to protect children, or does it fail to account for the importance of family ties?

Assignments

1. Locate the statute in your state that governs child abuse and neglect cases, as well as the applicable regulations. Answer the following questions:
    a. Who are mandated reporters?
    b. What are the sanctions for failing to report suspected abuse or neglect?
    c. What kinds of services must be offered to families?
2. Develop a set of questions and interview a person who is involved with child protection work, such as an attorney, a judge, or a protective service worker. Ask this person to describe his or her role in the system. Ask this person about some of the most difficult situations he or she has encountered and his or her perceptions of the major strengths and weaknesses of the protective system.
3. Assume that you are representing a child who was removed from her home at age 3 because of extreme neglect. At the time, the parents had serious drug and alcohol problems. The child has been in foster care for 12 months. During this time, the parents have tried to get their act together, but until recently their efforts had fallen short. However, they have recently both completed intensive treatment programs. The father has been at a new, steady job for about three

months, and the mother is working hard toward her high school degree. Both have completed a parenting class. The agency is pushing termination so the child can be adopted by her foster parents. The child has bonded with them and is thriving.

The judge has asked you to submit a memorandum outlining your position on behalf of the child. In doing do, you should research relevant case law to determine how your state approaches this kind of case and incorporate the results of your research into the memo.

Endnotes

1. *See* Prince v. Massachusetts, 321 U.S. 158 (1944); Pierce v. Society of Sisters, 268 U.S. 510 (1925); Meyer v. Nebraska, 262 U.S. 390 (1923); Wisconsin v. Yoder, 406 U.S. 205 (1972); Stanley v. Illinois, 405 U.S. 645 (1972).

2. *See* Elizabeth Pleck, Domestic Tyranny: The Making of American Social Policy Against Family Violence from Colonial Times to the Present 47-48 (1987). *See also* John Demos, Past, Present, and Personal: The Family and the Life Course in American History 41-64 (1986).

3. Pleck, *supra* note 2, at 72-87.

4. C. Henry Kempe et al., The Battered Child Syndrome, 181 JAMA 17 (1962).

5. Douglas J. Besharov, "Doing Something" About Child Abuse: The Need to Narrow the Grounds for State Intervention, 8 Harv. J.L. & Pub. Poly. 539, 546-547 (1985); Brian G. Frasier, A Glance at the Past, A Gaze at the Present, A Glimpse at the Future: A Critical Analysis of the Development of Child Abuse Reporting Statutes, 54 Chi.-Kent L. Rev. 650, 661 (1978).

6. *See* Pub. L. No. 93-247, 88 Stat. 4 (codified as amended in scattered sections of 42 U.S.C.).

7. Although beyond the scope of this chapter, it is important to be aware that parents may also be criminally prosecuted for abusing or neglecting their children, and that most states have a specific criminal abuse statute.

8. CAPTA, 42 U.S.C.A. §5106g, *as amended by* the Keeping Families Safe Act of 2003.

9. For further discussion of some of these issues, *see* William Y. Chen, Blue Spots, Coining and Cupping: How Ethnic Minority Parents Can Be Misreported as Child Abusers, 7 J.L. Socy. 88 (2005); Catherine J. Ross, The Tyranny of Time: Vulnerable Children, "Bad" Mothers, and Statutory Deadlines in Parental Termination Proceedings, 11 Va. J. Soc. Poly. & L. 176 (2004); Michael Futterman, Seeking a Standard: Reconciling Child Abuse and Condoned Child Rearing Practices Among Different Cultures, 34 U. Miami Inter.-Am. L. Rev. 491 (2003); Sandra Bullock, Low-Income Parents Victimized by Child Protective Services, 11 Am. U. J. Gender Soc. Poly. & L. 1023 (2003); Dorothy Roberts, Shattered Bonds: The Color of Child Welfare (2002).

10. With respect to medical neglect, most statutes include a religious exemption for parents who rely on spiritual means to cure their child. However, this exemption does not necessarily mean that a court is prohibited from ordering medical treatment if the child is in imminent danger, and, if the child dies, it may not shield the parent from criminal prosecution. For further detail and references, *see* Jennifer Stanfield, Current Public Law and Policy Issues: Faith Healing and Religious Treatment Exemptions to Child-Endangerment Laws: Should Parents Be Allowed to Refuse Necessary Medical Treatment for Their Children Based on Medical Beliefs? 22 Hamline J. Pub. L. & Poly. 45 (2000). Religious-based exemptions may also exist for what might otherwise be considered educational neglect. *See* Wisconsin v. Yoder, 406 U.S. 205 (1972) (allowing Amish parents to remove their children from the public schools at age 14 for religious reasons).

11. Child Maltreatment 2010, U.S. Department of Health and Human Services, Administration for Children and Families, Administration on Children, Youth and Families, Children's Bureau, http://www.acf.hhs.gov/programs/cb/resource/child-mal treatment-2010-1 (accessed Oct. 8, 2012).

12. *See generally* Bullock, *supra* note 9.

13. Pub. L. No. 96-272, 94 Stat. 500 (codified in scattered sections of 42 U.S.C.).

14. Dorothy E. Roberts, Is There Justice in Children's Rights? The Critique of Federal Family Preservation Policy, 2 U. Pa. J. Const. L. 112, 113 (1999).

15. *See* Ross, *supra* note 9, at 195-196. *See also* Will L. Crossley, Defining Reasonable Efforts: Demystifying the State's Burden Under Federal Child Protection Legislation, 12 B.U. Pub. Int. L.J. 259, 274 (2003).

16. Ross, *supra* note 9, at 195-196.

17. Pub. L. No. 105-89, 111 Stat. 2115 (1997) (codified in scattered sections of 42 U.S.C.).

18. Much has been written about these Acts in terms of their requirements and the different philosophies that they embody. In addition to the Roberts article cited *supra* note 14 and the Ross article cited *supra* note 9, *see* Kathleen S. Bean, Reasonable Efforts: What State Courts Think, 36 U. Tol. L. Rev. 321 (2005); Libby S. Adler, The Meaning of Permanence: A Critical Analysis of the Adoption and Safe Families Act of 1997, 38 Harv. J. on Legis. 1 (2001); Stephanie Jill Gendell, In Search of Permanency: A Reflection on the First Three Years of the Adoption and Safe Families Act Implementation, 39 Fam. Ct. Rev. 25 (2001); Rachael Venier, Parental Rights and the Best Interests of the Child: Implications of the Adoption and Safe Families Act of 1997 on Domestic Violence Victims' Rights, 8 Am. U. J. Gender Soc. Poly. & L. 517 (2000).

19. *See* 42 U.S.C.A. §671(a)(15)(D).

20. This discussion is intended to provide a very general overview of the process, which is quite complex. If you are working on a case, applicable state and federal rules governing both the substance and the procedures of these cases must be carefully reviewed.

21. ASFA includes other options as well, but reunification and adoption are the primary dispositional choices. *See* Adler, *supra* note 18, at 9-10.

22. Adler, *supra* note 18, at 10.

23. *See* Philip M. Gentry, Moving Beyond Generalizations and Stereotypes to Develop Individualized Approaches for Working with Families Affected by Parental Incarceration, 50 Fam. Ct. Rev. 36 (2012); Deseriee A. Kennedy, Children, Parents, and the State: The Construction of a New Family Ideology, 26 Berkeley J. Gender L. & Just. 78 (2011).

24. Roberts, *supra* note 14, at 118.

Chapter Thirteen

Adoption

Adoption allows for the creation of family relationships along nonbiological lines. Through adoption, the legal bond between a child and his or her birth parents is terminated, and a new relationship is established between the child and the adoptive parent or parents. In effect, the legal bond substitutes for the biological connection as the child is enfolded into a new family. (For exceptions to this general rule regarding termination of the biological parent's rights, see the discussion later in this chapter on stepparent and coparent adoptions.) After a brief historical overview, we examine the two major methods of adoption—agency adoption and independent or private placement adoption—and consider the adoption process. We then look at some of the issues that can arise in particular contexts, such as when a stepparent or a same-sex couple wishes to adopt a baby. Please note that the chapter does not address the issue of international adoption, and you should be aware that other policy and legal considerations come into play when the adoption process crosses national borders. Finally, we consider what happens when adoptive parents are unhappy with the child they have adopted and wish to abrogate or undo the adoption. Note that the terms "adoptive parents" and "adoptive parent" are used interchangeably, since both single persons and couples can adopt.

Adoption:
The legal process by which someone becomes a parent to a child with whom he or she does not have a biological relationship and assumes all the rights and responsibilities of parenthood

Historical Overview

As in England, the children of many American colonists were sent to live with other families, most commonly as servants or apprentices. Apprenticeships were formal arrangements by which a child was indentured to a person who was supposed to teach the child a trade and provide him or her with a place to live in exchange for the child's labor. This person stood *in loco parentis* and assumed the rights and responsibilities of a parent for the duration of the apprenticeship. These arrangements were found in all social classes, with children from middle and upper classes being indentured to persons from similar backgrounds in which they could "complete their social and professional training . . . while multiplying their connections and possibilities for advancement."[1] However, for the poor, these arrangements were born more from necessity and represented less of an opportunity for advancement; moreover, indenture was frequently imposed by officials in order to reduce the cost to towns of caring for the poor.

Thus, in the early part of our nation's history, it was not uncommon for children to spend part, or even most, of their youth living apart from their family of origin. Historians generally believe that the widespread acceptance of this practice, particularly that of apprenticeship, helped pave the way for the more modern practice of adoption.[6] In 1851, Massachusetts passed the nation's first general adoption statute. Under the law, each prospective adoptive family was to be scrutinized to ensure they were "of sufficient ability to bring up the child . . . and that it is fit and proper that such adoption should take effect." Upon approval by the court, the child would "to all intents and purposes" become the legal child of the adoptive parents, and the bond with the natural parents would be forever severed.[2] Intended in large measure to formalize the existing practice of incorporating nonbiological children into a household, the Massachusetts law quickly became a model, and similar statutes were quickly adopted in a majority of states.

Approaches to Adoption

Agency Adoption:
An adoption that is handled by a state or private agency

Independent Adoption/ Private Placement Adoption:
An adoption that is accomplished without an agency; parents can either place the child directly or utilize an intermediary

Adoption usually takes place in one of two ways. It can be accomplished either by an agency (**agency adoption**) or by the parents themselves acting with or without the assistance of a third-party intermediary (**independent** or **private placement adoption**). Agency adoptions are permitted in all states; however, due to some of the concerns discussed later in this chapter, a few states prohibit nonagency adoptions except where a stepparent or a close relative is the adopting parent. Before looking at the adoption process, this section begins with a brief overview of these two approaches and also takes a brief look at "safe haven" laws, which are intended to address the problem of infant abandonment.

Agency Adoptions

In an agency adoption, a state-licensed agency arranges the adoption and oversees the process. The precise contours of an agency's responsibilities are determined by the applicable state statutes, regulations, and licensing laws. An adoption agency can be either public, in that it is part of the state's child protective system, or private. In either instance, an agency can obtain custody of a child for purposes of adoption in one of two ways. First, an agency may obtain custody where a child has been freed for adoption following the involuntary termination of parental rights (see Chapter 12). Second, parents who wish to give up a child for adoption can surrender their child to an agency. Before accepting a **voluntary surrender** or **relinquishment**, an agency will usually provide the parents with counseling to help them understand their options and make sure that their decision is fully informed. A range of other services, such as legal referrals and financial assistance for basic legal and medical services, may also be available. The agency is then responsible for finding a suitable adoptive home for the child.

Voluntary Surrender/ Relinquishment: The surrender by a parent of a child to an adoption agency

Before placing a child with prospective adoptive parents, the agency will conduct a home study to determine the appropriateness of the placement. Once a placement has been made, the agency maintains some degree of supervisory responsibility to ensure that the placement meets the needs of the child. State rules often require an agency to make a certain number of home visits at specified intervals and to take remedial action, including removal, if the child is not adjusting well. In some states, the agency remains legally responsible for the child until the adoption is finalized.

Independent Adoptions

In contrast, in an independent adoption (also known as "private" or "direct placement adoptions"), a child is placed directly with the adoptive parents without a prior surrender to a licensed adoption agency. Most involve healthy, white newborns who are placed with the adoptive parents immediately after birth. Accordingly, adoption arrangements are usually made during pregnancy, often after an extensive search for an adoptable baby. If state law permits, searching parents may well launch a public campaign, which can include advertising in the classified section of a local paper, to help them locate a potential birth mother and demonstrate their qualifications as parents.

Some prospective adoptive parents hire an intermediary, who is often an attorney, to help them to find a child and arrange the placement. Where this is the case, the child may initially be transferred to this third party; however, unlike in an agency adoption, this is not a formal surrender — rather, the intermediary is simply serving as a conduit between the birth and the adoptive parents.

Unlike with agency adoptions, the birth parents are not usually provided with counseling prior to the relinquishment of the baby, and the prospective adoptive parents are not required to undergo a preplacement home study, although some states now require adoptive parents to be certified before they can accept a child into their home. In further contrast, once a baby is placed, the placement is not usually supervised, although a postplacement home study must be done before a court can approve the adoption. (Most adoptions must be approved by a court.)

Although as discussed next, birth parents must consent to the adoption, a number of concerns have been raised about the potential for exploitation that exists when adoptions occur without the involvement of a state-licensed agency, and a few states expressly prohibit independent adoptions. Other states have instead opted for increased control of the process, particularly with respect to the often closely related role of intermediaries and the payment of the birth mother's expenses.

Safe Haven Laws

Safe Haven:
Allows a birth parent, or an agent of the parent, to leave a baby at a safe location without fear of being prosecuted for child abandonment or neglect

In response to several highly publicized cases involving newborn babies who had been abandoned in dumpsters, garbage cans, and toilets, starting with Texas in 1999, most states have enacted what are known as "safe haven" laws (sometimes referred to as "Baby Moses" laws), which permit birth parents, or in some states only the birth mother, to leave a baby at a designated safe location, such as a hospital or fire station, as an alternative to abandonment. Some states also permit a party acting with the express consent of the birth parent or parents to surrender the child at the safe haven. Intended for the purpose of preventing the abandonment of newborns, as distinct from infants or older children, all laws contain an express limit on how much time can elapse between birth and the surrender of the child. Limits usually range from 72 hours to 30 days, although a few states provide for a period of up to a year.

Several common statutory features are designed to encourage parents to surrender their babies to a designated safe haven location rather than abandoning them. First, they are all structured to protect parental anonymity, and permit a parent to surrender a child without having to provide any identifying information. Some laws, however, do require that inquiry be made of the baby's medical and family history, but the parent is not required to provide this information. Second, many states offer parents complete immunity from prosecution for child abandonment or neglect. In other states, however, the protection is not as comprehensive, and the statute simply gives parents the right to raise safe relinquishment in accordance with the law as an affirmative defense to criminal charges.

Following relinquishment, the safe haven provider turns the infant over to the appropriate child protection agency. In some states, a parent is given a brief window of opportunity within which to change his or her mind and reclaim the child. The agency is then responsible for making an adoption plan for the child. A potentially complicating factor is that it is not always clear what steps must be taken by the agency in order to terminate the rights of the parents — the safe haven law may have specialized provisions, or it might reference the applicable provisions of the child protection law — and a number of cases have arisen over whether the agency had done enough to provide notice to the birth parents regarding the termination of their rights. This is most likely to be an issue with regard to the father, who may not have participated in or known about the decision to relinquish the baby, as it is usually the mother who avails herself of the safe haven option.[3] (A discussion regarding the rights of unmarried fathers follows.)

The Adoption Process

In this section, we will look at the stages of the adoption process. In the following section, we consider particular issues or exceptions to general principles that may arise in specific circumstances, such as where a same-sex couple wishes to adopt a child or the birth parents are unwed.

Adoption Based on Parental Consent or Relinquishment

Unless the rights of parents have been involuntarily terminated, an adoption cannot proceed without their consent. (See the next discussion, however, regarding unwed fathers.) In some states, the consent of the child also becomes necessary once he or she reaches a certain age, which is generally set somewhere between age 10 and 14. Although this section generally speaks in terms of the birth parents, it is important to recognize that the parents may not be participating in the adoption as a unit and that each may play a different role in the process.

Parental Consent to a Private Placement Adoption

Parental consent is an essential requirement in a private placement adoption. To be valid, consent must be fully informed and free from duress, fraud, or undue influence and given in a manner that conforms with all applicable state regulations, such as that it be in writing and signed before a public official.

Consent:
The requirement that a biological parent must assent to the adoption of his or her child, unless his or her parental rights have been terminated

In some situations, it can be difficult to determine if the consent was truly voluntary. For example, a young birth mother who is under pressure from her parents and friends to give up the child may be ambivalent but feel as if she has no choice but to give up her baby to a married couple who appears to be in a better position to raise the child. Although there may not be undue influence or duress in a strictly legal sense, under some circumstances, it may be difficult to characterize a decision to give up a child as a purely voluntary one.

In most states, a mother's prebirth consent is not binding, and a legally valid consent cannot be obtained until some time after the birth of the child; a typical waiting period is 48 or 72 hours after birth. This rule recognizes the impact of giving birth and the fact that it may be impossible to fully comprehend the import of a decision to give up a child until the child is actually born. Interestingly, in many states, a father's prebirth consent is binding. This differential treatment reflects both conventional views about fathers as less affected by the birth process and thus less likely to regret a prior decision to give up a child, as well as the practical concern that a father might not be around to give consent at the time of birth.

By itself, the consent does not actually terminate the rights of the birth parents or transfer them to the adoptive parents. In effect, by executing a consent, the birth parents are authorizing the court to proceed with the adoption.

Relinquishment to an Agency

In an agency adoption, the operative legal act is the relinquishment of the child to the agency, rather than the giving of consent to the adoption itself. By relinquishing their child, parents are effectively transferring their right to consent to the adoption to the agency. In many states, the act of relinquishment automatically terminates the rights of the birth parents. In other states, this result is not automatic, but relinquishment enables an agency to seek an immediate court order terminating parental rights. (Note: Keep in mind that these adoptions begin with a voluntary act and are thus different from adoptions that result from an involuntary termination of parental rights—these adoptions are discussed later in this chapter.)

What If a Parent Changes His or Her Mind?

What happens if, after either consenting to an adoption or relinquishing a child to an agency, a parent changes his or her mind about going forward with the adoption? Although this occurs only in a small number of cases, it can result in bitter litigation that pits the birth parents against the prospective adoptive parents.

Private Placement Adoptions.   Most states allow parents to revoke their consent within a specified time period, such as up until the time the adoption is approved by the court. Thereafter, consent is deemed irrevocable. In some jurisdictions, however, irrevocability is limited to validly obtained consents. This leaves open the possibility that even after the adoption has been finalized, a birth parent could seek to revoke his or her consent by establishing that it was improperly obtained.

In most states, the **revocation of consent** (including those within the applicable time period) requires court approval. The standards for determining whether to allow a revocation vary widely from state to state. Some states are fairly tolerant of parental changes of heart, and judges have considerable discretion. In other states, judges can approve revocations based only on specific statutory factors, which typically address the validity of the consent and do not allow for changes of heart that are not bound up with considerations of duress and the like. In these states, a birth mother who experiences profound regret about her decision would not be permitted to revoke her consent even if requested within the statutory time frame. But a young birth mother who could establish that the prospective adoptive parents in concert with her own parents repeatedly pressured her to give up the child might be allowed to revoke her consent.

Revocation of Consent: A parent's seeking to take back his or her consent to an adoption

Where a parent seeks to revoke his or her consent, the prospective adoptive parents may respond by asking the court to **dispense with the parental consent requirement**. In effect, the adoptive parents are asking the court to terminate the parental rights of the birth parents so that the adoption can proceed without their consent. In evaluating this request, the court may treat the consent as evidence of an intent to abandon the child and count it against the biological parents in evaluating their fitness. Thus, what began as a voluntary process may result in litigation and a possible involuntary termination of parental rights. (See the next discussion for greater detail on involuntary termination.)

Dispensing with Parental Consent: A decision by the court to proceed with the adoption without the consent of the parents based on a finding of parental unfitness

Agency Adoptions. Most states are stricter about revocations where a relinquishment has been made to an agency, and in many states, the relinquishment becomes irrevocable once the child has been placed with the prospective adoptive parents for a specified period of time. This stricter standard reflects the fact that greater safeguards, such as prerelinquishment counseling for the birth parents, are built into the agency process.

Adoption Based on the Involuntary Termination of Parental Rights

If the rights of parents have been involuntarily terminated because of abuse or neglect, an adoption can proceed without their consent because the termination frees the child for adoption. Following termination, custody is generally transferred to the state or, more specifically, to a public adoption agency, which must then try to find an appropriate adoptive home for the child.

If the rights of both parents have been terminated, the placement is virtually risk-free because they have been divested of any say in the matter.[4] If, however, the rights of both parents have not been terminated, such as situations where one parent has vanished, the agency may not be able to proceed with the adoption until that parent's status is resolved. However, if allowed by state law, an agency may choose to make an **at-risk placement**. These placements are subject to the risk of disruption if a parent whose rights have not been terminated subsequently seeks to assert his or her right to the child.

At-Risk Placement:
An adoption placement that is made before the rights of both parents have been terminated

Many children who are available for adoption following the termination of parental rights have been in the protective services system for considerable periods of time. Few are infants, and many have experienced severe abuse or neglect and have lived in a variety of foster homes and institutional settings. Although desperate for homes, these children are often passed over in favor of infants who are generally more available through the independent or private agency adoption route.

In most states, parental rights can also be terminated within the context of the adoption proceeding itself. Unlike a separate termination proceeding, which is almost always initiated by the state, here the request, generally referred to as "a request to dispense with parental consent," is usually initiated by a private party. These requests are made under a variety of circumstances. For example, a child may be living with relatives who then decide they want to adopt him or her, but the parents are opposed. The relatives would file an adoption petition and ask the court to dispense with the need for parental consent. Or an unmarried mother who places her newborn with prospective adoptive parents might seek to have the court dispense with the father's right of consent. Similarly, if a child was relinquished to an agency by one birth parent, the agency might seek to dispense with the consent of the other parent. In order to prevail, it must be shown that the parent is unfit; otherwise, his or her consent is legally required.

The Adoption Placement

Before an adoption can be finalized, a child must live with the prospective parents in a **preadoption placement**; however, many states exempt close relative, stepparent, and coparent adoptions from this requirement. The preadoption placement requirement applies to both agency and independent adoptions; however, as discussed next, important differences exist in the placement process.

Preadoption Placement:
The specified period of time that a child must live with his or her prospective adoptive parents before the adoption can be approved

The Home Study

Perhaps the most significant distinction in the placement process between agency and independent adoptions is the **home study**. Home studies, which are intended to weed out potentially unsuitable parents, are generally not required in independent adoptions, whereas an agency

Home Study:
An evaluation of a person or couple seeking to adopt a child to determine potential suitability, usually done only in agency adoptions

cannot place a child until a home study has been completed. During the home study, prospective parents are usually asked about the following:

- religious beliefs and practices;
- approaches to child rearing and discipline;
- child-rearing skills;
- the nature of relationships with extended family members;
- history of prior intimate relationships;
- career plans and how the child will be cared for;
- ability to provide for the child financially;
- history of criminal convictions; and
- emotional stability and maturity.

Most adoption professionals regard the home study as essential to protect the well-being of adoptive children. While recognizing its potential intrusiveness, it is widely believed that in the absence of a biological connection from which affective bonds are thought to naturally flow, prospective parents must be evaluated to determine their capacity for developing a loving relationship with an adoptive child.

Configuration of Relationships During the Placement

Private Placement Adoptions. As noted previously, in these adoptions, parental rights are usually not terminated until the adoption is approved by the court. This makes these placements somewhat riskier than agency placements because the possibility exists that a biological parent will change his or her mind and seek the return of the child. As discussed earlier, states vary in their approach to postplacement revocations—some are very strict, while others are more flexible and may permit a change of mind unless harm to the child can be shown.

Because the rights of the biological parents are not terminated until the adoption is approved, the authority of the prospective adoptive parents to make decisions on behalf of the child during the placement needs to be established. This is usually done through a voluntary transfer of temporary custody from the birth parents to the adoptive parents.

Agency Adoptions. Unless it is an at-risk placement, the rights of both parents will have been terminated by the time the placement is made; accordingly, the agency usually has legal custody of the child, although it may delegate some decision-making authority to the prospective parents. As the repository of legal authority, the agency retains supervisory control over the placement, and a social worker will make periodic visits to evaluate how the placement is working out. The agency has the right to remove the child if it determines that the placement is not in the child's best interest. Most states place some limits on the authority of an agency to revoke a placement, and aggrieved adoptive parents may have a form of redress, such as the right to an administrative hearing.

The Social Study

Postplacement Social Study:
An assessment of an adoption placement done to provide information to the judge who will be deciding if the adoption should be approved

Although preplacement home studies are characteristic of agency adoptions, a **postplacement social study** must be completed in both private placement and agency adoptions before an adoption can be finalized, although the requirement may be waived in certain situations, such as where a close relative or a stepparent is the adopting parent. These studies are intended to provide the judge with information to help him or her decide whether or not to approve the adoption. In some states, the evaluator must also make a specific recommendation in favor of or against the adoption. Although important, these studies tend to be less comprehensive than the initial preplacement home study.

The Adoption

Judicial Review and Approval

All adoptions must be approved by a judge, and proper notice of the proceeding must be given to all persons with an interest in the child, including, for example, foster parents, preadoptive parents, and relatives who have been caring for the child.[5] To protect the validity of the adoption, it is critical that notice rules be carefully followed.

The rights of the parents must be terminated before the adoption can be approved. As has been discussed elsewhere in this chapter, parental rights may already have been terminated in a separate proceeding, such as where the child has been in foster care, or termination may occur as part of the adoption proceeding itself. In a private placement adoption, termination is usually a formality, as the court is simply being asked to approve what the parties have agreed to; however, when a party is requesting that the court dispense with the parental consent requirement, the termination phase of the hearing may well be contested.

Open Adoption:
An adoption that permits some degree of contact with one or both biological parents

Once parental rights are terminated, the court determines whether the adoption is in the best interest of the child. If approved, the court may also at the same time approve an **open adoption** agreement, allowing for post-adoption contact between the birth parents, the child, and the adoptive parents (as discussed later in this chapter). If the court concludes that the adoption is not in the child's best interest, it is not approved. If it is an agency adoption, the underlying relinquishment remains in effect, and the agency can attempt a subsequent placement. However, in a private placement adoption, parents usually consent to an adoption by a specific person or couple, and if the adoption fails, the consent is nontransferable. This is a difficult situation, as the prospective adoptive parents lose the child they were hoping to adopt, and the birth parents may find themselves with custody of a child that they were planning to relinquish.

Making Adoption More Open

Once the adoption is approved (subject to any rights of appeal or post-judgment challenges), a child's legal ties with his or her family of origin are severed, and the child is now legally incorporated into a new family. Completing this transformation, the records of the proceeding are sealed along with the original birth certificate, and a new birth certificate is issued, naming the adoptive parents as the child's parents. The sealing of the records and the issuance of the new birth certificate exemplify the secrecy in which adoptions have traditionally been shrouded. As a rule, no information was shared either before or after an adoption, and adoptive parents were counseled not to disclose the fact of adoption to the child. This secrecy was thought necessary to protect the interests of all participants: Birth mothers would be protected from the taint of immorality or shame, adopted children could grow up with unquestioned ties to their adoptive parents, and adoptive parents would not be threatened with the lurking presence of a child's "true parents."

However, this began to change in the 1960s, in large part because secrecy was no longer thought to be in an adoptive child's best interest: "Social scientists accumulated evidence that attempts by adoptive parents to supplant the biological parents by pretending that the child had no biological ancestry could be damaging to the child's orderly, normal development as well as to the adoption family's stability."[6] Supporting these findings, adult adoptees began to speak out about how damaging and confusing the silence about their origins had been and of their deep longing to know of their past. Other considerations, such as the lessening of the stigma of unwed motherhood, also contributed to a lifting of the shroud of secrecy, and today, many states facilitate open adoption and increased access to adoption records.

Open Adoption

The central feature of an open adoption is that it anticipates some degree of continued contact between the birth parents and the adopted child, despite the severance of their legal bond. Open adoptions are generally associated with private placement adoptions and those in which parents voluntarily relinquish a child to an agency; however, in some states, an open adoption may be an option even if the rights of a parent have been involuntarily terminated, if continued contact is determined to be in the best interest of the child.

Open adoption offers a wide range of postadoption contact arrangements. For example, contact might simply consist of a yearly exchange of letters and photographs with no direct interaction between the child and his or her birth parents. On the other hand, it might consist of regular telephone calls or even regular visits. Where visits are involved, they are often arranged through an intermediary so there is no direct contact between the birth and the adoptive parents.

A growing number of states have adopted open adoption laws that permit birth parents and adoptive parents to enter into judicially enforceable agreements regarding postadoption contact, if such contact is deemed to be in the best interest of the child. Some states further extend this right to other birth relatives; however, they may impose a threshold showing before a contact agreement will be enforceable, such as that the relative had enjoyed a substantial relationship with the child prior to the adoption. In addition to laws recognizing the validity of contracts for postadoption contact, in some cases judges are authorized to order postadoption visits even where not expressly agreed to by the adoptive parents. In some states, the option of postadoption contact is not available to parents whose rights were involuntarily terminated.

Access to Adoption Records

Beginning in the 1970s, adult adoptees began to call for the opening of sealed birth adoption records, both so that they could fill in the missing pieces of their past and possibly also search for their birth parents. As a result, all states now permit the release of nonidentifying information about the birth parents to both adopted children and adoptive parents. Typically, a child who has been adopted cannot access this information directly until she or he is 18. Depending on the state, nonidentifying information may include medical information; information about the birth parents, such as their age, race, and religion; and information about the birth and the adoption process.

The pattern is considerably more complex when it comes to information that "may lead to the positive identification of birth parents, the adoptee, or other birth relatives," such as "current or past names of the person, addresses, employment, or other similar records or information."[7] At least some of this information is typically contained in sealed birth records.

States differ in the ease with which they permit adoptees to access their adoption records. At one end of the spectrum, a handful of states allow children who have been adopted to access their birth records once they reach adulthood, without needing either the consent of the birth parents or proof of good cause or best interest. Most of these states give birth parents who do not want to be contacted the option of filing a "contact veto," and states providing this option also subject adoptees who violate the veto to civil or criminal penalties.[8] At the other end of the spectrum, many states do not allow individuals who have been adopted to access their birth records without a court order, which typically must be premised upon proof of good cause or that disclosure is in the adoptee's best interest. In the middle of the spectrum, many states have created various kinds of registry systems through which adult adoptees and birth parents (and sometimes birth siblings and adoptive parents) may be able to access identifying information. Some states use a "passive" registry system, which requires that both parties register their consent to the release of information before a match can be attempted. In other states, search efforts can be initiated based on the request of one party. If the other party is located and gives his or her consent, identifying information can be released to the person initiating the search.

■ Adoption in Specific Situations

The previous section traced the general stages of the adoption process. However, given the myriad of family arrangements, certain situations involve more specialized rules or raise unique issues. In this section, we consider some, although certainly not all, of these situations.

Stepparent Adoptions

Many of the adoptions that take place each year involve stepparents. Typically, this occurs when a divorced custodial parent remarries, and the couple wishes to establish a formal parent-child relationship between the new spouse and the children from the previous marriage. Most states have a "streamlined" procedure that allows a judge to waive the home study requirement; however, in some states, the adoption cannot be approved until the parties have been married for at least a year.

The custodial parent must consent to the adoption, as must the noncustodial parent. If the noncustodial parent refuses to consent, the adoption can proceed only if there are grounds for dispensing with his or her consent (as discussed previously). Some states have relaxed the requirements for the dispensing of consent in the stepparent adoption context by either statute or judicial decision. Thus, for example, the failure of a parent to maintain communication with his or her children, although not usually by itself considered unfitness, may be enough in the stepparent context to allow the adoption to proceed over the objection of the noncustodial parent.

As you are now aware, adoption typically severs the legal rights of the birth parents. Thus, in a "regular" adoption situation, the custodial parent, by consenting to the adoption, is agreeing to a termination of his or her legal status. However, given that the entire point of a stepparent adoption is to create a new parental unit consisting of the custodial parent and his or her new spouse, it would make no sense to apply the **"cutoff"** rule in this situation. In recognition of the absurdity of this potential outcome, most statutes include an explicit exception to the cutoff rule for stepparent adoptions, making it clear that the parental rights of the biological spouse continue in full force and effect following the adoption.

"Cutoff" Rule:
Principle that operates to extinguish the parental rights of the biological parents at the time of adoption; may not be applied when a stepparent or a coparent is adopting the child

Adoption by Gay Men and Lesbians

As discussed in earlier chapters, over the past few decades, gay men and lesbians have struggled to secure legal recognition of their family relationships. As parents, they have fought to eliminate sexual orientation as a negative factor in custody disputes and to secure the parental status of coparents (see Chapter 5). Additionally, as discussed in this section, gay men and lesbians have sought the right to become parents through adoption, both as individuals and as couples.

Single-Parent Adoption

Although states generally permit single-parent adoption, many agencies and birth parents prefer to place a child with a married couple, thus potentially making it more difficult for any unmarried individual to adopt. However, the pathway to adoptive parenthood for single gay men or lesbians has historically been more difficult than it has been for their heterosexual counterparts.

However, a recent study indicates that attitudes are shifting, and that a growing number of adoption agencies are now willing to accept applications from prospective gay and lesbian adoptive parents. Somewhat tempering the significance of this finding, the study also showed that the most receptive agencies were those working with hard-to-place children, and thus in greater need of a pool of potential parents, while agencies that focused "on the placement of domestic infants and toddlers were found to be the least likely to have policies and practices supportive of homosexual adoption."[9]

Coparent Adoption

Coparent Adoption:
Adoption by a coparent; the adoption does not extinguish the rights of the biological parent

Coparent adoption, or as it is sometimes known, second-parent adoption, involves a situation where a same-sex couple is raising a child together, but only one is recognized as the child's legal parent (through birth or adoption). Accordingly, the couple seeks to have the second parent (or coparent) adopt the child so both partners are fully recognized as his or her legal parents.

In seeking adoptive rights for coparents, the stepparent adoption cases have been drawn on as analogous since, as with a stepparent, legal recognition is being sought for an established parent-child relationship that exists within the framework of a committed relationship with the child's legal parent. Recognizing this structural similarity, a number of courts have recently approved coparent adoptions as being in a child's best interest. In this regard, courts have also been influenced by the fact that adoption ensures the survival of the parent-child relationship in the event the couple splits up or one partner dies, which is important because many jurisdictions do not grant custodial or visitation rights to coparents (see Chapter 5). As with stepparent adoptions, in approving these adoptions, courts have agreed that it would be absurd to apply the cutoff provisions to terminate the rights of the legal parent. To avoid this result, courts have either read in a statutory exception based on the absurdity of the result or extended the stepparent exception to the cutoff rule by analogy. It is important to recognize that the story has yet to be written as to exactly how the Obergefell v. Hodges decision will impact the adoption rights of same-sex couples. However, there is little doubt but that it will open up the pathways to greater rights. For example, the ability to adopt as a stepparent will certainly become available as same-sex couples divorce and remarry. Moreover, the need for adoption is likely to diminish as a growing number of same-sex spouses come to be recognized as the legal parents of children they are raising with their spouse by way of marital presumptions (see Chapter 5).

Unwed Fathers

Historically, many jurisdictions permitted the adoption of a child born to unmarried parents based solely on the consent of the mother. Although the legal status of unwed fathers has improved, they do not have the same adoption consent rights as unmarried mothers. For women, consent rights vest automatically at the time of birth, whereas, as we saw in Chapter 11, under the "biology-plus" rule, men must take some steps to demonstrate their parental commitment to the child.

All states now provide consent rights to unwed fathers who have taken steps to actualize a relationship with their children. Once the right to consent attaches, an adoption cannot proceed over the father's objection unless he is proved unfit—at this point, he is legally indistinguishable from either an unmarried mother or a married father. Note that even if an unwed father has not demonstrated enough of a parental commitment to become a consenting party, he may still be entitled to receive notice of the adoption hearing as an interested party. As an interested party, although he lacks authority to approve or veto the adoption, he most likely will be permitted to give testimony on the issue of whether the adoption is in the best interest of the child.

Putative Father Registry:
Enables men who are or
believe they may be the
father of a child to register
with the state in order to
protect their potential
interest in the child

States take a variety of approaches with respect to what an unwed father must do to acquire consent rights. Over half of the states have established what are known as **putative father registries**, which enable men who are or believe they may be the father of a child to register with the state in order to protect their potential interest in the child. Registration must usually be accomplished within a statutorily prescribed time period following a child's birth; once registered, a man is entitled, at a minimum, to notice of any adoption proceeding involving the child. In some states, the failure to register cuts off the father's rights. Exceptions may be included, though (see Exhibit 13.1), for situations in which a man did not have a reasonable opportunity to comply with the statutory requirements, such as where the mother moved to another state before he knew she was pregnant, or where he did not know about the birth of the child under circumstances that do not suggest abandonment.[10]

Some states employ a more open-ended approach and look to see whether an unwed father has demonstrated a substantial commitment to developing a relationship with his child. Just what is meant by a "substantial commitment," however, is far from clear. In some states, a minimal level of involvement seems to be enough, while in others, the father must demonstrate that he participates in his child's life in a consistent, meaningful manner.

When the child is a newborn, there is considerable divergence over what constitutes the demonstration of a substantial parenting commitment. Some states will evaluate the father's conduct during pregnancy to determine if he demonstrated a commitment to becoming a parent through the financial and emotional support of the mother. A lack of involvement during the pregnancy may deprive him of consent rights, while an active, involved role may serve as the basis for finding a demonstrated commitment to the assumption of parental responsibilities. In other jurisdictions, the father's conduct during pregnancy is less important, and the focus is more on his conduct immediately following the birth of the child and whether he acted in a timely manner to demonstrate his commitment to assuming the responsibilities of parenthood.

Opportunity Interest:
The chance that the
biological link provides to an
unmarried father to develop
a meaningful relationship
with his child

What happens if the father has not been able to take advantage of the **opportunity interest** in developing a relationship with his child, either because the mother has prevented him from developing a relationship with the child or because he did not know about the pregnancy? If he somehow learns about the proposed adoption, will he be given the opportunity to consent or object to it going forward?

Most courts have permitted a father to participate in the adoption proceeding in the absence of an established relationship with the child where he can show that he sought to establish a relationship in a timely manner, even if his efforts failed. Thus, his rights will generally not be defeated in situations where the mother actively prevented the relationship from developing,

Exhibit 13.1
Intent to
Claim Parental
Rights

State of Minnesota   **District Court**

County	
Select County	

Judicial District:	
Court File Number:	
Case Type	Family Court

In the Matter of:

_____

Petitioner

vs.

_____

Respondent

**INTENT TO CLAIM
PARENTAL RIGHTS**

I, _____, state as follows:

1. I am _____ years of age; and reside at _____
    (Street Address)   (City)   (State)   (County)

2. I have been advised _____ is the mother of a _____ child
    (Male/Female)

    named _____ born or expected to be born on _____.

3. I declare I am the father.

4. I understand the mother wishes to consent to the adoption of this child. I do not consent to the adoption of this child, and I understand I must return this form to the court administrator within 30 days of receiving the adoption registry notice.

5. I further understand I must bring a paternity action under the Parentage Act (Minn. Stat. §§ 257.51 to 257.74) within 30 days of receiving the adoption registry notice, or, if the child is not yet born, within 30 days after the birth of the child, unless I am unable to do so. I understand a paternity action is separate from the mailing of this form. In the paternity action, I must state I am the father of the child for one or more of the reasons stated in Minn. Stat. § 257.55, subd. 1. I intend to retain my legal rights with respect to the child, and request to be notified of any further proceedings with respect to custody or adoption of the child.

6. I enter my appearance in this case.

DO NOT SIGN UNTIL YOU ARE BEFORE A NOTARY PUBLIC OR COURT ADMINISTRATOR.

OATH

I have been sworn and say under oath I have read and understand this form. The facts it contains are true and correct to the best of my knowledge, and I understand that by signing this document I admit paternity. I have signed this document freely and voluntarily.

Subscribed and sworn to before me this
_____ of _____, _____

_____
Notary Public/Court Deputy

Signature: _____
Sign only in presence of notary or court clerk
Print Name: _____
Street Address: _____
City/State/Zip: _____
Telephone: _____

ADO104   State   ENG   Rev 5/08   www.mncourts.gov/forms   Page 1 of 2

Exhibit 13.1 cont.

ACKNOWLEDGEMENT

Pursuant to Minn. Stat. § 549.211, the undersigned acknowledges that costs, disbursements, and reasonable attorney and witness fees may be awarded to the opposing party or parties for actions in bad faith; the assertion of a claim or a defense that is frivolous and that is costly to the other party; the assertion of an unfounded position solely to delay the ordinary course of the proceedings or to harass; or the commission of a fraud upon the Court.

Subscribed and sworn to before me this
_____ of _____, _____

_____
Notary Public/Court Deputy

Signature: _____
Sign only in presence of notary or court clerk
Print Name: _____

Street Address: _____

City/State/Zip: _____

Telephone: _____

ADO104   State   ENG   Rev 5/08   www.mncourts.gov/forms   Page 2 of 2

absent countervailing considerations such as a history of intimate partner abuse. Even less clear is what the result should be in situations where the putative father has no knowledge of the pregnancy and thus made no attempt to establish a relationship with the child. If he has no idea, should that be regarded as evidence of a lack of interest in or commitment to parenting? As one court concluded, a biological father who was "not interested enough in the outcome of his sexual encounter . . . to even inquire about the possibility of . . . pregnancy" should not acquire constitutionally protected rights to participate in an adoption proceeding.[11] On the other hand, is it really fair to expect someone to grasp an opportunity that he knows nothing about? Should courts really impose an affirmative duty on men to inquire about pregnancy, or should they instead focus on protecting the opportunity itself, even if not known about and therefore not acted upon?

These kinds of questions can also arise in the context of the safe haven laws (as discussed previously) if the father does not know either of the pregnancy or of the mother's decision to avail herself of this option. Many safe haven laws do not have clear notice provisions, and as a result, some courts have refused to terminate the father's rights. Others do include specific notice provisions, such as that a search be made for the father using any information that might be available; that service be made through publication in the paper, which includes any possible identifying information about the baby; and that a search be done of the putative father registry.[12]

Finally, and perhaps raising the most difficult questions, what should happen in a situation where an unwed father does not learn about the child until after an adoption has been approved by a court? Should the adoption be set aside in order to vindicate a father's right to develop a relationship with his child? Does this approach elevate the biological claims of fatherhood over the best interest of the child? What weight should be given to the adoptive parents? Should the outcome turn on the conduct of the mother, in terms of whether she lied to the father about the existence of the child? Is her conduct relevant from the perspective of the child's needs? Should the outcome turn on the conduct of the father — whether he did what he could to learn about and connect with the child?

These are agonizing questions to which there are no simple answers, and these cases highlight the tension between the long-cherished rights of biological parenthood and the need to secure stable adoptive homes for children where there does not appear to be a birth parent who is ready and able to assume the responsibilities of parenthood. Some courts have focused on the harm to the father and have been willing to set an adoption aside to vindicate his right to develop a relationship with his child. Here, his underlying biological connection to the child is given priority in determining which parenting relationships will be permitted to continue. In contrast, other courts have refused to set aside an adoption in this situation if it determines that it is in the best interest of the child to maintain the continuity of the adoptive relationships.

Transracial Adoption

Significant controversy surrounds the issue of the role that race should or should not play in the creation of families by adoption.[13] Until the 1950s, many states had laws prohibiting the placement of children across racial lines, and, even where not expressly prohibited, most agencies had explicit policies against such placements. Similar to laws banning interracial marriage, this prohibition reflected racial animus and a belief in the desirability of maintaining white racial purity. As courts began to strike down racial classifications in the late 1950s, these laws were eventually declared unconstitutional.

This constitutional direction, combined with other factors — including the increased numbers of children in the foster care system, the decline in the number of white infants available for adoption, and a greater societal acceptance of interracial relationships — led to an upsurge in the number of **transracial adoptions** during the late 1950s and 1960s. An additional contributing factor was that social workers had begun to question their generally held assumption that children should be placed in families that most closely matched their families of origin, based on the belief that children would do best if they blended into their adoptive families.[14]

Transracial Adoptions:
Adoption across racial lines

Most of these transracial adoptions involved the adoption of black children by white families.[15] In 1972, this trend was denounced by the National Association of Black Social Workers, and in an influential position paper, the organization argued that black children should be placed "in Black families where they belong physically, psychologically, and culturally in order that they receive the total sense of themselves and develop a sound projection of their future. . . ."[16]

This prompted a reconsideration of the role of race in adoption placements and in-racial placements again became the preferred approach. However, in contrast to the earlier policies that embodied notions of white racial supremacy, racial matching was now based on positive concerns for the well-being of black children. Regulations and agency policies were amended to reflect this preference for in-racial placements, which often meant that a child would not be placed with white families unless it was clear that no black adoptive home was available.

However, this shift in favor of in-racial placements also generated significant concern because it often meant that children remained waiting in foster care or institutional settings until a particular type of home became available. Additionally, a number of studies indicated that where adoptive parents are sensitive to the issue, transracially adopted children can develop a clear sense of racial identity and may be particularly adept at functioning in a world that is gradually coming to embrace the benefits of diversity.

Accordingly, in 1994, Congress passed the Multiethnic Placement Law (MEPA), which was amended in 1996 by the Interethnic Placement Provisions. Together, these enactments prohibit agencies that receive federal funding from denying or delaying adoption (or foster care) placements based on considerations of race, color, or national origin.[17] However, under very limited and compelling circumstances, an exception may be made where considerations of race, culture, or ethnicity are necessary in order to protect the best interests of a particular child.[18]

Although strictly limiting the role of race in the placement process, MEPA does recognize the importance of having a diverse pool of prospective foster and adoptive parents. Accordingly, the Act imposes a duty on states to make a diligent effort to recruit foster and adoptive parents who reflect the ethnic and racial diversity of the children for whom homes are needed within their borders.

Adoption Abrogation and the Tort of Wrongful Adoption

Adoption Abrogation: The undoing of an adoption by the adoptive parent or parents

Like any other parents, most adoptive parents are prepared to handle the daily vicissitudes that come with raising children, but what happens if they come to regret their decision because the experience proves far more difficult because, for example, unbeknownst to the adoptive parents, the child had previously experienced severe physical and sexual abuse or is genetically predisposed to a debilitating disease? Should they be permitted to abrogate or undo the adoption?

The majority view is that children cannot be "sent back" — that once finalized, adoptions cannot be undone based on parental dissatisfaction with the child. Underlying this position is the recognition that children are not goods who can be returned if they later are viewed as "damaged." However, this position is not universal. A few states, either by statute or judicial decision, permit parents to undo an adoption in what are deemed extraordinary circumstances, such as where a child is facing a lifetime of institutional care; however, most judges are wary of these actions because they effectively orphan the child. Note, however, that as with any parent, if adoptive parents cannot care for their child, they may eventually lose their parental rights due to abuse or neglect.

However, in contrast to situations involving an attempt to abrogate an adoption based upon the adoptive parents' dissatisfaction with the child or their concerns that they cannot provide the child with the kind of care needed, the law tends to be somewhat more lenient where the abrogation is premised upon procedural defects in the adoption proceeding. Most common in this category of case are claims by the adoptive parents that the agency engaged in fraud or deliberate misrepresentation by, for example, telling them that a child had no history of mental disorders when it knew the child had been institutionalized for mental illness in order to induce them to adopt a child that they might not have otherwise taken into their home. In this situation, some courts are willing to undo an adoption based upon their authority to vacate court judgments for fraud in accordance with the rules of civil procedure.

However, based on the recognition that this approach disregards the interests of the adopted child, a number of states no longer permit adoptive parents to set aside an adoption based upon fraud or misrepresentation, but, instead, permit them to sue the agency for **wrongful adoption** in order to recover damages for unanticipated expenses, which might include, for example, residential care or extraordinary medical treatments. In allowing these damage suits, courts have been careful to make clear that adoption agencies cannot be expected to guarantee that adopted children develop as happy and healthy children. At the same time, they have emphasized that adoptive parents are entitled to rely on the accuracy of the information they obtain from an agency when seeking to make an informed choice about whether they wish to proceed with the adoption of a particular child.

Wrongful Adoption:
An action that adoptive parents can bring against an adoption agency if the agency failed to tell the parents the truth about the child they adopted

Chapter Summary

Through adoption, a child acquires new parents who assume all of the rights and responsibilities previously vested in the biological parents, and the child's legal relationship with his or her birth parents is extinguished. This cutoff rule is subject to limited exceptions, most commonly in stepparent and coparent adoptions. Adoptions can be accomplished through an agency or by the parents themselves, acting with or without the assistance of a third-party intermediary. In addition, most states now have safe haven laws, which permit birth parents to anonymously drop a newborn off at a designated location without fear of being prosecuted for abandonment.

An adoption cannot proceed without the consent of the birth parents, subject to a limited exception for some unwed fathers, unless parental rights have been terminated or the court has approved a request to dispense with parental consent. In private placement adoptions, the consent attaches to the adoption itself; in an agency adoption, the consent attaches to the relinquishment of the child to the agency, which in turn acquires the right of consent. Most states allow birth parents to revoke consent under specific circumstances; some states give birth parents considerable latitude, while others are quite strict; however, in all jurisdictions, it is harder to revoke a relinquishment to an agency.

In most situations, the child must live with the prospective adoptive parents in a preadoption placement before the adoption can be finalized. In an agency adoption, placement will not be made until a home study has been completed, and the placement is supervised by the agency. Postplacement social studies are done in both agency and private placement adoptions in order to assist the judge in deciding whether to approve the adoption. This decision is based on the best interest standard.

A developing trend is to provide for greater openness in adoption. Many states now allow open adoptions, which permit postadoption contact between the adopted child and the birth parent. Additionally, most states now permit the release of nonidentifying information to adopted children, and many now permit the release of identifying information in accordance with specific procedures, which may result in communication between an adult adoptee and his or her birth parents.

Stepparent adoptions account for a considerable number of yearly adoptions. Here, in a significant exception to the cutoff rule, the parental rights of the custodial spouse survive the adoption. This same exception has been made in co-parent adoptions involving gay and lesbian couples.

Unwed fathers now have considerably more rights in the adoption arena than they had in the past and may be entitled to consent rights based on a substantial parenting commitment or an acknowledgment of paternity or the filing of notice in a putative father registry. If a father comes forward after an adoption has been finalized, some courts may allow the adoption to be disrupted, while other courts refuse to do this based on the best interest of the child.

There has been considerable controversy over the role that race should play in adoption placements. Presently, federal law prohibits delays in or denials of adoption placements based on considerations of race, color, or national origin.

When an adoption does not live up to parental expectations, most courts will not permit the parents to abrogate or undo the adoption, although abrogation has been permitted by some courts under extraordinary circumstances. Where the agency has breached its obligation to properly disclose information, parents may be able to sue the agency in tort for wrongful adoption.

Key Terms

Adoption
Agency Adoption
Independent Adoption
Private Placement
    Adoption
Voluntary Surrender/
    Relinquishment

Safe Haven
Consent
Revocation of
    Consent
Dispensing with
    Parental Consent
At-Risk Placement

Preadoption
    Placement
Home Study
Postplacement Social
    Study
Open Adoption
Cutoff Rule

Coparent Adoption
Putative Father
    Registry
Opportunity Interest
Transracial Adoptions
Adoption Abrogation
Wrongful Adoption

Review Questions

1. What is an agency adoption?
2. What is an independent or private placement adoption?
3. What role do intermediaries play in independent adoptions?
4. What concerns have been raised about the potential for exploitation or coercion in the context of independent adoptions? What solutions have been suggested?
5. What are some of the major differences between these two types of adoption?
6. Explain how safe haven laws work.
7. What role does consent play in an independent or private placement adoption?
8. What is the legal significance of relinquishment of a child to an adoption agency?
9. What happens if a parent wishes to revoke his or her consent to an adoption?
10. Why are states generally stricter about the revocation of a relinquishment made to an agency, as compared to the revocation of consent?
11. What is the purpose of the home study? When is it usually done? What is usually inquired into?
12. During an agency placement, who usually has legal custody of the children?
13. Does the execution of the consent document effectively transfer parental rights over to the adoptive parents?
14. During the placement in an independent adoption, who has authority to make decisions regarding the child?

15. What is the purpose of a postplacement social study?
16. What standard does the court use in deciding whether to approve an adoption?
17. Why have adoptions traditionally been cloaked in secrecy? Why has this been challenged?
18. What is an open adoption?
19. What approaches do states take with respect to open adoption?
20. What typically happens to the original birth records and the adoption records once an adoption is approved?
21. What approaches do states take to provide children who have been adopted access to their birth records?
22. Following a stepparent adoption, what is the status of the custodial parent?
23. In what ways are coparent adoptions similar to stepparent adoptions? In what ways are they different?
24. Explain the adoption rights of gay men and lesbians in each of the discussed types of adoption.
25. Historically, what rights did an unwed father have relative to the adoption of his child, and why?
26. How are unwed mothers and unwed fathers treated differently with respect to consent rights? What accounts for this differential treatment?
27. Under what circumstances will an unmarried father be entitled to consent rights?

28. Historically, what accounted for the policy against transracial placements? When and why did this policy begin to change?
29. Under federal law, what role, if any, can race play in the adoption placement process?
30. How do courts generally respond when parents seek to undo an adoption?
31. Explain the concept of wrongful adoption. How does it differ from adoption abrogation?

Discussion Questions

1. What do you think the result should be in a case where a father was wrongfully deprived of his opportunity to develop a relationship with his child who has subsequently been adopted? Should the adoption be set aside in order to vindicate the father's rights to develop a relationship with his child? Should the needs of the child take precedence if removal from his or her adoptive family would be harmful to the child?
2. If you were an adoptive parent, how would you feel about an open adoption plan that allowed the child to visit regularly with his or her birth parents? How would you feel about this if you were a birth parent?
3. What role do you think race should play in the formation of adoptive families? What about the sexual orientation of the parents?
4. Do you think safe haven laws make sense? What arguments can you think of in favor of and against this approach?

Assignments

1. Determine whether private placement adoptions are permitted in your jurisdiction. If they are, determine the following by consulting the relevant statutory and/or regulatory provisions:
   a. Are prospective adoptive parents subject to a certification requirement?
   b. Is the use of intermediaries allowed?
   c. If so, are they subject to any legal requirements, such as limitations of fees and costs or accounting requirements?
2. Determine what the rules are in your jurisdiction governing when a parent can revoke his or her consent to an adoption. In developing your answer, detail both the substantive standards as well as the procedural requirements. To do this, you may need to consult both the relevant statutory and regulatory provisions as well as case law.
3. Locate an adoption agency in your area and interview someone who works there. In your interview, see if you can determine the following:
   a. Does the agency specialize in a particular type of adoption?
   b. How does it screen parents who want to adopt?
   c. What is the cost of a typical adoption?
   d. How long does the typical adoption take?
   e. What areas of inquiry are of particular importance when conducting a home study?
   f. Does the agency ever revoke placements? Under what circumstances?
4. Assume that the attorney you work for has asked you to do some research on coparent adoptions, as he is seeking to file a petition on behalf of one of his clients. As there is no law in your jurisdiction on coparent adoptions, he has asked you to locate rulings from other jurisdictions that both permit and deny second-parent adoptions. Carefully read and analyze the cases you have located, and prepare a memorandum listing the essential reasons behind the court decisions.

Endnotes

1. Catherine J. Ross, Welfare Reform and Juvenile Courts: Families Without Paradigms: Child Poverty and Out-of-House Placements in Historical Perspective, 60 Ohio St. L.J. 1249, 1257-1258 (1999).

2. Stephen B. Presser, The Historical Background of the American Law of Adoption, 11 J. Fam. L. 443, 465 (citing Act of 1851, ch. 324).

3. For a discussion of some of the complexities of safe haven laws, *see* Susan Ayres, Kairos and Safe Havens: The Timing and Calamity of Unwanted Birth, 15 Wm. & Mary J. Women & L. 227 (2009); Jeffrey A. Parness, Deserting Mothers, Abandoned Babies, Lost Fathers: Dangers in Safe Havens, 24 Quinnipiac L. Rev. 335 (2006); Carol Sanger, Infant Safe Haven Laws: Legislating in the Culture of Life, 106 Colum. L. Rev. 753 (2006).

4. Courts in several states have recently grappled with the complex interplay between termination and adoption proceedings in situations where the adoption of a child was approved while a parent's appeal of the termination of her parental rights was under review. For a discussion of these cases, *see* Kate M. Heideman, Avoiding the Need to "Unscramble the Egg": A Proposal for the Automatic Stay of Subsequent Adoption Proceedings When Parents Appeal a Judgment Terminating Their Parental Rights, 24 St. Louis U. Pub. L. Rev. 445 (2005).

5. In interstate cases, the applicable jurisdictional requirements of PKPA, the UCCJA, and the UCCJEA must be complied with. For a general discussion of these Acts, *see* Chapter 9.

6. Lucy S. McGough and Annette Peltier-Falahahwazi, Secrets and Lies: A Model for Cooperative Adoption, 60 La. L. Rev. 13, 41 (1999).

7. Access to Adoption Records, Child Welfare Information Gateway, http://www.childwelfare.gov (accessed June 12, 2014).

8. *See* Rosemary Cabellero, Open Records Adoption: Finding the Missing Piece, 30 S. Ill. U. L.J. 291 (2006); Caroline B. Fleming, The Open-Records Debate: Balancing the Interests of Birth Parents and Adult Adoptees, 11 Wm. & Mary J. Women & L. 461 (2005).

9. The Evan B. Donaldson Adoption Agency, Adoption by Lesbians and Gays: A National Survey of Adoption Agency Policies, Practices, and Attitudes (2003). Available at http://www.childwelfare.gov/adoption/types/families/gay.cfm (accessed Oct. 2, 2012).

10. *See* Robbin Pott Gonzalez, The Rights of Putative Fathers to Their Infant Children in Contested Adoptions: Strengthening State Laws That Currently Deny Adequate Protection, 13 Mich. J. Gender & L. 39 (2006); Kimberly Barton, Who's Your Daddy? State Adoption Statutes and the Unknown Biological Father, 32 Cap. U. L. Rev. 113 (2003); Mary Beck, Towards a National Putative Father Registry, 25 Harv. J.L. & Pub. Poly. 1031 (2002); Rebecca Aizporu, Protecting the Unwed Father's Opportunity to Parent: A Survey of Paternity Registry Statutes, 18 Rev. Litig. 703 (1999).

11. In the Matter of A.A.T., 287 Kan. 590, 196 P.3d 1180, 1195 (2008) citing In re Adoption of S.J.B., 294 Ark. 598, 600, 745 S.W.2d 606 (1988).

12. *See* articles cited *supra* in note 3.

13. Most of the debate has focused on the adoption of black children by white families, and this chapter's discussion is based on the literature on this subject. Many of the same considerations will be present, though, whenever an adoption crosses racial or ethnic lines. *See* Stephanie R. Richardson, Strict Scrutiny, Biracial Children and Adoption, 12 B.U. Pub. Int. L.J. 203 (2002); Kim Forde-Mazrui, Black Identity and Child Placement: The Best Interests of Black and Biracial Children, 92 Mich. L. Rev. 925 (1994) (discusses placement issues relative to biracial children); Margaret Howard, Transracial Adoption: Analysis of the Best Interest Standard, 59 Notre Dame L. Rev. 503 (1984) (examines concerns relative to the placement of Native American children).

14. For detail, *see* Howard, *supra* note 13, at 505-516; Cynthia G. Hawkins-Leon and Carla Bradley, Mid-Atlantic People of Color Legal Scholarship Conference: Race and Transracial Adoption: The Answer Is Neither Simply Black Nor White or Wrong, 51 Cath. U. L. Rev. 1227 (2002); Valerie Phillips Herman, Transracial Adoption: "Child-Saving" or "Child-Snatching," 13 Natl. Black L.J. 147 (1993).

15. The gap between the number of black children needing homes and available black adoptive parents has been attributed in part to the failure of agencies to recruit black parents and to the use of screening criteria that are weighted in favor of white families. *See* Hawkins-Leon and Bradley, *supra* note 14, at 1233-1238.

16. National Association of Black Social Workers, Position Paper (Summer 1972), reprinted in Forde-Mazrui, *supra* note 13, at 926.

17. *See* the Multiethnic Placement Act of 1994, Pub. L. No. 103-382, 108 Stat. 405, as amended by the Removal of Barriers to Interethnic Adoption Provisions of the Small Business Job Protection Act of 1996, Pub. L. No. 104-188, 110 Stat. 1755, §1808.

18. *See* Dennis Hayashi, Director, Office for Civil Rights and Olivia Golden, Principal Deputy Assistant Secretary, Administration for Children and Families Memorandum: Interethnic Adoption Provisions of the Small Business Job Protection Act of 1996 (1997) http://www.hhs.gov/ocr/civilrights/resources/specialtopics/adoption/jointguidancewacf.html (accessed Oct. 6, 2012). This topic remains very controversial, and the current federal approach to transracial adoption has again been the subject of public hearings. For discussion of some of the issues, *see* Evan B. Donaldson Adoption Institute, Finding Families for African American Families: The Role of Race and Law in Adoption from Foster Care (2008); Laura Briggs, Somebody's Children, 11 J.L. Fam. Stud. 373 (2009); Ralph Richard Banks, The Multiethnic Placement Act and the Troubling Persistence of Race Matching, 38 Cap. U. L. Rev. 271 (2009).

Glossary

Abuse. Broadly speaking, abuse refers to the physical, sexual, or emotional harm of a child by a parent/caretaker.

Abuse prevention laws. Laws that enable domestic violence victims to obtain emergency protective orders.

Abuse reporting laws. Laws that establish a mechanism for the reporting of suspected cases of child abuse and/or neglect to a state protective agency. *See also* Mandatory reporter; Permissive reporter.

Acceptance of service. Assent by a defendant to being presented with the summons and complaint, and the defendant's willing acknowledgment of the receipt of the same.

Acknowledgment of paternity. Voluntary acknowledgment by the parents of the paternity of the father. This is accomplished through the completion of a notarized paternity affidavit.

Active listening. An engaged way of listening, involving reflection back of informational and emotional content.

Adjudication of paternity. Paternity determined through a court action.

Adoption. The legal process by which someone becomes a parent to a child with whom he or she does not have a biological relationship and assumes all the rights and responsibilities of parenthood. Adoption is premised on the termination of rights in the biological parents unless a co-parent or a stepparent is adopting the child, in which case the parental rights of that party's partner will remain in effect. *See also* Adult adoption; Agency adoption; Independent adoption; Open adoption; Transracial adoption.

Adoption abrogation. The undoing of an adoption by the adoptive parent(s).

Adoption placement. *See* Pre-adoptive placement.

Adult adoption. The adoption of one adult by another.

Adultery. Voluntary sexual intercourse between a married person and someone who is not his or her spouse; a fault divorce ground.

Affidavit. A factual statement that is signed under the penalties of perjury; often submitted to a court in support of a motion.

Affirmative defense for relief. A response to an allegation in a complaint in which the defendant seeks to establish that the plaintiff is not entitled to recover on his or her claim.

Age of capacity. The minimum age below which a young person may not marry—commonly set at age 14.

Age of consent. The age at which a young person becomes eligible to consent to his or her own marriage—usually set at the age of majority.

Agency adoption. As distinct from an independent adoption, an adoption that is handled by a state or private agency. A key component of these adoptions is that a home study is done prior to the placement of a child with a prospective adoptive family.

Alimony. *See* Spousal support.

Alimony pendente lite. Temporary support paid to one spouse by the other during the pendency of a divorce.

All-property. States that allow a couple's accumulated assets to be distributed at divorce without a formal distinction between separate property and marital property.

Annulment. A decree establishing that spouses were never actually married because an impediment existed at the time the marriage was celebrated.

Answer. The pleading filed by a defendant in response to a plaintiff's complaint, in which he or she seeks to avoid liability; component parts include responses to the plaintiff's factual allegations, affirmative defenses, and counterclaims.

Appeal. Resort to an appellate court for review of a lower-court decision; usually involves questions of law rather than of fact.

Appellate court. A court with jurisdiction to review lower-court decisions.

Appreciation. The increase in value of an asset.

Arbitration. A dispute resolution mechanism whereby parties agree to submit their disagreement to a neutral decision maker. The arbitrator's authority derives from the party's agreement, and his or her decision is usually binding subject to a limited right of court review.

Arrearage. Money that is overdue or unpaid; in this context, an outstanding support obligation.

At-risk placement. An adoption placement that is made before the rights of both parents have been terminated.

Attributed income. *See* Imputed income.

Bankruptcy. The filing of a court action in which a party seeks to be discharged from responsibility for paying his or her debts.

Batterer intervention program. A treatment or counseling program that works specifically with abusers.

Best interest. The predominant legal standard for resolving custody disputes between parents; the standard is child-centered, focusing on the needs of the child rather than on the rights of the parents.

Bigamy. The unlawful act of contracting a second marriage while one or both of the partners is already married to someone else.

Change in circumstances. A future event that arguably makes an existing order unfair and serves as the basis for a request for modification.

Child protection agency. Usually a state agency with responsibility for handling cases of child abuse and neglect.

Child support. The duty of financial support owed by a noncustodial parent to his or her minor children and to children over the age of majority in limited situations, such as in cases of disability.

Child support guidelines. Mandated by federal law, guidelines employing numeric criteria used to calculate the amount of child support to be paid by the noncustodial parent; under certain circumstances, deviations from the resulting amount may be allowed.

Child tax credit. Credit against tax liability provided to parents. Available to the parent with the dependency exemption.

Civil union. A formal status that provides same-sex couples with the rights, benefits, protections, and responsibilities that are available to married heterosexual couples under state (but not federal) law.

Clean break. Refers to the view that upon divorce, obligations stemming from the marriage should be kept to a minimum, leaving each partner free to start life anew, unencumbered by claims from the past.

Cohabitation. Two unmarried persons living together in an intimate relationship. The term applies to both same-sex and heterosexual couples.

Collaborative law model. An approach to the practice of law that stresses cooperation and the avoidance of litigation.

Collusion. Agreement by a couple to obtain a divorce in avoidance of the fault principle that requires a guilty and an innocent spouse.

Common law. The law of England as accepted by the colonies prior to the American Revolution; also refers to judge-made law.

Common law marriage. A marriage created by the conduct of the parties rather than through a formal ceremony. Creation usually requires agreement, cohabitation, and a reputation in the community as husband and wife.

Community property. A system of property ownership between husband and wife in civil law jurisdictions in which each spouse has a vested one-half ownership interest in all marital property regardless of title; excluded is all property classified as separate property.

Comparative rectitude. A doctrine that ameliorates the harsh effects of the traditional divorce defense of recrimination by allowing a divorce when one party's marital fault is regarded as less serious than the other party's.

Compelling state interest. A governmental interest of sufficient magnitude that it may justify limitations on fundamental rights.

Complaint. In a civil case, the pleading filed by the plaintiff to initiate a lawsuit; includes factual allegations, a statement of legal claims against the defendant, and a request for relief; called "petition" in some states.

Complaint for contempt. A parent's return to court following a divorce, to enforce existing arrangements about custody or visitation arrangements after a dispute.

Complaint for modification. A parent's return to court following a divorce, to change existing arrangements about custody or visitation arrangements after a dispute.

Condonation. A divorce defense, the essence of which is that the plaintiff has forgiven the acts of marital misconduct upon which his or her complaint for divorce is based.

Confidentiality. An ethical rule prohibiting attorneys and persons working with them from disclosing client information except under limited circumstances, such as to prevent the commission of a serious crime.

Connivance. A divorce defense, the essence of which is that the plaintiff consented to the wrongdoing upon which his or her complaint for divorce is based.

Consent. Relative to adoption law, the requirement that a biological parent must assent to the adoption of his or her child unless his or her parental rights have been terminated.

Consideration. The bargained-for exchange that underlies the formation of an enforceable contract; consideration serves to distinguish a contract from a promise.

Constructive desertion. Imputes the act of desertion to the spouse responsible for the other's departure.

Constructive service. Service of a summons and complaint on a defendant in a manner other than by delivering it to him or her in person, usually by publication, mailing, or both.

Contempt proceeding. A proceeding against a party who is in violation of a court order; contempt proceedings can be either civil or criminal in nature. The purpose of a civil contempt action is to obtain compliance with a court order, while the purpose of a criminal contempt action is to punish a party for his or her noncompliance.

Continuing jurisdiction. In the custody context, the continuation of the initial decree state's authority to modify a decree to the exclusion of other states.

Contract. A legally enforceable agreement between two or more parties. *See also* Express contract; Implied-in-fact contract.

Co-parent. A parent who shares the raising of a child with his or her partner in the absence of a formally recognized parent-child relationship.

Co-parent adoption. Adoption by a co-parent (*see above*); here, the adoption does not extinguish the rights of the biological parent.

Cost basis. The cost of an asset, used to calculate the amount of appreciation from the time of purchase.

Counterclaim. A claim made by the defendant against the plaintiff.

Covenant marriage. Developed in response to concerns about the prevalence and impact of divorce, covenant marriage laws emphasize the permanency of marriage and limit the availability of divorce.

Credit reporting. In the child support context, the provision of information to a credit agency about a party's failure to make child support payments.

Criminal nonsupport. The willful failure to pay child support when one has the ability to do so; may also apply to the willful failure to pay spousal support.

Cruelty. A fault ground for divorce based on mistreatment of a relatively serious nature; cruelty generally can include either physical or emotional wrongdoing.

Custody. Broadly, the care of and responsibility for a child. *See also* Joint custody; Legal custody; Physical custody; Sole custody.

Cutoff rule. A principle that operates to extinguish the parental rights of the biological parents at the time of adoption; may not be applied when a stepparent or a co-parent is adopting the child.

Cyberstalking. The use of the Internet or other mode of electronic communication to threaten or harass someone.

De facto parent. An individual who has no biological relation to a child but who has functioned as a family member; must show that he or she resided with the child and shared caretaking responsibilities with the consent and cooperation of the legal parent.

Decree *nisi*. A provisional judgment of divorce that automatically ripens into the final divorce decree absent a challenge or decision by the parties to vacate the divorce.

Default judgment. A judgment entered against a defendant who fails to respond to a complaint or otherwise defend the action.

Defense of Marriage Act (DOMA). A federal statute that allows states to deny recognition to marriages between same-sex partners that were validly entered into in a sister state. Additionally, DOMA, for purposes of federal law, restricts the definition of marriage to heterosexual couples.

Dependency exemption. Deduction that a taxpayer can take from gross income for a person who is principally dependent on the taxpayer for support.

Dependency proceeding. A court process to determine if a child's parents lack the present ability to care for him or her; may result in a transfer of custody to the state.

Deponent. The person whose deposition is being taken.

Deposition. A method of discovery in which the oral testimony of a witness is obtained through questions that are answered under oath.

Desertion. A fault ground for divorce; involves the voluntary, nonconsensual departure of one spouse without justification for a period of time defined by statute.

Diminished earning capacity. A decrease in a spouse's earning potential due to a lack of a sustained connection with the paid workplace, usually because of domestic responsibilities.

Discovery. The process by which each side is able to acquire information from the other side in advance of trial. *See also* Deposition; Interrogatories; Request for admissions; Request for physical and mental examination; Request for production of documents.

Discovery conference. A meeting at which the court develops a plan for how discovery will proceed in a case.

Dispensing with parental consent. In the course of an adoption proceeding, a decision by the court to proceed with the adoption without the consent of the parents based on a finding of parental unfitness.

Divisible divorce. A divorce in which the court has jurisdiction to dissolve the marriage based on a party's domicile but cannot resolve support and property matters because it lacks personal jurisdiction over the defendant.

Divorce. The legal dissolution of a marital relationship, such that the parties are no longer spouses. *See also* Divisible divorce; *Divorce a mensa et thoro*; Fault divorce; No-fault divorce.

***Divorce a mensa et thoro*.** A common law term meaning a "divorce from board and bed"; this is a decree of separation that permits spouses to live apart without dissolving the marital relationship.

Divorce hearing. The court hearing at which a marriage is dissolved and collateral issues are resolved; results in a divorce judgment. If the case is uncontested, the hearing is usually simple; the judge will inquire into the circumstances underlying the request for divorce and review the parties' separation agreement. If the case is contested, a trial on the merits will be conducted.

Divorce judgment. The court decree that dissolves the marriage; a decree *nisi* may be entered initially.

Docket number. The number assigned to each case by the court; the number is used for organizational and reference purposes and is included on all papers filed in a case.

Domestic partnership. Usually refers to a municipal ordinance allowing unmarried couples to register as domestic partners; provides some legal recognition and possible eligibility for benefits. Domestic partnerships are also recognized by some private employers.

Domestic violence. Abusive behavior toward someone with whom one is in a dating, familial, household, or intimate relationship. *See also* Intimate partner violence.

Domicile. A person's permanent home; the place to which the person intends to return when away.

Donor insemination. The process by which a woman is inseminated with or inseminates herself with sperm contributed by a donor, who may be known or unknown.

Dual property. States that distinguish between marital property and separate property for distribution purposes.

Due process clause. A clause found in both the fifth and fourteenth amendments to the U.S. Constitution that protects persons from arbitrary or intrusive governmental actions. The clause provides both procedural protections and substantive rights.

Economic self-sufficiency. The idea that after a divorce, both spouses should become self-supporting as quickly as possible.

Emancipation. The point at which a child is no longer considered a dependent of his or her parents; generally occurs at the age of majority or upon the occurrence of certain acts, such as marriage of the child.

Emergency jurisdiction. A jurisdictional ground that permits a court to assert jurisdiction over a custody dispute when a child is physically present in the state and has been abandoned or needs immediate protection from abuse or neglect.

Enhanced earning capacity. An increase in a spouse's earning ability attributable to a marital division of labor that enabled that spouse to concentrate on career development without major domestic responsibilities.

Equal protection clause. A clause in the fourteenth amendment to the U.S. Constitution that prevents states from imposing arbitrary and discriminatory legislative classifications.

Equitable distribution. The division of property at divorce based principally on considerations of fairness and contribution rather than title.

Equitable parenthood. A doctrine used to extend parenting rights to a stepparent when there is a developed, consensual relationship between the child and the stepparent, and he or she wishes to assume the rights and responsibilities of parenthood; may also be applicable when a co-parent is seeking custodial or visitation rights.

Ex parte. A hearing that is held without prior notice to the other side due to the urgent nature of the proceeding or the harm that such notice would cause.

Express contract. A contract that is created by the actual, articulated agreement of the parties. See also Implied-in-fact contract.

Extraordinary expenses. Large, discrete expenditures that do not recur on a regular basis, as distinct from the day-to-day expenses of raising a child.

Fair market value. The price that a willing buyer would pay to a willing seller when neither party is under compulsion to buy or sell.

Family preservation. A child welfare approach that stresses the use of "reasonable efforts" to keep family together or reunify them following a child's removal.

Fault divorce. A divorce that is premised on the marital fault of one spouse.

Federal Marriage Amendment (FMA). An amendment first introduced in Congress in 2003, stating that "[m]arriage in the United States shall consist only of the union of a man and a woman"; the FMA would prevent either the federal or any state constitution from being construed to require that "marriage or the legal incidents thereof be conferred upon any union other than the union of a man and a woman."

Filing fee. The administrative fee charged by a court for the filing of an action.

Financial affidavit. A document that discloses income and assets, which parties must complete in family court proceedings where property or support is at issue.

Foster care. The taking in and caring for a child who is unable to live at home, usually because of parental abuse and/or neglect.

Freedom of contract. The right of each individual to freely structure his or her own affairs.

Genetic testing. Performed when paternity is contested; can be done through a cheek swab and can prove or disprove paternity with virtual certainty. Unless an objection is made, the tests must be admissible without foundation testimony or proof of authenticity.

Gift. A voluntary transfer of property made with donative intent, meaning that the gift-giver (donor) simply wishes to give the recipient something without requiring anything in exchange. For a gift to be effective, the transfer must be complete—the donor must fully relinquish all vestiges of ownership and control.

Goodwill. An intangible asset, the good reputation of a business in the community that generates future patronage.

Guardian ad litem. A person who is appointed by a court to conduct a custody investigation; may also refer to a person appointed to provide legal representation to a child.

Harassment Order. Civil order that can be obtained by an individual who is being harassed without the requirement of a special qualifying relationship

Home state jurisdiction. A jurisdictional ground that enables a state to assert jurisdiction over a custody dispute based on the fact that the child lives or had lived in that state for the six months prior to the initiation of the action.

Home study. An evaluation of a person or couple seeking to adopt a child to determine potential suitability, usually done only in agency adoptions.

Illegitimate. An outdated term for a child born to unmarried parents.

Implied-in-fact contract. A contract that is inferred from the conduct of the parties. *See also* Express contract.

Imputed/attributed income. The attribution of income to a party who is deliberately unemployed or underemployed, based on earning capacity, for the purpose of establishing the amount of his or her support obligation.

Inception of title rule. A rule fixing title at the time an asset is acquired.

Incest. Unlawful sexual relations between persons who are closely related to each other; marriages contracted in violation of incest provisions are invalid.

Incorporation. In the divorce context, upon approval of a separation agreement, the inclusion of its terms into the divorce judgment such that those terms become part of the judgment. *See also* Merger; Survival.

Independent adoption. An adoption that is accomplished without an agency; parents can either place the child directly or utilize an intermediary.

Indissoluble. In reference to marriage, the belief that the legal relationship between spouses is permanent and can never be terminated.

Initial custody determination. The first custody decision in a case, as distinct from subsequent modifications.

In loco parentis. Common law doctrine conferring parental rights and responsibilities on someone who voluntarily assumes a parenting role.

Innocent spouse. Pertaining to fault divorce, the requirement that the petitioning spouse not have engaged in marital misconduct.

In rem jurisdiction. The authority of a court to resolve a case based on the presence of property within its borders.

Intangible assets. Property that lacks a physical presence and cannot be ascertained by the senses.

Interrogatories. A discovery method involving written questions to a party, which must be answered under oath.

Intimate partner violence. Violence between partners who are in a same-sex or heterosexual relationship, including dating relationships. *See also* Domestic violence.

Irreconcilable differences. A no-fault divorce ground, the essence of which is that the parties are no longer compatible and there is no hope of reconciliation.

IV-D agency. Under Title IV-D, the agency in each state responsible for administering that state's child support program.

Joint custody. As distinct from sole custody, the sharing of parental rights and responsibilities — can apply to legal or physical custody, or both.

Joint petition. A pleading filed in a no-fault divorce action by co-petitioners to initiate the divorce.

Judgment. *See* Default judgment; Divorce judgment.

Jurisdiction. The authority of a court to hear and resolve a case before it. *See also* Emergency jurisdiction; In rem jurisdiction; Personal jurisdiction; Subject matter jurisdiction.

Lack of capacity. Lack of ability of a party to enter into legally enforceable agreements.

Last resort jurisdiction. A relatively insignificant jurisdictional ground that enables a state to assert jurisdiction over a custody dispute when no other state has or is willing to assume jurisdiction, and it is in the best interest of the child for the state to do so.

Legal custody. As distinct from physical custody, legal custody confers on a parent the authority to make major decisions related to his or her child's life; legal custody can be sole or joint.

Legal separation. A judicial decree permitting parties to live apart, usually for cause, without dissolving the legal relationship of spouses. *See also* Separate maintenance.

Legitimate. In contrast to the term "illegitimate," refers to a child born to married parents.

Legitimation. The process of altering the status of a child born to unmarried parents so that he or she is the legal equivalent of a child born to married parents.

Lien. A nonpossessory interest in the property of another that operates as a cloud against title.

Living separate and apart. A no-fault divorce ground that requires the parties to have lived apart for a statutory period of time, with the separation serving as proof of marital breakdown.

Long-arm statute. A statute that spells out when a state may assert personal jurisdiction over a nonresident.

Lump-Sum Support/Alimony in Gross. A support award of a specific amount of money, usually payable in a single installment, although it can also be made payable in periodic installments until the full amount of the order is reached.

Mandatory reporter. In contrast to a permissive reporter, a person, usually a professional who comes into contact with children in the course of his or her work, who is legally obligated to report suspected cases of child abuse or neglect pursuant to an abuse reporting law.

Marital breakdown. *See* Irreconcilable differences.

Marital fault. Acts of wrongdoing by one spouse toward the other that serve as the basis of a fault divorce. *See* Adultery; Cruelty; Desertion.

Marital property. As distinct from separate property, assets acquired during the marriage as a result of marital efforts or funds, which are subject to division at divorce.

Marital unity. A common law principle espousing that upon marriage a husband and wife become one, resulting in the suspension of the wife's legal identity.

Marriage restriction laws. Laws that prevent certain people, such as close relatives, from marrying each other.

Married Women's Property Acts. The series of statutory reforms that gradually improved the legal status of married women, principally through extending rights of property ownership and control that had been denied at common law.

Mediation. A nonadversarial approach to dispute resolution in which a neutral third party—the mediator—helps parties reach a mutually satisfactory resolution to a conflict; an increasingly popular option in divorce cases.

Merger. Going beyond incorporation, merger refers to when a separation agreement, once approved by the court, loses its separate identity and thereafter exists only as part of the court's judgment; this contrasts with the concept of survival.

Minimum contacts. A jurisdictional concept enabling a state to assert personal jurisdiction over a nonresident when he or she has a sufficiently developed relationship with that state.

Modification. The alteration of an existing order based on a change in circumstances.

Modification jurisdiction. The authority of a court to modify a custody or support decree.

Motion. In general, a request made to a court for some kind of relief during the pendency of an action.

Motion for a new trial. A post-trial request that the court set aside the judgment and order a new trial because of prejudicial errors during the trial.

Motion for relief from judgment. A post-trial request that the court vacate or modify its judgment, usually because of an error, unfairness, or newly discovered evidence.

Motion to compel. A request to the court that it order the other side to comply with a discovery request.

Motion to dismiss. A request to the court that it dismiss the plaintiff's case for lack of jurisdiction, improper service, or the plaintiff's failure to state a valid claim entitling him or her to relief.

Mutual consent. The idea that a no-fault divorce should require the agreement of both spouses.

Mutual orders of protection. Orders of protection granted by some courts to both parties where only one party has sought court intervention.

Neglect. Broadly speaking, the willful failure by a parent/caretaker to provide for a child's basic needs.

Negotiation. The process through which attorneys seek to resolve a case outside court; often done at a settlement conference at which the clients are present.

Nexus approach. As distinct from the per se approach, this approach requires that parental conduct have a demonstrated detrimental impact on a child before it will be taken into account in a custody determination.

No-contact order. A protective order that prohibits someone from having any contact with the party he or she has abused.

No-fault divorce. A divorce that is based on the breakdown of the marital relationship rather than on the marital fault of one spouse. *See also* Irreconcilable differences.

Noncustodial parent. A parent who has been divested of both legal and physical custody, but is still a legal parent with enforceable rights, such as visitation.

Open adoption. An adoption that permits some degree of contact with one or both biological parents.

Opportunity cost. The loss of earning potential attributable to a lack of a sustained relationship with the labor force, often due to a spouse's primary investment in the domestic realm.

Opportunity interest. The opportunity that the biological link provides to an unmarried father to develop a meaningful relationship with his child.

Parens patriae. The authority of the state, as a sovereign power, to protect those who cannot protect themselves, most notably children.

Parent locator service. A federal or state agency that is responsible for locating absent parents in order to establish or enforce a child support award.

Parental unfitness. Parental abuse or neglect that is severe enough to warrant a termination of rights.

Parenting coordinator. A person who is appointed to assist parents in implementing their parenting plan following a divorce.

Parenting plan. A written agreement in which the parents detail how they intend to care for their children following a divorce.

Paternal preference. The common law doctrine that vested fathers with the absolute right to care and custody of their children.

Paternity disestablishment. The undoing/revocation of a determination that a man is a child's legal father.

Pension. Deferred compensation payable at retirement.

Permanency plan. A plan that either calls for the return of a child home following removal for abuse or neglect or for the termination of parental rights.

Permanency hearing. A hearing to determine if a child who has been removed from the home due to abuse or neglect can safely return home or whether parental rights should be terminated and the child freed for adoption.

Permanent alimony. An ongoing support award to a spouse who is unlikely to become economically self-sufficient; the award is subject to modification and is generally terminable upon death of either spouse or remarriage of the recipient.

Permissive reporter. In contrast to a mandatory reporter, a person who may report suspected cases of child abuse or neglect to a child protective agency but is not legally obligated to do so.

Per se approach. As distinct from the nexus approach, the idea that some behaviors are so inherently harmful that they should be the basis for denying custody to a parent without proof of actual harm.

Personal jurisdiction. The authority of a court over the person of a defendant.

Personal property. Broadly, all property owned by an individual other than real property; includes both tangible and intangible assets.

Personal service. In contrast to constructive service, delivering the summons and complaint by hand to the defendant.

Petition. *See* Complaint.

Physical custody. As distinct from legal custody, physical custody refers to where a child lives; a parent with physical custody usually maintains a home for the child and is responsible for the child's day-to-day care. Physical custody can be either sole or joint.

Polygamy. The situation where an individual (most commonly a man) has multiple spouses at the same time.

Postmarital agreement. Similar to a premarital agreement, but entered after rather than before a marriage. *See* Premarital agreement.

Postplacement social study. An assessment of an adoption placement done to provide information to the judge who will be deciding if the adoption should be approved.

Prayer for relief. *See* Request for relief.

Preadoption placement. The specified period of time that a child must live with his or her prospective adoptive parents before the adoption can be approved.

Premarital acquisitions. Property owned by a spouse prior to marriage.

Premarital agreement. A contract entered into by prospective spouses in which they seek to establish their respective rights in the event the marriage fails; most commonly, provisions address spousal support and the allocation of property.

Premarital counseling. Using incentives such as a reduced marriage license fee, some states now encourage potential spouses to participate in counseling as a way to reduce the divorce rate.

Presumption of paternity. The legal assumption that the father of a child born to a married woman is the woman's husband.

Pretrial conference. A meeting held by a judge with counsel prior to trial, mainly to streamline issues and determine the possibility of settlement.

Pretrial statement. A memorandum prepared by each side in advance of a pretrial conference; a key purpose is the delineation of issues still in contention.

Primary caretaker. The parent who has been mainly responsible for the day-to-day care and nurture of a child.

Primary caretaker presumption. A legal rule that gives preference to the primary caretaker parent in the event of a custody dispute.

Private placement adoption. *See* Independent adoption.

Procedural fairness. Fairness of the parties in their treatment of one another in the process of negotiating an agreement, as distinct from fairness in the resulting terms (substantive fairness).

Professional goodwill. The reputation of a professional practice in the community that generates future patronage.

Protective order. 1. In domestic violence cases, a court order to shield the victim from harm; although civil in nature, violation of these orders is a criminal offense in many states. *See also* No-contact order; Restraining order; Stay-away order; Vacate order. 2. A court order limiting discovery that is unreasonable or oppressive.

Qualified Domestic Relations Order (QDRO). A court order that allows the distribution of pension benefits to a nonemployee spouse.

Qualified Medical Child Support Order (QMCSO). A court order requiring that a child be covered by the noncustodial parent's group health insurance plan.

Real property. As distinct from personal property, real property refers to land and that which is growing upon or affixed to it.

Reasonable efforts. The effort that a child protective agency must make (in most situations) to prevent removal of a child from his or her home, or if the child has been removed, the effort that the agency must put toward reunification.

Recapture. The recomputation of a support obligor's gross income to include amounts that had been improperly deducted as spousal support payments, and the readjustment of his or her tax obligation.

Recrimination. A divorce defense that prevents a divorce from being granted on the basis that both parties are guilty of marital misconduct; may be ameliorated by the doctrine of comparative rectitude.

Rehabilitative support. Time-limited support intended to enable a spouse to obtain the education or training necessary to become economically self-sufficient.

Reimbursement alimony. A support award intended to reimburse a spouse for contributions to the professional education of the other spouse; in addition to reimbursing the financial contribution, it may also compensate for the loss of future income.

Relinquishment. The surrender by a parent of a child to an adoption agency.

Relocation disputes. A disagreement arising during or after a divorce in which the custodial parent seeks to move to another state with the children, and the noncustodial parent seeks to prevent the move.

Request for admissions. A discovery method in which a party asks the other side to admit to the truth of certain facts or to the authenticity of certain documents; done mainly to simplify matters for trial.

Request for mental or physical examination. A discovery method in which a party asks the court to order the other side to submit to a medical or mental evaluation, used when such information is arguably relevant to the outcome of the case.

Request for production of documents. A discovery method in which a party can obtain documents from the other side that are needed to prepare the case.

Request for relief. The portion of a complaint in which the plaintiff sets out the relief that he or she is seeking from the court.

Restraining order. A court order directing a perpetrator to refrain from committing further acts of domestic violence against the party seeking protection from abuse; may also protect the children.

Return of service. The acknowledgment to the court by the person serving the defendant that service was made; usually includes a notation of how and when the service was made.

Reunification services. Services that a child protection agency provides to a family following the removal of a child for the purpose of enabling the child to return home.

Review and adjustment procedure. The periodic assessment and potential revision of a child support order by an IV-D agency.

Revival. The restoration of certain rights deriving from a prior marriage following the annulment of a subsequent marriage.

Revocation of consent. A parent's seeking to take back his or her agreement to an adoption.

Safe haven. These laws allow a birth parent, or an agent of the parent, to leave a baby at a safe location, such as a hospital or fire station, without fear of being prosecuted for child abandonment or neglect.

Second glance doctrine. Review by a court of the terms of a premarital agreement to determine whether they are fair as of the time of enforcement.

Separate maintenance. Similar to a legal separation, but here the essence of the action is a request for support. *See also* Legal separation.

Separate property. As distinct from marital property, property that belongs to the acquiring spouse and is not subject to distribution at divorce. It usually consists of gifts, inheritances, and premarital acquisitions.

Separation agreement. A contract between divorcing spouses in which they set out the terms of their agreement relative to all collateral matters, such as custody, support, and the distribution of property.

Service of process. Delivery of a summons and complaint to a defendant; provides the defendant with notice of the action and informs him or her that a default judgment may be entered unless an answer is filed within a specified time. *See also* Constructive service; Personal service.

Service plan. A plan developed by the child protection agency in cases of substantiated abuse that sets out the services to be provided to the parents to help them care for their children; may also impose certain obligations on the parents.

Significant connection jurisdiction. A jurisdictional ground that permits a court to assert jurisdiction over a custody dispute based on the fact that a child and at least one contestant have a meaningful relationship with that state, and relevant evidence is available there.

Sole custody. The vesting of custodial rights in one parent — can apply to legal custody, physical custody, or both.

Source of funds rule. As distinct from the inception of title rule, an approach that ties the time of acquisition of an asset to the contribution of funds and permits the dual characterization of an asset as both marital and separate in proportion to contribution.

Special equity. A rule giving a spouse who contributed purchase funds to an asset titled in the name of the other spouse an interest in the asset, which is reachable at divorce; was relevant in jurisdictions that divided property according to title.

Spousal support. A monetary amount paid to one spouse by the other for support pending or after legal separation or divorce. *See also* Alimony pendente lite; Lump-sum support; Permanent alimony; Rehabilitative support; Reimbursement alimony.

Stalking. The malicious, willful, and repeated tracking down and following of another person; stalking is often a precursor to acts of serious bodily harm.

Standing. A jurisdictional concept requiring a person to have a sufficient stake in the outcome of a controversy in order to maintain a legal action.

Statute of frauds. A rule requiring that certain kinds of contracts be in writing in order to be enforceable.

Stay-away order. A court order, pursuant to an abuse prevention law, requiring the perpetrator to keep away from the victim's home or from other places where the victim regularly goes (e.g., work).

Stepparent. The legal relationship of a new spouse to the children of a prior marriage.

Subject matter jurisdiction. The authority of a court to hear a particular kind of case.

Subpoena. A writ commanding a witness to appear at a particular time and place to give testimony.

Subpoena duces tecum. A writ commanding a witness to produce books, papers, or other items, usually at a deposition or trial.

Substantive fairness. Fairness of the actual terms of an agreement, as distinct from procedural fairness.

Summons. Issued by the court at the commencement of an action for service on the defendant, a document that informs the defendant of the action and that he or she is required to respond within a certain period of time or risk the entry of a default judgment.

Support worksheet. A worksheet that is tied to child support guidelines and is used in calculating a support award.

Survival. In contrast to a merger, the incorporation of a separation agreement into the divorce judgment, but the retention of its significance as an independent agreement.

Tangible property. Property with a physical presence, which is capable of being felt and seen.

Temporary order. An order made during the pendency of a legal proceeding; temporary orders are superseded by the judgment.

Tender years presumption. The traditional custodial assumption that children of a young age should be raised by their mothers.

Termination of parental rights. The permanent severance of the parent-child relationship based on parental unfitness.

Testamentary capacity. The legal ability to dispose of one's property at death through the execution of a will.

Title. The right of exclusive ownership and control of an asset.

Title IV-D. A law that amends the Social Security Act to establish a cooperative federal-state program for the obtaining and enforcement of child support orders.

Tracing. The process by which a party seeks to establish the separate identity of an asset owned at the time of divorce so that it is not subject to distribution.

Transitional support. *See* Rehabilitative support.

Transmutation. The postacquisition change in the classification of an asset from marital to separate, or vice versa. Transmutation can occur through agreement, commingling, the taking of title in joint name, or use.

Transracial adoption. Adoption across racial lines.

Trial notebook. A binder containing everything needed to present a case in court.

Unallocated support. Child and spousal support awards combined in a single support amount without designation.

Unbundled legal services. Also referred to as "limited task representation." An attorney agrees to provide a client with limited assistance from a menu of options instead of providing the client with comprehensive representation. Typically, rather than entering into a retainer agreement, the client pays for each separate service at the time it is rendered. Unbundled services include the giving of legal advice, coaching on how to handle the case, assistance with drafting pleadings, and representation in court.

Unconscionability. When a contract is grossly unfair to one side; usually involves parties with a significant disparity in bargaining power.

Vacate order. A court order requiring a perpetrator of domestic violence to move out of the home that he or she shares with the party who has been abused; vacate orders do not affect title to property.

Valuation. The determination of what an asset is worth, most commonly by ascertaining its fair market value; usually done by an expert.

Venue. A geographical concept designating which locale an action is to be filed in.

Violence Against Women Act (VAWA). A federal law providing protection to victims of domestic violence and funding for antiviolence programs.

Virtual visitation. The use of electronic communication tools as a supplemental way for a child and a noncustodial parent to connect.

Visitation. The time that a noncustodial parent spends with his or her child.

Void. A marriage that is without any legal effect from its inception; a void marriage does not require a decree of annulment to invalidate it. *See also* Voidable.

Voidable. A marriage that is considered valid unless and until it is declared invalid by a decree of annulment. *See also* Void.

Void as against public policy. The invalidation of a contract on the basis that it violates deeply held community beliefs.

Voluntary surrender. *See* Relinquishment.

Wage withholding. An order directing a support obligor's employer to take support payments directly out of that party's paycheck.

Wrongful adoption. An action that an adoptive parent can bring against an adoption agency if the agency failed to tell the parents the truth about the child they adopted.

Index

Testamentary capacity, 2-3
Texas
    community property in, 3
    safe haven laws in, 392
Threats, domestic violence protective
        orders in cases of, 48
Title IV-D agencies
    child support and, 150-152
        eligibility for services, 151
        parent locator services, 152
    enforcement of spousal support
        through, 204
    Title IV-D agency, defined, 150
    Title IV-D law, defined, 149
Title to property, 214-215
    defined, 215
Tort of wrongful adoption, 409-410
Tracing to establish separate identity
        of asset, 227
Transitional support, 196-197
Transmutation, 228-229
Transracial adoptions, 408-409
Treasury Department, 172
Treatment. *See* Counseling
Trial notebook, 332

U

Unallocated support, tax
        consequences of, 182
Unauthorized practice of law in
        initial client interview,
        260-261
Unbundled legal services, 312
Unconscionability in contracts, 32
Uniform Child Custody Jurisdiction
        Act (UCCJA), 246-251
    emergency jurisdiction, 248-249
    home state jurisdiction, 248
    jurisdictional requirements, 247
    significant connection jurisdiction,
        248
Uniform Child Custody Jurisdiction
        and Enforcement Act
        (UCCJEA), 246-251
    emergency jurisdiction, 248-249
    home state jurisdiction, 248
    jurisdictional requirements, 247
    significant connection jurisdiction,
        248

Uniform Interstate Family Support
        Act (UIFSA)
    child support enforcement,
        173-174
    jurisdiction, 243, 245
    spousal support and, 204
Uniform Parentage Act (UPA), 141,
        363-365
Unvested pensions as marital
        property, 220-221
Unwed fathers
    adoption consent rights, 403-408
    paternity and, 349-353
        biology-plus approach, 351-353
        challenging exclusion of, 350
        defining fathers, 350-351
Use, transmutation by, 228-229

V

Vacate orders in domestic violence
        cases, 49-50
Vacation leave as marital property,
        221-222
Valuation of marital property,
        229-230
    defined, 229
    experts, role of, 230
    fair market value, 229-230
    methods of, 229-230
    overview, 216-217
    time for, 230
Venue, 273
Verbal abuse, domestic violence
        protective orders and, 48
Violence, domestic. *See* Domestic
        violence
Violence Against Women Act of
        1994 (VAWA), 72-75
    criminalization of interstate
        domestic violence, 73
    defined, 72
    firearms, relinquishment of,
        52-53
    full faith and credit for protection
        orders, 73
    immigrants, protection of, 74
    jurisdiction, 247
    overview, 72-73
    victims, working with, 74-75

Virginia
    anti-miscegenation laws in, 6
    pets as marital property in, 220
Virtual visitation, 132-134
Visitation
    amount of time, 123
    child support and, 161-162
    by co-parents, 138-140
    by de facto parents, 140-141
    defined, 101
    disputes regarding, 130
    domestic violence protective
        orders and, 50-51
    frequency of visits, 123
    by grandparents, 135-137
    motions for, 301
    "nonparents" and, 134-142
    overview, 123
    parameters, setting of, 124
    same-sex couples and, 138-140
    schedule, 123-125
    shared custody versus, 124-125
    sole custody versus, 124-125
    by stepparents, 137-138
    unrestricted visitation, problems
        with, 125
    virtual visitation, 132-134
Voidable marriage, 93
Void marriage, 93
Voluntary acknowledgment of
        paternity, 358-360
    form, 359
Voluntary surrender or relinquish-
        ment for adoption, 391

W

Wage withholding to enforce child
        support, 170-171
Washington
    community property in, 3
    de facto parents in, 141
    grandparent visitation in,
        136-137
West Virginia, primary caretaker
        presumption in, 116
Wisconsin
    de facto parents in, 140
    restrictions on marriage in, 6
Wrongful adoption, 409-410